NATURE'S WAY

A Complete Guide to Health through
Yoga & Herbal Remedies

K.R.I. JAGADISH

tara-india research press
new delhi

tara-india reserach press
B-4/22, Safdarjung Enclave, New Delhi – 110 029.
Ph.: 24694610; Fax : 24618637
bahrisons@vsnl.com; contact@indiartesearchpress.com
www.indiaresearchpress.com

2007

ISBN thirteen : 978-81-8386-040-5
ISBN ten : 81-8386-040-0 (South Asia Edition)

Nature's Way
K.R.I. JAGADISH
2007 © tara-india research press

Photo credits:
All photographs and illustrations supplied by author

Catalogue-in-data
1. Cure-Natural., 2. Care-Natural., 3. Nature., 4. Organic., 4. Health.
I. Title II. Author

*"This edition is published for sale in India, Pakistan, Sri Lanka, Bangladesh,
Bhutan, Maldives, Nepal and Afghanistan (Indian Subcontinent) only."*

Printed and Bound in India for *tara-india research press,* at Focus Impressions, New Delhi-110 003

Benediction

This is a good book on health. The author, K.R.I. Jagadish who comes from a family of traditional herbalists, has completed with proficiency the advanced course in herbal medicine conducted by the South Australian School of Herbal Medicine.

The beauty of this book lies in its successful effort to fuse the science and art of medicine with that of Yoga. The insatiable urge of the author to accumulate useful pieces of information from all possible sources and to assimilate them is amply evident here.

In today's world, it has become necessary to present ancient Indian concepts in modern terminology so that everyone can understand them. This, however, cannot be achieved in one day. It is an arduous task, which may perhaps require several generations. It is heartening to note that Jagadish is treading this path.

In the Western world, there is a tendency to assume that Yoga is merely the practice and perfection of Yogic postures (Asanas). This book has successfully presented various Yogic exercises with special reference to their therapeutic value. The reader need not wonder whether the author is acquainted with the true meaning and purpose of Yoga. It must be borne in mind that to use the great science of Yoga merely for its therapeutic value is like using a good milking cow just for its dung.

The great sciences of Yoga and Ayurveda have many secret techniques. They, however, will be handed down by the accomplished gurus only if they feel that the disciples will use them for the welfare of mankind, which means not only providing for good health but also aiding spiritual practice.

The effort put in by Jagadish into this book is indeed worthy of praise. We are confident that scientific-minded Yoga therapists will be greatly motivated by it. By the Divine Grace of Lord Dattatreya, may this book help mankind in every which way it can.

Jaya Guru Data.

His Holiness Sri Ganapathi
Sachchidananda Swamiji
Mysore

For my parents; wife Padma; daughters Laxmi, Latha,
Leka and Lovanya; son-in-law Gopi; granddaughter
Nikhila; sister and brothers; and all my Yoga friends.

Foreword
⨍

Ramaswamy Iyengar Jagadish, or "Jag" as he is affectionately known, comes from Mysore, an area in India where the value of Yoga therapy for healing has long been recognized. Yoga has been the guiding principle of Jag's family for generations and his youth was spent at his grandmother Pavalamma's side, learning the use of Yoga in the treatment of many ailments. This approach includes diagnosis with the pulse, Ayurvedic massage, Yogasanas, herbal remedies and dietary advice. From India Jag moved to Sabah, Malaysia, where he came into contact with both Chinese healing techniques and Western aromatherapy. He learnt to combine the Chinese system of nerve channels and Western essential oils with the Ayurvedic tradition.

Jag now lives in Brunei where his door is always open to those seeking relief from medical problems as well as to those who wish to keep their bodies toned or are interested in dietary advice. Nearly every day, a constant stream of people pass through his home, many suffering from conditions that Western medicine has no cure or treats with drugs that induce side effects. Jag can achieve total cures for most medical problems, including diabetes, cancer, arthritis, asthma and slipped disc, but he insists he is no magician. He uses a combination of manipulation, massage, herbal and essential oils, Yogasanas, meditation and dietary advice to achieve permanent beneficial results. However, the essential ingredient in this approach is the active participation of the patient. Jag's treatments only clear the way for the organism to resume its natural healthy state. For any real cure the patient must be mentally and physically involved, as well as effect the necessary changes in dietary habits. These must carry on over the long term. This sometimes entails adopting a whole new lifestyle, a fact some are reluctant to accept.

Jag's home itself goes a long way towards making these often difficult and stressful transformations in living practices possible. The atmosphere in his apartment could not be further from that of the hospital or clinic. The distinctions that normally exist between the "well" and the "ill" disappear in the constant flow of activities in the living room, bedroom and kitchen. These include Yoga classes, patients performing therapy routines for problems as varied as blood pressure and stress, diagnosis, massage and manipulation, as well as the preparation of herbal remedies. The atmosphere is an open door one (except for some delicate cases) with open discussions. New patients soon become used to sharing their problems and being part of a support network that is tremendously helpful when they have to give up much enjoyed but health threatening activities. Above all this, Jag reigns supreme, with his irrepressible wit and good humour. He cajoles the most depressed of the patients into adopting a positive frame of mind.

In the first seven chapters of this book easy-to-follow, detailed instructions are given for over a hundred Yogasanas and meditations. The well-illustrated Yogasanas are laid out according to level. There is also mention of the benefits of the Asanas and the caution to be practised. In chapter eight the Asanas are arranged into routines for the maintenance of general fitness and well-being, starting with those for beginners and progressing gradually to fairly advanced sequences. It must be emphasized that Yoga is not a system of glorified gymnastics. The focus is on the beneficial therapeutic effects rather than on spectacular positions. The poses are to be assumed slowly and gracefully so both the superficial and deep layers of muscles are toned equally. Avoid jerky, vigorous movements.

Chapters nine to eleven deal with the food we eat. The importance of a balanced diet is emphasized and food combinations are explained, as well as how the wrong combinations can block the absorption of vital nutrients. All the main nutrients necessary for healthy living are listed, together with their sources in fruit, vegetables, pulses and spices. Another point that is underscored is that, except in exceptional cases, it is not necessary to take vitamin supplements. As long as an individual has a varied intake of fresh foods in the correct combinations, the body will receive what it needs to function properly.

Chapter twelve deals with the signs and symptoms of many medical problems. This is followed by ten chapters covering all the major systems of the body. In each the problems of the system are described, Asana routines are listed together with specific variations for therapy, and recipes are suggested. Most of these recipes were passed down to Jag from his grandmother Pavalamma, and it is his wish that they now become available to all.

Finally, there are chapters on the endocrine and lymph glands and on massage. Jag's approach to medical problems is holistic. The whole organism is interconnected and any cure involves the way we move our muscles and joints, the food we put into our bodies and our mental attitude. While Jag can help by clearing blockages, releasing trapped nerves or stimulating sluggish organs, we too can do our part by knowing how to exercise and what to eat. This knowledge is here for us to acquire in this book. Seek the advice of a doctor advice before undertaking any particular therapy. At the very least, the doctor should be involved in a monitoring capacity as some exercises, if performed wrongly, can worsen a condition. It is also advisable to learn the Asanas under the guidance of Yoga instructor who is used to the variations and modifications entailed by therapy.

Jonathan Mossop
Brunei, September 1994

Acknowledgements

❥

Establishing the first Jag Therapy Centre   *K.H. Ang, Atasan Sdn Bhd, Brunei.*

Organising the first Jag Therapy Centre in Brunei   *Margaret Liew, Ng Boon Keat, Kim Ward, Pritam Singh, Pow Mee Ting, Satish Kumar, Shaila and Uma Muthiah.*

Business adviser and manager   *Ng Boon Keat*

For providing and upgrading the computer   *The Yoga family and Darren Onn*

For providing the printer   *Margaret Liew and Alphonsus Liew*

Photographs   *Laxmi, Latha, Leka, Lovanya, Bernadette and Anne Marie*

Drawings   *Margaret Liew and Latha Jagadish*

Scanning   *Margaret Liew*

Help in massaging   *Margaret Liew, (Jean) Gin Lian, Preetam Singh, Ian Stewart, Maureen and Andrea.*

Help in conducting Yoga classes   *Jonathan and Ann Mossop, (Jean) Gin Lian, Shaila, Monica Heywood Kenny, Preetam Singh, Satish Kumar, Shaila, Pow Mee Ting, Wendy and Ian Stewart.*

Proofreading the book   *Padma Jagadish, Jonathan Mossop and Latha Jagadish, who provided her expertise again before the book went to press.*

Gifts of essential massage oils and herbs   *The Yoga family and well-wishers*

Sourcing for oils and herbs   *Susie Ng*

For providing massage beds   *Darren Onn, Jung & Co (Singapore).*

Cooking lessons   *Padma Jagadish, Kim Ward and Uma Muthiah.*

Jag Therapy Branches   *Yoga Family*

And a special thanks to   *Ken Jung for his invaluable services.*

Contents

Author's Note

The responsibility for health should not be left exclusively in the hands of doctors. Patients too should do their part. This shared responsibility goes a long way in relieving feelings of helplessness and futility.

There is a tendency to equate alternate medicine with holistic medicine. This, however, is wrong. There is also no single method in any holistic approach. Diet, Asanas, meditation, massages, counselling, etc. work hand in hand for better health. These methods, however, cannot be tested scientifically because there is no apparatus as yet to test how they work on human beings.

Much of what I have been able to achieve depends on the attitude of the individual in accepting my technique or approach. The therapeutic effects of relaxation and meditation have no syllabus nor there is any rule to be followed. I encourage patients to find their own special way to adjust to the regime. In this book, I have given only a number of examples of therapies for specific problems, which are the starting point, just a rough idea of the different systems used in maintaining health. This, however, is neither the end nor the beginning.

Initially, I used to scribble down some guidelines for my patients, and my wife Padma and friends collected them. Over time, I was surprised that Padma had collected over three thousand sheets of paper. With the help of friends, she compiled them. The result — my first book called *Health through Yoga and Diet*. However, people who did not know me personally and had bought the book found it difficult to follow the instructions without proper illustrations. Others also contacted me and suggested that I give specific recipes. I aimed to do just that in my next book.

Over the past sixteen years, an extraordinary number of people in Brunei helped me produce my second book — *Nature's Way: Health through Yoga and Herbal Remedies*. Some gave advice and suggestions, while others gave material help, providing me with computers, printers, etc. There were others who gave me moral support and encouragement. Above all, my wife and daughters gave me their full support.

In this book, I have tried my best to give as much information as was requested by friends and readers of my first book. It aims to provide basic information about some of today's common problems as well as gives tips on the benefits and the risks involved. The book has many recipes; however, they are not complete. There are still volumes left in me that are yet to be published.

I must stress that this book is in no way a substitute for a doctor. It gives you an awareness of the problems so that you can take a far more active role in your health and those close to you.

I am ever grateful to my father K.Y.R. Iyengar (Muthanna) for encouraging me to spread this art, which was passed down to me by my grandmother, Pavalamma and my aunt, Thayamma. I am also grateful to Mr Tay for sharing his vast knowledge of acupressure, Shiatsu massage and Chinese herbs with me. My reverence and thanks to His Holiness Sri Sri Ganapathi Sachidananda Swamiji of Mysore for taking the time off his busy schedule to go through this book, as well as for his blessings. I endeavour to continue helping people in every which way I can.

My sincere thanks to all my well-wishers for their help. I love you all and will always be grateful for your kindness. I pray for the health and harmony of all.

K.R.I. Jagadish
No. 50 I Block,
Aniketana Road 3rd Cross South,
Kuvempunagar,
Mysore 570 023,
Karnataka, India
Phone/Fax: 91-821-560205

Introduction
❧

HEALTH

Among the many good things bestowed upon us by God, health is one of the most precious and sought after. Nevertheless, we tend to ignore its value when we are not suffering from any illness, believing that no illness can touch us. If only this were true! Even when witnessing the illnesses and suffering of our friends or relatives, many of us tend to think that the same could never happen to us. We only desire to be healthy when we ourselves suffer from some kind of illness.

The real cause of ill health lies in our failure to adhere to the principles and requirements of healthy living. Almost all our health problems arise from abusing the laws of nature. Good health is basically healthy living based on a balanced diet, adequate exercise and mental equilibrium. The food we eat plays a major role in our health. Yet, we tend to worry about its taste, appearance, and the way it is served over how it affects our body.

There are many ways to maintain good health and to recover from illnesses, but there is no one system of medicine that can keep us completely healthy. Our well-being depends on many factors, such as genes, exercise, mental health and attitude, lifestyle, as well as nutritional intake and balance. Rather than take these factors for granted, make an effort to learn why these factors are considered important in the first place. Usually, the results or benefits of being healthy are realised through experience, and the best way to demonstrate the value of anything is to see it work.

EXERCISE

Health, fitness and performance are three separate phenomena. Health is generally defined as freedom from disease; fitness is related to the ability to meet the demands of the environment; and performance is how successful an individual is in accomplishing a task. An individual can be healthy without being fit, and he or she can be of poor health and yet be able to perform superbly in certain athletic activities. There are several instances of physically fit athletes winning gold medals in competitions who are anything but healthy.

The mystique surrounding the cult of physical fitness has given rise to the mistaken belief that a good physical condition comes slowly and that a rigorous exercise routine is necessary for fitness. Exercise in itself is not a panacea. Exercising regularly does not mean you can eat any type of food and still remain healthy.

The science of physical fitness is primarily designed for athletes who focus on specific tasks. Another emphasis of physical fitness programmes is its use as a therapy for those recovering from illnesses. However, these programmes only focus on isolated body parts. When a specific area is put into action during an exercise, the body responds by sending more blood, nutrients and energy to that area. This response improves health and vitality in that area, but the system as a whole does not benefit from it.

I am not advocating that these fitness programmes not be followed; rather, I am suggesting that they be well understood. Most of these programmes put a lot of pressure on the individual, demanding a certain amount of exterior accomplishment. What happens is that he or she exerts more pressure than is possible and may overdo the exercise. This may result in uncomfortable breathing, difficulty in relaxing and tiredness. The programmes are organised on the basis of the competitive spirit and goals of an individual. Other parameters include the time devoted to it, physical load (pressure or effort channelled into a sport) and the amount of physiological effort exerted. The competition integral to these programmes results in stress at the cost of health. Most of the programmes meant for physical fitness are beneficial only to a certain degree, and no one exercise develops total fitness. Several types of exercises are necessary for all-round development.

Sport is certainly not unhealthy in itself but when indulged in excessively, may cause various ailments. Training to a very high level does not make an individual healthier. On the other hand, an inactive life is also detrimental to health. So, what must be sought after is the right kind of exercise that takes into account these factors: muscles strength, endurance, blood circulation and respiratory endurance.

The type of physical fitness programme embarked on depends on several factors — the age and vigour of an individual, the time he or she spends on the programme, weather conditions and his or her ability to afford special equipment for the exercise. Exercise, when properly selected to fit an individual's needs, becomes an enjoyable form of recreation. It relieves monotony and brings about a zest for living, optimism, enthusiasm, as well as a sense of relaxation. Exercise has a bearing on our ability to handle stress, weight control and the overall functioning of all our vital organs.

Any good exercise routine should cater basically for three areas of fitness: strength, flexibility and cardiovascular health. In addition, it should provide mental equilibrium by relaxing the mind and body. Without proper extension and stretching of muscles, the body cannot reach its highest potential. A thorough stretching programme exercises every muscle, nerve, organ and gland in the body. Hatha Yoga, one of the oldest philosophies, gives great benefits in these respects. The following is a list of some types of exercises and what they can or cannot do: Isometric exercise tightens the abdominal muscles, builds muscle size and strength in a particular region but does nothing for cardiovascular fitness; Isotonic exercise, such as weight lifting, contracts the muscles and helps build muscle size and strength but does not help the heart and lungs; Isokinetic exercise, which involves further weight lifting using the strength of the lower part of the body, builds muscular strength and provides cardiovascular fitness. However, it is performed without rest and results in both physical and mental strain. It does not bring about a feeling of relaxation; Aerobics is a form of exercise that requires a proper supply of oxygen for energy. It enhances the system that channels the oxygen supply and helps strengthen the heart and lungs; Anaerobic exercise, such as sprinting, because it is maintained for only a short while, does not require as much oxygen for energy. Consequently, it does not result in the same benefits as aerobics; and gymnastics, ballet and certain martial arts improve flexibility, speed and balance.

Whatever programme you choose, be clear about your goals. Is it flexibility, strength, stamina, stress reduction or anything else that you are seeking? Stick to the programme and try not to constantly switch from one type of exercise to another. Realise the dramatic changes taking place in your body and learn to appreciate them. After taking up a particular type of exercise, you may experience feelings of depression and restlessness, as well as discomfort when you discontinue it for a few days. This is very common among runners, swimmers or anyone who does workouts several times a week. On the other hand, even if you lead a sedentary lifestyle, you can reach an acceptable level of conditioning within a short period by selecting a suitable programme.

Apart from the physical effects, exercise has a tremendous psychological effect on the body. When performing vigorous exercise, the body produces hormones called beta-endorphins, which act as tranquillisers. They make the body immune to pain and enhance a sense of momentary well-being. This is the reason why some people are addicted to certain types of exercises.

The most primary motivations for exercise should be enjoyment and health. However, whatever you do, moderation is the best prescription for good health. Some exercises may not be suitable for the body condition of some people and should therefore be avoided. Do not attempt anything that brings about pain. It is best to consult a physical therapist if you are unsure which exercise programme to follow. It is also good to take the advice of a doctor if you are on medication.

Exercise does not insure us against disease, nor does it remedy disease. It has no magical ability to correct the effects of an unhealthy lifestyle. It does, however, make the body stronger and more capable of dealing with ill health.

Carefully selected exercises and a good diet are necessary for a happy, disease-free life. Set realistic goals; and make up your mind as to how you want to lead your life. The first step involves formulating what exactly you hope to achieve by taking up a fitness programme. Next, make a formal resolution. It is good to make the resolution only after a lot of thought and feeling. Only this way can you prepare your subconscious mind for the struggle ahead. Without the cooperation of your subconscious mind, little progress can be made. Let the cerebellum know what our cerebrum desires.

DIET

Wholesome living requires abstinence from foods or drinks detrimental to the body, and a healthy diet is designed to cleanse the body of accumulated waste matter.

When we are thirsty, cool water gives us immediate satisfaction. Just as we enjoy variety in foods so we derive pleasure by varying the taste of the fluids we drink. While pure water, fresh fruit juice and milk are healthy drinks, in a search for novelty, we sometimes go too far. Many of our beverages contain chemical substances such as sugar and other substances with drug effects, such as caffeine and theobromine. These substances affect our bodily functions.

The science of nutrition is not new and goes back many centuries. Before, man was not influenced by external factors, such as advertisements, social customs and the commercial business world, which controls the economy and indirectly the way we live today. In short, far healthier food was eaten then.

We developed originally as plant eaters and not as flesh eaters, and our teeth are not designed to eat meat. Our saliva has specific enzymes, which are meant for digesting the complex carbohydrates of vegetables, while the more acidic enzymes found in the saliva of flesh-eating animals are meant for breaking down protein. Our stomachs secrete far less hydrochloric acid compared to the animals that eat flesh. We do not have the enzyme uricase to break down uric acid. The digestive tracts of flesh-eating animals are shorter than ours, and this helps them expel putrefying flesh quickly.

More and more studies show that meat is not essential to a nutritionally balanced diet. In a study of man and laboratory animals, it was found that both did very well on diets free of meat. The knowledge and practice of a healthy way of living will do much to prevent disease; a balanced diet will provide the necessary nutrients, including vitamins and minerals. Many of us are led to believe that we will suffer from protein deficiency if we do not have diet rich in protein. This is not true.

However, even when we take all the precautions, illnesses and injuries sometimes do occur. Where possible, we should be able to give ourselves simple remedies that do not leave residuals in the body. However, it must be stressed that self treatment should be restricted to only minor symptoms of illnesses. The wave of enthusiasm that followed the discovery of vitamins in 1912 was quickly exploited by commercial interests and popular advertisements that gave the impression of "magical good health" through their intake. Only in special cases are additional vitamins necessary, but unfortunately, we tend to use medicines indiscriminately. Self medication has become a habit, and this is encouraged by advertisements.

Animals eat certain plants for cures. Similar instincts exist among us; however, we tend to ignore them. Whatever nutrient the body needs and cannot produce by itself can be obtained from the plant kingdom.

Many people today eat for taste and convenience and ignore the basic health factor. In other words, they fail to realise what is good for their body. A well-nourished person is one who exercises properly and follows a programme of healthy living. He or she also possesses the following: boundless vitality, clear and alert eyes, well-formed bones with a straight back, a good posture, graceful movements, a well-formed contour and healthy muscles without the unnecessary fat, efficient bodily functions, as well as good endurance and sleep.

This ideal state of health comes from sticking to a good diet, which should contain the right type of fat and protein, with sufficient minerals to ensure the formation, repair and reinforcement of tissues. There must also be sufficient carbohydrates for energy and the right amount of fat. In addition, there must be enough vitamins for the proper functioning of vital organs. When people are asked whether they are healthy and well nourished, amazingly a high percentage of them, even those from affluent countries, are not able to answer in the affirmative. Many people in fact are under nourished. This comes from eating more than the body requires; eating between meals, which disrupts the normal rhythmical functioning of the organs; and neglecting breakfast for reasons ranging from lack of time to lack of appetite.

These practices indicate an intake of excessive sugary foods, which supply the body with "empty" calories, as well as an intake of processed foods, which contain preservatives, artificial flavouring and colour. Although manufacturers add vitamins and minerals to food to compensate for the lost nutrients, these are often not really restored in the enriching process. Because of convenience, people often choose processed foods over fresh food, thus depriving themselves of important food elements lost in whole or in part at the processing stage. There is no adequate substitute for fresh foods.

There are three basic causes of malnutrition: an insufficient intake of food, a deficiency in certain nutrients and disorder in the body, which prevents proper absorption and utilisation of required nutrients. In some cases, the problem can be psychological in nature. We might have formed an aversion for food or developed preferences for certain types of food. It is important to establish firm discipline, either self or parental, and to try and enjoy the taste of all types of nutritious food in their natural state. Nutritious food grown in good soil and a good diet are the best guarantee for health and happiness.

Herbalists of long ago had answers for many common aches and pains. They used herbs as food and as medicine. These remedies worked. However, they could not give any chemical equations or formulas for these remedies as is required by today's scientific world.

We should not just take the average statistical values found in many diet books. We should understand the chemistry of digestion and assimilation and what effect the food will have on our body. In addition, know how much of a particular type of food should be eaten, where it can be bought and how best to combine the different types of food to get the best results. Knowing more about nutrition and studying how the body reacts to it is important.

A good diet and exercise are effective in so far as we are motivated to follow guidelines given by therapists who adhere to the holistic approach or as found in this book with sincerity, free from outside influences. The secret of lifelong health and happiness lies in our ability to dictate our own lifestyle. We are what we eat and what we do.

1

The Meaning of Yoga
∝

Yoga is an in-depth science and philosophy. It is as vast as an ocean and as such, it is impossible to cover all its aspects. This book will present its essence in simple language with well-illustrated examples. Yoga has come to where it is today from legendary Indian Yogis or Rishis. Translated into simple English, Rishis are holy men. Rishis enjoyed ideal physical and mental health by adhering to the Yogic principles. Yoga is not a vague doctrine but a practical system of self culture, an exact science based on the principles formulated by people who spent their lives studying its nature thoroughly. Yoga in Sanskrit means "union" or "binding together". This involves disciplining not only the body, but also the intellect, mind, will and emotions. In the *Bhagavad Gita*, Yoga is described as an equilibrium between success and failure, and a smart way of living in today's world.

Yoga is a philosophy that instils in the minds of people a hopeful and optimistic approach to life. Many believe that practising Yoga involves running away from home, giving up worldly pleasures and pursuits, turning vegetarian and putting an end to relationships with people when it is really a cultivation of an all-embracing love. A love that envelopes the Yogi or the Yogini and those surrounding him or her.

There are those who believe that Yoga is inextricably linked with religion. However, Yoga is neither a religion nor a magic formula. It is a method of realising one's true self by blending the body, mind and spirit into a harmonious whole.

For the Yogis, animals were their teachers. Many Yogic techniques were developed by studying the actions, movements and behaviour of animals in the wild. These animals, with no doctors or drugs to cure their ailments, found in nature their only true guide. They cured ailments by relying on their natural instincts. By studying these animals, Yogis realised that animals relaxed at will far more easily than the average man.

They discovered that:

- Animals live five times their growing span, while humans live only two to three times their maturity.
- Animals keep their vigour and appearance for five-sixths of their lives while humans do not.
- Animals breathe fully while humans use only one sixth of their lung capacity.
- Animals contract their muscles at will. All deep contractions are simply the prolongation of a natural instinctive stretch.

From these and many other observations, Rishis realised the importance of relaxation, deep contractions and breath control. Above all, they grasped the true value of concentration. A state of concentration cannot be achieved without mastering relaxation. Similarly, it is impossible to achieve deep relaxation without applying thought to the particular Yoga stretch involved.

The primary principles of Yoga supplement one another and are:

- Relaxation
- Contraction
- Breath control
- Concentration

The original purpose of Yoga seemed to provide sages with a rocklike steadiness in their sitting postures during meditation. It looks as though out of this beginning, there developed a comprehensive system of postures that were to be held for seconds, minutes, hours or even days. There are stories about holy Indian men who have been known to hold their Yoga positions for weeks. Their aim was complete mastery of body, mind and health.

Some postures are identical to the characteristic movements of birds, reptiles and insects. In fact, these postures are named after animals. Yogic postures are found in the earliest rock carvings in Harappa and Mohenjo-Daro. Archaeologists discovered these two cities in 1924. As far back as 326 B.C., soldiers in Alexander the Great's army wrote of the gymnastic philosophers they saw in India.

Over the course of Yoga's development, Yogis devised several branches or types of Yoga to suit people of different temperaments, attitudes and inclinations. This enabled any person to do Yoga.

In rigorous exercises like gymnastics, only some specific muscles are rapidly and repeatedly exercised. When doing such exercises, there is no influence on the mind. In Yoga, on the other hand, there is a harmonious development of both the mind and body. Most physical exercises cause what is known as phasic contraction of the muscles. Yogic postures create a static contraction. This maintains a muscle under tension without causing repeated motion.

The word *Asana* (literally meaning "the seat") was used by Patanjali of India, the sage and founder of Yoga, when he referred to the attainment of a comfortable position. To develop certain parts of the body at the expense of others is irrational. There must be a systematic development of mind and body, as well as no strain when a person practises the Asanas. In this context, the endocrine system plays a significant role in controlling the body. Yogasanas activate certain glands effectively and so help regulate the proper production of hormones. The metabolism of the body is, thus, maintained.

The Yogic student stores an abundance of *Prana*, which is "the life source". This is breath through the regular practice of Pranayama, meaning the "regulation of breath", the most important step in Yoga.

Yoga is a practical system of self culture. It is an exact science and a perfect system of self discipline for the mind, senses and physical body. Yoga helps develop coordination and control of all the forces within the body, leading to perfection, peace, harmony and lasting happiness.

The Yoga Sutra, written by Patanjali, is the basis for Raja Yoga or the "royal path of Yoga". It includes both the physical practices of Hatha Yoga, "the regulation of breathing and body control", and the meditative disciplines of Jnana Yoga, "the Yoga of knowledge".

Patanjali's Yoga Sutra aptly sums up the function of Yoga in the following way: "the body shell is the horse and the mind is the rider. It is the horse that takes the mind to the goal of life. It must therefore be kept healthy and strong."

The Yoga Sutra was written for people who were already treading the path of Yoga. Patanjali did not use flowery language, extolling the benefits of Yoga as he did not need to convince his readers who were his followers. His book merely emphasises the need for everyone to practise Yoga as a first step to self understanding and self analysis. To achieve this, he underscores discipline.

Patanjali gives the guidelines for practising Yoga as *angas* or "limbs". They are the Ashtanga Yoga or the eightfold paths or limbs or tools of Yoga:

- Yama (abstention)
- Niyama (observance)
- Asanas (postures)
- Pranayama (breath control)
- Pratyahara (control of the senses)
- Dharana (concentration)
- Dhyana (meditation)
- Samadhi (contemplation)

Yama and Niyama stress the ethics and morality that have to be practised in a person's daily life. They develop physical and mental purification. Asanas, Pranayama and Pratyahara are concerned with the body and the senses. Dharana, Dhyana and Samadhi deal with the mind.

CLASSIFYING THE DIFFERENT TYPES OF YOGA

While the different branches of Yoga can stand on their own, they also complement one another. It is difficult to separate them as all forms of Yoga seek to unite man, the finite with the infinite, the spirit with the matter and the mind with the body. The Yogas other than Hatha are mainly meditative and more directly aimed at Yoga as an end goal and union. However, even in performing the physical techniques of Hatha Yoga, to some extent, the practitioner cannot avoid performing the other Yogas.

1. JNANA YOGA
Union by Knowledge

This is the path to spiritual knowledge and wisdom corresponding to the intellectual temperament, in which the intellect penetrates the veils of ignorance and prevents a person from seeing his or her true self, the *atman* or "the soul". The disciplines of this path are knowledge, learning and meditation. It is the path to wisdom through the attainment and acquisition of knowledge, aided by a process of self analysis.

2. BHAKTI YOGA
Union by Love and Devotion

This is the Yoga that focuses strongly on love, devotion and worship. Its disciplines are the rites as given in the *Upanishads* and *Vedas* and songs sung in praise of the gods. By practising this Yoga, a Yogi or Yogini transcends his or her limited personality and aims to achieve cosmic consciousness.

3. KARMA YOGA
Union by Action and Service

This is the path of selfless action and service, with no thought given to the positive results that may be attained. It implies unconditional giving. The belief of a Karma Yogi is that his mind and thought are purified by actions of unconditional service. He loses his sense of identity as a doer and becomes united with consciousness. He becomes an instrument through which the divine plan is executed.

4. MANTRA YOGA
Union by Voice and Sound

The practice of Mantra Yoga influences consciousness through the repetition of certain syllables, words or phrases. This is now practised as Transcendental Meditation or TM for short. The rhythmic repetition of mantras is called japa.

5. YANTRA YOGA
Union by Vision and Form

Yantra Yoga employs the use of sight and form (the shape and design of an object). A yantra is a design with the power to influence consciousness. It can be an objective picture, an inner visualisation or a design that brings serenity, and is appealing to the mind.

6. LAYA YOGA
Arousal of Potential Energy

This is the method of obtaining mastery over the mind or will. It is studied only after mastering Hatha Yoga.

7. KUNDALINI YOGA
Arousal of Latent Psychic Nerve Force

Kundalini Yoga combines many techniques of Hatha Yoga, especially prolonged breath suspension and stable postures with intense meditative concentration. These techniques attempt to awaken the psychic nerve force latent in the body. The symbol of Kundalini is the serpent, which is coiled below the base of the spine. The force goes up the spine and passes through several *chakras* or "power centres".

8. TANTRIC YOGA
Union by Harnessing Sexual Energy

The term tantric is applied generally to distinguish physiological systems from non-physiological ones. The central tenet of this Yoga is to dissolve the individual ego and attain perfect relaxation for the purpose of merging with universal energy.

9. HATHA YOGA
Union by Body Mastery and Breath

Hatha Yoga is the most well-known form of Yoga. It is a physical Yoga composed of Asanas, Pranayama and relaxation. It regulates breathing and maintains body control. Done with disciplined practice, it enhances the supply of oxygen into the blood stream. By concentrating on certain nerve centres, it ensures the restoration of vital energy to the body.

A proper diet ensures a cleansing process for the body, where impurities and toxins are eliminated. In the process, essential minerals and vitamins are absorbed. The best-known feature of Hatha Yoga is the posturing, in particular Asanas, now known as Yogic postures but originally meaning "the seat". It is known for its practical benefits to the health of the nervous system, glands and vital organs. This Yoga can be viewed as a hygiene that takes into account the purification of the total organism.

10. RAJA YOGA
Union by Mental Mastery

Hatha Yoga is the most practical of all Yogas, with its emphasis on promoting vibrant health and the tapping of an individual's latent energies. It also has a calming effect on the mind.

However, the direct work of mastering consciousness and stilling thought to become aware of the "ground of being" belongs to Raja Yoga. It is called raja or royal because the Yogi who practices this Yoga becomes the ruler of his mind.

Patanjali lists Asanas and Pranayama in his eight limbs of Yoga, and such classic texts as the *Hatha Yoga Pradipika*, the *Gheranda Samhita* and *Siva Samhita* follow Patanjali in viewing Hatha Yoga practice as providing a physiological hygiene that prepares the body for effective mental control. Based on this view, Raja Yoga includes Hatha Yoga within its system.

While Hatha Yoga works on the body, purifying and perfecting it, and through the body on the mind, Raja Yoga works on the mind, refining and perfecting it, and through the mind on the body.

However, just as some people perform the physiological Yogas with little or no thought for mental discipline, so there are exponents of the mental Yogas who consider that the body will respond positively to control of consciousness without having to resort to anything more physical than a stable posture in sitting for meditation. Have good control over the body before attempting to practise Raja Yoga seriously.

YOGA AND HEALING

Investigations made at different medical centres comparing people who practised Yoga with other groups, who performed other types of physical exercises or none at all, show that there are significant differences between the two groups of people.

The implications have not been fully accepted by the orthodox medical fraternity and are regarded by many as mere theories. However, there are a few hospitals and clinics that encourage the use of the Yogic system of healing. Doctors here find the system appropriate for treating certain types of rheumatism, arthritis and some cardiac complaints, as well as for treating respiratory problems like asthma and metabolic disorders like diabetes.

Asanas are used to combat constipation, ease sciatica, normalise the thyroid gland and tone the liver and the pancreas. Doctors have found Yoga to be more beneficial than the standard anti-inflammatory drugs. The results of such treatment are significant. However, due to people's ignorance and other reasons, they are not popular treatment procedures.

The practice of Hatha Yoga is encouraged as it is an inexpensive, safe and natural way of preventing and, to a certain extent, treating certain diseases. It does not have any side effects. When practised together with orthodox medicine, it can cure or ease many physical ailments. Treatment is based on a set of Asanas, Pranayama and restraint on *ahara* or "food".

The effectiveness of Yoga depends on body conditions, the way it is accepted as a way of therapy, a person's age and other factors, including the person's attitude.

If the goal is health and an all-round development, then the daily routine should include Asanas that increase flexibility, improve blood circulation, develop the breathing capacity, as well as relax the muscles of the body and the mind.

In addition, to correct the body chemistry, stick to a proper diet. Be prepared to follow the principles involved in Yoga practice, otherwise it becomes no different from any other physical activity.

Beginners are advised to follow a progressive pattern: start with simple Asanas before going on to more advanced Asanas. Do not expect overnight results as Yoga therapy does not produce miracles. Be willing to go back on the progressive steps if you find the Asanas too hard to cope with, owing to age, condition of the body or other such limiting factors.

Do not attempt to set a world record in results, as Yoga is about relaxation, not competition. Try to do the Asanas to the best of your ability by following the illustrations. The daily programme given (see chapter 8) represents suggested activity for a moderately healthy adult.

Not everyone can do all the exercises, so do not be disheartened if you cannot do some of them. Think positively and develop a happy and relaxed frame of mind before trying out any of the exercises. There are no fixed programmes to be strictly followed.

Please consult a doctor before embarking on any exercise programme, Yoga included.

THE AIMS OF POSTURING

Almost every Asana directly or indirectly helps to relax the mind. A well-balanced programme of postures works on every muscle, nerve, gland and organ, thereby bringing optimum benefit to the entire body.
The *Hatha Yoga Pradipika* states that "Asanas should be practised for gaining steady posture, health and lightness of the body". This quotation points out the rewards of performing Asanas and is devoid of any fantastic claims to the occult and magical powers.

The primary purpose of Asanas is to achieve the highest possible standard of muscular tone, mental health and organic vigour, as well as to stimulate the nervous and glandular systems.

Hatha Yoga is interpreted as a method that achieves maximum results using minimum energy. The postures are not movements; rather, the postures are adopted and held. Most postures are relaxing rather than strenuous; refreshing rather than fatiguing; noncompetitive; require no special equipment or clothing; and can be performed by men, women and children of all age groups.

One physiological function that is intimately linked with life is breathing or what the Yogis call, "the breath of life". The practice of Pranayama is mainly for purification. Pranayama, the Yogic "science of breath control", is the very core of Hatha Yoga. Pranayama includes both "the mastery of body and control of breathing". Breath control is every bit as important as the Asanas.

Pranayama consists of two parts: Prana (meaning "life breath") and Yama (meaning "control"). When I ask my students to learn the correct way of breathing, they are amused as well as puzzled. No doubt breathing takes place every second, the Yogic way of breathing encourages deep breathing and develops the art of using the lungs to breathe fully.

Patanjali, in his eight Asanas of classical Yoga, points out that Pranayama comes after the bodily poses and before Pratyahara. Dharana then takes place, where attention is turned inwards for concentration after which Dhyana, the extension of Dharana into contemplation, occurs. Finally Samadhi, the super-conscious is experienced.

All techniques of Yoga aim for a state of tranquillity. Postures, breath control, mind-stilling meditation, physical, mental and spiritual purification have a relaxing influence, which is widely acknowledged to be Yoga's greatest advantage. Those who perform the postures in my evening classes report after only a few weeks of Yoga practice that they are more relaxed, and that their emotions are under control.

Each Yoga practice session should follow a sequence of postures recommended by the teacher. Postures are grouped according to their physical benefits and ease of performance.

For general practice, the following order has been known to offer maximum benefit:

• Complete Breath Standing
• Shavasana
• Suryanamaskar
• Standing postures
• Sitting postures
• Lying down postures
• Inverted postures
• Mudras
• Bandhas
• Pranayama
• Meditation

Between each Asana, perform Sahavasana. This is the corpse pose, where the Yogi or Yogini lies flat on the back with arms lying limp by the sides of the body. Generally, there is a counter-posture for each Asana, and these should be performed consecutively for maximum benefit.

THE DOS AND DON'TS

Remember that Yoga is neither a short cut nor a stepping stone to quick health. It takes time to practise the Asanas and achieve the best comfort level for the body. Patanjali calls Asanas *stiram sukam asanam* or postures that can be "maintained steadily with comfort".

Even though some Yoga instructors tend to teach their favourite Asanas, Patanjali advises students to choose those they are comfortable with and which complement their purpose.

It is necessary to adhere to the Dos and Don'ts when performing Yogasanas, although oftentimes, there may not be a scientific explanation available. Everyone, including beginners, must observe the basic principles of Yoga.

Abide by the following rules before performing a group of postures:

- The effectiveness of Yogasanas depends on the concentration you bestow on its practice as well as the correct adherence to its technique.
- Understand the principle behind each Asana and its benefits and try to follow the exact technique. Group the Asanas according to their physical benefits.
- The sequence and duration of each Asana must be strictly followed.
- Do not try to get into the final position of the Asana right away. Intermediate positions must be practised before the final position.
- After holding the final position of the Asana, be just as slow coming out of the posture as you did getting into it.
- In every Asana, the order of getting into the position is important. Returning to the original position is done in the reverse order.
- Do not stop abruptly in the middle of an Asana.
- Regular practice is essential to experience the best results. Avoid strained or jerky movements.
- If you are a beginner, do not feel distressed if you are not able to master the Asanas within a short period of time. It is better to go slow and secure maximum benefit by doing the moderate position of the Asana correctly rather than injuring yourself trying to achieve the extreme position quickly.

- It is extremely important that a beginner reveals any physical discomfort or illness to the Yoga instructor. This will help both the instructor and the beginner ascertain the suitability of the various postures.
- People with a history of serious illnesses should consult their doctor before taking up Yoga. There are sets of specific Asanas for particular ailments. Some Asanas cannot be performed because of certain illnesses. For instance, people with sinus problems should avoid inverted postures.

YOGA UNDER SUPERVISION

It is best to learn Yoga under supervision. Prepare yourself mentally before taking up Yoga as it is helpful to start with a good spirit. Patience and concentration are necessary for maximum benefit. Concentration calms a turbulent mind, strengthens the train of thought and clarifies ideas.

Do not perform Yoga in a competitive spirit as it is not a competitive sport. You are only competing with yourself.

When performed correctly, Asanas should not you cause any discomfort. Feel your way into the posture gradually, bearing in mind your limitations. If you do not feel pleasant after doing an Asana, something is wrong with your technique. You may have been straining or overstretching yourself too much.

If an Asana causes discomfort or pain, discontinue it for a while. You should have a clear idea between pain that results from muscle discomfort due to some problem in the region and pain that results from stretching or contraction of the muscles due to the incorrect way it is done.

Concentrating on the movement of an Asana will help you get into the final position and master the exercise. This increases muscular tone and flexibility. Mental discipline produces an awareness of each part of the muscular and skeletal systems. This is particularly true of the spine — you become aware of each and every vertebra.

During the holding period, tense only those muscles that are actually in use and relax all other parts of the body. The final holding position should be maintained and there should be no adjustments. There should be no strain or forceful movement. Pause for a few seconds until the breathing and blood circulation return to normal. To relieve the strain, perform Shavasana.

A minute's rest between Asanas will generally be enough, although much depends on the individual and the type of Asana being performed. However, there are some combinations such as Matsyasana (Fish in Lotus) and Sarvangasana (Shoulderstand) that should be performed without a long break.

When performing Asanas, relax between postures and between repetitions. Even a short period of relaxation can refresh both the mind and body. It also improves your ability to tackle everyday problems. The same benefits can also be experienced by people suffering from depression, stress and strain.

Asanas should not be performed during or immediately after any illness. Do not start a Yoga session feeling tensed. Rest for a while on a mat on the floor first before beginning the session.

Women are advised not to perform certain Asanas during menstruation. Some beneficial Asanas, though, can be performed during this time and these are highlighted in the respective chapters. Similarly during pregnancy, specific Asanas are to be performed for a specified period of time.

It is best to perform Asanas in the morning after emptying your bowels. Although you may feel slightly stiff in the morning and cannot reach the extreme positions of the Asanas, benefits are maximum at this time of the day. Alternatively, you can practise at night, in which case you must make sure that your stomach is empty for at least two to three hours before you start the Yoga session. Eat, if you must, an hour after the practice.

Asanas can be performed anywhere so long as the exercise area does not get direct sunlight or draught. Do not perform Asanas in an air-conditioned room or under a moving fan.

Use a thick blanket or a carpet on a hard even surface. Do not practise on a sofa or a bed as you cannot maintain proper balance. You should dress appropriately.

No warming-up exercises are necessary before you begin the Asanas. Have a warm shower first as a cleansed body promotes circulation and relaxes the muscles. There are some Asanas that are not appealing to the eyes, but learn to tackle them one step at a time. Perform Shavasana (the corpse position) or any other relaxation pose between each Asana and at the end of the session.

At the end of the session, after relaxing for at least 10 minutes, meditate for a while to further relax yourself.

2

The Pawanamuktasana and Shakti Vikasaka Series

A sanas, unlike other exercises, are postures to be held. They are performed slowly with deep abdominal breathing. There are three stages in each Asana — coming into the pose, holding the pose and coming out of the pose. Asanas work on all the major systems of the body. The Pawanamuktasana series ("wind releasing"), for instance, helps eliminate wind and acid from the joints and prevents stiffness of the muscles. The Shakti Vikasaka series ("strengthening exercises") loosens the joints and improves mobility. It also brings about the harmonious development of muscular tissues adjoining the joints.

The Pawanamuktasana and Shakti Vikasakas are mainly for beginners, helping them prepare for the more difficult Asanas later on. Performed at the beginning of the daily routines (see chapter 8), these Asanas are simple and require little physical effort. Yet, they are beneficial to the well being of the body. They regulate the *tri-doshas* (the three main constitutions of the body) and are used in therapy for arthritis and neuromuscular disorders. Furthermore, the Asanas for the eyes help strengthen eye muscles as well as help clear some eye disorders. Netra Shakti Vikasaka ("Asanas for strengthening the eyes") are to be performed without wearing glasses or contact lenses for maximum benefit.

Read the instructions for each Asana carefully first. Relax between each Asana, between each repetition of the Asana and at the end of the practice. Some of the Pawanamuktasana and Shakti Vikasaka Asanas involve rigorous breathing. Begin with normal breathing, and gradually introduce rigorous breathing. Never strain yourself (especially your eyes), and discontinue immediately if you are uncomfortable. Perform all Asanas with care and patience in a relaxed manner.

1. SAMASTHITI

This is a position of readiness for all Asanas performed in standing position.

- Stand straight with your feet together. The weight of the body is distributed evenly on your feet.
- Tighten your kneecaps and contract your hips.
- Push your chest out, and straighten your spine and neck.
- Keep your arms by the sides of your thighs.

2a

2. PURNA BHUJA SHAKTI VIKASAKA
[Developing the Arms]

Benefits: Strengthens the arms and shoulders. Relieves pain at arthritic joints. For better results, apply a hot towel to the affected region before doing the Asana. The hot towel loosens the joints, resulting in less restrictive movements.

<u>a</u>

- Stand or sit in Samasthiti.
- Keep your fingers and thumb together and stretch out your arms.
- Raise your arms sideways at shoulder level.
- Bring your thumb and fingertips together so that they touch and are tense.
- Bend your wrist and then your arms inwards, bringing your fingers and thumb close to your armpits. The elbows point sideways.
- Hold the position for a few seconds.
- Now straighten your arms by the sides at shoulder level.
- Stretch your wrists and then your fingers.

<u>b</u>

- At shoulder level, roll your arms so that your palms face up.
- Bring your fingertips and thumb together.
- Bend your wrist and then the elbows, bringing the bent fingers over your shoulders.
- Place the back of your fingers on top of your shoulders.
- Now raise your shoulders, and move the elbows towards each other behind your head.
- Hold the position for a few seconds.

2b

- Lower your shoulders and elbows.
- Straighten your arms at shoulder level.
- Stretch your wrists first and then your fingers.
- Roll your arms at shoulder level, and lower them by the sides of your body.
- Relax and repeat the Asana a couple of times.

3. BAHU SHAKTI VIKASAKA
[Strengthening the Arms]

Benefit: Improves the mobility of the wrist.

<u>a</u>

- Sit down, keeping your spine straight.
- Stretch out your arms in front, spreading your fingers.
- Clench your fists, with your thumbs inside, and hold them tight for a few seconds.
- Now stretch out your fingers with force.
- Repeat the Asana several times.

b
- Gently hold your left wrist with your right hand.
- Keeping your thumb and fingers together, move your left hand forwards and backwards several times.
- Similarly, holding your right wrist with your left hand, move your right hand forwards and backwards several times.

4. BHUJA VALLI SHAKTI VIKASAKA
[Strengthening the Arms]

Benefit: Eases stiffness in the arms and shoulder blades.

a
- Stand in Samasthiti
- Raise your left arm by the side so that the upper part of your arm touches your ear.
- Keep your fingers together and point them upwards.
- Now stretch your left arm as far up as possible.
- Hold the position for a count of 10, and then lower your arm.
- Perform the Asana with your right arm raised.

b
- Now raise both your arms.
- When your upper arms are by side of your ears, stretch your arms out upwards.

4b

5. BHUJA BANDHA SHAKTI VIKASAKA
[Strengthening the Upper Arms]

Benefit: Improves the flexibility of the elbows and shoulder joints.

- Stand in Samasthiti.
- Clench your fists, thumbs inside.
- Bending your arms at the elbows, raise your forearms. Keep your forearms parallel to the floor.
- Breathing normally, throw your arms forward, keeping them parallel to the floor at shoulder level.
- Now revert to the starting position.
- Repeat the Asana 10 to 15 times.

6. SKANDHA-TATHA BAHU-MULA SHAKTI VIKASAKA
[Strengthening the Shoulder Blades]

Benefits: Tones the nerves, blood vessels and shoulder muscles.

- Stand in Samasthiti.
- Clench your fists, thumbs inside.
- Keep your arms straight by the sides.
- Take a breath, and while holding your breath, blow out your cheeks.
- Now bring your chin close to the sternal notch (V-shape hollow area in front of your neck).
- Still holding your breath, move your shoulders up and down vigorously.
- Straighten your neck, and breathe out.
- Relax and repeat the Asana 5 times.

7. KAPHONI SHAKTI VIKASAKA
[Strengthening the Elbows]

Benefit: Improves blood circulation in the elbows and strengthens joints.

a
- Stand in Samasthiti.
- Clench your fists, thumbs inside.
- Raise your fists close to your shoulders with a jerk, and then lower them to the original position.
- Keep your upper arms still and stiff throughout.
- Repeat the Asana 10 times.

7a

b
• Perform the Asana in 7a again, but instead of clench-
  ing your fists, keep your hands with your palms facing
  up and fingers and thumb together.

8. MANI BANDHA SHAKTI VIKASAKA
   [Strengthening the Wrist]
Benefits: Tones the nerves and increases blood
circulation in the wrists.

a
• Stand in Samasthiti.
• Stretch your arms out in front at shoulder level.
• With loosely clenched fists, move your fists up and
  down with force 5 to 10 times before slowly lowering
  your arms to the sides.

b
• Stand in Samasthiti.
• Now raise your arms from the sides to shoulder level.
• Bend your arms at the elbows, bringing your wrists in
  front of your shoulders.
• Move your wrists as in 8a.

c
• Stand in Samasthiti.
• Now bring your arms in front at shoulder level.
• Clench your fists, thumbs inside.
• Rotate your fists in a clockwise and anti-clockwise di-
  rection 10 times.

9. KARA-PRUSTHA SHAKTI VIKASAKA
   [Strengthening the Palms]
Benefits: Stimulates the heart. Helps relieve and
strengthen tired wrists.

a
• Stand in Samasthiti.
• Stretch your arms out in front. Keep them parallel to
  the floor, with your hands open and fingers together.
• Bending your hands at the wrists, move them up and
  down 10 times.
• Lower your arms to the sides.

b
• Stand in Samasthiti.
• Stretch your arms out at shoulder level, keeping them
  parallel to the floor.
• Bend your arms at the elbows, bringing your hands in
  front of your shoulders.
• Bending your hands at the wrists, move them up and
  down 10 times.
• Stretch your arms to the sides and lower them.

c
• Now perform the Asana as in 9b, keeping your fingers
  spread as far apart as possible.

10. ANGULI MULA SHAKTI VIKASAKA
   [Strengthening the Finger Joints]
Benefit: Prevents stiffness in the fingers. Good for typists,
writers and musicians.

a
• Stand in Samasthiti.
• Raise your arms in front to shoulder level, keeping them
  parallel to the floor.
• Spread out your fingers, and tense your arms.
• Hold the position for a count of 20.
• Relax your fingers, and lower your arms.

b
• Stand in Samasthiti.
• Raise your arms in front to shoulder level, keeping them
  parallel to the floor.
• Spreading out your fingers and bending them at the
  knuckles, form the shape of a hooded cobra.

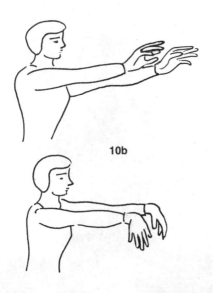

10b

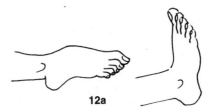

12a

- Keep your arms, including your fingers, stiff.
- Hold the position for a count of 20.

11. ANGULI SHAKTI VIKASAKA
[Toe Exercise]
Benefits: Keeps leg and toe tendons healthy and strong. Gives relief to arthritic conditions and gout. Relaxes hamstrings and relieves pain resulting from the inflammation of the sciatic nerve.

- Sit down with your spine straight and legs stretched out in front.
- Keep your heels and toes together.
- Without moving your ankle, move your toes backwards and forwards as many times as possible.

12. GULPASANA
[Ankle Exercise]
Benefits: Strengthens the ankles. Improves blood circulation. Good for people with arthritis and gout.

<u>a</u>
- Sit down with your spine straight and legs stretched out in front.
- Without moving your toes, move your ankles forwards and backwards several times.

<u>b</u>
- Now move feet apart, and make circles with your ankles, both in a clockwise and anticlockwise direction.

13. JANU SHAKTI VIKASAKA
[Knee Cranking]
Benefits: Strengthens the knees and relaxes the hamstrings. Good for sciatica and arthritis of the knees.

<u>a</u>
- Sit down with your spine straight.
- Bend your right leg at the knee.
- Hold any part of your right leg, preferably your foot or sole, with both your hands.
- Without bending your trunk forward, raise your leg, and try straightening it.
- If possible, bring your right knee towards your nose.
- Bend your right leg, and bring it down.

<u>b</u>
- Do the same with your left leg.
- Repeat the Asana 3 times.

14. NETRA SHAKTI VIKASAKA
[Strengthening the Eyes]
Benefits: Relaxes the nerves and prevents tension. Cures minor eye problems.

<u>a</u>
- Sit down with your legs stretched out in front.

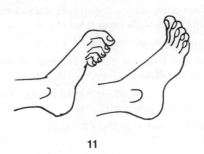

11

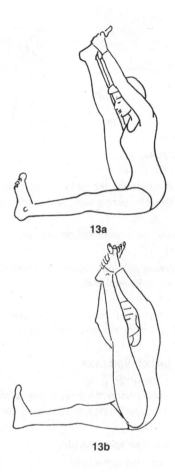

13a

13b

14d

- Place your left fist on your left knee, thumb pointing up.
- Raise your right arm to the side at shoulder level, thumb pointing up.
- Without moving your head, look at your left thumb and then your right thumb alternately.
- Repeat the Asana 10 times.
- Close your eyes, and visualise what was done during the Asana.
- Perform the Asana with your right hand on your right knee and your left arm raised at shoulder level.

d
- Sit down comfortably with your eyes closed facing the sunlight. Do not look towards the sun.
- Rub your palms until they become warm.
- Place your palms on your closed eyelids. Feel the warmth transmitted from your palms to your eyes.
- When your palms lose heat, rub them once more, and place them on your eyelids.
- Perform the Asana for about 2 minutes.

e
- Sit down with your legs stretched out in front.

- Place an object 3 metres away at eye level.
- Focus your eyes on the tip of your nose, and then shift your focus to the object.
- Repeat the Asana 5 times.

b
- Sit down with your legs stretched out in front.
- Raise your arms from the sides to shoulder level, thumbs pointing up.
- Without moving your head sideways, look at your left thumb, space in between your eyebrows and then your right thumb.
- Reverse the direction and repeat 5 times.

c
- Sit down with your legs stretched out in front.
- Keep your knees together.

- Place your left hand on your left knee and your right fist, thumb pointing up on your right leg.
- Keeping your right arm straight and without moving your head, hold your gaze on your right thumb.
- Raise your right arm to the front of your body. Keeping it straight and as high as possible and without tilting your head, move it to your left, down, right and back to the starting position again. In other words, make a complete circle with your stretched arm.
- Now move your arm in the opposite direction, making a similar circular movement.
- Perform 5 rounds both ways.
- Perform similarly with your left arm.

f
- Sit down with your legs stretched out in front.
- Keeping your arms straight, place your fists on your knees, thumbs pointing up.
- Without moving your head and keeping your eyes focused on your left thumb, raise your left arm as far up as possible.
- Still holding your gaze on your left thumb, lower your left arm onto your knee.
- Now shift your gaze to your right thumb, and raise your right arm as far up as possible.
- Repeat the Asana 5 times, raising and lowering your arms alternately.

Note: After performing each eye exercise, close your eyes, and rest them for at least 1 minute.

Relaxing the Jaw

- Yawn slowly, stretching your jaw muscles to the maximum.
- Hold the stretch for 5 seconds, and then release the pressure.
- Relax before repeating the Asana a couple of times.

Relaxing the Lips

- Purse and push forward your lips (the way you would when you kiss), concentrating on the sensation of tension felt.

- Hold the kissing position for 5 seconds, and then fully relax your lips.
- Repeat the Asana a few more times.

Relaxing the Tongue

- Close your mouth with the upper row of teeth touching the lower row. With the tip of your tongue, touch the roof of the mouth as far back as possible.
- Keep your tongue still for 5 seconds.
- Let go of the stretch so that your tongue "floats" in the mouth, its tip behind the lower row of teeth.
- Relax before performing this a couple of times.

Relaxing the Eyes

- Without moving your head, look to your left, right, up and then down as far as possible. Concentrate on the sensation of tension felt in the muscles that move the eyeballs, after which concentrate on the relaxation sweeping over you when closing your eyes.
- Relax and repeat the Asana 2 more times.

Relaxing the Brow
Benefit: Combats worries.
- Frown deeply, contracting the muscles of the brows.
- Maintain the frown for 5 seconds and then relax.

Relaxing the Scalp
Without moving your head and using conscious control, contract the muscles of your scalp forwards and backwards a few times with the help of your fingers and thumbs.

3

Asanas for Beginners

The Asanas in this chapter, because they are addressed to beginners of all ages, are simple. Yet, they are highly effective in regulating bodily functions. Mastering this group of Asanas will stand the beginners in good stead for the Asanas in chapters 4 and 5.

Learn the movements of each Asana by breathing normally. Once you have learnt how to do the movements correctly, try to synchronise your breathing with the movements. Closely follow instructions for breathing during a particular position. Do not try to assume the extreme positions from the start. The moderate and intermediate positions are just as important as the extreme ones. If you experience difficulty holding a position for the specified duration, come out of it immediately. The point of concentration for the holding position is given at the end of some Asanas. This is meant for those who can remain comfortable in a particular holding position for a longer period of time. Do not force yourself if you feel you are unable to hold for long.

Chapter Eight covers a 24-day programme for beginners. This is followed by 3 routines for beginners. The combination of Asanas that can be performed is also given. Follow the order. In addition, there are routines for the intermediate and advanced groups of learners.

Do not be discouraged if your progress seems slow at first, and your positions do not exactly resemble the photographs and illustrations. Regular practice will help bridge the gap.

1a   1b

1. BUMI PADA MASTAKASANA
[Headstand Modified]

Benefits: Brings calmness to the mind and increases the flow of blood to the brain and pituitary, helping to cure many forms of nervous and glandular disorders of the body. Improves the haemoglobin content of the blood, enhancing the general health and vitality of the mind and body. Perform the Asana after abdominal breathing Asanas (see chapter 6) and some form of relaxation. The following is a modified position:

a Stage 1
- Sit on your heels.
- Place your forearms with your fingers interlaced on a pillow or blanket.
- Place the top of your head (just above the forehead) on the blanket between your hands, with fingers intertwined behind your head. Remember to place the interlaced fingers and palms against the back of your head in order to keep the head in place. Arch your neck.
- Keep your elbows on the floor in front of your knees.
- Bend your toes inwards. Pressing them, raise your body slowly. Try to straighten your legs. Your entire body is resting on your toes, the top edge of your forehead and elbows or forearms.
- If the weight is not entirely felt on your head and arms or if your back is not straight, then walk your feet in as close as to your head as possible to reach a comfortable position. Hold the position for a count of twenty. Avoid straining your neck.
- By bending your knees towards your chest, lower them to the floor, and bring your trunk close to your thighs.

- Remain in this position for a count of twenty.
- Now perform Shavasana (refer to Asana 47) for 1–2 minutes.
- Once comfortable in the above position, move on to Stage 2.

b Stage 2
- Bend your knees a little, bringing them closer to your chest.
- Lift your feet off the floor and bring your heels close to the buttocks.
- Keep your spine straight. Feel the weight of your whole body on your head and elbows.
- Hold the position for a count of twenty.
- Slowly lower your feet to the floor.
- Again, by bending your knees towards your chest, lower them to the floor, and bring your trunk close to your thighs.
- Relax with your head down.
- Hold the position for the same length of time.
- Now perform Shavasana for 1–2 minutes.
- After mastering the balance, hold the position for a longer period of time. Bear the whole weight mainly on your head. Keep your elbows and shoulders in line, and elbows should not be wide apart. Do not push the waist and pelvic region forward. Make sure your legs are together while raising and lowering them.

Caution: People with high blood pressure, low blood pressure, vertigo, heart palpitations, thrombosis or chronic catarrh should not perform this Asana. Beginners are advised to perform this Asana at end of their Yoga

The ideas, suggestions, herbal remedies and diet contained in this book are not intended as a substitue for consulting with your doctor. All matters regarding your health require medical supervision.

session. If the Asana is performed before a Yoga session, do not perform any vigorous Asanas immediately after it. If there is any discomfort, discontinue the Asana. Do not repeat it in the same session.

Concentration: Sahasrara Chakra (the pituitary and pineal glands). For an explanation of the Chakras, see chapter 7. The brain is the centre of Sattvaguna qualities, which control mental power. The trunk has Rajoguna qualities, which control passion, while the body below the diaphragm is the centre for Tamoguna, which controls sensual pressure. The Bumi Pada Mastakasana and Shirasasana (see chapter 5) help develop harmony among these three *gunas* of the body.

2. VIPAREETA KARANI MUDRA
[Shoulderstand Preliminary Pose]

Benefits: Stimulates the thyroid gland, including the circulatory and reproductive systems.

Mostly practised by women, the Asana is performed before a complete Shoulderstand is attempted.

- Lie down flat on the floor, with your hands, palms down, by your sides.
- Exhaling, swing both your legs upwards.
- Rest your elbows on the floor, and lift your hips and trunk off the floor. Do not use force to bring your chin close to your chest. Also, do not use force to make your spine and back straight.
- Support your body with both your hands, placing them on either side of the spine.

To come out of Vipareeta Karani Mudra,

a
- Slowly lower your legs to the floor. Do not raise your head and do not jerk or bend your legs while lowering them.
- When your trunk and legs reach the floor, lie there for a while as you would in Shavasana.

or

b
- Slowly bend your knees towards your chest.
- Keeping your head close to your knees, roll back on the floor to a sitting position.

2

- Now stretch your legs and sit down for a while, keeping your head lowered for some time before lying down on your back.

Caution: Beginners should remain in the position for only a few seconds. Gradually increase the holding time.

3. SARVANGASANA
[Shoulderstand]

Benefits: Stimulates the thyroid gland and regulates the circulatory, nervous and reproductive systems. Activates the endocrinal glands.

Sarvangasana is called the "Mother of Asanas" because it brings about harmony and happiness to the body.

- Lie down on your back, keeping your arms, palms down, by your sides.
- Exhaling, swing both your legs upwards.
- Now lift your hips and trunk off the floor.

• Rest your elbows on the floor, and support your back with both your hands, placing them on either side of your spine. Press your chin firmly into the base of your throat. Keep your legs straight, with your toes in line with your eyes. Maintain a right angle pose with your chest and trunk, and neck. Rest the weight of your body on your shoulders.

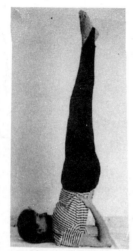

3

Caution: Breathe normally while holding the pose. The counter pose is Poorva Uttana Padasana [Simple Fish] in this chapter. Perform it after the Shoulderstand. The duration of the counter pose should be at least one third the time given for Sarvangasana. People with enlarged thyroid gland, liver or spleen, high blood pressure or heart ailments should not perform this exercise.

Concentration: Vishuddhi Chakra (the thyroid gland).

4. POORVA HALASANA
[Plough Preliminary Pose]

Benefits: Stretches the pelvis and activates the kidneys and intestines. Helps to normalise blood pressure.
The Asana is meant for people with weak backs and neck problems.

• Lie down on your back and place your arms, palms down and spread out a little, under your buttocks.
• Breathe out and raise your legs to a vertical position and bring them overhead.
• Keep your legs apart but straight.
• Breathe normally for a count of 30 or stay in the position until you are comfortable.
• Inhale and slowly lower your back and legs to the floor.
• Increase the holding time gradually and relax after the Asana.

Caution: People with a slipped disc or sciatica should not perform this Asana.

Concentration: Vishuddhi Chakra (the thyroid gland).

5. HALASANA
[Plough 1]

Benefits: Improves the functioning of the liver, kidneys and pancreas. Tones spinal nerves and regulates the functioning of the thyroid and adrenal glands. Good for those with diabetes, piles and digestive disorders like indigestion or constipation.

• Lie down on your back and place your arms by the sides with palms down.
• Breathe out completely and use the rectus muscles to lift up your legs, making sure not to bend them.
• Keep your arms on the floor and clasp your hands together if possible.
• Try to touch the floor with your toes without bending your knees. In the final position, press your chin firmly into the base of your throat. Do not strain your back. If you are not confident initially, place your hands on the back for support. If you cannot hold the position comfortably, then place your hands on the back itself.
• For starters, hold the position for a count of 30 and then increase the time slowly.

To come out of Halasana:

• Retain your breath out, bend your knees towards your forehead, and bring your heels close to your hips.
• Roll forward as in a Sarvangasana [Shoulderstand], bending forward into the Backstretch position.

or

• Stretch your legs up and without raising your head, slowly lower your back and legs to the floor.
• Relax until your breathing becomes normal.

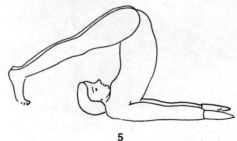

5

Caution: People with sciatica, back pain or slipped disc should not perform Halasana and all its variations. Halasana is best performed after Sarvangasana [Shoulderstand]. After Halasana, perform Poorva Uttana Padasana [Simple Fish] or Supta Vajrasana [Backward Bend] for at least one third of the holding period for Halasana.

Concentration: Vishuddhi Chakra (the thyroid gland) or on Manipura (the adrenal glands), depending on the position.

6. KANDARSANASANA
   [Plough 2]

Benefits: Same as Halasana.

• Perform Halasana.

• Now bring your arms over your head slowly.

• Bend your arms at the elbows and clasp hands together on top of your head.

or

• Lie down on your back.

• Clasp your hands together on top of your head.

• As in Halasana [Plough 1], breathe out completely and use the rectus muscles to lift up your legs, making sure not to bend them.

• Now touch the floor with your toes. Keep your legs straight and press your chin firmly into the base of your throat.

• Hold the position for a count of 30.

To come out of Kandarsanasana:
Come out as in Halasana.

6

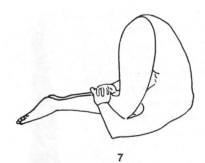
7

Concentration: Swadisthana Chakra (gonads/ovaries).

7. KARNA PEEDASANA
   [Plough 3]

Benefits: Activates the thyroid and adrenal glands. Stimulates the spinal nerves and massages the abdominal organs. Increases circulation in the abdominal area.

• Assume Kandarsanasana.

• Once in a comfortable position, bend your knees to touch your shoulders.

• Sandwich your head between your knees.

• Fold your arms behind your knees and clasp your hands together.

• Hold the position for a count of 30.

• Release the clasped hands, stretch your arms and bring them back to the floor.

To come out of Karna Peedasana:
Same as Halasana.

Concentration: Manipura Chakra (the adrenal glands).

8. POORVA UTTANA PADASANA
   [Simple Fish]

Benefits: Stimulates the adrenal and prostate glands. Improves the functioning of the reproductive and nervous systems.

The following is the simplest fish pose for beginners:

• Lie down on your back.

• Raise your shoulders and arch your neck backward so that the very top of your head rests on the floor.

- Keep your arms on the floor by the sides of your body. Look as far down as possible.
- Hold the position for at least a third of the time given for Sarvangasana [Shoulderstand].
- Now straighten your trunk and head.

9. SUPTA VAJRASANA
[Backward Bend]

Benefits: Improves blood circulation and tones the nervous system. Stimulates the prostate glands and kidneys.

a
- Sit in Vajrasana (see Asana 24) and keep your legs folded at the knees.
- Place your palms on the floor behind your toes.
- Arch your spine backward by expanding your chest and raising your shoulders.
- Now drop your head slowly.
- Stay in the position for a count of 15.

9b

b
- Now look to left and lower your left elbow to the floor.
- Look to the right and lower your right elbow.
- Arch the back until the top of your head touches the floor.
- Release the pressure on your elbows, and place your arms by the sides of your thighs.
- Keeping your neck arched backward, shift the weight of your body onto one of your folded legs, and stretch the other leg.
- Similarly release the leg.
- Now straighten your back, followed by your neck.

Concentration: Manipura Chakra (the adrenal glands).

10. JANGHA SHAKTI VIKASANA
[Dancers 1]

Benefits: Improves the balance and limbers up joints. Strengthens the feet, knees and thighs.

- Stand with your feet a foot apart.
- Stretch your arms out, palms down, at shoulder level.
- Now stand on your toes. Keep your spine erect and do not lean forward.
- Breathe out, and lower your trunk until you reach a squatting position.

10

- When your thighs are parallel to the floor, breathe in and raise your trunk.

Caution: People who suffer from constant headaches and high blood pressure should avoid performing this Asana.

11. URVASANA
[Dancers 2]

Benefits: Helps to prevent arthritis of the knees and hip joints.

a
- Stand in Samasthiti (see chapter 2).
- Breathe in, and while doing this raise your arms over your head.
- Breathe out and while doing this, bend your elbows, and place your wrists on top of your head, palms together.
- Keep your elbows by your sides, and push your chest slightly forward.
- Now slowly stand on your toes.

b
- Exhale, and while doing this keep your knees together and your spine erect. While exhaling, squat down until your thighs are parallel to the floor.
- Inhale and come to a standing position on your toes.

11a   **11b**

Caution: People who suffer from high blood pressure, tension or headaches should avoid this Asana.

12. PADANGULI SHAKTI VIKASAKA
   [Dancers 3]
Benefits: Strengthens the knees, shoulders, ankles and hip joints.

• Stand in Samasthiti.
• As in Dancers 2, bend your elbows, and place your wrists on top of your head, palms together.
• Keep your chin up and elbows pointing to your sides.
• Maintain an erect spine, and rise high on your toes.

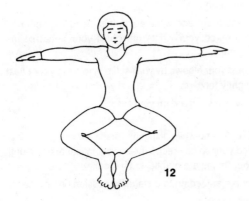

12

• Exhale, and while doing this lower your trunk, spread your arms by your sides. At the same time, spread your knees apart. Your arms and thighs must be parallel to the floor by the time the final squatting position is achieved.
• Still remaining high on your toes, inhale, and while doing this, raise your trunk and bring your knees closer together. At the same time, bend your arms to bring them to the original position.
• While squatting down, synchronise the spreading of your arms with your exhalation. While straightening your trunk, synchronise your arm movement with your inhalation.

Caution: People who suffer from high blood pressure or headaches because of tension should avoid this Asana.

13. URDHVA EKA HASTOTTANASANA
   [Side Bend Single Arm]
Benefits: Tones muscles and increases the flexibility of shoulder blades. Good for shoulder arthritis.

<u>a</u>
• Stand in Samasthiti.
• Breathe in, and while doing this raise your right arm.

<u>b</u>
• When your arm is at shoulder level, roll it so your palm faces up (when you start, your palm faces down). Continue raising it.
• When your upper arm is by the side of the right ear, breathe out, and while doing this pull your left arm down at the left side and stretch your right arm upwards.
• Keep the body in a vertical plane, and do not twist or bend your trunk forward. Alternatively, you can stand against the wall, and keep your shoulder blades and back touching the wall throughout the exercise.
• Feel the stretch on one side of the trunk.
• Hold the position for a breath.
• Inhale, and while doing this, straighten your trunk.

<u>c</u>
• Now exhale, and while doing this lower your right arm, rolling it at shoulder level. Raise your left arm.

<u>d</u>
• Bend towards the right.
• Repeat the Asana twice on each side.

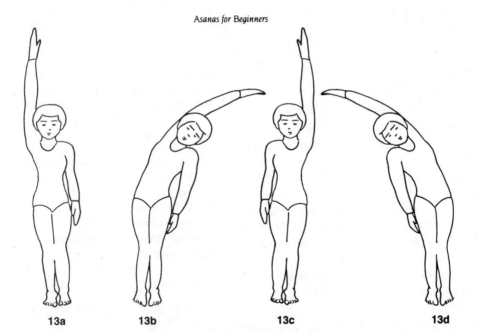

13a   13b   13c   13d

14. URDHVA HASTOTTANASANA
   [Side Bend]

Benefits: Same as Urdhva Eka Hastottanasana.

This is done the same way as Urdhva Eka Hastottanasana but with both arms raised.

<u>a</u>

• Stand in Samasthiti.

• Inhale, and while doing this raise your arms.

• When your arms are parallel to the floor, roll them at your shoulders, and bring them over your head.

• Keep your arms parallel to each other, palms facing each other.

<u>b</u>

• Exhale, and while doing this bend your body to the left to a moderate position. This can be achieved by stretching your right side and compressing the left.

• Hold the position for a count of 10.

• Inhale, and straighten your trunk.

• Exhale, and while doing this continue to bend the same way to the right.

• Hold the position for the same duration.

• Inhale and, straighten your trunk.

14a

• Increase the angle of the bend gradually. Do not strain.

• Repeat this twice on each side.

• When your trunk is upright, lower your arms, and breathe out.

15. TRIKONASANA
   [Triangle Simple]

Benefits: Good for people suffering from nervous depression. Relieves spinal nerves and lower back muscles. Makes the spine flexible. Increases the circulation of blood to the entire body. Helps to prevent arthritis in shoulders and hip joints. Activates the adrenal glands, and besides relieving constipation gives a gentle massage to the abdominal organs.

<u>a</u>

• Stand in Samasthiti.

• Stretch your arms out at shoulder level.

• Spread your feet apart by about two feet, with toes pointing slightly inward.

• Keep your arms straight, breathe out, and bend your trunk to the left side.

• Place your left hand on your left knee.

• Roll your right arm at your shoulder.

• Breathe in, and while doing this, bring your right arm over your right ear, palm facing down.

The ideas, suggestions, herbal remedies and diet contained in this book are not intended as a substitue for consulting with your doctor. All matters regarding your health require medical supervision.

- Relax your head on your left shoulder.
- Hold the position for a count of 10.
- Now breathe out, and raise your right arm.
- Bring your left arm in line with the right.
- When your arms are in a straight line, breathe in and straighten up.
- Repeat the Asana on the right side.

<u>b</u>
- Keep your trunk upright and your arms stretched out by your sides. Spread your feet apart slightly more.
- Breathe out, bend to the left, a little more than in 15a. Place your left palm on your shin.
- Breathe out, stretch the right side of your trunk, and bring your right arm over your right ear.
- Hold the position for a count of 10.
- Come up as in 15a, and perform Asana on the right side.

15b

<u>c</u>
- Now spread your feet as far apart as possible.
- Bend your trunk to the left.
- If you can, place your left palm on your ankle, and bring your right arm over the ear parallel to ground.
- Hold the position for 10 seconds, and come out as before.
- Perform the same way on your right side.
- When your trunk is upright, bring your feet together, breathe out, and lower your arms to your sides.

Caution: Pregnant women should not perform this Asana. In the beginning, do not perform the extreme bending position. Bend only to some extent but repeat the bend several times. Increase your bend gradually without holding. Continuous movement helps to increase the mobility. Do not lean forward to achieve the extreme bending position. Beginners must take care not to overstretch.

16. DWIKONASANA
   [Chest Expansion 1]
Benefits: Strengthens the muscles between shoulder blades, chest and neck.

<u>a</u>
- Stand in Samasthiti.
- Inhale, and while doing this stretch your arms out at shoulder level.
- Roll your arms so that your palms face the front.
- Bend your elbows, and bring your hands in front of your chest. The middle fingers must touch each other, with thumbs pointing downwards.
- Stretch your arms forward, and feel the tension in your elbows.

<u>b</u>
- As you breathe in deeply, spread out your stretched arms, and stretch them as far behind as possible.
- Now lower your arms.
- Clasp your hands together behind your back.

<u>c</u>
- As you inhale, raise your arms, and bend your spine backward to a moderate position.
- Hold the position for a count of 10.
- Straighten your trunk and keeping your arms raised, exhale. Bend forward to a moderate position.

<u>d</u>
- Drop your head, and raise your clasped hands as high as possible.
- Breathe normally, and hold the position for a count of 30.
- Breathe in, and slowly straighten your trunk.
- As you inhale, arch your back a little more than before.
- Hold the position for a count of 10.
- Straighten your trunk and keeping your arms raised and exhaling, bend forward a little more than before.

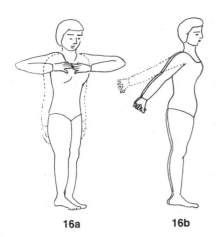

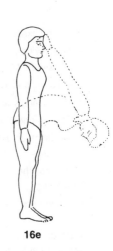

| 16a | 16b | 16c | 16d | 16e |

- Hold the position for a count of 30.
- As you breathe in, straighten your trunk.

e
- For the third time, arch your back to a comfortable extreme position.
- Hold the position for a count of 10.
- Straighten your trunk.
- Breathe out, and bend forward to an extreme comfortable position.
- Hold the position for a count of 30, and straighten your trunk as before.
- When you are in an upright position, release your clasped hands and relax.

Note: If you find it difficult to keep your arms straight, do not clasp your hands together. Instead, hold a wooden rod, and roll your arms at the shoulders.

17. ARDHA CHAKRASANA
[Chest Expansion 2]

Benefits: Improves your sense of balance. Helps relieve hip, shoulder and knee arthritis. Good Asana for relaxation, because it relieves tension in your neck.
This is similar to Dwikonasana [Chest Expansion 1]. The difference lies in the positioning of your feet.

a
- Stand in Samasthiti.
- As in Dwikonasana [Chest Expansion 1], clasp your hands together at the back.

- Keeping your knees together, bend your right knee, and extend your left leg forward.
- As you exhale, bend forward, and at the same time raise arms as high as possible.
- Bring your forehead towards your left knee.
- Hold the position for a count of 10.
- Straighten your trunk.
- Now bring in your left leg.
- Extend your right leg forward, and perform as before.
- Straighten your trunk, and release your clasped hands.

b
- Keeping your knees together, bend your right knee, and extend your left leg forward.
- As you press your left heel, roll your left leg so that your left toes point to the left side, and the back of your left knee touches the inner side of your right knee.

17a

- As you exhale, breathe out, bend your trunk to the front.
- Now swing your trunk, twisting at your waist, to the left so your forehead faces your left knee.
- Hold the position for a count of 10.
- Now swing your trunk to the front.
- As you inhale, straighten your trunk.
- Adjust your left foot, bring your feet together, and straighten your legs.
- Perform the Asana on other side by extending your right leg.
- Repeat once again on both sides.

Caution: Pregnant women should avoid this Asana, as should people with vertigo and high blood pressure.

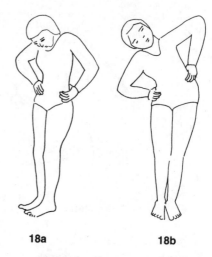

18a   18b

18. UTTITA CHAKRASANA
   [Circular Motion]
Benefit: Trims the waistline.

a
- Stand in Samasthiti.
- Place your palms on your waist.
- Keep your elbows in line with your body by your sides and your shoulders relaxed throughout.
- As you exhale, bend your trunk forward to a moderate position, compressing your abdominal area
- Hold the position for a breath.
- As you exhale, roll and twist your body to the left so that left side of the waist is compressed and the right is stretched. Remember that the chest must face the front.
- Now drop your head to the left side.
- Inhale and as you exhale, continue to roll, and twist your trunk at the waist to the back so that the abdominal area is stretched and the back of the waist is slightly compressed.
- Now drop your head back, and take a breath.
- As you exhale, roll your trunk to the right.
- Maintain the position and inhale. As you exhale, continue rolling your body to the front. Repeat this movement in the reverse order.
- After a complete clockwise and anti-clockwise rotation, compress your waist a little more on each side, and repeat the Asana again.

b
- Now perform the Asana once again by increasing the bending and compression on the right and left sides.
- Roll, and twist your trunk at the waist, not at the hip joint.

19. PADAHASTASANA
   [Legclasp]
Benefits: Tones the abdominal organs, activates the liver and spleen, relaxes the back muscles, stimulates the spinal nerves, clears constipation problems and improves the circulation to the brain.

a
- Stand in Samasthiti.
- Slowly bend forward.
- Place your palms behind your knees, and clasp your fingers together.
- Draw in your trunk slowly.
- Hold the position for a count of 10.

b
- Relax, and slide your palms further down your calf muscles.
- Again, draw in your trunk.
- Hold the position for a count of 10.

19a

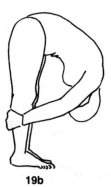
19b

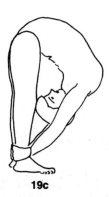
19c

<u>c</u>
- Relax, glide your palms behind the ankle, and draw in your trunk.
- Hold the position for a count of 10.
- Relax, and drop your arms.
- As you breathe in, come up to an upright position very slowly.

Caution: People with severe back ailments should avoid this Asana.

20. UTTITA LOLASANA
[Dangling]
Benefits: Relaxes the back muscles, stimulates the spinal nerves, clears constipation problems and improves the circulation to the brain.

<u>a</u>
- Stand straight with your feet apart.
- Drop your arms in front.

<u>b</u>
- Gently bend your trunk forward at the waist.
- While bending forward, sway your head and trunk.

<u>c</u>
- Once in a comfortable position, stretch your lower back gently by slowly swinging your trunk forward.
- Hold the position for a count of 10.
- As you breathe in, swing your trunk gracefully, and come up to an upright position.

Caution: People suffering from vertigo or high blood pressure should avoid this Asana.

21. MARJARIASANA
[Cat Pose]
Benefits: Improves the flexibility of the neck, shoulders and spine. Relieves menstrual cramps, and strengthens the reproductive system. Pregnant women get the most benefit from this Asana for the first 3 months of their pregnancy. They should, however, not suck in or snap the abdomen.

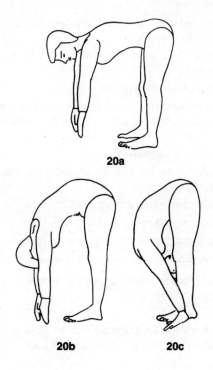
20a

20b   **20c**

The ideas, suggestions, herbal remedies and diet contained in this book are not intended as a substitue for consulting with your doctor. All matters regarding your health require medical supervision.

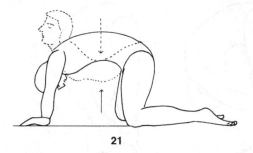

21

- Kneel down on your knees with your palms and spine parallel to the floor. Remember the following: your arms (at the shoulder width level) and thighs must be perpendicular to the floor and parallel to one another. Keep your arms straight throughout the Asana. The knees may be slightly apart.
- Keep your back arched upwards, and drop your head.
- Tilt your head by arching your neck back.
- As you breathe in, arch your back inward with your spine moving towards the floor.
- Raise your shoulders upwards, and move your trunk forward and up.
- Allow your chest to expand fully. Feel the stretch on the herniacal region.
- As you exhale, move your trunk backward and hunch your back.
- Now drop your head inward.
- Once you reach the starting position, continue to move your trunk further back. Notice that in this position your arms and thighs are at an angle.
- Breathe out completely.
- As you breathe out, pull your organs of the abdomen towards the rib cage.
- Hold the position for a count of 10.
- Do not strain yourself.
- Snap out of the pull with force, and breathe normally.
- Relax, and repeat the Asana 3 to 5 times.

Caution: For period therapy, perform the Asana without sucking in the abdomen.

Note: Asanas in the sitting position are done in Suka, Veera, Vajra, Padma, Siddha and Swastika. These

Asanas bring about steadiness. Generally, in these Asanas, the head, neck, and trunk are in one straight line. Stick to one that gives you the most comfort. If there is severe pain in the legs after some time, unlock them. To start with, sit for a few minutes, and gradually increase the time. Regular practice, improves the posture and brings about comfort.

22. SUKASANA
[Easy Pose]
Benefits: This Asana, a comfortable cross-legged position, is suitable for people who cannot sit in more complicated Asanas despite repeated attempts.
- Sit cross-legged on the floor.
- Keep your head, neck and trunk in one straight line for a while.

22

23. VEERASANA
[Hero, Warrior or Champion Pose]
Benefits: Relieves rheumatic pain in the knees and heaviness in the stomach. Good for people who are flat-footed.
- Sit down on the floor with your feet stretched out in front.
- Now bend your left leg outwards, bringing your left foot beside your left hip. Similarly bend your right leg, bringing your right foot beside your right hip.
- Keep your knees together, and rest your buttocks on the floor between your feet. The inner side of each calf touches the outer side of the respective thigh.

23

25

24. VAJRASANA
   [Sitting Thunderbolt]
Benefits: Improves the circulation and condition of nervous stability. Strengthens the pelvic and visceral regions.

- Kneel down on the floor.
- Rest your thighs on your legs and buttocks on the soles of your feet.
- Keep the spine straight, and point your toes of your left and right feet towards each other.
- Place your palms on your thighs.

25. PADMASANA
   [Lotus Pose]
Benefits: Tones the sacral nerves and calms the mind.

- Sit down on the floor with your legs stretched out in front.
- Fold one leg, and place its foot on top of the other thigh. The sole must face up. The heel must be as close to the pelvic area as possible.
- Fold the other leg, and place its foot on top of the folded thigh. Keep your spine straight throughout the Asana.

Caution: People with sciatica or sacral infections should avoid this Asana.

26. SWASTIKASANA
   [Auspicious Pose]
Benefits: Activates the nerve plexus of the reproductive system.

- Get into a comfortable sitting position.
- Fold the left leg, and place the foot near the right thigh.
- Similarly place the right foot, and push it in between the left thigh and calf. The toes must be between the thigh and calf of the other leg.
- Place your hands on your knees. Keep your spine straight.

Caution: People with sciatica or sacral infections should avoid this Asana.

26

27. SAMKATANASANA
   [Dangerous Pose]
Benefits: Renders hip joints mobile and clears arthritic conditions in the joints.

<u>a</u>
- Sit down on the floor.

- Place the right foot on the floor by the side of the left buttock. Your right knee must touch the floor.

b

- Bend the left leg, and bring the left foot to the floor by the side of the right buttock. Your left knee must be placed on your right knee.
- Hold the position for a while.
- Interchange the position of legs, and hold the position for the same period of time.

Caution: People who have inflammation of the knee or ankle joints should not perform this Asana.

27a   27b

28. NAUKA SANCAHALANA
[Rowing the Boat]

Benefits: Massages the abdominal organs and tones the muscles in the area. Pregnant women are encouraged to do this Asana for the first 3 months of their pregnancy.

- Sit with your legs stretched out in front. Keep them together.
- Bend the body forwards and backwards, and at same time, bend your arms at your elbows. Note that the motion is similar to rowing a boat.
- While bending forward, breathe out, and breathe in while moving backward to a leaning back position.
- Contract the abdominal area while bending forward.

Caution: People suffering from sciatica should avoid this Asana.

29. CHAKKI CHALANA
[Churning the Mill]

Benefits: Strengthens the uterine muscles and tones the abdominal muscles. Pregnant women are encouraged to do this Asana for the first 3 months of their pregnancy.

- Sit down comfortably with your legs stretched out in front.

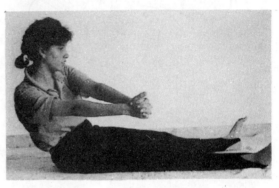

29

- Clasp your hands together in front of you.
- Keep your arms straight at shoulder level.
- Now move your body from the waist level so that your arms make a circular movement.
- Keep your arms taut and parallel to the floor throughout the Asana.
- Do the circular movement both clockwise and anticlockwise. Start with smaller circles, and gradually increase the radius of the circles.

30. DRUTA HASTASANA
[Chopping The Wood]

Benefits: Strengthens the sacral and vaginal muscles. For women, it develops their breasts. Good for pregnant women as it results in an easy childbirth.

- Sit down in a squatting position with your feet flat on the floor and your knees apart.
- Keeping your arms straight, clasp your hands together, and move your arms up and down as if chopping wood.
- Inhale while raising your arms and exhale while lowering them.

Note: If you find it difficult to squat, perform the Asana standing. Also, instead of moving your arms together, raise your arms up and down alternately as if pulling a vertical rope.

31. GOMUKHASANA
[Posture Clasp]

Benefits: Stimulates the abdomen. Strengthens the nerves and muscles of the legs and thighs. Increases the mobility of the shoulder blades. Relieves cramps in the legs and shoulders.

- Sit in Samkatasana, Padmasana or in any comfortable position.
- Keep your spine straight.
- As you breathe in, stretch your right arm out at shoulder level. Keep it straight.
- Roll your shoulder, and as you breathe in, continue raising your arm by the side of the right ear.
- Bend your right arm.
- Keep your right elbow behind your head.
- Bend your left arm, and bring it behind your back. It must face outwards between the shoulder blades.
- Lock your fingers. Use a towel if you find it difficult to do this.
- As you breathe in, pull your arms up.

30

- Hold your breath
- As you breathe out, pull your arms down.
- Hold your breath out.
- Repeat this twice.
- Lower your left arm.
- Straighten your right arm, and as you breathe out, bring it to shoulder level.
- Roll your shoulder, and lower your arm, palm facing down.
- Change the position of your legs if sitting in Samkatasana or in Padmasana.
- Now perform on the left side by raising your left arm and keeping your right hand behind your back.

Variation of Gomukhasana

This is a simpler version of the posture clasp for people who are unable to lock their fingers easily and who suffer from discomfort in the shoulder joints.

- Stretch your left arm out at shoulder level.
- Roll your arm so that the palm faces up, and raise your arm further.
- Bring your elbow behind your head, and bend your arm at the elbow so your palm is on the right shoulder blade.
- Similarly place your right palm onto the left shoulder blade.
- Pull your arms and shoulders, and bring your elbows closer together.
- Hold the position for a count of 10.
- Release the stretch.
- Raise and lower your shoulder blades a couple of times.
- Now stretch your right arm, and when your arm is at shoulder level, lower it to the side after rolling the shoulder.
- Similarly bring your left arm back to its original position.

Concentration: Ajna Chakra (the pituitary glands).

32. BADDHA KONASANA
[Knee and Thigh Stretch]

Benefits: Increases the circulation of blood to the pelvis,

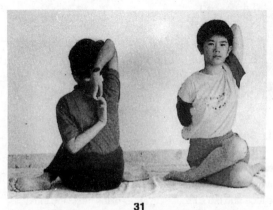

31

kidneys, back, prostate glands and abdomen. Good for those suffering from urinary disorders and back pain. Helps regulate menstrual disorders. Relieves sciatic pain and prevents hernia. Pregnant women are encouraged to perform this Asana regularly during the nine months of pregnancy to prevent varicose veins and strengthen the uterus muscles. Also good for an easy childbirth.

- Sit down, and keep your spine straight. If this is difficult, use a wall to sit straight.
- Bring the soles of your feet together.
- Hold your feet together with your palms.
- Pull your feet in towards the body without raising your heels from the floor.
- As you breathe in, lower your knees, bringing them as close to the floor as possible.
- Hold the position for a count of 10.
- Do not bend your body forward while lowering your knees to the floor.
- As you breathe out, raise your knees.
- Lower and raise your knees 2 more times.

Variation of Baddha Konasana

- When your knees are on the floor by your sides, breathe out.

32

- Bend your trunk forward, bringing your head close to the floor.
- Hold the position for a count of 10.
- As you breathe in, straighten your trunk.
- As you raise your knees, breathe out.
- Repeat the Asana 2 times.

33. DRUTA GRIVASANA
   [Neck Movement]

Benefits: Good for releasing tension and for relieving an arthritic condition in the neck.

a
- Sit down on the floor, keeping your palms by your sides on the floor. Keep your spine straight.
- Without moving your trunk and shoulders, bend your

neck forward, bringing your chin close to your chest.
- Hold the position for a count of 10.
- Now straighten your neck.
- Drop your neck backward, gently stretching the throat area.
- Hold the position for a count of 10.
- Again straighten your neck.

b
- Now, without twisting your neck to the left, bend your neck, placing your left ear above your left shoulder.
- Hold the position for a count of 10.
- For the last movement in this Asana, bring your neck to an upright position, and bend it to the right the same way as before.
- Hold the position for a count of 10.

33a

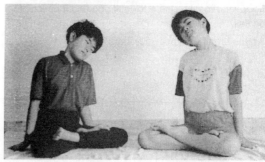

33b

34. SIMHASANA
   [Lion Pose]

Benefits: Stimulates the liver and thyroid gland and controls bile production. Increases blood circulation to the face and the surrounding areas of the neck and throat. Relieves pain in the coccyx region. Helps people suffering from asthma as well as those with a stutter. Prevents arthritic condition in the joints.

• Sit down on your feet with your toes bent, and place your palms on your knees.

• Keep your arms straight, and spread your fingers as far out as possible.

• Pull your shoulders back to push out your chest.

• Tilt your neck, and as you breathe out, stretch your tongue as far down as possible.

• Bring as much tension as possible to your face and neck.

• Breathe normally, and hold the position for a count of 20.

• As you breathe in through your nose and mouth, withdraw your tongue very slowly.

• Relax, and repeat the Asana twice.

Concentration: Anahatha Chakra (the thymus glands).

Simhasana in Padmasana

• Sit in the Lotus Pose.

• Extend your arms in front, and place your palms on the floor, fingers stretched out.

• Now stand on your knees, and arch your spine so your chest expands. Remember that the pelvic region and the front of your knees must be on the floor.

• Open your eyes wide.

• Open your mouth wide, and as you breathe out, stretch out your tongue as far down as possible.

• Breathe in and out through your mouth and nose.

• Hold the position with tension for a few seconds.

• As you breathe in through your mouth, withdraw your tongue very slowly.

• Now relax.

• Come back to the Lotus sitting position.

• Repeat the Asana twice.

Caution: People suffering from a slipped disc, sciatica, and high blood pressure should avoid this Asana.

Concentration: Anahatha Chakra (the thymus glands).

35. GUPTA PADMASANA
[Hidden Lotus Pose]

Benefits: Relieves back pain.

• After performing Padma Simhasana [Lion Pose in Lotus], slowly lower your body forward, bringing your chest and chin to touch the floor.

• Bring your arms behind your back and fold them like the Indian greeting *namaste*.

• Hold the position to your comfort.

36. ARDHA MATSYENDRASANA
[Half Twist]

Benefits: Stimulates the peristaltic motion in the intestines. Prevents bladder problems and the enlargement of the prostate gland.

35

a

• Stretch out your legs in front.

• Bend your left leg, and place your left foot on the outer side of your right knee. Keep your left knee in an upright position.

b

• Place your left hand on the floor by the side of your left hip or just behind it.

c

• Bring your right arm over your left knee such that your right hand holds your right knee or left ankle.

• Bring your chin close to your left shoulder.

• As you breathe out, twist your trunk, as far as possible, towards the left. Do not bend your left arm while doing this.

• Breathing normally, hold the position for a count of 20.

• As you breathe out, twist your trunk and then your neck forward. Do this twice, each time increasing the intensity of the twisting on the left side.

• Now change the position of your legs, and perform the Asana on the right side.

Note: If you find it difficult to hold your right knee or the left ankle, use your right palm to hold your left knee, and pull your left thigh towards your trunk. Alternatively, you can place your right elbow on the outer side of the left thigh, and press the thigh inward. In some cases, it may be difficult to bring your left foot to the outer side of your right leg. This may be due to arthritis of the hip joints or distention of the abdominal area. If you cannot hold your

36a

36b

36c

right knee with your right hand, then hold your left knee, which is an upright position.

Concentration: Ajna Chakra (the pituitary glands).

37. MATSYENDRASANA
   [Full Twist]

Benefits: Acts on the synovial fluid in the joints, thereby helping rheumatic patients. Tones the abdominal muscles and activates the pancreas. Improves the efficient functioning of the nervous system.

a
• Sit with your legs stretched out in front.
• Bend your right knee, and place your right sole against the inner side of your left thigh. Your right knee is on the floor.

b
• Bend your left knee, and place your left foot on the floor by the outer side of your right knee, all the while keeping your left knee in an upright position.

c
• Place your left hand on the floor behind the left side of your hip.

d
• Bring your right arm over your left knee, and hold your right knee.
• Bring your chin close to your left shoulder.
• As you breathe out, twist your trunk to the left.
• If possible, bring your left arm from the back to hold the right side of your waist.
• Hold the position for a count of 20.
• Lower your left arm to the floor.
• Twist your trunk and then your neck forward. Do this once more on the same side.
• Bring your trunk forward, and stretch your left and right legs.
• Reverse the position of your legs, and perform twice on the right side by twisting your trunk to the right.

Concentration: Ajna Chakra (the pituitary glands).

38. PASCHIMOTTANASANA
   [Backstretch]

Benefits: Improves the mobility of your hip joints and

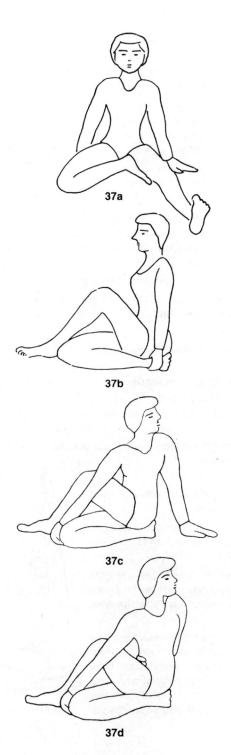

37a

37b

37c

37d

relieves tension in the hamstrings. Activates the kidneys, liver and pancreas. Helps lower blood pressure. Good for correcting disorders of the female reproductive system.

<u>a</u>

- Sit down on the floor with your legs stretched out in front.
- Keep your arms in front of you, palms on your thighs.

<u>b</u>

- Breathing in, slowly raise your arms until the upper part of your arms touches the sides of your ears.
- Tilt your head such that you see your fingers.
- Stretch your trunk.

<u>c</u>

- As you breathe out, bend forward.
- Bend your elbows, and place your palms on your knees, fingers facing inward.
- Keeping your knees straight, pull your trunk as far down as possible.
- Drop your head gently, forehead towards your knees and elbows pointing out.
- Relax your neck and shoulders.
- Hold the position for a count of 30.
- As you breathe out, keep your trunk and head down, and then stretch your arms
- As you breathe in, slowly sit up straight, keeping your arms by the sides of your ears.
- When your trunk is straight, look up at your fingers and lean back.
- As you breathe out, bend forward as before to bring your palms to the calf region.
- Pull down your trunk.
- Breathing normally, hold the position for a count of 30, relaxing your neck and shoulders.
- Stretching your arms as before, sit up straight.
- For the third and fourth time, perform the same way as before, but bring your palms to hold your ankles and then your heels.
- Now stretch your arms and trunk, and as you breathe in, straighten up.
- As you breathe out, lower your arms in front and relax.

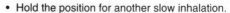

Caution: People suffering from sciatica, a slipped disc, sacral infections or chronic arthritis should avoid this Asana.

Concentration: Swadisthana Chakra (gonads/ovaries).

Variation of Paschimottanasana

- Sit with your legs stretched out in front.
- Keep your feet together and your spine straight, palms on your thighs.
- As you breathe in, raise arms over your head.
- Tilt your head back such that you see your fingers.
- Stretch your trunk and arms.
- As you breathe out, bend your body forward, curling your spine.
- As you bend forward, bend your elbows so your palms can be placed on your knees.
- Keep your legs straight, and relax your neck and shoulders.
- Hold the position for a slow inhalation.
- As you breathe out, slide your hands down your legs.

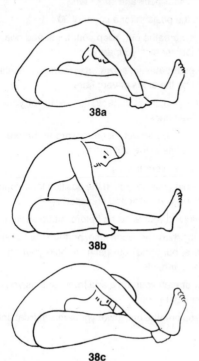

38a

38b

38c

- Bring your palms to the calf region, and pull in your trunk.
- Hold the position for a breath.
- As you breathe out, hold your ankle or toes with your palms.
- Push your trunk forward and down at the same time.
- Hold the position for another slow inhalation.
- Release the hold on your ankle, and stretch your arms so that the upper part of your arms are by the sides of your ears.
- As you inhale, resume the starting position.
- Repeat the Asana 3 to 5 times, each time arching your spine more.

38 (variation)

Concentration: On breathing.

39. SHASHANKASANA
   [Baby Pose]
Benefits: Calms the mind and lowers blood pressure. Relieves abdominal pain, abdominal cramps and discomfort in the surrounding region due to menstrual disorders.

a
- Sit in Vajrasana with your knees together.
- Keeping your spine straight, place your hands on your knees.
- As you breathe in, raise your arms over your head for a good stretch of your abdominal area.

b
- As you breathe out, bend your trunk forward such that your palms and forehead touch the floor. Your outstretched arms are on either side of your head. Your body rests on your thighs.

39a

Do not raise your buttocks from your heels.
- Hold the position for 2 minutes.
- As you breathe in, raise your trunk and arms.
- When your trunk is in an upright position, breathe out, and lower your arms onto your knees in front.

Caution: People suffering from hernia should not attempt this Asana.

Concentration: Manipura Chakra (the adrenal glands).

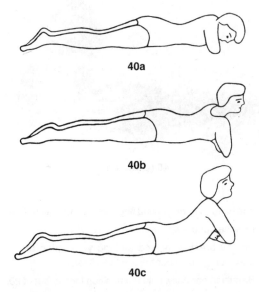

40a

40b

40c

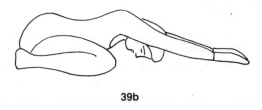

39b

40. BHUJANGASANA
[Cobra Pose]

Benefits: Stimulates the liver, pancreas and kidneys. Tones the ovaries and uterus. Helps correct female disorders like amenorrhoea as well as spinal disorders. Good for those suffering from a slipped disc or backaches.

<u>a</u>
- Lie down with your forehead on the floor.
- Keep your legs together and your arms by the sides of your thighs, palms down.
- As you breathe in, bring your arms to shoulder level.
- Now bend your arms at the elbows to bring your palms right below your shoulders.
- With palms placed on the floor, touch the second finger of one hand with the second finger of the other.

<u>b</u>
- Tilt your head.
- As you breathe in, arch your spine.

<u>c</u>
- Pressing your palms on the floor, raise your upper trunk off the floor. The lower abdomen rests on the floor.
- Breath normally, and remain in the position for a count of 20.

- Looking up, breathe out, and uncurl your spine by lowering your trunk.
- When your chest is on the floor, bring your forehead to touch the floor.
- Stretch your arms out at shoulder level.
- As you breathe out, place your arms by the sides of your thighs.
- Keep your cheek on the floor and relax.

Caution: People with hernia, ulcers in the abdomen and hyperthyroid should not attempt this Asana.

Concentration: Swadisthana Chakra (gonads/ovaries).

Variation of Bhujangasana
- Lie down with your forehead on the floor.
- Keep your legs together and your arms by the sides of your thighs, palms down.
- Tilt your head.
- As you breathe in and without the help of your palms, arch your spine, and raise your trunk.
- Now breathe out.
- As you breath in, place your palms on the floor right below your shoulder, and touch the second finger of

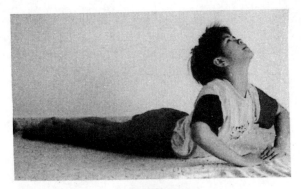

40 (variation)

one hand with the second finger of the other as before.
- Breathe out once more.
- As you breathe in, and arching your spine to the maximum, raise your trunk off the floor.
- Breathing normally, hold the position for a count of 20.
- Now take a breath.
- As you breathe out, lower your trunk to half the maximum stretch, and take a breath.
- As you breathe out, stretch your arms, and place them back by the sides of your thighs.
- Take a breath again.
- As you breathe out, uncurl your spine by lowering your trunk to the floor.
- Now bring your forehead to touch the floor and relax.

Caution: People with hernia, ulcers in the abdomen and hyperthyroid should avoid this Asana.

Concentration: Swadisthana Chakra (gonads/ovaries).

41. TIRYAKA BHUJANGASANA
   [Cobra Twist Pose]
Benefits: Helps the peristaltic motion of the intestines.
- Lie down with your forehead on the floor and arms by your sides.
- Place your palms right below your shoulders.
- Tilt your neck backward, and as you breathe in, arch your spine.
- Raise your trunk to half the maximum stretch.

- Now turn your neck to the right such that your chin is above your right shoulder.
- As you breathe out, twist the upper part of your trunk at the waist to the right, and look over your right shoulder towards the sole of your left foot.
- With the lower abdomen remaining on the floor, stay in the position for a breath.
- As you breath out slowly, twist your trunk and then your neck to the front.
- As you breathe in, arch your spine, and raise your trunk to the maximum.
- Breathing out, lower your trunk to the floor.
- Relax, and placing your palms right under your shoulders, touch the floor with your forehead.
- Perform similarly on the other side.

Caution: Do not perform this Asana without supervision.

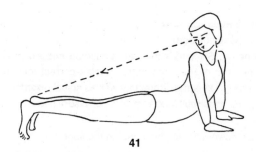

41

42. SHALABASANA
   [Locust Pose]
Benefits: Increases the blood supply to the prostate glands and keeps them healthy. Relieves pain in the lower back. Activates the thyroid gland. Good for people suffering from a slipped disc and sciatica.

a
- Lie down on your abdomen.
- Place your chin on the floor, and keep your feet together.
- Make two fists, and place them by your thighs.
- Raise your right leg to a moderate position, and hold the position for a count of 10. Keep your leg straight and still.

- Lower your right leg.
- Perform likewise with your left leg.
- Now raise your right leg to the extreme position.
- Lower your right leg after a count of 10.
- Perform likewise with your left leg.
- Relax with your cheek on the floor.

b
- Lie down with your head resting on your chin.
- Raise both your legs to a moderate position.
- Keep your legs straight and your knees together.
- Use your fists as support to balance your body.
- Breathing normally, hold the position for a count of 10.
- Lower your legs.
- Relax for a while before attempting the extreme position.
- Now raise both your legs to the extreme position.
- Keep your legs straight and together, and stay still while breathing normally.
- Hold the position for a count of 10, after which lower your legs.
- Relax until your heartbeat becomes normal.

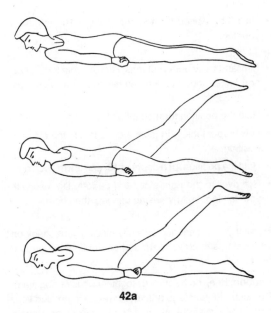

42a

Caution: Breathe normally, and do not hold your breath throughout the Asana. People with a weak heart, high blood pressure, hernia, peptic ulcers and intestinal disorders should avoid this Asana.

Concentration: Vishuddhi Chakra (the thyroid gland).

43. DHANURASANA
[Bow Pose]
Benefits: Tones the abdominal organs and brings flexibility to the spine. Gives relief to those suffering from a slipped disc when this Asana is performed in combination with Shalabasana [Locust Pose].

a
- Lie down on your abdomen, chin on the floor.
- Bend your knees up.

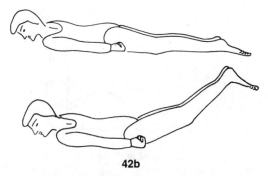

42b

b
- Stretch your arms backward, and clasp your ankles or feet.

c
- Raise your head and trunk.
- Pull your ankles or feet up, lifting your knees and thighs off the floor.
- Hold the position for a count of 10.
- Lower your knees, trunk and chin.
- Release the clasp on your ankles or feet, and relax with your cheek on the floor.
- Perform the Asana one more time.
- Relax until your heartbeat becomes normal.

Variation of Dhanurasana

After assuming the final position, rock forward as you breathe in and backward as you breathe out. Do not use your head to rock.

Caution: Do not hold your breath while performing this Asana. People with high blood pressure, hernia and spinal deformities should avoid this Asana.

Concentration: Vishuddhi Chakra (the thyroid gland).

44. UTTITA MERU DANDASANA
   [Side Raise Pose 1]

Benefits: Increases the flexibility of the hip joints. Relaxes the hamstring and redistributes fat from the hips and thighs to other parts of the body.

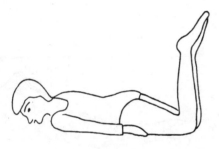

43a

43b

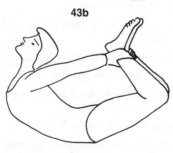

43c

<u>a</u>
- Lie down on your left side.
- Place your left arm under your head.
- Bend your elbow, and lifting up your head, place your cheek on your left palm.
- For balance, place your right hand on the floor in front of the navel region, and keep your whole body in one straight line.
- Stretch your right leg, and raise it to a moderate position.

44a

- Hold the position for a count of 10.
- Lower your leg, and raise it up again to an extreme position.
- Hold the position for another count of 10, and lower your leg.

<u>b</u>
- Similarly, raise both your legs, keeping your toes, heels and knees together. Remember that your legs must be straight.
- Hold the position for a count of 10.
- Lower your legs, and raise them again to the extreme position.
- Hold the position for a count of 10, and lower your legs.
- Roll over to the right side, and perform likewise with your left leg, first by raising one leg, then both.

Note: If you experience difficulty placing your cheek on your palm, stretch your arm out on the floor under your head.

Caution: Keep both your legs together while raising them. Do not bend your legs or lean forward. Do not curl your body when raising your legs to the maximum. People suffering from a weak heart or blood pressure should avoid this Asana.

45. ANANTASANA
[Side Raise Pose 2]

Benefits: Prevents hernia. Relieves pain in the pelvic region and back.

- Lie down on your left side.
- As in Uttita Meru Dandasana [Side Raise Pose 1], place your cheek on your left palm.
- Bend your right knee, and hold the right toe with your right hand fingers.
- Stretch your right leg up vertically without curling your body.
- Hold the position for a count of 10.
- Bending your right knee, return to the original position.
- Perform likewise on the other side.

46. EKAPADA JATARA PARIVARTANASANA
[Legover Single Leg]

45

Benefits: Improves the mobility of the hip joints and spinal column. Good for relief from sciatica, back pain and arthritic conditions of the hip joints.

- Lie down on your back.
- Keep your legs together, arms stretched out on either side at shoulder level.
- Bend your left leg towards your chest.
- Bring your knee close to your chin and your left heel close to your buttocks.
- Straighten up your left leg.
- Twisting at the pelvic joint, bring your left leg towards your right arm. Do not bend your knees.

- Try to bring your left foot as close as possible to your right hand on the floor.
- Hold the position for a count of 20. Do not raise your left shoulder off the floor, and do not twist your neck to the side.
- Now raise your left leg up, and when upright, bend your knee towards your chest.
- Place your toes on the floor, and stretch your leg down.
- Perform likewise with your right leg, bringing it over to your left side.
- Repeat this again with each leg.

47. SHAVASANA
[Corpse Pose]

This is an ideal way to relax after performing any Asana during a Yoga session.

- Lie down flat on your back with your arms by your sides, palms facing up.
- Keep your legs slightly apart.
- After tensing up your body, relax your body by stretching once.

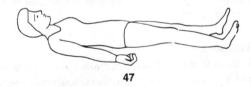

47

48. ADVASANA
[Reversed Corpse Pose]

Benefits: Relieves pain in the back due to a slipped disc or stiff neck.

This is one of the best ways to relax after performing Asanas.

- Lie down on your stomach.
- Stretch your arms over your head, with your palms facing down and your forehead touching the floor.
- Hold the position for a while.

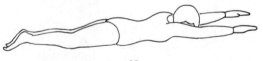

48

RELAXATION

For a total relaxation of mind and body, complement your Asanas and Shavasana with the following relaxation techniques. These imaginative techniques of enhancing relaxation have been practised by Yogis for many years.

One such technique is to imagine a tiny hole in the small of the back, from which tension drains away. This has the effect of flattening the back along the floor and encourages lying with one's full weight. Yet another technique is to think of a current of water slowly flowing through the body, cleansing it of all its tensions and impurities. Imagine it flowing through the neck, shoulders and along the arms into the chest, onto the abdomen, down to the spine, and through the buttocks filling the thighs, knees, calves and feet. Finally, the purifying water trickles away from the fingertips.

Skill in relaxation develops gradually and one can adapt any similar method. When practising relaxation, bear in mind that tension and relaxation are important in your body, and you cannot go against its natural functioning. For example, the heart and lungs contract, tense and then relax naturally. The same principle is applied to other parts of the body, but this time at your own command and control.

TECHNIQUE 1

Lie down on the floor, and close your eyes. Clear your mind of thoughts. Bring your attention to your legs. Stretch and tense your muscles as hard as you can, and hold the stretch for a few counts. Now let go of the tension, and feel your muscles go limp. Shift your thoughts to your hips, and repeat the process.

Also repeat the process with your waist, chest, arms, shoulders, neck, face and head. When you come to your head, without tensing any other part of the body, bring your thoughts (for a few seconds) to those parts of the body you first tensed and then relaxed. Repeat the entire process with a lesser degree of tension and a shorter holding period. After this, stay in the lying down position for 10 minutes.

TECHNIQUE 2

This is a continuation of Technique 1. Lie down on the floor. Tense the muscles of the body, from the legs to the head, and release the tension as in Technique 1 (do not hold for long).

When your thoughts reach the head region, make an attempt to think of any incident that has been the cause of a feeling of apprehension in you. Tighten your forehead and tense the region, keeping the thought as long as the feeling remains prominent. Now make your head and your tensed forehead go limp.

Practise this well enough to let the thought disappear with the tension of the muscles of the forehead. Continue to lie down for a while longer. Repeat the technique with a fearful thought, tensing the face accordingly and holding it for a while. Repeat the tensing and relaxing as before.

After practising this relaxation technique, recognise the fact that any part or parts of your body can be relaxed at will. Do not exert any effort when trying to relax. The moment you make an effort, it becomes contradictory to the idea of relaxing at will.

TECHNIQUE 3

As in Technique 1, shift your thoughts from your toes to your head, tensing and relaxing your muscles without any holding. Now focus your attention on your chest and abdominal region. Think of how the area has contributed to life in such activities as eating, smoking, etc. Try to recollect any incident relating to the field of your thought. At the same time, feel the tension corresponding to that thought. A warning at this stage: do not start assessing whether you are doing the right thing or not.

Concentrate on the thought without any judgement. Once the thought becomes pronounced, let go of it, along with the tension it has created in the muscles of the region. Lie down for a while, and try to think of various incidents relating to the different regions as a bundle of feelings. Once the thought becomes noticeably clearer, make the muscles go limp. At this stage, you should be capable of letting go of your thoughts without realising it.

Try repeating the technique on different regions by bringing in thought-related incidents or feelings or results. At the end of the technique, relax while lying down.

4

Asanas for Intermediate Learners

This group is meant for those who have completed the Asanas in the beginner's group and have undergone adequate training, particularly in performing the Asanas with ease. The Asanas here are intended for those of average health and who do not suffer from any disease or dislocation. In any case, it is best to consult a doctor before performing the Asanas.

Instructions given for each Asana are meant to be used as a general guide. They can be modified according to the age, occupation, physical condition and aptitude of the performer. The number of repetitions depends on the time the performer can set aside for the Asanas. The routines at the end of the chapter can be changed according to the need of the performer and need not be fixed. Through practice, it will become clearer as to how to select the Asanas and the daily programme that best suit you.

In this group, importance is given to breathing while performing the Asanas. Try to synchronise breathing with the movements involved in each Asana. Relax in between the Asanas.

1. NAMASKAR
[Salutation]

Benefits: Tones the nerves, thigh muscles, knee joints, shoulders and arms.

<u>a</u>

- Squat with your feet flat on the floor and knees wide apart.
- Place your hands together in a prayer position in front of your chest, with your elbows pressing against the inner sides of your thighs.
- As you inhale, tilt your neck back, and push your knees out.
- Hold the position for a few seconds.

1a

<u>b</u>

- Exhale, and stretch your arms to bring them parallel to the floor.
- Bring your knees together.
- Bend your head forward and all the way down.
- Now hold your toes with your fingers.
- Exhale, raise your hips up, and straighten your legs.
- Hold the position for a few seconds.
- Return to the starting position by bending your legs at the knees.

2. SURYANAMASKAR
[Salutation to the Sun]

Suryanamaskar, not traditionally regarded as part of the Yoga session, is a combination of seven Asanas performed twice in succession with unbroken rhythm for one complete round.

Suryanamaskar exercises every part of the body: it tones all the major muscles of the body. It puts the endocrinal, circulatory, respiratory and digestive systems into equilibrium. Furthermore, the synchronisation of breath with physical movements improves the clarity of the mind.

Suryanamaskar can be incorporated into the regular routine of Yogasanas or can be performed on its own.

Perform Suryanamaskar slowly, all the while concentrating on the movement. Once the movement becomes familiar, breathing coordination may be introduced into the practice. When you understand the sequence and breathing clearly, you can then concentrate on the Chakras (see figure in chapter 7), repeating the sequence several times.

Women should not perform Suryanamaskar during their period and after 3 months of pregnancy. Also avoid it if you have a fever or any other chronic infection. It is best to perform Suryanamaskar before any other Asana. It loosens the joints and prepares the body for other Asanas.

2A

A PRANAMASANA
[Prayer Pose]

Benefits: Prepares the body for other Asanas and develops the power of concentration.

- Stand in Samasthiti.
- Bring your hands together in front of your chest in a prayer position. The thumbs, pressed together, must touch chest.
- Hold the position for a few breaths.

Concentration: Anahata Chakra (the heart and lungs).

B HASTA UTTANASANA OR ADHO MUKHA HASTASANA
[Raised Arms Pose]

Benefits: Stretches the abdominal viscera and shoulder muscles, opens up the lungs and tones the spinal nerves.

- As you inhale, raise your arms over your head.

2B

- Stretch your arms, and arch as far back as you can from the waist. Keep your legs straight.
- Once in a comfortable position, hold the position for a count of 5, holding your breath if possible.

Concentration: Vishuddhi Chakra (the thyroid gland).

C   PADAHASTASANA OR UTTANASANA
[Hand to Foot Pose]

Benefits: Tones the abdominal muscles, improves blood circulation to the head and results in a supple spinal column.

- Straighten your trunk, keeping your legs straight.
- As you exhale, bend your body forward at the waist until your fingers touch the floor in front of your toes. If possible, place your palms on the floor in front of your toes.
- Bring your head towards your knees by contracting the abdomen.
- Hold the position for a couple of breaths.

2C

Note: You may initially feel strain on your calf muscles, the back of your thighs and the spine. After sufficient practice, such discomfort will disappear.

Concentration: Swadisthana Chakra (gonads/ovaries).

D   ASHWA SANCHALANASANA
[Horse Rider's Pose]

Benefits: Massages the abdominal muscles and strengthens the leg and neck muscles. Improves the balance of the nervous system.

- As you inhale, keep your left foot and palms in a firm position, and stretch your right leg as far back as possible, resting your toes on the floor. Your left leg must be bent in front of your chest by the side of your left arm.

- Raise your head and look in front, slowly arching your spine to bring your chest forward to a comfortable position. Keep your arms straight while doing this.
- Hold the position for a couple of breaths.

Concentration: Ajna Chakra (the pituitary glands).

2D

E   PARVATASANA
[Mountain Pose]

Benefits: Strengthens the nerves and muscles of your arms and legs. Keeps your spine supple and supplies fresh blood to it.

- Without altering the position of your palms and right toes, stretch your left leg backwards, and bring it by the side of your right leg.
- As you hold your breath, lift up your buttocks so that the weight of your body is on your palms and toes.
- Lift up your hips as high as possible, drop your head down, and bring it in.

2E

- As you breathe normally, hold the position for a couple of seconds.

Concentration: Vishuddhi Chakra (the thyroid gland).

F ASHTANGA NAMASKAR
[Salutation by the Eight Limbs]
Benefits: Develops the chest and strengthens the muscles of the limbs.

- As you breathe out, bend your arms, and bring your chin and knees to the floor. Remember that your toes, knees, chest, palms and chin must touch the floor.
- Keep your pelvis slightly raised from the floor.
- Hold the position for a couple of seconds.

Concentration: Manipura Chakra (the adrenal glands).

2F

G BHUJANGASANA
[Serpent Pose]
Benefits: Compresses the abdomen to drain out stagnant blood from the area. Relaxes the spinal muscles.

- Raise your head, keeping your palms and toes firmly on the floor.
- As you breathe in, raise your body from the waist by stretching your chest and straightening your arms.

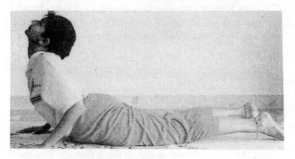

2G

- Tilt your head back and look up.
- Arch your spine slowly. Your thighs and knees need not be touching the floor.
- Hold the position for a couple of breaths.

Concentration: Swadisthana Chakra (gonads/ovaries).

H ASHTANGA NAMASKAR
[Salutation by the Eight Limbs] (see F)
Perform this Asana again by breathing out and bending your arms..

I PARVATASANA
[Mountain Pose] (see E)

- Pressing down on your palms and toes, breathe out.
- Bend your head down, and raise your buttocks up.
- Straighten your legs and arms, and drop your head further in.
- Hold the position for a couple of seconds.

J ASHWA SANCHALANASANA
[Horse Rider's Pose] (see D)

- As you breathe in, place your left foot behind your left palm.
- Lower your right knee to the ground.
- Tilt your neck back.
- Raise your head and look in front, slowly arching your spine to bring your chest forward to a comfortable position. Keep your arms straight while doing this.
- Hold the position for a couple of breaths.

K PADAHASTASANA
[Hand to Foot Pose] (see C)

- As you breathe, raise your hip outwards.
- Bring your right foot forward, and place it behind your right palm by the side of your left foot.
- Straighten your legs.
- Drop your head down, and bring your forehead towards your knees.
- Hold the position for a couple of seconds.

L   HASTA UTTANASANA
[Raised Arms Pose] (see <u>B</u>)

- As you breathe in, stretch your arms, and raise your body to an upright position.
- Bring your arms over your head.
- Tilt your back to look up, and arch your spine.

M   PRANAMASANA
[Prayer Pose] (see <u>A</u>)

- Straighten your body, breathe out, and lower your arms, bending them at the elbows.
- Bring your hands together in front of your chest. The thumbs, pressed together, must touch your chest.
- Lower your arms to your sides, and relax your body.

The second half of the Asana is as follows:

- Repeat in same way but with the following changes.
- Assume Ashwa Sanchalana (see <u>d</u>), and stretch your left leg back instead of the right one.
- Now in Ashwa Sanchalanasana (see <u>j</u>), bring your right foot forward behind your right palm.

This completes one full round of Suryanamaskar. Repeat as many complete rounds of Suryanamaskar as you possibly can.

Note: Never perform Suryanamaskar vigorously or you may strain your muscles. After completing Suryanamaskar, do Shavasana (Relaxation) for at least 2 minutes. Shavasana helps to normalise heartbeat and the respiratory process.

3.   EKA PADA SARVANGASANA
[Shoulderstand Single Leg]

Benefits: A specific therapy for the pelvic region, hip joint arthritis and piles. Aids in the process of weight loss and is also good for the kidneys. Gives relief to an asthmatic condition and tightness in calf muscles, which results from varicose veins.

Before doing this Asana, perform Sarvangasana or Shoulderstand (see chapter 3). Hold the position for a while, and then proceed as follows:

- Bend your right knee, and place your right foot on the upper part of your left thigh.

3

- Bend your hips forward, and place your right knee on your forehead. Your left leg must be parallel to the floor and resting on your right foot.
- Hold the position for a count of 30.
- Now remove your right foot from your left thigh, and straighten it by bringing it parallel to the floor by the side of your left leg.
- Hold the position for a few seconds.
- Raise your legs upwards to the Shoulderstand position.
- After holding the position for a few seconds, bend your left knee, and place your left foot on your upper right thigh.
- As before bring your left knee towards your forehead, keeping your right leg parallel to the floor.
- Again hold position for a few seconds.
- Straighten your left leg, and raise both your legs upwards to assume the Shoulderstand position.
- Come out as in Shoulderstand.

Caution: People with an enlarged spleen or liver should not perform this Asana. The Asana is also not to be attempted by those with high blood pressure or heart ailments.

Concentration: Vishuddhi Chakra (the thyroid gland).

4.   EKA PADA HALASANA
[Plough Single Leg]

Benefits: Stretches the pelvis and tones the kidneys. Activates the peristaltic motion of the intestines, thereby preventing constipation.

- Assume Halasana or Plough 1 (see chapter 3).
- Hold the plough position for 20 seconds, and then alternately raise and lower your legs in a continuous but slow motion as if cycling.
- If you prefer, you can place the toes of one of your legs on the floor while pointing the toes of the other leg towards the ceiling for a while instead of moving your legs continuously.

Note: At the end of the Asana, perform a backward bending counter pose like Paryanaka [Fish in Vajrasana]. After performing the counter pose (or any of the fish poses), perform Shavasana or Advasana before performing any other Asana.

Caution: People with a slipped disc, sciatica or high blood pressure should not attempt this Asana.

Concentration: Swadisthana (gonads/ovaries)

4

5. PARYANAKA
[Fish in Vajrasana]

Benefits: Strengthens your abdomen, back and chest. This is an advanced version of Supta Vajrasana or Backward Bend (see chapter 3).

- Sit in Vajrasana.
- With the help of your elbows, lie flat on your back.
- Stretch your arms over your head, and place them on the floor, palms facing up. Your head must be between your arms.
- Hold the position for a while.
- Using your hands, raise your shoulders to arch your neck and spine backwards. As you do this, drop your head backwards.
- Slowly rest the crown of your head on the floor.
- Now bend your arms at the elbows, and fold your arms in front of your forehead.
- Clasp your opposite elbows together with your hands.
- Hold the position for a while.
- Stretch your arms.
- Rest your trunk and then your neck on the floor.
- Place your arms by the sides of your thighs.
- Use your elbows to straighten up to sit in Vajrasana.

Caution: People with sacral problems should not perform this Asana.

Concentration: Swadisthana Chakra (gonads/ovaries), back and abdomen.

6. SETU BANDHASANA
[Bridge Pose]

Benefits: Tones the muscles of your back and relieves pain in the lower back due to sciatica. A useful exercise for pregnant women in that it strengthens the back and uterine muscles. Also good for women with menstrual problems.

<u>a</u>
- Lie down on your back.
- Bend your legs at the knees, heels touching your buttocks.
- Hold your ankles.

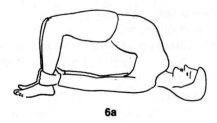

6a

- Keep your feet and shoulders firmly on the floor.
- Raise your buttocks, arching your spine to bring your chest close to your chin.
- Hold the position for a while.
- Lower your trunk, release the hold, and stretch your legs.

Concentration: Vishuddhi Chakra (the thyroid gland).

<u>b</u>

Benefits: Relieves back pain due to sciatica or disc problems. Improves the circulation of blood to the gonads and corrects irregular menstruation.

- Bend your legs, and bring your heels close to your buttocks as before.
- Place your hands on the floor by the sides of your ears, with your fingers pointing in the same direction as your head.

6b

- Raise your shoulders, and arch your neck and spine backwards.
- Place the top of your head on the floor. Keep the buttocks on the floor.
- Hold the position for a while.
- Using your hands for support, raise your buttocks, and balance on your head and feet.
- If possible, place your hands on your raised thighs, which are parallel to the floor.
- Hold the position for a few seconds.

Caution: People with high blood pressure, coronary problems and weak neck should avoid this Asana, as should pregnant women with a history of miscarriages.

Concentration: Manipura Chakra (the adrenal glands) and Vishuddhi Chakra (the thyroid gland).

7.   CHAKRASANA
   [Back Pushup]
Benefits: Helps the entire nervous system and influences hormonal secretions. Good for the female reproductive system. Pregnant women can perform this Asana in the early stages of their pregnancy.

The Asana is an excellent counter pose for Halasana [Plough 1]:

- Lie down on your back.
- Bending your knees, bring your feet close to your buttocks.
- Place your hands on the floor by the sides of your ears.
- Raise your shoulders, arch your neck backwards, and place the top of your head on the floor.
- Press your feet firmly on the floor.
- Lift up your buttocks so that your thighs are parallel to the floor.
- Use your palms to help maintain balance, and feel the entire weight of your body on your feet and head.
- Pressing on your hands and feet, raise your trunk, arching your spine further backwards so that your head no longer touches the floor. Remember that in this position, your neck must be further arched back toward the floor. The entire body must rest on your hands and feet.

7

- Hold the position until you are comfortable, then lower your body, bringing the top of your head to touch the floor.
- Keep your head arched, lower your buttocks to the floor, and bring your back to rest on the floor.
- Straighten your neck, stretch your legs and relax.

Note: Follow up Chakrasana [Back Pushup] with a forward bending Asana.

Caution: This Asana is not meant for those with high blood pressure, stomach ulcers, partial deafness, dilated eye capillaries or those who have undergone any abdominal operation.

Concentration: Manipura Chakra (the adrenal glands).

8. TARASANA
[Star Pose]

Benefits: Develops your breathing capacity. Good for those with an asthmatic condition, chest congestion and breathing difficulties.

a
- Stand in Samasthiti.
- Rolling your shoulders, bring your palms to face the front.
- Breathing in and making sure your arms are tight, slowly raise them to the front.
- Stretch your arms out at shoulder level, palms facing up.
- Hold your breath.

b
- Rolling your arms at shoulder level, turn your palms downwards, and spread your arms by your sides at shoulder level.

c
- Still holding your breath, roll your shoulders, and bring your palms to face the front at shoulder level.
- Bring your hands forward and parallel to each other.

d
- Still holding your breath, with palms facing each other, raise your arms upwards so that your upper arms are by the sides of your ears.

e
- Still holding your breath, bring your arms to shoulder level.
- Roll your shoulders so that your palms face down.
- Alternatively, you can roll your shoulders when your arms are over your head so that your palms face out. Now bring your arms down from the sides of your ears to shoulder level.

f
- As you breathe out, lower your arms to your sides.
- Relax before repeating the Asana.

Caution: Do not strain your lungs by holding your breath for too long.

9. UTTITA PAWANA MUKTASANA
[Standing Knee to Chest]

Benefits: Activates the pancreas. Limbers up the hip joints and strengthens the spine. Clears abdominal disorders and constipation.

- Stand with your feet slightly apart.
- With your left leg on the floor, lift up your right knee.
- Place your right hand on your ankle and your left hand on your knee.
- Keeping your spine straight, pull up your thigh close to your chest.
- Hold the position for a count of 20.
- Now release the pressure on your left leg.
- Repeat the Asana with the left leg bent.

9

Caution: Pregnant women should not attempt this Asana.

Note: If you experience difficulty doing the Asana standing up, do it lying down on your back

10. TADASANA
   [Stretch Pose]

Benefits: Promotes spinal alignment. Tones the rectus muscles, stretches the intestines, clears congestion in the spinal nerves and strengthens the abdomen, neck muscles and pelvic region. Pregnant women can perform this Asana during the first six months of their pregnancy.

<u>a</u>
- Stand with your feet apart.
- As you breathe in, raise your arms over your head from your sides.
- Keep your arms straight, and clasp your hands together.

<u>b</u>
- Bend your hands 90 degrees at your wrist.
- Arch your neck back to look up at your hands.
- Lift up your feet and balance yourself on your toes.
- Breathe in, and stretch your entire body.
- As you breathe normally, hold the position. Only advanced practitioners should hold their breath when the body is stretched.
- Relax, and place your feet flat on the floor.

<u>c</u>
- Bend your neck to the front and breathing out, lower your arms to your sides.
- Relax and breathe normally.

Variation of Tadasana
- Raise your arms over your head, and clasp your hands together.
- Roll your arms so that your hands face up.
- Tilt your neck back to look at your hands.
- As you breathe in, come up on your toes, stretching your arms and trunk.
- Hold the position to your comfort.
- Lower your feet to the floor.

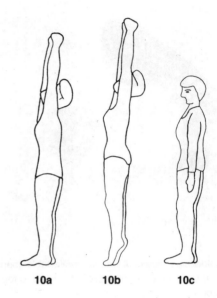

10a   **10b**   **10c**

- Roll your shoulders so that your palms face down.
- Release the clasp, and lower your arms to your sides.
- Return to the standing position and relax.

Caution: People with high blood pressure should not attempt to hold their breath.

11. TIRYAKA TADASANA
   [Swaying Palm Tree Pose]

Benefits: Tones the rectus muscles. Clears non-chronic intestinal blockage and helps restore spinal energy by clearing congestions. Pregnant women can perform this Asana for the first six months of their pregnancy.

- Stand in Samasthiti.
- Raise your arms over your head from your sides. If you are unable to keep your arms stretched and parallel to each other, clasp your hands together.
- As you breathe out, first swing your hips slightly to the left.
- Now bending your trunk slightly, swing your arms and upper trunk to the left.
- Hold the position for a breath.
- As you breathe in, swing your trunk and arms to an upright position.

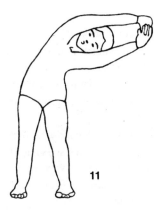

11

- Swing your hips bringing them to the starting position.
- Perform the Asana on the right side and relax.

12. KATICHAKRASANA
   [Cork Screw Pose]
Benefits: Limbers up the spine. Tones the back muscles and relaxes the lower back muscles. Helps relieve stiffness in the waist and hip joints.

a
- Spread your feet apart (to shoulder width).
- Place your left hand on your right shoulder, and bring your right arm from the back to hold the front of your left hip bone.
- Keep your chin close to your right shoulder.
- As you breathe out, twist the upper part of your body to the right.
- Breathing normally, hold the position for a count of 10.
- As you breathe out, twist your trunk and then your head to the front.
- Repeat the Asana again.
- Now perform the Asana on the left side.

b
- Stand with your feet apart (to shoulder width).
- Place your right hand in front of your left hip bone.
- Bring your left hand from behind and place it on your right hip bone.
- Bend your knees slightly, and tense your knee caps, contracting your buttocks at the same time.

- Turn your head to the left, and place your chin close to your left shoulder.
- As you breathe out and maintaining the tension in your knees, twist the upper part of your body to the left.
- Breathing normally, hold the twisted position for a count of 10.

12a   12b

- As you breathe out, twist your trunk and your head to the front.
- Begin releasing the tension in your knees and buttocks.
- Repeat the Asana on the right side.

13. MERU PRISHTASANA
   [Spine and Back Pose]
Benefits: Relieves stiffness in the spine. Tones the muscles of the back, waist and hip joints.

a
- Stretch your arms out at shoulder level, and roll your arms so that your palms face up.
- Bending your arms at the elbows, place your palms on top of your shoulders. If this is not possible, try clasping your hands together behind your head. Your elbows must point sideways.
- As you breathe out, lower your left elbow, and pull your trunk down to the left. Your right elbow must be pointing up.
- Compress the left side of your trunk, and stretch the right side.
- Hold the position for a count of 10.

13a

- As you breathe in, straighten your trunk.
- Repeat the Asana on the other side.
- Repeat the Asana again on each side and relax.

b
- Clasp your shoulder tops with your hands, keeping your elbows pointing sideways at shoulder level.

- Now bend your trunk forward so that your elbows and trunk are parallel to the floor.
- As you breathe out, swing your trunk to the left.
- Twist your trunk and bending down further, try to bring your right elbow towards your left knee.

13b

- Hold the position for a count of 10.
- Twist your trunk in reverse order so that it faces the floor.
- When your trunk and elbows are parallel to the floor, swing your trunk to the front.
- Swing your trunk towards the right and twist it, bringing your left elbow close to your right knee.
- Hold the position for a count of 10.
- Now twist your trunk in the reverse direction, and swing your trunk to the front.
- When your trunk is parallel to the floor, breathe in, and straighten your trunk.
- Release the clasp on your shoulders, and lower your arms.

14. PARIPOORNA TRIKONASANA
[Triangle Complete]

Benefits: Good for people suffering from nervous depression. Relieves constipation and tension in the spinal nerves and lower back muscles. Stimulates the circulation of blood to the entire body. Helps to prevent arthritis in the shoulders and hip joints. Activates the adrenal glands and gives a gentle massage to the abdominal organs.

This Asana has a few stages, which have to be performed in order. Keep your movements slow, and do not strain yourself.

a
- Stand in Samasthiti.
- Breathing in, stretch your arms out at shoulder level, palms facing down.
- Spread out your feet (about 3 to 4 feet).
- Keep your toes slightly facing inwards.

b
- As you breathe out, bend your trunk to the left.
- Slide your left hand down your left leg, and hold onto any comfortable part of your leg.
- Roll your right arm at shoulder level, and breathing in, bring it against your right ear.
- Without bending your knee, pull your trunk down to the left side, bringing your right arm parallel to the floor. Feel the stretch on the right side of your trunk.
- Hold the position for a count of 10.
- As you breathe out, raise your right arm, and rolling it at shoulder level, stretch it such that it is vertical to the floor.
- Straighten your left arm, and bring both your arms in one line.
- As you breathe in, raise your trunk.
- When your trunk is straight, keep your arms at shoulder level, palms facing down.
- Now perform the Asana on the right side.

c
- When your trunk is straight and your arms are at shoulder level, exhaling slowly rotate your trunk to the left.
- Let your head follow your trunk, and keep your arms at shoulder level, parallel to the floor. The hips stay twisted.
- Once you feel comfortable in the position, breathe in.
- Breathing out and without bending your knees, bend your trunk.
- Twist the trunk further towards the left, with your right hand holding your left ankle. Your left arm is raised, with its fingers and thumb pointing up.
- Keep your eyes focused on the fingers of your left hand.
- Try to keep your arms in one line, and hold the stretch for a breath.
- As you breathe in, straighten your twisted trunk. Your arms must now be parallel to the floor.

14a

14b

14c

- As you breathe out, twist your trunk to the front.
- Hold the position for a breath.
- Perform similarly on the right side.

<u>d</u>
- Keep your trunk straight with your arms at shoulder level.
- As you breathe out, bring your stretched arms in front at shoulder level, palms facing down. Remember that your arms are parallel to each other and to the floor.
- Pressing down firmly on your left foot, twist your trunk to the right, and take a breath.

<u>e</u>
- As you breathe out, bend your twisted trunk to the right.
- Place your hands by the side of your right foot and your head between your arms.
- Contract your abdomen, and pull your trunk towards your right leg.
- Hold the position for a breath.
- As you breathe in, straighten your trunk.
- As you breathe out, twist your trunk to the front.
- Repeat the Asana on the left side.

<u>f</u>
- When your arms are in front and parallel to floor, palms facing down, start breathing in, and at the same time, raise your arms over your head. While doing this, do not arch your spine.
- With your upper arms against the sides of your ears, tilt your head back, and look at your fingers.
- Stretching your arms and keeping them stiff, arch your spine back as much as possible.
- Hold the position for a few seconds, then straighten your trunk.
- As you breathe out, bend your trunk forward at your waist.
- Place your hands on the floor between your feet, and move your head in.
- Hold the position for a breath.
- As you breathe in, slowly raise your trunk and arms.
- When your are in an upright position, stretch your arms out in front, and keep them parallel to the floor.
- As you breathe in, stretch your arms out to your sides.

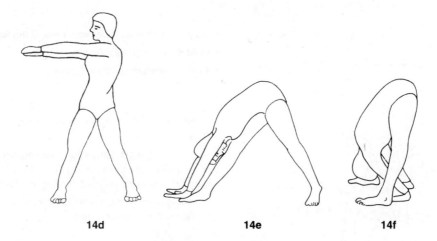

| 14d | 14e | 14f |

- Bring your feet together, and breathing out, lower your arms.
- Lie down, and relax for a while.

Caution: Beginners should not overstretch. Master the stages of Trikonasana or Triangle Simple (see chapter 3) before proceeding any further. If you initially experience difficulty bending to the extreme position, rectify this problem by repeating the Asana several times before bending more with each try (without holding the pose). Do not lean forward to achieve the extreme bending position. Pregnant women should not attempt this Asana.

15. UTTITA TRIKONASANA
[Triangle Stretched 1]

Benefits: Same as Trikonasana [Triangle Simple].
The Asana is an extended version of Trikonasana [Triangle Simple].

- Stand in Samasthiti.
- As you breathe in, stretch your arms out from your sides at shoulder level.
- Spread your feet as far apart as possible.
- Pressing down firmly on the toes of your left feet, move your left heel 90 degrees forward.
- Keep your right foot at an angle, toes pointing towards the left.
- Breathing out, bend your trunk to the left. Keep your trunk in the vertical plane. Do not bend your knees. Bring your left palm by the outer side of your left foot and right arm perpendicular to the floor.

- Roll your right arm at shoulder level, and breathing in, bring it over your right ear.
- Gently tilt your neck back, and look at your right hand.
- Hold the position for a count of 30.
- Look to the front by tilting your neck back.
- Raise your right arm so that your arms are in one line.
- As you breathe in, straighten your trunk.
- Once you are upright, adjust your feet to bring them to the starting position.
- Now repeat the Asana on the right side.
- When you come to an upright position, bring your feet together.
- As you breathe out, lower your arms.

Caution: Same as Trikonasana [Triangle Simple].

16. UTTITA PARIVRATA TRIKONASANA
[Triangle Stretched 2]

Benefits: Same as Paripoorna Trikonasana [Triangle Complete].

- Stand in Samasthiti.
- As you breathe in, stretch your arms out from your sides at shoulder level.
- Spread your feet as far apart as possible.
- Pressing down firmly on the toes of your left foot, move your left heel 90 degrees forward, and pressing down on your right toes, move your right heel 60 degrees.
- Keep your arms in one line, parallel to the floor, at shoulder level.

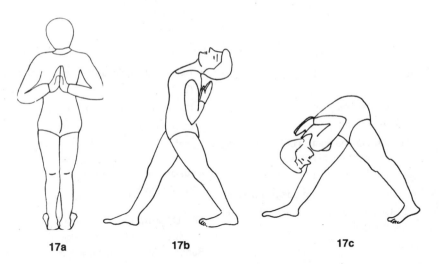

17a   17b   17c

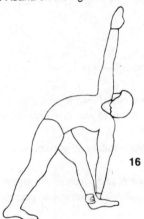

16

- As you breathe out, twist your trunk to the left, and take a breath.
- As you breathe out and twisting your trunk further to the left, bend it at your waist.
- Place your right hand by the outer side of your left foot.
- Raise your left arm, fingers pointing up.
- By tilting your neck towards your left shoulder, look up at your left hand.
- Hold the position for a breath.
- Arch your neck to bring your face to the front.
- Keep your arms in one straight line, and breathing in, straighten your trunk. While doing this, do not twist your trunk to the front. Your arms are now at shoulder level.
- As you breathe out, twist your trunk to the front. Adjust your feet, and bring them to the starting position.
- Repeat the Asana on the right side.

17. PARSHVOTTANASANA
[Back Namaste Pose]

Benefits: Removes stiffness in the hip muscles and tones the abdominal organs.

a
- Stand in Samasthiti.
- Place your hands together in namaste. If you are unable to do this, clasp your wrists together behind your back.

b
- Now spread your feet apart.
- Adjusting your feet, turn your trunk at your waist to the right.
- As you breathe in, tilt your neck back, and arch your spine backwards, keeping your knees taut.
- Hold the position for a count of 10.

c
- Straighten your trunk.
- As you breathe out, bend your trunk forward.
- Bring your forehead towards your right knee.
- Breathing normally, hold the position for a count of 20.
- Without raising your body and by adjusting your feet, exhale. While breathing out, swing your trunk slowly at your hips to bring your head towards your left knee. Remember that your forehead must point towards your left knee, and the trunk is bent on the left side. Keep your legs taut.
- Hold the position for a count of 20.
- As you inhale, raise your trunk, and continue to arch your spine backwards.

- Hold the position for a count of 10.
- Now straighten your trunk, and breathing out, bend forward.
- Bring your forehead towards your left knee.
- Hold the position for a count of 20.
- Swing your trunk towards the right as before, bringing your forehead towards your right knee.
- Hold the position for a count of 20.
- As you inhale, raise your trunk to an upright position.
- Turn your body such that your chest faces the front, and bring your legs together.
- Lower your arms.

18. PADA ANGUSHTASANA
[Legclasp Gorilla Pose]

Benefits: Activates the pancreas and abdominal organs. Prepares pregnant women for an easy childbirth. Good for those with back pain and sciatica. Persons with sciatica should perform this Asana under close supervision.

a
- Stand with your feet one foot apart.
- As you exhale, bend your trunk forward.
- Relax your head and arms, and feel the weight of your body on your toes.
- Bend to a comfortable position, and hold your big toes.
- By bending your elbows outward, pull your trunk down and inwards from the pelvic region. Do not bend your knees.
- Bring your head towards your knees.
- Hold the position for a count of 10.

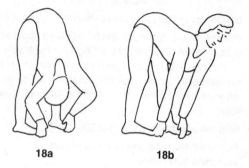

18a   18b

b
- Release the hold, and tilt your head back.
- Curl your back such that it curves in the middle.
- Push your trunk inwards and shoulders upwards.
- Looking up and keeping the pressure on your toes, breathe in, and straighten your trunk.

Caution: This Asana is not meant for those with high blood pressure.

19. UTTANASANA
[Legclasp Migraine Pose]

Benefits: Stretches the spine, tones the liver, slows down heartbeat and soothes brain cells. Releases tension and calms the mind. Relieves heaviness in the head. People who experience discomfort in the head while attempting Bumi Pada Mastakasana or Headstand Modified (see chapter 3) should perform this Asana to rectify the problem.

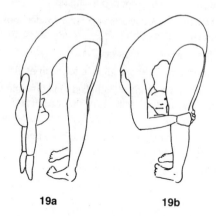

19a   19b

a
- Stand with your feet about one foot apart, toes pointing inwards.
- Arching your neck forward, move your chin close to your chest. Keeping your chin pressed to your chest, take a breath.
- As you breathe out, bend your trunk forward at your waist.
- Relax your arms, and put pressure on your heels. While doing this, assume a comfortable position.

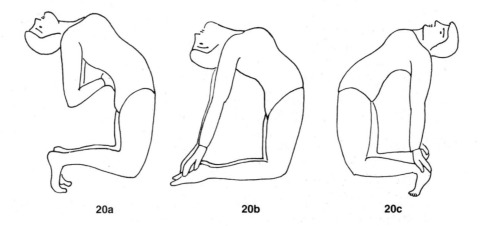

20a   20b   20c

b
- With both your hands, clasp your ankle or calf muscles firmly.
- Arch your neck further, and pull in your trunk to bring your forehead towards your knees.
- Hold the position for a while.
- Keeping your chin pressed to your chest, straighten up in one exhalation the moment you feel a tingling sensation behind your ears.
- When your trunk is straight, gently drop your neck back, and breathe out.
- Relax for a while, and repeat the Asana again.

Caution: This Asana is not meant for people with a slipped disc or high blood pressure.

20. USHTRASANA
[Camel Pose]

a
Benefit: Helps rectify deformity in the spine and shoulders.
- Kneel down on your toes, with your knees together and thighs perpendicular to the floor.
- Place your hands on your lower back, fingers pointing towards your buttocks.
- As you breathe in, stretch your abdominal area, and arch your spine back.

- Drop your neck back, making sure your thighs remain perpendicular to the floor.
- Breathing normally, hold the position for a count of 10.
- Now straighten your neck and your spine.
- Relax, and repeat the Asana.

Caution: This Asana is not meant for people suffering from tension, high blood pressure and abdominal ailments.

b
Benefit: Induces deeper breathing.
- Kneel down on the floor, feet flat on the floor.
- Keep your thighs perpendicular to the floor.
- Place your palms on your back, and arch your back as before. If you can, bring your palms to hold your heels or ankles.
- Hold the position for a count of 10.
- Now place your hands on your back again.
- Slowly straighten your neck and trunk.

c
Variation of Ushtrasana
Benefit: Good for asthmatics. Activates the muscles and connecting tissues of the face, nasal passage, neck, shoulders and back.
- Sit on your heels with your knees and feet apart.
- Keep your chin close to your chest.
- Hold your heels.

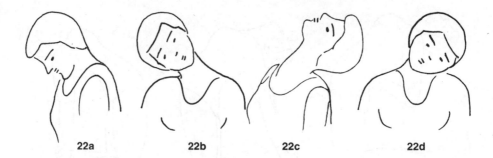

22a   22b   22c   22d

- As you breathe in, raise your trunk, and arch your back. Note that at this stage your thighs are perpendicular to the floor.
- Drop your head back.
- Hold the position for a count of 10. If possible, hold your breath in this position.
- Bend your neck to the front, and bring your chin close to your chest.
- As you breathe out, lower your trunk, resting your buttocks on your heels.
- Get into Shashankasana or Baby Pose

  (see chapter 3) and relax.

Caution: This Asana is not meant for those with stomach ulcers, high blood pressure or serious back ailments.

Concentration: Vishuddhi Chakra (the thyroid gland) and Anahata Chakra (the thymus glands).

21. PADMA PARVATASANA
[Traction]
Benefits: Relieves pain in the muscles due to rheumatism and arthritis in the shoulders. Helps those with disc problems.

- Sit down with your spine straight.
- As you breathe in, stretch your arms out at shoulder level, palms facing down.
- Roll your shoulders, palms facing up, and continue breathing in. While doing this, raise your arms, and bring them by the sides of your ears.
- Interlace your fingers so that your palms face down.
- Bend your hands at your wrists.

- Keep your arms straight, and without arching your spine, breathe out completely.
- As you keep your breath out, pull up your trunk, giving a maximum stretch to your spine. Feel the stretch on your back.
- Hold the position for as long as you can, and do not strain yourself while holding your breath.
- Relax your trunk, and breathe in.
- As you breathe out, lower your arms to your sides.
- Repeat the Asana with your palms facing up.

22. GRIVASANA
[Neck Roll]
Benefit: Relieves headaches and tension.

<u>a</u>
- Sit down with your spine straight, preferably in Padmasana or Veerasana.
- Place your hands by your sides.
- Keeping your arms straight, do not move your shoulders.
- Drop your neck to the front.

<u>b</u>
- As you breathe out, roll your head to the right. Your right ear is just above your right shoulder.
- Hold the position for a breath.

<u>c</u>
- As you breathe out, roll your neck, and drop your head back.
- Hold the position for a breath.

<u>d</u>
- As you breathe out, roll your neck to the left. Your left ear is just above your left shoulder.

- Hold the position for a breath.
- As you breathe out, roll your neck to the front.
- Again hold the position for a breath.
- As you breathe out, roll your neck to the left.
- Continue to move your head in the reverse direction.
- Repeat the Asana twice, rolling your head in both directions.

Caution: This Asana is not meant for people who have damaged their cervical bone.

23. SIMHA GRIVASANA
[Neck Lion Pose]
Benefit: Relaxes the facial muscles.

- Sit down in a comfortable position, with your spine straight and arms by your sides.
- Bend your neck to the front.
- Keeping your eyes closed, press your chin close to your chest.
- Hold the position for two breaths, and straighten your neck.
- Gently twist your neck towards the left such that your chin is above your left shoulder.
- Opening your eyes and mouth wide, bring your lower jaw towards your left shoulder.
- Close your mouth, followed by your eyes.
- Twist your neck towards the right.
- Perform the Asana on the right side.
- Twist your neck to the front, and tilt your head back slowly and as far back as possible.
- Now open your eyes and mouth as wide as possible.
- Close your mouth and eyes, and straighten your neck.

24. HASTA GRIVASANA
[Hand and Neck Pose]
Benefits: Relieves tension and rigidity in the neck and shoulders.

- Sit in Siddhasana or Sukasana.
- Place your palms on your knees.
- Keep your arms straight and eyes on the back of your left hand fingers.

- Very slowly raise your left arm high. Try to bring it perpendicular to the floor, with your fingers pointing up and palm facing the front. Your left arm is in line with the left side of your body.
- Roll your arm at the shoulder so that your palm faces the left.
- Without losing sight of your fingers, start lowering your arm to the left side.
- Once lowered to a comfortable position, start raising your arm. Fix your gaze still on your left hand fingers.
- When your arm is perpendicular to the floor (or raised as high as possible), roll it so that your palm faces the front.
- Lower your arm slowly, and place it onto your left knee.
- Now perform the Asana with your right arm.

Note: Always keep your eyes fixed on the back of your moving fingers. Do not twist your neck to follow the movement of your arms.

25. BHU NAMANASANA
[Spinal Twist]
Benefits: Stretches the spine and lower back. Stimulates the spinal nerves.

- Sit down with your spine straight and legs stretched out in front.
- Keep your feet slightly apart.
- Place your left hand behind your left hip, fingers pointing backwards.
- Place your right hand by the outer side of your left thigh, fingers pointing towards the left.
- Twist your torso to the left, and, at the same time, move your left hand back and your right hand towards the left so you can bend easily.
- Arching your spine, bring your nose close to the floor. Your left upper arm will be parallel to the floor. Feel the pressure on your left shoulder. Your buttocks must be on the floor.

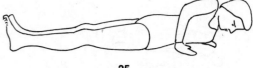

25

- Hold the position for a count of 10.
- Straighten your trunk, and perform similarly on the right side.

26. UPAVISHTA MATSYENDRASANA
[Seated Angle Twist]

Benefits: Acts on the synovial fluid in the joints, thereby helping rheumatic patients. Tones the abdominal muscles and activates the pancreas. Improves the efficient functioning of the nervous system.

- Sit down with your legs stretched out in front.
- Keeping your spine straight, spread your legs out at shoulder width.
- As you breathe in, raise your arms in front at shoulder level, keeping them straight.
- Fix your gaze on the back of your left hand.
- As you breathe out, twist your trunk to the left until your right arm is in line with your left foot.
- As you breathe in, stretch your left arm as far behind as you can.
- As you breathe out, bend your trunk so that you can hold your left foot with your right hand.
- Try bending your trunk as far down as possible.
- Stretch your left arm out, still holding your gaze on the back of your left hand.
- Hold the position for a count of 10.
- Release the hold on your left foot, and release the stretch on your left arm.
- As you breathe in, straighten your trunk, and make sure your right arm is parallel to the floor.
- As you breathe out, bring your left arm parallel to your the right arm, and take a breath. Your spine is erect.

26

- As you breathe out, twist your trunk to the front.
- Now shift your gaze back to the right hand.
- Perform similarly on the right side.
- Repeat the Asana twice on each side.
- After performing the Asana twice on each side, with your arms in front, breathe out, lower your arms and relax.

27. YOGA ANANDASANA
[Animal Relaxation Pose]

Benefits: Increases the flexibility of your hip and shoulder joints. Eases arthritis of your knees and pelvic joints. Relieves menstrual pain and abdominal cramps.

- Sit down with your legs stretched out in front.
- Place the sole of your right foot against the inner side of your left thigh. Your right knee touches the floor.
- Fold your left leg back such that your left heel is by the side of your left hip.
- As you breathe in, raise your arms, bringing them in front and parallel to the floor.
- As you breathe out, stretch your trunk forward and down to the floor.

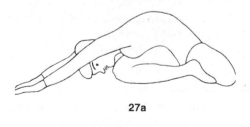

27a

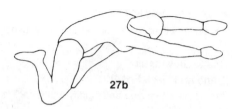

27b

- Bring your forehead forward to touch the floor.
- Now swing your trunk towards your right knee so that your right armpit is above your right knee.
- Stretch your arms out, and place them on the floor. Your head is between your upper arms.

- Hold the position for a count of 30.
- Keeping your trunk at the same level, swing your trunk and arms to the front.
- As you breathe in, raise your trunk. When your trunk is straight, your arms are parallel to the floor.
- Lower your arms, and change the position of your legs.
- Repeat the Asana by placing the sole of your left foot against the inner side of your right thigh.

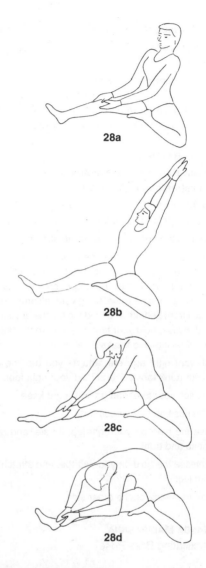

28a

28b

28c

28d

28. JANU SIRASASANA
[Alternate Leg Pull]

Benefits: Tones the liver, kidneys and spleen. Regulates blood pressure. Gives relief to those suffering from enlarged prostate glands. Those suffering from sciatic pain can perform this Asana instead of Paschimottanasana or Backstretch (see chapter 3).

<u>a</u>
- Sit down with your legs stretched out in front.
- Bend your left knee.
- Bring your left foot close to the inner side of your right thigh. Your left knee on the floor points to the left.
- Keep your right leg straight at a slight angle towards the right side. Place your hands in front of you.

<u>b</u>
- As you breathe in, raise your arms over your head.
- Tilt your neck to look at your hands.

<u>c</u>
- Stretch your trunk, and as you exhale, bend forward.
- Stretch out as far as you can, and swing your trunk to the right.
- Holding onto any part of your right leg, maintain the position for a count of 30.

<u>d</u>
- Without raising your trunk, stretch your arms out such that they are by the sides of your ears.
- Swing your trunk to the front.
- As you inhale, raise your trunk and arms together.
- Repeat the Asana twice, each time increasing your bending gradually.
- When you have finished, breathe out, lower your arms, and stretch out your left leg.
- Now perform the Asana by bending your right leg and stretching out your left leg.

Variation of Janu Sirasasana
[Alternate Leg Pull]

Benefits: Reduces high blood pressure and relieves menstrual pain.

- When your trunk is straight and arms are over your head, twist your trunk towards the side.
- Bend forward to hold onto any part of your stretched leg.
- Hold the position for a count of 30, and stretch your arms and trunk.

- Keeping the body twisted, breathe in, and come upright.
- Twist your trunk forward, and as you breathe out, lower your arms.
- Perform similarly on the other side.

Note: People with enlarged prostate glands benefit by holding the pose for a longer period of time.

29. ARDHA BADDHA PADMA PASCHIMOTTANASANA
[Backstretch in Half Lotus]

Benefits: Encourages blood flow in the abdominal region. Releases tension and helps lower blood pressure.

- Sit down on the floor with your spine straight.
- Bending your left leg at the knee, place your left foot on the upper part of your right thigh. Your left knee touches the floor, and your left heel presses against the navel region. If possible, bring your left arm around your back from behind, and hold the big toe of your left foot. Otherwise, hold your foot from the front, bringing your left heel close to the lower abdomen.
- Stretch your right arm out, and as you breathe out, bend your trunk forward, and hold your right foot.
- Try to place your forehead on your right knee.
- Hold the position to your comfort.
- Release the hold on you right leg, inhale, and raise your head and trunk.
- Now release the hold on your left toe, and stretch out your left leg.
- Repeat the Asana on the other side.

30. ANANDA MADIRASANA
[Intoxicating Bliss Pose]

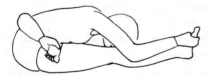

29

- Sit in Vajrasana.
- Place your hands on your heels, palms facing down and fingers pointing in.
- Keep your trunk straight, buttocks resting on the back of your hands.

- Keeping your eyes closed, fix your eyeballs on the centre of your eyebrows
- Hold the position for 1 minute.

31. DHYANA VEERASANA
[Relaxation Hero Pose]

Benefits: Relaxes the nervous system.

- Sit in Veerasana.
- Stretch your left leg out.
- Bend your left leg, and place your left heel by the side of your right knee.
- Place your right hand, palm down on your right knee.
- Keep your right arm straight.

31

- Rest your left elbow on your left knee.
- Place your left palm on your left cheek, fingers resting on the temple.
- Apply a slight pressure on the temple with your fingers.
- Breathing normally for 1 minute, hold the position.
- Change the position of your legs and hands, and perform similarly on the other side.

Concentration: Ajna Chakra (the pituitary glands).

32. PARIPOORNA NAVASANA
[Diamond Pose 1]

Benefits: Tones the liver. Prevents hernia and relieves back pain.

- Sit down with your spine straight.

- Stretch your legs out in front, keeping your palms by the sides of your thighs.
- Press down on your palms, and recline your trunk slightly.
- Raise both legs well above your head. The body assumes the shape of a V.
- Balancing on your buttocks, place your arms by the sides of your thighs. Your arms are parallel to the floor.
- Hold the position for a count of 20.
- Lower your legs, bring your trunk forward and relax.

Caution: This Asana is not meant for people with high blood pressure.

33. UBHAYA PADANGUSHTA
[Diamond Pose 2]

- Sit down with your legs stretched out in front.
- Reclining your trunk a little, flex your knees, and raise your legs.
- When your legs are well above your head, hold your toes with your fingers.
- Balancing on your buttocks, breathe out.
- Holding your breath, move your trunk and legs towards each other.
- Try to bring your forehead as close to your knees as possible.
- Hold the position to your comfort.
- Release the hold on your toes, and lower your legs and trunk to the floor very slowly.

Variation of Ubhaya Padangushta
Benefits: Activates the intestines and strengthens the abdomen.

This Asana is meant for those who find it difficult to balance themselves on their buttocks.

- Lie down on your back, and raise your legs over your head.
- Raise your arms to hold your toes with your fingers.
- Keep your legs straight, bringing them as close to your face as possible.
- Hold the position for a few breaths.

- Still holding your breath, bend your legs at the knees to bring your heels to the floor.
- Stretch your legs out.

34. NAUKASANA
[Saucer Pose]

a
- Lie down on your back with your feet together and head resting on the floor.
- Keeping your arms straight, place your hands on your thighs.
- Breathe out.
- Still holding your breath, raise your trunk and legs at the same time.
- Slide your hands down your thighs until your fingers are close to the top of your knees.
- Breathing normally, hold the position for a count of 20.
- Balancing your body on your buttocks, relax your neck.
- Now lower your trunk and legs at the same time and relax.

b

Benefits: Strengthens the back and tones the nerves, particularly the sciatic nerve.

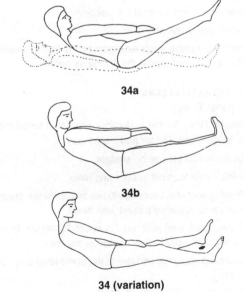

34a

34b

34 (variation)

- Repeat as before.
- When balancing your body on your buttocks, bring your chin close to your chest.
- Bend your ankle so that your toes point towards your head. This gives a maximum stretch on the back of your legs.
- Hold the position for a count of 10.
- Stretch your toes, relax your neck, and lower your legs and trunk together.

Variation of Naukasana

- Lie down on your back, keeping your legs apart at shoulder width level.
- Keeping your arms straight, put your hands on your thighs.
- Place an object on the floor between your legs.
- Without arching your neck forward, raise your trunk so the object is clearly visible.
- Hold the position for a count of 20.
- Lower your trunk and relax.
- Now place an object on the floor between your knees or calf region.
- Without arching your neck to the front, raise your trunk as before so that object is clearly visible.
- Breathing normally, hold the position.
- Lower your trunk and relax.
- For the third time, place an object on the floor between your thighs, and repeat the Asana as before.

35. ARDHA NAVASANA
[Boat Pose]

Benefits: Good for the abdominal area as it tones the liver, spleen, gall bladder and intestines.

- Sit down with your spine straight.
- Stretch your legs out in front and relax.
- Keeping your chest out and elbows by your sides, clasp your hands together behind your head.
- Recline back until your head is about 30–40 cm. from the floor. Your back does not touch the floor.
- Now raise your legs and feet to the same level as your head.
- Balance yourself on your buttocks.

- Breathe normally, and hold your chin up.
- Looking up, hold the position to your comfort.
- Now come out of the position, breathe out, and holding your breath, raise your legs.
- As in Diamond 1 (Asana 32), raise your trunk upwards.
- Lower your legs and relax.

Caution: In the final position, avoid holding your breath as the effect then will be on the stomach-muscles instead of the abdominal organs.

36. SARPASANA
[Snake Pose]

Benefit: Tones the uterus and ovaries.

a
- Lie down on your abdomen, forehead touching the floor.
- Place your hands close to the chest on either side of the floor, fingers pointing towards your head.
- Tilt your head back, and look up.
- Breathing in and arching your spine, raise your trunk to your comfort.
- Keep your lower abdomen on the floor.
- Hold the position for a count of 20.
- As you breathe out, relax your spine, and bring your trunk and then your forehead back to touch the floor.
- Now relax for a while.

b
- Keeping your arms by the sides of your thighs, tilt your head back, and look up.

36a

36b

- Without pressing down on your hands, breathe in, arch your spine, and raise your trunk.
- Now breathe out.
- As you breathe in, stretch your arms out by your sides, and breathing out, place them on the floor by the sides of your chest.
- As you breathe in, and keeping your chest out, arch your spine to the maximum.
- Breathing normally, hold the position for a count of 20.
- Breathing out, lower your trunk to the starting position.
- As you breathe in, stretch your arms out at your sides.
- As you breathe out, place your palms by the sides of your thighs.
- Take a breath, and as you breathe out, relax your spine, and lower your trunk.
- Now bring your forehead to touch the floor and relax.

c
- With your forehead touching the floor, place your palms by the sides of your chest. Your chin touches the floor.
- Stretch your arms back, and interlace your fingers.
- Keeping your arms straight, raise them so that your shoulder blades move towards each other.
- As you breathe in, raise your trunk, and keep looking up.
- Hold the position for a count of 20.
- As you breathe out, lower your trunk, and bring your chin to touch the floor.
- Lower your arms, and release the clasp.
- Bend your arms, and your place hands by the sides of your chest.
- Now bring your forehead to touch the floor.
- Stretch your arms out, and place them back by your sides.
- Keep your cheeks on the floor and relax.

Caution: This Asana is not meant for people suffering from peptic ulcers, intestinal problems, hypertension and hernia.

37. PARIPOORNA SHALABHASANA
[Swan Pose]
Benefits: Relieves pain in the sacral and lumbar regions.

Activates the pancreas and bladder.
- Lie down on your abdomen, forehead touching the floor.
- Keeping your legs together, stretch them out.
- Keeping your arms by your sides, tilt your head back, and arch your neck.
- Arching your spine, raise your trunk.
- Keeping your legs straight, raise them.
- Raise your arms until they are parallel to the floor.
- Hold the position for a count of 10.
- Lower your arms and then your legs and lastly your trunk and head.
- Relax with your cheek on the floor.
- For the second time, when you are in the final position after holding it for a few seconds, tense your legs, and stretch them out further.
- Contract your hips, and maintain the tension in your legs for a few seconds.
- Lower your arms, legs and then your trunk and head.
- Relax with your cheek on the floor.

Caution: Same as Sarpasana [Snake]

38. BEKASANA
[Frog Pose]
Benefits: Gives relief to the arthritic and rheumatic conditions of the joints. Strengthens the lower spine and back muscles.

a
- Lie down on your abdomen.
- Put your chin on the floor.
- Bend your knees, and hold your ankles.
- Pressing down on your legs, bring your heels to the outer sides of your hips. Your elbows are bent and point up.

b
- Arching your spine, press your feet down further toward the floor, and raise your head and then your trunk.
- Keep your knees on the floor and slightly apart if necessary.
- Breathing normally, hold the position for a count of 10.

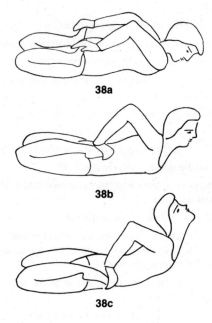

38a

38b

38c

<u>c</u>
- Lower your trunk and then your chin to the floor.
- Release the pressure and then the hold on your ankles.
- Stretch your legs back to the starting position.
- Relax with your cheeks on the floor, and repeat the Asana as before.

39. VAYU NISHANKASANA
   [Gas Releasing Pose]
Benefits: Activates the nerves and helps release excess gas.
- Lie down on your back.
- Bend your knees towards your chest.
- With the help of your arms, press your knees close to your chest.
- Raising your head, bring your chin close to your knees, and hold the position for a count of 10.
- Lower your head, and release the hold on your legs.
- Place your arms back by your sides, and stretch your legs out on the floor.

39

40. JATARA PARIVARTANASANA
   [Legover Both Legs]
Benefits: Tones the liver, spleen and pancreas. Strengthens the intestines. Relieves pain in the lower back. Good for people with sciatica.

<u>a</u>
- Lie down on your back, arms stretched out at shoulder level on both sides.
- Bring your knees towards your chest.
- Using your arms, pull your knees close to your chest.
- Bring your chin up to your knees.
- Hold the position for a count of 10.
- Lower your head to the floor, placing your arms at shoulder level on the floor.
- Raise your legs, and make sure they are straight.

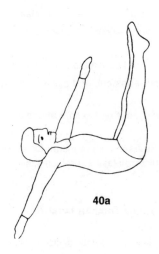

40a

The ideas, suggestions, herbal remedies and diet contained in this book are not intended as a substitue for consulting with your doctor. All matters regarding your health require medical supervision.

40b

b

• Keeping your upper back on the floor, bring your legs to the left side.

• Breathe out, and holding your breath, contract your abdomen.

• Moving your legs together inch by inch on the floor, try to bring them close to your left hand.

• Hold the position for a count of 20.

• Raise your legs, making sure they are straight.

• Bend your knees towards your chest.

• Bring your toes to the floor, and stretch your legs.

c

• Perform similarly on the right side.

Caution: Do not bend your knees or raise your shoulders. Do not twist your neck.

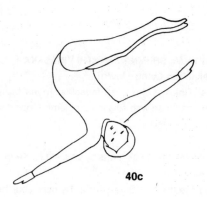

40c

41. JYESTIKA MAKARASANA
[Head Twist]

Benefits: Relaxes the neck. Gives relief to such problems as backaches, slipped discs and spinal disorders. Good for thyroid, voice box and tonsillitis problems.

a

• Lie down on your abdomen.

• Raise your head and shoulders, and place your elbows right below your shoulders on the floor.

• Bend your head so that your chin is close to your chest.

• Place your hands behind your head, pressing your chin close to your chest.

• Hold the position for a count of 10.

• Release the pressure by letting go of the left hand.

41a

41b

41c

b

- By pressing your head with your right palm to keep your chin close to your chest, twist your neck to the left. If possible, without moving your chin away from your chest, bring your chin onto your left palm by the side of your left shoulder. Do not move your elbows.
- Hold the position for a count of 10.
- Move your neck to the front, keeping your chin close to your chest.

c

- Bring your left hand back behind your head and this time, release your right hand.
- Continue to twist the neck to the right. Your chin is on your right hand, and your left hand is at the back of your head.
- Hold the position for a count of 10.
- Bring your neck to the front as before, and repeat the Asana once more on both sides.

Caution: Keep your chin close to the body. Do not lift your head when trying to twist your neck or when trying to place your chin on your hands.

42. SUPTA BADRASANA
[Knee and Thigh Stretch Lying Down]
Benefits: Clears arthritis in the hip joints. Helps backache problems due to slipped disc or sciatica. Good for strengthening the reproductive organs. Pregnant women get good results from this Asana.

a

- Lie down on your back.
- Bend your right leg, bringing your right heel close to your buttocks. Do not lift your heel off the floor.

42a

- When your right knee is pointing up, bend your thigh towards the right side, and try to bring your right knee to touch the floor.
- Hold the position for a count of 10.
- Raise your right knee, keeping your right foot close to the left thigh on the floor.
- Now stretch your leg.
- Perform similarly with the left leg.

b

- Now bend both your legs, bringing your heels close to your buttocks.
- When your knees are together in an upright position, spread them apart, and bring them by your sides. The soles of your feet touch each other.
- Try lowering your knees to your sides as close to the floor as possible.
- Hold the position for a count of 10.
- Raise your knees, place your feet on the floor, and stretch your legs out.

Caution: Do not lift your feet off the floor when your heels are close to your buttocks.

42b

43. SUPTA MUSHUMNA SHAKTHI VIKASAKA
[Pelvic Tilt Lying Down]
Benefits: Relaxes the back muscles. Tones the disc region. Helps those with sciatica problems. Good Asana for back problems.

a

- Lie down on your back, arms by your sides. Keep your legs together.
- As you breathe in, raise your arms over your head, and stretch them.

43

- Keeping your legs together and arching your ankles outward, stretch your toes. Your spine is arched away from the floor.

b

- Now breathe out, and at the same time place your arms by your sides.

- Arching your ankles inwards, point your toes towards you. Your shoulders are off the ground.

- Now move your spine toward the floor.

- Repeat the Asana 5 times.

Note: At every exhalation, try to place your entire back on the floor.

44. MATSYA KRIDASANA
   [Flapping Fish Pose]
Benefits: Relaxes the sciatic nerve and promotes hip joint mobility.

- Assume Advasana, and hold the position for a count of 30.

- Bend your right elbow, and place your right hand by the side of your chest.

- Turn your neck, and look towards the right.

- Bending your left arm at the elbow, place it under your head so that your cheek rests on it.

- Bend your right leg at the knee, and bring your right thigh towards your chest. Your right heel is close to your right buttock.

44

- By your clasping hands together, place your right elbow on your right knee.

- Keep your left leg straight.

- Hold the position for a count of 30.

- Release your clasped hands, and stretch your right leg out.

- Put your forehead on the floor, and stretch your left arm over your head. Now stretch your right arm overhead.

- Hold the position for another count of 30 before performing the Asana on the other side.

5

Asanas for Advanced Learners
❧

This chapter has additional benefits in store for the advanced group of Yoga learners. Include some Asanas from this group into your daily routine. The Asanas may be performed along with a daily routine or after the completion of the basic Asanas. During practice, bear the following in mind:

- Perform the Asanas slowly, with a pause in between them.
- Spend more time holding the postures.
- Avoid straining yourself, as this may cause more stress on your muscles.

1. SHIRASASANA
[Headstand]

Benefits: Clearer thoughts due to the supply of fresh blood to the brain. General improvement in health and growth as the pineal and pituitary glands are nourished by the Asana.

One of the most important Yogasanas, Shirasana has many variations. However, do not attempt them until you perfect Shirasana. Before getting into the final posture of this Asana, master the first and second stages of Bumi Pada Mastakasana [Headstand Modified] in chapter 3 first.

- Get into the final position of Bumi Pada Mastakasana [Headstand Modified].
- Slowly raise your legs, and keeping your spine straight, straighten them. Retain your breath while raising your legs off the floor.
- Staying in the final position depends upon your confidence level of comfort experienced. For starters, the recommended holding time is 30 seconds. Gradually increase the time by 30 seconds up to a maximum of 5 minutes.

To come out of Shirasana:

- Balancing on your forehead and elbows, bend your knees towards your chest. Slowly lower your feet to the floor.
- Rest your trunk against your thighs, and keep your forehead in front of your knees.
- Relax for 30 seconds.
- Now perform Shavasana [Corpse Pose] until your heartbeat becomes normal.

Caution: It is better to perform this Asana before Tadasana [Stretch Pose] (see chapter 4) at the end of the programme. Do it on an empty stomach. On a hot day, do not stay in the final pose for a long time. People who suffer from high blood pressure, heart palpitations, vertigo and constipation should avoid this Asana.

Concentration: Sahasrara Chakra (crown of the head).

1

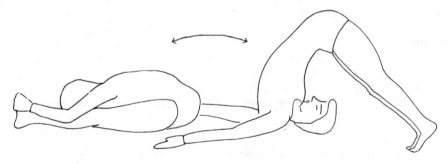

3

2. PADMA SARVANGASANA
[Shoulderstand in Lotus]

Benefits: Releases normal gravitational pressure on anal muscles, thereby relieving haemorrhoids. Tones the reproductive organs, spine and legs. Develops consciousness of body temperature.

- Perform Shoulderstand (see chapter 2).
- Folding your legs, assume the Lotus position in the final pose.
- Hold the position for about 30 seconds to 1 minute, depending on your comfort level.
- Release the Lotus lock, and straighten your legs upwards.
- Again hold the position for about 30 seconds to 1 minute.
- Again assume the Lotus position, this time changing the position of your legs.
- Hold the position to your comfort, then stretch your legs out.
- Lower your trunk, and come out as in Shoulderstand.

Variation of Shoulderstand in Lotus

- Sit down in the Lotus position.
- Recline your back, and lie down flat on the floor.
- As in Shoulderstand, raise your folded legs.
- Hold the position to your comfort.
- Lower your folded knees towards your chest, and roll forward to the sitting position in the Lotus Pose.

Caution: Shoulderstand in Lotus should only be attempted by those who can perform Lotus in the sitting position comfortably.

3. DRUTA HALASANA
[Plough Dynamic]

Benefits: Activates the intestinal peristaltic motion. Redistributes fats around the pelvic region.
This Asana involves rapid movements.

- Once you assume the Plough position, breathe out.
- Holding your breath, roll forward to the Backstretch position.
- Lower your trunk to the floor.
- Take a breath, and breathe out.
- Holding your breath again, swing your legs together into the Plough position.
- Repeat the entire to and fro motion continuously as many times as possible without any strain.

Caution: People with high blood pressure, sciatica and back pain should avoid this Asana.

4. SUPTA VEERASANA
[Fish in Veerasana]

Benefits: Stimulates the adrenal glands by putting pressure on the small of the back. Tones muscles by increasing circulation to the abdominal area, kidneys, liver and pancreas.

a
- Sit in Veerasana.

b
- By bending backwards and supporting your body with your elbows, lie down flat on your back.

c
- Raise your arms one at a time, and bring them over your head.
- Keep your arms on the floor by the sides of your ears.

- Hold the position for a few seconds.
- Now bend your elbows, and place your hands, palms down, by the sides of your head.
- Raising your shoulders, tilt your neck backwards.
- Arching your spine, raise your trunk.
- Arch your neck further, and place the top of your head on the floor.
- Interlace your arms.
- Hold the position to your comfort.
- Stretch your arms, bringing them forward to hold your toes.
- Using your elbows for support, raise your trunk to a sitting position.

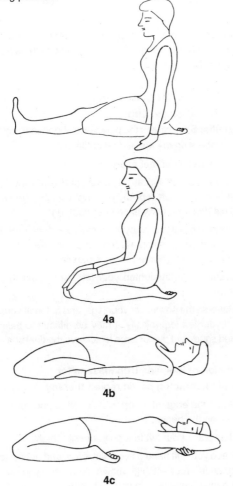

4a

4b

4c

Caution: Do not strain the muscles of your thighs by forcing your knees to touch the floor.

Concentration: Manipura Chakra (the adrenal glands) or Anahata Chakra (the thymus gland).

5. MATSYASANA
[Fish in Lotus]
Benefits: This Asana stretches the intestines and abdominal organs. Stretching the neck benefits the thyroid. The pelvic joint becomes flexible.

a
- Sit in Padmasana.

b
- Bending backwards and supporting your body with your elbows, lie down flat on the floor.
- Raise your arms one at a time, and bring them over your head.
- Keep your arms on the floor by the sides of your ears.
- Hold the position for a while.
- Now bend your elbows and place your hands, palms down, by the sides of your head.

c
- With the help of your hands, raise your shoulders, and arch your neck.
- Place the top of your head on the floor.
- Arch your spine to your comfort.
- Interlace your arms.
- Hold the positionto your comfort.

d
- Stretch your arms, and place them on your thighs.
- Now hold your toes.
- Using your elbows, raise your trunk to a sitting position.

Concentration: Manipura Chakra (the adrenal glands) or Anahata Chakra (the thymus gland).

6. UTTHANASANA
[Squat]
Benefits: Strengthens the uterine muscles, inner thighs, knees and ankles.

a
- Stand straight with your feet about 2 feet apart.

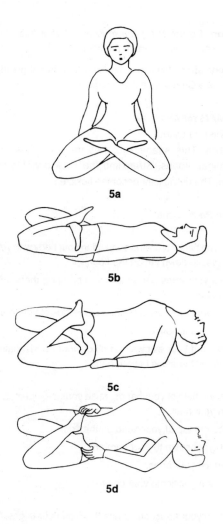

5a

5b

5c

5d

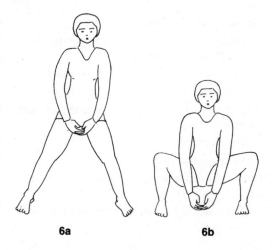

6a   6b

- Interlace your fingers in front of your abdomen. Your arms hang freely.

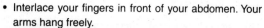

b

- Breathing out and keeping your heels pressed to the floor, slowly bend your knees, and lower your trunk to a squatting position.
- Hold the position for a breath.
- Once in a comfortable position, breathe in, and straighten your knees, assuming the starting position.
- Repeat the Asana as many times as possible.

Note: Keep your spine straight throughout the Asana.

Caution: Do not try to get into the extreme position immediately. Do this gradually, each time increasing the bending of your knees.

7. EKAPADA UTTHANASANA
[Squat Single Leg]

Benefits: Strengthens the pelvic and abdominal regions, and limbers up the knees and ankle joints.

- Stand with your feet apart.
- Bend your left leg at the knee, and place the outer side of your left foot on your right thigh. The whole weight of your body is on your right leg.
- Breathing out, squat by bending your right knee to a comfortable position. Keep your spine straight. In the final position, your left thigh is parallel to the floor.
- Breathing in, straighten your left leg by raising your trunk.
- Reverse the position of your legs, and balance yourself on your left leg. Initially, it may be difficult to balance and squat, but do not force to achieve the final position.

Variation of Ekapada Utthanasana for those undergoing pelvic region therapy

- Sit on the edge of a bench. Your left buttock does not rest on the bench.
- Now place your left foot on your right thigh.
- Place your left hand on your left knee, and gently apply pressure. Your left thigh moves down, and you will feel a gentle movement in your left pelvic joint.

- Hold the position for a few seconds, and then release the pressure.
- Repeat by pressing and releasing pressure a couple of times.
- Perform the same way on your right side.

8. GARUDASANA
[Eagle Pose]

Benefits: Helps reduce stiffness in the shoulders, strengthens the ankles and relieves cramps in the calf muscles.

- Stand in Samasthiti.
- Bend your right knee a little.
- Bring your left leg over your right thigh.
- Now twisting at your left knee, bring your left foot behind your right calf.
- Bend your elbows, and bring them in front of your chest.
- Entwine your left arm around your right arm.
- If possible, clasp your hands together.
- Hold the position to your comfort.

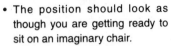

8

- Relax your arms, followed by your legs.
- Now perform the Asana by balancing yourself on your left leg.

Caution: It is not easy interlocking your legs. Forcing yourself to do this may cause discomfort in your knees. For starters, practise the Asana by sitting on a chair.

9. UTKATASANA
[Imaginary Chair]

Benefits: Removes stiffness in shoulders, lifts the diaphragm, and massages the apex of the heart.

- Stand with your feet 1 foot apart.
- Breathing in, raise your arms over your head from your sides.

9

- Keep your arms straight, and interlace your fingers, palms facing down. Keep your chin up and spine straight.
- Breathing out and holding your breath, lower your trunk to a squatting position by bending your knees (If you are unable to retain your breath for a considerable period of time without strain, do this in the final position. Alternatively, breathing normally, stay in the final position by putting pressure on your heels).
- The position should look as though you are getting ready to sit on an imaginary chair.
- In the squatting position, stretch your arms upwards.
- Without straining yourself, hold the position for as long as you can hold your breath out.
- Relax your arms, and then raise your trunk by straightening your knees.
- Breathe in, and relax before repeating the Asana again.

Caution: Do not force yourself to hold your breath for too long, as this may strain your lungs. Do not raise your heels from the floor during the course of the Asana.

10. VRUKSHASANA
[Tree Pose]

Benefits: Activates all the joints of the body, particularly the knee and ankle joints. Tones the thigh and leg muscles.

a
- Stand on your left leg, and fold your right leg at the knee.
- Place your right foot on the inner side of your left thigh, bringing it up as high as possible.
- If you can, press the toes of your right leg against your left thigh. If not, place the entire sole of your right foot on your left thigh. The folded leg is at a right angle to the other leg.

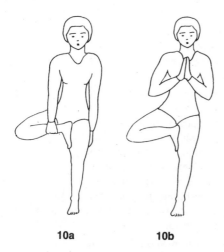

10a   **10b**

<u>b</u>

- Breathing in, raise both your arms sideways, and bring them over your head.
- Join your palms together.
- Breathing out, bend your arms at the elbows, and place your hands on your head. If you find it difficult to do this, place your hands in front of your chest.
- As you breathe in, try to give a backward push on the folded elbows, letting your chest expand.
- Move your right knee slightly backwards.
- Tense your entire body.
- Retain your breath, and maintain the tension for a few seconds.
- Loosen the tension, and breathe out.
- Breathing in, straighten your arms upwards, and breathing out, bring them by the your sides.
- Lower your right leg.
- Perform similarly with the other leg.

Caution: Do not strain your lungs by holding your breath for too long.

Variation of Vrukshasana

- Stand straight with your feet together.
- Bending your right leg at the knee, lift your right foot off the floor. Do not bend your left leg.

- Hold your right ankle, and place your right foot against the left side of your lower abdomen. Keep your right knee close to your left knee.
- As you breathe in, raise your arms overhead, until your palms touch each other.
- As you breathe out, bend your elbows, and place your wrists on top of your head.
- Breathe in, and let your chest expand.
- Tighten your whole body by tensing or keeping the body stiff.
- Hold the position for a few counts.
- Relax and breathe out.
- As you breathe in, raise your arms, and breathing out, lower them to your sides.
- Now bring your right foot down.
- Perform the Asana by bending your left leg and placing your left foot against the right side of your lower abdomen.

11. SANTULANA ASANA
   [Balance Posture]

Benefits: Improves blood circulation. Tones muscles and relieves pain in the knees, ankles, shoulders and elbow joints.

<u>a</u>
- Stand in Samasthiti.
- As you breathe in, raise your right arm in front of you over your head. The upper part of your arm is by the side of your right ear and fingers are together, pointing upwards.

<u>b</u>
- Shift your weight to your right leg, and bend your left leg at the knee.
- Hold your left ankle with your left hand.
- Keeping your knees together and bending your left elbow, pull your left foot close to your buttocks.

<u>c</u>
- Drop your head backwards to look at your right hand.
- Arch your spine a little.
- Hold the position for a count of 10.
- Straighten your spine.
- Repeat the Asana again.

11a	**11b**	**11c**	**11d**

- This time arch your spine more, pulling your left foot higher and stretching your right arm as far behind as possible.
- Hold the position without any strain.
- Straighten your spine.
- Lower your left foot, and breathing out, lower your right arm.

d
- Perform the Asana by balancing yourself on your left leg.

Note: If you find it difficult to balance yourself on one leg, use the side of a chair or table for support.

12. NATARAJASANA
[Shiva's Pose]
Benefits: Removes rigidity in the spine and joints.

a
- Stand in Samasthiti.
- As you breathe in, raise your left arm, and bring it near your left ear.
- Bend your right leg at the knee, and hold your right ankle firmly.
- Stretch your trunk and left arm.

b
- As you breathe out, bend your trunk and your left arm forward.

- At the same time, pull your right foot as high as possible, bringing your right knee behind.
- Look at your left hand.
- In the final position, your right thigh, trunk and left arm are parallel to the floor.
- Hold the position for a while.
- Straighten your trunk.
- Lower your right leg first and then your left arm.
- Now perform the Asana by balancing yourself on your right leg.

12a

12b

The ideas, suggestions, herbal remedies and diet contained in this book are not intended as a substitue for consulting with your doctor. All matters regarding your health require medical supervision.

13

13. SAMAKONASANA
[Right Angle Stretch Pose]

Benefits: Promotes spinal growth and relieves tension in spinal nerves.

- Stand straight, hands clasped together behind your head.
- Bend your body at the waist so the spine is horizontal to the floor.
- Look up and stretch your spine, and then spread your arms wide, keeping them in line with your shoulders.
- Bring your arms over your head as before, loosen your body, and assume the standing position.
- Lower your arms to your sides.

Note: If you find it difficult to perform this Asana with your hands clasped together behind your head, try stretching your arms over your head. Keeping your arms straight and bending your trunk forward, make sure your arms and trunk are parallel to the floor. Try looking up by tilting your head upwards. Relax your head and neck before straightening your trunk to the starting position.

14. MUSHUMNA SHAKTIVIKASAKA
[Pelvic Tilt]

Benefits: Improves mobility in the pelvic region. Relieves lower backache and pain resulting from sciatica.

a
- Stand one foot away from the wall.

- Bend your knees slightly so your buttocks rest against the wall.
- As you breathe in, expand your chest, and push your abdomen outwards so your spine curls away from the wall.

b
- As you breathe out, move your navel (by squeezing your abdomen while breathing out) towards the wall, pushing your abdomen inwards. This makes your lower back move towards the wall and your shoulders rounded.
- As you inhale, make your lower back curl, and move away from the wall.
- Repeat curling and straightening the spine as many times as possible. Coordinate these movements with your breathing.

Caution: Those who find it difficult to stand may perform Supta Mushumna Shakthi Vikasaka [Pelvic Tilt Lying Down] in the intermediate group for the same results.

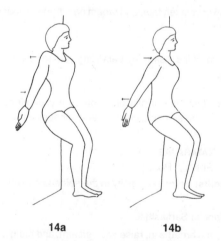

14a   **14b**

15. UTTITA PARSHVA TRIKONASANA
[Triangle Stretched Knee 1]

Benefits: Improves mobility and blood circulation.

a
- Stand in Samasthiti.
- Raise your arms from your sides to shoulder level.

- Spread your feet apart to the maximum.
- Adjust your left foot so your toes point towards your left (move your heel by using your toes as a pivot).
- Keep your right foot pointing inwards a little.
- Bend your left knee so your left thigh is parallel to the floor.
- Keep your chest facing the front throughout the Asana.

b
- Bend your trunk to the left, and place your left hand on the floor beside your left foot.
- Roll your right arm at shoulder level, and bring it over your right ear so your arm is parallel to the floor.
- Arch your neck backwards, and look at your hand.
- Hold the position for a count of 20.
- Straighten your neck.
- Raise your right arm, and roll it at shoulder level.
- Still keeping your left knee bent and arms in one line, raise your trunk.
- Now straighten your left leg.
- Adjust your feet, and bring them to the starting position.
- Perform similarly on the right side by bending your right knee. Relax for a while after the Asana.

15a

15b

16a

16b

16. UTTITA PARSHVA PARIVRATA TRIKONASANA [Triangle Stretched Knee 2]

Benefits: Improves blood circulation and mobility in the joints.

a
- Stand in Samasthiti.
- Raise your arms from your sides to shoulder level, and spread your feet.
- Adjust your right foot by moving your heel so that your toes point to the right.
- Twist your trunk to the right. By moving your left heel, adjust your left foot.
- When your trunk is twisted completely to the right, bend your right knee, keeping your right thigh parallel to the floor.

b
- Bend your trunk to the right.
- Place your left arm on the outer side of your right foot.
- Roll your right arm at shoulder level, bringing it over your right ear, and keep it parallel to the floor.
- Tilting your head backwards, look at your right hand.
- Hold the position for a count of 20.
- Raise your right arm, and roll it at shoulder level.
- Keeping your arms in one line, straighten your trunk. At this stage, your trunk is still twisted to the right.

- When your trunk is straight, straighten your right knee.
- Now twist your trunk to the front, and adjust your feet.
- Perform the Asana on the left side.

Variation of Uttita Parshva Parivrata Trikonasana
Instead of twisting your trunk first and then bending your knee to the side, bend your knee before twisting your trunk. When coming out of the pose, twist your trunk forward first, and then straighten your knee.

17. VEERA BHADRASANA
[Hero Posture]

There are four stages in this Asana. Perform each stage one at a time, holding the position for as long as you are comfortable. Come out of each of the final positions in reverse order. Once you understand the movements fully, all the four stages can be performed as one single Asana. The stages are as follows:

Benefits: Relieves cramps in the calves and thighs.

<u>a</u>
- Stand in Samasthiti.
- Inhaling, raise your arms to shoulder level, palms facing down.
- Spread your feet apart to the maximum.
- Move your left heel forward so your toes point to the left.
- Your right toes point inwards.
- Now bend your left knee.
- Keep your left thigh parallel to the floor. Your right leg is straight.
- Twist your head to the left, and look at your left hand.
- Hold the position for a few seconds.

Benefits: Relieves stiffness in the back and shoulders.

<u>b</u>
- As you exhale, bring your right palm to touch your left palm.
- Your arms are parallel to the floor and in line with your left thigh.
- Keep your left knee bent.
- Without bending your elbows, inhale, and raise your arms over your head so your fingers point upwards.
- By arching your neck back, look at your fingers.
- Expand your chest fully.
- Hold the position for few seconds.

<u>c</u>
- Keeping your head tilted back, lower your trunk forward so it rests on your left thigh.
- Keep your arms parallel to the floor and your right leg straight. Hold your gaze on your thumbs.

Benefits: Tones the abdominal and leg muscles. Enhances the feeling of harmony, balance, poise and power. Improves concentration and tones the nervous system.

<u>d</u>
- If possible, straighten your left leg by lifting your right leg off the floor.
- Keep your trunk, arms and right leg parallel to the floor.
- Hold your gaze on your thumbs.
- Your left leg supports the entire body. Do not strain yourself.
- By bending your left knee, lower your right leg to the floor, so your trunk rests on your left thigh, which is parallel to the floor.
- Keeping your left knee bent, breathe in, and raise your trunk.
- Your arms are parallel to the floor.
- Bring your right arm to the right side, and twist your head forward.

17d

- Straighten your left leg, and adjust your feet.
- Now perform the Asana on the other side.

Note: It is good to perform Uttanasana [Legclasp Migraine Pose] (see chapter 4) after this Asana to prevent tension.

18. ARDHA CHANDRASANA
[Half Moon Pose]

Benefits: Strengthens the knees and tones the nerves connected to the lower back.

a
- Stand in Samasthiti.
- Raise your arms from your sides to shoulder level.
- Bending your right knee, bend your trunk to the right.
- Place your right hand on the floor by the side of your right foot.
- Put your left hand on your left thigh.
- Drop your head towards the right, bringing your right ear close to your right shoulder.
- Adjust your right hand until you achieve a position of good balance.

18a

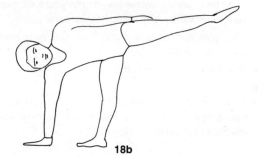

18b

b
- As you exhale, raise your left leg, and straighten your right hand.
- Feel the tension on your right foot and right hand. The right side of your body is parallel to the floor.
- Hold the position for as long as you are comfortable, and come out of it in reverse order.
- Now perform the Asana on the other side.

Caution: Attempt this Asana only when you are truly confident of performing it well. If done wrongly, it may cause more harm than good.

19. PARIGHASANA
[Triangle Kneeling]

Benefits: Tones abdominal muscles. Sideways spinal movement gives relief to a stiff back.
- Kneel down on the floor, keeping your thighs perpendicular to the floor.
- Breathing in, raise your arms from your sides to shoulder level.
- Stretch your right leg to the right side.
- Keep your right heel in line with your left knee.
- As you exhale, bend your trunk to the right.
- Place your right hand on your right leg.
- Roll your left shoulder, your left palm facing up.
- As you breathe in, bring your left arm over your left ear.

19

- Gliding your right hand further down your right leg, pull your trunk as far out to the right as possible.
- Drop your neck to the right so your right ear is on your right shoulder.
- Hold the position for a count of 20.
- As you exhale, raise your left arm.
- When your left arm is in line with your right arm, roll your left arm at shoulder level.
- As you inhale, raise your trunk.
- When your trunk is upright and arms are parallel to the floor, bring your right leg back to the starting position.
- Now stretch your left leg to left side, and perform the Asana again.

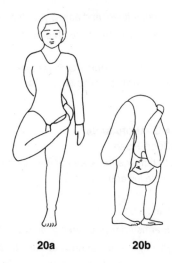

20a   20b

20. ARDHA BADDHA PADMA UTTANASANA
[Legclasp Single Leg]

Benefits: Relieves stiffness in the knees. Increases the peristaltic activity of the abdomen.

<u>a</u>
- Stand in Samasthiti.
- Bend your knee, and raise your right leg.
- Place your right foot on your upper left thigh or, if possible, place it on the left side of your lower abdomen.
- Bring your right arm from behind, and hold the big toe of your right foot. If you find this difficult to do, hold your right foot with your right hand from the front.

<u>b</u>
- As you breathe out, bend your trunk forward, all the way down.
- Place your left hand or your fingertips by the side of your left foot.
- Drop your neck until your forehead points to your left knee.
- Breathing normally, hold the position for a while.
- As you inhale (in a relaxed manner), raise your trunk.
- Release the hold on your right toe before lowering it.
- Now perform the Asana on the other side.

Caution: People with a slipped disc or sciatica should avoid this Asana.

21. RISHI
[Rishi's Posture]

Benefits: Stretches and tones the muscles and connective tissues. Releases stiffness in the spine. Stretches nerves that emerge from the spinal column. Removes tension in the neck. Develops the power of concentration. Good for poise and sense of balance.

<u>a</u>
- Stand in Samasthiti.
- As you breathe in, raise your arms to shoulder level in front, palms facing down. Your thumbs touch each other.
- Come up on your toes.
- Now concentrate on the back of your right hand, and breathing out, twist your trunk and arms at your waist to the right.
- If you find it uncomfortable standing on your toes, twist your trunk without coming up on your toes.
- Keep your arms parallel to the floor, and try to keep your heels together.
- Now lower your heels to the floor.

<u>b</u>
- As you breathe out, twist your trunk further, and bend it towards your right, all the while holding your gaze on the back of your right hand.

- Raise your right arm so your fingers point upwards, and, at same time, place your left hand behind your right knee.

c
- Bend your left arm at the elbow, and pull in your trunk further.
- Hold the position for as long as you are comfortable.
- Your neck is twisted slightly so your eyes can focus on the back of your right hand.
- As you breathe in, raise your trunk, which is twisted to the right.
- When your trunk is straight, your arms are at shoulder level to the right. They remain straight and are parallel to the floor, palms facing down.
- As you breathe out, and remaining on your toes, twist your trunk to the front the same way as before. Continue twisting to the left, and perform the Asana on the left side.
- Now perform the Asana on both sides, bringing your hands down to the calf region.
- Hold each position for as long as you are comfortable.

d
- Now increase the bending with a twist to the right side so your left hand is placed on your right ankle.

21c

21d

- Hold the position to your comfort, and with the twist, straighten your trunk.
- Now twist to the left, and perform the Asana again.
- After straightening your trunk, twist it to the front, coming down on the soles of your feet.
- Breathing out, lower your arms.

Note: You achieve better balance by coming up higher on your toes. In the beginning, perform without holding any position to get the movements and breathing order right. This helps you achieve more flexibility in the joints as well as builds your confidence to balance yourself on your toes. Increase the twisting and bending gradually each time.

Caution: People suffering from high blood pressure and vertigo should avoid this Asana, as should pregnant women and women going through their menstrual cycle. People with chronic abdominal disorders, spinal injury or sacral infections should also avoid this Asana.

Concentration: Vishuddi Chakra (the thyroid gland) and Swadisthana Chakra (gonads/ovaries).

22. SIRAS ANGUSHTA YOGASANA
[Chest Expansion 3]
Benefits: Stretches the hamstring muscles and gives a lateral stretch to the spine. Stimulates the nerves and improves blood circulation. Helps increase the appetite.

a
- Stand in Samasthiti.
- Clasp your hands together behind your back.
- Keeping your arms straight, raise them.
- Stretch your left leg to the side at an angle of about 45 degrees from your right leg. Your feet are placed diagonally on the opposite corners of an imaginary square. Your toes are pointing in the same direction.

b
- As you exhale, bend your trunk forward.
- Bend your left knee outwards so your left thigh is almost parallel to the floor.
- Raise your arms further.
- Swing your trunk to the left so your left shoulder is close to the inner side of your left knee.

22a

22b

- Lower your head, pointing your forehead towards your left ankle.
- Hold the position to your comfort.
- Still keeping your left knee bent, move your trunk to the front.
- Now straighten your knee.
- As you inhale, straighten your trunk, bringing your feet together.
- Now perform the Asana with your right knee bent.

Caution: People with back problems should avoid this Asana.

23. DRUTA USHTRASANA
[Camel Dynamic]

Benefits: Stretches the stomach and intestines. Relieves constipation.

- Kneel down on the floor, toes bent and thighs perpendicular to the floor.
- Place your hands on your back as in Ushtrasana [Camel Pose] (see chapter 4), and arch your spine backwards.
- Lower your hands one at a time to hold your heels.
- Now, breathing in, stretch your left arm forward.
- Keeping your arm straight, palm facing up, raise your arm, and bring it as far back as possible.
- Drop your head back without any strain.
- Bring your arm to the front, and look to the front.

- Lower your arm to hold your heel again.
- Now perform similarly on your right side.

Caution: Same as Ushtrasana [Camel Pose].

24. TIRYAKA USHTRASANA
[Camel Leaning]

Benefits: Good for getting rid of a rounded back and lumbago. Relieves arthritic condition in the shoulders.

- Sit in Veerasana.
- Keep your knees apart.
- Raise your trunk off the floor.
- As you inhale, stretch your arms out by your sides.

- Exhale and your twist torso to the right, bend backwards, and hold your left heel with your right hand.
- Raise your left arm in front as high as possible.
- Look at your left hand.
- Straighten your neck, and lower your left arm to shoulder level.

24

- Release the hold on your left heel, raise your right arm and twist your trunk to the front.
- Perform the Asana again, now twisting your trunk to the left.

Caution: People who suffer from high blood pressure and constant headaches should avoid this Asana.

25. VYGHRASANA
[Tiger Pose]

Benefits: Relieves pain due to sciatica and tones the reproductive organs. Helps strengthen the pelvic and uterus regions.

a
- Go down on all fours.
- Keep your arms and thighs parallel to each other and perpendicular to the floor. Your hands are on the floor at shoulder width level.

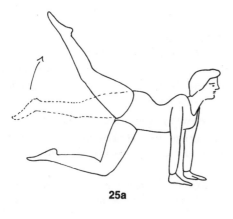

25a

25b

25c

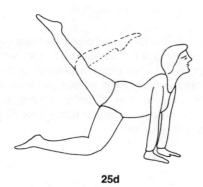

25d

- In this position, keep your back hunched and head lowered towards the floor.
- Now tilt your head up.
- As you breathe in, arch your back inwards.
- As you exhale, stretch out your right leg, instep facing the floor.
- Raise your leg as high as possible, keeping it straight.

b
- Now inhale, and bend your knee to bring your right heel close to your buttocks.
- As you exhale, hunch your back up, and drop your head inwards towards your chest.

c
- Bring your right knee close to your forehead and your right heel close to your buttocks.
- Hold the position as long as possible to hold out your breath.

d
- Tilt your head up while keeping your right heel close to your buttocks.
- As you inhale, raise your knee upwards, and, at same time, arch your back inwards. Your chest expands.
- As you exhale, stretch your leg upwards, straightening it.
- As you breathe in, bring your toes onto the floor, and bend your right leg at the knee, bringing it back to the starting position. Your head is arched. Keep looking up.
- As you exhale, raise your trunk to a hunched position before lowering your head
- Relax in Shashankasana [Baby Pose] (see chapter 3) for a while.
- Now perform the Asana again by raising your left leg.

Caution: People with high blood pressure must be careful when performing this Asana as it increases blood pressure. At the end of the Asana, perform Grivasana [Neck Roll] (see chapter 4) to avoid strain in the neck.

26. VEERASANA
[Hero Sitting Posture]
Benefits: Improves the mobility of the knee and ankle joints. Helps relax leg and thigh muscles.

- Sit in Vajrasana, legs folded and buttocks on your heels.
- Stretch your left leg, and place your left foot on your right thigh.
- Place your hands, palms facing each other, in front of your chest in namaste.
- Take a breath.
- Hold your breath, and using your right leg as a lever on the floor, raise your trunk off the floor.
- Raise your hands over your head, fingers pointing upwards.
- Breathe normally, holding the position to your comfort.
- Lower your buttocks onto the floor.
- Stretch your left leg followed by your right.
- Perform the Asana again, placing your right foot on your left thigh.

26

27. SIDDHA YONI ASANA
[Female Accomplished Pose]

Benefits: Tones the nerves that control the reproductive system and improves circulation to the region. Gives relief to menopausal problems.

- Sit down with your legs stretched out in front.
- Fold your left leg, and place the sole of your foot flat against your inner right thigh.
- Place your heel inside the labia majora.
- Fold your right leg, and place the foot on top of your left calf.

27

- Pull the toes of your left leg up into the space between your right calf and right thigh. The heels of your feet are on top of each other.

Caution: People suffering from sciatica should avoid this Asana.

28. SIDDHASANA
[Male Accomplished Pose]

Benefits: Tones the nerves and improves circulation to the prostate glands and gonads. Has a calming effect on the entire nervous system.

- Sit down with your legs stretched out in front.
- Fold your right leg, and place the sole of your right foot against your left thigh, heel pressing against the perineum.
- Fold your left leg, and place your left foot on top of your right calf. The left heel presses against the pelvic region.
- Push your left toes, and edge into the space between your right calf and thigh muscles.
- Grab hold of the toes of your right foot, and pull them upwards into the space between your left thigh and calf.

Caution: People suffering from sciatica should avoid this Asana.

29. LOLASANA OR TOLASANA
[Scale Balance Pose]

Benefits: Strengthens the hands and wrists. Tones the back and abdominal muscles.

- Sit in Padmasana.
- Place your hands on the floor by the sides of your thighs.
- Balancing yourself on your hands, raise your whole body off the floor.
- Hold the position for a count of 10.

Caution: Do not force yourself to sit in the Lotus Pose. If you are unable to sit in Padmasana, sit down with your legs stretched out in front. Place your hands on the floor by your sides, and pressing them, raise your trunk. Place your right sole under your left buttock. Folding your left leg, place your left sole under your right buttock. Sit down on the soles of your feet.

30. BARADWAJASANA

[Twist in Veerasana]

Benefits: Tones the abdominal muscles. Increases the peristaltic motion of the intestines. Relieves pain in the lower back due to postural problems.

- Sit down with your legs stretched out in front.
- Bend your left leg, and place your left foot against your upper right thigh. Do not lift your left knee off the floor.
- Bend your right leg, placing your right foot by the outer side of your right hip.
- Place your left hand behind on the floor. Your right hand is on your left knee. Keep your spine straight.

30

- Move your head so that your chin is close to your left shoulder.
- As you breathe out, twist your trunk towards the left, holding your left knee firmly.
- First twist the trunk, and then use your shoulders to twist further. Keep your spine straight.
- If possible, hold the front of your right thigh with your left hand from behind.
- Breathing normally, hold the position for a count of 20.
- Lower your left hand onto the floor.
- Breathing out, twist your trunk forward, then twist your neck to the front.
- Repeat the Asana.
- Change the position of legs, and perform the Asana twice on the right side.

31. MARICHYASANA

[Elbow to Knee]

Benefits: Stretches the muscles on the back and sides. Activates the abdominal organs. Tones the spinal column. This Asana is best performed in the Lotus position. If you experience difficulty sitting in this position, perform the Asana in the standing position. See Meru Prishtasana [Spine and Back Pose] in chapter 4.

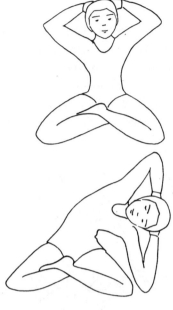
31a

<u>a</u>
- Sit in the Lotus position, keeping your spine straight.
- Raise your arms from your sides, and interlace your fingers behind your head.
- Keeping your chin up and elbows pointing sideways, take a breath.
- As you breathe out, stretch your trunk, and bend to the left.
- Bring your left elbow close to the floor. Do not lean forward. Keep your right elbow pointing up.
- Hold the position for a count of 10.
- Breathing in, straighten your trunk.
- Breathing out, twist your trunk to the left.
- Keep your elbows parallel to the floor, and breathe in.

<u>b</u>
- Now breathing out and your twisting further, bend your trunk, bringing your right elbow towards your left knee.
- Try raising your left elbow as high as possible.
- Breathing normally, hold the position for a count of 10.
- Breathing in, straighten your trunk with a twist, and breathing out, twist your trunk forward.
- Perform the Asana again on the right.

- When your trunk faces the front, take a breath, and breathing out, stretch your spine, and bend forward.
- Keep your elbows parallel to the floor.
- Bring your forehead close to the floor.
- Hold the position for a breath.
- Breathing in, straighten your trunk.
- Breathing out, release the clasp behind your head, and lower your arms.

31b

Variation of Marichyasana

- When bending to the left, instead of stretching your trunk, compress the left side of your trunk, bringing your left elbow to the floor. Your left elbow is placed close to your left hip.
- Bend similarly on the right side.
- When bending forward, begin compressing the abdominal area, and curl your spine.
- Breathing out, lower your trunk.
- Bring your forehead close to your legs.
- Hold the position for a count of 10.
- Straighten your trunk in a relaxed manner.

32. UDARAKARSHANA ASANA
[Abdominal Massage Twist]

Benefits: Compresses and stretches the abdominal organs and muscles, thereby eliminating abdominal ailments such as constipation.

32

- Sit down on the floor, and stretch your legs.
- Bend your left knee, and place your left foot by the side of your left hip. Your left knee is on the floor in front.
- Bend your right knee, and place your right foot on the floor by the side of your left knee. Your right knee is upright.
- Hold your right knee with your left hand.
- Place your right hand on the floor behind your right hip.
- Bring your chin close to your right shoulder.
- Pull your right knee towards the left with your left hand, and take a breath.
- Breathe out, and move your abdominal area to the right. Now twist the upper part of your trunk to the right.
- Adjust your right hand to achieve a maximum twist.
- Breathing normally, hold the position for a count of 20.
- Breathing out, twist your trunk forward first, release tension in the abdominal area, and then release the pull on your right knee.
- Repeat the Asana twice on the right.
- Change the position of your legs, and perform the Asana on the left side.

33. UPAVISHTA KONASANA
[Backstretch Seated Angle]

Benefits: Regulates the function of the ovaries.

a
- Sit down with your legs stretched out in front.
- Keep your feet apart, shoulder width level.
- Place your hands on your thighs, tilt your head back and look up.

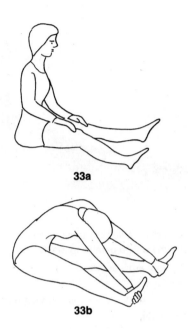

33a

34a   **34b**

34. VASISHTASANA
[Side Raise Pose 3]

Benefits: Strengthens the wrists and tones the back muscles. Relieves disorders of the coccyx region.

<u>a</u>
- Lie down on your left side, right leg above your left leg.
- Place your right hand on your right thigh.
- Put your left hand on the floor right below your left shoulder as you raise your trunk off the floor.
- Straighten your left elbow, and raise your upper torso.
- Using your toes as a pivot, raise your hips until your entire body is in one straight line. The weight of your body rests on your left hand and the outer part of your left foot.
- Keep looking to the front, and hold the position for a breath.
- Still balancing yourself on your left hand and foot, raise your right leg so it is parallel to the floor.
- Now raise your right arm, and bring it in line with your left arm.

<u>b</u>
- If possible, remain in the position without losing your balance, and turn your neck to look at your right hand.
- Hold the position to your comfort.
- First turn your head to the front, then lower your right arm and leg.
- Now lower your body.
- Roll onto the other side, and perform the Asana again.

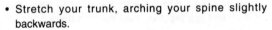

33b

- Stretch your trunk, arching your spine slightly backwards.

<u>b</u>
- As you exhale, glide your hands down your legs towards your ankles.
- Still looking up, pull your trunk towards your leg.
- Hold any extreme position on your legs.
- Relax your arms, and lower your head. Your forehead points downwards.
- For starters, hold the position for 30 seconds, and increase the holding time gradually.
- Tilt your head to look up.
- Push your shoulders back, and arch your spine.
- As you inhale, glide your hands on your legs towards your knees, and raise your trunk back to the starting position.
- Repeat the Asana 2 times.

Caution: People with a slipped disc should avoid this Asana.

35. SHASHANKA BHUJANGASANA
[Striking Cobra]

Benefits: Tones the reproductive organs. Relieves menstrual disorders. Good for people suffering from a slipped disc, sciatica and general back pain. Tones the liver and improves its functions.

<u>a</u>

- Sit in Vajrasana.
- Breathing in, raise your arms in front to shoulder level.
- Stretch your trunk without losing contact with your heels.

35c

35a

- Breathing out, bend your trunk forward until it rests on your thighs, and your palms and forehead are on the floor. Do not move your knees.
- Without moving your hands forward, press down on your hands.
- Now hold your breath out.

<u>b</u>

- Keeping your forehead close to the floor, stretch your trunk forward. Keep your hands pressed down on the floor by the side of your chest.
- Arch your neck backwards.
- As you breathe in, raise your trunk. Do not raise your lower abdomen off the floor.
- Hold the position for a count of 10.
- Keeping your neck arched backwards and breathing out, lower your trunk to the floor.
- Bring your forehead to the floor.
- Holding your breath out, pressing your hands and knees down on the floor, and keeping your forehead close to the floor, move your hips backwards so your chest rests on your thighs.

- Breathing in, raise your trunk up to a sitting position. Your arms will be parallel to the floor.
- Lower your arms and relax.

<u>c</u>

- As before stretch your trunk from Shashankasana [Baby Pose].
- Your lower arms are perpendicular to the floor. Your hands, palms down, are by the sides of your chest. Your feet are together, toes pointing away from your body.
- Tilt your head back to look up.
- Breathing in, raise your trunk.
- Straighten your arms, arching your spine as much as possible.
- When your arms are straight, your knees are off the floor. Your entire body is supported by your hands and toes.
- Curl your spine until you reach a comfortable stretch. Do not bend your legs at the knees.
- Hold the position for a count of 10.
- Keep looking up, and bringing your knees to the floor first, lower your trunk.
- When your trunk is lowered onto the floor, bring your forehead to the floor.
- Holding your breath out, go back to the sitting position as before.
- Relax before performing the Asana for the third time.

<u>d</u>

- This time sit on your heels, toes bent inwards. Your knees are together in front.

- Raise your arms in front, and lower your trunk forward so your chest rests on your thighs, and your forehead rests on the floor.
- Holding your breath out, stretch your trunk on the floor.
- Tilt your head backwards.
- As you breathe in, arch your spine to the maximum.
- Straighten your arms. At this stage your knees are off the floor.
- Now push your shoulders back so your chest expands, and simultaneously tense your buttocks, keeping your knees together. Do not hold this position.
- As before, lower your trunk and forehead onto the floor.
- Holding your breath out as before, rest your trunk on your thighs.
- Raise your trunk, and lower your arms before relaxing.

36. BHUJANGA TIRYAKA
[Swinging Cobra]
Benefit: Helps clear phlegm in the lungs.

- Lie down on the floor.
- Place your forehead on the floor, and keep your arms by the sides of your thighs.
- Bring your stretched arms to shoulder level.
- Bend your elbows, bringing your hands to the floor right below your raised elbows. Your lower arms make a right angle with your upper arms at the elbows. Your upper arms are parallel to the floor.
- Tilt your neck backwards and look up.
- As you breathe in, twist your trunk, and, at the same time, raise it towards the left until your right arm is straight.
- Your head follows the twist, and your chin is close to your raised left shoulder.
- As you breathe out, move your trunk to the front, swinging in reverse order.
- When your trunk is just above the floor, breathe in, and arching your spine, raise your back. Both your arms are now straight.
- Breathing out and bending your elbows, gently lower your trunk.
- Place your forehead on the floor.
- Perform similarly swinging your trunk to the right.

- Repeat the Asana a couple of times on either side, relaxing for a while in between.

Note: Breathing is an important aspect of this Asana, especially in therapy for asthma .

Caution: Do not perform this Asana without supervision.

37. UTTANA PADASANA
[Inverted Dog]
Benefits: Tones the muscles of the neck and back. Strengthens the rectus muscles. Activates the thyroid gland.

- Lie down on your back, keeping your legs together.
- Exhale, raise your shoulders off the floor, and arch your back.
- Arch your neck backwards, bringing the top of your head to the floor.
- Now look as far behind as possible.
- Raise both your legs until they are at an angle of 30 degrees from the floor.
- Raise your arms, keeping them taut until they are parallel to your legs.
- Breathing normally, hold the position for a count of 20.
- Lower your arms and legs, and straighten your neck.

Note: Instead of Poorva Uttana Padasana [Simple Fish] (see chapter 3), this Asana can be performed after Shoulderstand.

38. PURVOTTANASANA
[Hip Raise Pose]
Benefits: Improves the mobility of the shoulder blades. Develops the chest. Increases the breathing capacity.

- Sit down with your legs stretched out in front. Your hands are by your sides or just behind your hips. Do not keep your hands too far back.
- Keep your toes pointing up, heels on the floor.
- Pressing down on your hands and heels, raise your hips.
- Using your feet as a lever, stretch them forward, and raise your hips completely.
- Keeping your head tilted back, breathe normally for a count of 20.

The ideas, suggestions, herbal remedies and diet contained in this book are not intended as a substitue for consulting with your doctor. All matters regarding your health require medical supervision.

- Lower your hips to the floor and relax.
- Repeat the Asana again, but this time, when in the final position, bring your chin close to your chest, and adjust the height of your body line so you can see your toes.

39. SARVANGA PUSTI VIKASAKA
[Strengthening the Whole Body]

These three Asanas can be performed individually or together.

a
CHATURANGA DANDASANA

Benefits: Develops the wrists and improves the mobility of the joints.

- Lie down flat on your abdomen.
- Place your hands by the sides of your chest.
- Keep your feet slightly apart, toes bent inwards.
- As you exhale, raise your body, bringing it parallel to the floor. The weight of your entire body is on your hands and toes.
- Breathing normally, hold the position for 10 seconds.

b
ADHOMUKA SVANASANA

Benefits: Slows down heartbeat. Strengthens the abdominal muscles. Removes stiffness in the heels and ankles. Good for arthritis in the shoulder blades.

- After assuming Chaturanga Dandasana, raise your buttocks upwards.

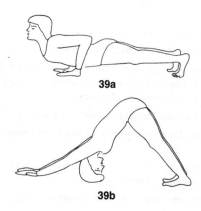

39a

39b

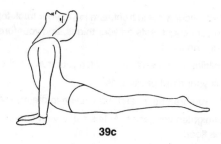

39c

- Now move your head inwards. Your body assumes the shape of an inverted V. Your hands are in the same position on the floor, but this time, your arms are straight, as are your legs. Your head is between your arms, and your forehead points towards the floor.
- Contracting your abdomen, bring your trunk as close as possible towards your legs.

c
URDVAMUKA SVANASANA

Benefits: Improves circulation and strengthens the spine. Good for people suffering from lumbago and other ailments of the back.

- After staying in the Adhomuka Svanasana position for a while, begin to dive forward by bending your elbows and stretching your trunk parallel to the floor.
- When your body is parallel to the floor, tilt your head back and look up.
- Stretch your trunk, and move forward by adjusting your feet so your toes point backwards.
- Arch your spine, and breathing in, raise your trunk until your arms are straight. Your spine is arched backwards to the maximum. Your knees do not touch the floor, and your legs are parallel to the floor.
- Lower your head and chest, and assume the pose of Chaturanga Dandasana.
- Now raise your buttocks until your body assumes an inverted V shape as in Adhomuka Svanasana.
- Perform all the three positions in sequence as many times as possible.
- At the end of the sequence, lower your body to the starting position, and assume Advasana.

40(i)a

40(ii)b

40c

40(I) UTTITA EKA PADASANA
[Thirty, Sixty, Ninety Single Leg]

Benefits: Strengthens lumbar region and abdominal muscles. Gives relief from gastric problems. Good for reducing abdominal fat.

<u>a</u>
- Lie on your back, arms by your sides.
- Raise your right leg such that it is 30 degrees from the floor.
- Keep your leg taut, and hold the position for a count of 20.

<u>b</u>
- Now raise your legs such that it is 60 degrees from the floor.
- Hold the position for a count of 20.

<u>c</u>
- Raise your leg once again to the maximum.
- Hold the position for another count of 20.
- Now breathe out.
- Bend your leg at the knee, and bring your thigh and knee towards your chest.
- Press down on your knee, and raising your head, bring your chin close to your knee.
- Hold the position for a few seconds.
- Lower your head, and stretch your leg, bringing your heel first to the floor.
- Perform the Asana again on your other leg.

(II) URDHVA PRASARITA PADASANA
[Thirty, Sixty, Ninety]

<u>a</u>
- Lie on your back, arms over your head on the floor. Keep your arms straight by the sides of your ears, palms facing up.
- Look up.
- Breathe out, and holding your breath out, raise your legs, 30 degrees from the floor.
- Breathing normally, hold the position without any strain.

<u>b</u>
- Breathe out, and holding your breath out, raise your legs further, about 60 degrees from the floor.
- As before, stay in the position while breathing normally for as long as possible without any strain.
- Breathe out, and holding your breath out, lift your legs further until they are perpendicular to the floor.
- Hold the position for a count of 20.
- Breathe out, and bend your knees towards your chest before stretching your legs to the floor or breathe out, and keeping your legs stretched, slowly lower your legs without bending your knees.

Variation of Urdhva Prasarita Padasana
If you experience difficulty performing the three levels of leg raise continuously, do them separately:

- First raise your legs 30 degrees from the floor, and hold the position.
- Bend your knees towards your chest before stretching your legs.
- Relax for a while, and raise your legs 60 degrees from the floor.
- After a while, raise your legs perpendicular to the floor.
- After holding the three positions to your comfort, come out as before.

41. SAMPOORNA SHAKTI VIKASAKA
[Slow Motion Firming]

Benefits: Firms the abdomen and thighs. Improves blood circulation and redistributes fat. Strengthens the back and abdominal muscles.

As its name suggests, this Asana must be performed as slowly as possible, with normal breathing.

41b

41c

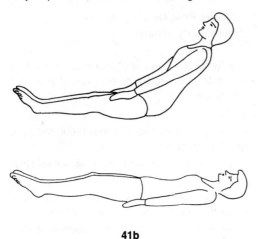

41b

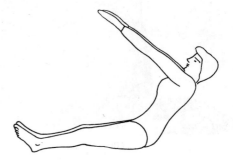

41d

a
- Sit down with your legs stretched out in front.
- Place your hands on your thighs, and relax your body.
- Slowly lean back.
- Relax your legs without raising them.
- Keep reclining your back as slowly as possible until your back rests on the floor. When your head and trunk touch the floor, your arms are by the sides of your body on the floor.

41e

<u>b</u>
- Raise your legs together so that they are slightly off the floor.
- Bend your knees slowly towards your chest. Keep the lower part of your legs parallel to the floor.

<u>c</u>
- When your thighs are brought close to your chest, straighten your legs slowly.
- When your legs are perpendicular to the floor, raise your arms, bringing them by the sides of your knees.

<u>d</u>
- Now slowly raise your head and trunk as high as possible from the floor. Your arms are up as well.
- Lower your legs slowly to the floor. Your trunk comes up while your legs go down.
- When your legs touch the floor, your trunk is upright.

<u>e</u>
- Bend your trunk towards your legs, and hold your feet.
- Straighten your trunk and relax.
- Repeat the Asana as many times as possible without straining your back.

Caution: Do not hold your breath at any point.

42. CHAKRA PAWANAMUKTA
JATARA PARIVARTANASANA
[Back Pushup Legover]

Benefits: This Asana is meant for those suffering from sciatica, lower backache and discomfort in hip joints due to arthritic conditions.

The Asana combines together in sequence such Asanas as Chakrasana, Vayu Nishankasana, Urdhva Prasarita Padasana and Jatara Parivartanasana.

<u>a</u>
- Lie down on your back.
- Bend your legs together at the knees, bringing your heels close to your buttocks.
- Hold your ankles with your hands. Use a towel if you experience difficulty doing this.
- By pressing down on your feet and keeping your shoulders on the floor, raise your body, and arch your spine. Your chest comes close to your chin.
- Hold the position for a while.

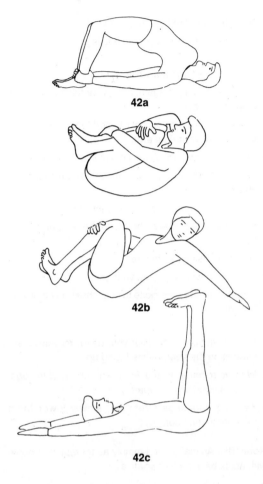

42a

42b

42c

- Still holding onto your ankles, lower your back.
- Release the hold on your ankles.

<u>b</u>
- Keeping your back on the floor, lift your buttocks a little to bring both your knees towards your chest.
- Wrap your knees with both your arms.
- Using your arms bring your knees closer to your chest.
- Lift your head to bring your chin close to your knees.
- Hold the position for a count of 10.
- Lower your head to the floor.

<u>c</u>
- Using your right arm to press down on your knees, release your left arm, bringing it to the left side at shoulder level.

- Turn your head to look to the left side.
- Roll your hips to bring your folded legs to the right side of your body.
- Hold the position for a while.
- By rolling your hips again, bring your folded legs back onto your chest.
- Place your left arm on your folded legs, and release the clasp of your right arm.
- Place your right arm by the right side at shoulder level.
- With your left arm, press your thighs towards your chest.
- Turning your head, look to the right side.
- Roll your folded legs as before to the left side of your body.
- Hold the position as before.
- Bring your legs back onto your chest.
- Once your knees are close to your chest, let go of your left arm.

<u>d</u>
- Place both your arms over your head. Your arms are straight on the floor, palms facing up.
- With your back on the floor, straighten your legs, keeping them slightly apart.
- Keeping your legs stretched, slowly lower them together to the floor.

Note: This Asana is used mainly as therapy for people with acute back pain or sciatica.

Caution: If possible, perform this Asana with some assistance.

43. MAKARASANA
[Crocodile Pose]
Benefits: Regulates heartbeat and relaxes the nervous system.

<u>a</u>
- Lie flat on your stomach, hands by your sides.
- Raise your head and shoulders, and place your elbows right below your shoulders.

<u>b</u>
- Now clasp your opposite elbows with your hands.

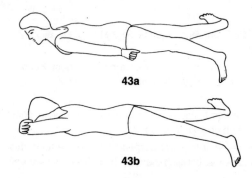

43a

43b

- Adjust the position of your neck and elbows so your forehead rests on your lower arms and chin on the floor.
- Stretch your legs, and raise them, keeping them apart. Your toes point to the floor. You may rest the soles of your feet against the wall so your legs are straight. This also helps you to hold the position for a longer period of time.

44. UTTHAN PRISHTASANA
[Lizard Pose]
Benefits: Tones the abdominal region. Relaxes the muscles and nerves of the back.

<u>a</u>
- Lie on your stomach.

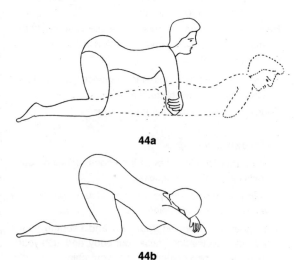

44a

44b

- Tilt your head back, and raise your shoulders.
- Hold your upper arms or elbows with the palms of your opposite hands.
- Place your crossed arms below your lower chest. Your upper body is inclined, with your chest resting on your forearms. Your toes are stretched out.

<u>b</u>
- Keeping your elbows in the same place, raise your buttocks and trunk backwards, using your knees and elbows for support.
- Stretch your torso backward by curling your spine.
- Continue moving backwards until your forehead rests on your folded arms. Your chin is on the floor.

6

Prana, Bandha and Mudra
⤴

Pranayama is more than just a breathing exercise. It is responsible for introducing an extra supply of oxygen to the lungs. In addition, it influences the flow of *Prana* or "vital energy" in the *Nadis* or "channels" of the Pranamaya Kosha (the bio-energy regions) and purifies the regions. Pranayama, therefore, improves physical and mental stability. *Kumbhaka* or "breath control" of the Pranayama helps in the mastery of the mind.

A *Bandha* means "to hold or tighten". Bandhas help control the different organs and nerves of the body. They massage the internal organs, removing stagnant blood and stimulating the area around the organs, thus improving overall health. Bandhas require Kumbhaka. The practitioner is advised to slowly develop the capacity to hold his or her breath.

This chapter also features some Mudras that are simple to follow. A *Mudra* — "a seal or lock" — is believed to arouse the dormant serpent power, the Kundalini Shakthi. Hasta Mudras are gestures of the hands, performed by using different positions of the fingers, wrists and arms. They are performed by joining together, folding, bending or opening the hands, fingers and fists. There are several types of Mudras, and they are used in such activities as dancing, prayer, meditation, consecration, bath, *Avahana* ("inviting God to merge with you") and food offering.

According to *Yogashastra* ("Rules of Yoga"), the universe consists of five elements. They are Agni or fire; Vayu or air; Akash or ether; Prithvi or earth; and Soma or Jal, which means water. The body is made up of the same five elements, and it is believed that an imbalance in these elements can cause illness or disease. An equilibrium in these elements is the key to good health. The Mudras, by reducing the toxins that cause the imbalance, restore this necessary equilibrium. The thumb and fingers represent these five elements as well, and in addition, they also represent the five Chakras corresponding to the endocrine glands of the body.

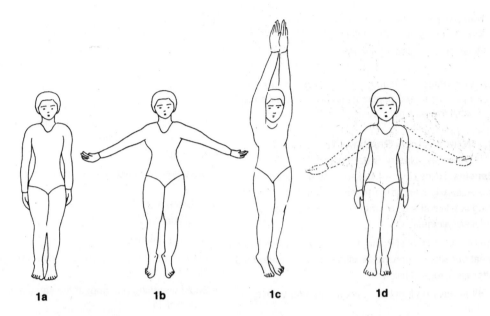

1a   **1b**   **1c**   **1d**

PRANAYAMA

1. HASTA UTTITA PRANAYAMA
   [Complete Breath Standing]

This Pranayama is normally done before any Yoga session.

<u>a</u>
- Stand in Samasthiti.

<u>b</u>
- Raise your arms from the sides as you breathe in.
- When your arms are at shoulder level, roll them at the shoulders so your palms face upwards.

<u>c</u>
- Continue raising your arms, and, at the same time, continue breathing in.
- Come up high on your toes.
- When your hands touch each other, complete your breathing in process.
- Hold your breath in, and remain on tiptoe for a few seconds.

<u>d</u>
- Begin lowering your arms, palms facing up, from the sides, and, at the same time, start breathing out.
- At shoulder level, unroll your arms, and continue lowering your arms, palms down. At the same time, continue breathing out.

- Lower the soles of your feet to the floor.
- Bring your body back to the starting position. Your breathing out process must be completed by now.
- Without resting, continue raising your arms, and breathe in at the same time.
- Repeat the entire process several times.
- Relax before performing any other Asana.

2. PADMA UJJAYI PRANAYAMA
   [Abdominal Breathing in Lotus]

Benefit: Regularises breath.

- Sit in the Lotus position.
- Place your hands on your knees. Keep your spine straight.
- Breathe in, and, at the same time, push your abdomen out.
- Continue breathing in, and expand your chest.
- Still breathing in, raise your shoulders to straighten your arms. By this time, your abdomen is fully expanded.
- Hold your breath for a while.
- Breathe out slowly, and, at the same time, draw in your abdomen slowly.
- Relax your shoulders first, and as you breathe out, relax your chest.

- Now pull your abdomen inwards with a force to expel any remaining air in the lungs.
- Relax before repeating the Pranayama again.

Caution: People suffering from high blood pressure, heart problems, and peptic or duodenal ulcers should avoid this Pranayama.

3. NADI SHODANA PRANAYAMA
   [Alternate Nostril Breathing]

Benefits: Helps clear a blocked nose (especially when the Asana is performed in the mornings). Corrects irregular breathing, normalises blood pressure and induces calmness.

This is one of the best Pranayama in Yoga. It brings about great benefits for general health. It must be performed after each Yoga session.

- Sit in any comfortable position, keeping your spine straight.
- Place the index and second fingers of your right hand on the centre of your forehead.
- Place your right thumb on your right nostril and your third finger on your left nostril.
- Close your right nostril with your right thumb.
- Inhale through your left nostril.
- Close your nostril with your left finger. Now both your nostrils are closed.
- Hold your breath.
- Release the pressure on your right nostril by removing your right thumb.
- Exhale through your right nostril. When you have finished exhaling, inhale through your right nostril.
- Close your right nostril, and retain your breath.
- Remove your finger from your left nostril and exhale.
- Continue breathing in and out alternately through your left and right nostrils for a few minutes and relax.

Caution: In the early stages of this Pranayama, do not force yourself to breathe in and out very slowly. Breathe according to your capacity. People suffering from high blood pressure should perform this Pranayama without breath retention.

4. PADADIRASANA
   [Balancing of Breath]

Benefits: Helps equalise breathing through both the nostrils. Keeps the body warm.

- Sit in Vajrasana.
- Cross your arms in front of your chest.
- Place your hands under your armpits, thumbs pointing towards your shoulders.
- Now close your eyes.
- Breathing normally, sit in the position for 1 minute.

5. BHASTIKA
   [Dynamic Breathing Standing]

- Stand in Samasthiti.
- Breathe in slowly, and, at the same time, push your abdomen out.
- Begin breathing out, and, at the same time, pull your abdomen in.
- Repeat this a couple of times so a rhythm develops. Slowly increase your speed of breathing. Start breathing in and out faster, making a bellowing sound. Your abdomen moves in and out in accordance with your breathing.
- Now slow down your speed of breathing.
- Slowly switch to normal breathing and relax.

Caution: People with high blood pressure should avoid this Pranayama.

6. MANDUKASANA RECHAKA PURAKA
   [Dynamic Breathing Sitting]

This Pranayama is the same as Bhastika [Dynamic Breathing]. The only difference is that it is performed sitting down.

- Sit on your heels, toes bent inwards.
- Place your knees as far apart as possible in front.
- Put your hands on your knees.
- Straighten your arms and spine.
- Synchronise the movement of your abdomen with your breathing.
- Repeat the Pranayama a couple of times.

Caution: People with high blood pressure should avoid this Pranayama.

7. BUDDHI TATHA DHARTI VIKASAKA
[Mind and Will Power Breathing]

Benefits: Pranayamas 7, 8 and 9, used exclusively in mental therapy, help develop mental health.

- Stand in Samasthiti.
- Tilt your head backwards, stretching your neck to your comfort.
- Keep your eyes wide open and mouth closed.
- Shift your thoughts to the crown of your head.
- Now slowly breathe in and out, gradually increasing it to a bellowing sound. Do this for 3 minutes first, and steadily increase the duration to 6 minutes.
- When it is time, slow down your breathing, and start breathing normally.
- Straighten your neck, and perform one round of neck roll.
- Relax for a while.

Caution: Pranayamas 7, 8 and 9 should not be done vigorously when they are first performed. Increase the momentum gradually. People suffering from high blood pressure or headaches due to tension should avoid this Pranayama.

8. SMARANA
[Memory Breathing]

- Place an object about a metre and a half from your feet. Stand at attention.
- Shift your thoughts to that part of your head, a soft spot, where the three bones of the skull on top of your head meet. At the same time, without tilting your neck, focus your eyes on the object on the floor.
- Slowly begin breathing through your nose, gradually making it vigorous (bellowing sound) for about 1 minute. Increase the duration to a maximum of 5 minutes.
- Slow down your breathing, and come out of the pose.
- Lie down on the floor, and relax for a while.

9. MEDHA PRANAYAMA
[Intellect Breathing]

- Stand in Samasthiti.
- Bend neck forward bringing chin close to sternal notch.
- Shift thought onto nape region of neck.
- Concentrate hard and then begin to breathe in and out in a rhythmic way but vigorously through nose.
- Perform for a minute to start with and later increase the time to your comfort.
- Slow down breathing and breathe normally.
- Straighten neck and relax.

10. BRAHMARI PRANAYAMA
[Humming of Bee Breathing]

Benefits: Relieves cerebral tension and reduces blood pressure.

- Sit in Sukasana.
- Close your eyes, and relax your entire body. Keep your mouth closed throughout the Pranayama.
- Take a breath through your nose.
- Hold your breath. Press your chin close to your chest near the sternum.
- Hold the position for a count of 3.
- Relax your neck.
- Still holding your breath, close your ears with your index fingers.
- Keeping your mouth closed, move your lower jaw down to separate your upper and lower sets of teeth.

10

- Breathe out slowly, producing a long continuous humming sound.
- Relax and repeat the Pranayama a couple of times.

11. SHEETALI PRANAYAMA
[Cooling Breath]

Benefits: Same as Sheetkari Pranayama.

- Sit down, keeping your spine straight.
- Open your mouth, and form the shape of an "O" with your lips.
- Fold your tongue into the shape of a fresh curled leaf about to open, and bring it between your lips. Suck in air through your curled tongue. If you find it difficult to do this, bring your tongue forward to touch your upper teeth from inside. Suck air into your mouth through the little gaps between your teeth.
- Now purse your lips, and exhale slowly through your nose.
- Repeat the Pranayama a couple of times before relaxing.

Caution: People with heart trouble should avoid this Asana.

12. SHEETKARI PRANAYAMA
[Hissing Breath]

Benefits: Induces muscular relaxation, eliminates thirst and purifies blood.

- Sit down, keeping your spine straight.
- Fold your tongue back so the under part touches the palate.
- Clench your teeth, and move your lips so they do not touch.
- Breathe in, letting the air flow in between your teeth.
- Hold your breath for few seconds before closing your mouth.
- Breathe out through your nostrils.
- Repeat the Pranayama a couple of times before relaxing for a while.

Caution: People with heart ailments should avoid this Asana.

13. EKA PADA UTTANASANA
[Single Leg Stretch Breathing]

Benefits: This is a good Pranayama for clearing nasal congestion, as well as for asthma and sinusitis.

- Lie down on your back.
- Stretch out your right leg and tighten it. Keep your left leg and left arm relaxed.
- Now stretch out your right arm.
- Start inhaling through your nose, and raise your tensed right leg. Do not twist your leg or turn it or use excessive force.
- When your right leg is at the highest position, hold your breath, and stay in the position for 5 seconds.
- Now, start breathing out through your nose, and, at the same time, lower your tensed right leg.
- Rest for 10 seconds, and perform the Pranayama again by raising your left leg.
- Repeat the Pranayama 5 times on each leg, relaxing in between.

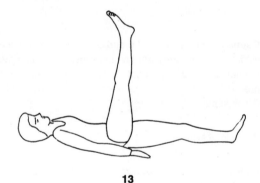

13

14. UJJAYI PRANAYAMA
[Abdominal Breathing]

a

- Lie down on your back. Keep your body straight, palms close to the body. Keep your heels together, and do not tighten your legs.
- Blowing out air slowly, exhale completely through slightly parted lips.
- Relax your body, and contract your abdomen.
- Inhale slowly through both your nostrils. Do not force yourself to inhale too much air. Let the abdominal area expand.

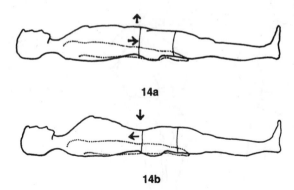

14a

14b

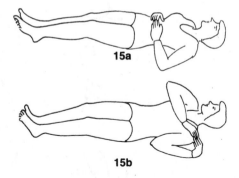

15a

15b

- Hold your breath, bringing your toes together and stretching them out.
- Tighten your legs, and pull in your stomach.
- Stretch your arms out gently, and tense your whole body.
- Hold the position for 3 seconds. Hold your breath without any strain.

b
- Now exhale steadily through your mouth.
- While exhaling, loosen the muscles of your body from top to bottom: first your chest then your stomach, thighs, arms and legs.
- Rest for 10 seconds before performing the Pranayama 5 times, resting between each repetition.

Caution: This Pranayama must be done on an empty stomach. Slowly increase the duration of breath held and the number of times the Pranayama is performed.

15. SURYA BHEDANA PRANAYAMA
   [Solar Plexus Breathing]
Benefits: Tones the muscles of your heart and lungs.

a
- Lie down on your back, and relax your body.
- Place the fingers of both your hands joined together on the solar plexus region of your body.
- Breathe in, and push out your abdomen.

b
- Holding your breath in, move your arms towards your head.
- When your fingers reach the forehead, breathe out, pulling your abdomen inwards.

- Once the breathing out process is complete, holding your breath out, move your fingers back to the solar plexus region.
- Repeat the Pranayama several minutes. When repeating the Pranayama, instead of bringing your fingers over your forehead, you can bring your fingers to any region where there is pain or discomfort and breathe out. While breathing out, imagine supplying energy to the region that hurts.

BANDHA

1. UDDIYANA BANDHA
   [Abdominal Lift]
Benefits: Firms, tones and trims the abdomen. Massages the viscera. Clears congestion caused by sedentary habits and an upright posture. Rids constipation problems. Improves digestion. Stimulates the liver, pancreas, kidneys, spleen and adrenal glands. Makes the diaphragm move much more easily, increases its elasticity, thus improving its movement. Improves the elasticity of the lungs. Gives the heart and the abdominal area a gentle massage. Lifts the viscera and presses them against the spine. Stimulates metabolism, circulation and digestion.

In this Bandha, the diaphragm is lifted high, which gives a massage to the muscles of the heart, thus toning them. The abdominal organs are pulled against the back towards the spine. No other Bandha comes close to its effect of squeezing and kneading the intestines, spleen,

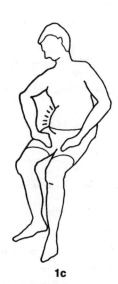

1a   1b   1c

pancreas, liver, kidneys and transverse colon. It also tones the supporting muscular "corset" (the connecting tissues of the diaphragm and the ribcage).

The Bandha involves the retraction of a relaxed abdominal wall on full exhalation. It is considered one of the cleansing processes of Yoga hygiene and as a "binding" (or the lock, which means to hold tightly) in Yogic breath control.

<u>a</u>

- Stand with your legs slightly apart and slightly bent at the knees, kneecaps in line with your toes (skiing position). This posture facilitates control when you first start performing the Bandha.
- Place your hands on top of your thighs, fingers pointing inwards.
- Your trunk is pushed slightly forward from the waist up. Your back is a little rounded.

<u>b</u>

- Empty your lungs by breathing out completely and as fast as possible. This is an important stage. If you empty your lungs slowly, you might have to fight the urge to take a breath, and this would hinder your performance of control.
- Relax your abdominal wall, keeping your lungs emptied of air.

<u>c</u>

- Now expand your thoracic cage without taking in air (the thorax is that part of the trunk between the neck and the abdomen) by lifting up your chest a little, with your shoulders drooping backwards and neck raised.
- Your diaphragm will now move up into the thoracic cavity, and your stomach will be pulled in, as though it were pulled by a wire attached to the base of your backbone.

<u>d</u>

- Hold the retraction for a few seconds, then release the abdominal wall gently. If you spring back with a jerk, the air that rushes in will be explosive. This is not the right way to perform this Bandha. There are 2 methods to be followed: the first way is to hold the retraction for 5 to 10 seconds. Then breathing normally, release the tension on the abdomen and relax. Exhale again, and repeat the retraction. The second way is to perform 5 to 10 fast retractions and releases on one emptying of the lungs. This counts as 1 cycle.

Variation of Uddiyana Bandha

<u>a</u>

- Assume an all-four position.
- Keep your knees apart and hands at shoulder width level.

b and c

- Relax your neck, and perform the sucking and snapping of the abdominal organs as described above. Perform it according to your breathing.

Caution: Perform this Bandha on an empty stomach and lungs. Women should avoid this during menstruation.

1a

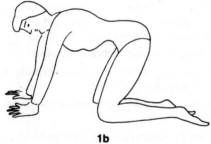

1b

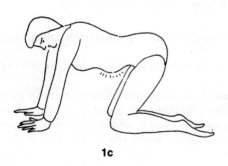

1c

variation

2. JALANDHARA BANDHA
[Chin Lock]

Benefits: An essential Bandha to prevent pressure on the heart, in the ears and in the area behind the eyeballs after performing Pranayama. Regulates the flow of blood to the heart and brain. Massages the thyroid and the parathyroid glands, thus improving their function. Relieves anxiety, stress and anger.

This Chin Lock assists in the suspension of breathing (Kumbhaka) in advanced yogic breath control.

- In this, your chin is lowered into the jugular notch between your collar bones. During breath retention, the Bandha is often combined with two other locks, Uddiyana Bandha and Moola Bandha.
- Sit in any comfortable position, allowing your knees to touch the floor.
- Place your hands on your knees.
- Relax your body, close your eyes, and inhale deeply.
- Hold your breath, bend your head forward, and press your chin against the chest near the sternum.
- Straighten your arms, locking so your shoulders are close to your cheeks.
- Hunch your shoulders.
- Hold the position, retaining your breath and lock for as long as possible.
- To come out of the posture, relax your shoulders, loosen your arms, and straighten your neck in that order before exhaling slowly.
- Relax before repeating the Bandha again.

2

Caution: People with high blood pressure or heart problems should avoid this Bandha. Women should avoid this during menstruation. Do not hold your breath beyond your capacity.

Concentration: Vishuddi Chakra (the thyroid glands).

3.   MAHA BANDHA
   [Great Binding Lock]

- Sit with your right heel against the perineum.
- Fold your left leg, placing your left foot high up on top of your right thigh, and breathe in.
- Contract the muscles in the region of the perineum, and draw them upwards.
- Hold your breath and contraction to your comfort.
- Relax and breathe out.
- Apply the Chin Lock (Jalandhara Bandha), lowering your chin to the jugular notch between your collar bones.
- Contract your anus strongly and repeatedly, and draw your abdomen back.
- Breathe in deeply, filling the thoracic cavity, and press the *Prana* or "life force" down (distend the abdomen area and breathe in).
- Another "life current" called the *Apana*, which belongs to the abdominal region, is pushed up, and two energy currents are united at the navel. The aim is to unite the upper and lower energy currents.
- Relax and stretch your left leg before you stretch your right one.

3

- Draw your left heel to the perineum, and place your right foot on your left thigh, and perform as before.
- Repeat the process several times, reversing the positions of your legs frequently during practice.

Caution: Same as Jalandhara Bandha [Chin Lock].

4.   MOOLA BANDHA
   [Perineum Retraction Lock]

Benefit: Stimulates the pelvic nerves.

Moola means "the root". For this Bandha it is customary to sit in the male or female Accomplished Pose (Siddhasana or Siddha Yoni Asana).

- Sit in the Easy Pose [Sukasana] if the suggested poses above prove difficult.
- Contract the perineum, the soft part between your anus and genitals.
- At the same time, squeeze tightly the sphincters controlling the opening and closing of the anus, as well as the genital muscles. The lower abdomen is pulled back towards the spine.
- Try pulling your anus and navel together.
- Hold the contraction for a few seconds without experiencing any discomfort.
- Contract your lower abdomen and the whole pelvic area.
- Repeat the Bandha 5 times, relaxing for 15 seconds each time between the contractions.

Caution: Same as Jalandhara Bandha [Chin Lock].

Concentration: Muladhara Chakra (base of the spine).

Note: It is dangerous to perform these Bandhas incorrectly. Uddiyana Bandha causes involuntary discharge of semen, while Moola Bandha increases sexual retentive power, which can be abused.

MUDRA

1. YOGA MUDRA
[Symbol of Yoga]

Benefits: Massages the abdominal area, stretches the vertebrae, and tones and activates the adrenal glands. Improves circulation, and releases anger and tension. Good for clearing nasal congestion, as well as for sinusitis and an asthmatic condition.

<u>a</u>
- Sit in the Lotus position. Otherwise, sit in Veerasana.
- Bring your hands behind your back.
- Hold your right wrist with your left hand. Do not hold your hand too tight.
- Keep the thumb and fingers of your right hand together and stretched out. Keep your arms loose.
- Exhale slowly, and hold your breath for a few seconds, concentrating on the base of the spine.
- Inhale slowly, and, at the same time, shift your concentration from the base of the spine to the pituitary glands.

<u>b</u>
- Now exhale slowly, and, at the same time, start lowering your trunk forward and down towards the floor. Synchronise the movements with your breathing. Do not jerk or strain yourself to bend more than is possible.
- Once in the position, breathe normally, holding the position for a couple of breaths. Concentrate on the base of the spine.
- Breathing in, raise your trunk to a sitting position.
- Shift your concentration to the pituitary glands.
- Holding your left wrist with your right hand, perform the Mudra again.
- Repeat the Mudra a couple of times, each time holding alternate wrists.

Variation of Yoga Mudra
- Bring your hands behind your back.
- Hold your right wrist with your left hand. Do not hold too tight.
- Keep the thumb and fingers of your right hand together and stretched out. Keep your arms loose.
- Exhale slowly, and, at the same time, lower your trunk forward and down towards the floor. Synchronise the

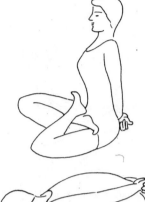

1a

movements with your breathing. Do not jerk or strain yourself to bend more than is possible.
- As you breathe in, raise your arms, keeping your right arm straight.
- Hold your breath for 5 seconds, after which breathe out, lowering your arms before relaxing them.
- Start inhaling, and raise your trunk to a sitting position.
- Rest for a few seconds.
- Hold your left wrist with your right hand, and perform as before.
- Relax and repeat the Mudra 5 times.

2. SHAMBAVA MUDRA
[Vision and Concentration Seal]

Benefits: This Mudra develops the mental faculties, in particular memory and the power of concentration.

- Sit down, keeping your spine straight.
- At eye level, place a bright object a metre away from where you are sitting.
- Now look at the object without blinking your eyes.
- Hold the position for 5 to 10 minutes.
- At this stage, you may begin to "see" small objects around the main one. Hold your gaze on the main object. You will soon notice that nothing but the main object is in view.

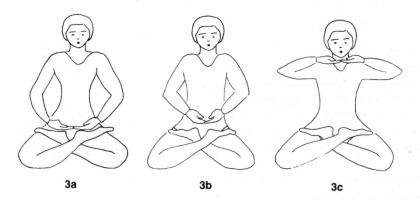

3a   3b   3c

Note: This Mudra may take several attempts before you perform it correctly.

Caution: Do not strain your eyes.

3. SHANTI MUDRA
[Invocation of Peace Seal]

Benefits: Calms the mind, increases strength and energises the entire body. Promotes general wellbeing.

a
- Sit in a meditative pose.
- Close your eyes, and place your palms, facing up and fingers pointing towards each other, on your lap.
- By filling your abdomen with air while breathing in and contracting it while breathing out, inhale and exhale as deeply as possible.

Concentration: Muladhara Chakra (base of the spine).

b
- Now inhale, fully expanding your abdomen.
- At the same time, raise your hands until they reach the front of your navel region. Coordinate the movement of your hands and abdominal expansion.

Concentration: Muladhara Chakra (base of the spine) to Manipura Chakra (the adrenal glands).

c
- Continue inhaling, and expand your chest region by raising your hands to the front of your heart.

Concentration: Manipura Chakra (the adrenal glands) to Anahata Chakra (the thymus gland).

- Draw in some more air, and raise your shoulders, bringing your hands in front of your throat.

Concentration: Anahata Chakra (the thymus gland) to Vishuddhi Chakra (the thyroid glands) to Ajna Chakra (the pituitary gland) and finally to Sahasrara (crown of the head).

- Retaining your breath, spread your arms to the sides, palms facing up.
- Holding your breath without any strain, stay in position for a few seconds.

Concentration: Sahasrara (crown of the head).

d
- As you exhale, lower your arms to the sides, and place your hands on your lap (starting position).
- At end of your exhalation, contract your abdomen, and bring your body to a limp position.
- Relax, and repeat the Mudra several times to your comfort. Synchronise your breathing and the movement of your arms without straining your lungs.

3d

4. MAHA MUDRA
[Great Seal]

Benefits: Helps clear abdominal disorders and menopausal problems.

- Sit with your right heel under your buttock near the anus and left leg stretched out in front:
- Bend forward, and with the fingers of both your hands, hold your left big toe.
- Relax your whole body, and breathe normally.
- Now arching your neck back, look up, and breathe in.
- Contract the muscles in the region of the perineum, and draw them upwards.
- Hold your breath and contraction to your comfort.
- Relax, and breathe out.
- Apply the Chin Lock (Jalandhara Bandha), lowering your chin to the jugular notch between your collar bones.
- Contract your anus repeatedly with strength, and pull your abdomen inwards.
- Breathing deeply, fill up the thoracic cavity, and press the *Prana* down. Another life current, the *Apana* from the abdominal region, is pushed up. The two energies currents unite at the navel.
- Release the hold on your left big toe, and stretch your right leg.
- Now perform the Mudra with your right leg stretched out.
- Repeat the Mudra several times.

Note: Reverse the position of your legs frequently during practice.

Concentration: Move your thought from Ajna Chakra (the pituitary glands) to Vishuddhi Chakra (the thyroid glands) and then to Muladhara Chakra (base of the spine).

5. BHOOCHARI MUDRA
[Gazing at Nothing Seal]

Benefit: Develops the power of concentration.

- Sit comfortably in front of a blank wall.
- Place your right hand on your right knee.
- Bring your left hand in front of your face, left elbow bent and pointing to the side at shoulder level. Your left palm faces the floor.

5

- Press your left thumb lightly against your upper lip just below the nose. Your fingers, which are together, point to the right.
- Fix your gaze on your left little finger and hold it.
- After 3 minutes, without changing the direction of your gaze, lower your left hand, and place it on your left knee. Do not change the direction of the gaze, and keep looking at the wall for another 3 minutes.
- Now close your eyes before lying down to relax.
- Perform the same way by bending your right arm in front of your face.

6. SHANMUKI MUDRA
[Psychic Source Seal]

Benefits: Stimulates sense of awareness and stops the mind from wandering.

- Sit in any meditative pose or in any comfortable position, keeping your spine straight.
- Raise your hands to your face, keeping your elbows at shoulder level.
- Place your right thumb lightly into your right ear hole or on the tragus. Do the same with your left thumb and ear.
- Close your eye gently, and place your index finger just below your eyebrows near the bridge of your nose.
- Place your middle finger at the base of your closed eyelid without exerting any pressure on the cornea.
- Place your ring finger on your outer nostril.
- Press against your nostril slightly. Do this gently, so your breathing is not affected.

- Place your little finger just above your lip.
- Hold the position, breathing rhythmically to your comfort.

Concentration: Bindu Chakra (the back top end corner of the head).

THERAPEUTIC HASTA MUDRAS

1. THE ANGUSHTA OR JYESTA (Thumb)
Represents Agni (fire) and is connected to the Manipura Chakra (the adrenal glands and the solar plexus).

2. THE TARJANI OR PRADARSHANI (Forefinger)
Represents Vayu (air) and is associated with the Anahata Chakra (the thymus gland and the cardiac plexus).

3. THE MADHYAMA OR JAIKARANI (Middle finger)
Represents Akash or Shunya, which means void and is related to the Vishuddhi Chakra (the thyroid glands and the pharyngeal plexus).

4. THE ANAMIKA OR PRANTAVASINI (Ring finger)
Represents the element Prithvi (earth) and is associated with the Muladhara Chakra (base of the spine).

5. THE KANISHTIKA OR RATHNI (Little finger)
Represents Soma or Jal (water) and is connected to the self-dwelling aspect or the Swadisthana Chakra and the organs of excretion, as well as the hypogastric plexus.

The following Mudras can be performed anywhere while walking, sitting or standing, and the longer they are performed, the better are the results. Problems, however, arise if they are performed wrongly, so follow the instructions closely. It is not necessary to perform Asanas before doing the Mudras, although any of the appropriate therapy Asanas can be done prior to the Mudras.

1. GNANA MUDRA
Benefits: Good for fatigue, sleeplessness, drowsiness and mental disorders. Improves memory and intelligence.

- Join together the tip of your forefinger and your thumb.
- Keep your other three fingers together and your arms straight. This Mudra can be done in conjunction with Shambava Mudra.
- Sit far away from a lit candle, preferably in a dark room, and gaze at it steadily for 10 minutes. If possible, do not blink.

2. PRANA MUDRA
Benefits: Improves energy circulation. Also improves eyesight and general health.

This mudra is related to Prana. Every action of the body depends on it.

Join together the tips of your little finger, ring finger and thumb, concentrate on your breathing.

3. VAYU MUDRA
Benefits: Activates the air element and helps clear Vataroga (Vata diseases), such as rheumatism, cramps, arthritis, paralysis and pain in the joints.

For maximum benefit, perform the following Mudra together with Prana Mudra.

- Bend fore finger and place its tip on the root of thumb.
- Now place thumb over fore finger and gently press.
- Concentrate on abdominal breathing.

4. PRITHVI MUDRA
Benefits: Activates the earth element and helps eradicate general weakness by stimulating the *tejus* (aura) and *kanti* (grace). Broadens the mind.

- Join together the tip of your ring finger and the tip of your thumb.
- Concentrate on the adrenal glands for as long as you are comfortable.

5. VARUN MUDRA
Benefit: Helps eradicate diseases caused by a reduction of the water element in the body.

Join together the tip of your little finger and thumb for as long as you are comfortable.

6. LINGA MUDRA

Benefits: Increases body heat and helps develop resistance to colds and coughs. Rids the body of phlegm and a congested chest. Helps fight obesity.

- Join your palms together, and lock facing fingers together. Keep one thumb upright.
- Encircle this thumb with the other thumb and forefinger.
- Concentrate on your chest for as long as you are comfortable.

Note: As heat is generated during this Mudra, drink some form of liquid during practice.

7. SHUNYA MUDRA

Benefits: Relieves earache and improves hearing ability.

- Place the tip of your middle finger at the base of your thumb. Press your finger with your thumb.
- Concentrate on the rhythm of Brahmari Pranayama.

8. SURBHI MUDRA

Benefits: Effective for people with poor memory, especially students. Helps control rheumatic swellings.

- Join your palms together.
- Bring the tip of your left little finger to touch the tip of your ring finger of your right hand.
- Now bring the tip of your left middle finger to touch the tip of your right forefinger. The tip of your right little finger touches the tip of your left ring finger. The tip of your right second finger touches the tip of your forefinger.

Caution: Do not perform this Mudra if you have a cough.

Variations

<u>a</u>
Benefit: Helps check urinary problems.

Bring angushta (fire element) to the root of kanishtika (water element).

<u>b</u>
Benefits: Help check stomach and digestive problems.

Bring angushta to the root of anamika (earth element).

<u>c</u>
Benefit: Help check mental problems.

Bring angushta to the root of tarjani (air element).

<u>d</u>
Benefit: Helps concentration, but perform carefully as it may affect hearing.

Bring angushta to the root of madhyama (ether element).

9. SURYA MUDRA

Benefit: Good for obesity

Place the tip of your right ring finger at the base of your thumb, and press.

10. APANA MUDRA

Benefits: Checks constipation. A combination of Vayu Mudra and Apana Mudra controls diabetes and heart disease.

Bring together the tips of your middle finger, ring finger and thumb.

11. SHAKAT MUDRA

Benefit: Controls anger.

- Spread your palms, which face outwards.
- Bring together the tips of your thumbs. Keep your forefinger straight.
- Bring together the tips of your other three fingers towards their base.

12. PYASA SHANTI MUDRA

Benefit: Quenches thirst.

- Bend your forefinger to touch the tip of your little finger.
- Now bring your thumb to touch your forefinger and little finger.

13. BHOOK SHANTI MUDRA

Benefit: Fights hunger.

Touch the tip of your little finger with your thumb to form a circle.

14. SHAKA MUDRA

Benefit: Keeps the body warm in a cold climate.

- Stretch your left hand, palm facing down, in front.
- Place your right ring finger at the base of your left ring finger (back of your left palm).

- Bring your right thumb to the base of your left ring finger (front of the palm).
- Now with your left forefinger and left thumb, make a circle around your right thumb.

Hands are reversed for ladies:

- Stretch your right palm in front, palm facing down.
- Place your left ring finger at the base of your right ring finger (back of your right palm).
- Place your left thumb at the base of your right ring finger (front of your palm).
- With your right forefinger and right thumb, make a circle around your left thumb.

Mudras to Increase a Reduced Tatva

Bring the tip of your finger representing the particular tatva to the tip of the thumb, and make it look like a circle.

- To increase the earth element, bring the tip of your ring finger to the tip of your thumb.
- To increase the air element, bring the tip of your forefinger to the tip of your thumb.
- To increase the water element, bring the tip of your little finger to the tip of your thumb.
- To increase the ether element, bring the tip of your middle finger to the tip of your thumb.
- To increase the fire element, place your right hand on your left palm. Bend your right thumb towards the little finger of your right hand. Press it on its first joint with your left thumb.

Mudras to Reduce an Increased Tatva

Bend the finger representing the particular tatva, and place its tip at the root of the thumb of the same hand. Place your thumb over that finger, using gentle pressure.

- To reduce the earth element, bring your ring finger to the root of your thumb.
- To reduce the air element, bring your forefinger to the root of your thumb.
- To reduce the water element, bring your little finger to the root of your thumb.
- To reduce the ether element, bring your middle finger to the root of your thumb.

- To reduce the fire element, place your left hand on your right palm. Bend your left thumb towards the little finger of your left hand, then press on its first joint with your right thumb.

Note: These Hasta Mudras are best done along with meditation.

7

Meditation

∽

Meditation is ancient and is part of the Yoga system. According to Maharishi Patanjali, meditation or *dhyana* "is an unknown flow of thought towards the object of concentration". It is described as a continuous process similar to that of oil flowing in an unbroken stream. The thought process is described as *vritti* or "waves" in the mind. Generally, these thought waves enter and stay in the mind for a short while until others take their place. In meditation, the waves flow so fast that there is no room for any one wave to remain as a thought. The effect is continuous.

Dhyana, as described by Patanjali, is different from what we normally think of as meditation. Dhyana is the process of keeping the mind focused on a central idea. It is the gathering of wandering thoughts to a concentrated focal point, and this expands awareness. In meditation, there is continuous systematic thinking without deviation from the main thought or object. Harmonious observation is thinking, while systematic analysis becomes meditation. In effect, dhyana does for the mind what Asana does for the body.

Meditation is useful as a therapy to combat both physical and emotional problems. Strong mental commands can act as medicine as well as food and pain relievers, and they can also improve blood circulation.

Meditation also brings about a gradual integration of the personality and has an influence on the nervous system. It helps to improve the way we use our senses and is a positive vital dynamic flow of thought on a subject or object.

In addition, meditation opens and improves our memory, and more than anything, it helps us get into contact with ourselves, something we think we already know how to. Those who practise meditation regularly are capable of coping with any kind of situation. People are constantly being tossed about both emotionally and intellectually in today's hectic world. The goal of successful meditation is to bring fluctuating emotions, temperaments and thoughts to a point of stillness.

Mechanical thinking is opposite of mindfulness. If you are already engaged in mindfulness, then you will consider each step an infinite wonder and take joy in it. No matter what position your body takes, you must be conscious of that position. You must live in direct and constant mindfulness of the body and be conscious of each breath, movement, thought and feeling. In short, you must be aware of everything that has any relation to yourself.

Your mind has a habit of wandering, but with regular practice, this "drifting" slows down and eventually disappears. There arises the feeling of returning to the focal point of the object without effort. Before you start meditating, you are advised to perform Yogasanas and Pranayama for maximum benefit. Regularised breathing not only helps meditation, but frees you from discomfort and disturbance caused by irregular breathing.

In meditation, you also need to be aware of the attitude you bring to the Asanas, which will be magnified during practice. If you bring an attitude of aggression, the pose will become aggressive. If you doubt your ability, then that doubt will be magnified in the mind. But if you bring an attitude of surrender and release, then you will surrender and release into the pose. The last thought you have before practising an Asana will be reflected throughout the body and mind during practice. By cultivating positive thoughts, you can create a situation that allows the Asana to become positive and beneficial.

By learning to create self-awareness during the practice of Asanas, you learn to practise self-awareness. The continued discipline of releasing where necessary, stilling what needs to be stilled, and focusing the mind on the task at hand is tremendously valuable not only in the practice of any one Asana but in life as well.

The essence of practising Asana is to realise one's purpose in life. To achieve this, proper understanding of each Asana, its movements, qualities, as well as its actions on the body and mind should be studied in detail. Mastery of an Asana is simple only if you put your mind to it. Meditation can be easy or hard depending upon your ability. Some find it difficult to construct mental images from feelings, and in such cases, it is better to focus on an object.

DIFFERENT GUIDELINES FOR MEDITATION

- Be practical as well as idealistic so your practice does not become hypocritical. Rather, have a solid commitment to your practice.
- To create the right kind of atmosphere, choose a place that is both clean and peaceful.
- Assume the right kind of posture that is both relaxing and comfortable. Perform simple Asanas just before the start of your meditation.
- There should be no conflict between your thoughts. Nor should there be any attempts to stop your mind from wandering. Thoughts will come and go. Do not be distracted by them, but do not reject them either. Merge your thoughts with the idea of meditation.
- Select a technique you like most.

HOW TO MEDITATE

- Spend a few moments focusing on your thoughts before you start meditating.
- Get comfortable with those thoughts.
- Observe your breath.
- Sit in an upright position. Make sure you are comfortable.
- Slowly, turn your attention to your breathing.
- Feel the exhaustion and tension flowing out as you exhale, and fresh and renewed energy entering your body as you inhale.
- After concentrating on your breathing for a while, factor in the following observations one at a time:
- (a) The difference in temperature between the inhaled and exhaled breath.
- (b) Your heartbeat and its rhythm.
- (c) The movements of your chest, abdomen and breath during respiration.

MEDITATION USING YANTRA

A mandala is a visual aid used in meditation. It is usually a geometrical shape that is symmetrical. The whole is a symbol of completion, harmony and integration. Everything is contained in the circle. It is timeless, with no beginning nor end. The inner circle is a reflection of the outer one, symbolising the inner spirit within the outer spirit's supreme nature. The point in the centre represents *bindhu*, which is "everlasting". The hexagon represents the six centres of consciousness. The triangle represents a pyramid, symbolising a mountain with a strong base reaching the top where all is one. This mandala represents the pairs of opposites, raised and transcended by the uniting principle.

Sri-Chakra

Yantra Meditation 1

- Place the Yantra 1 metre away from you in front at eye level.
- Look at the entire Yantra for 2 minutes.
- Start looking at a point on the circumference, and move your gaze round the circle.
- Once you reach the starting point, move your gaze to the centre.
- Continue doing this for 2 minutes.
- Now close eyes, and visualise the same Yantra.
- Remain comfortably seated, and, at the same time, concentrate on your breathing.
- Hold the position for 3 minutes. You can visualise constructing the circle, and placing a dot in the centre.
- Lie down and remain still in the position. Concentrate on your abdominal breathing to your comfort.

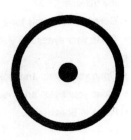

YM 1

Yantra Meditation 2

<u>a</u>

YM 2a

- Place the first Yantra in front of you as in YM1.
- Start looking at a point on the circumference, and move your gaze round the circle.
- Once you reach the starting point, move your gaze to the centre.
- Continue doing this for 2 minutes.
- Now close eyes, and visualise the same Yantra.
- Remain comfortably seated, and, at the same time, concentrate on your breathing.
- Hold the position for 3 minutes, and try reconstructing the circle, finally placing the dot in the centre.

<u>b</u>

YM 2b

- Now open your eyes, and replace the first Yantra with the second.
- Fix your gaze on the new Yantra for 2 minutes.
- Close your eyes, and visualise the same Yantra for 3 minutes.
- If the image is weak, open your eyes for a fraction of a second to manifest the vision.
- Lie down, and hold the position. Concentrate on your abdominal breathing to your comfort.

Yantra Meditation 3

The triangle symbolises the qualities of integration and visualisation. It is used to unify one's physical, emotional and mental faculties. The integration diminishes inner turmoil and conserves energy.

<u>a</u>

YM 3a

- Place the Yantra in front of you as described before.
- Direct your eyes from the apex of the triangle to the bottom right side.
- Now direct your eyes across the base, from right to left, and from there to the apex of the triangle.
- Continue doing this for 2 minutes.
- Close your eyes, and visualise the triangle for 3 minutes.

<u>b</u>

YM 3b

- Open your eyes, and look at the encircled triangle for 2 more minutes.
- Close your eyes, and visualise the same triangle for 3 minutes.
- Relax in Shavasana.

Yantra Meditation 4

This is to awaken or help an individual remember the objectives of life. The spiral movement serves both to remind and to help the mind elevate and refine consciousness to the degree necessary to merge with Yoga. YM4 is used in the awakening of Kundalini.

YM 4

- Place the Yantra in front of you as described before.
- Direct your eyes from the bottom of the spiral and along the curves to the top.
- Now shift your gaze to the bottom, and repeat the process of directing your eyes up the curves.
- Observe the spiral for 5 minutes.
- Now close your eyes, and visualise the same figure for another 5 minutes. Do not strain your eyes.
- If the image fades, open your eyes, and look at the Yantra briefly before continuing.
- Relax in Shavasana.

Yantra Meditation 5

This Yantra is related to the Anahata Chakra (the thymus gland). It represents the heart and mind. These faculties are improved during this meditative Asana. The Yantra also corresponds to love and compassion.

<u>a</u>

- Place the Yantra in front of you as described before.
- Start looking at the Yantra star as a whole, without dissecting it.
- Hold the gaze for 2 minutes.
- Close your eyes, and visualise the same Yantra for 3 minutes. In the beginning, it may be necessary to reinforce the image by opening your eyes and looking at the Yantra for a short while before closing your eyes immediately.

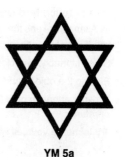

YM 5a

<u>b</u>

- Open your eyes to see an encircled star with a triangle in the centre.
- Hold the gaze for 2 more minutes.
- Close your eyes, and try to mentally visualise the whole picture before relaxing.

YM 5b

Meditation Using a Flower

This Asana brings unity between two or more things, that is, it terminates the subject-object relationship and develops oneness. The flower helps in the merging because the mind and vision can easily become involved with the elements of design, colour, texture and fragrance. Do not be impatient if you are distracted. Instead, try to bring the mind back to the flower gracefully.

The following is the method used to tame a "wild" mind, for when the mind attaches itself to something outside, a similar reaction is generated in the body. In other words, the nature of the reaction is the same as the nature of the involvement. This ability to control the mind and channel it in a chosen direction is achieved through proper practice.

- Place the flower in a position where you can look at it comfortably.

- Sit in a comfortable position.
- Observe the flower, study its nature and attempt to know its smallest details. Get yourself involved with its characteristics.
- Look at the flower for 10 minutes.
- After 10 minutes, close your eyes and relax.
- Visualise the flower you observed earlier.

If you find it difficult to observe the flower for a long time without blinking your eyes or if you feel pain in the eyes, do the following:

- Look at the flower for 30 seconds.
- Close your eyes and visualise the flower.
- Open your eyes after another 30 seconds, and repeat the process. While doing this, some people may be fascinated by the images that flash through their minds. However, this is just a distraction and not the desired goal.

Note: Do not let your mind wander from the objective of developing oneness.

Sense of Touch Meditation

This Asana awakens the tactile awareness and helps an individual become sensitive to touch. First of all, choose an object you would like to touch or feel.

- Sit comfortably, and close your eyes.
- Pick up the object, and use the fingers of both your hands to feel it.
- Fix your attention on it for 10 minutes, observing its quality, texture, shape and temperature.
- Try to merge yourself with the object.

Sense of Smell Meditation

People respond differently to different types of scents. Their moods may change accordingly.

- Select a soothing, scented incense that you like.
- Light the incense, and place it in front of you.
- Sit in a comfortable position, and close your eyes gently. Do not close them completely.
- Concentrate on the incense, and try to find out whether the scent is strong, light, heavy or sweet.
- Feel the effect of the scent on you before relaxing.

Concentrating on an Object

- Select an object, subject or even an idea, and think of everything about it without losing sight of its entirety.
- Review its characteristics, such as its shape, size, colour, texture and so on.
- Do not stop until you know it intimately. In other words, stop only when you know everything about it.

- Now record everything noted down about the object, subject or idea.
- In the second sitting, observe the same things about the object, subject or idea.
- After several sittings, you will learn that the mind, instead of wandering, learns to keep the characteristics of a subject when directed to do so.

Trataka — Candle Concentration

Many meditative Asanas involve the use of a candle flame. One of the reasons behind this is the idea of trinity expressed by the wick, wax and flame of the candle. The three cannot exist without the presence of at least two of the attributes. Similarly, the trinity comprises our body, mind and spirit. For a purposeful life, the three should have a harmonious coordination.

- Light a candle in quiet darkened room.
- Sit in comfort one arm's length away, so the flame is at eye level.
- Observe the flame for 3 minutes.
- Study its texture through observation as well as the shapes it takes. You may blink.
- Close your eyes for 3 minutes, and try to visualise the flame before relaxing.

Om Meditation

This meditation is associated with the Ajna Chakra (pituitary glands).

- Sit comfortably, and look at the Om for 5 minutes. Absorb yourself in it without breaking it into segments.
- Close your eyes, and visualise the Om in its entirety for about 5 minutes before relaxing.
- Repeat the process of sitting comfortably and looking at the Om. During your observation, perform audible rhythmical intonations of the Om for 5 minutes.
- Close your eyes, and visualise the Yantra.
- Continue with the silent repetitions of the Om without any change in rhythm before relaxing.

Om

Meditation Observing Smoke

- Light a joss stick, and place it some distance from where you are sitting.
- Start observing how the smoke curls in the air as it rises. Spend some time concentrating on this.

Solar Plexus Meditation

In this meditation, we learn how to consciously direct breath to any area that is not functioning properly.

- Sit comfortably, and place the thumbs and fingers of both your hands on the solar plexus region.
- Breathe in deeply, and while doing this, visualise your breath as a white current that is drawn into your lungs, subsequently filling them up.

- Now hold your breath.
- Visualise using your fingertips to "collect" this solar energy from your lungs.
- Move your fingers and thumbs to your forehead or to the region to which this energy needs to be transferred.
- Now start breathing out, and while doing this, visualise transferring the white Prana into the region.
- Hold your breath out, and bring your fingertips back to the solar plexus region.
- Repeat the entire process for 10 minutes.
- Now keeping your eyes closed, direct your attention to the region where the solar energy was distributed.
- Hold the thought for another 3 minutes before relaxing.

Meditation for Solving Problems

- Select a problem that worries you.
- Express it clearly either by repeating it in words or by writing it down.
- Now go back in time, and search for any event, information or ideas that may help solve the problem.
- Find out with thoughts on the problem at hand if this information offers any solution to the problem.
- Again express the solution if you find one or state why it may not work.
- Bring back your thoughts to the problem.
- Now feel how your present situation has changed.

Symbolic Meditation

In this Asana, an object is selected and used as a starting point for developing the power of contemplation. The object can be a flower, a candle flame or anything that pleases your mind.

- Study the physical characteristics of the object, such as its shape and beauty.
- Now concentrate on the functions of the object.

Colour Meditation

Although many people do not usually pay close attention to colour, it has important effects. From ancient times until now, colour therapy has been an accepted part of mental and physical treatment in Egypt, China and India.

Colour can affect both body temperature (pastels make you feel much cooler than rich tones) and the mood (red and yellow make you more cheerful than dark colours) and can, therefore, be indicative of the emotional state of an individual.

People who want to attract attention wear clothes in bright shades of purple, magenta, red or orange. It has been shown that young children learn best when surrounded by bright colours, such as red, yellow and blue.

Indian yogis associated colours with different states of the mind. They believed that red signifies vitality; saffron or yellow promotes meditation; green denotes harmonious relations; and blue represents coolness and tranquillity. What yogis knew then is, in fact, being rediscovered by modern doctors, who now use colours in operating theatres. There are colours even in psychiatrists clinics.

When you start meditating, the lights of different colours appear in your mind. They represent individual *Tatvas* or elements. The relationship is as follows: water is white; fire is red; the air is green; and ether is blue.

Other Characteristics of Colours

- Black is perceived as a negative colour, indicating surrender, hatred and malice.
- Bright green signifies tolerance, tact, adaptability and intelligence.
- Bright grey is associated with selfishness.
- Bright orange translates as pride and ambition.
- Brilliant golden yellow stands for intellectual qualities of a high status.
- Crimson is for love.
- Dark blue denotes calm and tranquillity.
- Dull grey shows fear.
- Dirty green stands for jealousy.
- Deep and dull yellow is indicative of the intellect.
- Dark clear blue conveys religious feelings.
- Grey is about concealment, and the person who chooses grey tends to be uncommitted and uninvolved.
- Green signifies pride, tension and the desire to impress.
- Red stands for an increase in pressure, rate of respiration as well as the desire to succeed.
- Red without black signifies righteousness.
- Red on a black background is indicative of anger.
- Red flashing on a green background is thought of as anger mixed with jealousy.
- Rose red is for love.
- Scarlet translates as anger.
- Slimy green signifies deceit and cunning.
- Violet with blue stands for spiritual thoughts.
- Violet is magical, erotic and unreal.
- Yellow stands for cheerfulness and is indicative of the desire for happiness.

The following are a few examples of problems that can be partially solved through the effective use of colour:

Melancholia or Acute Depression
Through the ages, red has been a popular colour for stimulating the optic nerves to produce an instant reaction from the mind. From the physical point of view red, light rays purify the blood and increase blood circulation. Red surroundings help patients heal faster.

Anxiety
Surroundings of green or amber yellow are helpful.

Toothache
Visualise the colour orange filling the area where there is toothache.

Fatigue
When tired, imagine a stream of white light, starting from the toes and reaching the skull, flowing through your body. This makes you feel energetic again. Any yellow material (like a scarf or a cap) on the head increases the outflow of energy, while purple on any part of the body helps limit the outflow of energy.

Stress
Blue is soothing and is good for mental peace.

High Blood Pressure
A blue light is used for treating high blood pressure.

Low Blood Pressure
Because of its stimulating effect, red is beneficial.

The seven colours of the rainbow spectrum are commonly used in meditation. Each of the seven colours corresponds to the different parts of the body.

- Red — limbs.
- Orange — lower back and pelvic region.
- Yellow — upper abdomen, covering the kidneys, pancreas and liver.
- Green — chest, including the heart and lungs.
- Blue — neck, throat and the thyroid.
- Indigo — eyes and the pituitary.
- Violet — brain and crown of head

These therapeutic colours also address many specific ailments, such as the following:
- Red — skin allergy
- Pink — lymph glands, ovaries and to tone down the effects of wearing red clothing.
- Orange — backache.
- Yellow — energising.
- Green and white — stress, to lower blood pressure and to help with respiratory problems
- Blue — general well-being, thyroid and intestinal problems.
- Indigo — healing, memory and insomnia
- Violet and purple — memory

In a rainbow, colour intensity increases from red to violet, that is, red has the lowest intensity, while violet has the highest intensity. If you meditate from low intensity to high intensity, this has a warming effect, which may, depending on the situation, require further visualisation of another colour to counteract the warmth.

On the other hand, meditation from high intensity to low intensity has a cooling effect on the body. After visualising the spectrum of colours, you can focus on any particular area of the body that needs healing, and let the energised colour of that area spread. Instead of meditating on a whole spectrum of colours, you can meditate on any one colour or a few colours.

Patients with heart ailments when meditating from low intensity to high intensity should always stop meditating at any colour intensity above the green colour but never lower. Similarly, when meditating from high intensity to low intensity, heart patients are advised not to meditate beyond the green colour.

Music during meditation serves as an anchor to bring you back to reality. Sound vibrations, imaginary or real, are used in some meditations to activate certain glands or Chakras. Sound meditation is used to activate the adrenals and the thyroid gland.

All meditations should ideally be done in the company of a good friend or partner. It is important for the instructor who guides the meditation to be a part of the learner's routine. However, always learn to rely on yourself. Do not be dependent on the voice of a teacher for every step of the meditation.

CHAKRA MEDITATION

Each Chakra is associated with a corresponding colour and function. The effect of an Asana can be greatly enhanced by focusing your mind on the region of the Chakra.

When you hold a position still for some time, a form of massage takes place. The Asana exerts pressure on the Chakra, each of which is associated with the major nerve plexuses of the body. The Chakras are the main relay and control centres of the human organism, and many psychological institutions use them in the healing process of their patients .

In Yoga, these Chakras are depicted symbolically as lotus flowers, each with a certain number of petals. The seven major energy centres located close to the glands, which we refer to as Chakras, are energy centres, through which we receive, transmit and process life energies.

Colours used in Chakra meditation are slightly different from meditation on the endocrine glands as the following box shows:

Chakra	Colour	Location
Sahasrara	colourless	crown of the head
Ajna	pale grey	pituitary
Vishuddhi	violet	thyroid
Anahata	smoky blue	thymus
Manipura	yellow	adrenals
Swadhisthana	crimson red	ovaries/gonads
Muladhara	red	base of the spine

Muladhara (the Root): Base of the Spine

Located in the perineal point. Second segment of the coccyx. It is represented by a deep red lotus with 4 petals, a yellow square in the centre and a red triangle with an apex upwards inside the square. By nature, the Chakra comprises the earth and skin elements. The triangle stands on an elephant, which represents stability. The Chakra also represents the skin element. It is concerned with survival and is the origin of energy.

Swadhisthana (Self Dwelling): Gonads/Ovaries

Located below the navel, it is represented by a crimson red lotus with 6 petals. In the centre is a white crescent moon, which is on the back of a crocodile. This represents the water and blood elements, involving excretion and reproduction. The Chakra can be represented by a deep vast lake with turbulent waves under a dark sky at night. The tides represent our awareness and its ebb and flow. This is the Chakra that helps us perceive others' thoughts.

Manipura (City of Jewels): The Adrenals

It is symbolised by 10 bright yellow petals and a red triangle inside them. The Chakra helps create a sense of harmony and balance. It is associated with the fire element and the flesh of the body. It is related to the digestive system and glandular problems.

Anahata (Unstuck): The Thymus

It is located near the heart and represents love, compassion and affinity. It is symbolised by a smoky blue lotus with 12 petals. In the centre is a hexagon. The Chakra can be represented by a tiny flame inside a dark empty cave. It is the air element and is associated with the fat element of the body. The Chakra is related to the heart and lungs.

Vishuddhi (Purification): The Thyroid

This deals with communication and telepathy and is symbolised by a violet lotus with 16 petals. In the centre is a white circle standing on a white elephant. The elephant symbolises ether. The Chakra may be represented by cold drops of sweet nectar dripping into a pot. It represents ether and is connected to the bone element of the body.

Ajna (the Command): The Pituitary

This concerns visualisation and clairvoyance. It is symbolised by a pale grey or white lotus with 2 petals and is associated with the mind and brain. The Chakra controls the mind.

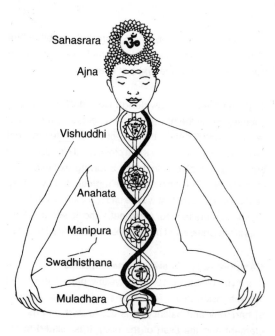

Position of the Chakras in the body

In addition to these, there are two more Chakras in the head:

Bindu

This is also known as the Soma Chakra and is at the top rear corner of the head. It is symbolised by a tiny crescent moon on a full moon. The Chakra is associated with the production of *Bindu*, which means "semen".

Sahasrara: Crown of the Head

This is associated with intuition and connection to the universe and is the pathway or a contact point to the universe. Strictly speaking, this is not considered a Chakra. Rather, it is the abode of the highest consciousness. It is visualised as a shining lotus with 1,000 petals.

Nadi

The *Nadi* (channels), which are associated with the nerves, are a flow of current. Ancient texts say that there are 72,000 such currents of light in a psychic body. Among them 14 are considered vital. Of these, three are the most important, and they are *Ida*, *Pingala* and *Sushumna*. The Sushumna Nadi, which is silver in colour, runs within the spinal cord from the base of the spine to the pituitary. To its left is a curved path called Ida, which is blue. To the right of Sushumna is Pingala, which is red. In Hatha Yoga, these two are to be unified harmoniously, so energy flows through Sushumna.

The method of meditation that follows is used widely in psychic healing workshops. The real relaxation that it gives is indescribable. It relieves tension after a hard day's work.

Colour Meditation 1

- Sit in a comfortable position, feet in contact with the floor.
- Breathe uniformly and rhythmically, and maintain this throughout the period of meditation.
- Close your eyes.
- Imagine the centre of the earth as a ball of fire. If you find it difficult to visualise this, try looking at a bright light or candle flame for a few seconds. Now close your eyes to recreate the image.
- Feel the energy flow from the source to your body. The energy flow is from your feet to the base of your spine.
- Visualise a bunch of red flowers filling the area from your feet to the base of your spine.
- Water the flowers, smell their fragrance and appreciate their beauty.
- When you have completed the previous step, shift to Swadhisthana.
- Now imagine orange-coloured fruit, and sense their nature fully.
- Shift to the adrenals, where energy from the golden yellow sunlight pours into the adrenals or the surrounding region, and sense the energy.
- Now move to your heart region, where green leaves fill the space.
- Imagine small shoots coming out of a plant, and their growth filling the entire region of the heart.
- Bring your thoughts to the thyroid, where crystal clear blue water is poured on the growing plant. Feel the beauty of the flowing stream.

- While your thoughts move upwards from the thyroid to the pituitary, start visualising a beautiful sky of indigo. Enjoy the aura.
- Gradually shift your thoughts to the crown of your head, and feel how the entire region is filled with violet and a sense of tranquillity.
- If you have the time, go through the energy Chakras once again in sequence.
- Feel totally relaxed and an inflow of energy.

Colour Meditation 2

This meditation is based on an Indian folklore. King Indra asked a celestial architect called Viswakarma to make a weapon, a bow. So, Viswakarma went to the forest to find suitable wood. He fashioned a plain but beautiful bow. However, he wanted to make it more elegant, thus began his search for this quality in the bow. Draw a parallel in meditation, where you begin the search to create a more beautiful bow.

- Sit in a comfortable position, and close your eyes.
- Imagine that you are going to make a colourful bow, and you go to the high mountains and select good wood.
- Now make a bow, and you want it to be painted with beautiful colours.
- Look up at the sky at dawn, and see its violet colour. Paint a strip of violet on the bow. Once complete, go in search of other colours.
- While walking on an imaginary road, picture weavers using the dye from the indigo plant to colour clothes. Now paint a strip of indigo on the bow.
- After completing this, wander around the woods and come across a handsome peacock dancing under the sun, its tail spread out like a magnificent fan. Paint a strip of peacock blue on the bow.
- Keep wandering in search of more colours.
- Look out for a beautiful grove of mango trees with healthy looking green mangoes.
- Paint a strip of green on the bow.
- Still wandering in the woods, notice newly born lion cubs with golden yellow fur.
- Paint a strip of yellow on the bow.

- Walk in the direction of a village near the woods.
- Imagine village women applying henna, which is natural orange in colour, on a traditional Indian bride's hand and feet.
- Paint a strip of orange on the bow.
- Finally come across a Flame of the forest tree with brightly coloured red flowers that are blossoming.
- Paint a strip of red on the bow.
- Now hang the bow in a place where there is sunlight for the paint to dry. The bow is now ready.
- Continue visualising the beauty of each colour and how they were found for as long as you can.

Colour Meditation 3

This is a continuation of Colour Meditation 2.

- In your mind, draw the bow you created, which has been placed under direct sunlight to dry.
- Now there appears a light shower, which will prevent the bow from being cracked.
- Lie down on the ground, and watch raindrops hit the bow.
- Visualise drops of red colour falling at your feet and entering the body, and spreading to your limbs.
- Next orange drops enter your groin and fill the pelvic and lower abdominal area.
- Yellow enters your navel region and fills your abdomen and back.
- Green enters the solar plexus and fills the chest and lungs.
- Blue enters the thyroid through your neck and fills the whole region.
- Indigo enters the eyes.
- Violet enters the crown of your head and fills the brain.
- Feel the toxins removed from your body, which is now revitalised.

Note: Every time a colour enters your body, feel the new sensation it produces. Similarly, for health problems connected to the different organs, choose situations that correspond to the respective colours, and visualise them.

Colour Meditation for Relaxation
(Trakata or Candle Concentration)

- Sit in an upright comfortable position 1 metre away from a lighted candle.

- Look at the flame for 3 minutes, and close your eyes for another 3 minutes. If you so desire, increase the meditation time a little.
- See the rainbow spectrum in the flame, starting from red at the top to orange, yellow, green, blue, indigo and finally violet at the bottom.
- Take in the different colours one at a time and then as a beam of light.
- As they enter through the pupils of your eyes, the colours are inverted. Violet will be at the top, and it will reach the pituitary, filling it completely.
- Close your eyes, and visualise the violet colour of the pituitary.
- Feel the decreasing pressure of tension before relaxing.

Meditation for Stress

a
- Imagine a beautiful and peaceful garden filled with lush green trees.
- Breathe in the fresh air.
- Visualise a lake, then a white swan coming into view. See its graceful movements on the water.
- Go towards it.
- Travel on the swan's back to any desired destination.
- Feel the relaxation seeping into your body.

OR

b
- Lie down under a lush, green tree.
- Look up at the blue sky.
- Consider the characteristics of the sky — its vastness, depth and beauty.
- Imagine the "blueness" of the sky falling to the earth in the form of blue drizzle.
- Fine soft drops fall on your neck and are absorbed into your body through your neck.
- Imagine the blueness spreading to your entire body.
- Feel the relaxation taking over you.

OR

c
This meditation aims to clear confusion in your mind caused by stress and tension. Three colours are visualised together.

- Imagine sitting in a park or garden filled with beautiful flowers. There is a light breeze. You feel relaxed in this place even though you are troubled.
- See the different colours of the flowers and smell their fragrance.
- Above your head a bunch of violets, whose petals touch your head and skin.
- A gentle breeze causes the violet petals to "dance" on your head, giving a massage to specific areas of your scalp and easing tension away from your skull.
- Now look at the indigo plant in front of you. The indigo colour enters your eyes to colour your brain and pituitary indigo. This creates a soothing effect.
- Surround your neck and shoulders with sky blue flowers. They gently "rub" your neck, throat and shoulders, activating the thyroid.
- You notice the three types of flowers and their three colours very clearly. Your mind now sees things clearly, helping you further to have clear thoughts.
- Enjoy this clarity of the mind and the relaxation it brings.

Meditation for Insomnia
"Sleep is a mental activity. The body may be tired, but if the mind is not relaxed, you will not sleep." The pituitary controls the metabolism of involuntary movements, and this includes sleep. The colour best suited for relaxed meditation is indigo, the colour of tranquillity. As indigo is a "hot" colour, it induces a feeling of heaviness. Purple offsets this feeling of heaviness.

- Visualise being in the high mountains and looking up at the clear indigo sky.
- Imagine light rays of indigo emanating from the sky and entering your eyes.
- Let the indigo rays enter your pupils to converge on the pituitary, colouring it completely indigo.
- Visualise purple sky around the indigo sky. Let the purple sky now colour the entire crown of your head so your head is now purple.
- Let the purple spread to your entire brain, enveloping the indigo pituitary.
- Let the purple and indigo merge into one.
- Now let the colour flow around your body before relaxing.

Meditation for Brain Power

- Sit in a comfortable armchair, and listen to your favourite, soothing music.
- Imagine a crystal bowl, and fill it with your favourite things, such as flowers, fruit, mementoes, etc.
- Look at the things in the bowl. A door opens into the bowl.
- Enter through the door so you can be among your favourite things.
- Inside the bowl is violet all around.
- Enjoy the violet as it bathes all your favourite things in this colour.
- Pick up one of your favourite things, and study it thoroughly. The object is bathed in violet, and there is a streak of silver grey across the violet.
- Pick up your other favourite objects one by one to study them closely. Each is bathed in violet with a silver streak across it. The objects surround you, floating about as you look at each one of them thoroughly.
- Feel the relaxation taking over you.

Note: Music is used as an anchor to bring you back to reality or signal the end of the meditation. The purple/violet/indigo colour family is used to activate brain cells. Silver grey streaks represent the brain centre.

Meditation for Concentration

This meditation encourages concentration and reduces "interference" from external stimuli.

- Imagine being in a quiet place, which you know and love well.

  There are other people in this place with you who are moving about quietly.
- Imagine listening to your favourite music.
- Now visualise a much-loved object, concentrating on its colour, while, at the same time, listening to the music and watching the people around you move about quietly.

Meditation for Improving Memory

- Lie down in a secluded, beautiful place.
- It is a clear moonlit night. The sky above is purple and speckled with bright stars.

- Imagine having a straight and strong vibrant spinal column.
- Visualise red, orange and yellow energies at the base of the spine.
- Now the colours rise, separately and distinctly, from the base to the top of the spine in the shape of a fountain.
- As each colour rises, the energy activates the endocrine glands.
- The brain at the top of the spinal column is illuminated by the colour purple. Just as the purple sky is above you, so is the purple brain above your spine. Just as the stars are like bright spots of light in the purple sky, so are the bright spots of light in the purple-coloured brain. One of the stars is the most brilliant, so is one of the spots on the left side of your brain. This is where the memory of everyday life is stored.
- Let the brain and sky merge into one. Also, let the brilliant star and bright memory spot be one, which radiates light and energises you.
- Select the memory surrounding any incident.
- Enjoy the sense of relaxation and well being.

Meditation for Mental Strain and Headaches

- Imagine looking at the blue water in a large aquarium. See pink coloured gold fish swimming in the water, and look at its colour.
- Notice how it swims effortlessly, with not a worry in world.
- See the bubbles from its gills as it breathes rhythmically.
- Notice the green algae in the aquarium, and the fish swimming towards it before eating it.
- Observe how the fish nibbles at the algae, moving in and out of it to take a bite.
- Feel the relaxation creeping into you.

For further visualisation:

Notice a pink lotus on the surface of the blue water. Its stem is green, and the fish swims towards it.

Note: The colours for this meditation range from blue to pink, starting from the neck, the spine and then the lower back. This meditation is also suitable for people suffering from backache.

Meditation for Over-excitement, Hyperactivity and Migraine

- Lie on a bed of velvety pink roses.
- A gentle breeze blows. It blows the petals around your temples, gently massaging them.
- The breeze blows the petals around your neck, gently massaging the area.
- Now the breeze blows the petals around your shoulders, gently massaging the area. Also, imagine green leaves blowing around your shoulders. The leaves spread their colour to your body, colouring it green. The colour then spreads to all parts of your body.

Meditation for Headaches

- Imagine being in your favourite place that is on high ground. It is dusk, and the sky is purple.
- Visualise imaginary fingers giving you a massage on your head for relief from headaches or tension.
- Imagine the scent of lavender enveloping your body and caressing it.
- Feel the relaxation seeping into your body.

Vishuddhi Chakra Meditation

- Lie down on a rock under a violet sky at dusk.
- Imagine a violet coloured curtain hanging from the sky.
- Allow the curtain to float towards you, as it wraps itself around your throat region, colouring it violet.
- Inside the violet-coloured throat is a violet lotus with 16 petals. It is budding.
- While inhaling the fragrance, the petals open up, and while exhaling, the petals close. Visualise this activity, and synchronise it with your breathing.
- Feel the relaxation seeping into you.

For further visualisation:

- When the 16 petals open up, an elephant puts its trunk into the stamens to suck the sweet nectar.
- The elephant then spouts out the sweet nectar like a fountain to every part of your body.
- You may concentrate on any part of the body that requires healing. Work slowly and systematically towards this goal. Always remember to relax.

Note: The 16 petals represent the 16 hormones produced by the thyroid gland. The meditation regulates the hormone-producing thyroid.

Anahata Chakra Meditation

- Imagine looking at fish in a pond, and pick out a colourful fish of your choice.
- Watch how the fish swims effortlessly and gracefully.
- Watch how the fish takes in gulps of water through its mouth as it breathes in oxygen from the water.
- See air bubbles being expelled from its gills.
- Imagine your lungs breathing in air just like the fish breathing in air through its mouth. Your breathing is to be in harmony with the breathing of the fish.

For further visualisation:

- Imagine a smoky-blue pond (corresponds to the pleura).
- Look at an imaginary lotus with 12 petals on the pond. The 12 petals of the lotus correspond to the 12 ribs in the thoracic cavity of your body.
- Look at fish with quick rhythmic breathing move around the lotus.
- Notice green algae in the smoky-blue pond (corresponds to the trachea, alveoli).

Heart Anahata Chakra

- It is dusk. Imagine lying down on a big rock on the beach.
- Look up at the smoky-blue sky.
- Listen to your heartbeat.
- Imagine waves breaking against the rock. Listen to them as they splash against the rock. There is harmony between your heartbeat and the breaking of the waves.
- Imagine your heart to be smoky blue in colour and in the shape of a lotus with 12 petals. The lotus opens and closes its petals in harmony with the waves.
- As waves break on the shore, the lotus opens. As they ebb, the lotus closes.
- Imagine two overlapping black triangles inside the lotus that form a six-pointed star.

- As waves break on the shore again, the lotus opens, and blood is pumped to every part of your body through the six-pointed tips of the star.
- Let the blood flow to any area that needs cleansing, and feel its soothing effect.
- Feel the relaxation seeping into your body.

Meditation for the Heart and Blood Circulation

The colours used here are red, blue and pink (colour of the rose bud).

- Imagine looking at the earth's core, which is a red fiery ball. Radiant energy emanates from the core.
- Draw the red hot energy up to your feet and thighs, colouring your legs red.
- Go back to the red core for more radiant energy. Again it moves up your legs, which are red, and to the pelvic region, which is orange.
- Once more go back to the red core for more radiant energy, now drawing it up your kidneys and adrenals, colouring them yellow.
- Now go back to the red core for more radiant energy, drawing it up to your lungs.
- See the energy spread young green leaves all over your lungs, colouring the lungs green. In midst of the green leaves is a lovely pink rosebud. Look at it swaying in the breeze together with the leaves.
- Feel the relaxation seeping into your body.

For further visualisation:

- Look at the rosebud closely.
- The bud is about to open. Nurture it with blue raindrops that fall from the sky.
- As each raindrop touches the petals of the rosebud, imagine the drop synchronising with your heartbeat.
- Let the droplets be carried along the stem of the rosebud to every part of your body.
- Feel the relaxation seeping into your body.

Meditation for High Blood Pressure

- Lie down under a tree with lush green leaves.
- Imagine a gentle breeze caressing your body.
- Listen to the birds singing.

- Feel the sound energy vibrating in your ears.
- Look at the green colour of the leaves, and draw in their green energy through the solar plexus.
- The energy flows in waves through the lungs to every part of the body, refreshing it and flushing out the toxins to the surface of the skin, where the gentle breeze blows them away.
- Feel cleansed and relaxed.

Meditation for the Chest and Lungs

- Lie on your back in a pool of crystal clear blue water.
- There are green creepers floating in the blue water. Imagine swimming among them.
- The green creepers embrace your chest, holding your body up in the water. Relax yourself in the embrace.
- Feel the green colour of the creepers seeping into your chest, lungs, bronchi and alveoli.
- Feel the healing powers of the green creepers fill your lungs as they expel the mucous and toxins that clog them.
- Emerge feeling healed, cleansed and relaxed.

Relaxation for the Pectoral Muscles

- Lie down under a lush green tree.
- A gentle breeze blows, and birds sing in the tree.
- Green leaves fall on your chest, colouring it green. The leaves draw out the toxins and pain from the pectoral muscles.
- The breeze now blows away the green leaves from your chest. The pain and toxins are blown away, disappearing with the leaves.
- Feel healed, cleansed and relaxed.

Meditation for the Adrenals (with Adrenals Massage)

- Imagine lying body down in a peaceful beautiful place with many trees.
- Listen to the music of the wind as it wafts through your relaxed body.
- A nearby stream flows gently. Listen to the musical notes of the flowing water. Birds chirp merrily in the trees. The musical notes of the wind, stream and birds float towards you, touching and caressing you.

- Feel the vibrations, and let them enter your body as waves. These energy waves travel through your body to your kidneys. As the waves gather here, a yellow glow emanates from both sides of the spine.
- Visualise a red triangle at the top of each of your kidneys. The vibrations cause the triangles to dance and vibrate.

Note: The kidneys will have a yellow glow. The adrenals are the red triangles.

Colour Meditation for the Adrenals

- Lie down in a favourite place, looking at the clear sky.
- This place has imaginary trees and birds.
- A beautiful rainbow spans the horizon.
- Enjoy yourself looking at the beautiful colours of the rainbow.
- A slight drizzle starts around the rainbow.
- Tiny droplets fall from the rainbow.
- The droplets have a golden yellow colour taken from the rainbow.
- The fine golden raindrops are falling down onto your abdominal area, colouring the area golden yellow.
- The colour spreads all around the adrenals. Both sides of the spine are also golden yellow.

Colour Meditation for the Ovaries

- Imagine lying down on a soft bed of pink flowers.
- Imagine waves of pink colour approaching your feet.
- Allow the pink colour to enter your body, filling your whole abdominal area and ovaries with pink energy. This washes away the toxins and pain in the back, including any "knots" in the abdominal region.
- Visualise pink flowers all over the abdominal region, and feel its colour there.

Colour Meditation for the Uterus

- Imagine looking at the centre of the Earth, a red fiery ball. Draw radiant energy from it into your body.
- Bring the energy up your limbs, colouring them red.
- As the energy travels up to the uterus, it colours it pink. Imagine pink roses in the uterus area flushing out the toxins.

- Imagine an orange colour surrounding the pink uterus.
- Now bring the energy of the yellow colour up to the adrenals/kidneys; the energy of green colour in the form of green leaves to your chest; and blue energy as blue water to your throat. Let this blue water be poured onto the leaves and pink roses.
- Indigo energy enters through your eyes and filters down, healing the affected area.
- Feel the energy and relaxation taking over your body.

Colour Meditation for Menstrual Problems

Let blue waves flow over your body in a perfect harmonious rhythm.

Colour Meditation for Menopausal Problems

- Imagine sitting in your favourite place.
- Look at the bright red/brilliant yellow setting sun on the horizon. Imagine the red and yellow rays entering your body and energising your ovaries.
- Visualise a glowing red and yellow six-petalled lotus with a white crescent and a white crocodile representing the blood element.
- The sun sets, but its energy remains, just like the energy of the ovaries.

Colour Meditation for Stress and Menopausal Problems

- Imagine being in your favourite garden on a beautiful day. There are flowers blooming everywhere.
- See the beautiful colours of the flowers, and smell their refreshing fragrance.
- Look at the white jasmine, and smell its fragrance.
- Look at the purplish blue lavender. There are also red and pink roses everywhere. The violets are deep violet, while the sunflowers are bright yellow. Absorb the colour and fragrance of the flowers.
- Observe two colourful birds, flitting from flower to flower. They seem to reflect the colours of the flowers. Just like you, they too enjoy the colourful display of flowers.
- Watch the birds flit from jasmine flowers to lavender flowers, and from roses to violets and sunflowers in their apparent eternal flight of joy.

- Enjoy the colours and movements, and absorb them into your body.
- Feel totally relaxed.

Muladhara Chkara Meditation and the Skin Element

- Lie down in a room.
- Visualise a red lotus with 4 petals at the base of your spine. In the centre of the lotus is a yellow square. On the yellow square is an elephant. The petals cover the elephant on the yellow square.
- The lotus grows bigger, reaching out to touch every part of your body and colouring it red. The petals touch your skin, colouring it red.
- Look at the 4 smooth petals, and feel the soft smooth texture. Imagine your skin to be as smooth as the petals. The petals and skin merge into one.

Colour Meditation for Skin Problems

- Imagine being in a green meadow under a blue sky.
- You are beside a brook. Feel the texture of the grass. Spend some time concentrating and feeling the texture.
- Imagine green leaves gently falling on your body and brushing against it. Spend some time visualising this.
- Imagine the sky turning into indigo. Enjoy the texture of indigo as it touches your skin all over.
- Feel totally healed and relaxed.

Meditation for Hearing Difficulty

This meditation improves your sense of hearing. It helps focus the mind to hear in a particular direction.

- Focus on the rhythm of relaxed breathing.
- Listen to your heartbeat carefully.
- Place your palm over your heart to listen to your heartbeat.
- Relax your arm.
- Feel the sensation of sound, and listen to your breathing.
- Feel how every inhalation supplies nutrients to your body, and every exhalation removes the toxins.
- Feel your heartbeat pumping oxygen to every part of your body.

- As the heart beats, listen to the flow of the blood.
- Harmonise your breathing with your heartbeat and flow of blood. Focus on this for a while.
- Focus on the auditory aspect of your breathing, heartbeat and flow of blood to achieve clarity of sound.
- Feel the relaxation taking over you.

Meditation for Concentration of Vision

In this Asana, you may choose any colour you like.

- Imagine being in a scenic place where the air is fresh.
- Besides you, there are other people with a similar desire for relaxation. You are, however, undisturbed by their presence.
- Look at the sky, trees, colourful birds and the soft grass before looking at yourself.
- One particular colour from any of the four mentioned things attracts you.
- Draw in this colour to merge it with your body for enrichment.
- You do not notice anything but the colour you like.

Meditation for Focusing on Hearing and Vision

- Be in a crowded yet beautiful place with people, trees, flowers and colourful birds. Enjoy the scenery.
- Look at all the things mentioned above, but you are attracted to the colour of the object you most like. Spend some time admiring it. Other things do not seem to matter to you now.
- Listen to the humming music that comes from another object you like.
- You are attracted to two things at once: favourite colour and favourite music. Focus on them, allowing both to enter your body. The coloured wavelength and sound waves produce vibrations in your body. You are now relaxed and energised.

Meditation for Activating the Immune System

- Visualise an aquarium in which a pink fish is swimming.
- Observe how it nibbles the green algae off the pebbles. Draw a parallel to your body, where immune cells eat away at your infection.

Meditation for Cancer

a

- Imagine lying down in a blue room where the walls and ceiling are blue.
- Think of your favourite music.
- Imagine a pink rope hanging down from the ceiling above your chest. It is knotted and rough.
- Go through the process of untying the knots so the pink rope becomes untangled and smooth.
- Feel the healing waves wash through your mind and body.

b

- Imagine lying down in a completely blue room where the walls and ceiling are blue.
- Now imagine a pink fish swimming in an aquarium in the blue room.
- Look at the fish eating the greenish-yellow algae on the weeds and stones in the aquarium.

Note: The knot in (a) is just above the affected area. If the knot is just above your chest, the meditation is good for breast/lung cancer. The meditation supervisor keeps reminding patient about blue room, which represents the thyroid. The pink fish represents the lymph glands. The colour greenish-yellow represents cancer cells.

Meditation for Relaxation

- Imagine being a doctor, selflessly helping people in search of healing. You are happy that they listen to your instructions for successful healing.
- Think of examining an unwell patient.
- Place your thumbs at the centre of the patient's forehead, and gently massage the temples, using circling movements.
- Move your fingers up and down behind the ears several times for a gentle massage.
- While massaging the patient, experience a similar massage on your own forehead, temples and ears.
- Place your thumbs just below the eyebrows near the bridge of the nose, and then move it outwards below the eyebrows towards the temples.
- Use your fingers to gently tap the back of the neck, moving downwards to the base of the neck and shoulders.
- Experience the scent of lavender. The flowers follow the direction of the massage as they move on your body.
- Feel the texture of the lavender flowers on your body and skin as they gently massage you.
- Enjoy the relaxation.

Meditation for Energy and Vitality

- Sit in a comfortable position.
- Look at the spiral column (Yantra meditation 4) for 2 to 3 minutes. If you wish, you may visualise the spiral column without looking at it.
- Relate the spiral column to your own spinal column, moving upwards in a whirlwind motion.
- Your feet now touch the surface of the Earth, at whose centre is a red ball of energy.
- Imagine drawing energy from the red core to the surface before it reaches your feet. The feet channel the energy into your body, filling up your legs with red.
- Draw in more energy from the glowing core for energy to accumulate at the lower pelvic area. The red energy changes to orange.
- Draw in more energy to bring up to the base of the spine, coccyx and lower back. The energy changes to yellow.
- The base of the spine collects all the three distinct colours and accumulates the energy collected from Earth's core.
- Visualise the spiral column spinning upwards. The accumulated energy also spins upwards in a whirlwind motion, with the three colours spinning up together, distinct, separate.
- Let the coloured energy pass through the adrenals, the thoracic and cervical regions, the atlas (the first cervical vertebra), pituitary, as well as the entire brain.
- As energy spins up, it activates the endocrine glands, which in turn energise all the other parts of the body and create a healthy system.
- Go back to the core for more energy. Feel the energy seeping into your body.

Meditation for Recovery and Recuperation

- Imagine being in a blue room.
- Listen to the soft sound of tinkling bells, which are as tiny as grapes. The tinkling bells represent the lymph glands.
- Imagine that the ceiling has now changed its colour to pink. The pink colour colours your entire body in that colour.
- Experience the healing. You should feel as if you are in the pink of health.

Meditation for Addiction

This meditation is suitable for people with a confused mind as a result of an addiction, such as alcohol addiction.

- Imagine sitting or lying beside a lagoon as the sun sets.
- Look at the setting sun and its orange rays. It is dipping into the horizon, but you know it will return.
- Now visualise your addiction to alcohol.
- You think that getting drunk always makes you feel better.
- You hope to submerge your thoughts just as the sun submerges into the horizon. You know that the setting sun disappears into the horizon, and yet it will always rise.
- Feel how good it is to see the sun and how beautiful the sunset is.
- As the sun's rays pass through the clear water, visualise seahorses illuminated by orange light.
- The orange illuminates the seahorses from the top to bottom in a single column.
- Now feel the sun's rays entering your spinal column, the orange energy ascending from the coccyx to the pituitary. Feel the reassuring warmth.
- Let the energised orange colour pour itself into the cerebellum, turning into the colour of magenta and activating it. Bear in mind that the cerebellum is related to sense organs of speech, hearing, taste, touch, smell and sight.
- Experience the energy unclouding your mind, ridding it of the urge to suppress. You feel a sense of clarity.
- The body also feels energised as the orange energy from the spine radiates outwards and down the body, giving it a gentle massage.

- You now have a positive frame of mind and feel very relaxed.

Note: The colour orange can be employed for less serious addicts. Please note, however, that orange must be substituted with red for those with a very serious case of alcohol addiction.

Meditation for Irritation

- Imagine being in a quiet place. It is a peaceful evening.
- Suddenly, flies come towards you. They buzz around your head and annoy you.
- Pity them as they are ignorant and cannot help what they are doing.
- Look up at the sky, and see stars in the sky. One is brighter than the rest.
- Two bright lights emanate from the star, one red and one blue. Concentrate on these lights.
- The flies cannot see the lights or the star, as such things are beyond their comprehension. Pity the flies.
- Visualise that you are with the star. Now the flies cannot reach you, and so they disappear.

Meditation for Decision Making

The purpose of this Asana is to create the best mental condition for intelligent decision making.

- Imagine lying down in your favourite comfortable and secluded place.
- Imagine violets dancing lightly on top of your entire scalp.
- Imagine indigo colour going into your eyes and reaching the pituitary.
- Imagine hyacinths growing around you.
- Look at their blue colour, and smell their perfume.
- Imagine the blue colour and perfume reaching your thyroid region.
- Experience a positive feeling of relaxation.

Meditation for Muscular Cramps

This is best done after the Asanas for muscle cramps (see chapter 21).

- Imagine lying down on a big rock on the beach.

- Look at the waves as they hit the rock.
- Watch the waves break into foam against the rock, and listen to the sound of the breaking waves.
- As the waves hit against the rock, wave energy is transformed into sound energy.
- Listen to the sound as it has a soothing and calming effect.
- Feel the sound energy travel to the rock you are lying on, and feel its vibrations.
- Let the vibrations pass from the rock to your body. This has a soothing and calming effect on every part of your body.

Meditation for Constipation and Indigestion

- Imagine lying on the beach, looking up at an all-encompassing blue sky. The sea too is blue.
- Drink in the colour from your throat, visualising the thyroid to be blue.
- The golden sun is now about to set.
- Feel streaks of gold streaming into the blue sky to touch your body, settling on your abdominal region and adrenals.
- Visualise the blue thyroxins spreading down your body to the abdominal region, which is golden yellow. The blue colour floats down.
- As the sun sets, the sky slowly loses its golden yellow light. The blue slowly and gently pushes the golden yellow away.

Meditation for the Neck and Shoulders

a

This meditation uses autosuggestion to massage the neck, shoulders and arms. It is especially useful for inner muscles and nerves that require attention.

- Imagine being in a place where there is white snow under blue skies.
- Look at the wide expanse of the snow-covered slopes. You feel the desire to ski.
- Wear goggles to block out the glare before readying yourself to ski.
- Feel the movement in each part of your body with the movement of the skis and ski poles.
- Feel your arms, head, neck and trunk move back and

forth while skiing down the slope. Feel the muscles and nerves working actively.
- Feel the blood circulation in your body, which is both warming and energising.
- Feel the breeze.
- Spend ample time skiing down the slopes.
- You notice a chalet.
- Sit down near it.
- You can still feel the warmth in your arms, neck and shoulders.
- There is a light drizzle under the blue skies. Look at the fine blue raindrops. As they fall onto your neck and arms, the blue colour spreads, washing away the toxins to the surface, where the breeze blows them away.

b
- Lie down or sit down on the floor.
- Place your hands at the back of your neck, and give yourself a gentle massage.
- Relax your arms.
- Imagine being in the woods with a friend on a beautiful day.
- Birds chirp merrily in the trees, and the sun's rays fall on the leaves.
- Your friend's hand is on your neck and shoulders. He/she gives you a gentle massage in these areas while walking with you.

c
- Imagine looking at a pool of water at night.
- There is a fountain in the pool. The water is illuminated by multi-coloured lights.
- Watch the water rise from the pool up a tube to a certain height before falling down like a shower.
- Imagine your spine to be the fountain.
- A red column of water rises up your spinal column to a certain height around the pelvic region before radiating outwards and energising the area.
- The fountain water changes its colour from red to orange.
- Notice the orange-coloured water rise a little higher up your spine.
- Just as water rises, so does the energy, revitalising the area as it rises.

- The fountain water changes its colour to yellow.
- Notice the yellow-coloured water go higher up your spine to the adrenals, activating the area.
- From the fountain, blue water rises to reach the top of your spinal column, activating the thyroid gland.
- Blue droplets of water pour out like a shower, radiating outwards and downwards, washing away the pain in your neck and soothing the shoulder area.
- Enjoy the relaxed feeling in your neck and shoulders.

Meditation for General Aches and Pains

- Imagine being in your favourite picnic spot with a close friend.
- The sky is blue, and the grass green. The birds sing merrily in the trees.
- Imagine warm blue water flowing over the waterfall into a beautiful stream.
- Imagine that the blue water is cascading over your head, bathing it as well as your body.
- Feel the aches and pains melt away, and feel totally relaxed.

Now visualise and create any type of situation for meditation. Feel and experience the benefits gained. Colour meditation is very powerful, and it transforms everything it surrounds. Enjoy the reaction. Let daily activities be associated with this wonderful environment so that every action is imbued with a heightened sense of comfort.

8

Routines

❧

Before starting on these routines, it is best that you do any of the Pawanamuktasana or Shakti Vikasa Asanas (see chapter 2). The Asanas will loosen stiff joints and muscles. It will also enable you to perform the routines here more effectively.

Always start out with the moderate position the first time you perform any of the Asanas. When repeating the same posture on another day, get into the intermediate position on the second or third attempt. As you progress, attempt the extreme position.

The holding time given for each position is only a guideline. Depending on your own comfort level while performing the Asanas, either increase or decrease the duration. Take a recommended 5 minutes to perform Pranayama and Asanas for relaxation (see chapter 20). Concentrate on the movements. Relax in between each Asana by performing Advasana or Shavasana (see chapter 3). Remember to adhere to the Dos and Don'ts in chapter 1.

TWENTY-FOUR-DAY PROGRAMME

What the following abbreviations mean:

mod: moderate

int: intermediate

ext: extreme

sec.: seconds

Day 1

1. Dwikonasana
   [Chest Expansion 1]
   2 times (mod)
   back (5 sec.), front (20 sec.)
2. Paschimottanasana
   [Backstretch]
   Knee position
   2 times, 20 sec.
3. Bhujangasana
   [Cobra Pose]
   (with palms)
   2 times, 20 sec.

Day 2

1. Trikonasana
   [Triangle Simple]
   (knee position 2 times) 10 sec.
2. Dwikonasana
   [Chest Expansion 1]
   2 times
   back (5 sec.), front (20 sec.)
3. Baddha Konasana
   [Knee and Thigh Stretch]
   2 times, 20 sec.
4. Ardha Matsyendrasana
   [Half Twist]
   2 times, 10 sec.
5. Paschimottanasana
   [Backstretch]
   2 times, 20 sec.
6. Bhujangasana
   [Cobra Pose]
   (with palms)
   2 times, 20 sec.
7. Repeat all the above Asanas once without holding.

Day 3

1. Urdhva Eka Hastottanasana
   [Side Bend Single Arm]
   (mod)
   2 times, 20 sec.
2. Trikonasana
   [Triangle Simple]
   2 times, 20 sec.
3. Baddha Konasana
   [Knee and Thigh Stretch]
   2 times, 20 sec.
4. Ardha Matsyendrasana
   [Half Twist]
   2 times, 20 sec.
5. Paschimottanasana
   [Backstretch]
   (knee and calf)
   2 times, 20 sec.

6. Bhujangasana
   [Cobra Pose]
   (with palms)
   2 times, 20 sec.
7. Ekapada Jatara Parivartanasana
   [Legover Single Leg]
   2 times, 10 sec.
8. Repeat the Asanas again without holding.

Day 4 (Meditative Poses)

1. Padma Ujjayi Pranayama
   [Abdominal Breathing in Lotus]
2. Hasta Uttita Pranayama
   [Complete Breath Standing]
3. Nadi Shodana Pranayama
   [Alternate Nostril Breathing]
4. Shavasana [Corpse Pose]
   [Relaxation]

Day 5

1. Hasta Uttita Pranayama
   [Complete Breath Standing]
2. Trikonasana
   [Triangle Simple]
   (knee, calf and ankle) once, 10 sec.
3. Baddha Konasana
   [Knee and Thigh Stretch]
   2 times, 20 sec.
4. Simhasana [Lion Pose]
   2 times, 10 sec.
5. Supta Vajrasana
   [Backward Bend]
   (first position)
   2 times, 20 sec. each
6. Paschimottanasana
   [Backstretch]
   (knee, calf and ankle) 20 sec.
7. Bhujangasana
   [Cobra Pose]
   (with palms)
   2 times, 20 sec.
8. Nadi Shodana Pranayama
   [Alternate Nostril Breathing]

Day 6

1. Hasta Uttita Pranayama
   [Complete Breath Standing]
2. Dwikonasana
   [Chest Expansion 1]
   once (mod and int)
   back (10 sec.), front (20 sec.)
3. Urdhva Eka Hastottanasana
   [Side Bend Single Arm]
   (mod and int) once, 20 sec.
4. Ardha Matsyendrasana
   [Half Twist]
   2 times, 20 sec.

The ideas, suggestions, herbal remedies and diet contained in this book are not intended as a substitue for consulting with your doctor. All matters regarding your health require medical supervision.

5. Paschimottanasana   (knee, calf and ankle)
   [Backstretch]   3 times, 20 sec.
6. Bhujangasana   (with palms)
   [Cobra Pose]   2 times, 20 sec.
7. Ekapada Jatara
   Parivartanasana
   [Legover Single Leg]   2 times, 20 sec.
8. Nadi Shodana Pranayama
   [Alternate Nostril Breathing]

Day 7

1. Ujjayi Pranayama
   [Abdominal Breathing]
2. Supta Vajrasana   (first position)
   [Backward Bend]   2 times, 20 sec.
3. Bumi Pada Mastakasana
   [Headstand Modified]   30 sec.
4. Advasana
   [Reversed Corpse Pose]
5. Bhujangasana   (with palms)
   [Cobra Pose]   3 times, 20 sec.
6. Ekapada Jatara
   Parivartanasana
   [Legover Single Leg]   2 times, 20 sec.
7. Nadi Shodana Pranayama
   [Alternate Nostril Breathing]

Day 8

1. Ujjayi Pranayama
   [Abdominal Breathing]
2. Urdhva Eka
   Hastottanasana   2 times, 10 sec.
   [Side Bend Single Arm]   (mod, int and ext)
3. Uttita Lolasana
   [Dangling Pose]   2 times
4. Marjariasana [Cat Pose]   2 times, 10 sec.
5. Uddiyana Bandha
   [Abdominal Lift]   3 times, 10 sec.
6. Yoga Mudra

Day 9

1. Hasta Uttita Pranayama
   [Complete Breath Standing]
2. Urdhva Hastottanasana   once each, 10 sec.
   [Side Bend]   (mod, int and ext)

3. Supta Vajrasana
   [Backward Bend]   20 sec.
4. Ardha Matsyendrasana
   [Half Twist]   2 times, 20 sec.
5. Paschimottanasana   (knee, calf and ankle)
   [Backstretch]   once each, 20 sec.
6. Bhujangasana
   [Cobra Pose]   2 times with palms, 20
                             sec. and once without
                             palms, 20 sec.
7. Shalabasana   (single leg only)
   [Locust Pose]   2 times, 10 sec.
8. Advasana
   [Reversed Corpse Pose]
9. Nadi Shodana Pranayama
   [Alternate Nostril Breathing]

Day 10

1. Hasta Uttita Pranayama
   [Complete Breath Standing]
2. Dwikonasana   2 times (mod
   [Chest Expansion]   and int)
                             back (10 sec.), front (20
                             sec.)
3. Urdhva Eka
   Hastottanasana
   [Side Bend Single Arm]   2 times, 10 sec.
4. Urdhva Hastottanasana
   [Side Bend Both Arms]   3 times, 10 sec.
5. Baddha Konasana
   [Knee and Thigh Stretch] 2 times
6. Simhasana [Lion Pose]   2 times, 10 sec.
7. Ardha Matsyendrasana
   [Half Twist]   2 times, 20 sec.
8. Paschimottanasana   (3 positions)
   [Backstretch]   20 sec. each
9. Bhujangasana
   [Cobra Pose]   (2 times with palms, 20
                             sec. and once without
                             palms, 20 sec.
10. Shalabasana
    [Locust Pose]   (one leg and both legs)
                             2 times, 10 sec.
11. Ekapada Jatara
    Parivartanasana
    [Legover Single Leg]   2 times, 10 sec.

12. Uddiyana Bandha
    [Abdominal Lift]   3 times, 10 sec.
13. Yoga Mudra

Day 11
1. Bumi Pada Mastakasana
   [Headstand Modified]   1 min.
2. Shashankasana
   [Baby Pose]   1 min.
3. Vipareeta Karani Mudra
   [Shoulderstand
   Preliminary Pose]   30 sec.
4. Poorva Uttana Padasana
   [Simple Fish]   10 sec.
5. Poorva Halasana
   [Plough Preliminary Pose]   30 sec.
6. Supta Vajrasana
   [Backward Bend]   10 sec.
7. Gomukhasana
   [Posture Clasp]   2 times, 10 sec.
8. Paschimottanasana
   [Backstretch]   3 times, 20 sec.
9. Bhujangasana
   [Cobra Pose]   3 times, 20 sec.
10. Nadi Shodana Pranayama
    [Alternate Nostril Breathing]

Day 12
1. Bumi Pada Mastakasana
   [Headstand Modified]   1 min.
2. Shashankasana
   [Baby Pose]   1 min.
3. Vipareeta Karani Mudra
   [Shoulderstand
   Preliminary Pose]   1 min.
4. Supta Vajrasana
   [Backward Bend]   20 sec.
5. Poorva Halasana
   [Plough Preliminary Pose]   30 sec.
6. Poorva Uttana Padasana
   [Simple Fish]   10 sec.
7. Uttita Meru Dandasana   (single leg)
   [Side Raise Pose 1]   2 times, 10 sec.
8. Advasana
   [Reversed Corpse Pose]
9. Marjariasana [Cat Pose]   3 times
10. Yoga Mudra

Day 13
1. Bumi Pada Mastakasana
   [Headstand Modified]   1 min.
2. Shashankasana
   [Baby Pose]   1 min.
3. Sarvangasana
   [Shoulderstand]   1 min.
4. Poorva Uttana Padasana
   [Simple Fish]   20 sec.
5. Halasana [Plough 1]   30 sec.
6. Supta Vajrasana
   [Backward Bend]   10 sec.
7. Druta Hastasana
   [Chopping the Wood]   5 times
8. Gomukhasana
   [Posture Clasp]   3 times, 10 sec.
9. Paschimottanasana
   [Backstretch]   3 times, 20 sec
10. Bhujangasana
    [Cobra Pose]   3 times, 20 sec
11. Advasana
    [Reversed Corpse Pose]
12. Yoga Mudra

Day 14
1. Trikonasana
   [Triangle Simple]   3 times, 10 sec.
2. Uttita Chakrasana
   [Circular Motion]   3 times, 10 sec.
3. Baddha Konasana
   [Knee and Thigh Stretch]   3 times, 10 sec.
4. Simhasana [Lion Pose]   2 times, 20 sec.
5. Ardha Matsyendrasana
   [Half Twist]   2 times, 10 sec.
6. Paschimottanasana
   [Backstretch]   3 times, 20 sec.
7. Bhujangasana
   [Cobra Pose]   3 times, 20 sec.
8. Shalabasana   (one leg and both legs)
   [Locust Pose]   2 times, 10 sec.
9. Dhanurasana [Bow Pose]   2 times, 10 sec.
10. Nadi Shodana Pranayama
    [Alternate Nostril Breathing]

Day 15

1 Jangha Shakti Vikasaka
   [Dancers 1]   2 times
   Urvasana [Dancers 2]   2 times
   Padanguli Shakti Vikasaka
   [Dancers 3]   2 times
2. Uttita Chakrasana
   [Circular Motion]   3 times, 10 sec.
3. Ardha Matsyendrasana
   [Half Twist]   2 times, 20 sec.
4. Paschimottanasana
   [Backstretch]   3 times, 20 sec.
5. Sarvangasana
   [Shoulderstand]   2 min.
6. Poorva Uttana Padasana
   [Simple Fish]   45 sec.
7. Halasana [Plough 1]   30 sec.
8. Supta Vajrasana
   [Backward Bend]   30 sec.
9. Bhujangasana
   [Cobra Pose]   3 times, 20 sec
10. Uttita Meru Dandasana
   [Side Raise Pose 1]   2 times, 10 sec.
   Anantasana
   [Side Raise Pose 2]   2 times, 10 sec
11. Ekapada Jatara
   Parivartanasana
   [Legover Single Leg]   3 times, 10 sec.
12. Nadi Shodana Pranayama
   [Alternate Nostril Breathing]

Day 16

1. Bumi Pada Mastakasana
   [Headstand Modified]   1 min.
2. Advasana
   [Reversed Corpse Pose]   1 min.
3. Jangha Shakti Vikasaka
   [Dancers 1]   once
   Urvasana [Dancers 2]   once
   Padanguli Shakti Vikasaka
   [Dancers 3]   once
4. Druta Grivasana
   [Neck Movement]   2 times
5. Matsyendrasana
   [Full Twist]   2 times, 20 sec.
6. Shashankasana
   [Baby pose]   1 min.

7. Bhujangasana
   [Cobra Pose]   3 times, 20 sec.
8. Shalabasana
   [Locust Pose]
   (one leg and both legs)   2 times, 10 sec.
9. Dhanurasana [Bow Pose]   2 times, 10 sec.
10. Nadi Shodana Pranayama
   [Alternate Nostril Breathing]

Day 17

1. Bumi Pada Mastakasana
   [Headstand Modified]   1 min.
2. Shashankasana
   [Baby Pose]   1 min.
3. Druta Hastasana
   [Chopping the Wood]   5 times
4. Nauka Sanchalana
   [Rowing the Boat Pose]   5 times
5. Druta Grivasana
   [Neck Movement]   2 times
6. Paschimottanasana
   [Backstretch]   3 times, 20 sec.
7. Bhujangasana
   [Cobra Pose]   3 times, 20 sec.
8. Tiryaka Bhujangasana
   [Cobra Twist Pose]   once, 20 sec.
9. Uddiyana Bandha
   [Abdominal lift]   3 times, 10 sec.
10. Yoga Mudra

Day 18

1. Bumi Pada Mastakasana
   [Headstand Modified]   1 min.
2. Advasana
   [Reversed Corpse Pose]
3. Dwikonasana   (3 positions)
   [Chest Expansion 1]   back (10 sec.), front
                                 (20 sec.)
4. Ardha Chakrasana
   [Chest Expansion 2]   once, 20 sec.
5. Padahastasana
   [Legclasp]   2 times, 20 sec.
6. Uttita Lolasana
   [Dangling Pose]   once
7. Chakki Chalana
   [Churning the Mill Pose]   5 times

The ideas, suggestions, herbal remedies and diet contained in this book are not intended as a substitue for consulting with your doctor. All matters regarding your health require medical supervision.

8. Nauka Sanchalana
   [Rowing the Boat Pose]   5 times
9. Bhujangasana
   [Cobra Pose]   2 times, 20 sec.
   Tiryaka Bhujangasana
   [Cobra Twist Pose]   once, 20 sec.
10. Uddiyana Bandha
    [Abdominal Lift]   3 times
11. Yoga Mudra

Day 19

1. Bumi Pada Mastakasana
   [Headstand Modified]   1 min.
2. Shashankasana
   [Baby Pose]   1 min.
3. Trikonasana
   [Triangle Simple]   3 times, 10 sec.
4. Matsyendrasana
   [Full Twist]   2 times, 20 sec.
5. Paschimottanasana
   [Backstretch]   3 times, 20 sec.
6. Uttita Meru Dandasana
   [Side Raise Pose 1]   2 times
   (mod and ext), 10 sec.
   Anantasana
   [Side Raise Pose 2]   2 times, 10 sec.
7. Bhujangasana
   [Cobra Pose]   3 times, 20 sec.
   Tiryaka Bhujangasana
   [Cobra Twist Pose]   once, 20 sec.
8. Shalabasana
   [Locust Pose]   2 times, 10 sec.
9. Dhanurasana [Bow Pose]   2 times, 10 sec.
10. Nadi Shodana Pranayama
    [Alternate Nostril Breathing]

Day 20

1. Sarvangasana
   [Shoulderstand]   3 min.
2. Poorva Uttana Padasana
   [Simple Fish]   1 min.
3. Halasana [Plough 1]   30 sec.
   Kandarsanasana
   [Plough 2]   30 sec.
   Karna Peedasana
   [Plough 3]   30 sec.

4. Supta Vajrasana
   [Backward Bend]   30 sec.
5. Gomukhasana
   [Posture Clasp]   3 times, 10 sec.
6. Druta Grivasana
   [Neck Movement]   3 times
7. Baddha Konasana
   [Knee and Thigh Stretch]   3 times
8. Matsyendrasana
   [Full Twist]   3 times, 20 sec.
9. Paschimottanasana
   [Backstretch]   3 times, 30 sec.
10. Uttita Meru Dandasana
    [Side Raise Pose 1]   2 times, 10 sec.
    Anantasana
    [Side Raise Pose 2]   2 times, 10 sec.
11. Bhujangasana
    [Cobra Pose]   3 times, 20 sec.
12. Uddiyana Bandha
    [Abdominal Lift]   3 times
13. Yoga Mudra

Day 21

1. Bumi Pada Mastakasana
   [Headstand Modified]   1 min.
2. Jangha Shakti Vikasaka
   [Dancers 1]   once
   Urvasana [Dancers 2]   once
   Padanguli Shakti Vikasaka
   [Dancers 3]   once
3. Trikonasana   (knee, calf and ankle)
   [Triangle Simple]   once each, 10 sec.
4. Padahastasana [Legclasp]   2 times, 10 sec.
5. Druta Hastasana
   [Chopping the Wood]   5 times
6. Baddha Konasana
   [Knee and Thigh Stretch]   2 times
7. Shashankasana
   (Baby Pose)   1 min.
8. Bhujangasana
   [Cobra Pose]   3 times, 20 sec.
9. Shalabasana
   [Locust Pose]   2 times, 10 sec.
10. Dhanurasana [Bow Pose]   2 times, 10, sec.
11. Nadi Shodana Pranayama
    [Alternate Nostril Breathing]

The ideas, suggestions, herbal remedies and diet contained in this book are not intended as a substitue for consulting with your doctor. All matters regarding your health require medical supervision.

Day 22

1. Bumi Pada Mastakasana
   [Headstand Modified]   1 min.
2. Urdhva Eka
   Hastottanasana
   [Side Bend Single Arm]   2 times, 20 sec.
3. Uttita Chakrasana
   [Circular Motion]   3 times, 5 sec.
4. Chakki Chalana
   [Churning the Mill]   5 times
5. Ardha Matsyendrasana
   [Half Twist]   2 times, 20 sec.
6. Uttita Lolasana
   [Dangling Pose]   2 times
7. Uttita Meru Dandasana
   [Side Raise Pose 1]   2 times, 10 sec.
   Anantasana
   [Side Raise Pose 2]   2 times, 10 sec.
8. Bhujangasana
   [Cobra Pose]   3 times, 20 sec.
9. Uddiyana Bandha
   [Abdominal lift]   3 times
10. Nadi Shodana Pranayama
    [Alternate Nostril Breathing]

Day 23

1. Dwikonasana
   [Chest Expansion 1]   Back (10 sec.) and front
                               (20 sec.)

   Ardha Chakrasana
   [Chest Expansion 2]   20 sec.
2. Urdhva Eka
   Hastottanasana
   [Side Bend Single Arm]   2 times, 10 sec.
   Urdhva Hastottanasana
   [Side Bend]   2 times, 10 sec.
3. Nauka Sanchalana
   [Rowing the Boat Pose]   5 times
4. Simhasana [Lion Pose]   2 times, 10 sec.
5. Druta Grivasana
   [Neck Movement]   2 times
6. Paschimottanasana
   [Backstretch]   3 times, 30 sec.
7. Sarvangasana
   [Shoulderstand]   3 min.
8. Halasana [Plough 1]   30 sec.
   Kandarsanasana

[Plough 2]   30 sec.
Karna Peedasana
[Plough 3]   30 sec.
9. Poorva Uttana Padasana
   [Simple Fish]   1 min.
10. Yoga Mudra
11. Nadi Shodana Pranayama
    [Alternate Nostril Breathing]

Day 24

1. Bumi Pada Mastakasana
   [Headstand Modified]   1 min.
2. Jangha Shakti Vikasaka
   [Dancers 1]   2 times
   Urvasana [Dancers 2]   2 times
   Padanguli Shakti Vikasaka
   [Dancers 3]   2 times
3. Matsyendrasana
   [Full Twist]   2 times, 20 sec.
4. Advasana
   [Reversed Corpse Pose]
5. Gomukhasana
   [Posture Clasp]   3 times, 5 sec.
6. Supta Vajrasana
   [Backward Bend]   2 times, 20 sec.
7. Ekapada Jatara
   Parivartanasana
   [Legover Single Leg]   2 times, 10 sec.
8. Uddiyana Bandha
   [Abdominal Lift]   3 times
9. Marjariasana [Cat Pose]   2 times
10. Yoga Mudra
11. Nadi Shodana Pranayama
    [Alternate Nostril Breathing]

THREE ROUTINES FOR BEGINNERS

ROUTINE 1

1. Jangha Shakti Vikasaka [Dancers 1]
2. Urvasana [Dancers 2]
3. Padanguli Shakti Vikasaka [Dancers 3]
4. Uttita Lolasana [Dangling Pose]
5. Trikonasana [Triangle Simple]
6. Druta Grivasana [Neck Movement]
7. Baddha Konasana [Knee and Thigh Stretch]
8. Paschimottanasana [Backstretch]
9. Nauka Sanchalana [Rowing the Boat Pose]
10. Bhujangasana [Cobra Pose]
11. Shalabasana [Locust Pose]
12. Dhanurasana [Bow Pose]
13. Ekapada Jatara Parivartanasana
    [Legover Single Leg]
14. Nadi Shodana Pranayama [Alternate Nostril Breathing]

ROUTINE 2

1. Hasta Uttita Pranayama
   [Complete Breath Standing]
2. Uttita Chakrasana [Circular Motion]
3. Urdhva Eka Hastottanasana
   [Side Bend Single Arm]
4. Urdhva Hastottanasana [Side Bend]
5. Padahastasana [Legclasp]
6. Chakki Chalana [Churning the Mill]
7. Shashankasana [Baby Pose]
8. Matsyendrasana [Full Twist]
9. Paschimottanasana [Backstretch]
10. Uttita Meru Dandasana [Side Raise Pose 1]
11. Anantasana [Side Raise Pose 2]
12. Padma Ujjayi Pranayama [Abdominal Breathing in Lotus]
13. Bumi Pada Mastakasana [Headstand Modified]
14. Shavasana [Corpse Pose]

ROUTINE 3

1. Dwikonasana [Chest Expansion 1]
2. Ardha Chakrasana [Chest Expansion 2]
3. Ardha Matsyendrasana [Half Twist]
4. Paschimottanasana [Backstretch]
5. Simhasana [Lion Pose]
6. Gomukhasana [Posture Clasp]
7. Sarvangasana [Shoulderstand]

8. Poorva Uttana Padasana [Simple Fish]
9. Halasana [Plough 1]
10. Supta Vajrasana [Backward Bend]
11. Ekapada Jatara Parivartanasana
    [Legover Single Leg]
12. Marjariasana [Cat Pose]
13. Uddiyana Bandha [Abdominal Lift]
14. Yoga Mudra
15. Advasana [Reversed Corpse Pose]

BASIC ROUTINES

Perform any one of the following routines once a day:

BASIC ROUTINE 1

1. Suryanamaskar [Salutation to the Sun]
2. Sarvangasana [Shoulderstand]
3. Poorva Uttana Padasana [Simple Fish]
4. Halasana [Plough 1]
   Kandarsanasana [Plough 2]
   Karna Peedasana [Plough 3]
5. Matsyasana [Fish in Lotus]
6. Shavasana [Corpse Pose]
7. Paschimottanasana [Backstretch]
8. Bhujangasana [Cobra Pose]
9. Uddiyana Bandha [Abdominal Lift]
10. Yoga Mudra
11. Nadi Shodana Pranayama

BASIC ROUTINE 2

1. Suryanamaskar [Salutation to the Sun]
2. Sarvangasana [Shoulderstand]
3. Paryanaka [Fish in Vajrasana]
4. Halasana [Plough 1]
   Kandarsanasana [Plough 2]
   Karnapeedasana [Plough 3]
5. Chakrasana [Back Pushup]
6. Bhujangasana [Cobra Pose]
7. Uddiyana Bandha [Abdominal Lift]
8. Yoga Mudra

BASIC ROUTINE 3

1. Suryanamaskar [Salutation to the Sun]
2. Sarvangasana [Shoulderstand]
3. Ekapada Sarvangasana
   [Shoulderstand Single Leg]

4. Poorva Uttana Padasana [Simple Fish]
5. Halasana [Plough 1]
6. Ekapada Halasana [Plough Single Leg]
7. Kandarsanasana [Plough 2]
8. Karna Peedasana [Plough 3]
9. Paryanaka [Fish in Vajrasana]
10. Paschimottanasana [Backstretch]
11. Bhujangasana [Cobra Pose]
12. Uddiyana Bandha [Abdominal Lift]
13. Yoga Mudra

BASIC ROUTINE 4

1. Bumi Pada Mastakasana [Headstand Modified]
2. Sarvangasana [Shoulderstand]
3. Ekapada Sarvangasana [Shoulderstand Single Leg]
4. Matsyasana [Fish in Lotus]
5. Paschimottanasana [Backstretch]
6. Halasana [Plough 1]
7. Paryanaka [Fish in Vajrasana]
8. Advasana [Reversed Corpse Pose]
9. Bhujangasana [Cobra Pose]
10. Shalabasana [Locust Pose]
11. Dhanurasana [Bow Pose]
12. Shavasana [Corpse Pose]
13. Ardha Matsyendrasana [Half Twist]
14. Padahastasana [Legclasp]
15. Trikonasana [Triangle Simple]

BASIC ROUTINE 5

1. Hasta Uttita Pranayama [Complete Breath Standing]
2. Suryanamaskar [Salutation to the Sun]
3. Trikonasana [Triangle Simple]
4. Udarakarshana Asana [Abdominal Massage Twist]
5. Sarvangasana [Shoulderstand]
6. Matsyendrasana [Full Twist]
7. Paschimottanasana [Backstretch]
8. Halasana [Plough 1]
9. Chakrasana [Back Pushup]
10. Bhujangasana [Cobra Pose]
11. Shanmukhi Mudra [Psychic Source Seal]
12. Nadi Shodana Pranayama

ROUTINES FOR INTERMEDIATE LEARNERS

In these routines, the number of times each Asana is repeated or the duration for holding each position is not given as this depends on the individual.

Follow the order given in each routine. Find the position that you are most comfortable with and stay in that position for a while.

While in the holding position, make sure you are comfortable and are enjoying yourself. Before taking the final position, stay in the moderate and intermediate stages for a few seconds.

The following nine routines cover most of the Asanas mentioned in the text:

ROUTINE 1

1. Sarvangasana [Shoulderstand]
2. Halasana [Plough 1]
3. Paschimottanasana [Backstretch]
4. Chakrasana [Back Pushup]
5. Shavasana [Corpse Pose]
6. Parshvottanasana [Back Namaste Pose]
7. Uttita Lolasana [Dangling Pose]
8. Upavishta Matsyendrasana [Seated Angle Twist]
9. Shashankasana [Baby Pose]
10. Druta Hastasana [Chopping the Wood]
11. Ananda Madirasana [Intoxicating Bliss Pose]
12. Bhujangasana [Cobra Pose]
13. Shalabasana [Locust Pose]
14. Dhanurasana [Bow Pose]
15. Yoga Mudra
16. Nadi Shodana Pranayama
17. Meditation

ROUTINE 2

1. Urdhva Eka Hastottanasana [Side Bend Single Arm]
2. Urdhva Hastottanasana [Side Bend]
3. Pada Angushtasana [Legclasp Gorilla Pose]
4. Grivasana [Neck Roll]
5. Chakki Chalana [Churning the Mill]
6. Ardha Matsyendrasana [Half Twist]
7. Yoga Anandasana [Animal Relaxation Pose]

8. Naukasana [Saucer Pose]
9. Paripoorna Shalabasana [Swan Pose]
10. Matsya Kridasana [Flapping Fish Pose]
11. Yoga Mudra
12. Nadi Shodana Pranayama
13. Meditation

ROUTINE 3

1. Paripoorna Trikonasana [Triangle Complete]
2. Gomukhasana [Posture Clasp]
3. Simha Grivasana [Neck Lion Pose]
4. Bhu Namanasana [Spinal Twist]
5. Paschimottanasana [Backstretch]
6. Jyestika Makarasana [Head Twist]
7. Bhujangasana [Cobra Pose]
8. Shalabasana [Locust Pose]
9. Dhanurasana [Bow Pose]
10. Yoga Mudra
11. Nadi Shodana Pranayama
12. Meditation

ROUTINE 4

1. Jangha Shakti Vikasaka [Dancers 1]
2. Urvasana [Dancers 2]
3. Padanguli Shakti Vikasaka [Dancers 3]
4. Uttita Chakrasana [Circular Motion]
5. Baddha Konasana [Knee and Thigh Stretch]
6. Nauka Sanchalana [Rowing the Boat Pose]
7. Druta Grivasana [Neck Movement]
8. Paschimottanasana [Backstretch]
9. Bhujangasana [Cobra Pose]
10. Ardha Navasana [Boat Pose]
11. Paripoorna Shalabhasana [Swan Pose]
12. Yoga Mudra
13. Nadi Shodana Pranayama
14. Meditation

ROUTINE 5

1. Dwikonasana [Chest Expansion 1]
2. Ardha Chakrasana [Chest Expansion 2]
3. Simhasana [Lion Pose]
4. Gupta Padmasana [Hidden Lotus Pose]
5. Matsyendrasana [Full Twist]
6. Janu Sirasasana [Alternate Leg Pull]
7. Supta Mushumna Shakthi Vikasaka
   [Pelvic Tilt Lying Down]

8. Bhujangasana [Cobra Pose]
9. Ekapada Jatara Parivartanasana
   [Legover Single Leg]
10. Vayu Nishankasana [Gas Releasing Pose]
11. Jatara Parivartanasana [Legover Both Legs]
12. Yoga Mudra
13. Nadi Shodana Pranayama
14. Meditation

ROUTINE 6

1. Sarvangasana [Shoulderstand]
2. Ekapada Sarvangasana
   [Shoulderstand Single Leg]
3. Halasana [Plough 1]
4. Poorva Uttana Padasana [Simple Fish]
5. Uttita Trikonasana [Triangle Stretched 1]
6. Uttanasana [Legclasp Migraine Pose]
7. Padma Parvatasana [Traction]
8. Ardha Matsyendrasana [Half Twist]
9. Paschimottanasana [Backstretch]
10. Bhujangasana [Cobra Pose]
11. Shalabasana [Locust Pose]
12. Bekasana [Frog Pose]
13. Yoga Mudra
14. Nadi Shodana Pranayama
15. Meditation

ROUTINE 7

1. Sarvangasana [Shoulderstand]
2. Ekapada Halasana [Plough Single Leg]
3. Halasana [Plough 1]
4. Poorva Uttana Padasana [Simple Fish]
5. Uttita Parivrata Trikonasana
   [Triangle Stretched 2]
6. Hasta Grivasana [Hand and Neck Pose]
7. Ardha Baddha Padma Paschimottanasana
   [Backstretch in Half Lotus]
8. Dhyana Veerasana [Relaxation Hero Pose]
9. Supta Badrasana
   [Knee and Thigh Stretch Lying down]
10. Bhujangasana [Cobra Pose]
11. Tiryaka Bhujangasana [Cobra Twist Pose]
12. Marjariasana [Cat Pose]
13. Uddiyana Bandha [Abdominal Lift]
14. Yoga Mudra
15. Nadi Shodana Pranayama
16. Meditation

ROUTINE 8

1. Tarasana [Star Pose]
2. Uttita Pawana Muktasana
   [Standing Knee to Chest]
3. Meru Prishtasana [Spine and Back Pose]
4. Upavishta Matsyendrasana [Seated Angle Twist]
5. Yoga Anandasana [Animal Rlaxation Pose]
6. Uttita Meru Dandasana [Side Raise Pose 1]
7. Anantasana [Side Raise Pose 2]
8. Sarpasana [Snake Pose]
9. Ekapada Uttanasana
   [Single Leg Stretch Breathing]
10. Yoga Mudra
11. Nadi Shodana Pranayama
12. Meditation

ROUTINE 9

1. Tadasana [Stretch Pose]
2. Tiryaka Tadasana [Swaying Palm Tree Pose]
3. Katichakrasana [Cork Screw Pose]
4. Uttita Lolasana [Dangling Pose]
5. Ushtrasana [Camel Pose]
6. Paripoorna Navasana [Diamond Pose 1]
7. Ubaya Padangushta [Diamond Pose 2]
8. Janu Sirasasana [Alternate Leg Pull]
9. Sarvangasana [Shoulderstand]
10. Paschimottanasana [Backstretch]
11. Poorva Uttana Padasana [Simple Fish]
12. Halasana [Plough 1]
13. Chakrasana [Back Pushup]
14. Bhujangasana [Cobra Pose]
15. Yoga Mudra
16. Nadi Shodana Pranayama
17. Meditation

ROUTINES FOR ADVANCED LEARNERS

These routines are for those who have already completed the basic and intermediate routines. At the end of each routine, perform Shavasana (see chapter 3), Yoga Mudra and Nadi Shodana Pranayama (see chapter 6). Follow up with any type of meditation.

ROUTINE 1

1. Jangha Shakti Vikasaka [Dancers 1]
2. Urvasana [Dancers 2]
3. Padanguli Shakti Vikasaka [Dancers 3]
4. Vrukshasana [Tree Pose]
5. Parshvottanasana [Back Namaste Pose]
6. Parighasana [Triangle Kneeling]
7. Upavishta Matsyendrasana [Seated Angle Twist]
8. Yoga Anandasana [Animal Rlaxation Pose]
9. Setu Bandasana [Bridge Pose]
10. Sarvangasana [Shoulderstand]
11. Matsyasana [Fish in Lotus]
12. Paschimottanasana [Backstretch]
13. Halasana [Plough 1]
14. Chakrasana [Back Pushup]
15. Sarvanga Pusti Vikasaka
    [Strengthening the Whole Body]
16. Sampoorna Shakti Vikasaka
    [Slow Motion Firming]
17. Matsya Kridasana [Flapping Fish Pose]
- Shavasana
- Yoga Mudra
- Nadi Shodana Pranayama
- Meditation

ROUTINE 2

1. Utkatasana [Imaginary Chair]
2. Paripoorna Trikonasana [Triangle Complete]
3. Gomukhasana [Posture Clasp]
4. Simhasana [Lion Pose]
5. Baradwajasana [Twist in Veera]
6. Upavishta Konasana [Backstretch Seated Angle]
7. Purvottanasana [Hip Raise Pose]
8. Bhujangasana [Cobra Pose]
9. Shalabasana [Locust Pose]
10. Dhanurasana [Bow Pose]
11. Makarasana [Crocodile Pose]
12. Sarvangasana [Shoulderstand]
13. Paryanaka [Fish in Vajrasana]
14. Paschimottanasana [Backstretch]
15. Halasana [Plough 1]
16. Chakrasana [Back Pushup]
- Shavasana
- Yoga Mudra
- Nadi Shodana Pranayama
- Meditation

ROUTINE 3

1. Katichakrasana [Cork Screw Pose]
2. Veera Bhadrasana [Hero Posture]
3. Uttanasana [Legclasp Migraine Pose]
4. Dhyana Veerasana [Relaxation Hero Pose]
5. Baddha Konasana [Knee and Thigh Stretch]
6. Marichyasana [Elbow to Knee]
7. Janu Sirasasana [Alternate Leg Pull]
8. Sarvangasana [Shoulderstand]
9. Paryanaka [Fish in Vajrasana]
10. Paschimottanasana [Backstretch]
11. Halasana [Plough 1]
12. Chakrasana [Back Pushup]
13. Jyestika Makarasana [Head Twist]
14. Ardha Navasana [Boat Pose]
15. Paripoorna Shalabhasana [Swan Pose]
16. Shambava Mudra [Vision of Concentration Seal]
17. Sheetali Pranayama [Cooling Breath]

- Shavasana
- Yoga Mudra
- Nadi Shodana Pranayama
- Meditation

ROUTINE 4

1. Urdhva Hastottanasana [Side Bend Both Arms]
2. Dwikonasana [Chest Expansion 1]
3. Ananda Madirasana [Intoxicating Bliss Pose]
4. Matsyendrasana [Full Twist]
5. Yoga Anandasana [Animal Rlaxation Pose]
6. Paripoorna Navasana [Diamond Pose 1]
7. Ushtrasana [Camel Pose]
8. Sarvangasana [Shoulderstand]
9. Supta Vajrasana [Backward Bend]
10. Paschimottanasana [Backstretch]
11. Halasana [Plough 1]
12. Chakrasana [Back Pushup]
13. Shashanka Bhujangasana [Striking Cobra Pose]
14. Jatara Parivartanasana [Legover Both Legs]
15. Paripoorna Shalabhasana [Swan Pose]
16. Uddiyana Bandha [Abdominal Lift]

- Shavasana
- Yoga Mudra
- Nadi Shodana Pranayama
- Meditation

ROUTINE 5

1. Santulana Asana [Balance Posture]
2. Uttita Parshva Trikonasana [Triangle Stretched Knee 1]
3. Padahastasana [Legclasp]
4. Padma Parvatasana [Traction]
5. Udarakarshana Asana [Abdominal Massage Twist]
6. Upavishta Konasana [Backstretch Seated Angle]
7. Marjariasana [Cat Pose]
8. Sarvangasana [Shoulderstand]
9. Halasana [Plough 1]
10. Paschimottanasana [Backstretch]
11. Chakrasana [Back Pushup]
12. Sarpasana [Snake Pose]
13. Bekasana [Frog Pose]
14. Urdhva Prasarita Padasana [30°, 60° and 90°]
15. Padadirasana [Balancing of Breath]

- Shavasana
- Yoga Mudra
- Nadi Shodana Pranayama
- Meditation

ROUTINE 6

1. Uttita Chakrasana [Circular Motion]
2. Rishi [Rishi's Posture]
3. Vyghrasana [Tiger Pose]
4. Shashankasana [Baby Pose]
5. Grivasana [Neck Roll]
6. Ardha Matsyendrasana [Half Twist]
7. Janu Sirasasana [Alternate Leg Pull]
8. Sarvangasana [Shoulderstand]
9. Matsyasana [Fish in Lotus]
10. Paschimottanasana [Backstretch]
11. Halasana [Plough 1]
12. Chakrasana [Back Pushup]
13. Uttita Meru Dandasana [Side Raise Pose 1]
14. Uttana Padasana [Inverted Dog]
15. Paripoorna Shalabhasana [Swan Pose]
16. Shanti Mudra [Invocation of Peace Seal]

- Shavasana
- Yoga Mudra
- Nadi Shodana Pranayama
- Meditation

ROUTINE 7

1. Tadasana [Stretch Pose]
2. Tiryaka Tadasana [Swaying Palm Tree Pose]
3. Katichakrasana [Cork Screw Pose]
4. Bhujanga Tiryaka [Swinging Cobra Pose]
5. Udarakarshana Asana
   [Abdominal Massage Twist]
6. Mandukasana Rechaka Puraka
   [Dynamic Breathing]
7. Shavasana [Corpse Pose]
8. Tarasana [Star Pose]
9. Ananda Madirasana [Intoxicating Bliss Pose]
10. Sarvangasana [Shoulderstand]
11. Matsyasana [Fish in Lotus]
12. Paschimottanasana [Backstretch]
13. Halasana [Plough 1]
14. Chakrasana [Back Pushup]
15. Sarpasana [Snake Pose]
16. Naukasana [Saucer Pose]
17. Paripoorna Salabhasana [Swan Pose]
18. Matsya Kridasana [Flapping Fish Pose]
- Shavasana
- Yoga Mudra
- Nadi Shodana Pranayama
- Meditation

FURTHER ROUTINES FOR ADVANCED LEARNERS

These routines are for those who have completed the above routines and wish to spend more time on Yoga.

ROUTINE 1

1. Jangha Shakti Vikasaka [Dancers 1]
2. Urvasana [Dancers 2]
3. Padanguli Shakti Vikasaka [Dancers 3]
4. Santulana Asana [Balance Posture]
5. Paripoorna Trikonasana [Triangle Complete]
6. Padahastasana [Legclasp]
7. Dhyana Veerasana [Relaxation Hero Pose]
8. Udarakarshana Asana
   [Abdominal Massage Twist]
9. Yoga Anandasana [Animal Relaxation Pose]
10. Padma Parvatasana [Traction]
11. Sarvangasana [Shoulderstand]

12. Halasana [Plough 1]
13. Paschimottanasana [Backstretch]
14. Chakrasana [Back Pushup]
15. Jyestika Makarasana [Head Twist]
16. Shashanka Bhujangasana [Striking Cobra Pose]
17. Yoga Mudra
18. Nadi Shodana Pranayama
19. Surbhi Mudra
20 Meditation

ROUTINE 2

1. Tarasana [Star Pose]
2. Urdhva Hastottanasana [Side Bend]
3. Katichakrasana [Cork Screw Pose]
4. Dwikonasana [Chest Expansion 1]
5. Simhasana [Lion Pose]
6. Matsyendrasana [Full Twist]
7. Shashankasana [Baby Pose]
8. Paripoorna Navasana [Diamond Pose 1]
9. Ushtrasana [Camel Pose]
10. Sarvangasana [Shoulderstand]
11. Matsyasana [Fish in Lotus]
12. Halasana [Plough 1]
13. Chakrasana [Back Pushup]
14. Paschimottanasana [Backstretch]
15. Bhujangasana [Cobra Pose]
16. Shalabhasana [Locust Pose]
17. Dhanurasana [Bow Pose]
18. Shambava Mudra with Gnana Mudra
19. Yoga Mudra
20. Meditation

ROUTINE 3

1. Shirasasana [Headstand]
2. Tadasana [Stretch Pose]
3. Rishi [Rishi's Posture]
4. Vyghrasana [Tiger Pose]
5. Marichyasana [Elbow to Knee]
6. Ananda Madirasana [Intoxicating Bliss Pose]
7. Janu Sirasasana [Alternate Leg Pull]
8. Sarvangasana [Shoulderstand]
9. Halasana [Plough 1]
10. Paschimottanasana [Backstretch]
11. Paryanaka [Fish in Vajrasana]
12. Paripoorna Shalabhasana [Swan Pose]
13. Matsya Kridasana [Flapping Fish Pose]

The ideas, suggestions, herbal remedies and diet contained in this book are not intended as a substitue for consulting with your doctor. All matters regarding your health require medical supervision.

14. Surbhi Mudra with Jalandhara Bandha
    and Ujjayi Pranayama
15. Shavasana [Corpse Pose]
16. Meditation

ROUTINE 4

1. Utkatasana [Imaginary Chair]
2. Veerasana [Hero Sitting Posture]
3. Siras Angushta Yogasana [Chest Expansion 3]
4. Gomukhasana [Posture Clasp]
5. Baddha Konasana [Knee and Thigh Stretch]
6. Upavishta Matsyendrasana [Seated Angle Twist]
7. Upavishta Konasana [Backstretch Seated Angle]
8. Maha Mudra [Great Seal]
9. Shavasana [Corpse Pose]
10. Sarvangasana [Shoulderstand]
11. Uttana Padasana [Inverted Dog]
12. Paschimottanasana [Backstretch]
13. Halasana [Plough 1]
14. Chakrasana [Back Pushup]
15. Sarpasana [Snake Pose 1]
16. Bekasana [Frog Pose]
17. Prana Mudra with Surya Bhedhana Pranayama
18. Shavasana [Corpse Pose]
19. Nadi Shodana Pranayama
20. Meditation

ROUTINE 5

1. Bumi Pada Mastakasana [Headstand Modified]
2. Shashankasana [Baby Pose]
3. Yoga Mudra
4. Matsyasana [Fish in Lotus]
5. Sarvanga Pusti Vikasaka
   [Strengthening the Whole Body]
6. Pranamasana [Prayer Pose]
7. Hasta Uttanasana [Raised Arms Pose]
8. Padahastasana [Legclasp]
9. Brahmari Pranayama
   [Humming of Bee Breathing]
10. Padadirasana [Balancing of Breath]
11. Shanti Mudra [Invocation of Peace Seal]
12. Shaka Mudra and Shambava Mudra

9

Approach to Diet

❧

Most of us develop eating habits early in life, and it is difficult to adjust or modify this habit at a later stage. It is, thus, important to cultivate a good eating habit that you do not break with age. There are, however, many people among us with poor eating habits who suffer from nutritional deficiencies. Some people do not have a balanced diet due to ignorance, while others are simply food faddists who do not pay attention to what they eat. Nutritional deficiencies also result from any interference with the absorption, storage and utilisation of food in the body by some disease. Another reason is excess excretion of nutrients from the body. Likely causes include chronic diseases of the gastrointestinal tract, including the liver, kidneys or the endocrine glands.

In today's fast-paced world, most people opt for convenience and eat more refined, processed and preserved foods. The food eaten is rich in fat, salt, sugar and have little dietary fibre and basic complex carbohydrates. It is ironic that, despite being affordable, many people give complex carbohydrates the snub. Sales in junk food, soft drinks and vitamin supplements, including dietary fibre pills, are at an all-time high. On the other hand, the consumption of unprocessed whole grain foods and cereals has fallen steadily.

Diet now has come to be mainly associated with weight loss or gain. With the emphasis on the intake of calories, essential nutrients that are absorbed naturally by the body are ignored. Any diet that omits carbohydrates will lead to an initial weight loss — the result of a drop in the body's normal water content and loss of glycogen in the muscles. There is, however, very little loss in "real fat". Taking extra vitamin supplements without the basic carbohydrates is useless.

To make sensible food choices for optimum health, it is important to arm yourself with some general information about the link between nutrition and health. A nutritious and balanced diet is indispensable for vital functions of the body, including the wear and tear of the body; an energetic lifestyle; and for protection against common diseases. Cultivate healthy eating habits from young. In this regard, children must be encouraged to eat the right kind of food. Eat food with love, and make eating a pleasure. After all, we are what we eat.

Although there has been a growing awareness of natural remedies in recent years, it is still not very popular, and in some cases, looked upon with suspicion. In my experience, only those told by doctors that they have to learn to live with their disease seek help from alternative nutritional medicine and Yoga therapy. It is lamentable that alternative medicine is often seen as the last resort. However, its ability to heal naturally is slowly gaining momentum among many. Concerned with the side effects and long term effectiveness of some Western medicines, these people are drawn to the age-old, tried and tested systems of natural cures. There is a growing awareness that health is linked directly to the food that is eaten.

Natural remedies help maintain good health by encouraging the body to regain its equilibrium. The natural cure does not claim to heal by itself, but it is a cleansing process that the body adopts for a cure. Nature takes its course in the healing. It removes the cause of the disease and, thus, roots out the disease itself. The answer is to eat food the way nature meant for it to be eaten.

For many sicknesses, home remedies work as effectively as modern medicines or even better. Certain ailments, however, can be treated better with modern medicines — no system of medicine is complete. This is especially the case for serious infections like appendicitis, typhoid, tetanus and pneumonia.

Most health problems have many causes, one leading to another. To eliminate the problem, get to the root of the problem and not just its symptoms. Because herbal remedies are prepared naturally, their actions are gradual. This is unlike medical drugs, which are in a highly concentrated form and thereby work much faster. Whatever the case, despite its slowness, natural medicines work and are safe.

YOGA AND AYURVEDA

The great attraction of Yoga today is its therapeutic aspect. It shows great potential in the life of an individual — it cures ailments and maintains a sound mind and body. Traditionally, Yoga and Ayurveda went hand in hand. Therefore, in applying Yoga therapeutically, an understanding of Ayurveda is essential.

Ayurveda means the "science of life", or the "knowledge of life". When Rishis and people who lived in the wild explored human problems through observation, they noticed a connection between animals, plants and man. They observed that when an animal was ill, it found a certain type of plant to cure itself. The Ayurvedic system evolved when such ideas were applied to human beings.

Ayurveda focuses on the idea of becoming healthy, retaining the intention of being healthy and passing this information to others. It focuses on physical health, while Yoga focuses more on mental health.

Yoga and Ayurveda share some similarities: both evolved as holistic systems, drawing on the same philosophical roots. The basic principle of these systems is that human beings are reflections of the universe. All the properties that exist in an individual are also found in the universe. There are, thus, five elements corresponding to the five sense organs.

Ayurveda informs each individual of his or her unique pattern of energy and matter. Within this pattern, one or more of the five elements may predominate. It is, therefore, important to understand each person's tendencies so that general defects of the body can be regulated or corrected.

Even today, Ayurvedic medicine uses fresh herbs, fruit and vegetables to make precious juices, pastes, warm and cold decoctions, teas, pills and tablets. Contrary to popular belief, it is strictly not vegetarian in nature. Like other systems of medicine, it uses animal-based products at times.

Just as those in the West, who firmly believe in the "back to nature" concept to rid the body of its aches, pains and problems, the exponents of Ayurveda also believe in the wholesome goodness of fresh products. Whenever possible, freshly prepared medicines are used.

TRI-GUNAS
(THE THREE QUALITIES)

Ayurveda aims at a healthy lifestyle in harmony with nature. The science of Ayurveda believes that there exists in all things the power of manifestation, which is natural (Prakruthi) and the principle of division, which gives rise to the ego that is unnatural (Vikruthi).

Nature has three Gunas or "basic qualities" known as the "three qualities" or Tri-Gunas. They are Rajoguna, Tamoguna and Sattvaguna. Gunas express the temperament, specific differences in psychology and the behavioural patterns of an individual. They are necessary in the right combination in order that the individual has a healthy, harmonious and happy life.

Rajoguna represents the principles of energy, activity and emotional disturbance. Tamoguna represents the principles of inertia, dullness and resistance. Sattvaguna represents the sense of equanimity, perception and intelligence. From these Tri-Gunas arise the five elements, which consist of:

- Agni (fire)
- Prithvi (earth)
- Akash (ether)
- Vayu (air)
- Soma or jal (water)

The five elements represent both the visible and invisible five states of matter in nature: solid, liquid, gaseous, radiant and ethereal. The five elements are present in every living being, including plants.

PANCHA MAHA-BUTA AND PANCHANGAM
(THE FIVE ELEMENTS AND THE FIVE ORGANS)

Rajoguna gives rise to Agni (fire), Tamoguna gives rise to Prithvi (Earth) and Sattvaguna generates Akash (ether). The combination of Sattvaguna and Rajoguna, in the right proportion, brings about Vayu (air), and the right combination of Tamoguna with Rajoguna develops Soma or Jal (water).

There is a fixed relation between the five elements and the structure of the human body and plants as the following illustrates:

1. AGNI OR FIRE

- Represents parts that are penetrating, light, dry, rough, and where sight predominates.
- Body parts are bile, digestion, body heat, colour and sight.
- The flowers of plants and trees.

2. PRITHVI OR EARTH

- Represents parts that are firm, heavy, inactive, rough, hard, and where smell predominates.
- Body parts are nails, bones, gums, flesh, skin, teeth and muscles.
- The roots of plants and trees.

3. AKASH OR ETHER

- Represents parts that are soft, smooth, transparent, and where sound predominates.
- Body parts are cavities and pores.
- The fruit of plants and trees.

4. VAYU OR AIR

- Represents energy, where touch predominates.
- Body parts are inhalation and exhalation.
- The leaves of plants and trees.

5. SOMA OR JAL

- Represents parts that are fluid, moving, slow, oily, soft, cold, slimy, moist, and where taste predominates.
- Body parts are blood, fat, phlegm, lymph, urine, bile and sweat.
- The stem and branches of plants and trees.

The seed of plants contain all these five elements, which are understood by their characteristics. The tools used to understand these characteristics are the sense of cognition and the sense of action.

Ayurveda classifies food according to its tendency to increase or decrease one or more of the elements. Food consists of the base elements — earth and water. The other three elements provide differences in shape and divergence of physical and mental activities.

Element (Maha-buta)	Expression (Karma Indriya)	Quality (Guna)	Physical Organ (Jnana Indriya)
Space/Ether	Speech	Sound	Ear-hearing
Air	Absorbing	Touch	Skin-feeling
Fire	Movement	Form	Eyes-seeing
Water	Regeneration	Flavour	Tongue-tasting
Earth	Elimination	Odour	Nose-smelling

The movement of these elements are an important consideration in Ayurveda. Air can move up and kindle fire. It can also move down and excrete waste. Water, being heavy, moves down to regulate fire. If there is too much air, the fire burns brightly; if there is too much water, the fire becomes dull and dies down. There must, thus, be a balance between the three Gunas. When the elements are not in harmony, the basic constitution of the individual is disturbed, resulting in various illnesses.

TRI-DOSHAS
(THE THREE CONSTITUTIONS)

From the elements arise three constitutions or *doshas*:

- When ether and air elements predominate, Vata-dosha sets in.
- From fire and water, Pitta-dosha results.
- The combination of water and ether results in Kapha-dosha.

The three doshas express the movement of energy within the body.

Ayurvedic treatment is based on the Tri-doshas: Vata, Pitta and Kapha. An even proportion of these three doshas in the body is considered healthy. Most people lean towards one or more of the characteristics of the Tri-doshas. This, in turn, gives them membership to that particular constitution.

The treatment of a disease is based on the constitution of an individual as well as on the specific nature of the disease. Problems are treated according to the individual's constitution by going to the root of his or her physiological and psychological make-up and not according to the symptoms. This is because symptoms may vary from one constitution to another, that is, from one person to another.

VATA OR AIR

Vata or air exists between the navel and feet of the body. It circulates in the lungs, heart, colon, bones and joints, nervous system and the alimentary canal. Its main seat is in the pelvic area and large intestines, from which it can be expelled easily.

Tastes connected with Vata are astringent, pungent and bitter. Vata induces action and is responsible for the activity of breaking down food for assimilation. Creation of Vata results from the pelvis; thus, Vata is termed the creator.

Vata helps to maintain equilibrium in energy flow through balanced breathing. It results in the formation of healthy tissues, proper functioning of the sense organs and discharge of impulses. However, when Vata is aggravated (due to unhealthy eating habits), it causes dryness (in any part of the body), chills, abdominal distension, insomnia, fatigue, constipation and loss of sensory faculties. When Vata obstructs channels, arthritis, rheumatism, abdominal disorders and constipation may occur.

Sweet, sour and salty foods are nutritive and reduce the problems of Vata. Pungent foods do not aggravate Vata, unless consumed in excess. When used in moderation, however, they dispel Vata. Diaphoretics, drugs and any agent that help create perspiration, can heal skin problems caused by Vata with their moistening property. Carminatives and laxatives dispel gas caused by Vata and clear abdominal disorders while nervines and antispasmodics help relieve muscular tension caused by Vata.

ASANA ROUTINE FOR VATA

People with Vata should concentrate on Asanas that put pressure on the abdomen and pelvis, as well as on those that strengthen the back muscles. The following Asanas are recommended:

- Padmasana (Lotus Pose)
- Yoga Mudra
- Bhujangasana (Cobra Pose)
- Halasana (Plough 1)
- Shavasana (Relaxation)
- Paripoorna Shalabasana (Swan)
- Veerasana (Hero Sitting Posture)
- Matsyasana (Fish in Lotus)
- Vayu Nishankasana (Gas Releasing Pose)
- Jatara Parivartanasana (Legover Both Legs)
- Meditation

Note: People with Vata should not do Sarvangasana (Shoulderstand) and spinal twists

PITTA OR FIRE

Pitta or fire has its seat in the abdomen above the navel and below the diaphragm and small intestines. It circulates in the liver, spleen, bile duct, pancreas, blood, eyes, brain and the skin.

Tastes associated with Pitta are pungent, sour and salty. Pitta represents metabolic activity. Its main functions are pigmentation, digestion, heat, cheerfulness, anger and jealousy.

Pitta is responsible for the proper digestion and assimilation of food, proper development of intelligence and perception, as well as for the maintenance of skin tone and muscles.

When disturbed (due to unhealthy eating habits for instance), Pitta causes yellowness of the skin, urine and eyes, a burning sensation in the tissues, irritability, fever, inflammations, acidity, excess thirst, and an increased appetite. Warm diaphoretics can cause perspiration and, thus, aggravate Pitta.

Sweet, astringent and bitter foods, alteratives, antibacterials, diuretics and bitter tonic herbs help clear problems caused by Pitta.

ASANA ROUTINE FOR PITTA

People with Pitta should perform Asanas that put pressure on the navel and the solar plexus area to release the energy in the liver and small intestines. The Asanas to be performed are as follows:

- Padmasana (Lotus Pose)
- Dhanurasana (Bow Pose)
- Supta Vajrasana (Backward Bend)
- Sarvangasana (Shoulderstand)
- Chakrasana (Back Pushup)
- Tadasana (Stretch Pose)
- Sheetali Pranayama (Cooling Breath)

Note: People with Pitta should avoid Shirasasana (Headstand) and Kandarsanasana (Plough 2).

KAPHA OR WATER

Kapha or water has its seat in the chest. It circulates between the head and the chest. Tastes associated with Kapha are sweet, sour and salty. It is anabolic and is responsible for stamina and the shape of the body. Its main functions are nourishment, binding of the joints, sexual vigour, fortitude and patience.

When present in the right proportion in the body, Kapha gives stability, maintains body fluids and provides comfort in the movement of joints. When not in the right proportion, it leads to the accumulation of phlegm, increases cold sensations, gives rise to difficulty in breathing, coughing and weak joints.

Pungent foods help treat the problems caused by Kapha. Diaphoretics, expectorants or mucous-dispelling herbs expel fluids caused by too much Kapha, which is mainly accumulated in the lungs and stomach. Emetics or agents that induce vomiting are good for treatment but must be used with care. Bitter foods help reduce fat in the body, thereby decreasing Kapha. Astringents, due to their drying effect, reduce the occurrences of Kapha.

ASANA ROUTINE FOR KAPHA

People with Kapha should do Asanas that bring energy to the chest and head, open up the lungs, clear the stomach, increase flexibility, and reduce fat. The Asanas are as follows:

- Ardha Matsyendrasana (Half Twist)
- Ardha Navasana (Boat Pose)
- Simhasana (Lion)
- Vrukshasana (Tree Pose)
- Chakrasana (Back Pushup)
- Paschimottanasana (Backstretch)
- Sarvangasana (Shoulderstand)
- Matsyasana (Fish in Lotus)
- Halasana (Plough 1)
- Siddhasana (Accomplished Pose)

Note: People with Kapha should not do Bow, Locust or Padmasana (Lotus Pose) as they put pressure on the kidneys and adrenal glands, thereby weakening them.

In many herbal remedies, problems are treated according to the constitutions, by going to the root of the physiological and psychological aspects of the individual and not according to the symptoms.

The three doshas express the movement of energy within the body. The following summarises the basic characteristics of an individual according to the three doshas:

The above characteristics, although broadly classified, are useful in knowing the Prakruthi (the natural constitution of an individual).

According to Ayurveda, the disease-producing factors in the body are disturbances in the constitution of the body Vata, Pitta and Kapha, while those in the mind are Rajaguna, the activity, and Tamoguna, the inertia.

Air, water and fire are the three basic principles most fundamental to life. When the equilibrium of these three doshas is disturbed, disease results. This can be due to an excess or a deficiency of one or more of the five elements. The body is supported entirely by these doshas.

Doshas also exist in plants and even here, they are classified accordingly. Soil conditions and geographical zones are taken into consideration when determining the characteristics:

- Plants with good growth, heavy and abundant leaves, good retention of water and plenty of sap are Kapha (water) plants.

ASPECTS	KAPHA PRADHANA	PITTA PRADHANA	VATA PRADHANA
Stature/Frame	Stout, Dwarfish	Average, lean	Thin, tall
Weight	Overweight	Average	Low
Skin	Thick, oily, cool	Soft, oily, warm	Dry, rough, cool
Hair	Thick, oily, wavy	Soft, oily	Dry, kinky
Teeth	Strong, white	Soft, bleeds	Spaced, crooked
Eyes	Attractive, large	Sharp	Small, dry
Appetite	Low, steady	Good, excessive	Very low, varies
Diseases	Oedema, mucous	Heaty, infections	Nervousness, pain
Thirst	Average	Excessive	Low variable
Stools	Thick, heavy, slow	Soft, loose	Dry, constipated
Activity	Lethargy	Average	Excessively active
Mental	Calm, slow, grateful, religious, serious, forgiving	Aggressive, sharp, ungrateful, ambitious	Restless, curious, intelligent, angered easily
Emotion	Greedy, selfish	Irritable, jealous	Fearful, insecure
Memory	Persistent, slow	Sharp	Variable
Sleep	Heavy	Clear	Interrupted
Speech	Slow, melodious	Sharp, clear	Fast, average
Pulse	Smooth, slow	Jumpy	Feeble
Likes	Hot, dry, pungent	Hot, oily	Cold
Sweat	Medium	Scanty	Profuse

- Plants with few leaves that are rough and crooked with little sap are Vata (air) plants.
- Plants that are average in height with brightly-coloured flowers and contain sap but not in excess, as well as possess a burning effect (to the touch), are Pitta (fire) plants.

DHATU AND ITS CHARACTERISTICS

Ayurveda classifies plants and herbs according to the *dhatu* or "the action (of plants and herbs) upon our tissues". The combination of the five elements is responsible for creating dhatu. In Ayurveda, the human body and plants are made of seven tissues or dhatu. These dhatu assist or construct the organs of the body. Ayurveda incorporates the knowledge of minerals present in herbs that act on these tissues.

The seven dhatu are as follows:

- **Rasa** (plasma): This is nourished by nutrients from digested food.
- **Raktha** (blood): This is nourished by Rasa and governs oxygenation of the tissues.
- **Mamsa** (muscle): This is nourished by Raktha. It allows for joint movements and increases strength.
- **Meda** (fat): This is nourished by muscles and maintains lubrication of the tissues.
- **Asthi** (bones): They are nourished by Mamsa and give support to the body structure.
- **Majja** (marrow): This is nourished by Asthi and fills the cavities.
- **Sukra** (Reproductive tissue): This is nourished by Majja. It contains the ingredients of all the tissues.

In plants, the dhatu or tissues are the following: the juice of the plant is the plasma; the resin of the plant is the blood; the softwood is the muscle; the gum is the fat; the bark is the bones; the leaves are the marrow and nerve tissues; and the flowers are the reproductive tissues.

The dhatu of a plant works best upon the corresponding dhatu of the human body. When one dhatu is defective, it affects the corresponding dhatu. This explains Ayurveda's emphasis on proper eating habits.

Eating the wrong kinds of food results in toxins, which enter the system through absorption. They are channelled to the weaker parts of the body. This causes clogging, blockage, obstruction, stagnation and contraction.

In Ayurveda, food entering the body should be effectively assimilated or eliminated. This is of prime importance to proper bodily functions. From these dhatu or "tissues", which form the organs, several systems develop. These systems are called srota or "channels". The main cause of any disease is due to obstruction in these channels, which are similar to the systems, such as the skeletomuscular system, in physiology.

Pranavaha srota is the channel for Prana (breath), Aharavaha srota is for food, Rakthavaha is for blood, Asthivaha and Majjavaha are for bones and bone marrow respectively, Mamsavaha for muscles, Sukravaha for semen, Arthavaha for the reproductive system in women, Stanavaha for lactation, and Manovaha for the nerves and mental capacity.

Ayurveda underscores the importance of keeping the systems clean, particularly the channels through which waste products pass. There are three mala or "waste products produced in the body", which are:

- Sakrit or "faeces"
- Mutra or "urine"
- Swedha or "sweat"

The channels that govern the elimination of waste products from the body are:

- Purishavaha srota or "the channel for faeces to pass through"
- Mutravaha srota or "the channel for urine"
- Swedhavaha srota or "the channel for sweat"

In its herbal treatment, Ayurveda uses:

- Raktha shodhaka or "blood and lymph purifiers"
- Krimi Vinashaka or "destroyer of germs"
- Vata Visarjaka or "eliminating gas"
- Swedha Visarjaka or "inducing perspiration"
- Mutra Visarjaka or "increasing urination"
- Ruthusravaka or "promoting menstruation"
- Kapha Visarjaka or "clearing phlegm and mucous"
- Malashuddhika or "laxatives"
- Unmadhaka or "nervines"
- Dipana or "stimulants"
- Agnimandyka or "digestive"
- Bruhana or "nutritives"
- Rasayana or "rejuvenatives"

- Vajikarana or "promoters of vitality"
- Stambakha, which in a broad sense can be considered astringents, is divided into three categories, namely those that stop bleeding or haemostatic, those that stop diarrhoea and those that promote healing of the tissues. Depending on the problem, they are combined in the right order. Precautionary measures are given importance in every treatment.

Our body is classified into two categories of hot and cold according to its constitution. By this classification, there are four sections: the internal organs, body coverings like the skin, upper body (above the waist) and lower body (below the waist).

Ayurveda therapy does not cure the symptom of any disease directly, but it helps to remove the root cause of the symptom so that every individual can attain health and harmony the natural way.

The approach is holistic treatment. By knowing the doshas of the individual, Ayurveda treats the problem using herbs of an opposite dosha to neutralise the effect. It is also necessary to know which remedies are beneficial and which are harmful well before administering the treatment.

Herbalist healers and Ayurvedic pundits have been analysing food according to its medicinal purposes for many centuries. Through experience, they have a system of classification for various types of food. For example:

- Nutmeg (a small amount) in food prevents abdominal spasms due to putrefaction. Nutmeg in excess can cause dullness of the brain.
- Anthelmintic herbs and antiparasitical herbs can weaken the tissues and can reduce sperm production if used in excess.
- Asafoetida prevents stagnation of food in the intestines, releases gas and destroys tapeworms when used as seasoning in food. When used with lentils, kidney beans, common beans, navy beans, green beans, pinto beans, string beans, etc. it makes food feel "light" by reducing gas formation.
- Bitter foods help increase appetite, but this works only for those having fever or pitta (fire) diseases. However, they slow down the digestion process, as well as weaken the assimilation of food and body's tissues when consumed in excess.

- By adding the powder of cardamom seeds to milk, the mucous forming property of milk is neutralised. The power detoxifies caffeine when added to coffee.
- By seasoning food with fennel seeds, abdominal cramps caused by consuming spice in excess can be prevented.
- Comfrey rootstock causes congestion in the lungs. With clove flower buds, cardamom or ginger root, it acts as an expectorant.
- Cooling alteratives like goldenseal and indigo, which are used as raktha shodhaka (blood purifiers), have a strong antibiotic effect; thus, they should be used sparingly, particularly when the patient is weak. If taken in excess, they may have the same detrimental effect as antibiotics, where useful bacteria are destroyed.
- Coughs are mainly due to the wet or dry conditions of the body. Wet coughs usually have yellow phlegm while dry coughs have little phlegm. For wet coughs, drying expectorants like cardamom, cinnamon, clove flower buds, black mustard and orange peel are used. For dry coughs, moistening demulcents like comfrey rootstock, liquorice root, marshmallow, milk and raw sugar are used.
- Cumin is an antidote for the effects of tomatoes, chillies and other hot pungent herbs. The combination of cumin, coriander seeds and fennel seeds acts as a catalyst to promote proper assimilation of food and other nutrients.
- Dandelion root detoxifies the effects of meat, as well as fried and fatty foods when eaten in excess.
- Eating cold foods like cucumber and raw foods in excess can cause cold sensations, thereby resulting in rheumatism. Black pepper, an antidote for symptoms of cold, should be added to food before consumption.
- Hawthorn herb can aggravate mucous formation and increase weight. It is good to mix the herb with a powder of cardamom seeds or cinnamon to neutralise the effect.
- Diuretics that are heaty like juniper berries are diaphoretics. They can cause more harm than good if used in the wrong proportions on kidney and bladder infections.
- Juniper berries aggravate Pitta or fire. They are to be mixed with demulcent diuretics like marshmallow to prevent them from causing any irritation.

- Heaty carminatives like ajowan or omum, asafoetida, basil, bay leaves, cardamom, cinnamon, clove flower buds, ginger, juniper berries, nutmeg, orange peel and turmeric may promote Pitta or fire. They contribute to acidity when used in excess.

- Buckwheat, being heaty, can cause severe itching. For some people, their faeces becomes so glutinous that expulsion is difficult.

- Hot and pungent herbs like black pepper, cayenne, cinnamon and ginger may aid bleeding (in the nose, arms, vagina, etc.) when used for a long period.

- Nutritive herbs like almond, dates, raisins and sesame seeds are restorative for conditions of weakness. However, they are difficult to digest. They should be combined with carminative herbs like cardamom, ginger or with sweet flavoured herbs like comfrey roots to aid assimilation.

- Parsley, because it is heaty, should be used with care when treating kidney problems. Its effect can be neutralised by mixing it with herbs like marshmallow.

- Saffron is a good catalyst for promoting absorption of nutrients present in food. A few threads of saffron added to food does the trick.

- Stimulants and digestive herbs like black pepper, cayenne, cinnamon, horseradish and mustard should not be used in conditions like dehydration, fluid insufficiency and inflammatory conditions because of the herbs' strong drying property. They should not be directly applied on mucous membrane as they reduce Kapha and destroy the mucous membranes.

- There are certain nervine herbs like dhatura or marijuana that contain chemicals or alkaloids. Due to their being poisonous and their strong effect on the nerves, their use is limited.

- To counter the emetic property of chamomile, add ginger.

- Turmeric is one of the best antibiotics. It helps to multiply healthy intestinal bacteria. However, pregnant women should avoid it. It should be used sparingly otherwise.

- When suffering from severe fatigue, avoid neem as it lowers the blood sugar.

- When there is ulceration in the intestinal membrane, avoid herbs with a strong purgative property. This is because they suppress the ability to digest and weaken peristaltic motion.

CLASSIFICATION OF FOOD

THE traditional Asian way of classifying food depends on many factors. These include the flavours of food, the type of sensation they produce, the way they act on body secretions, the reaction by the organs of the body to the food, the effect of food on the organs during different seasons, as well as their tastes and usefulness.

Ayurveda recognises six rasa or "tastes". Each taste has a definite virya or "potency". The six tastes are pungent, sweet, sour, bitter, astringent and salty.

Each flavour has a prabhava or "specific action" on both the internal organs of the body and emotions of the individual. The six tastes are associated with the different types of energies they produce within the body.

Sweet, bitter and astringent tastes are cooling, while salty, sour and pungent tastes are heaty. Food has an inherent tendency to cause "heat" or "cold" in the body. Accordingly, it is classified into different groups. When we talk about the energies of food we are talking about the sensations they produce like hot, warm, cool, cold and neutral. In addition, there is the reaction or post-digestive effect. This has nothing to do with the body temperature but with the elemental composition of the ratio of body elements.

The flavours of food have been identified by our ancestors from their experiences in India and China over the course of many centuries. Some types of food are classified as either strong in flavour or as flavoured. Others have been classified as having more than one flavour. The following is a useful list of flavours, which also details what they do:

- **Pungent flavours** act on the lungs and large intestines, induce perspiration, and aid energy circulation. They promote secretions, particularly in the nasal cavity, cure intestinal disorders, abdominal swelling and oedema, and eliminate waste easily, thereby preventing obesity. They also kill worms, improve blood circulation, stop anal itching and alleviate Kapha. When used in excess, pungent tastes cause weariness, dizziness and tremors, diminish strength, and induce pain.

- **Sweet flavours** act on the stomach and spleen, and neutralise the toxic effects of food. They alleviate Pitta and Vata. They are nourishing and prevent general weakness. They soothe the five senses, are responsible for a good complexion, relieve thirst, and promote the health of the skin and hair. Sweet flavours in excess, create obesity, laziness, excess sleep, loss of appetite, weak digestion, difficulty in breathing and urinating, swelling in the abdomen and lymph glands, goitre, and increase mucous in the throat and eyes. They cause Kapha diseases.

- **Sour flavours** act on the liver and gall bladder, and obstruct movement, thereby checking excess perspiration or diarrhoea. They dispel gas, aid digestion, as well as invigorate the sense organs and the mind. In excess, they result in thirst, build toxins in the blood, cause oedema and a burning sensation in the throat and heart, and prevent the healing of wounds and fractures. They liquefy Kapha and aggravate Pitta.

- **Bitter flavours** act on the heart and small intestines, reduce body heat, and induce movement, thereby causing diarrhoea. They are best for detoxifying all the systems of the body, act as antibacterial agents, help reduce body temperature when feverish, relieve fainting spells, itch and inflammations, and promote digestion and lactation. They are beneficial to those with Pitta and Kapha-related diseases. In excess, they result in tissue wastage and produce roughness in the blood vessels, thereby causing dizziness and dryness of the mouth, which in turn cause Vata diseases.

- **Salty flavours** act on the kidneys and bladder, and soften the muscles. They promote digestion, act as mild sedatives and laxatives, relieve stiffness and soften tissues. They alleviate Vata and help liquefy Kapha. When taken in excess, they cause thirst, blood stagnation, gout, muscle wastage, aggravate infections and inflammations, particularly in the skin, as well as increase bleeding and hyperacidity. They cause Pitta diseases.

- **Astringent properties** come from tannin in plants. They help prevent diarrhoea and bleeding, as well as promote healing of wounds and joint disorders. They alleviate Kapha and Pitta. When consumed in excess, they create pain in the heart, cause constipation and premature ageing, and disrupt blood circulation. They increase Vata diseases.

In general, a combination of sweet and pungent flavours is good for Vata diseases. Sweet and astringent flavours (mix well but are difficult to digest) and sweet and bitter flavours are good for Pitta diseases. A combination of sweet and sour flavours is good for Vata diseases.

Pungent and astringent flavours work better on Kapha diseases while bitter and pungent flavours work as diuretics, thereby curing Kapha diseases.

There are some exceptions as well. The actions of some types of food do not follow the pattern. For example:

- **Honey:** It has a sweet taste and is viscous. Its post-digestive effect is also sweet. Honey controls phlegm and reduces Kapha. This is because the virya or its "potency" is heating.

- **Lemon:** It has a sour taste, a sour post-digestive effect and a cooling potency. It produces phlegm and increases the element, water.

- **Ginger root:** It has a pungent taste and is heaty. However, the post-digestive effect is sweet, thereby reducing the element, air.

Food is classified into four groups according to its action on body secretions. Food makes body fluids move either inward, outward, upward or downward. Generally these classifications are based on nature. The leaves and flowers of plants are classified as upward while the roots and fruit are classified as downward. However, this is not always the case as illustrated by the following:

- Food that induces perspiration and reduces body heat is called outward action foods.

- Food that acts on a swollen stomach or eases bowel movements is called inward action foods.

- Food that relieves diarrhoea or a prolapse of the uterus is grouped as upward action foods.

- Food that relieves vomiting is called downward action foods.

The movement of food can be changed according to the way food is prepared. Generally, warm and hot food with pungent and sweet flavours are considered upward or outward moving. Cold and cool foods that have sour or salty or bitter flavours are considered downward or inward foods.

Food is also classified as obstructive or sliding according to their property to stop or induce fluid movements in the body.

Olives and guava, which result in diarrhoea when taken in excess, tend to obstruct the fluid channel, and this slows down movement. Others like honey activate fluid movement.

The season in which a particular food type is good or bad for consumption is also taken into consideration. In spring, have food that tends to move upward and has neutral energy with a pungent, sweet or bitter flavour. In summer, have pungent or sweet flavoured foods that move outward and have hot energy. In autumn, have sweet or sour flavoured foods with a downward movement that have cold, cool and warm energies. In winter, have bitter or salty flavoured foods with an inward movement and cold energy.

Food has different actions on different organs or parts of the body due to its chemical composition. This is the most important aspect of the Asian system of a balanced diet. It is the organic action caused by food that makes it an important means of maintaining health. This has been proven true by the experiences of our forefathers over the centuries.

FOODS THAT ACT ON THE BLADDER
Cinnamon, fennel, grapefruit and watermelons.

FOODS THAT ACT ON THE HEART
Bitter gourd, green and red pepper, milk, mung beans, musk melons, red beans, saffron, wheat and watermelons.

FOODS THAT ACTS ON THE INTESTINES
Black pepper, cabbages, castor beans, mushrooms, cucumbers, eggplant, figs, honey, lettuce, nutmeg, rice bran, salt, soya beans, squashes, sword beans and sweet basil.

FOODS THAT ACT ON THE STOMACH
Barley, bitter gourd, brown sugar, cabbages, caraway, celery, Indian corn, cucumbers, dates, eggplants, fennel, garlic, ginger, milk, mung beans, olives, radish, rice bran, salt, squashes, sword beans, vinegar and watermelons.

FOODS THAT ACT ON THE KIDNEYS
Ajowan, black sesame seeds, grapes, caraway, chestnuts, cinnamon, fennel, grapefruit, plums, salt, soya beans, star anise, string beans, wheat and wine.

FOODS THAT ACT ON THE LIVER
Black sesame seeds, brown sugar, celery, plums, saffron and vinegar.

FOODS THAT ACT ON THE LUNGS
Carrots, coriander, garlic, ginger, grapes, honey, mustard, maltose, milk, onions, olives, peanuts, pears and radishes.

FOODS THAT ACT ON THE SPLEEN
Ajowan, barley, soya bean curd, bitter gourd, brown sugar, carrots, coriander, cucumbers, dates, eggplants, figs, garlic, ginger, grapes, green pepper and red pepper, honey, nutmeg, peanuts, radish leaves, rice, soya beans, squashes, string beans and wheat.

CLASSIFICATION OF FOOD BY TASTES

Bitter foods generally, through perspiration and body fluids, reduce body heat. They induce urination and diarrhoea, as well as activate the heart and small intestines.

Examples include agrimony, apricots, asparagus, barberries, bitter gourd, celery, chamomile flowers (both types), chicory, chrysanthemums, coffee, coriander, cumin, dandelions, dill, echinacea rootstock, fenugreek, garlic, goldenseal, gooseberries, grapefruit, hops, jasmine, juniper, lettuce, lemongrass, liquorice, limes, lotus plumule, mullein leaves or flowers, resin of myrrh, neem, orange peel, pomegranates, pumpkins, radish tops, rose flowers, rosemary, saffron, sandalwood, sarsaparilla, shepherd's purse, St. John's wort and turmeric.

Pungent foods promote blood circulation and induce perspiration. They act on the lungs and large intestines.

Examples include ajowan, allspice, anise seeds, apricots, basil, asafoetida, bay leaves, black pepper, caraway, cayenne, chamomile flowers (both type), seeds of cherry also known as black cherries, cinnamon, clove flower buds, coriander, cumin, dill, eucalyptus leaves, fennel, fenugreek, garlic, ginger, gooseberries, grapefruit, ground ivy, honey, horseradish, juniper, lavender, leek, lemon balm or karpooravalli, lemongrass, marjoram, mustard, myrrh, nutmeg, onions, orange peel, parsley, peppermint, pumpkin, radishes, rice bran, rose flowers, rosemary, saffron, spearmint, St. John's wort, thyme and turmeric.

Salty foods soften the muscles and glands and act on the kidneys and bladder.

Examples include barley, garlic, kelp, milk, salt, seaweed and most animal products.

Sour foods are obstructive and help prevent diarrhoea, and excess perspiration. They stimulate the liver and gall bladder.

Examples include apples, apricots, gooseberries, grapes, grapefruit, hawthorn herbs, lemons, limes, oranges, mangoes, olives, peaches, pears, pineapples, plums, raspberries, red beans, rose hips, starfruit, strawberries, tamarind, tomatoes and yoghurt.

Sweet foods neutralise the toxic effect of other types of foods. They act on the stomach and spleen.

Examples include alfalfa leaves, almonds, apples, apricots, asparagus, bananas, barley, greens of beetroot, cabbages, carrots, celery, cherries, chestnuts, cinnamon, coconuts, coffee, comfrey rootstock, Indian corn or corn silk, cucumbers, chrysanthemums, dandelions, dates, eggplants, fennel, fenugreek, figs, garlic, ginger, gooseberries, grapes, grapefruit, guavas, hawthorn herbs, hibiscus flowers, honey, horse beans, juniper, kelp, kidney beans, lemon balm, lettuce, liquorice, malt, oranges, mangoes, marshmallow, milk, mullein, mung beans, musk melons, olive, onions, papayas, peaches, peanuts, pears, pineapples, plums, pomegranates, potatoes, pumpkin seeds, radishes, raspberries, red beans, rice, rose flowers, saffron, sandalwood, sarsaparilla, sesame seeds, soya beans, spearmint, spinach, squashes, starfruit, strawberries, string beans, sugar cane, sunflower seeds, sweet potatoes, tamarind, tomatoes, walnuts, watermelons, wheat, yam and yoghurt.

CLASSIFICATION OF FOOD BY ENERGIES

Cold foods are aloe, bananas, bitter gourd, chamomile flowers, grapefruit, kelp, musk melons, salt, starfruit, sugar cane, tomatoes and watermelons.

Cool foods are agrimony, alfalfa, apples, asparagus, barley, soya bean curd, coconuts, coriander, corn silk, cucumbers, cumin, dates, eggplants, fennel, gooseberries, hops, lettuce, lemons, lemon balm, lemongrass, limes, oranges, mangoes, marjoram, mung beans, neem, pears, peppermint, pomegranates, radishes, raisins, sarsaparilla, rose petals, sesame seeds, spinach, strawberries, wheat and yoghurt.

Warm foods are ajowan, almonds, asafoetida, asparagus, basil, caraway, cardamoms, cherries, chestnuts, clove flower buds, coconut milk, coffee, coriander, dates, dill, orange peel, fenugreek, garlic, ginger, grapefruit, onions, guavas, hawthorn herbs, mustard, myrrh, leek, malt, goat's milk, nutmeg, parsley, peaches, pumpkin seeds, raspberries, rice, rose hips, rosemary, spearmint, squashes, sunflower seeds, tamarind and walnuts.

Hot foods include black pepper, cinnamon, cayenne, eucalyptus, ginger, soya bean oil and turmeric.

Neutral foods are apricots, greens of beetroot, cabbages, carrots, celery, Indian corn, figs, grapes, guava leaves, honey, horse beans, lotus, milk, olive, papayas, peanuts, plums, potatoes, radish leaves, rice bran, saffron, soya beans, string beans, sweet potatoes and yams. A person with a cold physical constitution does not feel thirsty, has a pale complexion, a light or thin whitish coating on the tongue, discharges colourless or whitish urine and passes soft stools. Such people should increase eating hot or warm energy foods, sweet and pungent foods and reduce cool, cold and bitter foods.

A person with a cool constitution feels heavy, possibly a result of water retention. He or she also feels tired and has a glossy tongue. Such people should have foods that remove fluids from the body.

Ayurveda does not force anyone to become a vegetarian. It gives sound advice on what should be eaten and what that food does to the body. In many ways, vegetarian diets are good as diseases found in animal meat are avoided. It is quite possible that if vegetarian food is prepared in a tasty way, many people would not mind turning vegetarian.

People fail to understand the actual requirements of the body and the fact that the body's needs can be best catered for by natural foods. All vegetables contain proteins and carbohydrates; most contain little fat. They have a high water content and thus not many calories. More than anything, it is the minerals, vitamins and fibre contents that are necessary for healthy living. We are not conditioned to eat raw meat, so we cook and season it to get rid of the smell.

Meat has little water content and so does not move easily in the intestines, resulting in constipation and toxins in the body. Bearing in mind that human intestines are much longer than those of carnivorous animals, just imagine how long and tedious a journey the consumed meat takes before reaching the elimination process.

Animals have a special enzyme called uricase, which neutralises the uric acid present in meat. Unfortunately, man is not blessed with this powerful enzyme. No doubt meat is a good source of protein, iron and vitamin B, yet when consumed in large quantities, it does more harm than good. There is little roughage in meat to help the system clear the waste that builds up, resulting in both arthritic diseases and arteries that are clogged with cholesterol.

TOWARDS HEALTH

The perfect diet is simple and consists of fruit, juices, sprouts, salad and vegetable juices, yoghurt, honey, nuts, cottage cheese, dried fruits, figs, dates and vegetables cooked for a few minutes.

To help the body fight or overcome a sickness, most often than not, all that is needed is to keep it clean by having sufficient rest and nutritious food. Apart from a balanced diet, you need to have good thoughts, be in healthy surroundings and exercise adequately.

The science of Ayurveda emphasises the preventive and curative aspects of food, Asanas, the right attitude and a comfortable environment for complete health. It teaches us to heal ourselves by coming to terms with the needs of our body. In fact, Ayurveda lays claims to the saying that "all food is medicine and all medicine is food".

10

Nutrients for Health

Being healthy does not mean abstaining from all types of appetising food. It is about developing sensible eating habits and maintaining the balance between eating for joy and eating for health. In order to live healthily and in physical and mental harmony, it is essential to protect ourselves against diseases. We, therefore, have to be extremely careful about the type of food we eat.

Nature for one has its own way of giving us the most beneficial nutrients. As long as we do not ignore the basic requirements for sustenance, in line with nature's gift of healthy living, most of the problems of today will not even arise. They start only when we deviate from nature in order to please our taste buds. If we reduce eating food for pleasure and taste, and increase our intake of natural foods, then we are already on our way towards healthy living.

A carefully planned diet should be rich in the required proteins, carbohydrates, fats, minerals and vitamins. Nutrients are important for maintaining a healthy mind and body. They are interdependent and work together for the well-being of our body. For example, the healing quality of vitamin A is enhanced by the intake of vitamin E. Lecithin helps vitamins A, D, E and K as well as fat to be absorbed by the body. It is important to know the nutrient supplements required, their functions in our body and their source for a truly healthy diet.

PROTEINS

These form enzymes, which carry out the living process, such as the growth of cells, tissues, etc. They form the structural elements of the cells and are sources of energy.

Most types of food contain protein. Rich sources of protein are eggs, fish, meat, milk and legumes. Animal proteins have a high protein efficiency ratio. They are also rich in cholesterol. An active person requires more protein than an inactive one. However, a high intake of protein overworks the liver and kidneys, as well as increases water and calcium loss. To combat the effects of a high protein intake, supplement your diet with vitamin B6 (an absence of this affects your moods and behaviour).

Proteins required for good health are made of three types of amino acids: nonessential amino acids, semi-essential amino acids and essential amino acids.

The following are nonessential amino acids that the body itself can synthesise:

- **Alanine** is used as fuel by the brain, nerve and muscle tissues. It builds up the immune system by producing antibodies.
- **Aspartic acid**, involved in the formation of RNA and DNA (the chemical bases of heredity and carriers of genetic information), increases resistance to fatigue. Salts of aspartic acid increase stamina. The acid is abundant in sugar cane and greens of beetroot.
- **Glutamic Acid** is important for nerve functions. It is used as the basis of the flavour enhancer, monosodium glutamate. It increases the blood sugar and is used to treat hypoglycaemia.
- **Glutamine** is responsible for the metabolism of the brain. It is used to treat alcoholism and senility.
- **Glycine** is needed for the proper functioning of the nerve, skin and muscle tissues. It helps to mobilise glycogen from the liver and builds up the immune system.
- **Hydroxyproline** is isolated from gelatine for nutritional supplement.
- **Ornithine** helps to build the immune system, as well as promotes the functioning and healing of the liver. It is important in the formation of urea and detoxifies ammonia, which is poisonous to living cells. It is used in an anti-cholesterol diet.

- **Proline** is important for the proper functioning of joints, tendons and heart muscles. It is abundant in gelatine.
- **Serine** helps to build up the immune system. It is an energy storage source of glucose by the liver and muscles.
- **Taurine** is present in high concentration in the tissues of the heart, skeletal muscles and nervous system. It treats some types of epilepsy by controlling seizures. It is present in bile and shark.

The following are semi-essential amino acids needed by infants (not by adults):

- **Arginine** stimulates the release of growth hormones and builds up the immune system. It increases muscle growth and reduces body fat.
- **Cysteine** is important for hair growth and is good for the skin and nails. It is an antioxidant and is useful in the treatment of rheumatoid arthritis.
- **Cystine** is the main constituent of hair and is an oxidised form of cysteine. It is used in the treatment of respiratory disorders.
- **Histidine** is important for the formation of red and white blood cells. It is used by the body to counteract allergic reactions, as well as treat ulcers, anaemia and rheumatoid arthritis.
- **Tyrosine** is needed for the proper functioning of the adrenal, pituitary and thyroid glands. It is used for treating anxiety and insomnia.

Essential amino acids that the body cannot manufacture by itself are the following:

- **Isoleucine** is necessary for the formation of haemoglobin. It is found in beans, seeds, nuts, egg yolks and chicken.
- **Leucine** promotes the healing of the skin and broken bones, as well as lowers the blood sugar. It is found in cereals, beans, seeds, milk, cheese, beef and chicken.
- **Lysine** is needed to inhibit the growth of viruses and metabolise calcium. It is found in wheatgerm, beans, beef, chicken, eggs and fish.
- **Methionine** is necessary for preventing the buildup of excess fat in the liver. It is found in seeds, brazil nuts, meat, eggs and cheese.
- **Phenylalanine** is necessary for a positive mood, as well as to enhance memory and the learning capacity.

It also helps to suppress the appetite. It is found in wheatgerm, almonds, dates, beans, pistachio nuts, meat and cheese.

- **Threonine** helps to build up the immune system. It is needed for proper growth of the mind and body, and is important for the formation of specialised proteins like collagen. It is generally low in a vegetarian diet. It is found in wheatgerm, beans, seeds, meat and fish.
- **Tryptophan** is involved in the regulation of moods and metabolism. It is required in the production of hormones and is used to treat migraines, insomnia, stress, anxiety and depression. It is found in seeds, beans, meat, eggs. fish and turkey.
- **Valine** is an energy storage source of glucose by the liver and muscles. It is found in oats, wheatgerm, beans, seeds, chicken and cheese.

Protein foods are good for the body. The purest form of protein is found in egg white, milk, yoghurt and fat-free meat. Not all proteins contain the necessary amino acids in sufficient amounts. Certain types of food like whole milk, buttermilk, eggs, brewer's yeast, wheatgerm, cottage cheese and soya beans are considered "complete" as they supply nearly all the eight amino acids that the body is unable to produce. Vegetable proteins were considered second best until it was found that the right combination of nuts, legumes, cereals, fruit and vegetables supplies the equivalent of first-class protein.

When eaten together, the following types of food contribute all the essential amino acids:

- **Eggs** contain all the essential amino acids.
- **Milk** contains nearly all the essential amino acids and is a rich source of lysine.
- **Legumes** and **dhal** are rich in lysine and isoleucine but lack tryptophan, methionine and cystine.
- **Grains** are rich in tryptophan, methionine, cystine but not lysine and isoleucine.
- **Nuts** and **seeds**, except cashew nuts and pumpkin seeds, are good sources of tryptophan, methionine and cystine but lack lysine and isoleucine.
- Most **vegetables** are rich in tryptophan and lysine but lack isoleucine, methionine and cystine.
- **Wheat** lacks lysine, while peas and beans lack methionine and cysteine.

For the required protein, combine food groups so that the amino acids of one group compensate for their lack in another.

Some good combinations of food that give all the required amino acids are the following:

- Bean curd with sesame seeds
- Bean soup with whole wheat bread
- Broccoli with cheese
- Cereals and milk
- Chickpeas with sesame seeds
- Corn and beans
- Cream of pumpkin soup
- Creamed soup (containing vegetables) with rice or noodles
- Eggs and french fries
- Legumes (any type) with wheat
- Mashed potato with milk
- Oatmeal with milk
- peanut butter with whole wheat products
- Rice with fresh green peas
- Rice with black-eyed beans
- Rice with lentils (dhal)
- Rice and soya products
- Spinach with egg
- Wheat and dairy products
- Wheat with seeds (any type), nuts and beans

CARBOHYDRATES

These are the main sources of energy. They provide 4 calories per gram, form cell surface coating to prevent cell damage and have many other important functions.

Those from grains, legumes, wholemeal bread, wheat products, homemade muesli, rice, potatoes, corn, baked beans, kidney beans, lima beans and starchy tubers are complex carbohydrates. Modern diets are rich in simple sugars, so minimise the intake of such sugars.

FAT

This is a high energy food. Certain types of fat (the essential fatty acids and steroids) form hormones, prostaglandins and other substances. These regulate such functions of the body as body temperature, cell division, cell multiplication, immune function, blood pressure and fluid controls. They also help in transporting fat soluble vitamins A, D, E and K.

Oil extracted by cold press from soya beans, peanuts and the germs of grains are the best form of unsaturated fat and polyunsaturated fat. Fish is a rich source of polyunsaturated fat while meat, milk and egg yolks are sources of saturated fat.

Avoid taking hydrogenated fat, saturated fat and cholesterol. Bear in mind that a high intake of saturated fat and cholesterol are detrimental to the heart and circulatory system. A high intake of polyunsaturated fat requires a high intake of vitamin E.

FIBRE

This is the indigestible portion of vegetables, grains and fruit. It is essential for maintaining important intestinal functions. A low intake of fibre results in diverticulosis (abdominal pain, diarrhoea and constipation), cardiovascular diseases, colon cancer and diabetes.

Fibre from vegetables, whole grains and fruit increase faecal bulk. Insoluble cellulose, hemicellulose and lignin fibre increase intestinal transit time. Soluble fibre like gum and pectin absorb unwanted elements from the intestines and help reduce the cholesterol level.

Coconuts, wholemeal bread, bran, muesli, wheat, kidney beans, soya beans, Indian corn, lentils, peas, potatoes with skin, blackberries, figs, passion fruit, prunes and raspberries are rich in fibre.

WATER

This regulates body temperature, constitutes the bulk of the blood and lymph, as well as transports nutrients. Water deficiency can cause shock, cardiac failure and an imbalance in electrolytes.

MINERALS

Together with vitamins, minerals play a vital role in keeping the body fit and healthy. Though required in small quantities, minerals may affect the proper functioning of vital organs if taken in too small a quantity. They help build enzymes and maintain the viscosity of the blood. Minerals also help neutralise acids and prevent food from rotting in the stomach.

Sources of minerals include vegetables, fruit and nuts. Even though we tend to skin fruit and vegetables before eating them, we should try to eat them with the skin. This is because the skin contains the maximum number of minerals.

Many substances in the wrong combination block the absorption of minerals like calcium, magnesium, zinc and iron. Exercise care when consuming such foods. They include bran, whole grain wheat like pastry, biscuits, *chapatis*, tea, coffee and liquorice. Phytates in grains bind minerals, making them unavailable for the body. You, therefore, lose precious minerals when you tuck into a breakfast of cereals thinking that they have more fibre.

Soft drinks and some food additives contain phosphates. Consuming these upsets the calcium-phosphorus and magnesium-phosphorus ratio in the body, resulting, for instance, in calcium deficiency.

For the optimal use of minerals, the irritating or poisonous drug of salts of potassium, iron, copper, zinc should be consumed after digestion. If consumed immediately after food, chemicals destroy and impair the action of the minerals. Also affected are certain active elements, including the enzymes of the gastric juice, and their action will be ineffective in the process of digestion.

VITAL MINERALS

Calcium is needed for strong bones, a regular heartbeat, muscle contraction, to prevent blood clotting, as well as to metabolise the body's iron and vitamin B12. Calcium deficiency causes bone and teeth degeneration, muscular pain, general weakness, as well as circulatory, vascular and stomach disorders.

Rich sources of calcium are almonds, asparagus, bananas, blueberries, broccoli, brussels sprouts, butter, cabbages, carrots, cauliflowers, cheese, cucumbers, dandelions, grapefruit, honey, kelp, leeks, legumes, lemons, lettuce, lima beans, limes, mangoes, milk, mustard, oranges, parsley, peaches, pineapples, sesame seeds, soya beans, sprouts, strawberries, tuna, turnips and yoghurt.

A high intake of protein, antibiotics and anti-inflammatory steroids necessitate an increase in calcium intake. Aluminium-based antacids interfere with calcium absorption. Phytates of bran and other high fibre diet bind calcium. Taking excess bran during breakfast results in calcium deficiency, as does a high intake of phosphorus or fat. Similarly, excess protein drains off calcium in the urine. Exposure to aluminium or lead requires a calcium supplement. Harmful effects of excess calcium can be counteracted by consuming large amounts of salads and green vegetables. Consuming more than 2,000 milligrams of calcium per day, however, can cause hypercalcaemia (presence of an abnormally high concentration of calcium in the blood).

Chlorine acts as an electrolyte and is essential for maintaining the body fluid's osmotic pressure and acid-alkali balance. It is an essential constituent of gastric juices. It aids in digestion as well as in the flexibility of the joints.

Lack of chlorine causes inflammations, infections, congestion of tissues, cysts and swellings, glandular disorders, and poor fertility in women.

Rich sources of chlorine are avocados, bananas, beef, greens of beetroot, butter, cabbages, celery, cheese, chicory, coconuts, common salt, cucumbers, dandelions, dates, duck, eggs, eggplants, lamb, lettuce, mangoes, papayas, radishes, raisins, spinach and tomatoes. Modern diets and processed foods are rich in salt, which, in excess, can cause hypertension.

Chromium is necessary for controlling the blood sugar and for glucose tolerance. It also helps in the production of insulin. It is found in black pepper, brewer's yeast, butter, cheese, green leafy vegetables, meat, pulses and wheatgerm.

Copper is required for the formation of connective tissues and haemoglobin, as well as for iron absorption, nerve functions and indirectly protects the body against oxidation damage. Good sources of copper are apricots, whole grains, nuts, legumes, egg yolks and seafood.

A high intake of vitamin C, zinc, raw meat, molybdenum and lead or mercury contaminated food prevent copper absorption.

Fluorine is necessary for proper bone and tooth structure. It reduces the risk of osteoporosis. Fluorine is found in greens of beetroot and horseradish.

Aluminium-based antacids interfere with fluorine absorption. A high intake of fluorine is toxic.

Germanium activates the immune system and may induce the production of interferon (a protein with potential use for treating acute viral infections). It is found in beans, tuna, garlic, green tea and dried fish.

Iodine synthesises the thyroid hormone, which regulates the metabolic rate. It is found in seafood and iodised salt. Iodine is also found, in traces, in asparagus, blackberries, blueberries, brussels sprouts, cardamoms, carrots, eggs, eggplants, fish, garlic, kelp, mushrooms, oats, pineapples, squash and tuna.

Iron is present in haemoglobin and other enzymes involved in the generation of energy. It helps in the growth of the body and promotes resistance to diseases. It cures and prevents anaemia and maintains a good skin tone.

Iron deficiency results in blood disorder, inflammations, fever, throbbing pain, infections, congestion in the lungs and brain, headaches, and menstrual disorders. Vitamin C enhances the absorption of iron.

Foods rich in iron are asparagus, beans, greens of beetroot, blackberries, broccoli, cherries, chicory, cucumbers, dried apricots, dried peaches, eggs, fish, kidneys, lentils, lettuce, lima beans, liver, meat, oats, oysters, parsley, peas, potatoes, pumpkins, raspberries, salad vegetables and wholemeal bread.

As foods rich in iron like spinach contain oxalic acid, the iron is made unavailable. This is because the oxalic acid binds the iron. Oxalic acid in spinach makes the cartoon character Popeye, who gains immense strength after eating spinach, very much a myth.

Cereal grains, due to the presence of phytic acid, "tie up" the iron and make it unavailable to the body. Tannin in tea and caffeine in coffee deprive iron absorption, particularly when drunk after meals.

Whole grain cereals are much more rich in iron than their processed counterparts such that, despite the effect of the phytic acid, they contribute iron to the diet. Antacids and laxatives hinder the absorption of iron. It is not advisable for children to have an excess of antacids and laxatives.

The non-haem iron is better absorbed if some haem iron is present in a meal or fruit containing vitamin C. For example, if you have poached egg on a slice of wholemeal toast, no iron is absorbed from either food types. By adding a fruit to it, the iron in the egg as well as the toast will be made available.

Lithium is used to treat manic-depressive disorders. Large quantities of lithium, however, are toxic.

Magnesium is needed for energy generation, muscle contraction, nerve functions, bone and tooth formation, as well as for the metabolic processes of various types.

It helps to fight depression, assists the cardiovascular system, as well as prevents calcium deposits and the formation of kidney and gall stones. Magnesium deficiency causes nervous disorders and shooting headaches, as well as cramps and pain in any part of the body, which are aggravated by the cold.

Neomycin type antibiotics and thiazide diuretics increase the requirements of magnesium in the body. Magnesium is found in abundance in figs, lemons, grapefruit, almonds, seeds, dark green vegetables, apples and brown rice.

Other foods rich in magnesium include bananas, greens of beetroot, blackberries, blueberries, bran, celery, cherries, coconuts, Indian corn or corn silk, blackcurrants, dried fruit, dried beans, eggs, grapes, limes, milk, mustard greens, oats, oranges, papayas, peas, pineapples, plums, pomegranates, potatoes, prunes, radishes, rye, sardines, squash and walnuts.

Consuming large amounts of magnesium with a large amount of phosphorus and calcium is toxic. Refined foods are deficient in magnesium and are one of the causes of cramps. A high intake of protein, calcium, phosphorus and vitamin D causes magnesium deficiency and hyperactivity in children.

Manganese is needed for healthy cartilage. It also protects the body from oxidation. Manganese is found in almonds, string beans, dandelions and walnuts.

Manganese deficiency causes stress, headaches, muscular pains and nervous excitability.

Phosphorus is a component of nucleic acid, bones and teeth. It is necessary for maintaining the acid-alkali balance and aids body repair. It provides energy, helps to metabolise fats and starches, lessens the pain of arthritis, as well as maintains healthy gums and teeth. Phosphorus is good for people suffering from nervousness and for women going through postnatal depression. It is also good for those who have lost their mental and physical efficiency and for those with low resistance to infections.

It is found in whole grains, nuts, seeds, milk, cheese, legumes and almost all types of food. It is also found in almonds, apricots, avocados, lima beans, beef, cheese, coconuts, corn, cucumbers, currants, duck, eggplants, honey, lamb, lentils, milk, mushrooms, olives, peaches, peanuts, pears, peas, potatoes, prunes, pumpkins, radishes, raisins, rice, rye, walnuts and wheat.

Potassium is essential for maintaining the intra-cellular acid-alkali balance, nerve signal transmission and muscular functions. It cannot be stored and has to be in balance with sodium intake. It is one of the main brain tonics and aids clear thinking by sending oxygen to the brain. Potassium is helpful in allergy treatment and is useful in reducing blood pressure.

Potassium is found in abundance in all green leafy vegetables, bananas, sunflower seeds, bamboo shoots, raisins, potatoes, mushrooms and garlic. Other foods rich in potassium include apples, apricots, barley, beef, greens of beetroot, blackberries, blueberries, broccoli, brussels sprouts, cabbages, carrots, cauliflowers, celery, cherries, chickpeas, chicken, chicory, coconuts, corn, cucumbers, currants, dandelions, dried fruit, duck, eggplants, figs, fish, grapes, grapefruit, honey, horseradish, lamb, lemons, lentils, lettuce, lima beans, limes, mangoes, milk, mustard, nuts, olives, onions, oranges, parsley, peaches, peanuts, prunes, radishes, spinach, tomatoes, turnips and zucchinis.

Potassium deficiency symptoms are stomach disorders, the presence of kidney stones, fluid retention, odorous perspiration, anal itching and morning headaches. Deficiency in potassium results in depression, irritability, diarrhoea, hysteria, a big appetite, continuous yawning and stretching, and degeneration of the cells.

Strict vegetarians have a high percentage of potassium in their body. If not enough salt is added to their diet, there will be a low level of sodium in the body. This will upset the sodium-potassium ratio, thereby resulting in deficiencies.

Selenium protects the body from oxidation damage and its deficiency increases the risk of cancer. Sources of selenium are garlic, brazil nuts, fish and seafood, whole grains, cereals, cucumber skin, and dairy products.

Silicon is necessary for keeping body tissues elastic. It is good for menopausal distress and dandruff problems.

Natural foods rich in silicon are onions, tomatoes, broccoli and cucumbers. Silicon is also found in abundance in alfalfa, apricots, asparagus, barley, greens of beetroot, carrots, cauliflowers, corn, cucumber skin, kelp, oats, peanuts, potatoes, rice polishing, spinach, sprouted seeds, unrefined nuts and wheat.

Silicon deficiency causes arthritis, skin diseases, head and scalp problems, brittle nails, and mastitis.

Sodium works together with potassium, phosphorus and chlorides to maintain the acid-alkali balance, blood pressure, water content and nerve conductance of the body. Natural sodium prevents heat prostration or sunstroke. Sodium helps the nerves and muscles to function properly.

Rich sources of sodium are bananas, tomatoes, okra, dried figs, carrots, apples, raisins and coconuts. Other foods include greens of beetroot, broccoli, brussels sprouts, butter, cabbages, cashew nuts, celery, chickpeas, dandelions, dates, dried peaches, garlic, goat's milk, grapefruit, horseradish, leek, lettuce, olives, oranges, papayas, parsley, pears, pineapples, prunes, pomegranates, pumpkins, radishes, raspberries, raw milk, rice, sesame seeds, squash, strawberries, water chestnuts and whey.

A high sodium diet leaches out potassium.

Sulphur is present in the skin, hair and nails. It tones the skin, hair and helps fight bacterial infections. Foods rich in sulphur produce gas.

Sulphur is found in green leafy vegetables, eggs, dried beans, eggplants, tomatoes, avocados, brussels sprouts, carrots, cauliflowers, chicory, horseradish, mustard greens, onions, papayas, parsley and rye.

Sulphur deficiency results in liver ailments, skin diseases, dandruff problems, dropsy, frequent urination, cystitis and gout.

Zinc is crucial to the immune system. It maintains the thymus gland, spleen and lymph nodes (organs of the defence system) in a healthy condition. Sources of zinc are fish and eggs.

Zinc deficiency reduces antibodies. A high intake of zinc harms the immune system as it interferes with iron absorption.

Certain types of food impair the absorption of zinc from the body. These are peanuts, soya beans, cereals, beans, bran, brazil nuts, hazel nuts, lentils, oats, oysters, sardines, steak and walnuts. High fibre and protein-rich foods like soya products and cheese, coffee, cow's milk, and iron supplement also prevent the absorption of zinc from the food we eat if combined together with those from the earlier list.

Some minerals harm the immune system, lower the body's resistance to viral diseases, suppress the effect of interferon and are toxic to the white blood cells. They include:

- **Cadmium** found in cigarettes, canned fruit, margarine, sugar and alcohol.
- **Lead** found in paints, cigarettes, smoke, tin cans and polluted air.

- **Mercury** found in tuna fish and shark. Dressings used in salads, chemicals used to prevent moulding and fungicides contain mercury. Exercise care when using them.
- **Nickel** found in vegetables and meat, cigarette smoke and margarine. However, small amounts of nickel are needed for certain enzymes in the brain.

VITAMINS

Vitamins are easily destroyed when you wash or heat vegetables. Preserve the natural goodness of vegetables by

- Eating them raw whenever possible.
- Not peeling the skin as it is a source of fibre. A concentration of vitamins and minerals is found just beneath it.
- Not soaking the vegetables before cooking them.
- Steaming and not boiling them.
- Not using bicarbonate.

Vitamin A (Retinol) builds resistance to infections. It maintains healthy skin and healthy membranes of the respiratory, digestive and urinary tracts. It is necessary for good eyesight and the development of cells, including immune and bone cells.

Main sources of vitamin A are liver, green vegetables, green pepper, egg yolk, dairy products and milk. Vitamin A deficiency results in night blindness, dry skin, acne, loss of appetite, sinus trouble and increased susceptibility to infections. It also increases the risk of cancer.

A high intake of vitamin A can cause fatigue, lethargy, headaches, insomnia, brittle nails, skin changes and loss of body hair.

Zinc must be present for the proper functioning of vitamin A. Laxatives used over a long period of time reduce the absorption of this vitamin. Others that nullify its positive effects are caffeine, alcohol, vitamin D deficiency and iron consumed in excess.

In the **Vitamin B Group**, each vitamin is linked to the other. All are water soluble and are excreted in the urine when taken in excess.

Vitamin B1 (Thiamine) is an anti-ageing vitamin. It promotes growth and prevents air or sea sickness. It aids digestion and improves mental faculties like the capacity to learn and the nervous system and the muscles, as well as the functioning of the heart.

Thiamine is found in whole grain, brewer's yeast, meat, legumes, nuts, rice bran, sunflower seeds and fish. Vitamin B1 deficiency results in loss of appetite, gastro-intestinal problems, memory loss, muscle cramps, beri-beri, depression, irritability, concentration lapses, as well as numbness and tingling in the hands and feet. It also causes calf muscles to become tender, reduces tolerance to pain, results in insomnia, night sweats, chest pains, cardiac failure, rapid pulse, ankle swelling (in alcoholics, it causes a ruddy face and warm hands and feet) and shortness of breath.

Thiamine is easily destroyed by tea, coffee, oral contraceptives and stress. Cooking also destroys part of this vitamin. Thiamine is associated with folic acid.

Vitamin B2 (Riboflavin) is stable under heat but deteriorates when exposed to light. Riboflavin is needed for healthy skin and hair. It is also needed for eliminating mouth sores, as well as for metabolising fats and carbohydrates. It is necessary for red blood cell and antibody formation, and for the formation of enzymes in the liver. It helps pregnant and breast-feeding women to produce healthy amounts of milk. Lactating women require this vitamin.

Riboflavin is found in milk, almonds, green leafy vegetables, brewer's yeast, fish, liver, kidney, eggs and cereals.

Vitamin B2 deficiency causes dryness and cracking of lips, a greasy and red face, burning feet, an excess of tear production, diarrhoea, mouth sores, dermatitis, loss of hair and vaginal itching.

Use of oral contraceptives, sulfa-drugs and diuretics increases the requirements for vitamin B2. When consumed in excess, though rare, vitamin B2 can cause poisoning, a burning or prickling sensation and numbness.

Vitamin B3 (Niacin), also known as the courage vitamin, is important for mental health and the nervous system, particularly for depression and insomnia.

It relieves indigestion caused by a lack of hydrochloric acid. It is necessary for the formation of certain enzymes, the production of sex hormones and the metabolism of cholesterol. It helps pregnant women with a poor protein intake and who have blood fats and arthritis. Niacin is good for osteoarthritis of the knee.

Niacin is found in fish, brewer's yeast, beans, nuts, milk, cheese, vegetables and whole grains.

Vitamin B3 deficiency results in headaches, irritability, loss of memory, pigmentation on the back of the hands and face, a sore tongue, and diarrhoea.

Vitamin B6 (Pyridoxine) is a nerve relaxer and an anti-stress vitamin. Pyridoxine is required for the metabolism of proteins, amino acids, body histamine, serotonin (brain chemistry), and for the proper absorption of minerals like magnesium and zinc. It is also required for the synthesis of haemoglobin and neuro transmitters like adrenaline. It is essential to maintain a healthy immune defence.

Pyridoxine is found in wheat bran, wheatgerm, cabbages, molasses, unpolished rice, sunflower seeds, bananas, avocados, milk, fish, egg yolks, whole grains and green leafy vegetables.

Pyridoxine is good for people with kidney stones, kidney failure, diabetes, premenstrual syndrome and also benefit hyperactive children. It plays a vital role in the biosynthesis of RNA and DNA present in all cells. Without these, no new cells are formed, thereby resulting in no antibodies. Pyridoxine reduces muscle spasms, leg cramps and numbness in the hands.

Pyridoxine deficiency results in bad breath, nervousness, insomnia, irritability, dermatitis near the nose, corners of the eyes and the mouth, loss of appetite, weight loss, anaemia, dandruff problems, mouth sores, abdominal cramps, rashes in the genital area, muscle cramps, nervousness, water retention, and depression.

As vitamin B6 works well in combination with magnesium, it is recommended it be added to food rich in magnesium. Consumption of vitamin B6 should not exceed more than 50 milligrams per day.

Pantothenic Acid is an anti-stress vitamin. It is not heat stable. Natural bacteria present in the body also produce this vitamin in the gastro-intestinal tract. Pantothenic acid is necessary for the production of antibodies, as well as for the metabolism of fat and sugar. A high intake of antibiotics, however, affects the formation of the vitamin.

Pantothenic Acid is found in dark green vegetables, wheatgerm, pumpkins, legumes, brewer's yeast, egg yolks and whole grains. Deficiency in the vitamin causes hypoglycaemia, depression, stomach ulcers, allergic reactions, asthma, headaches, emotional mood swings, general weakness and numbness of the body, a tingling sensation in the hands and feet, as well as abdominal cramps.

Folic Acid (Folacin) is vital for cell division and blood production. It is also required for the synthesis of DNA and certain amino acids, formation of red blood cells, and the maintenance of healthy glands and liver.

Folic acid is found in dark green vegetables, fruit, brewer's yeast, soya beans, mushrooms, wheatgerm and whole grains. A deficiency in the vitamin results in anaemia and tiredness. Aluminium-based antacids deplete folic acid, while cooking destroys foliates. Vitamin C prevents this destruction of foliates.

Vitamin B12 (Cyano Cobalamin) regenerates red blood cells, thereby preventing anaemia. It increases energy, maintains a healthy nervous system, as well as improves memory and balance. White blood cells function best in the presence of this vitamin.

Vitamin B12 is found in milk, meat, cheese, liver, fish, dairy products, brewer's yeast and eggs. Vitamin B12 is not found naturally in any plant food.

Vitamin B12 deficiency results in anaemia, exhaustion, pale skin, numbness and a tingling sensation in the hands and feet, depression, heart palpitations, menstrual problems, nervousness, body odour, brain damage, as well as a confused mind. Oral contraceptives, cholesterol-reducing drugs and anti-inflammatory drugs increase the requirements of vitamin B12.

Inositol is required for the metabolism of fats and cholesterol, as well as for the formation of lecithin. It is involved in all bodily functions.

Inositol is found in citrus fruit, wheatgerm, whole grains, nuts, milk, meat and brewer's yeast. Inositol deficiency causes high cholesterol in the blood, constipation, as well as skin and eye problems.

PABA (Para Amino-benzoic Acid) is an important component of folic acid. It is one of the best ultra violet screening compounds. It protects the skin, aids in the metabolism of protein as well as in the formation of red blood cells.

Biotin is required for healthy skin and proper hormone production. It is also required for the metabolism of carbohydrates, amino acids and fatty acids, formation of antibodies, as well as for the proper absorption of B12, folacin and pantothenic acid.

Biotin is found in brewer's yeast, nuts, fruit, unpolished rice, dairy products, meat, egg yolks and whole grains. Biotin deficiency causes weakness, depression, anaemia, skin disorders and muscle pains.

Vitamin C (Ascorbic Acid) is required for collagen synthesis, blood vessel integrity and bone strength. It is necessary for synthesising adrenal hormones and for the proper functioning of white blood cells.

Vitamin C helps heal wounds and bleeding gums, prevents viral and bacterial infections, lowers the incidence of blood clots, prevents colds and scurvy, as well as eliminates harmful chemicals and radicals that cause cancer. It plays a role in the production of interferon, which helps fight viral diseases.

It is found in citrus fruit, green leafy vegetables, green pepper, kale, broccoli, papayas, parsley, tomatoes, cauliflowers, potatoes, cabbages and okra.

Vitamin C deficiency results in loss of appetite, fatigue, nose bleeding, slow healing wounds, easy bruising and scurvy. Nitrate and nitrite preservatives are converted into carcinogenic nitro samines in the stomach, which could lead to cancer. Vitamin C in the diet may prevent their formation. Cooking vegetables in copper vessels or any other metal utensils destroys vitamin C. Drugs like steroids and antibiotics, as well as smoking increase the requirements of vitamin C.

Vitamin D (Cholecalciferol) regulates the absorption of calcium and phosphorus, maintains the blood calcium level and helps in bone formation. It is also responsible for the proper functioning of the thyroid.

Vitamin D is naturally available in sunlight. It is also found in milk, tuna, sardines, fish liver oil, egg yolks and dairy products. Symptoms of deficiency are fatigue, muscle cramps and rickets.

A high intake of vitamin D (more than 5000 i.u.) may affect adults. Signs include excess thirst, drowsiness, sore eyes, itchy skin and vomiting. In the long run, too high an intake of vitamin D causes soft tissue calcification and kidney damage. Harmful effects of vitamin D can be counteracted by eating plenty of salads and green vegetables.

Vitamin E (Tocopherol) is an anti-oxidant that stops the deterioration of body tissues. It is more of a protective vitamin because it slows down the ageing process, prevents blood clots, reduces the risk of cancer, opens smaller blood vessels and improves blood circulation to the nerves. It also improves the process of urination and helps the body fight off swollen feet.

Vitamin E is applied to muscular cramps. As an ointment, it is used to treat burns, cuts and skin problems.

Vitamin E is found in wheat germ (first extracted from wheat germ), nuts, soya beans, vegetable oil, green leafy vegetables like spinach, cereals, egg yolks and whole grains.

Vitamin E deficiency destroys the red blood cells. It also causes muscle degeneration and reproductive disorders. It should be used with caution on patients with high blood pressure since it improves the heart tone, thereby increasing the pressure further. Consumption of polyunsaturated fatty foods, use of oral contraceptives and mineral oils increase the requirements of vitamin E.

Vitamin K (Phylioquinone) aids in the vital task of blood clotting. It promotes the growth of the body and the healthy functioning of the liver.

Vitamin K is found in green leafy vegetables, liver, fish liver oil, cauliflowers, soya oil, yoghurt, kelp and cheese. Vitamin K deficiency causes haemorrhaging, nose bleeding, miscarriages, diarrhoea and poor absorption of food into the body. An intake of laxatives, antibiotics and cholesterol-reducing drugs increase the requirements of vitamin K.

Some health conscious people consume vitamin pills daily without doctor's advice. These people, although perhaps armed with a knowledge of the problems that arise due to vitamin deficiency, may not be aware of the dangers of taking them in excess. It is, therefore, worthwhile to outline some of the ill-effects of vitamin overdose:

- Vitamins A, D, E, and K are fat soluble and do not get excreted in the urine. If vitamins A and D are stored in excess, the kidney cannot be protected from its toxic effects.
- Vitamins A and D, if present in the body in excess, can cause liver damage, headaches at the back of the head (occipital headache) and easy fracture of bones.
- Vitamin D promotes the absorption of calcium, leading to the accumulation of the mineral in the blood. In excess, soft tissues can be formed and kidneys injured, resulting in constipation, general weakness, lethargy and anorexia nervosa.
- Even water soluble vitamins B and C are toxic when taken in excess. They can lead to a dependency state.
- A high intake of vitamin B complex can cause headaches, insomnia, irritability, nausea, and peptic ulcers due to the presence of nicotinic acid (vitamin B3).
- A high intake of vitamin C can causes acidosis. It can also interfere with the absorption of vitamin B12.

A normal, healthy person who has a balanced diet does not need vitamin supplements. If you are sick and have a restricted diet due to various problems or if you take antibiotics that deplete vitamins, then supplements may be needed. You should preferably consult a doctor first before deciding to pop vitamins into your mouth.

OTHER ESSENTIAL NUTRIENTS

Acidophilus is responsible for a healthy intestinal environment. It prevents the growth of disease-causing organisms and is useful in fermenting dairy products like yoghurt.

Beta Carotene is associated with vitamin A. Beta Carotene deficiency may increase the risk of cancer. It is not toxic. Although some people have a yellow tinge on their skin due to a high beta carotene intake, this is easily controlled by reducing the dosage. Bata Carotene is found in green leafy vegetables, green pepper and in orange-coloured vegetables like carrots and pumpkins.

Bioflavonoids work in conjunction with vitamin C, and are required to prevent colds, influenza and bruising. They strengthen the blood vessels.

A deficiency in this nutrient results in easy bruising, varicose veins and an increased susceptibility to infections. Bioflavonoids are found in small quantities in buckwheat, cherries, grapes and other fruit

Brewer's Yeast is highly nutritious, with significant amount of vitamins, minerals, carbohydrates, amino acids, as well as RNA and DNA. Brewer's yeast is rich in zinc and vitamin B2. It is used to control the blood sugar. When taken regularly, the nutrient help to combat arthritis, headaches and migraines.

Choline is required for fat metabolism. It is important for nerve functions, the thymus gland as well as for a healthy liver. Choline deficiency results in cirrhosis of the liver, hardening of the arteries and high blood pressure. Sugar, caffeine and alcohol, when taken in excess, can destroy it.

Choline is found in wheatgerm, nuts, soya beans, lecithin, brewer's yeast, meat and green leafy vegetables. Free choline is available only in food supplement form.

Coenzyme (Coq10) plays the role of a catalyst to create cellular energy. It is found in rice bran, wheatgerm, beans, nuts, fish, meat and eggs.

Essential Fatty Acids include linoleic acid, alpha linolenic acid, gamma linolenic acid and arachidonic acid. Essential fatty acids act as heat insulators in the body and regulate the cholesterol metabolism.

They are essential for maintain healthy cells and a healthy nervous system, as well as to help the body produce hormones, particularly prostglandin E1. The latter is needed to regulate vital functions of the body. Essential fatty acids are found in vegetable oil and fish oil.

Evening Primrose (Oenothera biennis) is rich in essential fatty acids, particularly gamma linolenic acid. It helps to regulate a faulty immune system, thereby preventing illnesses like asthma and hay fever.

It regulates nerve damages commonly found in diabetes. It prevents atopic eczema by raising the level of EFA (Essential Fatty Acid). It lowers the cholesterol level and also regulates the blood clotting process.

Pre-menstrual tension (PMT) is mainly due to the imbalance of the hormones, oestrogen and progesterone in the second half of the cycle. EFA in evening primrose is easily converted to prostglandins, thereby relieving PMT symptoms, such as tender breasts, fluid retention and irritability. It also gives relief to people suffering from multiple sclerosis and rheumatoid arthritis.

Lcarnitine is needed for building up energy in the body, and for stimulating the production of enzymes in the stomach and pancreas. It is found in meat, milk and brewer's yeast.

Lecithin is a natural emulsifier. It occurs together with cholesterol and helps to keep fats in suspension. It is, for instance, needed to transport elements required or produced by the cells from one place to another, as well as for metabolism. It is also necessary for the assimilation of vitamins A, D and K, and for the correct functioning of the glands. Lecithin is found in abundance in the heart, kidneys, brain, the endocrine glands, eggs and soya beans.

Lecithin is produced by the liver in the body. It is the source of two vitamins, choline and inositol. Ideally, it should be obtained from unrefined foods like cold pressed oil, whole wheat cereals, wheatgerm, nuts and liver. Soya lecithin in granular form is a rich source of polyunsaturated fatty acid and is a useful addition to the diet. Exercise will further increase the lecithin content of muscles.

11

Herbs, Health and Harmony
∝

More and more people are now beginning to understand the importance of including fruit, vegetables, and herbs in their diet. Some are even using natural products for medicinal purposes.

Active people who follow a proper diet are generally healthier and happier than those who do not follow one. Herbal treatment, for one, demands a healthy lifestyle. The effects of medicating with herbal medicines, however, are negated by excess junk food, alcohol and smoking.

Changing the diet by including organically-grown natural foods that provide nutrients guarantee health without any side effects. Taking up gentle exercises like Yogasanas develops the ability to concentrate on the body's total functioning while spending a few minutes on meditation gives you peace of mind.

Increasing the daily consumption of fruit and vegetables, especially in their raw form is good as more minerals and vitamins will be absorbed into the body. This will enable the body to defend itself against infections. Vegetables are good sources of minerals. Green vegetables, especially are rich in vitamin A while vegetables rich in chlorophyll are natural blood builders. "Sun ripened" fruit are good sources of vitamins and sodium.

When cooking vegetables, it is better to use stainless steel utensils with as little water as possible to preserve the nutrients in vegetables. Do not remove the peelings of vegetables that can be eaten. This is because most of the nutrients are present close to the skin of vegetables. Wash vegetables in salted water so that insecticide residue will be eliminated.

As most fruit nowadays are picked before they ripen, they are low in vitamins. Avoid fruit sprayed with sulphur dioxide as sulphur causes skin and bowel problems. Because of the processing, the sugar in dried fruit becomes concentrated. Before eating such fruit, soak them in cold water overnight to reduce the concentrated sugar content. To rid the fruit of insect eggs, soak dried fruit in boiling water for a few seconds.

Nuts are rich in protein (although most of them lack the essential amino acid — lysine), fat, fibre, some minerals and vitamins. They are also nutritious. Besides lysine, almonds and peanuts are deficient in methionine. Having nuts along with pulses, dairy products, grains and green vegetables is a complete protein diet.

Nuts are a rich source of vitamins apart from vitamin B12 and vitamin E, as well as minerals like calcium, magnesium, iron, zinc and phosphorus. Some nuts like cashew nuts increase the cholesterol level. They must therefore be consumed sparingly by those with a high cholesterol problem.

The seeds of fruit and vegetables have been used both as food and medicine since ancient times. They can be used to season food or be mixed with other foods for added flavour. Many edible seeds are rich in natural oils. Polyunsaturated oils obtained from edible seeds are better than hard animal fats, which are saturated. Cold pressed oils are better than those extracted chemically using preservatives and other additives.

Pulses are rich in vitamin C, vitamin B, iron, calcium and potassium. They are low in fat and are a source of fibre. Sprout pulses as they provide excellent nutrients.

Interest in herbs has been growing in the last few years due to their medicinal value and nutritional content. It is interesting to note that nearly 30 percent of all the known species of the plant kingdom have been used in traditional medicines for ages. So far, about 1,500 types of herbs are classified as good for health. Herbs can be used safely as part of the diet rather than as medicine in daily life. Specific herbs strengthen specific organs of the body. The duration of treatment varies according to the degree of the ailment.

This chapter includes some basic information about plants commonly used for medicinal purposes. Many herbs, such as baneberries, black bryony, buttercups, columbine, common buckthorn, ivies, meadow saffron, mistletoe leaves and yew are poisonous. Yet some other plants, which have limited use as medicine, are important in maintaining good health.

The danger of self-diagnosis and treatment cannot be overemphasised. When in doubt or if you experience discomfort, stop the treatment. Consult an expert in natural therapy immediately. Where possible, seek the advice of a doctor.

The healing qualities of plants and herbs have long been used in the Ayurvedic system and Chinese medicine. Modern western medicine also has its roots in the use of herbs. Until the development of chemical technology and chemotherapy, most medicines had herbal origins. The wonder "steroid drugs" are synthesised from a chemical extracted from the West African wild yam. Aspirin is made from meadowsweet and willow bark.

PRINCIPAL GROUPS OF ACTIVE CONSTITUENTS

- Alkaloids are chemically related to tropane and both affect the involuntary muscles of the body (e.g. the muscles of the eyes, etc.).
- Glycosides, of which cardiac glycosides increase the efficiency of heart muscles and are potent even in small doses. Anthraquinone glycosides, which are as not as toxic as cardiac glycosides, are found in plants and are used as laxatives. Thiocyanate glycosides found, for instance, in mustard irritate the skin but improve the circulation of blood. Phenolic glycosides are least toxic in this group. They are disinfectants and have anti-inflammatory and diuretic effects on the body.
- Saponins produce soapy lather with water. Their therapeutic value is expectorant in catarrh of the respiratory passage. Saponins break down red blood cells and are blood poisons. They are present in many plants of the Solanaceae family, such as horse chestnut.
- Bitters are the most beneficial food group. They promote digestion, as well as act as sedatives and tonics.
- Tannins are astringent, and promote rapid healing and formation of new tissues.
- Mucilages reduce irritations, fermentation and act as mild laxatives.

HERBAL PREPARATIONS

Collecting your own herbs ensures quality. Be careful to avoid plants contaminated with lead or sprayed with toxins.

All herbs taken internally should be grown organically. Care should be taken when drying them so that their medicinal properties in the volatile oil are not lost due to overexposure to heat and light.

In Ayurveda, there are many different types of herbal preparations. In addition to the standard infusions, decoctions and poultices, there are also herbal wines or tincture, jellies, ghee, pills and resin preparations.

Infusions and decoctions can be drunk either cold or hot. The general practice is to drink them hot to induce perspiration for the treatment of a fever or a cold. As diuretics, they are drunk cool.

Infusions can made from leaves, flowers, tender shoots, bark, roots, seeds or from the entire plant. Infuse either the fresh or dried parts of the herb. If the infusion is from the seeds, roots, or bark, use them either crushed or powdered for maximum benefit. Fresh herbs should be cut into small pieces.

Utensils used to make the infusion should be glassware, ceramic or earthenware.

Milk is sometimes used in place of water to make an infusion. However, exercise care as milk produces an allergic reaction in some people. Some herbs are sensitive to heat or contain highly volatile oils in which case cold infusions are recommended.

It is best to have an infusion unsweetened. If you must, add honey, brown cane sugar or liquorice for taste. A pinch of herb weighs approximately 2 grams, while a tablespoon of herb weighs 10 grams. Usually, 1 part dried herb is equivalent to 3 parts fresh herb.

HOT INFUSIONS

- The ratio of herbs to water is 1 : 8.
- To 1 teaspoon of dried herbs or 3 teaspoons of fresh herbs, add 1 cup (about 8 teaspoons) of boiling water. Cover the mixture with a lid and let it stand for about 3–5 minutes.
- Filter the solution and drink it hot.

Do not let the volatile oil escape. Do not use aluminium pots.

COLD INFUSIONS

- To 1 teaspoon of dried herbs or 3 teaspoons of fresh herbs, add 1 cup of clean cold water.
- Cover the mixture and let it stand overnight or at least for 8 hours.
- Filter the solution and drink it.

DOSAGE

Have one glass of infusion at a time. Unless otherwise stated, the specified quantities given in the text are for adults. For children, dilute the infusion according to their age. For children between the ages of one and three, add 3 parts water to 2 parts infusion. For children between the ages of three and five, add 2 parts water to 3 parts infusion. For those between the ages five and ten, add 1 part water to 4 parts infusion.

DECOCTIONS

Decoctions are stronger and preferred by most people. They are usually prepared using the woody or hard herbal parts. It is good to powder or crush the parts used. The ratio of herbs to water is usually 1 : 16.

- To 1 teaspoon of dried herbs or 3 teaspoons of fresh herbs, add 2 cups of water.
- Bring the mixture to boil over a low flame until the water reduces to a quarter of the original volume.
- Let it simmer for two minutes and then leave it aside for ten minutes.
- Strain the tea while it is hot.

If large quantities of decoctions are prepared, use a litre of water for every 60 grams of the dried herbs.

MILK DECOCTIONS

- To 1 part dried herbs or 3 parts fresh herbs, add 8 parts fresh milk and 16 parts water.
- Boil the mixture over a low flame until the liquid reduces to a quarter of the original volume.

DOSAGE

In general, have 2 tablespoons of the decoction with half a cup of water unless specified otherwise.

EXTRACT

The essence obtained by partial evaporation of an aqueous solution of any type of medicinal plant can be used instead of its decoction.

MACERATION

The solution obtained by steeping a plant in cold water or wine to extract its properties may also be used in treatment. This may take a few hours to a few weeks depending upon the herbs used.

Externally, herbs can be used as a compress, in a poultice or in the bath.

Among some of the treatments in which drugs are not used, the application of cold and heat treatment on the body is one of the most important. Careful application of common non-toxic agents can bring about relief. However, it should be remembered that not all ailments can be treated by home remedies. You should be discerning enough to know when to seek the help of a doctor.

APPLICATION

Hot application, alternating with cold, increases blood circulation. When cold water is applied to a region, the circulation of blood in that region increases significantly. Similarly by applying a hot towel, blood is drawn to the skin surface. This, in turn, gives greater energy to the muscles and stimulates the brain.

HOT APPLICATION

Hot application relieves internal congestion, lung congestion, pleurisy and inflammation of the feet.

COLD APPLICATION

A cold application relieves swelling and congestion, inflamed breasts, and appendicitis. When the head is hot and throbs, a hot foot bath and a cold towel on the head brings about relief.

FOMENTATION

A fomentation is a local application of a heated liquid using small towels. It is usually done on the skin surface.

HOT FOMENTATION

- To the chest and throat region as a means of relieving sore throats, tonsillitis, coughs, bronchitis and chest congestion.
- To the sides of the chest under the arms from the breast bone to the spine for relief from pleurisy.
- Across the small of the back for relief from problems related to the kidneys and lumbago.
- Applied moderately on the spine induces sleep.

- Applied alternately with cold fomentation over the abdomen stimulates digestion and movement of the bowels.

COLD FOMENTATION

- Over inflamed areas around the joints relieves pain due to sprains.
- Over the heart area relieves rapid heartbeat due to high fevers.
- Over the forehead relieves headaches.
- Over the abdomen relieves pain due to acute appendicitis.

Take the necessary measures to avoid catching a cold while doing either a hot or cold fomentation. Towel dry immediately after a cold fomentation. Heat must not be applied after a cold fomentation on the legs or on any area with poor blood vessels like varicose veins or acute swelling.

BATHS

Infuse 500 grams of herbs in 3–4 litres of boiling water. Let it stand for about 20 minutes unless stated otherwise. Add this infusion to a hot water bathtub. Soak in bath for 10–20 minutes. Repeat this once every three days.

ALTERNATE HOT AND COLD ARM BATHS

Immerse your arms alternately in hot water (note that the temperature of the hot water must not be too high and the temperature of the cold water must not be too low) for 5 minutes and then in cold for a minute for a maximum of 5 rounds. Finish always with the cold bath. Pat yourself dry with a towel after the baths. This helps clear infections in the arms.

ALTERNATE HOT AND COLD FOOT BATHS

This is very much the same as the arm baths. The difference is that the temperature of the hot water should be increased gradually each time to reach the best of comfort. Soak in hot water for 2 minutes and then in cold for 30 seconds for eight rounds. Always end with the cold water. This clears congestion in the upper part of the body as well as treats foot infections.

EMBROCATION

Sprinkle the affected region with the appropriate liquid and massage gently.

COMPRESS

Soak a towel in an infusion or decoction. Wring out the excess liquid, and apply the towel to the affected region. It can be hot or cold depending on the problem.

JUICE THERAPY

Raw fruit and vegetables are rich in vitamins, minerals and trace elements (required for metabolism). Some raw fruit and vegetables contain natural medicines, vegetable hormones and antibiotics. For example, string beans, cucumbers and onions contain insulin-like substances, while radishes, garlic, onions and tomatoes contain substances that act like antibiotics.

Specific juices are beneficial for specific conditions. The fruit and vegetable juice therapy (also known as the juice fasting therapy) is beneficial both as a treatment and as a preventive measure.

Although a juice fasting therapy is to be continued for a period of 30 days, it is not recommended for working people or students. This group of people are advised to go on the juice fasting therapy once a week followed by juice and milk the next day and then a balanced diet for the rest of the week. This process cleanses the system.

During raw juice therapy, the ability of the various organs of the body to eliminate toxins increases. Most ill health conditions are due to overacidity. However, by drinking the alkali-forming juices of fruit and vegetables, the body achieves an acid-alkali balance naturally. This increases the healing ability as uric and other inorganic acids are eliminated. At the same time, the natural sugars in fruit and vegetables provide strength.

NECESSARY PRECAUTIONS

All juices must be drunk fresh. Except for the seeds, almost the entire skin of fruit and vegetables can be used to make juices. If possible, use organically-grown fruit and vegetables than canned or frozen juices. If the juices are too sweet, they should be diluted with an equal amount of water.

Owing to their differing actions, fruit and vegetable juices should not be used at the same time or mixed. The following gives a list of juices that may be mixed together:

- Juices of sweet fruit (prunes, grapes) may be combined with the juices of sub-acid fruit (apples, plums, pears, peaches, apricots and cherries). Sweet fruit must not be mixed with acid fruit like oranges, lemons, grapefruit, strawberries and pineapples.
- Juices of sub-acid fruit can be combined with the juices of acid fruit.
- Juices of vegetable fruit like tomatoes and cucumbers can be combined with acidic fruit or green leafy vegetable juices, which are made from cabbages, celery, lettuce, spinach, parsley and watercress.
- Juices of green leafy vegetables can be combined with the juices of root vegetables (beetroot, carrots, onions, potatoes and radishes).

Where possible, try not to mix the juices. If the juice is not to your taste, add honey. The juices must be taken once every two to three hours. The quantity of juice taken on each occasion should be 250 millilitres. Juice therapy can be continued for up to 30 days at a stretch. Plenty of rest is recommended during the therapy.

At the start of the juice therapy, you may experience discomfort in the abdomen as well as the following problems: diarrhoea, loss of weight, headaches, fevers, sleeplessness and bad breath. This is common because of the large deposits of toxins in the body.

Many ailments can be treated with juice therapy, and it is important to select the right juices to treat specific ailments. For instance, the juices of carrots, cucumbers and cabbage are useful for asthma, arthritis and skin problems. Orange juice, however, either aggravates these problems or acts negatively on them.

JUICE THERAPY FOR SPECIFIC AILMENTS

Acidity: grapes, oranges, mosambi, carrots and spinach.

Acne: grapes, pears, plums, tomatoes, cucumbers, carrots, potatoes and spinach.

Allergies: apricots, grapes, carrots, beetroot and spinach.

Arteriosclerosis: grapefruit, pineapples, lemons, celery, carrots, lettuce and spinach.

Anaemia: apricots, prunes, strawberries, red grapes, beetroot, celery, carrots and spinach.

Arthritis: apricots, lemons, pineapples, peaches, carrots, radishes and celery.

Asthma: apricots, lemons, pineapples, peaches, tomatoes, carrots, onions and spinach.

Bladder Ailments: apples, apricots, lemons, cucumbers, carrots, celery, parsley and watercress.

Colds: lemons, oranges, grapefruit, pineapples, carrots, onions, celery and spinach.

Colitis: apples, apricots, pears, peaches, pineapples, papayas, carrots, beetroot, cucumbers and spinach.

Constipation: apples, pears, grapes, lemons, carrots, onions, celery and spinach.

Diabetes: citrus fruit, carrots, celery, lettuce, spinach and bitter gourd.

Diarrhoea: papayas, lemons, pineapples, carrots and celery.

Eczema: red grapes, carrots, spinach, cucumbers and beetroot.

Epilepsy: red grapes, figs, carrots, celery and spinach.

Eye Disorders: apricots, tomatoes, carrots, celery, parsley and spinach.

Gout: red sour cherries, pineapples, tomatoes, cucumbers, beetroot, carrots, celery and spinach.

Halitosis: apples, grapefruit, lemons, pineapples, tomatoes, carrots, celery and spinach.

Headache: grapes, lemons, carrots, lettuce and spinach.

Heart Disease: red grapes, lemons, cucumbers, carrots, beetroot and spinach.

High Blood Pressure: grapes, oranges, cucumbers, carrots and beetroot.

Influenza: apricots, oranges, lemons, grapefruit, pineapples, carrots, onions and spinach.

Insomnia: apples, grapes, lemons, lettuce, carrots and celery.

Jaundice: lemons, grapefruit, pears, carrots, celery, spinach, beetroot and cucumbers.

Kidney Disorder: apples, oranges, lemons, cucumbers, carrots, celery, parsley and beetroot.

Liver Ailments: lemons, papayas, grapes, carrots, tomatoes, beetroot and cucumbers.

Menstrual Disorders: grapes, prunes, cherries, spinach, lettuce, turnips and beetroot.

Neuritis: oranges, pineapples, apples, carrots and beetroot.

Obesity: lemons, grapefruit, oranges, cherries, pineapples, papayas, tomatoes, beetroot, cabbages, lettuce, spinach and carrots.

Piles: lemons, oranges, papayas, pineapples, carrots, spinach and turnips.

Prostate Problems: carrots, asparagus, lettuce and spinach.

Rheumatism: grapes, oranges, lemons, grapefruit, tomatoes, cucumbers, beetroot, carrots and spinach.

Stomach Ulcers: apricots, grapes, cabbages and carrots.

Sinus Trouble: apricots, lemons, tomatoes, carrots, onions and radishes.

Sore Throat: apricots, grapes, lemons, pineapples, prunes, tomatoes, carrots and parsley.

Tonsillitis: apricots, lemons, oranges, grapefruit, pineapples, carrots, spinach and radishes.

Varicose Veins: grapes, oranges, plums, tomatoes, beetroot, carrots and watercress.

ACTION OF HERBS

Abortifacient induces premature expulsion of a foetus.

Examples: celery, cotton roots, horseradish, mistletoe leaves, papayas, pineapples, pennyroyal and shepherd's purse.

Acrid causes hot sensation and irritation to the skin.

Examples: milky juice of the stems and leaves of the fig plant, and the fresh roots of turnip.

Adjuvant aids in the effects of the main ingredients of herbs when mixed with them.

Examples: allspice, almonds, caraway, cardamoms, cayenne, cloves flower buds, coriander, figs, ginger, juniper, peppermint leaves and spearmint leaves.

Alteratives restore health by improving the nutritional level of the body.

Alteratives (Cooling) are good for Pitta (fire).

Examples: alfalfa, aloe, burdock, coriander, chrysanthemum, dandelions, echinacea, goldenseal, neem, pomegranates, jasmine, rose flowers, sandalwood and sarsaparilla roots.

Alteratives (Warming) are good for Vata (air).

Examples: barberries, bayberries, black pepper, cayenne, cinnamon, garlic, myrrh and turmeric.

Analgesic/Anodyne lessens or relieves pain in the body.

Examples: allspice, asafoetida powder, chamomile flowers (both Roman and German), cinnamon, clove flower buds, comfrey roots and leaves, ginger, piper longum, hops, juniper, lettuce, myrrh, peppermint leaves, saffron, and St. John's wort dried herb and leaves.

Anthelmintic/Vermicide/Vermifuge destroys or expels intestinal worms.

Examples: aloe gel, asafoetida, barberries, black pepper, carrot roots and seeds, cayenne, clove flower buds, cucumber seeds, elecampane roots, garlic, goldenseal, mulberry bark, neem, onions, papayas, pennyroyal, piper longum, plums, pomegranates, pumpkin seeds, tamarind, and thyme.

Antibilious removes excess bile and aids biliary and jaundice conditions.

Examples: barberries, dandelions and goldenseal roots.

Antibiotics prevent the growth of or destroys bacteria.

Examples: clove flower buds, garlic, honey, horseradish and turmeric.

Anticancerous prevents cancerous growths.

Examples: agrimony dried herbs, comfrey rootstock, carrots, drumstick leaves, ground ivy and loofa.

Anticatarrhal helps remove excess catarrh from the nose and other areas.

Examples: cayenne, elecampane, garlic, goldenseal roots, ground ivy leaves, hyssop herbs, marshmallow roots and leaves, okra, peppermint leaves, thyme leaves and flowering top and yarrow herbs.

Antidepressant helps relieve depression.

Examples: evening primrose plant, oats, lavender flowers, lemon balm and rosemary leaves.

Antidiarrhoeal helps prevent diarrhoea.

Examples: apples (peeled), blackberries, comfrey rootstock, ginger, lotus seeds, nutmeg, poppy seeds and raspberries (Yoghurt is also an antidiarrhoeal).

Anti-emetic helps relieve vomiting and nausea.

Examples: asparagus seeds, barberry root bark, cayenne fruit and leaves, clove flower buds, dill, fennel, ginger, lavender, lemon balm, neem, peach leaves, as well as raspberry fruit and leaves.

Antifungal prevents fungal growth.

Examples: Marigold petals, garlic, turmeric and neem.

Anti-inflammatory eases inflammations.

Examples: borage leaves, chamomile flowers (German), honey, lady's mantle leaves, liquorice roots, marigold petals, St. John's wort leaves and turmeric.

Anti-irritant soothes skin irritation.

Examples: evening primrose plant and thyme.

Antilithic reduces stone formation in the kidneys and gall bladder.

Examples: barberries, beans, carrot seeds, corn silk, cucumbers, ground ivy and plums.

Antimicrobial resists the formation of pathogenic microorganisms.

Examples: barberries, caraway, cayenne, clove flower buds, coriander, elecampane, eucalyptus, garlic, guavas, juniper, marigolds, marjoram, olive, peppermint, rosemary and thyme.

Antiperiodic counteracts intermittent diseases like malaria.

> Examples: angelica roots and leaves, eucalyptus and goldenseal.

Antipyretic/Febrifuge reduces fever.

> Examples: alfalfa, angelica roots and leaves, barberries, barley, basil, black pepper, borage, burdock, cayenne, chrysanthemums, red currants, eucalyptus, garlic, hops, lady's mantle, marigolds, neem, okra, olives, peppermint, raspberries and thyme.

Antirheumatic prevents rheumatism.

> Examples: apple peel, asparagus shoots, celery seeds, black currants, dandelions, fenugreek, juniper and sarsaparilla.

Antiseptic destroys microbes.

> Examples: ajowan, asafoetida powder, basil, bilberry leaves, chamomile flowers, cayenne, clove flower buds, eucalyptus, garlic, goldenseal, honey, hops, horseradish, juniper, marjoram, myrrh, neem, nutmeg, olive leaves, onions, peppermint, rosemary leaves, sandalwood and yarrow.

Antispasmodic prevents spasms.

> Examples: ajowan, angelica, aniseed, sweet fennel and caraway seeds, asafoetida powder, basil, calamus roots, caraway, chamomile flowers (both types), coriander, chrysanthemums, dill, eucalyptus, fennel, garlic, grapefruit, hawthorn fruit and leaves, hyssop, jasmine, lavender, lemon balm, lettuce, lily of the valley, liquorice, marjoram, mistletoe leaves, myrrh, nutmeg, oats, onions, okra, peppermint, parsley, radishes, rosemary leaves, saffron, sandalwood, sarsaparilla roots, spearmint, St. John's wort, and thyme.

Antitoxic is an antidote for poison.

> Examples: dandelion plant, cinnamon, cumin, garlic and grapefruit.

Antitumour prevents the growth of tumours.

> Examples: garlic and mistletoe twigs.

Antitussive/Bechic relieves coughs.

> Examples: elecampane, ginger and thyme.

Antiviral prevents viruses.

> Examples: clove flower buds, evening primrose, eucalyptus, garlic, limes, marjoram, onions and peppermint.

Aperient is a gentle purgative, which helps in the evacuation of the bowels.

> Examples: asparagus shoots, borage, cucumbers, dandelion plant, as well as rose flowers and hips.

Aphrodisiac increases sexual desire.

> Examples: clove flower buds, fenugreek, gooseberries, jasmine, nutmeg, piper longum, saffron and winter cherries.

Appetiser stimulates the appetite.

> Examples: ajowan, alfalfa, angelica roots and leaves, anise, basil, black pepper, caraway, cardamoms, cayenne, celery plant, chicory, coriander, cumin, fennel, figs, ginger, gooseberries, ground ivy, hops, malt, peppermint, mustard, parsley, plums, saffron, strawberries, and tomatoes.

Astringent causes contraction of tissues.

> Examples: agrimony dried herbs, amaranth, avocado leaves, bananas (unripe), betel leaves, bilberry leaves, blackberry leaves, caraway, celery, celery seeds, chicory, cinnamon bark, comfrey roots, elecampane, evening primrose plant, gooseberries, grapefruit, ground ivy, guava, hops, horse chestnut, lady's mantle, lemons, marigolds, myrrh, nutmeg, olive leaves, pomegranates, radishes, raspberry fruit and leaves, rose flowers and hips, rosemary, spinach, St. John's wort, thyme, winter cherries, and yarrow.

Bitter reduces toxins and fats, as well as stimulates the appetite for Pitta conditions.

> Examples: aloe, barberries, calamus, chamomile flowers (Roman), goldenseal, hops, loofa and neem.

Calmative produces a mild tranquillising effect.

> Examples: Chamomile flowers (German), dill, hops, jasmine, lemon balm leaves or herbs and marjoram.

Cardiac stimulates the heart.

> Examples: bananas, cayenne, black currant leaves, hawthorn fruit and leaves, lily of the valley, mistletoe leafy twigs, raspberry fruit and leaves, and tomatoes.

Carminative relieves flatulence.

> Examples: Ajowan, allspice, angelica roots and leaves, star anise, aniseed, asafoetida powder, basil, bay leaves, betel leaves, black pepper, caraway, cardamoms, carrot roots and seeds, cayenne, celery seeds, chamomile flowers (both types), cinnamon, clove flower buds, coriander, cumin, dill, fennel, fenugreek, garlic, ginger, horseradish, hyssop, juniper, lavender, lemon balm, marjoram, mustard, nutmeg seeds, onions, orange peel, bitter oranges, parsley plant, peppermint, piper longum, rose flowers, saffron, sandalwood, sarsaparilla roots, spearmint, thyme, and turmeric.

Cathartic is a purgative.

> Examples: aloe and mulberry bark.

Cholagogue stimulates the secretion of bile.

> Examples: agrimony dried herbs, apples, barberries, chamomile flowers (both types), chicory, dandelion plant, elecampane roots, garlic, goldenseal, olive oil, peppermint, marigold petals, radishes, rosemary leaves and turmeric.

Decongestive relieves mucous.

> Examples: calamus, camphor, eucalyptus and spearmint.

Demulcent soothes the mucous membrane.

> Examples: barley, chamomile flowers (German), calamus, comfrey roots, corn silk, cucumbers, fenugreek, figs, liquorice, marshmallow, oatmeal, okra, olive oil, leaves of peaches and sesame seeds.

Depurative detoxifies the blood.

> Examples: coriander, black or red grapes, grapefruit and sarsaparilla.

Diaphoretic promotes perspiration.

> Examples: ajowan, angelica, asparagus, basil, bayberries, borage, burdock, cardamoms, cayenne, chamomile flowers (German), chrysanthemums, cinnamon, coriander, black currants, elecampane, eucalyptus, fennel, garlic, ginger, hyssop, juniper, lemon balm, marjoram, peppermint, pennyroyal, safflower, sarsaparilla, tamarind, thyme and yarrow.

Digestive aids digestion.

> Examples: ajowan, allspice, angelica roots and leaves, anise, apples, asafoetida, basil, barberries, beetroot, black pepper, caraway, cayenne, chamomile flowers (both types), chicory, cinnamon, clove flower buds, coriander, dandelions, dill, fennel, fenugreek, roasted garlic, ginger, grapefruit, grapes, ground ivy, horseradish, juniper, lemons, lemon balm, mangoes, mustard, nutmeg, roasted onions, papayas, parsley, pears, peppermint, pineapples, red dates, rosemary, sage, starfruit, and strawberries.

Diuretic aids in the flow of urine.

> Examples: dried herbs of agrimony, alfalfa, angelica seeds, asparagus shoots, barley kidney beans' pods, beetroot, borage, burdock, carrot roots and seeds, celery plant, cinnamon, coffee, coriander, corn silk, cucumbers, black currants, dandelion plant, dill, elecampane roots, fennel, fenugreek, garlic, hawthorn, hops, horseradish, Indian corn, juniper, lady's mantle, lily of the valley, onions, parsley plant, leaves of peaches, pumpkin seeds, radishes, safflower, sarsaparilla roots, shepherd's purse, spearmint, turmeric, and yarrow.

Emetic induces vomiting.

> Examples: calamus and chamomile flowers.

Emmenagogue induces menstruation and stimulates the reproductive system.

> Examples: aloe gel, caraway, celery plant, chamomile flowers (both types), chrysanthemums, fenugreek, ginger, hibiscus, jasmine, juniper, lady's mantle, lemon balm, limes, marigolds, marjoram, myrrh, parsley plant, peppermint, raspberries, rose petals, rosemary leaves, saffron, shepherd's purse, tamarind, thyme and yarrow.

Emollient softens the skin. While demulcent acts internally, this acts externally.

> Examples: almond sweet oil, aloe, avocados, comfrey roots, elecampane, liquorice, fenugreek, figs, marshmallow, okra leaves, olive oil, rose petals and sesame seeds.

Expectorant removes mucous, especially from the respiratory system.

> Examples: angelica roots, aniseed, apricots, asafoetida powder, black pepper, calamus, camphor, caraway, cardamoms, cayenne, cinnamon, clove flower buds, comfrey roots, elecampane roots, eucalyptus, fennel, fenugreek, garlic, ginger, goldenseal, ground ivy, hyssop, lettuce, liquorice, marjoram, mustard, myrrh, onions, parsley plant, eaves of peaches, saffron, St. John's wort, thyme and turnips.

Flatulogenic produces a lot of gas.

> Examples: apples, apricots, bananas, beans, bran, broccoli, brussels sprouts, cabbages, carbonated beverages, carrots, cauliflowers, celery, citrus fruit, coffee, cucumbers, eggplants, raw and leafy vegetables, lettuce, onions, pears, green pepper, potatoes, prunes, radishes, raisins, soya beans, sweet pumpkins, tomatoes, and wheat products.

Galactagogue promotes milk production.

> Examples: aniseed, basil, borage, caraway seeds, cayenne, dill, eucalyptus, fennel, fenugreek, marigolds, peppermint, raspberries and thyme.

Germicide destroys germs.

> Example: ajowan.

Hallucinogenic causes delusion when used in excess.

> Example: nutmeg seeds.

Haemostatic stops bleeding in any part of the body.

> Examples: agrimony, alfalfa, cayenne, comfrey rootstock, goldenseal, gooseberries, hibiscus, jasmine, marshmallow, mullein, pomegranates, saffron, sandalwood, shepherd's purse, turmeric and yarrow.

Hepatic tones the liver.

> Examples: agrimony dried herbs, aloe, apples, asafoetida, asparagus, lemon balm, barberry root bark , carrot seeds, celery, chamomile flowers (both types), dandelion roots, elecampane, fennel, goldenseal, horseradish, hyssop and yarrow.

Hypocholesterolaemic reduces cholesterol in the blood.

> Examples: garlic and onions.

Hypoglycaemic lowers the blood sugar.

> Examples: bitter gourd, eucalyptus, garlic and onions.

Hypotensive lowers blood pressure.

> Examples: asafoetida, bitter gourd, curry leaves, elecampane, garlic, hawthorn berries, mistletoe twigs and yarrow leaves.

Irritants to the Skin

> Examples: cayenne, horseradish, juniper, mustard seeds and thyme.

Laxative promotes bowel movements.

Examples: apples, asafoetida powder, asparagus shoots, barberry roots or seeds, dandelions, fennel, figs, goldenseal, gooseberries, horseradish, lily of the valley, liquorice, peach leaves, plums, raspberry fruit and leaves, rose hips, black sesame seeds, tamarind, and turmeric.

Leucocytosis increases the production of white blood cells.

Examples: chamomile flowers (German) and garlic.

Lipolytic splits body fats.

Example: coriander.

Mucilage acts as a demulcent and as an emollient.

Examples: comfrey rootstock, fenugreek and marshmallow.

Nervine tones and strengthens the nerves.

Examples: asafoetida, basil, camphor, celery seeds, chamomile flowers (German), eucalyptus, fenugreek, garlic, hops, jasmine, lavender, lemon balm, lettuce, lime, mistletoe leaves, nutmeg, oats, pennyroyal, peppermint, rose flowers, rosemary, sandalwood, spearmint, St. John's wort, thyme, valerian and winter cherries.

Oxytoxic/Parturient contracts the uterine and aids childbirth.

Examples: goldenseal and jasmine.

Pectoral prevents respiratory and other chest diseases.

Examples: angelica roots and leaves, borage, comfrey rootstock, elecampane, garlic, goldenseal, ground ivy, hyssop, liquorice, and marshmallow.

Purgative

Examples: aloe and plums.

Refrigerant lowers body heat.

Examples; barberries, comfrey roots, red currants, lemons, raspberry fruit and leaves, and tamarind.

Rejuvenative revitalises the organs, prevents the decay of tissues and keeps premature ageing at bay.

Examples: aloe, calamus, gooseberries, myrrh, saffron, sesame seeds, and winter cherries.

Relaxants soothes and relaxes the tissues.

Examples: Comfrey, hops, marshmallow and oats.

Examples (relaxants for muscles): allspice and carrot seeds.

Restorative revives the body's function after an illness.

Examples: apples, fenugreek, limes and rosemary.

Rubefacient causes redness of the skin.

Examples; cayenne, clove flower buds, fennel, ginger, garlic, horseradish, juniper, lavender, marjoram, mustard, rosemary leaves and thyme.

Salicylates contain substances that are similar to aspirin.

Examples: alfalfa, almonds, aniseed, apples, apricots, asparagus, avocados, beetroot, brazil nuts, broad beans, broccoli, carrots, cayenne, cherries, chicory, chillies, cinnamon, coconuts, coffee, Indian corn, cucumbers, cumin, currants, dates, dill, eggplants, fenugreek, figs, grapefruit, grapes, guavas, honey, lemons, liquorice, musk melons, mustard, okra, olives, onions, oranges, peaches, peanuts, pear skin, peppermint, green pepper, pineapples, plums, potatoes, prunes, pumpkins, radishes, rosemary, sage, sesame seeds, spinach, squashes, tea, thyme, tomatoes, turmeric, walnuts, and watermelons.

Sedative reduces functional activity.

Examples: asafoetida powder, chamomile flowers (both types), celery seeds, hawthorn fruit and leaves, hops, hyssop, lettuce, nutmeg, olive leaves, peach leaves, saffron, sandalwood, St. John's wort, and winter cherries.

Sialogogue stimulates the secretion of saliva.

Examples: betel leaves, cardamoms, cayenne, red currants, ginger, lemons and tamarind.

Stimulant quickens the functioning of the organs.
The following is a list of stimulants and what they affect:

Asafoetida: the mucous membrane

Basil: the adrenal cortex

Black pepper: the nervous, circulatory and digestive systems

Cardamoms: the nerves

Carrots: the stomach and the eyes

Cayenne: the circulatory, nervous and respiratory systems

Celery seeds, jasmine, parsley, shepherd's purse and spearmint: the uterine

Chamomile (German): the production of leucocyte

Cinnamon: the circulatory, cardiac and respiratory systems

Coffee: the nervous system
Coriander: the cardiac, circulatory and nervous systems

Black currant leaves: the kidneys

Dandelions: the liver and gall bladder

Elecampane: the stomach

Evening primrose plant: the liver, spleen and the digestive system

Fennel seeds: the intestines and the circulatory system

Garlic: the liver, gall bladder and the digestive, respiratory and circulatory systems

Ginger: the digestive system and for blood circulation and cleansing

Goldenseal roots: the muscles

Grapefruit: the lymphatic and digestive systems

Lemons: white blood cells

Nutmeg: the stomach for the production of gastric juice

Oranges: the digestive and lymphatic systems

Palmarosa: the digestive and circulatory systems

Peach leaves: the bladder

Rosemary: the circulatory system, adrenal cortex and the liver

Thyme: the circulatory and immune systems

Stomachic tones the stomach.

Examples: angelica roots and leaves, aniseed, basil, chamomile flowers (both types), caraway seeds, cardamoms, cinnamon, clove flower buds, coriander, red currants, dandelion plant, dill, elecampane, fennel, garlic, gooseberries, horseradish, juniper, lemon balm, marjoram, onions, bitter oranges, papayas, peppermint, plums, rose flowers and hips, rosemary leaves, saffron, and spearmint.

Tonic nurtures the tissue elements and nourishes the mind and body.
The following is a list of tonics and what they affect:

Horse chestnut: the circulatory system

Hawthorn and lily of the valley: the heart

Elecampane and piper longum: Kapha

Almonds, angelica, coconuts, comfrey rootstock, dates, liquorice, marshmallow, myrrh, oat straw, onions, raisins and sesame seeds. Honey, milk, jaggery, yoghurt are also nutritive tonics: nutritive

Cardamoms and rosemary: the nerves

Comfrey roots and saffron: Pitta

Angelica, asafoetida, asparagus, clove flower buds, fenugreek, garlic, hibiscus, raw onions, rose flowers and saffron: the reproductive system

Aniseed: the stomach

Lemon balm or karpooravalli (anisochilus carnosus), parsley and rose: the uterine

Garlic: Vata

Tranquillisers have a calming effect.

Examples: olive leaves.

Vasoconstrictor narrows blood vessels.

Examples: coffee and peppermint.

Vasodilator widens blood vessels.

Examples: Barberries, as well as hawthorn fruit and leaves.

Vulnerary heals wounds or sores by external application.

Examples; agrimony dried herbs, aloe, chamomile flowers (both types), comfrey roots, cucumbers, elecampane, fenugreek, garlic, goldenseal, hyssop, lady's mantle, marigolds, marshmallow, oats, papayas, rosemary, shepherd's purse, St. John's wort, thyrne, turmeric and yarrow (honey is also a vulnerary).

Acidic Foods leave behind acidic salts, upsetting the ph value of the body.

Examples: asparagus, barley, beef, blackberries, blueberries, butter, cashew nuts, cereals, cheese, chestnuts, chicken, chocolates, cider, cocoa, cod liver oil, cow peas, cream, currants, eggs, refined flour, grapes, hazelnuts, honey, horseradish, huckleberries, millet, molasses, oats, fresh peaches, peanuts, pears, plums, pomegranates, pork, prunes, raspberries, rice, rye, sago, strawberries, sugar, tapioca, tomatoes, walnuts and wheat.

Alkaline Foods leave behind alkaline salts after the digestive process.

Examples: agar-agar, almonds, apples, apricots, bananas, beans, beetroot, bran, broccoli, brussels sprouts, buttermilk, cabbages, carrots, cauliflowers, celery, cherries, coconuts, Indian corn or corn silk, cranberries, cucumbers, dried currants, dandelions, dates, dill, eggplants, figs, garlic, grapefruit, guavas, herbs, leek, lemons, lentils, lettuce, mangoes, milk, mushrooms, mustard greens, okra, olives, onions, oranges, parsley, dried peaches, peas, pineapples, potatoes, pumpkins, peppermint, radishes, raisins, spinach, squashes, raw sugar, raw tomatoes, turnips, watercress and watermelons.

Gluten-rich Foods

Examples: wheat, oats, barley, rye and their products.

HERBS AND DOSAGE

Do not underestimate the potency of herbs. Do not take medication for long periods and never exceed the prescribed dosage. The following is a useful list of herbs to avoid or to consume with care:

Agrimony should not be used if you have constipation and are under tension.

Ajowan (Omum) should be avoided during pregnancy due to its high thymol content.

Alfalfa Leaves have a strong drying effect and should be taken with other nutrients.

Aloevera juice taken on its own tends to cause gripe (pain in the bowels) and constipation. Hence, take fruit juice with it. Avoid it during pregnancy as it can contract uterine muscles and also during breastfeeding as it is a powerful purgative. It also induces piles.

Angelica Roots should not be consumed by pregnant women or diabetics as they increase the sugar level in the urine.

Apples produce gas in the intestines when the bowels do not move easily. Do not overeat apple seeds as they are toxic. Do not mix them with protein either.

Apricots (dried) are rich in sugar, so do not overeat them. Diabetics, especially must be extra careful. The seeds are toxic, so do not mix them with food. Eat them on their own.

Arecanuts should not be eaten if the liver is sluggish or weak. It increases the production of saliva, vomiting, diuresis (increased discharge of urine) and stupor.

Asparagus should never be eaten raw. Use only its tender part. In excess, it irritates the kidneys. Asparagus should also not be eaten when the kidneys are inflamed.

Avocados should be eaten ripe without the skin.

Bananas should only be eaten when they are ripe, cooked or baked. They are not good for people with asthma, bronchitis and sinusitis.

Barberries are very heaty and should not be taken during pregnancy.

Black Beans (Urhad dhal) produce a lot of gas when consumed in excess. Mix them with fenugreek to counteract gas production. People suffering from skin problems, varicose veins and arthritis are advised not to consume black beans.

Beans String are not good for gout and arthritis. People with rheumatoid arthritis or rheumatism should avoid it completely.

Bitter Gourd should be avoided when the stomach is weak or does not function properly or when you feel nauseous.

Black Cherries are narcotic and can cause paralysis by affecting the nervous system.

Black Pepper should be avoided if you suffer from an eye disease, an inflamed digestive tract or a sore throat.

Blueberries/Bilberries should not be consumed over a long period as they can cause blood poisoning. Taking these herbs with meals induces coughs. Blueberries or bilberries are best taken two hours after meals. They should be mixed with salt, pepper and ginger for maximum benefit.

Borage can cause degeneration of the nervous system when taken in excess. It is not to be taken during pregnancy.

Bread (white), especially fresh bread, produces acid in the system. So, the best way to eat it is to toast it dry.

Brussels Sprouts produce a lot of gas.

Buttermilk should not be taken if you are an epileptic.

Cabbages produce gas. They also contain substances like isothiocyanates, which inhibit the thyroid and cause goitre.

Calamus Roots or Sweet Flag is considered toxic by the Food and Drug Administration (FDA). It should not be taken internally if you have a bleeding disorder like haemorrhoids.

Camphor acts like a narcotic poison when used in excess.

Cashew Nuts are rich in fats, uric acid and contribute to an increase in the cholesterol level. People who are overweight and have heart problems should avoid cashew nuts.

Castor Beans help prevent constipation, but in excess, they are bad for the stomach. They cause severe purging and vomiting, and contain a poisonous substance that is not good for the blood. Castor oil is safe as the poison remains in the seed.

Cauliflowers produce gas.

Cayenne irritates the mucous membrane and can cause dermatitis. It should be applied in a mild form as it is very hot. Excess consumption internally can cause gastroenteritis and kidney damage. It should not be used when you have ulcers, gastritis or if there is an inflammation in the digestive tract.

Celery is a strong diuretic. It should not be used if you have an acute kidney problem. Its high sodium content also spells trouble for people with high blood pressure. During pregnancy, celery must be taken in moderation. A high intake of celery in the late stages of pregnancy can cause premature expulsion of the foetus. To neutralise its effects, it is better to take celery in combination with apples and carrots.

Chestnuts should be eaten either roasted or boiled.

Chickpeas produce gas, which result in indigestion. Due to the high oxalic acid content, they form oxalates of lime in the bladder. Mixing them with black pepper or roasting them before use reduces the effects of the oxalic acid content.

Chikoo, especially the unripe ones, result in diarrhoea and weakness when taken in excess.

Chillies cause gastroenteritis and kidney problems when taken in excess.

Cinnamon should be avoided if you are suffering from common colds and coughs. Women with excess menstrual flow and pregnant women should avoid it. Blood in the urine and nose bleeding are also signs not to consume it. Do not take cinnamon if you have abdominal pain associated with dry lips, thirst, a sore throat, vomiting of blood, fever, ulcers, discharge of dry stools, voice loss and haemorrhoids.

Clove Flower Buds aggravate inflammatory conditions and hypertension.

Coconuts, when consumed in excess (particularly the white milky extract) are not beneficial as they increase the cholesterol level.

Coffee is not good for ulcers and in excess, causes insomnia.

Coriander should not be taken if you have cracked lips, suffer from constipation and are constantly thirsty.

Cow Peas, when consumed in excess, cause constipation. Dry fry the cowpeas before eating them.

Cucumbers, when consumed in excess, cause rheumatism. Unripe cucumber causes coughs.

Dates are not to be mixed with fruit like lemon, oranges, grapefruits and watermelons.

Fennel is not good for men who suffer from premature ejaculation. Fennel should not be taken if you have diarrhoea. In excess, fennel causes spasmodic contraction and delusion.

Fenugreek promotes vaginal bleeding and for pregnant women, it may result in an abortion.

Figs are difficult to digest and increase mucus unless used with milk. They should not be mixed with acidic fruit like tomatoes, grapefruit and oranges.

Garlic should be cooked or diluted for people with a weak constitution. People who develop certain allergic reactions to sulphur should not take it. It should not be placed on open wounds. It should also not be taken when there is any disease of the eyes or sore throat. Garlic produces wind. A high concentration of garlic can lead to haemolysis. Garlic should not be mixed with mangoes as it can cause liver problems, itchy skin and jaundice. When consumed with natural brown sugar, it causes obesity.

Goat's Milk is easier to digest than cow's milk. Filter and boil the fresh milk before drinking it.

Gooseberries are best eaten in the form of pickles or jelly. Sweeten them with date sugar or honey first.

Goldenseal Roots are good as an antibiotic but only in moderation. Otherwise, they destroy the intestinal flora.

Grapefruit should not be mixed with sweet fruit.

Grapes are not good for diabetes when consumed in excess. Soak them in salt water for half an hour before eating them so as to rid the grapes of sprayed pesticides.

Ground Ivy, in excess, can be poisonous.

Guavas or ripened guavas should be eaten with a little salt for better results to the body.

Hops can be dangerous when consumed over long periods of time.

Horseradish, in excess, causes diarrhoea and night perspiration.

Juniper stimulates the kidney nephrons and in excess or after prolonged use, can irritate the kidneys and urinary tract. Juniper berries, when taken in excess, can destroy useful bacteria in the intestines. Women should avoid juniper during pregnancy.

Lettuce loses its medicinal value rapidly after picking. It produces gas.

Lima Beans' skin can irritate the intestines. Lima beans also increase heartbeat and thirst, as well as produce gas. Replace the water used in cooking or dry fry them before consuming the beans.

Lily of the Valley has glycosides, which act like digitalis. It can cause irregular heartbeat and upset the stomach when consumed in excess.

Mangoes, when eaten with onion or garlic, can cause itchy skin and jaundice. After eating a mango, drink a glass of milk so that the nutrients are absorbed properly by the body.

Melons (all types), when consumed on an empty stomach, produce excess bile, resulting in giddiness and fever. When melons are eaten before milk, diarrhoea results.

Mistletoe Berries, in excess, are poisonous and have an adverse effect on the heart.

Motherwort can cause dermatitis. Women should avoid it during pregnancy.

Mulberry Fruit that is unripe and produces a milky juice can cause hallucinations. Too much of this may result in death.

Mustard Greens , in excess, can be toxic. Frequent consumption inhibit the absorption of iodine and aggravate goitre.

Nutmeg, when added in small quantities to food, prevents abdominal spasms due to putrefaction. Nutmeg, in excess, can cause stomach aches and dullness. People with haemorrhoids and toothache should avoid it.

Oats should not be eaten too often. Because of the avenin content in oats, skin may erupt in pimples or rashes.

Onions are best taken with greens like parsley to counteract the effect of the sulphur produced by them in the intestines. Cooked onions produce more gas than raw onions.

Sweet Oranges that are unripe oranges can upset the stomach.

Papaya (raw) is an abortifacient and when eaten as a chutney, prevents pregnancy at an early stage. When applied to the mouth of the uterus, the juice of the raw papaya as a pessary induces abortion.

Parsley must not be taken when the kidneys are inflamed. However, when combined with marshmallow, it reduces its effect on the inflamed kidneys.

Peanuts/Groundnuts should be eaten dry, roasted or boiled with the skin.

Peas (dried) produce gas.

Pennyroyal induces abortion.

Pineapples should not be eaten during pregnancy as they result in abortion. They are not good for ulcers of the digestive tract. Pineapples cause phlegm and affects the voice box. Adding sugar and ginger powder to washed pineapples reduces these effects.

Plums (fresh) should not be eaten in excess as they can cause stomach cramps and diarrhoea.

Pomegranate juice, in excess, can cause stomach cramps and vomiting.

Potatoes lose most of their nutrients when they are peeled and soaked in cold water before cooking. They are best eaten with the skin.

Sweet Potatoes are very fibrous, ferment easily and cause flatulence (too much gas in the intestines).

Sweet pumpkins, especially the tender ones, cause rheumatism. They produce a lot of gas, a swelling feeling in the stomach and are difficult to digest. They are not good for people suffering from chronic constipation.

Prunes must be avoided by those with uric acid problems (gout, calculi or acidosis).

Raspberries should not be mixed with sugar. They can cause constipation.

Rosemary, when taken internally in excess, can cause poisoning.

Salt, in excess, increases blood pressure, causes heart problems and kidney disorders. As most vegetables have enough salt present in them, try not to add too much salt when cooking them.

Saffron contains poison that acts on the central nervous system. It damages the kidneys when taken in excess. Too much saffron acts as a narcotic and for pregnant women, a miscarriage may result.

Sesame Seeds of the black variety are the best for medicinal use. They, however, are difficult to digest and very heaty. For pregnant women, the seeds may terminate the pregnancy.

Soya Beans, in excess, can cause coughs and thirst. They are not good for jaundice and gout.

Spinach has oxalic acid and when taken in excess, affects the joints.

Strawberry seeds cause inflammation of the bowels.

Tomatoes, when eaten in excess, cause arthritis, rheumatism, piles, stones and heartburn. If you have arthritis, rheumatism or diarrhoea, avoid tomatoes altogether.

Thyme infusion, taken in excess internally, overstimulates the thyroid gland.

Turmeric is not good on dry skin as it dries it further. In excess, avoid using it as it is carcinogenic (likely to cause cancer). Do not use it during pregnancy or when you have jaundice.

Valerian, in excess after extended use, can cause poisoning. The infusion of valerian should not be taken more than 2 times a day and not more than 2 weeks at a stretch.

Wheat is an allergen. Many people develop allergic reactions to wheat. In excess, it can cause stomach disorders.

Yarrow should not be taken during pregnancy.

12

Physical Signs and Symptoms
&

Oriental diagnosis, in particular Chinese traditional methods of diagnosis, and Ayurveda are studies of biological changes. In allopathy, diagnosis is the classification of symptoms that can be seen. In homeopathy, on the other hand, it is based on the totality of symptoms and causes. In some diseases, symptoms appear late in the course of the illness and are therefore called "silent diseases".

The four most commonly used forms of oriental diagnosis are based on the following:

- Observation of the skin, posture, colour, eyes and habits
- Listening to the sound, such as the tone, pitch and tempo of the voice
- The art of touch, such as the skin, pulse and the use of diagnostic points and meridians
- Analytical questioning

In oriental medicine, proper diet is the principal source of health and vitality.

A difficult but important aspect of preventive care is to be well-informed of the sensible and limited use of medicine. Some medicines are important and can save lives, but if you take the necessary steps to prevent sickness, the need for medication is altogether done away with.

Health is the well-being of the mind and body. We interpret causes of sickness according to our own experiences and points of view. To prevent any sickness or to treat it successfully, we must fully understand its causes and symptoms.

INFECTIOUS DISEASES

BY BACTERIA MICROBES OR GERMS

In tuberculosis, the germs commonly known as tubercle bacilli enter the body by air. Droplets of water coughed out by an infected person may also harm the people next to him or her.

Tetanus wounds spread through dirty wounds and contact with rusty objects, metallic instruments and so on. Some types of diarrhoea spread through water, while some kinds of pneumonia spread through air.

Gonorrhoea and other sexual diseases spread through sexual intercourse. Sores with pus spread through direct contact. Earaches spread with colds.

For the above diseases, antibiotics is the principle medicine used.

BY VIRUSES

Colds, influenza, measles, mumps, chicken pox, infantile paralysis and virus diarrhoea spread through air, insects or from a sick person. Rabies spreads from animal bites, while warts spread by direct contact.

There is no medicine on the market that effectively fights the above viruses. Antibiotics, for instance, are ineffective. Vaccination, on the other hand, prevents only some diseases like measles.

BY FUNGI

For example, ringworm and athlete's foot, which are spread through contact.

BY INTERNAL PARASITES

Diseases caused by internal parasites in the intestines, such as worms or amoebae spread due to a lack of cleanliness. Parasites in the blood, such as in malaria, spread through mosquito bites.

BY EXTERNAL PARASITES

Diseases caused by external parasites like lice, fleas, bedbugs and scabies spread through contact.

NON-INFECTIOUS DISEASES

Non-infectious diseases, as the name suggests, do not spread from one person to another. They have many different causes. Antibiotics or medicines that fight germs do not cure non-infectious diseases.

Non-infectious diseases are caused by:

- The wearing out of something within the body. Examples include rheumatism, heart attack, epileptic fits, stroke, migraines, cataract and cancer
- External factors. Examples include allergies, asthma, poisoning and stomach ulcers
- Lack of something essential to the body. Examples include malnutrition, pellagra, anaemia, goitre and cirrhosis
- Mental illnesses. Examples include anxiety, depression and fear

To help the body overcome an illness, often all that is needed is to keep clean, get good rest and have nutritious food. Use medicine only when it is absolutely necessary after a consultation with a doctor.

In this chapter some of the common causes of diseases and their symptoms are given. It is beyond the scope of this book to give all the possible causes, so the most common ones are given. The purpose is to give a clue as to why a person has certain symptoms. They are, however, not intended as diagnostic measures.

Let a specialist in the field examine you, decide on the problem and prescribe the medicine. Information on the causes and symptoms of illnesses is oftentimes a grey area. A given symptom may mean one thing in one person's case but something altogether different in another person's case. Special examinations and laboratory tests help diagnose a disease more accurately.

Although some sicknesses may seem very much alike, they have different causes and, therefore, requirement different treatments. The history and a careful examination are necessary before treating. Signs and symptoms help a great deal in diagnosing the sickness, but they are not complete in themselves. By knowing certain symptoms, we get an idea of the possible causes. The possible cause can, to a certain extent, be studied by looking at the external appearance of a patient.

THE SKIN

Colour and texture play an important role in determining a person's health. The following is a useful list:

- Skin that is bluish or purplish in colour may indicate carbon dioxide poisoning, pneumonia, lung disease, heart failure or an excess of red blood cells with an insufficient supply of oxygen.
- Skin with a bronze pigmentation may indicate a high absorption of iron.
- Skin that is brownish in colour indicates poor absorption of food.
- Skin with an unnatural brown colour shows liver and gall bladder disorders.
- Skin that is moist and greyish-white in colour indicates that the person may be suffering from shock.
- Skin that is greyish in colour may indicate a swollen liver.
- Skin that is orangey-yellow in colour may be a result of overeating carrots.
- Skin with a patchy pigmentation may be a result of leucoderma.
- Skin that is wet and prone to constant perspiration may indicate overburdened kidneys and a heavy heart (difficulty in pumping blood).
- A chalky white complexion indicates that the person is suffering from lung problems.
- A greenish colour on the face may indicate cancer of the lungs.
- A greenish colour on the back of the hands and between the fingers may indicate cancer of the intestines.
- Other than normal skin colour or skin that is tanned by the sun, if skin appears dark with black freckles all over the body, this may be due to diseased adrenal glands.
- Pale skin may be a result of anaemia, heart and lung

diseases, poor blood circulation, cancer or tuberculosis.
- Paleness of the lips and the insides of eyelids indicate anaemia.
- An unnatural reddish colour on the face is caused by the dilation of the capillaries during fever, intoxication, emotional anger, sunburn or heart disease.
- An unnatural reddish colour on the skin indicates that the heart is overworking.
- Yellowness of the skin may indicate a problem with the pancreas, liver or gall bladder. The person may most probably be suffering from jaundice.
- Yellow skin and eyes may indicate liver problems.
- Spotty pigmentation appears naturally during pregnancy.
- Oily skin results from overeating.
- A rough skin texture may indicate an excess of animal fat.

Itching (and dryness) is common in the later part of pregnancy.

- It can be due to an allergy or the presence of irritants (chemicals that come into contact with the skin and tissues and irritate them). Liver damage, diabetes, anxiety, kidney disorders, lack of cleanliness, infections and pinworm are other causes.

Rashes appear in various forms, but the most common are the following:

- Chicken pox are small pinkish spots. They first appear on the trunk and spread to the face, neck and limbs. They enlarge into bulbs with serous fluid at the apex. New spots keep appearing for ten days. It is infectious.
- German measles start off as patches of rashes and soon become discoloured pink or red spots just below the skin. They appear first on the face and then spread to the limbs and trunk.
- Measles are pink spots that appear on the skin usually after two days of fever with symptoms of a cold. These spots become red and brown within two weeks, after which the skin scales off. They appear first on the neck, face and chest. Later, they spread to all parts of the body.

Red or pale skin patches that are itchy may appear due to:

- Allergy to certain foods like shellfish, nuts, berries and eggs. They appear within 12 hours after eating the aforesaid foods.
- Taking medication containing protein when you are sensitive to protein.
- Allergy to silk, wool, poison oak, ivy or certain animals
- Bites by insects like lice or bugs.
- An imbalance in hormone production as for instance during menstruation.

THE FACE

- A wide square jaw with a small crown may indicate that the person is aggressive or active.
- Swelling of the face may indicate inflammation of the sinus. The person is prone to heart attacks.
- A swollen, running nose that looks soft may indicate an enlarged heart.
- Vertical lines between the eyes indicate liver or gall bladder problems.
- A weak jaw and a wide crown indicate the characteristics of a thoughtful, inactive person.

BREATHING

- Wheezing or a whistling sound while breathing may mean asthma.
- A crackling noise while breathing may indicate the presence of fluid in the airsacs.
- Absence of breath sound may indicate an accumulation of fluids in the pleura.

MOUTH

- The mouth shows the condition of the stomach and intestines.
- Cracks and sores on the lower lip may indicate ulcerated colon and intestines.

- Bluish or dark lips and fingernails may indicate a problem with breathing or the heart.
- Cracked lips, redness at the corners of the mouth or nose may indicate an inflammation of or excess acids in the digestive system.
- Inflammation of the mouth may appear as a symptom of certain blood diseases like leukaemia or skin disease, syphilis or dental problems. It may be due to deficiency in vitamins B and C.
- A sore mouth and ulcerated lips can be caused by germs and local irritants. They indicate deficiency in folic acid.
- Puffy and tender gums with bleeding may indicate a lack of vitamin C.
- Red, inflamed gums indicate a deficiency in vitamins and minerals and the presence of excess acids.

THE TONGUE

The tongue is a reliable indicator of the digestive system. It also indicates the state of the other systems. A normal tongue has an even red colour and is not shiny. Below is a list of tongue conditions that are not considered normal:

- A pale tongue may indicate weakness, anaemia and fluid retention.
- A deep red tongue may indicate an inflammatory condition or niacin deficiency.
- A red and smooth tongue may indicate vitamin B deficiency.
- A purple tongue may indicate vitamin B2 deficiency.
- A layer of white coating on the tongue can be due to bacteria thriving on it, which in turn is the result of an excess of putrefactive bacteria growing in the intestines. This may indicate an excess alkaline condition, poor digestion and internal congestion both in the digestive tract and the lungs.
- A heavy coating on the tongue is found in users of alcohol or in people suffering from high fever or dehydration.
- A yellow coating on the tongue may indicate excess acidity, toxicity or inflammation.
- A trembling tongue may indicate a nerve problem.

- A stiff and rigid tongue may indicate that the person is under tension.
- Tooth marks on the edges of the tongue observed after sleep may indicate water retention and low energy.

EYES

- If the eyes protrude in a short period of time, this may indicate a disease of the thyroid or toxic goitre.
- If the pupils are of different sizes, injury to the skull resulting in a blood clot is suspected.
- Spots blotting in any eye may indicate an early stage of cataract.
- Sparks in the field of vision may indicate a possible detachment of the retina.
- A greenish or yellowish eye may indicate a problem of the liver or spleen.
- If the pupils are small and they hurt, you could be suffering from iritis. This is a serious eye infection.
- If the pupils are large and they hurt, causing you to vomit, you could be suffering from glaucoma.
- If the eyes are red, this could be due to a heart problem.
- Swelling and dark coloration of the region directly below the eyes indicate weak kidneys.
- A burning sensation in the eyes can result because of a polluted environment or conjunctivitis.
- Deposits — fatty yellow accumulation containing cholesterol — can often be seen in the skin around the eyes. They disappear after a change in the diet.

EYELIDS

- Puffiness can be due to kidney problems, hay fever or allergy.
- Itching in the eyelids can be due to hay fever.
- Drooping of the eyelids can be due to congenital defects. If this happens to only one eyelid, the probable cause is a damaged nerve.

EARS

- The ears represent the circulatory, digestive and nervous systems. The rim of the pinna (the visible portion of the ear that projects from the head) represents the circulatory system, the middle portion represents the nervous system and the inner part of the pinna the digestive system. A slight touch results in pain in these areas due to problems in the corresponding circulatory, digestive and nervous systems.
- Ringing in the ears is caused by infections, the use of certain drugs like quinine or salicylate, excess smoking, drinking or in certain cases heart ailments.

Besides external appearances, examining the stools, urine, lymph nodes and pulse will help to identify possible causes of certain problems.

STOOLS

- Normal stools, not loose or hard but which float (move easily), indicate a healthy diet.
- Loose stools indicate indigestion or poor assimilation of food.
- Light or chalky stools indicate the improper production of bile due to stones in the gall bladder or a high cholesterol intake.

URINE

- Discharge of urine despite efforts to hold during coughing, sneezing or laughing may indicate enlarged prostate glands in men, and in women it could be due to torn muscles, possibly during delivery.
- It can also be due to a tumour in the spinal cord.

LYMPH NODES

- These protective nodes fight germs and toxins in our body. When an infection develops, they will be inflamed and enlarged. They will also be tender and painful to the touch.

- Scalp infection results in an enlargement of the lymph nodes at the back of the neck.
- Eye, ear, tooth, mouth and throat infections enlarge the nodes beneath the jaw.
- Infections on the hands or breasts tenderise the nodes below the armpit.
- Infections on the legs, thighs and genitals activate the nodes at the groin.
- When infections result from diseases like measles, all the nodes in the body are affected.
- If the lymph nodes are situated on the path of a cancerous region, their drainage can spread cancer to other regions of the body.

PULSE

The normal frequency of the pulse beat is 4–5 beats per respiration. This is about 70–75 beats per minute. For an athlete, the heart beat per minute may be slower, for a woman slightly fast and for a child, the fastest of the three.

In using the pulse for diagnosis, the regularity and rate at which it varies contribute to the amplitude. The noises, if any, are recorded.

The pulse acts as a mirror, indicating the illnesses and disharmony in the body. Feeling the pulse at different locations of the body indicates the specific conditions of an individual.

- When checking the pulse, place three fingers on the wrist. The pulse closest to the thumb indicates the condition of the heart and lungs. The pulse on the second finger indicates the state of the stomach, spleen and liver. The pulse on the third finger indicates the condition of the bladder, kidney and colon.
- If you feel the pulse at a greater depth nearer the thumb on the right hand, this indicates the condition of the lungs. If you feel it on the surface, this indicates the condition of the colon. The deep position of the same area on the left hand indicates the condition of the heart and the surface pulse that of the small intestines.
- The middle deep position of the right hand indicates the state of the spleen and pancreas, while the middle surface of the right hand indicates the condition of the stomach.

- The middle deep position of the left hand indicates the state of the liver, while the surface pulse in the same region indicates the condition of the gall bladder.
- The furthest deep point on the right hand indicates the state of the circulatory system, while the surface pulse indicates the condition of the lymphatic system.
- The furthest point from the thumb on the left hand, if it is deep, indicates the condition of the kidneys and adrenal glands. If you feel the pulse more on the surface, this reflects the condition of the bladder.
- A pulse rate of over 80 indicates a high metabolic rate, fever, hyperacidity, anxiety, stress, as well as heart and lung problems.
- A pulse rate of less than 60 indicates general weakness, anaemia, low thyroid activity, poor circulation and poor immunity.
- A weak, rapid pulse may indicate a state of shock.
- A very rapid, very slow or irregular pulse may indicate heart trouble.
- A relatively slow pulse with high fever may be a sign of typhoid.
- If the pulse feels stronger and is closer to the surface, the general tendency is to identify the problem as an external one and as acute.
- If the pulse is fast, then there is too much heat in the body. A strong and fast pulse may indicate cold, influenza or even a skin problem.
- If the surface pulse is weak or slow, this indicates a cold body type.
- If the pulse is felt deeper than usual on the surface, the problem is internal and of a chronic nature.
- If the deep pulse is stronger than usual, this indicates an internal problem due to heat.
- If the deep pulse is slow, this indicates problems related to colds, such as anaemic, low energy, etc.
- If the pulse is slippery or jellyfish-like, this indicates water retention or an accumulation of phlegm. Pregnant women will have slippery pulse.
- If the pulse feels like a bow string, this indicates that the person is nervous and tensed.
- If the pulse is tight, it indicates pain in the body.
- Audible murmurs, caused by a disturbance of the blood flow in the heart, signify valve diseases. Additional sounds may indicate other heart problems.

- Over a normal lung, there is usually a soft rustling sound. When the same sound becomes harsh, this indicates an infection under the area of the lungs.
- The pulse can reveal a person's allergy to certain types of food. Take the pulse before eating the food that is alleged to cause an allergic reaction. Check the pulse again every 10 minutes after eating the food. If the pulse rate varies by 10, this confirms the allergy. Repeat the check at least 2–3 times.

OTHER SYMPTOMS

ABDOMINAL PAIN

- If you have constant pain in the stomach, feel nauseous and have not been able to move the bowels, listen out for gurgles in the intestines. If there is no sound, even a faint one, then this indicates the malfunctioning of the intestines.
- If the pain is near the stomach region and is accompanied by nausea and vomiting, and occurs soon after consuming food, this can be due to an allergic reaction to certain foods.
- If the pain is in the middle of the upper abdomen near the umbilical region and shifts to the right side of the abdomen, accompanied by tenderness in the region, this may indicate appendicitis.
- If the pain is in the lower abdomen and is linked with the desire to urinate frequently, accompanied by a burning sensation during urination, this may indicate a bladder problem.
- If the pain is in the middle of the upper abdomen and spreads to the right shoulder blade, this can be due to an infection of the gall bladder or the presence of gall stones. Nausea and vomiting may result.
- Pain behind the breast bone, which spreads to the left arm and upper abdomen, indicates heart problems.
- Excruciating pain across the abdomen, which spreads to the groin and upper thigh may indicate kidney stones in the ureter. Chills and shock are associated with this problem.
- Pain just after meals at the lower end of the breast bone, which eventually spreads to the back and right shoulder, may indicate duodenal ulcers.
- Pain that appears more to the left of the upper abdomen when the stomach is empty may indicate gastric ulcers.

ABDOMINAL CRAMPS

Abdominal cramps are usually a symptom of gastroenteritis, excess alcohol, food poisoning, typhoid fever, dysentery, intestinal obstruction or cholera. When heavy work (as in manual labour) is done, cramps result from loss of salt. For women, abdominal cramps are common during pregnancy and menstruation.

ABDOMINAL MASS

During pregnancy, you can feel the uterus as a mass in the middle of the lower abdomen. If the bladder is full, you can feel the mass as something soft above the pubic area. If there is constipation, you can feel it on the left side of the abdomen. Abdominal mass can be caused by the enlargement of the liver, spleen or kidney. Cancer of the colon, tumours or cysts in the reproductive organs are other causes. If there is any inflammation, the muscles may become tight, resulting in spasms.

ABDOMINAL SWELLING

This is caused by the presence of gas as a result of swallowing air or due to the putrefaction of food in the stomach and intestines, as well as due to abnormal bacterial growth in the upper part of the bowels. It can also be due to gastritis or intestinal obstruction. It can be a complication in congestive heart failure, cirrhosis of the liver or kidney disorders.

APPETITE INCREASE AND LOSS

An increase in the appetite is common during pregnancy and can be a habit as well. Appetite increase can also occur as a result of hyperthyroid or tumour in the pancreas. When associated with weight loss, increase in appetite may indicate the presence of tapeworms.

A loss of appetite is symptomatic of tension, dislike of certain types of foods or chain smoking. When associated with weight loss, loss of appetite can be due to cancer of the stomach or hepatitis.

BACK PAIN

Skeletal abnormalities, muscular problems or systemic ailments can cause back pain. Cancer of the vertebrae, protrusion of discs, fibrositis, lumbago, menstruation, osteoarthritis, osteoporosis, pelvic problems, pregnancy and sciatica can also lead to back pain.

BAD BREATH

This problem may be due to the presence of putrefactive bacteria (from undigested foods) in the digestive tract, diseased gums or any deficiency that causes indigestion.

Stale breath may indicate poor digestion, acidity and sluggish intestines. In certain diseases, volatile substances may be eliminated through the lungs, such as sweet odour in diabetes or musty odour in liver failure. Stale breath may also be a result of poor oral hygiene or emotional problems like anxiety.

BEDWETTING

This may indicate weakness in the bladder and hindrance or infection in the urethra. It may also mean enlargement of the prostate glands or loss of bladder control due to damaged nerves.

BELCHING

This occurs as a result of swallowing air while eating. It is also caused by dyspepsia.

BLEEDING FROM THE LUNGS, MOUTH AND NOSE

Bleeding from the lungs becomes evident when there are traces of blood in the sputum. This may be due to infections in the lungs, tuberculosis or cancer.

If bleeding occurs when brushing teeth, this may be due to pyorrhoea. Bleeding in the gums indicates vitamin deficiency. If blood is vomited out, this can be due to peptic ulcers, gastritis, cancer or cirrhosis of the liver. Blood may also ooze from the nose or pharynx.

If the nose bleeds, this may be due to external injury, excess blowing of the nose, breathing dry air, tumour in the nose, high blood pressure, measles or rheumatic fever.

BLEEDING IN THE RECTUM AND VAGINA

Blood in the rectum may be due to polyps, benign tumour in the colon, and cancer of the colon or rectum. If the blood is a bright red, then this may be due to haemorrhoids. If the blood is black and tarry, this may indicate ulcerative colitis.

For women, bleeding is normal during menstruation. Unusual bleeding, other than menstruation, may be due to polyps of the uterus, cervix or fibroid. It may also be due to hormonal imbalance or a complication during pregnancy.

BLOOD IN THE URINE

This may indicate cancer of the bladder, urethra or kidneys. It may also be due to kidney stones or nephritis.

BREAST MASSES

Tiny nodules in the breasts become firm but tender before menstruation and in the third week after conception.

Extreme tenderness during breastfeeding indicates an infection. Otherwise, tenderness may also be due to a cyst. Abnormal lumps in the breasts may be due to cancer, where the pain does not appear until the last stages. For men, breasts may enlarge due to hormone treatment, which is given for cancer, cirrhosis of the liver or tumours.

BREATHING DIFFICULTY

During rigorous exercise, shortness of breath is normal. Breathing difficulty can be due to obstruction in the air passage or dust inhalation. It may also be due to pneumonia or pulmonary diseases. Breathing difficulty can also occur when the heart fails to keep up with the circulation as the body demands for more oxygen. Yet another cause is emotional disturbances.

CHILLS

These may occur in the early stage of pneumonia. If the temperature of the body rises in a regular pattern and you feel chilly, then you may be having malaria.

COLD HANDS AND FEET

You feel cold in the hands or feet due to poor blood circulation. This condition may result when you are in deep shock, suffer from a heart disease, arteriosclerosis or are emotionally disturbed.

CRAMPS IN THE LEGS

When you stretch the leg muscles, a muscular spasm often results. Cramps in the legs during pregnancy indicate a deficiency in calcium and phosphorus.

DELIRIUM

This is a state of mental instability, which may be due to the metabolism of nerve cells in the brain, diabetes, loss of fluids, poisoning, heart failure, head injury or alcohol intoxication.

DEPRESSION

This state is the result of a mental problem or sickness.

DIZZINESS

This may be due to disturbances in the semicircular canals of the ear, which are caused by problems like mumps, excessive use of the eyes, indigestion or migraines. It may also be due to head injury and brain tumour, in which case dizziness will be accompanied by ringing in the ears. Arteriosclerosis, haemorrhage, anaemia, tension or drug overuse are other causes of dizziness.

FAINTING

This occurs because of poor circulation of blood to the brain, thereby depriving it of oxygen or glucose. It may also be due to an inactive heart, haemorrhage, artery disease, emotional shock, atherosclerosis, anaemia, carbon monoxide poisoning or low blood sugar. Alcoholism, a heavy dose of sedatives, head injury, stroke, epilepsy, diabetes and hysteria are other possible causes.

FEVER

Fever results from infections, inflammations or destruction of body tissue. It may also be due to heatstroke or strenuous physical exertion. In infants, a fever may indicate dehydration.

HEADACHES

These occur because of stress, tension or toxins in the body. If you have a headache after waking up from sleep, this may indicate that you have high blood pressure. Headaches also occur as a result of eyestrain or a sinus infection or if you have a tumour in the neck or head. Do not ignore them or delay consulting a specialist if the headaches occur at a specific area, with increased intensity each time or if they are accompanied by high fever or fainting spells.

IRREGULAR HEARTBEAT

This may happen because of a rheumatic heart, injury to the heart, coronary artery disease, thyroid malfunction, arteriosclerosis or heart disease.

JAUNDICE

In this, the skin and the whites of eyes become yellow. Jaundice may also result from the destruction of red cells in excess, such as in anaemia, malaria, pneumonia or yellow fever or when you suffer from liver diseases like hepatitis or cirrhosis. Obstruction in the flow of bile by gall stone or cancer may yet be another cause.

LEUCORRHOEA

Also known as "white discharge", leucorrhoea may result from an inflammation of the reproductive organs, ovarian hormone imbalance, gonorrhoea, syphilis or cancer of the uterus.

MENSTRUATION

If menstruation fails to start beyond a certain age, this may be due to faulty endocrine glands. It may also be due to congenital reasons. Other than pregnancy, if menstruation stops suddenly, then the cause may be mental disturbance or endocrinal disturbance. Excess flow may indicate a fibroid tumour of the uterus or endocrinal disturbance. Painful menstruation may be a result of emotional problems.

NAUSEA OR VOMITING

There are many causes for nausea or vomiting, such as food poisoning, an infected appendix, low blood pressure, emotional disturbance, toxin accumulation or magnesium deficiency. For women, nausea or vomiting is common during pregnancy.

If nausea or vomiting is accompanied by bloating, cramps or pain in the stomach, this may be due to vitamin B6 deficiency or irritation of the digestive organs. Increased pressure in the head or disturbance in the semicircular canals of the ears may also cause nausea. Psychic reaction may yet be another cause.

NECK PAIN

This may occur when the lymph nodes enlarge. Neck pain occurs due to arthritis or head injury. Rigidity may indicate meningitis. An audible rush of blood indicates the enlargement of the thyroid.

NERVOUSNESS

This may be due to a psychological condition, fatigue, an overactive thyroid, malnutrition or head injury.

OEDEMA

Fluid accumulation occurs when the heart is unable to supply enough blood to meet the demands of the body's tissues.

Oedema may also result from kidney problems, which allow the blood albumin to leave the body during urination. Oedema usually appears first in the ankle. The swelling becomes bigger towards evening.

Cirrhosis of the liver also causes oedema in the abdominal area. A low protein diet, inflammations and allergies like hay fever or anaemia are other causes. For women during pregnancy, due to insufficient protein or pressure on the veins, ankles become swollen.

PERSPIRATION

This is normal when it happens due to heat or strenuous exercises. Perspiration also occurs during heart attack, shock, passing of kidney stones, pregnancy or menopause. Taking drugs like salicylates and the aftermath of a fever are other causes.

SALIVA

Excess saliva production may be due to poisoning involving mercury, arsenic acid, mushrooms or tobacco. It also occurs during teething in children. Motion sickness, migraine, hysteria or neural problems are other causes.

13

The Gastrointestinal System

❦

There are many causes of abdominal disorders. Common abdominal disorders are a result of psychosomatic factors, such as nervousness, stress, tension and strain. Most other problems are due to the body's defective digestion and absorption of food. These can be due to either hormonal imbalances or bad eating habits.

By learning to relax through Yogasanas, psychosomatic problems can be prevented. This requires a conscientious and deliberate effort on the part of the individual, and in some cases, it involves a significant change in habits. Yoga helps achieve these objectives. To maintain good health, it is important to eat the right type of food and to learn to relax and be free from emotional problems.

Ordinarily, children fall prey to abdominal diseases because of malnutrition, inadequate food or improper food. This can start in the womb itself. Most mothers want their children to be round and chubby and so may "force feed" them with the wrong diet. The children's system, however, cannot take this burden and digestive problems can result.

Examples of bad eating habits are as follows:

- Eating fruit with or immediately after meals. Fruit require nearly a quarter of the time taken for digestion when compared to other types of food, such as fresh vegetables or meat. This disrupts the digestive system and gives it more work.
- Eating fruit with sugar. Sugar makes fruit ferment, resulting in the production of gas and heartburn.
- Drinking water during meals or immediately after meals. The digestive juices become diluted and slow down the digestive process.
- Boiling vegetables in too much water or cooking or frying vegetables (except tomatoes). This results in the loss of essential nutrients.

Vitamin K and most types of vitamin Bs are synthesised by bacteria in the intestines. These are similar to the ones present in yoghurt. The growth of these bacteria depends on diet. Garlic, fibre foods, carrots, cabbages, and all vegetables with cellulose increase the growth of these organisms. Eating natural home-made yoghurt regularly helps destroy putrefactive bacteria in the intestines and improves the digestive process. Fresh fruit and vegetables help maintain the acid-alkali balance of your body. For gastritis, ulcers, colitis and gastroenteritis, as a result of excess heat in the body, increase the intake of soothing okra, fruit and yam. For digestive weakness, increase the intake of hot foods, such as ginger, fennel and aniseed.

By developing good eating habits and following certain simple rules, such as eating the right type of food for adequate nutrients, eating at regular intervals, avoiding excessive spicy and fried foods, eating in moderation, not going to bed immediately after eating, many gastrointestinal disorders can be prevented or even treated. Eating young and fresh vegetables grown without chemical fertilisers supply more vitamins, minerals and other nutrients than those in stored or canned foods.

Selecting the right type of food is considered an art, and with some interest, effort and patience, it can be easily developed. Certain types of foods and herbs prevent many disorders of the body, and, when taken in the right combination, are key ingredients in a healthy lifestyle. For a healthy digestive system, the food we take should primarily include:

- Bitters as all bitter foods and herbs increase the appetite and aid in the digestive process.
- Hepatics as they strengthen and activate the liver.
- Laxatives as they ease bowel movements.
- Relaxants as they help relax the tissues.
- Carminatives as they increase the peristaltic motion and prevent the production of excess gas.
- Astringents as they firm the tissues of the system.
- Antispasmodics as they prevent spasms or colic.
- Anti-microbials as they prevent infections.
- Sialogogues as they stimulate the production of saliva, thereby helping in the digestive process.
- Emetics as they induce vomiting to eliminate toxins from food.
- Anthelmintics as they prevent any parasitic worms.
- Demulcents as they prevent any possible inflammations in the digestive tract.

THE MOUTH

BAD BREATH (HALITOSIS)

Poor oral hygiene, abscess or infection, putrefying bacteria in undigested food, infected tonsils or gums, inflamed sinus, lung diseases, diabetes and lung cancer can cause bad breath. The nearly invisible film of bacteria that forms in the mouth is yet another cause.

Increase the intake of food that improve digestion and prevent putrefaction. Have food that help fight plaque, such as celery, carrots and peanuts. If bad breath is a result of a digestive disorder, avoid eating acid-producing foods, such as fried foods and red meat. Also avoid coffee and alcohol.

Recipes

- Chew a few parsley leaves, a teaspoon of caraway seeds or a teaspoon of dill seeds after each meal to clear bad breath due to indigestion.
- Chew a few red dates or fresh parsley leaves to clear bad breath that results from having garlic in food.

Gargle

Gargling your mouth with the right liquid helps control bad breath. Gargle after every meal:

- With a glass of warm water in which a drop of thyme oil or clove oil has been added.
- With the infusion of aniseed, sage leaves, cinnamon, juniper berries or rosemary.
- With the herbal infusion of myrrh and goldenseal mixed together in equal quantities.

BLEEDING GUMS

Ulcers, tumours, poor hygiene habits or severe vitamin deficiency, particularly vitamin K, can cause gum bleeding. Vitamin K deficiency is commonly caused by the lack of bile salts in the intestines. It also results from an excess intake of antibiotics, which causes the destruction of bacteria responsible for producing vitamin K. Bleeding of the gums when brushing the teeth is usually caused by pyorrhoea. If the problem persists, consult a dentist.

Include food that contains vitamin K, such as green leafy vegetables, in your diet. Also include food that improves bile production.

Recipes

- Gooseberry is rich in vitamin C. Eating it in the form of pickles, helps combat gum bleeding.
- Chew blackberry leaves a couple of times a day on a regular basis.
- Chewing eucalyptus leaves hardens spongy and bleeding gums.

Gargle

- Gargle with blueberry, bilberry or myrtle berry juice or use them as a mouthwash for inflamed gums.
- Gargle with salt water or with the warm infusion of bayberries after each meal.
- Use the infusion of dried blackcurrant berries, plums, mangoes or sesame seeds as a mouthwash. Keep a mouthful of the infusion for few minutes before spitting it out.

You may also brush your teeth with the fresh leaves of fennel, thyme leaves, neem twigs, the fresh juice of barberries or lemon juice once a week to strengthen the gums.

CANKER SORES

These are non-malignant lesions in the oral cavity caused by microorganisms. The sores appear when the body's resistance is low. An allergy to certain kinds of food containing citric and acetic acids can also cause canker sores.

They appear as small red swellings, as blisters or as single or multiple sores near the molar teeth, inside the lips or in the lining of the mouth. A canker sore has a yellow or greyish white centre with a red border.

Avoid eating acidic and pickled foods, walnuts, strawberries and tomatoes.

Recipes

Macerate a few rose petals and honey in a glass of warm milk. Add honey to taste. Alternatively, have a teaspoon of the paste of rose petals with honey 3 times a day.

Gargle

Gargle with warm water in which a pinch of salt and turmeric powder has been mixed. Do this after each meal.

MOUTH DRYNESS

This can be due to a local infection of the mouth, teeth or stomach. Inhaling hot smoke through the mouth can also cause dryness in the mouth.

An effective dose of vitamin C can help build up resistance and improve the healing process. Avoid dry foods, cinnamon and excess salt in food. Perform Sheetali Pranayama [Cooling Breath] as it can clear mouth dryness.

Recipe

Mix together 2 tablespoons of blackcurrant syrup, a teaspoon of olive oil and a few drops of lemon juice. Sip a tablespoon of this 3 times a day. Acts as a lubricant for the mouth.

MOUTH ULCERS

Oral ulcers can result from food allergies, particularly sensitivity to gluten found in wheat, rye, oats and barley.

Recipes

- Take 2 tablespoons of the decoction of red rose petals 2 times a day.
- Take a teaspoon of the jam of rose petals with ghee once a day after a meal.

Gargle

- Gargle with the juice extract of shepherd's purse or watercress once a day.
- Add 2 plums soaked in vinegar to boiling water. Add a pinch of salt. Use the warm water as a gargle 2 times a day.
- For inflammation of the tongue that produces white patches and for inflamed gums, use blueberry, bilberry or myrtle berry juice as a gargle or mouthwash.

MUMPS

Mumps is one of the inflammatory diseases of the salivary glands. It is contagious. It is more common among children. The incubation period is 2 to 3 weeks, and the swelling reduces in about 5 days. There will be inflammation and swelling of one or both of the upper salivary glands, including pain in the jaw, fever, chill and headaches. In severe cases, the pancreas may be inflamed, resulting in abdominal pain and vomiting. In adult males, it can result in serious complications, such as inflammation of the testes, which leads to sterility.

Have a bland diet and food rich in vitamin C in the form of a porridge. Take extra care to prevent the child from getting chilled. Apply a hot water bottle to the affected area.

Infusion

Mullein leaves or flowers are good for mumps. Have a glass of the infusion of mullein leaves 3 times a day for 5 days.

Applications

- Grind 1 acorus calamus root with a few drops of water on a stone. Add a drop of any anti-inflammatory oils, such as chamomile or entrops and white clay. Apply the paste to the neck 3 times a day until the swelling subsides.
- Apply a thick paste of asafoetida, made with water and white clay, to the swollen part 3 times a day.
- For swollen testes in the case of male adults, cushion the testes with cotton, and apply an icebag. Bed rest is essential.

INFLAMMATION OF THE SALIVARY GLANDS

This may be caused by an infection in the oral cavity as well as by liver problems or malnutrition.

Infusion

Sip a glass of the hot infusion of mullein flowers or the infusion of parsley leaves 3 times a day.

Decoction

Take 2 tablespoons of the decoction of yellow dock (Amla vetasa) once a day.

Gargle

Gargle with the infusion of sage. This is also good for tonsillitis.

Applications

- Grind the root of calamus with a few drops of water on a stone. Add a drop of any anti-inflammatory oil like chamomile flowers or entrops, as well as some white clay (enough to make a paste with water). Mix well. Apply the paste to the neck 3 times a day until the swelling subsides.
- Apply a thick paste of asafoetida made with water and white clay in equal proportion to the swollen part 3 times a day.

STOMATITIS

This is an inflammation of the lining of the mouth. It is mainly caused by vitamin deficiency, poor hygiene habits and eating highly seasoned or spicy foods. The membranes of the mouth appear red, the cheeks get puffy, and saliva flow increases. Symptoms of a fever may also appear.

Increase the intake of vitamins, minerals and nutritious liquid foods, such as tomato juice and orange juice, as well as yoghurt.

Recipe

Keep a teaspoon of the jam or marmalade of rose petals made with honey and ghee in the mouth. Suck the juice slowly. Do this once a day.

Infusion

Have the infusion of fresh blackcurrants as they are rich in copper, manganese and iron. Alternatively, you can eat some blackcurrants every day before meals.

Gargle

- Gargle with the infusion of blackcurrants or myrrh.
- Add a tablespoon of baking soda to a litre of cold water. Gargle with this solution.
- Gargle with the hot infusion of geranium, after which take a tablespoon of rose honey.

- Add lemon juice and honey in a glass of water. Use this as mouthwash once a day.

THRUSH

This is a fungus infection of the mouth that is common among infants. It is caused by malnutrition and vitamin deficiency. Excess use of antibiotic lozenges can destroy the natural healthy bacteria and allow fungus to grow. Poor hygiene habits and lack of sufficient nutrients that build up natural resistance in the body can worsen the condition. A white patch appears in the inside of the cheeks, particularly in babies. When left untreated, the patches turn yellow in colour.

To prevent thrush, take food rich in vitamin Bs. Also, wash the mouth well after each meal.

Gargle

- Gargle with the hot infusion of geranium, after which take a tablespoon of rose honey.
- Add lemon juice and honey in a glass of water. Use this as mouthwash once a day.
- Gargle with water in which a pip of garlic has been boiled. Do this after each meal.

For infants:

To prevent thrush in infants, the pregnant mother should follow hygiene as well as take nutritional supplements, especially if she is going to breastfeed the child later.

THE OESOPHAGUS

HIATUS HERNIA

This occurs when the lower end of the oesophagus or stomach protrudes through the diaphragm. The stomach is pushed upwards into the diaphragm and there can be an abnormal pouch in the region. Hiatus hernia is common among overweight people and pregnant women. Causes include increased pressure in the abdomen caused by vomiting, coughing, straining the bowels, pregnancy or obesity. It can be weakness of the muscles leading to the stomach. Too much stooping forward can increase pressure in the stomach and thus herniates the region. It can be a congenital problem. In hiatus hernia, pressure or pain will be felt behind the lower end of the breast bone. The pain increases when lying down. Other symptoms are vomiting when the stomach is full, rapid heartbeat, heartburn with pain spreading to the ears, neck and arms, and difficulty experienced in swallowing.

Have small portions of food frequently. Eat food prepared with the least amount of fluids. Avoid lying flat on the bed. Use pillows to prop up yourself. Avoid drinking fluids during meals and eating spicy foods. Overweight people are advised to reduce their weight. When standing, sitting or walking, avoid stooping.

Recipes

- Add 2 clove flower buds to tea. Drink this once a day.
- Have a peach fruit half an hour before each meal. This gives relief in the early stages.
- Take a tablespoon of bran in yoghurt before meals daily.

Infusion

At the early stage, hiatus hernia can be cured by drinking a glass of the infusion of fennel seeds or its soup or the infusion of caraway seeds once a day after meals.

Asana Routine

- Vayu Nishankasana [Gas Releasing Pose].
- Mushumna Shakti Vikasaka [Pelvic tilt]
- All relaxing Asanas.

Avoid all Asanas that involve forward bending and stretching of the region around the hernia. Do not attempt the following Asanas:

- Bhujangasana [Cobra Pose]
- Shalabasana [Locust Pose]
- Dhanurasana [Bow Pose]
- Paschimottanasana [Backstretch]
- Padahastasana [Legclasp]
- Naukasana [Saucer Pose]
- Paripoorna Navasana [Diamond Pose 1]
- Uddiyana Bandha [Abdominal Lift]

THE ABDOMEN

ABDOMINAL PAIN

Pain in general is a natural way of signalling that something is wrong with our system. It is not advisable to suppress or deaden the pain without rooting out its real cause. Abdominal pain is a symptom that appears during the course of many illnesses. Causes include food allergies, appendicitis, indigestion, gall bladder diseases and excess bacterial growth in the upper part of the bowel. Vitamin B1 deficiency, excess intake of vitamin D and calcium, and an overdose of medication like aspirin and antacids can also cause abdominal pain.

Seasoning food with ginger, liquorice or nutmeg on a regular basis prevents pain. If pain results from overeating, chew dry roasted fennel seeds with a pinch of rock salt or sea salt after meals for relief.

ABDOMINAL SWELLING

Like abdominal pain, abdominal swelling is also a symptom. It shows the presence of fluids in the abdominal area. Once Vata is aggravated due to an excess intake of sweets, the abdomen swells. Causes include gastritis, obstruction in the intestines, an excess of fried foods or food that produce gas, as well as an excess of fizzy drinks. Kidney and bladder problems and constipation can also cause swelling, particularly among children. In a malnourished child, the abdomen gets bloated, making the child weak. Too much food appears as fullness of the abdomen and veins can be seen on the surface.

Herbs that are pungent and carminative, such as basil, sarsaparilla, asafoetida, hippali and nutmeg taken together with buttermilk, help prevent abdominal swelling.

Asana Routine

For general toning and strengthening of the abdomen:

- Trikonasana [Triangle Simple]
- Tadasana [Stretch Pose]
- Tiryaka Tadasana [Swaying Palm Tree Pose]
- Katichakrasana [Cork Screw Pose]
- Ushtrasana [Camel Pose]
- Shashankasana [Baby Pose]
- Ardha Matsyendrasana [Simple Twist]

- Supta Vajrasana [Backward Bend]
- Halasana [Plough 1]
- Paschimottanasana [Backstretch]
- Bhujangasana [Cobra Pose]
- Jatara Parivartanasana [Legover Both Legs]
- Uddiyana Bandha [Abdominal Lift]
- Yoga Mudra.

THE STOMACH

ACIDITY AND HYPERACIDITY

This is the presence of excess acids in the stomach. Common causes include stress and poor eating habits, which create an imbalance in the acid-alkali combination within the body, thereby disrupting the digestive system. It is the result of excess Pitta. There will be discomfort in the pit of the stomach, a burning sensation in the abdominal area when the stomach is empty, and frequent belching with bad breath.

Increase the intake of alkalisers like carrots, celery, spinach and acid neutralisers like barley and peach. Citrus fruit like lemon have a net alkaline effect because their citric acid is quickly broken down in the body, leaving behind the alkaline salts. So, lemon juice can be used as an alkaliser in moderation.

Avoid alcohol, coffee, cola and aerated drinks, all types of meat, oily fish, eggs, cheese, cream and fried foods. Heaty carminatives like ajowan, asafoetida, bayberries, garlic, juniper berries, cinnamon may promote acidity. Avoid smoking.

Recipe

To prevent acidity, have a raw radish or carrot before each meal.

Juice

- Have a glass of ash gourd juice every morning on an empty stomach for a week.
- Have a glass of cucumber juice once every 2 hours without any other food.
- Drink only the fresh juice of either grapes, oranges, carrots or spinach once every 2 hours.

- Drink a glass of fresh carrot juice, fresh celery with apple juice, fresh lemon juice, raw beetroot juice, raw red potato juice or raw tomato juice before meals.
- Dissolve half a spoon of baking soda in a cup of water. Drink this after meals.
- Drink the fresh juice extract of red currants with apples or celery.

Infusion

Have a glass of the hot infusion of peppermint or chamomile flowers before each meal for a week.

Decoction

Have 2 tablespoons of the decoction of liquorice roots 2 times a day for 2 weeks.

APPETITE

Loss of appetite and increase in appetite indicate an unhealthy state of the body. Loss of appetite can be due to emotional tension, insufficient nutrients in the body as a result of disliking certain types of food, stomach cancer or hepatitis. Increase in appetite can be due to a developed habit. It can also be due to the presence of tapeworms, hyperthyroid or tumour in the pancreas. Instead of treating the symptoms, find out the problem and treat it with the right food.

Season food with herbs that are appetisers or begin a meal with a soup. Include in the diet figs, garlic, juniper berries, lemons, nutmeg and strawberries. They help improve the appetite. What follows are ways to increase the appetite.

Recipes

Blend 2 tomatoes in a glass of water with a pinch of salt, coriander leaves and green chilli without the seeds, as well as a teaspoon of tamarind water. Bring it to the boil. Drink a glass of this soup before meals.

Juice

- Add a tablespoon of the juice of celery petiole to a glass of apple and carrot juice. Drink this before meals.
- Have a tablespoon of the fresh juice of redcurrant berries mixed together with water twice a day.

- Have a tablespoon of the juice of chicory leaves with a glass of milk 3 times a day.
- Have a glass of water in which a teaspoon of ginger juice, a teaspoon of lemon juice and a pinch of salt have been mixed before meals. You can also add a pinch of the powder of cardamom seeds for flavour.

Infusions

- Have a cup of the hot infusion of chamomile flowers, fennel seeds, dill seeds, cardamom seeds, cardamom leaves or angelica seeds for a week.
- For children, half a cup of the warm infusion of caraway seeds or stinging nettle sweetened with honey 3 times a day is beneficial. You may also give them a thyme bath once every 2 days. This increases their appetite.

Decoction

Have 2 tablespoons of the decoction of caraway seeds mixed with milk or the decoction of ajowan or the decoction of gooseberry fruit diluted with water 2 times a day after meals for 3 days.

Asana Routine

All Yogasanas promote a healthy appetite. Some specific ones improve the appetite by strengthening the organs of the digestive system. This allows for the production of enzymes and digestive juices to aid in the digestion of food. The Asanas are:

- Naukasana [Saucer Pose]
- Paschimottanasana [Backstretch]
- Ushtrasana [Camel Pose]
- Paripoorna Shalabasana [Swan]
- Uddiyana Bandha [Abdominal Lift]
- Yoga Mudra

To help reduce the appetite, chew a few clove flower buds or have plenty of fresh grapes or peanuts before meals.

BELCHING

Like indigestion, belching results from a digestive disorder. Causes include swallowing air due to eating food too fast, **stress or anxiety**. It can also be due to the cold, virus, habit of drinking through straws, eating food that putrefies easily and produces a lot of gas.

Learn to relax. Avoid carbonated drinks, smoking, chewing gum or sucking candy. They can stimulate the swallowing of air.

Recipes

- Have a fresh grapefruit 3 times a day.
- Boil a glass of milk with 10 grams of dry ginger and 20 grams of rock sugar. Strain. Drink the milk once a day for 2 weeks.

FLATULENCE

This is the accumulation of gas in the stomach and intestines. Causes include the absence of the enzyme lactase, which is necessary for the digestion and assimilation of milk. Swallowing in too much air as a result of anxiety is another cause. Certain types of food and fermented foods tend to result in gas formation. Eating them regularly causes this problem. An excess of milk is yet another cause of flatulence in people who are lactose intolerant. An excess of laxatives and antacids also produce too much gas. It is the gas produced by bacteria that gives the characteristic odour when expelled.

Increase in the daily diet, bland foods, high protein and low-fat foods. It is better to eat cooked vegetables than raw ones. Season food with asafoetida and other spices, such as cumin, black pepper, garlic and turmeric, sauteed in a teaspoon of olive oil to help prevent gas formation. Soak vegetables, especially lentils, in water overnight. The next day, throw away the water, pour in fresh water and cook for a few minutes. Throw away the water again. Add some fresh water and continue cooking with a pinch of turmeric powder.

Avoid eating fruit with sugar, fried foods and protein with carbohydrates. Starchy foods and fruit, when eaten together, produce gas. This becomes worse when followed with a cup of creamed coffee. Oatmeal, together with fruit juice, also produces a lot of gas. Avoid aerated drinks.

Recipes

- Chew a few caraway seeds or cardamom seeds after each meal for relief.
- Eat a ripe papaya before meals.
- Add a drop of fennel oil or a drop of lavender oil to a spoon of sugar. Have this 2 times a day after meals.
- Fry a teaspoon of ajowan seeds in olive oil. Add 2 tablespoons of warm cooked rice and a pinch of salt. Have this before the main meals for 3 days.
- Heat a pot, and add a teaspoon of ginger juice and sugar. Pour in a cup of water, and bring it to the boil until the mixture becomes syrupy in texture. Add some saffron strands, cardamom, nutmeg and a clove bud. Take a teaspoon of this after meals.

The following recipes get rid of flatulence in children:

- Get the children to take 1 teaspoon of the infusion of aniseed after meals for 5 days.
- Add a teaspoon of honey to 2 teaspoons of the infusion of coriander leaves. Get the children to take this after meals for a week.

Juice

Have a glass of radish juice before meals.

Infusions

- Have a glass of infusion of the mixture of 1 part fresh ginger, 1 part chamomile flowers and half a part of fennel seeds with or without honey after meals.
- Have a glass of the infusion of fennel seeds, caraway seeds, angelica root and coriander seeds mixed together in equal proportions with honey 2 times a day after meals.
- Have a glass of the infusion of any of the following after meals: allspice, angelica roots, aniseed, betel leaves, caraway, cardamoms, Roman chamomile, cinnamon, coriander, lemon balm leaves, dill seeds with honey, neem leaves with honey, parsley, pennyroyal, peppermint leaves, sarsaparilla or yarrow.

Decoction

Have the decoction of coriander in milk. Add some sugar.

Applications

The following applications are suitable for children:

- Apply lavender oil or ginger and juniper oil to the abdomen. Massage gently.
- Apply olive oil to the abdomen, then place a warm betel leaf or lemon balm leaf or garden balm leaf on the abdomen for a few minutes. Do this 2 times a day.

Asana Routine

Sometimes, the digestive tract may be obstructed, resulting in flatulence. Performing the following Asanas helps rectify the problem:

- Ekapada Jatara Parivartanasana [Legover Single Leg]
- Shashankasana [Baby Pose]
- Supta Vajrasana [Backward Bend]
- Shashanka Bhujangasana [Striking Cobra]
- Tadasana [Stretch Pose]
- Tiryaka Tadasana [Swaying Palm Tree Pose]
- Katichakrasana [Cork Screw Pose]
- Bhujanga Tiryaka [Swinging Cobra]
- Udarakarshana Asana [Abdominal Massage Twist]
- Yoga Mudra
- Matsyasana [Fish in Lotus]
- Halasana [Plough 1]
- Uddiyana Bandha [Abdominal Lift]
- Meditation on solar plexus

GASTRITIS

Acute gastritis is an inflammation of the mucous membrane of the stomach. Aspirin misuse, overeating, food poisoning, stress, allergy and alcohol can cause acute gastritis. It can also be caused by the activity of the digestive juices, such as the secretion of hydrochloric acid in excess, the presence of yeast organisms called candida and drinking too much coffee or tea. Swelling in the abdomen, nausea and headaches may appear as symptoms.

Chronic gastritis may develop from acute gastritis, resulting in the degeneration of the glands that produce hydrochloric acid and pepsin. Symptoms include coating on the tongue, lack of appetite, belching, discomfort in the upper abdomen with distention of the abdomen immediately after eating food, nausea and weight loss. If untreated, the pain can be felt in the back. Vomiting with severe abdominal pain may also occur.

Be selective about the food you eat. Season food regularly with herbs, such as parsley, coriander leaves or seeds and asafoetida.

Avoid eating spicy foods, refined carbohydrates, food that is too cold or hot, food that produces excess gas, such as cabbages, drinking too much fluids during meals, such as aerated water with lime and citrus fruit juices or alcohol, and eating hot and pungent foods, such as cayenne. If gastritis occurs after swallowing corrosive substances, see a doctor immediately.

Recipes

See recipes suggested for improving the appetite and flatulence. The following is also helpful:

Have a thin broth with well cooked rice and cooked potatoes once a day. Helps in the speedy recovery once symptoms subside.

For gastritis due to excess gas:

- Have carrot soup once a day to prevent putrefaction.
- Have the flesh of a young coconut with coconut water once a day.
- Have a clove of garlic, which contains allistatin that protects against gastritis, in the morning, followed by a glass of fruit juice diluted with hot water.

For abdominal pain due to excess gas:

- Add a tablespoon of fresh yoghurt to 10 grams of ginger. Blend well. Add a pinch of salt to taste. Now mix it with cooked rice. Have this before meals. Add some brown sugar if you find the taste too pungent.
- Add 2 drops of lavender oil and a teaspoon of sugar to a cup of warm water. Drink this once a day.

For abdominal pain due to excess gas in children:

- Give the children sun ripened chikoo fruit once every other day for 2 weeks to prevent gas formation.
- To alleviate discomfort, give a teaspoon of gripe water that has been mixed with a teaspoon of warm water.

For abdominal swelling due to excess gas:

- Have a sweet ripe mango an hour after food followed by a glass of milk.

- Chew some cardamom seeds, caraway seeds or fennel seeds after each meal.

Infusion

To get rid of gastritis, have a glass of the cold infusion of dried basil leaves with a teaspoon of honey or the infusion of gooseberries or half a glass of the warm infusion of cinnamon powder after each meal for a week.

For abdominal pain due to excess gas:

Have a cup of the infusion of peppermint leaves twice a day for a week.

For abdominal pain due to excess gas in children:

Give them a teaspoon of the sweetened infusion of aniseed after food once a day.

For abdominal swelling due to excess gas:

Have a cup of the hot infusion of peppermint leaves 2 times a day after meals.

Decoction

For abdominal pain due to excess gas:

Have a tablespoon of the decoction of any of the following herbs after meals for 3 days: fennel seeds, allspice or angelica root.

Applications

Apply a hot fomentation to the abdomen every 2 hours.

For abdominal pain due to excess gas in children:

- Apply St. John's wort oil to the navel and lower abdominal region.
- Warm a leaf of lemon balm or garden balm to a comfortable temperature. Place it on the abdomen for a few seconds. Repeat this 3 to 4 times a day using fresh leaves.
- Gently rub a drop of castor oil in and around the navel. Warm a fresh betel leaf over a fire. Place the warm leaf on the navel region for a few seconds. Repeat this a couple of times, using fresh leaves each time.

HEARTBURN

This is a burning sensation that occurs in the lower oesophagus. It is caused by the backward flow of gastric juice from the stomach. When the sphincter, a tight valve between the stomach and oesophagus relaxes, it allows the gastric juice to flow back into the oesophagus. This can literally burn the oesophagus. Painkillers containing ibuprofen, such as aspirin, can also burn the oesophagus. Heartburn can interfere with breathing. If the heart burn persists, it could be because of hiatus hernia, ulcer in the stomach or duodeum, and in the elderly, it could be the sign of cancer or heart trouble. Peptic ulcers and eating too fast can also result in heartburn. In heartburn, a burning sensation in the chest or pain behind the breast bone, accompanied by a feeling of pressure in the stomach, appears.

A low fat, high bulk diet that is also rich in complex carbohydrates is best suited to deal with this problem. Add to the daily diet olives, papayas, warm milk and ginger. Have frequent but smaller portions of food. Take a calcium supplement after each meal. Sleep with pillows so your head and chest are elevated.

Avoid sugar, food containing caffeine, salt, alcohol, chocolates, spicy foods, fried and fatty foods, and food that causes obesity as they take longer time to digest. Drinking carbonated drinks can produce distention of the stomach, and thus cause acid to move into the oesophagus. Also avoid bending forward, lifting heavy objects, lying down immediately after having food and eating in a hurry.

Recipes

Have a raw onion with a slice of wholemeal bread 2 times a day.

Juice

Have a glass of carrot juice or celery juice extracted from fleshy petioles regularly once a day.

Caution: Pregnant women should avoid taking too much celery.

Infusion

Have a glass of the infusion of raspberries or peppermint leaves 3 times a day for 5 days.

INDIGESTION

Indigestion is a symptom of many problems, the mildest being poor digestion with a lack of natural appetite. Other symptoms are gas formation, with discomfort in the upper abdomen after eating, belching, headaches and mental dullness. If indigestion persists, consult a doctor. One of the causes of indigestion is the lack of pepsin or lactase, the enzyme needed to assimilate lactose. Non-ulcer dyspepsia characterised by heartburn, nausea and pain in the upper abdomen is associated with sugar indigestion. Indigestion can also be due to gastritis, food intolerance, cancer, angina or chronic pancreatitis. Stress is yet another cause of indigestion, as is food taken in excess or in the wrong combination.

Fasting once in 15 days is beneficial. Cooking meat in cider vinegar also helps prevent indigestion. Avoid eating food too fast. Take a high protein diet that is low in carbohydrates. Include in the daily diet food and herbs that are digestive, including yoghurt. Avoid milk as it increases acid production, starchy and sugary foods, unripe fruit and uncooked vegetables.

Recipes

To prevent indigestion:

- Have plenty of red grapes before meals to cure dyspepsia.
- Chew a small piece of ginger or some black pepper corns. These act as an appetiser before meals.
- Have lemon pickle with meals on a regular basis. Cut some fresh lemons and add salt and chillies to taste. Season with cumin and mustard seeds. Store the pickle in an earthen pot, stirring it regularly with a wooden spoon. After a month, the pickle is ready to be eaten.

For indigestion caused by overeating:

- Bananas: chew a whole cardamom 3 times a day.
- Ghee: suck a slice of lemon 3 times a day.
- Mangoes: drink a glass of milk immediately.
- Watermelon seeds: drink a glass of sugarcane juice.
- Brinjals: sip a teaspoon of pure ghee mixed together with sugar.
- Walnuts: drink a glass of pomegranate juice.
- Overdose of drugs: take a spoonful of maltose with warm water.

For abdominal swelling due to putrefaction and indigestion:

- Boil a teaspoon of malt in a glass of water. Drink this warm 2 times a day for a week.
- Have pepper soup. The following is the method of preparation: roast separately equal quantities of black pepper, cumin seeds, split chickpeas and split black beans. Grind until they become a powder, and add a little bit of asafoetida powder. Add a teaspoon of this to a cup of boiled water. Mix well, and add salt to taste. Add a teaspoon of fresh lemon juice. Drink or have this with rice 2 times a day for 2 days.
- Have grapefruit cooked in tamarind water once a day for a week. Fry a few mustard and cumin seeds in a teaspoon of olive oil. Add a few chillies. Now add finely cut pieces of grapefruit and fry. Add a glass of tamarind water, a pinch of salt and some brown sugar. Cook well. Eat this with rice before the main meals. You can also use an unripe papaya or bitter gourd instead of a grapefruit.

For abdominal pain due to indigestion:

- If pain results from eating the wrong type of food, add to a glass of warm water a quarter teaspoon of fried common salt. Drink this once after meals. Repeat if necessary.
- If the abdominal pain is associated with swelling, have 50 grams of unripe papaya soaked in vinegar 2 times a day.
- Cook a few cloves of garlic in water. Mix this together with soya sauce or molasses. Have the garlic with meals, and drink the liquid after meals. Continue doing this for at least 3 weeks.
- If there is abdominal pain as well stomachache and diarrhoea, mix together 5 dates, 100 grams of yam and 10 grams of ginger. Boil until the ingredients are cooked. Have this once a day for a week.

To prevent chronic indigestion:

- For acid indigestion (diverticulitis), have a radish every night.
- Add 0.5 grams of the powder of cardamom seeds to a teaspoon of the juice of basil leaves. Drink this 2 times a day to relieve vomiting due to improper digestion.
- Powder equal quantities of dry ginger and sesame seeds. Add a teaspoon of this powder to warm milk. Drink this in the morning for 7 days.

- Powder equal parts of dry ginger and black pepper powder. Mix them together with 2 parts aniseed and the same amount of honey. Blend well with some cinnamon, clove flower buds and cardamom seeds. Take a quarter teaspoon of this once a day.
- Add a teaspoon of fresh lemon juice and a pinch of baking powder to a glass of warm water. Drink this once a day. Lemon, however, is not to be taken by people with gastric or duodenal ulcers.
- Powder equal quantities of dry fried asafoetida, rock salt or sea salt, cumin seeds, black cumin seeds, ajowan seeds, dried ginger, hippali (piper longum) and black pepper. Mix a teaspoon of this powder with a small portion of cooked rice. Add a little pure ghee or olive oil. Have this before the main meals for 4 days. This recipe is also good for stomach pain, vomiting, diarrhoea, flatulence and gastric pain.

Juice

Have a glass of fresh coconut water just before meals to prevent indigestion.

For abdominal swelling due to putrefaction and indigestion:

- Add a teaspoon of fresh lime juice to warm water. Add a pinch of salt. Have this after each meal.
- Add a teaspoon of powdered dried orange peel to a glass of fresh orange juice. Drink this 2 times a day before meals.

Infusions

Have a cup of the hot infusion of ajowan, angelica roots, aniseed, basil leaves or chamomile flowers just before meals to prevent indigestion.

For abdominal pain due to indigestion:

- Have a cup of the hot infusion of dried herbs and the leaves of agrimony, fresh aerial parts of marjoram, or coriander or fennel seeds after meals 2 times a day.
- Have a cup of infusion of the mixture of 1 part cinnamon, 1 part clove flower buds and 10 parts blackcurrant leaves after each meal.

For indigestion caused by overeating:

Have a glass of the infusion of ordinary tea leaves in water with few clove flower buds once a day for 3 days.

To prevent chronic indigestion:

- Have a glass of the infusion of allspice for flatulent indigestion.
- Have a glass of the hot infusion of basil leaves with lemon and honey after meals.
- Have a glass of the infusion of cardamom seeds once a day for relief from vomiting due to indigestion.
- Have a glass of the infusion of ordinary tea leaves with clove flower buds to clear stomachache due to indigestion.

Applications

- Make a poultice of garlic mixed together with wheatgerm or almond oil. Apply it to the abdominal region once a day for a week to prevent chronic indigestion. Do not apply the poultice in concentrated form as it burns the tissue. Dilute the paste with base oil, one clove of garlic mixed together with 2 tablespoons of wheatgerm oil. If garlic oil is used instead of base oil, dilute 6 drops of garlic oil with 2 tablespoons of wheatgerm oil.
- Soak your feet in a garlic foot bath. This soothes the stomach and aids in the digestive process.

STOMACHACHES

Season food with fennel seeds and ginger, caraway seeds, basil, dill seeds, aniseed, peppermint, fenugreek, cinnamon, lemon balm or garden balm and parsley. Alternatively, you can use the above in salads regularly. Avoid nutmeg as it can cause stomachache when taken in excess.

Recipes

After each meal, keep a teaspoon of dill or aniseed in your mouth. Savour the juice slowly. This prevents stomachaches.

For relief from stomachaches:

- Make a syrup out of lemon balm and sugar. Take a teaspoon of this 2 times a day.
- Fry ajowan seeds in a teaspoon of ghee. Mix it with hot cooked rice. Add a pinch of salt. Have this before the main meals.
- Mix a few tender leaves of guava, a small piece of

ginger and a pinch of salt together. Have this mixture just before meals.

For stomachaches caused by other problems:

- Boil 5 red dates in water with a piece of yam and ginger until they become soft. Have this once a day for 10 days for relief from stomachaches and diarrhoea due to a weak stomach.
- For stomachaches associated with vomiting and giddiness, mix together a teaspoon each of tamarind fruit, jaggery (natural, uncrystallised brown sugar) and cumin seeds. Keep the mixture in your mouth, and swallow the juice slowly. Do this until the giddiness and vomiting stop.

Juice

Add a pinch of salt to half a teaspoon of ginger juice mixed together with a teaspoon of the juice of peppermint leaves. Drink this in the morning on an empty stomach for a few days to get rid of chronic stomachaches.

Infusions

- Have a glass of the infusion of fenugreek seeds or cinnamon bark half an hour after meals.
- Have a glass of the infusion of lime flowers and peppermint leaves mixed together in equal proportions. Have this once a day after meals for relief from stomachaches.

Decoctions

- Take 2 tablespoons of the decoction of caraway seeds diluted with water after meals for relief from stomachaches.
- Take 2 tablespoons of the decoction of dry ginger and coriander seeds mixed together in equal proportions once a day for 3 days.

STOMACH DISORDERS

If the problem persists, consult a doctor. Stomach disorders that result from eating the wrong type of food are likely to be temporary.

Having food and herbs that are stomachic and digestive on a regular basis help prevent stomach disorders. Avoid plums, bitter gourd and root vegetables, such as radish, as they can cause vomiting if the stomach is weak. Unripe oranges can upset the stomach. Avoid food that produces gas and results in constipation. Also avoid apples, dates, muskmelons and watermelons when the stomach is upset.

Recipes

For a weak stomach:
- For toning the stomach, eat a few red grapes or dates 2 times a day before meals.
- If you have difficulty digesting milk because of a sensitive stomach, add a glass of water in which dates have been soaked overnight to 2 glasses of boiled milk. This will help digest the milk better.

For stomach irritation:
Sprinkle a teaspoon of the powdered seeds of asparagus on food before eating. This clears stomach irritation associated with nausea.

For an upset stomach:
- Make a soup from cornflour, okra and white sugar. Drink this once a day for relief from stomach discomfort.
- Have a glass of fresh cow's milk to which a tablespoon of fresh ginger juice has been mixed. Have this hot. It relieves discomfort in the stomach due to indigestion.
- Fry lemon balm or garden balm leaves, cumin seeds and a few peppercorns separately on a dry pan. When they are cool, add yoghurt and a pinch of salt. Blend them together. Have this with rice for a week. Relieves discomfort in the stomach due to indigestion.
- Fry a few black peppercorns and a piece of grated dry ginger in a teaspoon of olive oil. Add water and a pinch of salt, and let it boil until the water reduces to a third of the original volume. Take 2 tablespoons of this, on its own or with sugar, 2 times a day.
- Season food with curry leaves, asafoetida and allspice to promote digestion, to prevent production of gas and thus prevent stomach disorder.

For babies with stomach upset:
- Give a teaspoon of the infusion of fennel seeds mixed together with a teaspoon of gripe water.
- If the pain is associated with cramps in the stomach or in the intestines, give a teaspoon of the infusion of chamomile flowers before meals.

For increasing the digestive power:
- Add the fresh juice of lime or bergamot orange to food to improve digestion.
- Soak 2 fresh figs in a glass of warm milk for an hour. Drink this before going to bed.
- Have a glass of tender coconut water with the flesh every morning for a week.
- Have a ripe papaya every day an hour after meals or cooked unripe papaya with a teaspoon of fresh lemon juice and a pinch of salt before meals.
- Simmer 3 cloves of garlic in water together with a small onion. Drink this as a soup before meals or eat it with well-cooked brown rice once a day.
- Have a few strawberries, a fresh grapefruit, peach, pear or star fruit and 2 cloves of diced garlic with honey or a small piece of tender ginger before each meal.

For increasing the digestive power in children:
- Give them a glass of the infusion of dill seeds or food seasoned with dill seeds.
- Give them 2 teaspoons of the infusion of fennel seeds followed by gripe water 2 times a day.

Juice
Have lemon juice and honey in hot water on an empty stomach in the morning. This relieves an upset stomach.

For increasing the digestive power:
- Have a few drops of the fresh milky juice of an unripe papaya in water, a glass of fresh pineapple juice or a glass of half-ripe apple juice before meals for 3 days.
- Have a glass of pomegranate juice in which a teaspoon of cumin seed powder and a dash of clove powder has been added. Have this once a day for 3 days.

Infusions
Have a glass of the infusion of agrimony, alfalfa leaves or lavender flowers with honey after meals. This relieves an upset stomach.

For a weak stomach:
Drink two cups of the infusion of dried leaves and seeds of basil for relief from stomach disorders like cramps, gastric catarrh, vomiting, etc. once a day.

For stomach cramps:

- Have a glass of the infusion of any of the herbs, such as dried basil, with a little honey, dried marigold flowers or bilberry leaves 3 times a day after meals.
- If the stomach cramp is associated with fever, have a glass of the infusion of chamomile flowers 2 times a day before meals.

For stomach spasms:

- Have the infusion of Roman chamomile flowers or horseradish 3 times a day before meals.
- Add a tablespoon of the infusion of basil leaves and marjoram herbs mixed together in equal quantities to a cup of the infusion of lime blossom sweetened with sugar. Have this after meals for a week.

For relief from digestive disorders:

- Mix equal quantities of basil leaves, basil seeds, lemongrass and peppermint leaves. On an empty stomach, have a glass of infusion of this mixture with lemon and honey.
- Have a glass of the infusion of any of the following herbs: dill seeds, peppermint leaves, leaves of fennel or comfrey leaves. Have this 3 times a day for a week.

For increasing the digestive power:

- Add a few clove flower buds to a cup of ordinary tea leaves. Have this 2 hours after meals.
- Have a glass of the infusion of barley that has been fried until brown 2 times a day.
- Have a cup of the infusion of powdered cardamom seeds, ginger, clove flower buds and coriander seeds mixed together in equal quantities. Have this 2 times a day before meals.
- Have a cup of infusion of any of the following herbs 2 times a day: the leaves of lemon balm, angelica roots, coriander seeds, peppermint leaves, aniseed, barberry leaves, marjoram herbs, dandelion roots, the dried rind of bitter oranges, sun dried unripe apples or caraway seeds.

Decoctions

For increasing the digestive power:
Take a tablespoon of the decoction of coriander, cumin and fennel seeds mixed together in equal proportion once a day for 3 days or elecampane roots once a day for 5 days.

Bath
Use the infusion of rosemary leaves for a warm bath every other day.

ULCERS

An ulcer is a raw area in which the natural covering of the underlying tissue is destroyed. A peptic ulcer is a sore on the walls of the stomach (gastric ulcer) or duodenum (duodenal ulcer). The region gets irritated by the acid of the stomach. The greatest dangers from untreated peptic ulcers are obstruction, where tissues around the affected region get inflamed before being obstructed, and haemorrhage. In most complicated cases, perforation can occur.

Gastric ulcer is one of the early signs of stomach cancer. It is common among people with the blood group A. Duodenal ulcer is more common among men, among people with the blood group O, as well as among alcoholics. There is usually a deficiency of iron, folic acid, vitamin B12 or vitamin B6 in an ulcer patient. Causes of ulcers include stress, overeating acid-forming foods, such as cereals, bread, meat, cheese, eggs and coffee, as well as an excess of pungent or hot foods. Irregular meals, alcohol consumption and chain smoking can also cause ulcers. The presence of parasites in the body is yet another cause, as is steroid abuse. Symptoms of ulcers include pain on a sensitive spot just below the breast bone, heartburn, belching of acid, loss of appetite and loss of weight. Vomiting is the primary symptom. When the tissue is damaged, it can affect an artery and this can result in bleeding. Vomiting out blood due to a haemorrhaging ulcer can pose a danger to life. The pain of duodenal ulcers appears a few hours after a meal and subsides when more food is taken. If there is anal bleeding and the colour of the blood is black and tarry, it can be due to peptic ulcers.

Diet plays a major role in treating peptic ulcers. The important aim is to neutralise the acidity of gastric juices by having a high protein, gluten-free diet. Include more milk and eggs. Skinned pulses, such as thor dhal and mung dhal, are beneficial. Refrigerated foodstuffs, such as cold yoghurt or even cold water, are also beneficial.

Food rich in vitamin C, vitamin A and zinc are necessary for treating ulcers. Raw cabbage contains chlorine and sulphur and is an anti-ulcer agent. It helps clear the mucous membrane of the stomach or duodenum. Honey and okra neutralise the acid. Sesame oil, sweet potatoes, carrots, pumpkins, winter squashes, spinach, broccoli and apricots are rich in vitamin A. Wheatgerm and black-eyed peas contain zinc. Barley, a demulcent, soothes the mucous membrane, and its mucilaginous content forms a barrier, preventing the acid from reaching the ulcers.

Food that helps to clear ulcers include cow's milk, goat's milk, coconut milk, radishes, papayas, cucumbers, pineapples, avocados, bananas, dates, eggplants, soya beans, black sesame seeds, alfalfa leaves, lemon balm, fenugreek, garlic, arrowroots, red currants, apples, custard, parsnip, as well as the juice of raw carrots, tomatoes and celery.

All types of food should be well cooked, except cabbages, which should be taken as raw juice. Avoid food that irritates ulcers, such as excess salt, sweets and spices. Avoid meat, whole cereals, raw onions, garlic, high fibre vegetables, tea, coffee and cola drinks. Also avoid all types of raw foods, even tender vegetables, hot and pungent herbs, such as cayenne, ginger, and hawthorn berries, citrus fruit and any food high in acid, cinnamon, lemons, plums, excess rice and antacids. Most antacids contain aluminium, which when consumed in excess impairs the absorption of iron and calcium. This, in combination with excess milk, can result in the formation of kidney stones.

Recipes

- For peptic ulcers, have some tender coconut flesh before meals as it is soothing.
- Steam a tablespoon of honey. Sip it warm 2 times a day for 3 days.
- Have a bowl of porridge made of barley before every meal.
- Take a teaspoon of maltose in a glass of water daily.
- Soak 3 dates in a cup of milk for an hour. Have them before each meal.
- Thick slimy okra is good for treating stomach ulcers and inflammation of the colon. Place some okra on cooked rice and cover the pot. When steamed this way, okra does not lose any of the main nutrients. Eat this every day until the symptoms clear.

For gastric ulcers:
Have soya bean milk instead of other types of milk daily.

For duodenal ulcers:
- Have some walnuts 3 times a day after meals.
- Blend peanuts that have been well soaked in water. Add fresh milk. Blend well. Boil the mixture until it becomes thick. Add honey to taste. Have this every night for 15 days.

For bleeding ulcers:
Have twice a day for 2 weeks meals consisting of any types of sprouts, fruit juice, eggs, cottage cheese, home baked bread, brewer's yeast, wheatgerm and buttermilk.

Juice

- Have a glass of warm raw cabbage juice 2 times a day for 2 weeks.
- Grate unpeeled potatoes, and squeeze out the juice. Simmer the juice in an earthen pot until the water evaporates. Drink the protein-rich sticky juice.

For duodenal ulcers:
Mix together a few drops of fresh lemon juice and a teaspoon of soya bean oil. Drink this on an empty stomach in the morning.

Infusion

Have a glass of the infusion of any of the following herbs after meals: alfalfa leaves, dried marigold flowers, mistletoe leaves or comfrey. Continue having the infusion on a daily basis for 2 weeks.

For duodenal ulcers:
- A strong tea of chamomile flowers is one of the best cures for ulcers. Drink this once a day before meals for a week.
- Have a glass of the infusion of lemon balm, lavender flowers or lime blossoms 3 times a day for a week.

For gastric ulcers:
Have a glass of infusion of comfrey roots, golden seal roots and marshmallow mixed together in equal proportion 3 times a day to soothe as well as to have a healing effect on the mucous membrane.

For bleeding ulcers:
Have a glass of the infusion of comfrey and parsley leaves mixed together in equal proportion 3 times a day. In addition, have only a milk-based diet so the bleeding ulcers heal.

Asana Routine
The following Asanas are beneficial:
- Shashankasana [Baby Pose]
- Ujjayi Pranayama [Abdominal Breathing]
- Nadi Shodana Pranayama [Alternate Nostril Breathing]
- Sheetali Pranayama [Cooling Breath]
- Bhoochari Mudra [Gazing at Nothing Seal]
- Trataka [Candle Concentration]

INTESTINES

APPENDICITIS
This is an inflammation of the appendix and is more common among the young. The appendix is located on the right side of the abdomen, midway between the hip bone and navel. The appendix may get jammed with stray pieces of food, resulting in infection, swelling and rupture. Constipation and pelvic maladjustments can also cause appendicitis. Common symptoms are pain and tenderness in the umbilical region and a slight fever. Sometimes, the pain is not felt in the umbilical region but all over the abdomen. Coughing and deep breathing increase the pain. Nausea and vomiting may follow. The pulse rate will increase while blood pressure will decrease. Consult a doctor on suspicion of any of these symptoms. Chronic infection can cause recurring attacks of abdominal pain on the lower right side of the abdomen, with a rise in temperature that is associated with nausea and vomiting.

Have a high fibre diet, such as green vegetables, to prevent constipation and appendicitis. When the appendix gets inflamed, avoid all types of food. Avoid laxatives or enemas as well. Laxatives can rupture the appendix.

Infusion
To prevent irritation of the appendix, have a cup of the infusion of fresh blackberry leaves once a day.

Application
Apply an ice bag to the affected region for temporary relief.

CHOLERA
One of the severest diseases of the intestines, cholera is an infectious water-borne disease. Caused by germs known as vibris cholerate, it affects the lower part of the intestines. Common symptoms of cholera appear as mild diarrhoea, vomiting, severe stomach cramps from loss of salts and fever. Later, the skin becomes dry, wrinkled and purple. Urine becomes scanty.

Rest and hospitalisation are advised. At the recovery stage, drink plenty of fluids, such as tender coconut water, to restore the loss of fluids as well as to supplement the loss of salts.

Ajowan, because of its thymol content, is good for cholera patients. Avoid solid foods and uncooked vegetables.

The following measures help prevent cholera, especially when there is a cholera epidemic:

Recipes
- Make a paste from 1 medium-sized onion and a few peppercorns. Have this 3 times a day.
- Fry a teaspoon of ajowan seeds in a teaspoon of olive oil. Mix it with rice and yoghurt. Have this once a day.
- On a clean betel leaf, place one teaspoon of honey and 0.1 grams of edible camphor. Burn it gently over a lighted candle. When it sublimes completely, eat it, including the leaf. Have this once a day.

Decoction
The root bark of guava contains tannins. Have its decoction 3 times a day to prevent vomiting and symptoms of diarrhoea.

Juice

- Have a glass of the juice of bitter gourd or of its leaves once a day (it is also a curative).
- Add 5 drops of the essence of cinnamon to a glass of water. Have this every hour.
- Have a glass of sweetened or salted lemon juice 3 times a day. This destroys the cholera bacilli present in the body.
- Add a teaspoon of the juice of drumstick leaves mixed together with honey to a glass of tender coconut water. Have this 2 times a day.
- Add 2 teaspoons of bitter gourd juice to an equal amount of onion juice. Mix well. Add a teaspoon of lime juice to coconut water, and add this to the onion and bitter gourd juice. Have the mixture 3 times a day.
- Have a glass of cucumber juice mixed together with coconut water from a young coconut. This supplies sufficient minerals during a cholera attack and restores the electrolyte liquid balance of the body.

Refer also to juice suggested under diarrhoea and dysentery.

COLIC

This is a digestive discomfort that affects infants. However, older children and adults may also experience it. It can be an intestinal spasm, spasmodic contraction of the bowel due to gas accumulation. Colic results in infants because of the swallowing of air during feeds, overfeeding or irregular feeding as well as the poor diet of the breastfeeding mother. Other causes are food allergies, an excess intake of sweet foods, indigestion, overeating, as well as the presence of round worms and gall stones or kidney stones in the duct. Symptoms of colic are similar to appendicitis. It produces severe pain in the abdominal area or in the region where the kidneys are located. If it is intestinal colic, the pain is felt in waves, while renal colic causes a steady pain. The abdomen becomes hard and feet turn cold. In general, there will be constipation. Children draw their legs towards their chest to take a position that gives relief from abdominal pain due to colic.

Seasoning food with asafoetida is one of the best ways to prevent and to get relief from intestinal colic. Feed the baby regularly, and make it 'burp' after each feeding, giving warm water in between feeds. In infants, the best way to prevent this is to carry them on the shoulders and tap their backs gently so that they develop proper breathing. If the child is suffering from repeated colic, this means there is a lot of gas in his or her intestines.

To prevent colic include in the diet ajowan, allspice, lemon balm, chamomile flowers, caraway seeds, cinnamon, dill seeds and fennel seeds. Avoid food that produces gas, such as cabbages, meat and aerated drinks. Nursing mothers should also avoid garlic, legumes and onions, as well as food that putrefy easily.

Recipes

For relief from colic:

- Roast cumin seeds in a pan. Add lemon balm leaves to the hot cumin seeds. Cover the pan until it cools down. Blend well with a tablespoon of yoghurt and a dash of salt. Eat this with rice or wholemeal bread.
- Have a few fresh basil leaves or peppermint leaves or drink the warm water in which they have been soaked for a few hours. Having this after meals relaxes the intestines.
- Boil a teaspoon of ginger juice and sugar in a cup of water to make a syrup. Add some saffron strands, cardamom, nutmeg and clove buds. Take a teaspoon of this after meals.

For children:

- If colic pain is associated with kidney problems, give them a tablespoon of blackcurrant juice 4 times a day.
- Peppermint water or infusion relaxes the intestines and is good for colic. Give the children a teaspoon of this 3 times a day.

Juice

For relief from colic:
Have half a glass of spearmint juice with a pinch of black pepper and honey to taste.

Infusions

For relief from colic:
Have a glass of the hot infusion of any of the following for a week: lemon balm or garden balm leaves or fennel seeds 3 times a day before meals; thyme leaves once a day; peppermint leaves after meals 2 times a day; cinnamon bark 2 times a day if colic is associated with eating the wrong type of food; aniseed or cardamom seeds after meals if colic is associated with gripping pain in the abdomen; and dill seeds, allspice, chamomile flowers or peppermint leaves before meals to get rid of colic that results from excess gas.

For children:

- Give them a tablespoon of the infusion of aniseed after meals.
- Give them a cold infusion of fried coriander seeds with sugar after meals.
- Give them a tablespoon of the infusion of Roman chamomile flowers every hour. If colic is associated with flatulence, add an equal amount of the infusion of angelica seeds.

Decoction

For relief from colic, take the decoction of any of the following after meals for a week:

- Two tablespoons of the decoction of angelica seeds and chamomile flowers mixed together in equal proportion, and diluted with a glass of warm water. Have this 3 times a day.
- One tablespoon of the decoction of caraway seeds or ajowan in warm water. Have this 3 times a day.

For children:

- Give them a teaspoon of the milk decoction of fennel seeds 3 times a day before meals.
- To a teaspoon of the decoction of caraway seeds, add half a glass of milk and sugar to taste. Get the children to drink this 2 times a day after meals.

For infants:
Give them a teaspoon of the decoction of anise in milk.

Applications

For children:

- Apply the paste of calamus roots mixed together with castor oil to the abdominal area.

- Wrap dry fried caraway seeds in a cloth while they are warm, and it place on the lower abdomen.
- Gently massage the abdomen using diluted oil of chamomile flowers, lavender flowers, marjoram, peppermint or spearmint.
- Place a hot water bottle on the abdominal area. This relieves pain. If the abdominal discomfort persists, make the child lie on the hot water bottle wrapped in a cloth. This should be followed by giving the child a few spoonfuls of lukewarm water.

For infants:
Warm a lemon balm or garden balm leaf over a hot plate, and apply it to the navel region of the baby for a few minutes. Repeat if necessary.

COLITIS

This is an irritation of the large intestine and affects infants (due to the wrong type of food consumed by breastfeeding mothers), children and adults. Mucous coilitis is the abnormal functioning of the colon. The main cause is emotional tension or stress. Constipation, headaches, sleeplessness and abdominal discomfort result. Increase the intake of "bulk-producing" foods. Learn to relax through yoga and meditation.

Ulcerative colitis occurs when the tissues of the colon get inflamed or ulcerated. Causes can be emotional in nature as well as physical, such as bacterial or viral infections. Allergic reactions to some types of food is another cause. Stools will be bloody and watery, and there will be an urgency to evacuate the bowels. Ulcerative colitis can be accompanied by fever, loss of appetite, anaemia, pain in the lower abdomen or abdominal cramps.

Drink lots of water, and have a bland diet in the form of a porridge. Increase in the diet food that is rich in protein and vitamins. Apples, apricots, beetroot, carrots, cucumbers, grapefruit, marigold, papayas, peaches, pears, pineapples and spinach help get rid of colitis. Eggplants, spinach and small red beans help stop bleeding that results from ulceration.

Avoid food rich in fibre, such as whole cereals, pulses and uncooked vegetables, as well as cold foods, spicy foods, gas-producing foods, food that is difficult to digest, and fruit juice. Also avoid hawthorn herb.

Recipes

- Okra with its mucous-like juice is the best-known remedy. Refer to recipe under peptic ulcers.
- Grind sun-dried broad beans into powder form. Dissolve 2 teaspoons of the powder in warm water. Drink this 3 times a day to control bleeding that results from diarrhoea.

Infusion

Have a glass of the infusion of dried marigold flowers 3 times a day for a week.

Juice

- For colitis due to putrefaction, take 2 teaspoons of the fresh juice of horseradish an hour after meals. Do this until the problem clears.
- Drink a cup of radish juice to which a teaspoon of brown sugar has been added 3 times a day. This is good for bleeding that results from ulceration.

CONSTIPATION

This is the clogging of the small or large intestines, resulting in irregular bowel action. It is also a sign that the involuntary contraction of the intestine that moves the waste matter is weak. Causes include poor eating habits, lack of sufficient bulk in the diet, oral medication and lack of exercise. Excess coffee or caffeinated drinks can force too much water out of the intestines, resulting in constipation. Cancer or tumour in or around the intestine, displacement of the bowel, as well as improper functioning of the liver, gall bladder and thyroid gland can cause sluggish intestinal action. Constipation also occurs when the abdominal muscles are weak, and there is no control over the nerves and muscles of the colon wall. This leads to an obstruction of the bowel, insufficient bile secretion, and no peristaltic motion due to nerve paralysis. Consult the doctor if the problem persists for several weeks, and if there is severe pain during bowel movement, abdominal swelling or blood in the stools.

Spastic constipation, characterised by spasms in the intestinal area, can result from calcium, magnesium, potassium or vitamin B6 deficiency. In children, this is a result of excess milk, insufficient bile production or drug toxicity. In infants, prolonged use of nappies, and nappies not changed soon after they are soiled, cause nappy rash and the growth of bacteria. Research shows that at the psychological level, this makes the child develop constipation.

During constipation, food stagnates and ferments in the body. If the toxins are absorbed from the colon, this can cause headaches, backaches, lethargy, insomnia, colic, a coated tongue, bad breath, loss of appetite, haemorrhoids and hernia. Children who suffer from constipation have bad breath and coated tongues. They grind their teeth in their sleep and may have nightmares It is interesting to note that vegetarians seldom suffer from this problem.

The best way to prevent constipation is to eat food in the right combination. Include in the daily diet food rich in fibre. Vegetables, either cooked or raw, nuts, seeds, fruit (especially blueberries, apricots, grapes, pears and pineapples), cereals and herbs are rich in fibre and act as natural laxatives. Meat, chicken, fish and fats are empty in fibre. The mild acid in fruit stimulates the production of digestive juices and induces antiseptic action in the digestive tract, thereby reducing the fermentation process. Also include, chicory, figs, raisins, sage leaves, dried beans and legumes, bran and whole wheat bread. Seasoning food with herbs, such as allspice or curry leaves, is beneficial.

Avoid laxatives as they make the stomach and intestinal walls weak and only give temporary relief. Also avoid eating excess meat, freshly-made bread, white bread, agrimony, cheese, peas, fresh potatoes, corn flour, pomegranates, raspberries, tapioca, tea, coriander, cream, milk, butter, eggs, refined foods and starchy foods as they are fully digested and absorbed into the body, leaving no bulk. Although castor beans are good for constipation, they are bad for the stomach. They cause abdominal pain and should therefore be avoided.

Recipes

To prevent constipation:

- Have a ripened banana blended with some black sesame seeds once a day.

- Soak a few plums or prunes overnight in water. Eat the fruit first thing in the morning. Drink the water as well.
- Drink buttermilk mixed together with 2 tablespoons of brewer's yeast 3 times a day for a week.
- Roast some black sesame seeds, and blend them with honey or sugar. Take a teaspoon of the mixture 2 times a day after meals.
- Once a week, eat leafy herbs, such as agase, cooked together with lentils before the main meals. This regularises the movement of the bowels.
- Add a teaspoon of cold pressed olive oil, fresh lemon juice and a pinch of salt to a salad. Eat the salad with evening meal to increase bile production. The salad acts indirectly as a laxative.
- Eat a raw tomato every morning. Follow with a ripened banana an hour after every meal. This improves the digestion of having eaten the wrong type of food, thus preventing constipation.

For relief from constipation:

- Begin and end the day by eating a well-ripened banana.
- Have a couple of dried figs, preferably with hot milk before going to bed.
- Have a grated white radish mixed together with honey once a day for 30 days.
- Have an unskinned apple with a glass of warm water before breakfast or eat a baked apple before going to bed.
- Have a glass of warm water before breakfast and a glass of fresh orange juice after breakfast for a week.
- Have a glass of warm water mixed together with powdered sunflower seeds and a tablespoon of honey once in the morning and once at night.
- Add a cup of black sesame seeds to a cup of crushed rice and boil in water to make a soup. Add salt to taste, and have the soup once a day until the problem disappears.
- Have the flesh of a coconut every morning and evening for a week to regulate the movement of the bowels. People suffering from high cholesterol should avoid this.
- Make a salad with a grated unripe papaya, and flavour it with powdered cumin seeds, green chilli, salt and fresh lemon juice. Have this before the main meals once a day for a week.

For children:

If children do not show any sign of an allergic reaction to milk, give them a glass of fresh milk before they go to bed. Make them drink the milk while it is hot.

For infants:

Give infants a teaspoon of grape juice once in the morning and once in the evening. This also gives them relief from thrush, fever or colds.

Juice

To prevent constipation:

- Have only fresh tomato juice every 2 hours for a day.
- Have the juice of raw apples mixed together with celery or carrots for proper digestion.
- Have a glass of the fresh juice of a cucumber, celery and an apple in equal proportion before each meal.
- Have unsweetened fresh lemon juice or grapefruit juice mixed in hot water before breakfast on a daily basis. This reduces acidity of the blood as the citric acid is converted into alkaline carbonates in the blood.
- To increase faecal bulk, have a glass of juice of any of the following before breakfast for a week: asparagus, cabbages, figs, olive, radishes, senna, tamarind, papayas, green onions, spinach or pears.

For relief from constipation:

- Have a glass of angle gourd juice or grapefruit juice with a pinch of salt once everyday on an empty stomach for 2 weeks.
- Have a glass of the juice of blackberry leaves and cherries or prunes mixed together in equal proportion 2 times a day.

Infusions

To prevent constipation (as mild laxatives):

- Have half a cup of the infusion of dandelion roots, greens of beetroot, apple peel or plum seeds 2 times a day.
- Have a glass of the hot infusion of dried basil herbs with honey; spinach with 5 drops of sesame seed oil;

or radish seeds sweetened with sugar 3 times a day after meals for a week.

- Mix 1 part barberries (an aid for the liver), 2 parts dandelion roots (for improving the digestion), 1 part cascara sagrada (to increase the peristaltic movement) and 1 part of ginger or fennel seeds (to prevent colic) together to make an infusion. Have a cup of this before retiring at night.

Applications

For relieving abdominal swelling in babies that results from constipation:

- Apply alternately a hot compression followed by a cold one to the abdomen 2 times a day.
- Apply camphorated oil or warm castor oil to the abdomen and navel region.

Asana Routine

Sitting in the Vajrasana position for 10 minutes after every meal helps. Other Asanas that are beneficial include the following:

- Suryanamaskar [Salutation to the Sun]
- Supta Vajrasana [Backward Bend]
- Shashankasana [Baby Pose]
- Ushtrasana [Camel Pose]
- Trikonasana [Triangle Simple]
- Tadasana [Stretch Pose]
- Matsyasana [Fish in Lotus]
- Halasana [Plough 1]
- Naukasana [Saucer Pose]
- Urdhva Prasarita Padasana [Thirty, Sixty, Ninety Both Legs]
- Jatara Parivartanasana [Legover Both Legs]
- Udarakarshana Asana [Abdominal Massage Twist]
- Uddiyana Bandha [Abdominal Lift]
- Yoga Mudra

DIARRHOEA

This is one of the body's most natural way of telling us that it has been loaded with unacceptable food. Diarrhoea can be caused by an inflammation of the intestines, the presence of bacterial parasites in the intestines, indigestion, intestinal weakness or nervousness. Other causes include chills, allergic reactions to certain types of food, inability to assimilate milk, inability to digest gluten found in wheat, food poisoning, an excess intake of soft drinks and pastries, eating unripe fruit, eating food with artificial sweeteners and eating contaminated food. It can also be due to a viral infection. Antibiotics containing magnesium can cause diarrhoea as a side effect. Common symptoms are abdominal pain, bloody stools, fever, loss of appetite and an increase in thirst. In children, diarrhoea can cause lethargy, cold feet, sunken eyes, a reduced urine flow, dry skin and dry tongue.

Fasting is highly recommended. Astringent foods, bitter foods, food that helps bile secretions and food rich in tannin help prevent diarrhoea. Take plenty of fruit juice with yoghurt, sago or rice water, coconut water and soup made of lentils. During the period of convalescence, have buttermilk and barley water with glucose. Plenty of fresh orange juice also helps. On further improvement, bland foods, along with oranges or grapefruit juice, is advised. In cases of dehydration, a glass of water with a pinch of salt and a teaspoonful of sugar every 2 hours is recommended.

Children are to be given plenty of water and food containing electrolytes like sodium chloride or potassium chloride and other nutrients, which are lost during diarrhoea. Adding bitter foods to the diet improves the digestive power.

Avoid milk, muskmelons, plums, coffee, tea, iced drink, fruit other than those mentioned above, all green leafy vegetables, horseradish, as well as food rich in fibre.

Recipes

For improving the digestive power:

- Have carrot soup before meals for a week.
- Make a paste from fresh curry leaves and honey. Have a tablespoon of this 2 times a day for a week.

To relieve diarrhoea:

- Have nutmeg fruit sweetened in sugar once or twice a day until the problem disappears.

- Boil cut guava in a little water. Eat this 3 times a day.
- Add the slices of a well-ripened banana to a cup of ordinary tea. Drink this 2 times a day.
- Mix dried yam powder together with some butter. Have a teaspoon of this once or twice a day until the diarrhoea stops.
- Have diced garlic with buttermilk 3 times a day. This destroys the germs that cause putrefaction.
- Grind a small piece of dried ginger, and add it to a glass of warm water. Mix well. Drink this once a day.
- Fry fennel seeds in ghee. Add anise and salt. Take a teaspoon of this with rice or yoghurt.
- Grind nutmeg seeds on a smooth stone to extract the milk. Add half a teaspoon of the milk to half a cup of yoghurt or buttermilk. Drink this once a day. Add rock sugar to taste.
- Have the white pulp of a pomegranate with its seeds 2 times a day. Add natural brown sugar to taste.
- Have rice with yoghurt or buttermilk. Yoghurt contains live lactobacillus bacteria, which are good for the intestines.
- Have a peeled and grated unripe or half-ripe apple 3 times a day for 3 days. Or dry some unripe sliced apples in the sun. Grind them until they become a powder. Add 1 tablespoon of the powder to a glass of warm water. Mix well. Drink this 2 times a day.
- To a bowl of cooked arrowroot add a teaspoon of malt, whey and a pinch of the powder of cardamom seeds. Have this once a day. Instead of arrowroot, mung beans, wheat, polished rice or soya beans can be used.
- Make a soup of okra. Add small red beans and salt to taste. Season it with a pinch of cinnamon, clove flower buds and cumin seeds. Drink this once a day. A small piece of green or red pepper can be added for flavour, but this is optional.
- Simmer potato peel, an onion, an unpeeled carrot and a few cloves of garlic over low heat until the water reduces to a third of the original volume. Add a pinch of salt and any seasoning herbs, such as black pepper, before drinking the soup.

For diarrhoea with blood:

- Have a soup made from sunflower seeds and rock sugar 3 times a day for 3 days.

- Blend 10 grams of black sesame seeds and 10 grams of raw sugar in a glass of goat's milk. Drink this 2 times a day.

For other types of diarrhoea:

- For diarrhoea due to food poisoning, add a tablespoon of tomato pulp to a baked apple. Mix well. Have this 3 times a day.
- For watery and smelly diarrhoea, mix together equal quantities of powdered coriander seeds and cumin seeds. Add 5 tablespoons of water and filter. Drink the filtered water with rock sugar once a day.

For dehydration due to diarrhoea:

- Boil 2 fried figs and a piece of fried ginger in a glass of water. Drink this 3 times a day.
- In a glass of coconut water, add sugar and a pinch of salt. Drink this 3 times a day. It is also good for diarrhoea with blood or vomiting.

To relieve diarrhoea in children:

Add 1 gram of raw sugar to a tablespoon of fresh lemon juice. Make the children take this 2 times a day.

Juice

To prevent and relieve diarrhoea:

- Have the fresh juice of strawberries or pomegranates before meals.
- Have a glass of tender coconut water with cucumber juice 3 times a day.
- Blend 50 grams of raspberries in buttermilk. Drink the juice 2 times a day for 3 days.
- Blend 10 grams of cumin seeds and 10 grams of sea salt or 10 grams of ginger with 5 grams of sea salt or 10 grams of fenugreek in glass of buttermilk. Drink this 3 times a day for 2 days.
- Have a glass of the juice of apples, watermelons, blackcurrants or celery. If desired, add an equal part peppermint, blackberry leaves, raspberries, carrots, radishes, figs, guavas, pineapples, olives, string beans, apricots, papayas or lemons. Drink this once every 2 hours for 3 days.

For diarrhoea associated with vomiting and abdominal swelling:

- Have fresh pineapple juice 2 times a day for 3 days.
- Mix together a teaspoon of honey, a teaspoon of fresh ginger or lemon juice and a pinch of cardamom powder. Drink this 2 times a day.

For dehydration due to diarrhoea:
Have a glass of red radish juice 3 times a day.

Infusion

For improving the digestive power:
Drink a hot or cold infusion of caraway seeds, comfrey rootstock or elecampane rootstock 2 times a day after meals for a week. Alternatively, you can have a decoction of any of the above.

For improving the digestive power in children:
Give them 2 tablespoons of the infusion of aniseed, chicory or elecampane rootstock 2 times a day.

To relieve diarrhoea:
- Have the infusion of St. John's Wort.
- Have a glass of the infusion of basil leaves 3 times a day.
- Have a glass of the cold infusion of amaranth leaves, apple peel, barley or comfrey rootstock 3 times a day.

To relieve diarrhoea in children:
Give them 2 tablespoons of the infusion of the dried fruit peel of guava that has been powdered, marshmallow, shepherd's purse herb, coriander seeds or coriander leaves, dried agrimony aerial part with rock sugar or dried agrimony mixed with an equal quantity of caraway seeds. Make the children take this 2 times a day before meals for 3 days. This also improves digestion.

Decoction

To prevent and relieve diarrhoea:
Take 2 teaspoons of the decoction of dried avocado leaves or lady's mantle 3 times a day.

To relieve diarrhoea in children:
Make a decoction from dried herbs (or the leaves) of lady's mantle and the dried roots of meadowsweet. Mix them together in equal proportion. Add a pinch of salt or sugar to taste. Give the children a tablespoon of this 2 times a day.

Application

For relieving diarrhoea in children:
Rub some ginger juice on the region of the navel.

Asana Routine

These Asanas are good, especially for chronic diarrhoea caused by intestinal parasites:
- Tadasana [Stretch Pose]
- Tiryaka Tadasana [Swaying Palm Tree]
- Katichakrasana [Cork Screw]
- Bhujanga Tiryaka [Swinging Cobra]
- Udarakarshana Asana [Abdominal Massage Twist]
- Meditation

DYSENTERY

This is the inflammation of the mucous membrane of the large intestine. It is characterised by bloody stools, abdominal cramps and fever. There are 2 types of dysentery: amoebic and bacillary. Amoebic dysentery is an infection caused by amoebae It is more common. Bacillary dysentery is caused by bacteria. The infection can spread from person to person through the infected excrement that contaminates food or water. Causes of dysentery include eating contaminated food and drinking water contaminated with parasites. The infection mainly occurs in the colon and can spread to the lungs and liver. If left untreated, the infection can cause the intestinal walls to erode, resulting in many complications. Common symptoms of dysentery are frequent stools with blood or stools with mucous or both with abdominal pain, as well as cramps and gripping pain in the bowels. Also one feels a frequent tendency to answer the call of nature and a sense of heaviness in the rectum. The pulse also becomes rapid.

Developing a healthy eating habit is the best way to prevent dysentery. Bed rest and hospitalisation are advised for acute dysentery. Have a high protein, low-residue diet and supplement it with vitamins. Also include garlic in your food regularly. This can prevent both amoebic dysentery (early stage) and bacillary dysentery. Have papayas, radishes, figs, red currants or bitter gourd on a daily basis. Avoid gooseberries, drinking tap water and eating food prepared in an unhygienic way. Once diagnosed with dysentery, avoid eating raw salads.

Recipes

To prevent dysentery:
Have sliced onions with yoghurt regularly to prevent diarrhoea with mucus.

To control bacillary dysentery:

- Add buttermilk to cooked rice.
- Eat raw curry leaves until the dysentery is under control.
- Mix ginger with brown sugar. Eat this 3 times a day for 7 days.
- Add half a teaspoon of butter to a cup of hot tea. Drink this 2 times a day.
- Add a teaspoon of honey to a steamed potato. Eat this once a day until the problem is under control.
- Powder a tablespoon of fried fenugreek. Add a teaspoon of raw sugar and a glass of yoghurt. Mix well. Drink this 2 times a day for 2 days.

To relieve dysentery with blood discharge:

- Eat a baked eggplant once a day for a week.
- Eat a radish cooked and mixed with buttermilk once a day for a week.

Juice

To control bacillary dysentery:
Have bitter orange juice mixed with an equal quantity of water until the problem clears.

Infusions

To prevent dysentery:
Have an infusion of roasted fenugreek before meals.

To control bacillary dysentery:

- Have a glass of the cold infusion of guava leaves, blackberry leaves or berries, or the infusion or garlic 3 times a day.
- Have a glass of the warm infusion of coriander and cumin seeds mixed together in equal proportion 3 times a day until the dysentery subsides.

For dysentery with blood discharge:
Have an infusion of peppermint leaves 3 times a day for 5 days.

Decoctions

To control bacillary dysentery:

- Take a tablespoon of the decoction of pitted olives and ginger mixed together in equal proportion 2 times a day.
- Take 2 tablespoons of the decoction of amaranth leaves, comfrey rootstock, motherwort leaves or radish leaves diluted with water before meals 3 times a day.

FOOD POISONING

This is caused by eating contaminated food, careless handling of food as well as by improper storage, canning or cooking of food. When food is not kept properly, bacteria multiply in it at room temperature. For instance, potato salads and creamy coleslaw breed bacteria if they are not properly refrigerated. Eating them can cause food poisoning. Eating fatty foods when the stomach is irritated can also cause food poisoning. It can also be caused by the poisoning of certain plants and animals. Food poisoning can be caused by a disease in the animal itself.

Symptoms of food poisoning caused by:

Eating poorly preserved foods (botulism):
Dim vision and difficulty in talking because of the paralysis of the larynx and throat muscles.

Eating mushrooms:
Abdominal pain, vomiting, diarrhoea and liver damage.

Eating shellfish:
May cause paralysis of the neck and chest muscles, as well as a reddish blue rash.

Eating contaminated meat:
Results in abdominal cramps, nausea, diarrhoea and fever.

Eating contaminated food other than meat:
Results in nausea, vomiting and abdominal pain.

Develop a healthy eating habit. Eating freshly prepared garden products prevents food poisoning. Drink plenty of warm water. The best antidote for food poisoning is ginger. Avoid gas-producing, off-colour, funny smelling food, as well as food from bulging and dented cans.

The following measures help relieve food poisoning:

Recipes

- Chew caraway seeds for relief from upset stomach and nausea.
- Crush a piece of ginger. Add it to vinegar, preferably rice vinegar, and drink the mixture to control food poisoning that results from having eaten fish, fruit or vegetables.
- To remedy fish and meat poisoning, add a quarter teaspoonful of dry fried common salt to a cup of warm water and drink.
- Induce vomiting for food poisoning caused by eating shellfish by adding a teaspoonful of powdered mustard seed to a glass of water. Drink this immediately.

Juice

- Add a teaspoon of fresh ginger juice to a glass of fresh orange juice. Drink this 3 times a day.
- The juice of the leaves and berries of sarsaparilla is a very good antidote. Drink a glass of either of this 3 times a day.
- Apple juice or the juice of blackberries are rich in pectin, which absorbs toxins. They are good for food poisoning that results from eating meat and eggs.

Infusions

- Have a glass of the hot infusion of borage, burdock or dandelion roots 3 times a day.
- For food poisoning due to spoilt or stale food, drink a strong tea of cinnamon bark mixed together with a teaspoonful of honey 2 times a day. Do not use cinnamon if the pain is associated with a sore throat, dry lips, thirst, vomiting of blood, fever or ulcers.

GASTROENTERITIS

This is an inflammation of the mucous membrane that lines the stomach and intestines. Inflammation in any part of the small intestines is called enteritis. It is given a different name when it appears in different sections of the digestive tract. For example, it is called duodenitis if it appears in the duodenum region. Enteritis can also result from food poisoning, excessive alcohol intake, viral or bacterial infection or food allergies. Common symptoms are diarrhoea (infrequent), abdominal cramps, abdominal pain, vomiting and fever.

When the symptoms cease, a bland liquid diet is advised. Introduce well-cooked food gradually. Alfalfa leaves, aloe, aniseed, beet greens, caraway seeds, cardamom seeds, carrots, celery, comfrey, coriander, garlic, goldenseal, lemon balm, oats, okra, ordinary tea, papayas, parsley, peppermint, pomegranates, spinach, squashes, tamarind, watercress, whey and yoghurt help clear gastroenteritis.

Avoid food and fluids as long as you experience nausea and vomiting. Drink plenty of fluids with electrolytes once the nausea and vomiting stop. Avoid eating plums, hard and fibrous foods, raw vegetables and fruit. Also avoid black pepper and cayenne as they aggravate gastroenteritis.

Recipes

To prevent gastroenteritis:

- To a cup of ordinary tea, add a ripe banana. Mix well. Drink this once a day.
- Cut a fresh guava into slices. Boil the slices in water until well cooked. Eat this 3 times a day.
- Boil 1 tablespoon of washed barley in a cup of water for a few minutes. Discard the water. Boil this half cooked barley again in 2 pints of fresh water until the water reduces to half. Strain the water, and add half a cup of the barley water to half a cup of fresh water. Drink this 3 times a day to get rid of stomach and intestinal irritation.

For relief from abdominal pain due to gastroenteritis:

- Take a tablespoon of the powder of a sun dried apple in warm water 2 times a day before meals.
- If abdominal pain is below the navel region, have a glass of water mixed together with a teaspoon of vinegar and a pinch of salt to taste 2 times a day for 2 days.
- Saute half a teaspoon of crushed black peppercorns in a teaspoon of olive oil with 1 gram of grated dried

ginger and a few curry leaves. Now add a glass of water. Bring the mixture to the boil until the water reduces to a third of the original. Add a pinch of salt. Drink this as a soup. Alternatively, mix with rice and eat it 2 times a day for 3 days. If desired, add fresh lemon juice to taste.

Juice

To prevent gastroenteritis:
Have a glass of the juice of chicory flowering herbs 2 times a day.

For relief from abdominal pain due to gastroenteritis:
Have the fresh juice of apples, dates or pineapples once every 2 hours.

Infusions

To prevent and relieve gastroenteritis:

- Have a glass of the infusion of tea leaves with half its weight of ginger once a day.
- Have the infusions of any of the following 3 times a day after meals: (i) Two teaspoons of the infusion of dried basil leaves with a teaspoon of honey, (ii) A cup of infusion of the mixture of basil leaves and blackcurrant berries mixed together in equal quantities, (iii) A cup of the infusion of 2 olives and 10 grams of ginger, (iv) A cup of the infusion of powdered nutmeg, cinnamon and clove flower buds mixed together in equal quantities for a week or (v) A cup of the infusion of lady's mantle leaves.

For relief from abdominal pain due to gastroenteritis:
Have a cup of the hot infusion of chamomile flowers 2 times a day before meals for a week.

For inflammation in the digestive tract:
Have an infusion of fennel with cardamom.

Decoctions

To relieve gastroenteritis:
Have the decoctions of any of the following 3 times a day after meals:

(i)   Two teaspoons of the decoction of sarsaparilla roots diluted with water,

(ii) Two teaspoons of the decoction of fennel seeds with honey or

(iii) Two teaspoons of the decoction of the mixture of 20 grams of fresh guava leaves, 10 grams of ginger and a pinch of salt.

For relief from abdominal pain due to gastroenteritis:

- Take 2 tablespoons of the decoction of fennel seeds diluted with water 3 times a day for 3 days.
- Take 2 tablespoons of the decoction of sarsaparilla roots diluted in water 2 times a day for 3 days.

HAEMORRHOIDS/PILES

If there is anal bleeding and if the blood is bright red, bleeding is from the rectum itself. Bleeding might be a common symptom of benign tumours or cancer of the colon as well. Ulcerative colitis can also cause anal bleeding but with diarrhoea, which is more common. Examination is required to determine the cause. Haemorrhoids is the swelling inside or around the anus due to the varicose condition of the rectal veins. Veins around the rectum do not have much support from any other tissue, so they distend easily. Causes of haemorrhoids include constipation, pregnancy, blood congestion, liver problems, abdominal tumours, prolonged standing or sitting, excess laxative use, and coughing and sneezing, which increase pressure on the rectal veins. It can also be due to congested blood. Symptoms of haemorrhoids are painful evacuation of the bowels, along with streaks of blood. In some cases, the blood may be black. There will be rectal bleeding and a feeling of fullness in the anus as well. Piles may protrude from the rectum, and when they do, the sphincter muscle of the rectum tightens, preventing the return of the rectal veins.

The most important way to heal haemorrhoids is to effect a change in the diet. If the haemorrhoids is associated with constipation, treating constipation is the best way to solve the problem. Include in the daily diet food and herbs that prevent constipation like fruit and vegetables, butter, curry leaves, horseradish, prunes, buttermilk, coconut water and yoghurt. Drink lots of water. Certain types of food like red beans, lotus, papayas, spinach, lemons, olives, parsley and guavas are very beneficial in treating piles.

For all types of anal bleeding avoid heaty foods, especially mustard seeds and mustard leaves. Also avoid food and drinks that induce constipation, such as spicy foods, wine, malt, coffee, tea, sugar and condiments and nutmeg.

Recipes

To relieve haemorrhoids/piles:

- Soak dried figs in water overnight. Eat them with the water before each meal for a week.
- Dry fry black sesame seeds. Add rock sugar and blend well. Take a teaspoon of this mixture with a glass of goat's milk every night for 15 days.
- Have a starfruit, 2 figs, ripened bananas or steamed bananas with rock sugar before meals. Alternatively, have a guava with a pinch of salt 2 times a day on an empty stomach for 2 months.
- Grate a raw and tender white radish. Add honey. Eat this on an empty stomach in the morning. Alternatively, have the juice of a white radish with a pinch of salt.

Infusions

To relieve haemorrhoids/piles:
Have a glass of the infusion of amaranth leaves, barberries, curry leaves, dandelion roots, goldenseal roots or parsley leaves 2 times a day regularly. These act as natural laxatives.

Applications

To relieve haemorrhoids:

- Dab the anal region with an infusion of agrimony leaves.
- If the skin around the rectum is cracked, apply honey.
- For rectal itch, apply a wad of cotton dipped in vinegar to the rectum. Leave it on overnight.
- If there is ulceration, apply lavender oil to the affected area.
- After washing the area well, dry the region thoroughly. Apply wheatgerm oil.
- Make a paste made from the rind of pomegranate fruit softened in water. Apply it to the area for a week.
- Cut some cranberries and wrap them in a piece of cloth. Tuck it gently into the affected area for relief.

- Place some ice cubes on the region for a few minutes, after which apply glycerine or cocoa butter to the rectum.
- Dice a green onion. Mix it with wheat flour, and fry the slices in animal fat. Spread the slices on a cloth and apply to the anus just before going to bed. This clears enlarged haemorrhoids.

Bath

- Sit in 6 inches of warm water on a towel twisted into a circle for half an hour. This soothes the inflamed tissues and relaxes the muscle spasms.
- Add to warm water chamomile flowers, crushed chestnut or oak bark. Infusions of these can be used instead of the herbs. Sit in this herbal water for 20 to 30 minutes for relief.

Asana Routine

To relieve haemorrhoids :

- Gomukhasana [Posture Clasp]
- Janu Sirasasana [Alternate Leg Pull]
- Sarvangasana [Shoulderstand]
- Matsyasana [Fish in Lotus]
- Paschimottanasana [Backstretch]
- Ekapada Jatara Parivartanasana [Legover Single Leg]
- Ekapada Halasana [Plough Single Leg]
- Chakrasana [Back Pushup]
- Supta Badrasana [Knee and Thigh Stretch Lying down]
- Shashanka Bhujangasana [Striking Cobra]
- Shalabasana [Locust Pose]
- Dhanurasana [Bow Pose]
- Matsya Kridasana [Flapping Fish Pose]
- Moola Bandha [Perenium Retraction Lock]
- Uddiyana Bandha [Abdominal Lift]
- Yoga Mudra

Inverted Asanas release pressure on the rectal veins, help drain the blood and induce the peristaltic motion. Try out the following:

- Ushtrasana [Camel Pose]
- Matsyasana [Fish in Lotus]

- Paschimottanasana [Backstretch]
- Vajrasana [Siting Thunderbolt]
- Shashankasana [Baby Pose]
- Shashanka Bhujangasana [Striking Cobra]
- Meditation

HERNIA

This is a protrusion of any part of the body tissue through the wall that contains it. The main cause is imperfect growth of the wall of that region or injury due to physical strain that results from lifting heavy objects, constipation, obesity or bad posture.

There are three type of hernia. Femoral hernia — a bulge that appears on the upper thighs; inguinal hernia — protrusion of the intestines near the groin; and umbilical hernia — a protrusion of the abdominal area around the navel. It can be cured in the early stages by doing Asanas that strengthen the region.

Ventral hernia is a projection of part of the intestines into the abdominal wall.

Recipe for ventral hernia

Mix star anise seed powder together with some rice wine and cinnamon. Add a pinch of salt. Have a cup of this 2 times a day.

Infusions for umbilical hernia

To relieve hernia:
Have a glass of the infusion of fennel seeds 3 times a day for a week.

Decoctions for umbilical hernia

To relieve hernia:

- Take 2 tablespoons of the decoction of orange seeds and caraway seeds mixed together in equal proportions daily after meals.
- Mix 2 tablespoons of the decoction of grapefruit seeds together with the same amount of caraway seeds. Add a glass of water. Take this daily after meals.

Applications

For all types of hernia:

- Apply a hot fomentation of the infusion of oak bark and vinegar.
- Apply a poultice of comfrey leaves to the affected area for a few hours a day.

Asana Routine

To prevent hernia:

- Supta Badrasana [Knee and Thigh Stretch Lying down]
- Ekapada Jatara Parivartanasana [Legover Single Leg]
- Halasana [Plough 1]
- Sarvangasana [Shoulderstand]
- Yoga Mudra, without bending forward too much

INFLAMMATION OF THE INTESTINES

The intestines are where the vital digestive processes of the body take place. Malabsorption of digested food stems from an allergic reaction to some types of food, causing problems on the intestinal walls.

Include in the daily diet demulcents and anti-inflammatory and carminative foods. For inflammation of the small intestines, pectin is necessary to stimulate intestinal action and to combat intestinal infections. Apples, for instance, contain pectin. They also assist in the production of pectin in the body. Avoid white radishes and gluten-rich foods, such as wheat as well as milk, sugar, tea and coffee.

Recipes

To relieve inflammation of the intestines:

- For toning the intestines eat red grapes.
- Drink a cup of the juice extract of cucumbers or okra. If desired, mix both together.
- Drink barley water mixed with milk to clear the irritation.
- Dry fry equal quantities of fennel seeds and black pepper. Grind them. Take a teaspoon of this with the water in which rice has been cooked 2 times a day.

- Mix a teaspoon of cold pressed soya bean oil together with a quarter teaspoon of fresh lemon juice. Drink this on an empty stomach daily for a week.

Infusions

To control and relieve inflammation of the intestines:

- Take 3 tablespoons of the hot infusion of dried German chamomile flowers 3 times a day.
- Have a glass of the infusion of aniseed, caraway seeds and fennel seeds mixed together in equal proportions 2 times a day. This is also an excellent way to cleanse the intestines.

INFLAMMATION OF THE COLON

The thick gooey aspect of okra is good for treating inflammation of the colon. Avoid strawberry seeds as they can cause inflammation.

WORMS

Worm infestation in the intestines is common due to water pollution and poor hygiene. There are different types of parasites that can enter the body. Stomachache, vomiting, dizziness, fever, anaemia, loss of weight and distention of the stomach are common symptoms.

Threadworm thrive in the rectal area and cause itchiness. Loss of weight, bad breath and loss of appetite are noticed.

Roundworm thrive in the small intestines; the larvae present in dirty surroundings can be ingested through water or raw vegetables. Usual symptoms are itchiness at the tip of the nose and excess secretion of saliva. A child with roundworm feels very hungry in the early stages but later loses his appetite and develops nervousness and irritability.

Hookworm thrive in the small intestines and suck the blood. They cause severe anaemia. The urge to eat sweets and yellow tinge on the skin are symptoms.

Increase the intake of the following in the daily diet: coconuts, squashes, aloe, carrots, garlic, arecanuts, mulberries, unripe walnuts, onions, papayas, pomegranates, pumpkins and tamarind.

Recipes

- Have a cooked squash with its seeds daily for a week with meals.
- Take a tablespoon of onion juice mixed together with a teaspoon of honey in the morning.
- Take a teaspoon of fresh ginger juice mixed together with warm water 3 times a day for a week.
- Take a teaspoon of jaggery, followed by a tablespoon of spearmint juice mixed together with honey in the morning.
- Crush the rind, pulp and seeds of a lemon. Steep them in cold water for few hours. Drink a glass of this before going to bed.
- Have a glass of milk in which 2 grams of grated clove flower buds have been boiled in the morning.
- Have an unripe papaya soaked in vinegar. Alternatively, drink the fresh milky juice of an unripe papaya diluted with water.
- Crush a tablespoon of pumpkin seeds. Add 250 ml of any fruit juice. Mix well and drink. An hour later, take a glass of the infusion of any herbal purgative. Alternatively, have pumpkin seeds regularly for 21 days.

Infusion

Have a glass of the infusion of black peppercorns with honey twice a day for 2 weeks.

Decoction

Take a tablespoon of the decoction of a whole lemon.

To eliminate tapeworms:

- Eat tender coconut meat mixed with coconut water first thing in the morning Do this for 3 days.
- Take a tablespoon of pomegranate seeds once daily.
- Drink half a glass of infusion of root bark of mulberry plant.

To eliminate roundworm:

Have a raw carrot on an empty stomach for 2 weeks.

To eliminate threadworm:

Grind 2 grams of the pips of a lemon and add a teaspoon of honey. Mix well. Have this in the morning before breakfast.

14

The Gall Bladder, Liver and the Pancreas
❧

THE GALL BLADDER

The gall bladder stores bile, concentrates it and releases it to the small intestine during digestion. It is one of those organs where stones form and cause infections. One of the main reasons for gall bladder problems is food intolerance. Whether it is a stone, chronic inflammation of the bladder or an infection, gall bladder problems can be most distressing. Abdominal pain occurs just under the ribs on the right side of the body. Ominous as this may sound, once diseased the gall bladder cannot be cured. For a healthy gall bladder increase in the diet food with cholagogue property.

GALL BLADDER CANCER

Gall stones in the gall bladder are associated with cancer of the organ. If left untreated in the early stages, this cancer spreads easily to the liver and adjacent organs. Indigestion accompanied by pain under the ribs in the upper right section of the abdomen is a common symptom. Due to the obstruction, the flow of bile is restricted and thus jaundice appears. Prevention is the best cure, so good eating habits and a lifestyle are recommended.

GALL STONES

Gall stones, formed from the materials found in bile, are a mixture of calcium carbonate, cholesterol and bile salts. Cholesterol found in animal fats is the biggest contributor to the formation of gall stones. Another contributor is bile pigments. Infection accelerates the process of stone formation. Overweight and light-skinned people are more susceptible to developing stones in the gall bladder, as are women.

A small or single stone may live silently in the gall bladder without causing any problem. When the stone moves into the opening of the gall bladder or into the bile duct, sharp pain is experienced to the right of the abdomen soon after eating fatty or fried foods. When inflammation occurs because of the stone, belching and diarrhoea with nausea result. Some people may feel a sense of fullness in the region of the liver and suffer from pain similar to that of colic.

Gall stones in the gall bladder are associated with cancer of the organ. The cancer spreads easily to the liver and adjacent organs if not treated in the early stages.

Proper food habits are most effective in preventing gall stones. Take the necessary measures to prevent persistent indigestion and flatulence. Increase the intake of food that produces bile salts to help decrease the size of the stone. Barberries and parsley are helpful in reducing the size of the stone, though they act slowly.

As a preventive measure, avoid all animal fats, including egg yolk and butter. As the body can manufacture cholesterol out of fats that do not contain it, do not increase your intake of fats. Every effort must also be made to counter the problem of obesity.

The following measures are for a healthy gall bladder:

Recipes

These also improve bile production:

- Have a clove of garlic every morning. Follow this with a glass of warm water in which a teaspoon of fresh lemon juice and honey have been mixed.
- Have 2 tablespoons of cold pressed olive oil before each meal.
- Boil 3 starfruit. Add 2 teaspoons of honey to it to make a paste. Have this once a day.
- Add to your daily diet beetroot, cherries, chicory, coconuts, oats, onions and peppermint. These are good cleansing agents.

Juice

- Have 3 tablespoons of undiluted lemon juice with honey before breakfast for a week.
- Have a tablespoon of olive oil with half a cup of lemon juice or grapefruit juice just before going to bed. If you feel nauseous in the morning, have any hot beverage.
- Have a glass of radish juice once a week.

To prevent formation of gall stones:

- Have a glass of raw carrot juice twice everyday.
- Have 2 tablespoons of chicory flowering herb juice diluted with milk twice a day.

Infusions

- Have a glass of hot infusion of chamomile flowers (this may help dissolve gall stones) or barberry leaves 3 times a day before meals.
- Have a tablespoon of the infusion of dandelion roots 2 times a day to cleanse the liver and gall bladder. It also prevents bile stagnation.
- Have a glass of hot infusion of chicory flowering herbs twice a day.

To prevent formation of gall stones:

Have a glass of hot infusion of dandelion roots, rosemary leaves, lavender flowers, parsley leaves or parsley seeds.

Other herbs that help prevent the formation of stones include barley, garlic, grapes, grapefruit, lettuce, lemons, pears, polished rice, radishes, starfruit, strawberries, string beans and watermelons. Try including some of these in your daily diet.

INFLAMMATION OF THE GALL BLADDER

This can happen suddenly with severe pain in the upper right abdomen. An increase in the pulse rate, fever, nausea and vomiting may follow. In case of pus formation, there will be chills with fever.

Recipes

To prevent inflammation of the gall bladder:

- Have grated fresh horseradish mixed with cider vinegar and grape sugar 3 times a day.
- Have a cup of infusion of barberries 3 times a day.
- If there is bleeding (evident in vomit), have celery and eggplant cooked together or separately 3 times a day.

Asana Routine

- Trikonasana [Triangle Simple]
- Urdhva Hastottanasana [Side Bend Both Arms]
- Padahastasana [Legclasp]
- Janu Sirasasana [Alternate Leg Pull]
- Paschimottanasana [Backstretch]
- Matsyendrasana [Full Twist]
- Bhujangasana [Cobra Pose]
- Dhanurasana [Bow Pose]
- Jatara Parivartanasana [Legover Both Legs]
- Uddiyana Bandha [Abdominal Lift]
- Yoga Mudra

Specific Asanas

- Pada Angushtasana [Legclasp Gorilla]
- Janu Sirasasana [Alternate Leg Pull]
- Bhujangasana [Cobra]
- Jatara Parivartanasana [Legover Both Legs]
- Maha Mudra [Great Seal]
- Uddhiyana Bandha [Abdominal Lift]

OBSTRUCTIVE JAUNDICE

The presence of stones or tumour restricts the free flow of bile from the liver. When the blood absorbs the bile, the "yellowness" is seen in the skin, mucous, urine and the whites of the eyes. Constant itching is another symptom, and vomit with bile appears green and tastes bitter. Consult a specialist to distinguish this from jaundice caused by inflammation of the liver.

Drink plenty of water to flush out bile through the urine. Season food with asafoetida regularly as a preventive measure. Figs and dandelion roots are also beneficial, so include them in your diet.

THE LIVER

The liver is a large glandular organ with many functions. These include processing blood and regulating its composition, storing sugar and releasing it in its assimilable form — glucose, as well as secreting bile.

More than any other organ in the body, the liver enables our body to benefit from the food we eat. Malnutrition is one of the chief causes of liver problems. Iron deficiency and anaemia can disrupt the proper functioning of the liver; a high intake of fatty foods can overburden it; and constipation or amoebic dysentery can cause the liver to be sluggish.

Common problems of the liver are cirrhosis (degeneration of the liver), viral hepatitis (inflammation of the liver), hepatitis A (caused by contaminated food and water) and hepatitis B (caused by body fluids).

Symptoms of a sluggish liver include loss of appetite, tiredness, weight loss, jaundice, swelling in the feet, red lines on palms, pain on the right side of the thoracic region with headaches, nausea and indigestion, a bitter taste in the mouth, belching, and feeling full after light meals due to stored bile that is not eliminated. Along with these, the spleen may enlarge.

Herbs like agrimony, bitter gourd, garlic, grapefruit, asparagus, plums and spearmint detoxify the liver. Gooseberries, oats, onions, peppermint and soya beans contain choline, a member of vitamin B complex that is necessary for a healthy liver. Radishes, barberries, borage, burdock, apple cider vinegar, evening primrose cherries and pomelos are cleansing agents for the liver. Carrots, celery, cherries, chicory, grapes, garlic and red beans, help combat liver disorders and jaundice by stimulating the flow of bile.

Another essential nutrient is zinc, which is found in wheatgerm, brown rice, black-eyed peas, brewer's yeast, chicory, sprouted seeds and grains, raw nuts, beetroot and beetroot greens, celery, radishes, garlic, lemons, and cucumbers. Vitamin E found in whole grain breads, wheatgerm and cereals and vitamin C found in citrus fruit are also necessary for a healthy liver. To stimulate the function of the liver, add lime or lemon juice and salt to taste in food.

The following measures rejuvenate the liver:

Recipes

- Have a clove of garlic with a teaspoon of olive oil at night for 14 days.
- Have almond milk. (Refer to recipe for colds).
- Eggplant is excellent for liver problems. It is good for treating enlargement of the liver, especially in children. Give them only whole wheat bread and roasted eggplants for 14 days.

Juice

- Have a glass of the juice of raw bitter gourd, celery, cherry or grapes daily before breakfast. This improves metabolism. It is also good for the normal functioning of the liver as well as for toning it.
- Have the fresh juice of the leaves of radishes once a day for the treatment of an indolent liver.
- Have a glass of warm lemon juice with honey every morning.
- Have a glass of the juice of chrysanthemum flowers once a day.
- Add a teaspoon of fresh aloe gel into a glass of apple juice. Mix well. Add a pinch of turmeric. Have this drink 3 times a day before meals.

Decoction

Have a tablespoon of the decoction of dandelion roots or plants after meals 2 times a day.

For congestion in the liver:

- Add a pinch of cardamom to 1 teaspoon of jaggery. Have this 3 times day.
- Have watermelon juice with cumin and suger cane juice once a day.
- Infuse chopped onions overnight in a glass of boiling water. Drink the liquid first thing in the morning until the problem clears.

Asana Routine

To tone the liver:

- Rishi [Rishi's Pose]
- Tadasana [Stretch Pose]
- Tiryaka Tadasana [Swaying Palm Tree Pose]
- Katichakrasana [Cork Screw Pose]
- Ardha Baddha Uttanasana [Legclasp Single Leg]
- Padahastasana [Legclasp]
- Udarakarshana Asana [Abdominal Massage Twist]
- Paripoorna Navasana [Diamond Pose 1]
- Paschimottanasana [Backstretch]
- Bhujanga Tiryaka [Swinging Cobra]
- Shashanka Bhujangasana [Striking Cobra]
- Yoga Mudra

CANCER OF THE LIVER

Primary cancer of the liver is often associated with cirrhosis. It can also be the result of exposure to carcinogenic chemicals or aflatoxin moulds that grow on unprotected grains and legumes like peanuts. Secondary cancer can be due to cancer of other abdominal organs. This can be easily transmitted to other parts of the body. Weight loss, pain in the upper abdomen, pain in the right side of the chest, accumulation of fluid in the abdomen and jaundice are common symptoms.

Prevention is the best cure. Eat the right types of food and herbs to maintain a healthy liver. Animal proteins in the form of dairy products, yoghurt, cheese and onions (either taken raw or with milk) are essential. A low salt diet, which can be easily digested, will also help. The most important types of food that help the liver in its cleansing and detoxifying operations are green vegetables and carrots.

Recipe

Have a glass of infusion of agrimony 3 times a day together with a glass of carrot juice to prevent liver disorders. These two may be complemented by an infusion of the leaves of ground ivy in equal proportion to agrimony.

CIRRHOSIS OF THE LIVER

This is the hardening of the liver that destroys the liver cells. When the liver cells gradually lose their function, the liver itself shrinks in size. Alcohol is the main cause of this problem. Other causes include malnutrition, inflammation of the liver (hepatitis), intestinal parasites, jaundice, disrupted blood circulation to the liver, syphilis and inflammation of the bile tract. A restriction in the free flow of blood in the portal vein results in the swelling of the abdomen and lower limbs. Due to an inflammation of the liver, the bile duct can be obstructed, resulting in jaundice and anaemia. Large veins over the abdomen near the navel region and reddish spots on the face caused by dilated capillaries, blood in vomit, thinning hair, bulging of the eyes or clubbed fingers may result. Breasts enlarge in men and menstruation becomes irregular in women.

To maintain a healthy liver animal protein in the form of dairy products, yoghurt and cheese are essential. A low salt diet that can be easily digested also help. The most important types of food that help the liver in its cleansing and detoxifying operations are green vegetables and carrots. Onions, either eaten raw or with milk, help maintain a healthy liver.

Organic proteins that are beneficial for the liver are brewer's yeast (2 tablespoons with each meal), goat's or cow's milk (preferably unheated and drunk fresh), cheese (not processed), sprouted seeds and grains, raw natural nuts, lychee berries, fennel seeds, and chamomile flowers.

Other supplements that help are lecithin (a source of choline), multivitamin supplements, vitamins C and E to heal and prevent scarring, as well as vitamin B6 and magnesium to prevent the accumulation of ammonia (yoghurt has the same function).

Avoid all meat and fatty foods, tea, coffee, spices, alcohol, carbonated beverages, all types of refined foods, animal fats, oil, salt, sugar, white sugar, cream, chocolates, canned foods, artificial flavouring and colouring, as well as eggs. Although egg yolk contains choline that is good for the liver, avoid it as it has a high cholesterol content.

Recipes

- Mix 2 tablespoons of olive oil and the juice of 1 lemon in a large glass of water. Add 4 cloves of garlic and blend them together. Take a tablespoon of this every morning for a week.

- Cut a pineapple into small cubes and soak them in honey for a few days. Have a few cubes every evening for a month.

- Cook drumstick (murunge) with the leaves to make a soup. Have this once a day for 4 weeks.

Infusions

- Have a glass of hot infusion of the black seeds of papaya, cumin seeds or dandelion roots 3 times a day.

- Pour a glass of boiling water over one heaped teaspoon of common club moss (lycopodium clavatum) and let it soak for 5 minutes. Sip the infusion slowly on an empty stomach once in the morning and once in the evening for 2–3 months.

- Add a teaspoon of juniper berries into a cup of boiling water. Let it stand for 10 minutes. Have the infusion three times a day. If the tincture is used, mix 15 drops in any infusion of choice and drink after meals.

- Have a cup of infusion of rosemary leaves or flowers 2 times a day or have 3 drops of rosemary essence in a cup of water with honey 3 times a day.

Applications

- For a warm compress of Swedish bitter moisten gauze or cotton wool in it and apply to the liver area in the morning. Follow this by applying marigold ointment to the liver area and bandaging it. Leave it on for 2–4 hours. Apply non-inflammatory oil to the skin before touching the gauze. If your skin is sensitive, rashes will develop in which case leave the compress on for a shorter period.

- For a warm poultice of horsetail, take some horsetail in a sieve and hang them over boiling water. When the herb becomes warm and soft, wrap it in a cloth and apply the poultice to the right side of the body covering the liver area. Keep the poultice warm and leave it on your body for a few hours. This is best done at night and should be left on your body overnight. Continue applying the poultice for a period of 30 days.

Tonics

Add 2 ounces of olive oil, a tablespoon of lemon juice and a clove of garlic into half a cup of water. Stir well. Have one-eighth of this mixture every morning before breakfast.

HEPATITIS

This occurs due to inflammation of the liver. There are two types: Hepatitis A and Hepatitis B. Hepatitis A is an infectious disease transmitted from person to person through poor hygiene. It is common among children. Common causes are viruses and bacterial infections. Jaundice, high fever, problems with the kidney and hypersensitivity are other causes. Symptoms show up between 2–6 weeks after the virus has been transmitted.

Hepatitis B is a serum hepatitis that is transmitted through blood transfusion and infected instruments like needles and blades. Symptoms will appear 4–20 weeks after the virus has been transmitted. In Hepatitis B, the liver can become tender and enlarged. It is more common in young adults.

For both types of hepatitis, symptoms in the early stage include loss of appetite, nausea and fatigue. Later, with the abnormal functioning of the liver, the skin and eyes may yellow. Jaundice, dark coloured urine or light stools are other effects.

To prevent hepatitis, make sure your diet consists of easily digestible foods in the form of soups. A low fat diet is recommended. For protein, consume carrots, green vegetables (green vegetables and carrots are also detoxifying agents), wheatgerm, black soya, and fresh yoghurt. Stick to a salt-free diet as hepatitis is associated with fluid retention in the body. Also add asafoetida as seasoning to your food.

Whenever possible, add dandelion roots and leaves, beetroot and beetroot tops, carrots and carrot tops, celery, burdock roots, garlic, onions, cucumbers and lemons to your diet. Avoid fatty foods. Even after recovery, it is better to avoid fatty, fried foods for at least a year depending upon the seriousness of the problem. Avoid turmeric as well. Refer also to food to include and exclude for cirrhosis of the liver.

Juice

- In a blender, add a cucumber, beetroot, carrot, onion or spring onion and lemon with or without water. Blend well. Drink plenty of this juice.
- Refer to tonic for cirrhosis of the liver on how to make a hepatitis tonic.

JAUNDICE

When an excess of bile circulates in the blood, this gives the skin a yellow tinge. Gall stones, tumours, cirrhosis or hepatitis obstruct the free flow of bile. Congenital closure of the bile duct causes jaundice in infancy. "Yellowness" in the skin and the whites of the eyes, vomiting green fluids, and the enlargement of the liver with pain in the upper right side of the body are common symptoms.

Recipes

- Cook dry figs in water until they become soft. Add sugar or honey. Cook it over a low flame until it becomes a jelly. Have a teaspoon of this twice a day. Drink milk afterwards as this activates the liver and clears the "yellowness" on the skin.
- Have ripe bananas with asafoetida (a small piece) to help clear the "yellowness".
- Add a teaspoon of lemon juice and honey to a well-ripened banana. Have this just before meals for a week.
- For infectious hepatitis, boil 90 grams of dried rice plants, including the stem and leaves and 10 grams of dandelion roots in a litre of water until the liquid reduces to 200 millilitres. Have 100 millilitres of this 2 times a day for 30 days.
- Boil 10 grams of sun dried mulberry fruit in a glass of water until the water reduces to half the original volume. Drink the water 2 times a day before meals for 14 days.

Juice

- Have a cup of celery juice with honey, parsley, crushed grapes or bitter gourd every morning.

- Have beetroot juice once a day for 3 days to clear excess "yellowness" in the urine and skin.
- Have 2 tablespoons of the juice of chicory leaves with milk 3 times a day.
- Have 5 drops of the extract of barberries 3 times a day.
- Have 2–3 glasses of fresh sugar cane juice daily for a week.

Infusions

- Have a glass of infusion of parsley leaves and seeds, safflower seeds, dandelion roots or mulberry roots 2 times a day for a week.
- Have a glass of infusion of malt and orange peel to relieve the after-effects of acute hepatitis.
- Mix in equal quantities cumin seeds, coriander seeds and dried pieces of lemon balm leaves. Have the infusion in boiled milk sweetened with honey twice a day for a week.

THE PANCREAS

This organ produces insulin and glucagon and secretes pancreatic juice to the duodenum (part of the small intestine below the stomach). An imbalance in the production of insulin in the pancreas causes problems like diabetes and hypoglycaemia.

Some ways to prevent the malfunction of the pancreas include the regular use of neem leaves in the diet as seasoning. Also, have a glass of infusion of fenugreek seeds or neem leaves once a day or have a glass of bitter gourd juice every morning.

DIABETES

The fundamental problem in diabetes is our system's inability to metabolise glucose completely. This results in an accumulation of sugar in the blood stream. There are two types of diabetes: Diabetes Mellitus and Diabetes Insipidus.

Diabetic Mellitus (sweet) is a common disorder of the metabolism of carbohydrates. In more than 50 percent of patients, it is linked with a hereditary background.

Diabetes Mellitus is associated with an insufficient production of insulin and excess glucose in the blood and urine. When the pancreas does not produce enough insulin, unused sugar enters the blood steam and the urine. Even if there is no sugar in the urine, it is possible to have excess sugar in the blood. Glucose accumulates in the blood and is eliminated through the urine instead of being used for producing energy.

Diabetes Insipidus is a rare but chronic disorder of the pituitary gland. When sufficient antidiuretic hormone is not secreted, an excess of dilute urine is produced. This can be genetic or constitutional. The urine does not contain sugar in this case. A person with this disease tends to drink a lot of water.

A CLOSER LOOK AT DIABETES MELLITUS

This is not always caused by a defective pancreas. Other organs or tissues can interfere with the metabolism of carbohydrates to cause it. More common among those who are overweight, this type of diabetes generally worsens in the presence of an infectious illness, such as the common cold, when the pituitary, thyroid and adrenal glands malfunction, during pregnancy, as well as during emotional stress. When the sugar level reaches a certain point (the body pH drops below 7.0), the body has to metabolise stored fat for energy. The by-product of this is the formation of ketones and acetones, resulting in fainting spells, coma and even death.

In the early stages, fatigue, weakness and frequent urination appear and usually in mild form; if left untreated, there is danger ahead. In adults, if sugar develops in the blood stream, the cells crave for it, resulting in weakness, dizziness, cold sweats, excessive thirst, frequent and excessive discharge of urine with or without sugar, numb feet, dryness in the mouth, tiredness, blurred vision, vaginitis in women and erectile dysfunction in men, skin disorders, hypertension, weight loss, as well as a tendency for the arteries to narrow. This may disrupt circulation, especially in the feet, resulting in advanced gangrene of the feet. Another possible side effect is ruptured capillaries of the eyes, resulting in blindness. Women may experience persistent genital itch. In children, the symptoms include excessive thirst and urine,

bedwetting, rapid weight loss, weakness, itching of the skin and an increase in appetite.

The disorder stems from the way the body processes carbohydrates. A proper diet is essential in controlling diabetes. Keep the intake of protein, fat and cholesterol low and increase the intake of high fibre.

A general diet for the early stages includes high complex carbohydrates and low-calorie foods, with plenty of fibre and nutrients from whole grains, lentils, nuts and seeds. A diet like this coupled with Yogasanas help prevent or even cure diabetes. A diabetic person must, however, regulate his or her physical exercise.

Insulin, adrenaline and glucagon are important hormones that help metabolise carbohydrates. Insulin helps to lower the blood sugar while the other two raise it. Chromium, one of the most important minerals for diabetics, helps to metabolise the proper sugar and glucose tolerance levels. With increased levels of insulin, the demand for chromium increases. With a deficiency in chromium, a person with a normal amount of insulin, may not be able to utilise it.

A small dosage of chromium, given especially to children, has shown a great improvement in the metabolism of the pancreas. Chromium is found in brewer's yeast, black pepper, wheatgerm and whole wheat bread. At least 3 teaspoonful of brewer's yeast must be taken daily.

Like people with low blood pressure, diabetic patients are generally deficient in potassium. They should, therefore, increase their intake of food rich in potassium. Zinc is a component of insulin; a lack of it results in diabetes.

Apart from zinc, sulphur is also present in pancreatic insulin. Manganese is responsible for glucose tolerance and removes excess sugar from the blood. It can become deficient due to excess urination. This loss may contribute to kidney problems, which are very common among diabetics. Diuretics increase the frequency urination, resulting in potassium or magnesium deficiency.

Vitamin C deficiency results if there is a lack of insulin. This reduces the fragility of tiny blood vessels. Lack of vitamin C, however, increases the risk of developing serious eye damage because of haemorrhages in the eye. Gooseberries, besides neutralising sugar, are one of the richest sources of vitamin C. Patients also benefit from taking vitamin B12 and honey. Blueberries or bilberries, too, are beneficial as they are rich in silicon, which helps to rejuvenate the pancreas.

Besides knowing what to eat, it is essential to know when to eat. Half the energy-supplying food should be eaten during lunch as this is when the body is the most active. The major part of the remaining food should be eaten during breakfast, with the least during dinner.

It is good to consult a doctor before changing the diet as the percentage of sugar level required varies from person to person. Once the insulin treatment starts, it cannot be halted. This is because the pancreas gets used to the insulin treatment and fails to produce what little it used to before the insulin was given. Check your feet regularly to make sure that there are no sores, blisters or cuts as they may spell trouble later on.

THE RIGHT FOOD AND HERBS

There are many types of food that contain an insulin-like substance (glukinins), which is a good substitute for pancreatic insulin. Patients can be treated effectively with this natural substance at the early stages.

Bitter gourd, fenugreek, onions and bean pods are rich in glukinins, which is also found in minute quantities in the raw juice of green beans, cucumbers, celery, lettuce, garlic and citrus fruit. Cucumbers and onions contain hormones that can activate the pancreas. These are essential in treating diabetes, so add them to your daily diet.

Infusion of blueberries or blackberries either from the seed powder or from the leaves is most beneficial as they control the blood sugar. An excess of blueberries, however, can result in "low sugar", so monitor its intake. In general, eating fresh fruit, such as lemons, oranges, plums, tomatoes, guavas, grapefruit, gooseberries, green leafy vegetables like spinach, string beans and whole wheat bread are good.

Nuts in their natural form, mung beans, green grams as sprouts, kidney beans, soya beans and their products, yoghurt, cakes made of bran, cabbages, the green part of asparagus, cauliflowers, mushrooms, cottage cheese, cumin, pepper, curry leaves, as well as the infusion of juniper berries as a drink can provide all the necessary nutrients for the body.

DIET RESTRICTIONS

Some people try to control their intake of sugar by not at all adding sugar to their food. They eat processed foods instead. Unfortunately, these processed foods contain more sugar than the required amount for the body.

As far as possible, avoid a high intake of starch and sugar, especially cooked starch as it is easily absorbed. Refined and processed foods contain empty calorie sugar, so avoid them as well.

Diabetics must reduce the intake of alcohol, animal fats, arrowroot, barley, biscuits, chestnuts, cornflour, fruit syrup, ginger, lemonade, macaroni, noodles, oats, potatoes, preserved fruit, prunes, puddings, red pumpkins, rice, sago, salt, sugar, sweet tapioca and turnips.

As there is a link between diabetes and high blood pressure, avoid food rich in cholesterol. Plant products are the safest. However, coconut and palm oils are rich in saturated fats and should therefore be avoided. It is best to avoid fried foods altogether.

In addition, to prevent gangrene of the feet, stop smoking as it further constricts the arteries. Do not wear nylon stockings, elastic tights or tightfitting socks. People who are not overweight, like their overweight counterparts, are advised to avoid soft drinks and simple sugar products. Child diabetics should avoid sugar concentrated foods.

The following measures reduce the blood sugar:
Recipes
- Add to your daily diet raw or cooked garlic, parsley leaves or watercress.
- Take 5 grams of garlic and 3 teaspoons of brewer's yeast during breakfast.
- Have a sliced banana with wheatgerm, ground sunflower seeds, a teaspoon of brewer's yeast and milk daily.
- Dry fry the sun-dried seeds of blueberries and make a powder out of them. Add a teaspoon of this powder into a glass of water and drink it on an empty stomach for 21 days.

The ideas, suggestions, herbal remedies and diet contained in this book are not intended as a substitue for consulting with your doctor. All matters regarding your health require medical supervision.

- Neem is one of the best blood purifying and detoxifying herbs. Add a few neem leaves as seasoning to food daily.

Juice

- Have a glass of raw bitter gourd juice every morning.
- Crush a guava and squeeze out the juice. Have this before meals.
- Have unsweetened lemon juice after meals.
- Have a glass of grapefruit juice in the morning regularly.
- Have 2 tablespoons of warm celery juice 3 times a day.
- Have ginger juice sweetened with honey daily.

Infusions

Have a glass of infusion of any of the following:

- Blueberry leaves 2 times a day with other essential vitamins and food.
- Neem leaves or bilberry leaves once a day.

Decoction

- Add 1 part barberry to 2 parts turmeric powder and make a decoction. Have 2 teaspoons of this 2 times a day.

Recipes

To reduce sugar in the urine:

- Drink the water in which the outer skin of kidney beans has been cooked or the soup of string beans once daily.
- Dry a few neem leaves in the shade and powder them. Add half the quantity of omum powder (ajowan). Mix well. Have a teaspoon of this mixture in hot milk every night for a month.
- To a glass of water add a teaspoon of ground juniper berries. Drink this once a day for 2 weeks. Repeat after a break of 2 weeks if necessary.

Recipes

For nutrient supplements:

- Steam potato leaves with an ash gourd. Have this regularly with meals.
- Drink soup made of mung beans soaked overnight.

- Boil fresh radish in water with a few abalones. Drink it as a soup once in 2 days to help overcome fatigue due to lack of insulin.
- Have tender coconut water regularly as this helps supplement lost minerals.

Recipes

To compensate for the lack of insulin:

- Have half a glass of juice of bilpatre (aegle marmelos) leaves on an empty stomach for 21 days.
- Eat 10–20 curry leaves for 3 months.
- Have a teaspoon of the juice of fenugreek leaves every morning for 90 days.
- Have 25–100 grams of fenugreek seeds daily in any form. The Central Food Technological Research Institute at Mysore, India, has released findings that eating fenugreek seeds regularly also reduces cholesterol in the body.

Recipes

For high blood pressure and diabetes:

Add 2 parts neem to 1 part basil and 2 parts curry leaves. Have a glass of an infusion of this mixture with some pure honey 2 times a day before meals.

Some Measures and Tips

During pregnancy, there is an increase in the blood sugar. Frequent checks are necessary to monitor the sugar level in the blood and urine. When the diabetic mother has to have surgery or when infection develops in any part of her body, she has to pay more attention than usual to the sugar level in the blood and urine to forestall any problems.

Due to control on the diet, strenuous exercises and an overdose of medication, it is possible to lower the sugar level of the body. To make sure that there is no hypoglycaemic reaction, it is good to be prepared with a packet of raisins. Pop these into your mouth whenever giddy.

Juvenile insulin dependent diabetes appears in the early ages. It does not affect the growth rate or intellectual development. A diet high in complex carbohydrates is beneficial but animal fats, candies containing fats, chocolate mixtures and similar fat-containing foods, sweet (aerated) drinks, dried cereals and ice cream should be totally avoided. Substitute these with sesame seeds, candies with no animal fats, food prepared with honey, natural plant protein, vegetable oil and nuts.

Children's main diet should include oranges and grapefruit (rich in potassium, vitamin C and vitamin A), eggs (without frying), soya lecithin (prevents cholesterol from building in the blood), fresh fish, chicken, peanut butter from freshly ground peanuts, whole wheat bread, millet, fresh cereals and cooked vegetables.

Asanas

The following Asanas to help control diabetes relate to the pancreas:

- Uddiyana Bandha [Abdominal Lift]
- Yoga Mudra
- Sarvangasana [Shoulderstand]
- Halasana [Plough 1]
- Paschimottanasana [Backstretch]
- Chakrasana [Back Pushup]
- Bhujangasana [Cobra Pose]
- Dhanurasana [Bow Pose]
- Padahastasana [Legclasp]
- Uttita Lolasana [Dangling]

HYPOGLYCAEMIA

This is a condition when the glucose level drops below 50 milligrams per 100 millilitres of blood. Just as too much sugar in the blood causes a host of problems, so does too little sugar. Because the brain gets insufficient glucose, this affects the nervous system. When the body tries to compensate for the lack of glucose, it produces epinephrine, resulting in sweating, chills, trembling, hunger and palpitations. It can result from excessive dosage of insulin, strenuous exercise, failure to eat properly after taking insulin, anxiety and stress. Apart from hereditary factors, an excess of white sugar and stress can overstimulate the adrenal glands. This in turn makes the pancreas work harder to produce an excessive amount of insulin to burn off the sugar, thereby weakening the pancreas.

Refined and processed foods cause a rapid increase in the blood sugar. This, in turn, increases the production of insulin. This causes a strain on the pancreas, liver and other endocrine glands in combating excess sugar. When the pancreas produces too much insulin, there will be a sudden and abnormal drop in the sugar level. This is called reactive hypoglycaemia or insulin rebound. Adding sugar to food makes things worse, as does too much exercise. After fasting, hypoglycaemia can occur and causes similar symptoms. It can also appear two to four hours after eating high carbohydrate foods.

Symptoms include anxiety, mental confusion, fatigue, depression, irritability, difficulty in concentrating, muscular pains, recurring headaches, weight problems, allergies, exhaustion, as well as cold hands and feet. There will also be the urge to overeat, especially food rich in sugar.

By eliminating refined sugar from your diet, many of the problems associated with sugar can be avoided. It is better to take complex carbohydrates that allow for slow absorption of nutrients. Have a good protein diet with eggs, dairy products, whole grains, nuts and seeds. Have cooked whole grains and vegetables, brown rice, sesame oil, peas and black beans.

Have frequent meals, adding some olive or sesame oil to cooked food. Never skip meals. Have fruit baked or stewed. Azuki or small red beans (soaked for several hours and cooked) are a good source of many trace elements. Adding roasted sesame seeds with husk to the food is beneficial as they provide extra calcium and proteins.

Zinc, necessary for a healthy pancreas (an unhealthy pancreas affects the production of insulin in the pancreas, which, in turn, causes hypoglycaemia), is found in whole grains, seeds and nuts.

Chromium — important in metabolising the proper sugar and glucose tolerance levels — is found in brewer's yeast, black pepper and whole grains.

Magnesium, required for blood sugar stabilisation, is found in whole grains, apple, green leafy vegetables (beet green), nuts, brown rice and soya beans.

Vitamin B complex, necessary for normal sugar metabolism, is found in whole grains, leafy vegetables, nut butters and brown (unpolished) rice.

Pantothenic acid, the deficiency of which results in a sudden drop of blood sugar is found in wheatgerm, cereals, beans, peas, liver, egg yolk and green vegetables.

In addition to a proper diet, perform Asanas that activate the pancreas and regulate the metabolism of the body.

Recipes

• Add a tablespoon of brewer's yeast, 2 tablespoons of wheatgerm, a tablespoon of sunflower seeds, a tablespoon of any desired nuts and a cup of parsley or guava leaves into a container. Add 2 cups of milk. Blend well. Drink this twice a day.

• Eat 2 peeled apples 2 times a day to maintain the sugar level.

Asana Routine

The following help combat low blood sugar:

• Suryanamaskar [Salutation to the Sun]
• Supta Vajrasana [Backward Bend] or Ushtrasana [Camel Pose]
• Halasana [Plough 1]
• Sarvangasana [Shoulderstand]
• Paryanaka [Fish in Vajrasana]
• Sarpasana [Snake Pose]
• Shalabasana [Locust Pose]
• Dhanurasana [Bow Pose]
• Padahastasana [Legclasp]
• Ardha Matsyendrasana [Half Twist]
• Paschimottanasana [Backstretch]
• Naukasana [Saucer Pose]
• Ekapada Jatara Parivartanasana [Legover Single Leg]
• Uddiyana Bandha [Abdominal Lift]
• Yoga Mudra
• Shavasana [Relaxation]

The best time to perform Uddiyana Bandha is in the morning. It is best to perform Uddiyana Bandha followed by Yoga Mudra. Refer also to the anxiety group.

CANCER OF THE PANCREAS

This is more common among men. Prevention is the best cure. Symptoms include abdominal pain, loss of appetite and pain on the back when lying down. A change in eating habits and lifestyle is necessary.

PANCREATITIS

This is the inflammation of the pancreas. Alcohol, peptic ulcers, gall stones or intestinal obstruction are some causes. Common symptoms are pain or tenderness in the abdominal area that radiates to the back, rapid pulse, fever, nausea, vomiting and excessive perspiration.

Have a glass of the infusion or 2 tablespoons of the decoction of fenugreek, bitter gourd and neem once a day for 3 weeks.

15

The Cardiovascular System
❧

For a number of problems that affect the heart and blood vessels (the cardiovascular system) the term "heart disease" is commonly used. Coronary diseases, such as congenital heart disease, coronary artery disease, hypertensive heart disease and rheumatic heart disease, are serious ailments that can lead to death. The major cause of cardiovascular ailments are illnesses resulting from strain and stress. Because a cure becomes uncertain once the disease sets in, every effort should be made to prevent heart disease, and prevention should begin during childhood. What is learnt and practised in childhood goes a long way in preventing heart problems at a later age.

The Yogic system of discipline helps to develop mind control, which governs and activates the body's actions and functions. Yoga treatment involves following certain principles and using the body as a tool of the mind. Many cardiologists are now recommending Yoga therapy for their heart patients. It has proven to be the most reliable rehabilitative and even to a certain extent curative system for recovery.

Yoga therapy deals with three major areas in regard to heart and circulatory diseases:
- A nutritious diet free from fat and other toxins that might affect the system;
- Relaxation therapy to rid the mind of stress; and
- Specific Asanas to increase the tone of the heart and improve blood circulation.

Congenital heart disease is the deformity of the heart or the major blood vessels and exists from birth. It must be evaluated and treated by a specialist. Symptoms of the disease depend on the nature of the defect. The term "blue baby" is usually used to describe babies with a defective heart. Dusky colour of the skin, delayed growth and shortness of breath when the child exerts itself are some possible symptoms. Coronary artery disease occurs as a result of obstruction in the coronary vessels. This interferes with the supply of oxygen to the heart. Most heart attacks resulting from coronary heart disease are unexpected. Hypertensive heart disease is the inefficient pumping of the heart due to hypertension (high blood pressure). Rheumatic heart disease is the inflammation in the heart's lining or valves or covering of the heart or inflammation of the heart muscles caused by rheumatic fever. It is common among children. It is important to prevent the recurrence of the disease after treating it.

The ideas, suggestions, herbal remedies and diet contained in this book are not intended as a substitue for consulting with your doctor. All matters regarding your health require medical supervision.

FOOD AND HERBS FOR
THE CARDIOVASCULAR SYSTEM

To stimulate the heart muscles, lily of the valley, figwort, hawthorn and food rich in chemicals called cardiac glycosides are beneficial.

To improve blood circulation, exponents of the natural theory recommend the following: angelica, buckwheat, cayenne, chamomile flowers, chillies, cinnamon, dandelions, ginger, lime blossom, marigold, hawthorn, mistletoe leaves and yarrow.

To prevent fluid accumulation due to a weak heart, take cucumbers, dandelions, lily of the valley and yarrow. They are diuretics.

To calm nerves or to prevent cardiovascular problems that result from stress or strain, lemon balm, lime flowers and chamomile flowers are beneficial.

To protect the tissues against decay, take the following protective foods: raw garlic and oranges.

To strengthen the heart and for a rich source of nutrients, alfalfa leaves, angelica root (in small doses), lemon balm, soya, bananas, cardamoms, guavas, lentils, peppermint, pomegranates, ash gourd, motherwort, shepherd's purse, tomatoes and wheat are good.

To prevent degenerative diseases of the heart and arteries, take sunflower seeds as they contain about 80 percent linoleic acid

To normalise the heartbeat, papayas are good.

CORONARY HEART DISEASE

Most coronary attacks come unexpected. Immediate treatment after the attack may prevent death but enough damage has already been done to the heart tissues. The best way to prevent coronary heart problems is to correct the risk factors. They are as follows:

- A high level of cholesterol in the blood
- Uncontrolled high blood pressure
- Low metabolism of the body
- Excessive smoking
- Lack of exercise
- Emotional stress
- Obesity

A CLOSER LOOK AT CHOLESTEROL

Cholesterol insulates the nerves, helps to produce hormones, metabolises fats and contributes to the manufacture of new body cells. Our body produces 500–1000 milligrams of cholesterol daily, which can be made in the body from fat, sugar or indirectly from protein present in food.

Cholesterol is only found naturally in food of animal origin like meat, poultry, seafood and dairy products, including eggs. Apart from these types of food, smoking and obesity can also cause the body to produce more cholesterol.

Lipoprotein is of two types: low density and high density. The low density lipoprotein, called "bad cholesterol", tends to deposit cholesterol and causes coronary problems. The high density one is called "good cholesterol".

Blood cholesterol is in the blood and high levels are strongly linked to the risk of coronary diseases. Coronary arteries blocked as a result of cholesterol can cause heart attacks; blocked arteries in the ear can cause deafness; and blocked arteries in the penis can lead to impotence.

Cholesterol is a problem only when it is present above the normal level in the body. Exercise alone cannot reduce the cholesterol level. It is a combination of diet and exercise that produces results.

CARE AND PREVENTIVE MEASURES

Be aware of the kinds of fat present in the diet. Due to the way animals are reared today and the effects produced on the human body after eating their meat, try to cut down on meat. Avoid all saturated oils as they are derived from an animal source as well as coconut oil and palm oil.

Polyunsaturated oils help lower the cholesterol level while mono-unsaturated oils like olive oil and vegetable oils like sesame oil reduce "bad cholesterol" in the body. Food rich in fibre like beans, because of pectin, also helps to lower the cholesterol level.

Fruit contain pectin but should be taken in large quantities. Soluble fibre found in pinto beans and oats help flush out excess cholesterol, as do fish from unpolluted waters like salmon, yoghurt, onion and garlic. Chromium, magnesium, calcium, zinc and copper in the right proportion help keep the level of cholesterol down. Niacin helps to normalise the cholesterol level while Vitamin C and vitamin E help raise the high density cholesterol level.

Avoid taking more than 3 grams of salt daily as salt absorbs water and causes oedema. Also avoid caffeine as it causes heart fluttering as well as sugar, especially refined sugar, as it increases the blood fat or triglycerides and builds up excess fat. Reduce the intake of animal fat to control the blood fats. Dangerously high levels of dietary cholesterol are found only in animal products. Mistletoe berries are poisonous and have an adverse effect on the heart if used in excess. Muskmelons and dried calyx act negatively on the heart. In addition, stop smoking and watch your weight.

Select exercises or Asanas that use the large muscles of the body in a systematic manner. Exercise these muscles for healthy arteries.

An adequate amount of potassium, found in grapes, bananas, cider vinegar and tomatoes, maintains the balance between the tissues and blood to strengthen the heart. Food rich in manganese helps to keep excessive vitamin B1 from reacting in the body tissue. Garlic has traces of manganese and also helps to reduce cholesterol and fibrinogen, a clotting agent. Kelp, mung beans, bananas and celery help soften the blood vessels. Red or black grapes, sarsaparilla and neem are blood purifiers.

To help alleviate water retention, add diuretics like dandelion root to the daily diet. To avoid tension, have food that calms the mind like lemon balm. Food rich in vitamin B complex, such as fish oil, honey, olive oil, papayas, safflower oil and brewer's yeast, as well as vitamin A and vitamin C, are essential.

Soya beans contain lecithin, an unsaturated fatty acid. It dissolves cholesterol and soothes the liver and gall bladder. It also prevents blood clotting in the arteries. Lecithin from soya beans is available in the form of capsules, syrup and powder.

Other types of food that are beneficial include cooked vegetables like asparagus, beetroot, bitter gourd, corn silk, eggplant, green peppers, lettuce, mustard, onions, red peppers, spinach, squashes, uncooked carrots, cucumbers, watermelons, seeds and cereals like pumpkin seeds, small red beans, wheat, oat bran, and herbs like saffron, cinnamon, cardamoms, hibiscus flowers and hawthorn.

Recipes

- Take a teaspoon of cold pressed olive oil regularly with salad to control cholesterol.
- Boil 125 grams of peanuts in a cup of water. Drink the water 3 times a day to get rid of cholesterol.
- Take vitamin B complex, 2 tablespoons of lecithin (from soya beans), 2 tablespoons of soya oil as salad dressing and wheatgerm daily.
- For a weak heart associated with nervous disability have a mixture 200 grams of papaya, 1 tablespoon of honey and 5 tablespoons of milk daily.
- Boil 15 grams of corn kernels in 500 ml of water until the water reduces to a third of the original volume and becomes reddish brown. Have half a glass of the water 2 times a day to relieve the strain on the kidney and thus on the heart.
- Eat dates either on their own or soaked in water to reduce heart palpitations.
- Soak 100 grams of gooseberries in water for 12 hours. Throw away the water and cook the berries in fresh water until they become soft. Add 300 grams of sugar and grind. Eat 2 grams of the mixture 3 times a day. This relieves heart palpitations.
- Swallow a clove of garlic daily in the mornings, after which drink a glass of warm water in which a teaspoon of fresh lemon juice and honey have been mixed. This reduces blood pressure and eases the strain on the heart.

Juice

- Have the fresh juice of lettuce for heart palpitations.
- Have a glass of cucumber juice 3 times a day on a regular basis or have a glass of juice from a cucumber, apple, celery and carrot mixed in equal proportion.

• Fresh juice of black or red grapes prevents heart attacks and averts pain and palpitations. The juice of dark grapes is rich in iron, and this makes it a good purifier and blood enricher.

Infusion
Have a glass of infusion made of 2 parts of hawthorn, 2 parts of motherwort leaves and 1 part of lily of the valley. Add freshly extracted orange juice, black or red grapes, parsley or pomegranate with rock sugar. Mix well. Have this 2 times a day.

Decoction
Mix 1 teaspoon of hawthorn berries together with a teaspoon of cinnamon powder. Add a pinch of the powder of cardamom seeds. Add a litre of water and bring to the boil. Take 2 teaspoons of the decoction 3 times a day.

Bath
For a hand and foot bath, add a clove of garlic, a handful of single seed hawthorn blossoms, greater celandine leaves and chopped common broom flowers to 1 litre of boiling water. Let it stand for a few hours. Pour the liquid into a clean bottle and use it as a hand and foot bath daily.

HEART ATTACK

Arteriosclerosis, the deterioration of the walls of the arteries, is the basic cause of heart attack. When any one of the coronary arteries develops an abnormal amount of fibrous tissues in the walls due to calcium and cholesterol buildup, it becomes narrow and eventually closes. Blood circulation to that part of the heart stops and that part of the heart dies. The shock caused by the chemical change in the area is the first symptom of heart attack. There can be uncontrolled functioning of the heart, which can cause death after a couple of hours or days after the first symptom. For those who survive the attack, the affected muscles will heal slowly or be replaced but not without scar tissue. Until the blockage in the arteries is cleared, there is always the possibility of another attack. It is also caused by a clot or thrombus caught in the narrow artery and may strike without any symptoms. Under stress, a surge in adrenalin stimulates respiration

and the blood pressure. This, in turn, may cause a heart attack. Strain on the kidneys and liver can cause the heart to overwork. This, too, can also cause an attack. More men than women suffer from heart attack. Women seem to be immune to the disease until after menopause.

Pain is felt behind the breast bone and often radiates to the left shoulder and arm. Sometimes, it can be felt in the right arm as well, and this should not be neglected. There is a feeling of strangulation. The pain is so severe that the following may occur: difficulty in breathing, excessive perspiration and pale and moist skin. Nausea and vomiting may follow. If the symptom of the heart attack results from the gradual reduction of blood supply to the heart, pain will be felt immediately after exertion. This, however, subsides after some rest. This is angina pectoris. If you think someone is having an attack, do not hesitate and call for an ambulance immediately.

CARE AND PREVENTIVE MEASURES
Rest is an absolute necessity at the time of an attack. The patient should sit in a half reclined position with the head slightly elevated. This helps to ease the breathing process.

Nutrition plays an important role in causing or preventing heart diseases. Include in the daily diet polyunsaturated fats, especially linoleic acid found in vegetable oils. This is good for the normal metabolism and reduces the level of cholesterol in the blood.

Also include in the diet essential fatty acids (EPA) commonly found in fish oil and food for the heart like alfalfa leaves, barberries, black currants, brewer's yeast, carrots, chickpeas, cottage cheese, cucumbers, garlic, grapes, guavas, honey, lemons, kelp, non-meat protein (like pulses), oats, onions, oranges, pomegranates, primrose, rosemary, saffron and yoghurt. Also exercise and meditate regularly to avoid stress.

Avoid food rich in cholesterol as well as those that may cause a high production of cholesterol. Egg yolk, meat, coconuts, chocolates, avocados, macadamia nuts, cashew nuts and palm oil are some types of food rich in cholesterol. Saturated animal fats like butter, cheese and cream raise the cholesterol level. Minimise the intake of salt and stop smoking.

Recipes

- Have the fresh juice of red or black grapes 3 times a day to purify the blood.
- Chew a clove of garlic in the mornings, after which have a glass of warm water with a teaspoon of honey. The garlic and the water strengthen the heart muscles and improve circulation.
- Together with regular food, have fresh asparagus soup without any additives 3 times a week. This reduces the rate of the heartbeat.
- Grate ash gourd and steam it. Add honey and cook over a low fire until it becomes a jelly. Take a tablespoon of the jelly once a day for 40 days. Ash gourd is a tonic for the heart muscles.
- Blend a ripe cucumber and carrot together to make a juice. Have a glass of this 2 times a day to improve circulation. The juice also stimulates the heart muscles.

Infusion

Have a glass of the infusion of rose petals with honey or the leaves of the fig plant with honey or lime flowers with honey or tender neem leaves with honey or dates. Have the infusion 3 times a day to help relieve heart pain and palpitations.

Asanas Routine

- Hrudaya Stambana Pranayanama [Slowing the Heart Breathing]. Practice this breathing exercise 2 times a day for 5 minutes and then perform Shavasana. If possible, sit erect in Lotus Pose. Inhale through both the nostrils and fill the lungs with air. Contract the throat by bringing the chin close to the neck (chin lock). Force the air upward by pulling the stomach and abdomen upward and backward (stomach lock). Hold the breath for 2 or 3 seconds. Release the stomach lock first and then the chin lock. Close the left nostril and breathe out slowly through the right nostril. Perform again. Now close the right nostril and breathe out through the left nostril. Repeat the entire process for a maximum time of 30 minutes. Do not strain yourself while doing this Asana. Relax in between if necessary.
- All relaxing exercises are beneficial. Refer to the Relaxation Therapy group (see chapter 20).
- Meditate preferably using the heart Chakra. Refer to Yantra meditation 5 (see chapter 7).

Note: Avoid Asanas that are strenuous.

ANGINA PECTORIS

A gradual narrowing of the coronary arteries leads to angina, which results in the heart having to work harder. The heart exerts itself more than usual and the heart muscles may require more blood for their own needs. Naturally, when the coronary arteries narrow, the collateral vessels continue to grow larger and wider and reduce anginal symptoms. It is a chest pain and described as if a vest is tightened around the chest. It lasts for a few minutes only. Pain is felt behind the breast bone and often radiates to the left shoulder and arm. Sometimes, it is felt in the right arm, and this should not be neglected. This is because the nerve fibres originate from the same area on the spine. Usually, the pain results from undue excitement, tension or stress, after strenuous or sexual activity and during the digestion process of a heavy meal.

CARE AND PREVENTIVE MEASURES

Doctors prescribe nitroglycerine tablets to be placed under the tongue to relax the tiny muscles of the coronary arteries. The workload of the heart is to be reduced while the damaged muscle is being healed. Rest relieves the pain. The aim of the therapy is to bring more blood rich in oxygen to the heart through the coronary arteries by dilating the arteries. It also clears any blockage in the arteries.

While recovering from angina pectoris, stick to a nonfat, low protein, bland diet low in calories to reduce the risk of an attack.

Recipes

- Bananas are rich in potassium. Eat at least 3–5 bananas a day.
- Pop raisins into the mouth whenever possible. Raisins prevent weakness and giddiness.
- Add capsicum or hot pepper to the daily diet as it helps to prevent blood clots.
- Have oat bran for breakfast daily. It acts like a sponge and absorbs cholesterol.
- Take a tablespoon of liquid lecithin or 2 tablespoons of powdered lecithin with meals daily.
- To a small papaya (the fruit contains carpin, which relieves pain due to angina pectoris) add a teaspoon

of olive oil and 2 cloves of garlic. Blend well to make a juice. Drink this once a day for 2 weeks.

Infusions

- Have a glass of the infusion of aniseed after meals.
- Have a glass of infusion made from the mixture of the following herbs: 3 parts hawthorn flower (hawthorn berries dilate the arteries) to 3 parts motherwort leaves or flowering tops to 2 parts lime blossom (lime blossom is excellent for clearing cholesterol accumulations in the arteries) to 1 part lily of the valley. Have the infusion 3 times a day.

Asana Routine

- Shavasana [Relaxation, tensing & relaxing]
- Ujjayi Pranayama [Abdominal Breathing]
- Meditation using colour (see chapter 7)
- All relaxing sitting down and lying down Asanas

ENLARGEMENT OF THE HEART

In Asia, enlargement of the heart occurs mainly due to the oxidation of lactic acid in the heart muscles. Vitamin B1 is the catalyst. Muscles become weak without it.

The leaves of the fig plant are good for heart pain and swelling. Include garlic, onions, parsley, nutmeg, black currants, cucumbers, guavas, oats, saffron, honey and tomatoes to the daily diet.

HYPERTENSIVE HEART DISEASE

When the heart overworks itself to maintain a higher blood pressure, the resulting damage is known as hypertensive heart disease. To prevent this disease prevent high blood pressure.

HEART FAILURE

When an unhealthy heart is made to work beyond its capacity, it may not be able to pump enough blood to the arteries. Heart failure results. Symptoms include weakness in the legs, discomfort in the stomach without any specific cause related to digestive disorders, swelling in the ankles (it usually subsides during rest periods) and heart palpitations. If the left side of the heart is affected, breathlessness, excessive coughing with sputum and fatigue result. If the right side is affected, pain and pulsation near the liver, symptoms similar to appendicitis or gall bladder problems result.

Have sufficient rest. Control oedema by taking diuretic foods and develop a healthy eating habit to reinforce the action of the heart muscles.

CIRCULATORY DISEASES: PROBLEMS OF THE BLOOD AND BLOOD VESSELS

Circulatory problems deprive a part of the body of necessary blood. Arteries that carry blood can change shape, and this can lead to clogging, constriction, hardening and obstruction. The risk increases with age. Common symptoms are cold hands and feet, numb or tingling hands (due to narrowing of the arteries or impaired blood supply and can occur in the limbs), fingers or toes becoming white and then purple when exposed to the cold and cramps in the legs.

CARE AND PREVENTIVE MEASURES

Introduce into the daily diet dark grapes, neem and sarsaparilla, the alkaline salts of which act as blood purifiers. Also include alfalfa, echinacea, hibiscus, pomegranates, beetroot, pineapples, basil, blueberries, burdock, carrots, celery, dandelion roots and leaves, lotus, stinging nettle, parsley, peaches, olive oil, onions, strawberries, grapefruit, oranges, pears and honey. Because of their mineral content, copper, manganese, iron and black currants also act as good blood purifiers. Blackberries, besides being blood purifiers are also blood builders.

Introduce food that promotes circulation and softens blood vessels like red or green pepper. Food that improves circulation include bitter foods, angelica, basil, soya beans, brussels sprouts, cayenne, ginger. Horseradish, when used externally as a poultice, stimulates the flow of blood. In addition, include the following:

- Apricots, cucumbers, tomatoes and turmeric as they are blood cleansers.
- Avocados, which contain copper and iron, as they aid in the process of red blood rejuvenation.
- Blackberries as they are blood builders and purifiers, and chickpeas and asparagus as they are blood enrichers.
- Tomatoes and ginger as they help prevent the coagulation of blood.

  Above all, relax through meditation.

General Tonics

- Have a glass of the juice of chicory, celery and parsley mixed in equal proportion.
- Have a glass of either the juice or infusion of sarsaparilla roots twice daily.
- Simmer a few cloves of garlic in water. Add a small onion. Drink it or have the soup with cooked brown rice. Add steamed spinach and tomatoes to soup if desired.
- Take equal parts of dried ginger and black pepper powder and mix them with 2 parts aniseed to 2 parts of honey. Blend well. A little cinnamon, clove flower buds and cardamom may be added for flavour. Take a teaspoon of this once daily.
- Chyavanaprasha, made of gooseberries, honey and forty different types of herbs, is an excellent tonic for circulatory problems and general debility. It is available commercially in any shop that sells Ayurvedic medicine.

Recipes

- To improve blood circulation, season food regularly with red pepper.
- Have a ripe mango, after which drink a glass of warm milk to purify the blood.
- Oily fish like mackerel or herring, because of their magnesium, vitamin B3, vitamin C and vitamin E content, are beneficial for circulation if consumed daily.
- Have soup made of cooked asparagus at least 3 times a week. The chlorophyll in asparagus enriches blood and is good for the formation of red blood cells.

Juice

- For circulatory problems, have a glass of the juice of sarsaparilla roots, one of the best blood purifiers, regularly.
- Have a glass of the juice of red/black grapes or pomegranates or cucumbers, which are also good blood purifiers.
- Have a glass of the juice of tomatoes and ginger to prevent blood coagulation.

Infusions

- To improve blood circulation, have a glass of the infusion of 3 parts of prickly ash to 3 parts of hawthorn to 1 part of ginger. Have the mixture 3 times a day.
- On an empty stomach, have a glass of the infusion of the mixture of a teaspoonful of basil seeds with a tablespoon each of the mixture of the crushed leaves of basil, lemongrass and peppermint leaves. Add lemon and honey if desired to improve the taste of the infusion. Have it once a day.
- Have a glass of the infusion of alfalfa leaves, echinacea rootstock, hibiscus flowers or neem with honey once a day.

Baths

To stimulate circulation:

- Use rosemary leaves or fresh shavegrass in the bath 3 times in a week.
- Alternate between a hot and cold water bath 3 times a week.

Asanas

All Yogasanas help improve blood circulation. Meditation, on its part, has a better effect on the heart and its functions. It promotes the harmonious circulation of blood.

ANEURYSM

This is the bulging of the arteries and can result from weak arteries, infections or injuries to the arteries or due to high blood pressure. Shortness of breath and pain in the chest on exertion are experienced. If it is in the skull area, sudden headaches can occur on exertion. In the abdominal area, it results in arteriosclerosis. Relaxation therapy of Yogasanas with meditation is beneficial.

ARTERIOSCLEROSIS

The most important cause of coronary heart disease and stroke, arteriosclerosis is the gradual deterioration of the walls of the arteries through the hardening and thickening of the artery walls. Hardening may be caused by an increased proportion of fibrous tissues and excess calcium or cholesterol in the blood. High blood pressure, diabetes, obesity and excessive nerve strain, consuming eggs, cream and other animal fats in excess can act as catalysts and harden the arteries. If the problem is not treated at an early stage, it can affect the functions of the kidneys and cause stroke and paralysis. Common symptoms are mental deterioration, severe chest pain and pain in the leg muscles. If the disease is associated with diabetes, there will be a cold sensation in the feet.

CARE AND PREVENTIVE MEASURES

Take food and herbs that prevent the hardening of the arteries like garlic, lime blossom and blood purifiers. Proper exercise improves blood circulation and controls cholesterol accumulation.

To stop overworking the heart, avoid fats, including hydrogenated fats and fatty foods, dairy butter, cream, cheese, eggs and food with concentrated sugar. Quit smoking.

Infusions

- Have a glass of the cold infusion of garlic 2 times a day.
- Have a glass of the hot infusion of hawthorn flowers or hawthorn fruits or black currant leaves (not petiole) or orange peel 3 times a day.

ATHEROSCLEROSIS

This is the hardening of the inner walls of the arteries, resulting in loss of elasticity. It is a form of arteriosclerosis, which thicken and harden the walls of the arteries. Atherosclerosis is the basic cause of coronary heart disease and the risk factors favour the development of arteriosclerosis. When fats, including cholesterol accumulate, the walls become narrower and restrict the blood flow. As a result, the heart muscles send signals of distress in the form of chest pain of angina pectoris to indicate that they lack oxygenated blood. If there is a total blockage, the heart muscles may die, resulting in heart attack.

CARE AND PREVENTIVE MEASURES

Include in the daily diet blood purifiers. Refer also to recipes given under blood circulation.

ATHEROMA

Atheroma is another form of arteriosclerosis. When fats accumulate in the thin membrane lining the inner walls of the arteries, the arteries become narrow. Plaques of atheroma collect and may ulcerate through the lining, leaving a raw surface. Platelets from the blood may accumulate on those areas to form a clot. Should a clot form in one of the coronary arteries, this will block that artery. This is called coronary occlusion. The pain is similar to that of angina but cannot be relieved by rest.

If the heart muscle supplied by that artery is deprived of its supply of blood, the muscle will die. The result is myocardial infarction. An impaired supply of blood to any tissue is termed Ischaemia. If the blockage is in a large artery, paralysis and even death may occur.

There are many factors that lead to the formation of atheroma: hereditary factors, high levels of blood fats (lipids) like cholesterol and triglycerides, high blood pressure, obesity, nervous tension and lack of physical exercise. Most of these problems are reversible and coronary problems can be prevented. Common symptoms are absence of urine and angina pain.

CARE AND PREVENTIVE MEASURES

Monitor the type of fats eaten. The right intake of vitamin E, vitamin C and garlic on a daily basis is beneficial. To maintain the cholesterol level in the blood, exercise regularly.

Avoid hydrogenated vegetable fats and fats derived from animal sources, which increase the cholesterol level, food rich in refined carbohydrates and concentrated refined sugar and its products as they increase triglycerides. Avoid a diet rich in calories, which can lead to obesity, and smoking, which increase triglycerides in the blood stream.

Recipes

- Take a teaspoon of fish oil 3 times a week to reduce the accumulation of fats in the arteries.
- Make a syrup with garlic (one of the most effective herbs for atheroma) and honey. Take a teaspoon of this daily. Prevent garlic odour by adding some parsley.
- Take iodine supplements with brewer's yeast, which is rich in B-complex, 3 times a day. This prevents high blood pressure and eases the hardening of the arteries.

BLOOD CLOTTING (EMBOLISM AND THROMBUS)

Clotting involves a complex chemical change. A blood clot may form in a vein, artery or heart. The blood platelets can become excessively sticky due to certain problems of the body like asthma, rheumatoid arthritis, migraine and high blood pressure. This is not usually found in diabetics. If the clot is in the vein, it moves towards the heart and then lodges in the lungs. Sudden chest pain, difficulty in breathing and coughing out blood are some symptoms. If the clot is in the artery, it moves away from the heart and may become lodged in any smaller artery. If the clot is in the limbs, sudden severe pain appears, with paleness and a sensation of cold and numbness. If it happens in the legs, it is called phlebitis and eventually, gangrene may set in. If the arterial clot lodges in the brain, stroke results.

CARE AND PREVENTIVE MEASURES
Minimise clotting by taking fish oils, evening primrose oil, garlic oil, pineapples, wheatgerm and ginger regularly in combination with vitamin B6 and vitamin C supplements. Soya beans, capsicum, ash gourd, and hot pepper prevent blood clotting in the arteries. Selenium in garlic helps to prevent platelet adhesion and clot formation. Onions slow down platelet clogging, thereby preventing the formation of blood clots.

Infusion
To unblock the arteries and veins, have an infusion of cinnamon bark or ginger or black pepper either on its own or in combination 3 times a day.

The best treatment for all arterial problems is prevention. This is because by the time is the disease is diagnosed, there may already be damage to the tissue.

HIGH BLOOD PRESSURE
(HYPERTENSION)

Blood pressure is the measurement of the pressure of blood on the walls of the arteries, varying with the resilience of the blood vessels and with the heart's contraction (systole) or relaxation (diastole). The average normal blood pressure in children of six years of age is 90/60; in adults, it may range from 120/80 to 140/90. A persistent reading above 140/90 indicates hypertension. The more difficulty the blood has in flowing, the higher the number will be. Arterial walls tighten due to cholesterol deposits and harden due to both cholesterol and calcium deposits, resulting in high blood pressure.

Hypertension is not related to nervous tension. A calm person may also have high blood pressure. This depends on his or her attitude and lifestyle. People who live under stress or pressure should change their way of life to prevent aggravating the situation. Complication arising from blood pressure reduces as soon as it is brought under control. Overeating and obesity are the common causes of high blood pressure. Hereditary factors, constant worrying, unreleased stress and physical strain may also contribute to high blood pressure.

In the majority of the cases, the cause of hypertension is not easily identified. This is known as primary or essential hypertension and is inherited. In addition, environmental factors also play a role.

Hypertension with an identifiable cause is secondary hypertension, which, in most cases, is due to the ingestion of drugs and chemicals. Oestrogen, progesterone and oral contraceptives rank first among many other drugs. Anti-inflammatory drugs and certain appetite-killing agents have a similar effect. Derivatives used in treating peptic ulcers or liquorice found in sweets result in water and sodium retention, which, in turn, can increase the blood pressure. A diet rich in fat and carbohydrates can cause extra fat to be deposited on the walls of blood vessels, resulting in atheroma, which increases the blood pressure. Pollution due to chemicals like lead, cadmium and chemicals in hair blackening cosmetic substances can increase the blood pressure. Infections, such as tonsillitis and typhoid fever, can lead to kidney failure, resulting in high blood pressure.

There is usually no symptom in hypertension. However, some people experience the following: heaviness in the head, a ruddy face or redness in the eyes, an uneasy feeling towards crowds and noise, trembling hands and legs, constipation, noises in the ears and a desire for cold foods and drinks. Some of these symptoms may not be due to hypertension itself. If unsure, consult a doctor.

CARE AND PREVENTIVE MEASURES
High blood pressure can be controlled. Stick to a salt-free, low protein and fat diet rich in carbohydrates and fibre. When cooking, use vegetable cold pressed oils instead of animal fats in moderation.

Calcium helps to keep the pressure under control and stabilises the arterial blood flow. It acts as a natural diuretic because it clears excess sodium. Calcium is found in yoghurt, milk, cottage cheese, soya bean curd, turnips, mustard greens and broccoli.

Potassium, besides keeping the pressure under control indirectly, is essential for strengthening the cellular walls. Potassium is lost in refined foods and when cooking vegetables in large quantities of water. If the sodium intake is low, potassium supplements increase the pressure. If diuretics are taken, along with sodium, potassium is washed away and may cause an erratic blood pressure. Vegetarians tend to have a lower rate of this problem because of the dietary intake of potassium.

Potassium is found in avocados, bananas, brown rice, brussels sprouts, cauliflower, cherries, cooked oatmeal, cooked lentils, dates with pits, grapefruit, milk, molasses, oranges, peaches, pineapples, potatoes boiled in their jackets, prunes, raw fruit, spinach, watermelons, wheatgerm and winter squash.

Garlic is the safest way to reduce blood pressure and relieve strain on the heart. Garlic contains allicin (which is rich in sulphur and helps reduce fats in the blood and liver), selenium (which prevents clotting) and the trace mineral, manganese. It also brings down the level of cholesterol and fibrinogen, a clotting agent.

Lecithin, like cholesterol, is produced in the liver. To synthesise lecithin, essential fatty acids, choline and inositol, vitamin B compounds and other nutrients are necessary. When there is a deficiency in choline or inositol, the lecithin will not be manufactured in the right quantities. In the absence of vitamin B6 and magnesium, the lecithin cannot be synthesised efficiently. Similar to the one manufactured in the body, lecithin is found in all unrefined foods containing oil, such as soya beans, nuts, wheat, liver.

Choline can be made in the body from the amino acid, methionine if enough protein is present in the diet. Blood cholesterol drops when there is sufficient choline.

Liver, brewer's yeast, wheatgerm and soya lecithin are the richest natural sources of choline and inositol. Include food and herbs in the daily diet that help to dilate the blood vessels like kelp, sprouts of mung beans, black currants, garlic, nutmeg, bean pods, parsley, aniseed, tomatoes and celery, radishes, olives, onions, bitter gourd and honey.

Orange peel is an antihistamine, which will also contribute to lowering of the pressure. Other blood pressure reducing foods are alfalfa, beans, blueberries, cinnamon, celery, hawthorn fruit, banana, pods of lima beans, lime flowers, low sodium milk, mistletoe leaves and yarrow. Onions prevent blood clotting.

Avoid alcohol, canned and preserved foods, egg yolks, liver, kidney and all kinds of meat, angelica root in excess, bayberries, clove flower buds, liquorice and shepherd's purse. Reduce the intake of celery if the pressure is high as it is rich in sodium.

Do not discontinue any medication without the advice of the physician. Rest, both physical and mental, is a valuable remedy for blood pressure. Achieve this through Yoga meditation.

Recipes
To prevent blood pressure:
- Have watermelon seeds regularly.
- Have 1–2 tomatoes on an empty stomach for 15 days. This is not meant for people with arthritis.
- Add a tablespoon of honey to a glass of warm water. Mix well. Drink this every morning.

- Blend a banana with a teaspoon of black sesame seeds and a teaspoon of honey. Have this once a day.
- Soak mung beans in water overnight. Cook this with an equal amount of rice. Have a portion of this daily with regular meals.
- Take a tablespoonful of natural liquid lecithin daily or add a tablespoon of lecithin powder to food.

To control blood pressure:

- Include plenty of cooked bean pods in the daily diet.
- Eat peanuts soaked in vinegar and drink the vinegar twice a day for 40 days.
- Boil a glass of milk with 2 threads of saffron and drink it hot once a day for 3 days.
- Add a teaspoon of unsalted butter to 1 gram of black pepper powder. Have this every morning for 21 days. Repeat if necessary.
- Simmer over a low fire a potato with its jacket, an onion, a few cloves of garlic and an unpeeled carrot until the water reduces to half. Add any permitted seasoning. Drink the soup for two weeks.

For blood pressure associated with other problems:

- Have celery cooked in vinegar once in two days (do not take this if the pressure is too high). This helps to reduce hypertension and relieves headaches due to hypertension. It also lowers the cholesterol level.
- Have a banana with honey daily if hypertension is associated with dizziness and constipation.

Juice

To prevent blood pressure:

Have a glass of fresh carrot juice once a day.

To control blood pressure:

- Have a raw fruit and vegetable juice therapy of grapes, oranges, cucumbers, carrots and beetroot for 21 days. Follow this with a balanced salt-free diet.
- Have a glass of the juice of chestnuts and radish with honey mixed in equal proportion twice a day.

    For blood pressure associated with blood sugar, take 3 tablespoons of the juice of bitter gourd or neem leaves every morning. This helps reduce blood sugar and thus blood pressure.

Decoctions

To control blood pressure:

- Take 2 tablespoons of the decoction of barberry root bark 2 times a day. It dilates the blood vessels and thus lowers blood pressure.
- Take 2 tablespoons of the decoction of bean pods, hawthorn fruit, mulberry roots or powdered peanuts 3 times a day to reduce blood pressure.
- Take 2 tablespoons of the decoction of mistletoe leaves once a day. Note that this lowers blood pressure by raising it first, followed by a fast pulse rate.
- Boil 3 dried peach fruit or 100 grams of watermelon peel in 2 glasses of water until the volume reduces to half. Have a glass of the water for 21 days.

    Have a broth in which a small green onion and 2 cloves of garlic have been boiled. Have this 2 times a day.

Asana Routine

The following Asanas are for relaxing purposes:

- Matsya Kridasana [Flapping Fish Pose]
- Jyestika Makarasana [Head Twist]
- Advasana [Reversed Corpse Pose]
- Paschimottanasana [Backstretch]
- Nadi Shodhana Pranayama [Alternate nostril breathing without retention of breath]
- Meditation

These Asanas help lower the pressure:

- Paschimottanasana [Backstretch]
- Ardha Baddha Padma Paschimottanasana [Backstretch in Half Lotus]
- Janu Sirasasana [Alternate Leg Pull]
- Yoga Anandasana [Animal Relaxation Pose]
- Shashankasana [Baby Pose]
- Poorva Halasana [Plough Preliminary Pose]
- Matsyasana [Fish in Lotus]
- Nadi Shodana Pranayama [Alternate Nostril Breathing, without retention]
- Sheetali or Sheetkari Pranayama [Cooling or Hissing Breath]
- Meditation
- Shavasana [Relaxation]

LOW BLOOD PRESSURE

This should not be considered a disease. A person's life span is lengthened by it. This means lowered systolic pressure relative to age. The difference between systolic and diastolic should be between 30 and 40 mm of mercury. In some cases, low blood pressure is caused by an impoverished diet or some chronic disease. This can be corrected easily by a nutritious diet. In such cases, low blood pressure is an indication of low metabolism, hypothyroidism and tiredness. Other causes include the following: excess fasting, malnutrition, too much worrying and a passive life. Exhaustion, headaches, shortness of breath, dizziness, inability to concentrate, digestive disorders, irritability and cold sensations are common symptoms.

CARE AND PREVENTIVE MEASURES

A diet rich in protein is beneficial. It is better to go for smaller meals but take them more frequently to keep the blood sugar level up. Include in the daily diet ginger, cinnamon and garlic. Have a sun bath for 5–10 minutes daily. Avoid fasting and purgatives.

Recipe

To normalise blood pressure, munch on an unpeeled carrot once a day.

Infusions

To normalise blood pressure:

- Have a glass of the infusion of shepherd's purse once in 2 days. It regulates the function of the heart.
- Have a glass of the infusion of lavender leaves or rosemary leaves 2 times a day.
- Boil a banana stem in water. Have the infusion 3 times a day for 2 weeks. Exercise care as the infusion may increase the blood pressure to above normal.

Asana Routine

Do not strain yourself while doing these Asanas:

- All Sitting Pawanamuktasana
- All Forward Bending Asanas
- Suryanamaskar [Salutation to the Sun]
- Sarvangasana [Shoulderstand]
- Halasana [Plough 1]
- Karna Peedasana [Plough 3]
- Matsyasana [Fish in Lotus]
- Paschimottanasana [Backstretch]
- Bhujangasana [Cobra Pose]
- Shalabasana [Locust Pose]
- Bhastika Pranayama [Dynamic Breathing Standing]
- Meditation

STROKE

This is an attack of paralysis caused by a ruptured artery or haemorrhage in the brain or by an obstruction of an artery as from a clot. Any interruption in the blood supply to the brain can cause permanent damage to the brain cells within 5 minutes. If the patient survives, he or she will be handicapped to some degree by the paralysis of muscles. The onset of a stroke is usually sudden. It can be caused by an interruption in the blood supply due to a blood clot either from the heart or in the major blood vessels of the neck, a rupture in the wall of an artery due to high blood pressure or through a weak artery.

Blood pressure is a good warning sign for stroke, heart disease and kidney problems. It also indicates the malfunction of the adrenal glands. When the blood pressure is too high, the blood vessels may burst. If this happens in the heart, it can cause a heart attack. If it happens in the brain, it can cause a stroke. The patient may collapse, lose consciousness and experience sudden weakness or numbness in the arms or legs or on one side of the face. Usually, before a stroke really occurs, there are some indications, such as restlessness, dizziness, anxiety and a distorted face. Depending on the part of the brain affected, the stroke can impair speech, hearing, taste or sight. It can cause dizziness, vomiting, migraines, paralysis or numbness in the arms.

CARE AND PREVENTIVE MEASURES

To reduce the chances of a stroke, keep the blood pressure low, the weight normal, avoid smoking and becoming stressed, cut down on salt and stick to a diet rich in the following: fibre, magnesium (to prevent blood clots and for the proper functioning of the circulatory system) and potassium (to prevent the arteries from hardening, thereby avoiding a slow flow of blood. Potassium is also important in the transmission of nerve impulses, nutrient intake and for waste removal in cells and to keep the sodium level in balance.

Bananas are beneficial due to their potassium content. Aspirin is a preventive drug that reduces the stickiness of blood. Other supplements are selenium to reduce platelet clotting and vitamin C to strengthen blood vessel walls. Regular exercise is a must.

The following types of food rich in salicylates help a person recuperate from a stroke:

Fruit like apples, cherries, dates, figs, grapefruit, grapes, guavas, lemons, mandarin oranges, musk melons, peaches, pears with their skin, pineapples, plums, prunes, raisins and watermelons.

Vegetables like asparagus, beetroot, broad beans, broccoli, carrots, cucumbers, green peppers, okra, onions, potato skin, radishes, spinach and tomatoes.

Herbs like alfalfa, aniseed, celery seeds, cinnamon, cumin, dill, fenugreek, mustard, paprika, rosemary, sage leaves, turmeric and thyme.

Nuts like almonds, brazil nuts, coconuts, peanuts and sesame seeds.

Soya beans, which dissolve cholesterol and improve circulation, thereby preventing a stroke.

Other types of food like honey, peppermint and cottage cheese.

Infusions

To prevent the occurrence of a stroke:

• Have a cup of the infusion of sage leaves regularly. Sage leaves strengthen the body and prevent any chances of a stroke. They are also good for trembling limbs.

• Mix lavender leaves, marjoram herb, rosemary, sage leaves and sweet violet together in equal proportion in a pot. Add a cup of cider vinegar. Bring it to the boil. Have a glass the infusion once a day to clear symptoms of a stroke.

For rehabilitation after a stroke:

Take mistletoe leaves (cold infusion) twice a day. Although slow, this helps in the recovery process from a stroke. Begin with 3 cups a day for about six weeks, 2 cups a day for another 3 weeks, and 1 cup for another 2 weeks. This is the normal treatment period in the early stages of a stroke. The treatment is not suitable for people with high blood pressure.

Applications

Massage using any of the following essential oils mixed together with a base oil:

• Thyme oil (for those suffering from paralysis, stroke and multiple sclerosis).

• Thyme oil and St. John's wort oil in equal proportion.

• Chamomile oil, thyme oil and basil oil in equal proportion.

Asana Routine

For rehabilitation after a stroke, try out the following Asanas:

• All the Pawanamuktasana and Vikasaka series are beneficial.

• Ekapada Jatara Parivartanasana [Legover Single Leg] with help if necessary.

• Shavasana [Relaxation]

• Meditation

• Ujjayi Pranayama [Abdominal Breathing-lying down]

• Nadi Shodhana Pranayama [Alternate Nostril Breathing]

THROMBOPHLEBITIS

This disease, which mostly affects women, occurs when a vein develops a clot and this gets inflamed. The veins of the thighs and legs are the ones that are commonly affected. Thrombophlebitis may occur during pregnancy, after childbirth, surgery or influenza. Symptoms include pain in the groin area and calf muscles and frequent swelling in these areas. Rest is essential. Have food that retards clots.

Note: Massaging or even rubbing a clot can cause it to spread to other parts of the body. This can cause serious damage and even lead to death.

VASCULAR DISEASE

This is the narrowing of the arteries in the legs. It is linked to smoking and lack of exercise. Symptoms are pain in the calf and thigh muscles or cramps while walking. The skin appears pale and cool to the touch and hair on the toes may drop. Eating soya beans helps.

VARICOSE VEINS

This is a condition in which the veins become enlarged, dilated or thicker. The walls of the veins become relaxed and press inwardly upon the nerves, resulting in the formation of ulcers on the veins. Varicose veins can occur in any part of the body but are most common in the legs.

Varicose veins are caused by the sluggish circulation of blood due to the following reasons: a low intake of dietary fibre, constipation, wearing tight clothes and obesity. Standing stationary for long periods of time and successive pregnancies are other factors. During pregnancy, due to increased pressure on the pelvis and abdomen, the circulation of blood slows down. The first sign of varicose veins is swelling along the course of a vein, followed by muscular cramps and a feeling of tiredness in the legs, particularly behind the knees. In some cases, the region becomes purplish and pigmented and this is called varicose ulcers.

CARE AND PREVENTIVE MEASURES

Have a diet rich in fruit and green vegetables, vitamin B complex, vitamin C and vitamin E. In addition, have cayenne, ginger (stimulates blood circulation in the legs), horse chestnuts, buckwheat (strengthens the blood vessels) and dandelion (gets rid of water retention). Vitamin B6, folic acid and an extra dose of vitamin E help relieve varicose veins. They may even clear the condition.

Go on a juice therapy for a week, then an all fruit therapy diet for another week. After this, follow a strict diet consisting of orange juice and lemon juice for breakfast, raw vegetable salad with olive oil and lemon juice as dressing for lunch, steamed vegetables like spinach, cabbages, carrots, cauliflower, potatoes, raisins and figs for supper.

At the end of this, stick to a balanced diet, with emphasis on grains, seeds, vegetables and fruit. In particular, include garlic, honey, barberries and comfrey rootstock in the diet. Sleeping with the feet raised above the level of the heart also helps.

Avoid condiments, alcohol, white flour, white sugar and their products. Avoid massaging the affected region.

Recipe
Have a clove of garlic and a glass of warm water with honey every morning.

Infusion
Have a glass of the infusion of barberries with vitamin E 3 times a day.

Applications
* Apply honey to the affected area on a regular basis.
* Apply an ice pack to the enlarged veins twice a day on a regular basis.
* Apply basil oil and expose the affected area for five minutes to the early morning sun.
* Apply geranium or cypress oil with wheatgerm or almond oil as base oil for relief.
* Apply a paste of ground cabbage and apply once daily.
* Make a poultice from blended comfrey leaves and apply.
* Use chestnuts externally as a poultice or in the bath.

Baths
* Have an alternate hot and cold hip bath.
* Have a hot epsom salt bath.
* Mix chamomile flowers in boiling water and add this to the bath. Take the bath once in 2 days.
* Add a decoction of crushed chestnuts to hot bath water and soak for 15 minutes.
* Soak legs in warm water in which a decoction of male fern has been mixed for 15 minutes every other day.

- Add a decoction of oak bark to a hot bath and soak for 15 minutes.
- Add a decoction of fresh shavegrass to bath. Do this every other day.

Asana Routine

Besides these Asanas, all inverted Asanas will help in the draining of stagnant blood:

- Pawanamuktasana
- Gomukhasana [Posture Clasp]
- Vajrasana [Sitting Thunderbolt]
- Bhujangasana [Cobra Pose]
- Shalabasana [Locust Pose]
- Meditation

BLOOD DISEASES

ANAEMIA

Anaemia occurs when the blood cannot carry as much oxygen as it can due to insufficient red blood cells or a reduced amount of haemoglobin in these cells. It can also mean that the body does not produce enough haemoglobin, thereby causing a lack of iron indirectly. This is oxygen and iron starvation. Lack of iron or the inability of the body to absorb it are some causes. It can also occur due to defective ingestion or absorption, loss of blood, depression of the red blood cells forming tissues of the bone marrow, toxins and overexposure to radiation like X-ray.

TYPES OF ANAEMIA

Iron-deficiency Anaemia results in the bone marrow producing smaller red blood cells with less haemoglobin in them. This eventually causes a low red blood cell count. Causes include excessive loss of blood during menstruation, gastro-intestinal bleeding due to ulcers, lack of hydrochloric acid in the stomach, cancer of the stomach, pregnancy, haemorrhoids, hookworm, vitamin B6 deficiency, rheumatoid arthritis and tuberculosis. Common symptoms are fatigue, fainting spells, palpitations, shortness of breath, headaches and deformed finger nails.

A well-balanced diet is necessary to rectify the problem. Vitamin B12, proteins and iron are necessary for the cells to function better. Do not drink too much tea as it destroys iron and do not strain yourself.

In another type of anaemia, red blood cells are larger than normal. This is caused by a deficiency in folic acid (fast food, alcoholism and diarrhoea can lead to a deficiency in folic acid or vitamin B12), the presence of tapeworms, bacterial infections in the intestines or a degenerated stomach that prevents vitamin B12 from being available to the cells.

Symptoms include fatigue, a smooth tongue, breathlessness on exertion, poor appetite and indigestion. Deficiency in vitamin B12, folic acid and protein will lead to a tingling sensation and numbness in the hands and feet.

For treating this type of anaemia, follow a diet rich in protein. Also, take vitamin B12 supplements with folic acid. Folic acid is available in abundance in fresh vegetables. Expectant mothers are advised to eat a lot of fresh green vegetables.

In the third type of anaemia called haemolysis, red blood cells are destroyed while they are in circulation. They occur as a result of burns and infections. The disease may also be congenital. Symptoms include jaundice of the skin and eyes and dark coloured urine.

Finally, anaemia may also result from nutritional deficiencies in iron, protein, folic acid, vitamin B12, vitamin C, iodine, cobalt, copper and vitamin B6. This is known as nutritional anaemia.

Symptoms include pale skin, listlessness, tiredness, rapid heartbeat, a sore tongue, cracks at the corners of the mouth and concave nails. Other symptoms are headaches, dizziness, palpitations, shortness of breath on exertion and brittle finger nails. In children, symptoms are poor appetite and low resistance to infections. If you eat beetroot and the urine turns out red, this suggests a deficiency in iron.

CARE AND PREVENTIVE MEASURES

Garlic is beneficial. Cherries and spinach are a rich source of iron and are good blood builders Although spinach is rich in iron, the iron cannot be absorbed by the body because of the presence of oxalic acid. However, part of this can be obtained when cooked with tamarind water.

Alternatively, cook spinach leaves with egg. Because of their mineral content, copper, manganese and iron, black currants are useful in treating anaemia.

Food that helps in the production of red cells — alfalfa, apricots, avocados, barberries, beetroot, blueberries, carrots, comfrey rootstock, dark grapes, dates, kelp, fenugreek, stinging nettle and raspberries. Food that rebuilds the blood — almonds, cucumbers, garlic, honey, leek, milk, molasses, oranges, parsley, prunes, raisins, saffron, sarsaparilla, wheatgerm, brewer's yeast and yoghurt..

Recipe

Add 2 saffron strands to boiled fresh milk. Have this once a day.

Juice

- Have a cup of the juice of chicory in combination with celery and parsley mixed together in equal proportion.
- Mix equal quantities of fresh grape juice and orange juice. Drink this 2 times a day. This is especially good for children suffering from anaemia.
- Mix the fresh juice of 2 parts spinach and 1 part parsley. Add an equal quantity of fresh orange juice. Have a glass of this 2 times a day.

Infusions

- Mix equal quantities of thyme and stinging nettle together. Have the infusion 3 times a day with honey.
- Have a glass of the light infusion of St. John's wort flowers before breakfast and before turning in for the night.

Asana Routine

- Suryanamaskar [Salutation to the Sun]
- Bhujangasana [Cobra Pose]
- Shalabasana [Locust Pose]
- Sarvangasana [Shoulderstand]
- Halasana [Plough 1]
- Matsyasana [Fish in Lotus]
- Paschimottanasana [Backstretch]

- Ujjayi Pranayama [Abdominal Breathing]
- Shirasasana [Headstand]
- Nadi Shodhana Pranayama [Alternate Nostril Breathing]
- Sheetali Pranayama [Cooling Breath]
- Sheetkari Pranayama [Hissing Breath]

Note: Asanas involving deep breathing are essential.

POLYCYTHAEMIA

This is a disease that results from an excess of red blood cells and the amount of haemoglobin in the blood. This may cause the blood to thicken, causing blindness and mild strokes. The secondary problem may result from heart and lung disorders. Common symptoms are purple lips, headaches, dizziness, fainting spells, nose bleeding and ankle swelling. Correcting the problem of the lungs and heart helps secondary polycythaemia.

LEUKAEMIA

Diseases that affect the white blood cells are called leukaemia. Anaemia is the first symptom, followed by headaches and a weak feeling. Pain in the bones and joints also appear. There will be bleeding, especially from the nose and gums, as well as infections in the mouth and throat. These will be accompanied by fever. The lymph nodes may enlarge and at a later stage, the spleen may also enlarge.

Treatment depends on the type of leukaemia and the individual's age. A heavy dosage of vitamin C and other supplements is advised, while fruit and vegetables are to be eaten fresh. A regular checkup is necessary. Consult a doctor for further advice.

Depending on the type of leukaemia, herbal treatment prevents and may even help cure the disease at an early stage. Some orthodox medicines, such as vinblastine and vincristine used to treat leukaemia, are extracted from Madagascar Periwinkle. This is an example of an instance where herbs may be used as a source of active ingredients.

CARE AND PREVENTIVE MEASURES

Have plenty of stewed apples, red or black grapes, carrots and non-acidic fruit and vegetables with wheatgerm, oats, barley, whole wheat bread, yoghurt, honey or milk. Avoid acidic fruit, animal protein, too much salt, spices and fast food (especially oil or fried foods).

A cancer patient should have a meal of grapes every 2 hours for 2 weeks, after which he or she should fast for a day or two and then continue with the meal of eating grapes. For a start, have 30 grams of grapes for every meal and increase it gradually to 180 grams. After this diet, have fresh fruit, tomatoes, buttermilk and cottage cheese for 2 or 3 weeks.

Follow up with raw vegetable juice, fruit, nuts, milk, yoghurt and honey. However, grapes should still be the main food eaten. Dr. Lambe, an English dietician, treated cancer in England 100 years ago with grapes. Today, Germany has become the centre for this type of natural healing therapy.

Remedies for leukaemia work through the liver by activating its detoxifying property. These include greater celandine, walnut or burdock. Since in most cases leukaemia is found in the spleen, take herbs that activate the spleen: speedwell (Veronica officinalis), dandelion roots or stinging nettle (Urtica dioica).

A cleansing action on the lymphatic system from herbs like cleavers (Galium aparine), also known as bedstraw, is beneficial. Similarly, select the type of tea with herbs that not only acts as a calming agent but also helps in digestion and circulation.

The following are some fruit and vegetables that help prevent the formation and spread of cancer cells:

- Avocados (due to their copper and iron content aid in the process of red blood regeneration)
- Blackberries (one of the best-known nerve tonics and blood builders)
- Olives (prevent cholesterol accumulation)
- Beetroot (rich in B2. Beetroot greens are a rich source of calcium, vitamin A and iron and are a source of catalase for protection against cancer)
- Beta carotene (has anticancer properties)
- Cold pressed olive oil

Recipe

Make a herbal mixture from 80 grams of speedwell, 100 grams of cleavers, 100 grams of yarrow (which act on blood marrow and stimulate blood renewal), 80 grams of wormwood (Artemisia absinthum) for activating the digestive system, 120 grams of elder shoots (Sambucus nigra), 120 grams of marigolds (act as a blood cleanser), 120 grams of greater celandine, 120 grams of stinging nettle (a blood builder and rich in iron), 60 grams of St. John's wort (for anxiety) and 60 grams of dandelion roots. Store in a cool, dry place.

To prepare, add a cup of boiling water to a heaped teaspoon of the above mixture. Cover and let it steep for 10 minutes. Strain, add honey (if too bitter) before drinking it. Have about 16 cups of this freshly made, warm tea at regular intervals daily.

For cleansing the entire system:

- Soak a teaspoon of shredded calamus roots overnight in a cup of water. Warm it the next morning and strain. Take a sip before and after every meal (6 sips for a day).
- Take 3 teaspoons of Swedish bitter diluted in 3 cups of herbal mixture (prepared as above) tea half an hour before each meal 3 times a day.

Applications

- Apply Swedish bitter as a compress to the liver and spleen area once a day for 4 hours if the liver and spleen are not normal in size.
- Apply the essential oil of marjoram diluted with a base oil like wheatgerm oil or almond oil or grape seed oil (6 drops of marjoram to 4 teaspoons of the base oil) to the area after a bath once daily.

Bath

Steep 200 grams of thyme in cool water. Heat and strain. Add the water to a bathtub of warm water. Soak with the chest above water for 20 minutes. Do not dry yourself. Wrap body well and lie down for an hour well-covered.

BLOOD POISON

Bacteria can enter the blood stream from local infections and cause poisoning.

Juice
Have as much as possible the juice of black or red grapes as they cleanse poisoned blood.

Infusions
- Have a glass of the warm infusion of yarrow, sage leaves and horsetail herbs mixed together in the ratio of 9:9:5 once a day for 21 days.
- Have a glass of the warm infusion of cowslip, elder flowers, stinging nettle, dandelion roots and speedwell mixed together in the ratio of 3:3:1:1:1 once a day.

BLEEDING

Eggplant stops bleeding in the anus and nose, as well as bleeding during urination.

Juice
- Have the fresh juice of white pumpkins.
- Take 4 teaspoons of the fresh juice of a lemon or bergamot orange 3 times a day. This is also good for internal haemorrhage of the lungs.

Infusion
Have an infusion of Shepherd's purse tea. It acts as a blood coagulant and treats internal and external bleeding.

16

The Respiratory System

❧

Any disease of the muscles and bones of the chest wall, lungs or air passage will interfere, to some extent, with the normal functioning of the respiratory system. This leads to a lower than normal supply of oxygen to all other organs and tissues of the body, thereby affecting their performance.

While muscle and nervous diseases weaken the capacity to breathe properly, diseases of the air passage narrow the tubes and reduce the efficient functioning of the gas exchange process.

Infections are the most common forms of lung diseases. When the defence mechanisms of the respiratory system, like the hair in the nose and mucous membranes in the bronchi, are affected, chances of infections increase. Streptococcus germs affect the whole human system. They may infect the throat and cause septic sore throat, swollen lymph glands, sinusitis, pneumonia and meningitis, among others.

Most respiratory diseases begin with a viral infection like a common cold. When the patient's resistance to infections is low, localised infections of the tonsils, adenoids and tissues of the throat develop. The tissues become swollen, with dead germs and dying cells, and cause pain.

Respiratory stimulants that help the nerves and muscles like bittersweet and daisy; respiratory relaxants that help to relax the tissues of the system by easing tension like aniseed, hyssop and thyme; and demulcents that clear inflamed mucous membranes like comfrey rootstock, mullein and marshmallow should be included in the daily diet. Also, include food that belongs to the expectorant and pectoral groups.

It is equally important to develop a healthy way of breathing through Pranayama and other Asanas. The following pages list ailments specific to the respiratory system and suggest ways of remedying them.

For respiratory problems like colds, flu, bronchitis and asthma:

- Boil 6 teaspoons of crushed mustard seeds in water to make a decoction. Add the decoction to warm water and have a foot bath.
- Add the infusion of thyme to hot bath. Use this to bathe once a day.

NOSE
NOSEBLEEDING

Nosebleed occurs when the capillaries inside the nose get ruptured due to injury or for no apparent reason. Some people get nosebleed because of nasal infection or hay fever. If you get nosebleed after an operation of the tonsils or adenoids, you should see a specialist immediately.

Increase the intake of amaranth, chestnuts, horseradish and spinach in your daily diet as these stop bleeding. Avoid cinnamon as it aggravates bleeding.

Juice

- Drink a glass of radish juice with brown sugar once a day for a week.
- Add a few lemon slices or lemon juice to half a glass of sugared water. Have this 2 times a day for a week. Repeat if necessary after a short break.

Applications

- Apply the juice of radishes or spinach to the bridge of the nose.
- Rub a cotton bud on the inner surface of a tender onion leaf. Dab the juice onto the inner walls of the nostrils.
- Crush a clove of garlic. Add a teaspoon of coconut oil. Mix well. Apply the oil to the soles of the feet. Apply once every 3 days for 3 weeks.
- Apply a wad of cotton soaked in lemon juice to the nostrils.

COMMON COLDS

This is a viral inflammation that affects only the upper part of the respiratory tract, nose, throat and sinuses. Lack of sleep, exposure to cold and wet, lack of exercise and living in poorly ventilated areas can lower the body resistance. Unless local resistance and general immunity are increased, the individual is likely to catch colds often. If not treated in the early stage, complications like bronchitis, infected sinuses, middle ear diseases and tuberculosis can set in. Sneezing, running nose, teary eyes and stuffiness in the head appear. Nasal membranes swell, making the individual breathe through the mouth. The sense of smell and taste reduce. Sore throat results, and if the cold becomes chronic, fever and pain in the joints are felt, resulting in influenza. Allergens like pollen, dust, smoke, perfumes and chemicals also give similar symptoms like sneezing, coughing and breathing difficulty.

At the early stage, a heavy dosage of vitamin C is considered to be a preventive measure. Eating sensibly, getting enough rest, avoiding exposure to chills and learning to relax can ward off common colds. Drink plenty of water for 24 hours. Follow up with liquid foods mainly of fruit juices until the acute symptoms subside. "Flu shots" are effective against a particular virus only for a limited period but do not cure the problem. Continue with a diet rich in vitamin C and which has antihistamine property. A spoonful of honey a day keeps cold and other infections away.

If the nose is blocked due to a cold, do not blow the nose because forceful blowing may spread infection into the sinuses and eustachian tube. Nose drops or antihistamine can give temporary relief, but using them too often may result in greater congestion of the nose. Avoid food that triggers cold symptoms like cinnamon, cold drinks, cucumbers and pineapples. Cinnamon is good for cold limbs but not for chest colds.

The following measures help prevent colds:

Recipes

- After a hot bath, have a cup of hot lemon juice with honey before going to sleep.
- Add a pinch of turmeric powder that has been sauteed in a teaspoonful of ghee to the soup of either black beans or mung beans. Season with ginger and cumin seeds. Have the soup before meals at least twice a week. This builds up the resistance to colds.
- Apply mustard oil diluted in base oil to the nose bridge daily.
- Take a teaspoon of honey in warm water daily before meals.
- Increase the intake of food and herbs like sweet basil, figs, ginger, lemons, blackberries, sarsaparilla, onions, radishes, peppermint, grapefruit, garlic, rice, vinegar, lemon balm, rose flowers, safflower, saffron, peppermint and spearmint in your daily diet.

- Add a quarter teaspoon of black pepper powder and rock sugar to hot milk. Have this for the duration of the cold.
- In a small pot of water, put a few cloves of garlic and a small onion. Bring it to a simmer. Add a pinch of salt and powdered black pepper. Drink this directly or mix it with brown rice and have it during the period of the cold.

For relief from colds:
- Soak 7 almond nuts in water, remove the skin and grind them in water. The mixture looks like milk. Add a few threads of saffron or a pinch of turmeric powder and a few seeds of cardamom. Add 2 black pepper corns, a pinch of edible camphor and sugar to taste. Bring this to a boil. Drink the liquid hot for 5 days. Repeat if necessary after a week.
- Mix powdered black pepper, ginger, aniseed and honey together until it becomes a paste. Take a teaspoon of this with rice once a day for 3 days.
- Eat fresh starfruit daily.
- Have black pepper soup with ginger and lemon once a day.
- Have a glass of milk that has been heated with a pinch of turmeric powder and a teaspoon of sugar.

Juice
- Have 2 tablespoons of lemon juice mixed with honey before going to bed.
- Have 2 tablespoons of lemon juice in a glass of hot water before going to bed.

Infusions
Have a glass of infusion of any of the following until the cold stops:
- Dry ginger with brown sugar or of basil leaves once a day after meals.
- Eucalyptus leaves in cold water once a day before going to bed.
- Ginger, clove flower buds, coriander seeds and nutmeg mixed in equal proportion with a few drops of fresh lemon juice and honey 3 times a day.

- Leaves of hyssop, rosehips, safflower, cinnamon or of echinacea rootstock 3 times a day for 3 days. This produces perspiration and gets rid of the cold.

Decoctions
Have 2 tablespoons of decoction of any of following:
- Dried figs diluted in water 3 times a day.
- Clove flower buds mixed with rock sugar once a day.

Asana Routine
Do not strain your lungs while performing the following Asanas:
- Suryanamaskar [Salutation to the Sun]
- Simhasana [Lion]
- All breathing asanas

Inhalation
Inhale vapours of turmeric powder sprinkled on hot water before going to bed. After inhaling, do not drink water for a minimum of 2 hours.

CHRONIC COLDS

Recipes
- If cold is severe and chest is congested, warm in a frying pan a teaspoon of ghee, castor oil and sesame oil. Add to the warm oil, a teaspoon of powdered black pepper and bring the mixture to the boil. Have the pepper with rice and apply the oil on the chest, throat and back.
- Crush 2 cloves of garlic, add a teaspoon of mustard seeds and have this with rice wine once a day.
- Blend equal parts of dried ginger and black pepper powder with 2 parts aniseed and honey. Take a teaspoon of this diluted in water once a day after meals with a few cardamom seeds.

Infusions
- Have a glass of infusion of garlic, ginger and black pepper mixed in equal proportion with a teaspoon of honey 3 times a day.

- To a glass of hot infusion of half a teaspoon of ginger powder, add a teaspoon of honey. Have this once a day for 2 weeks.

Decoctions

- Add a pinch of mustard powder to 2 teaspoons of the decoction of garlic. Have this in water once a day.
- Have 2 teaspoons of the decoction of walnuts and ginger mixed in equal quantities to induce perspiration during a cold.
- Powder 3 clove flower buds, a small piece of liquorice root, half a teaspoon of black pepper, a small piece of dry ginger, a blade of lemongrass, a piper longum (hippali) and some natural brown sugar. Boil the mixture in 2 glasses of water until it reduces to a third of the original volume. Have a teaspoon of the decoction 3 times a day.

Applications

- Make a paste from one spring onion, 15 grams of fresh ginger and 3 grams of salt. Wrap this in cloth and rub over chest, back, soles of feet, palms and arms.
- Apply a hot fomentation to the face and chest and a cold compress to the back of the neck while soaking feet in hot water. Do this once a day. Once perspiration starts, remove fomentation pads, stop the foot bath and cover yourself so that you will not get any chills.

Other Recipes

For colds due to infections:
Blend a clove of garlic with a teaspoon of honey. Take this 2 times a day after meals.

For colds due to congestion in the chest:
Sprinkle turmeric powder over lighted coal and inhale smoke a few times with a break of a day for 3 days. This helps clear a blocked nose.

For colds due to allergies:

- Have a glass of infusion of orange peel and ginger mixed in equal proportion with honey once a day for 2 weeks.
- Have soup made from 2 tablespoons of fresh peppermint, a tablespoon of soya bean curd and a

quarter teaspoon of grated fresh ginger with meals once a day for 2 weeks.

For a stuffy nose:
Have a small raw onion twice a day before meals.

To clear head colds:
Have a hot infusion made from verbascum flowers, lime flowers, chamomile flowers, agrimony leaves, fennel seeds or sage leaves 3 times a day.

For colds with fever:
Have a glass of infusion of elder flowers, peppermint and yarrow mixed in equal proportion 3 times a day or the infusion of unripe pineapples once a day for 3 days.

For colds and bronchial fever:
Inhale the vapour of peppermint or spearmint leaves in hot water just before sleeping.

For colds associated with coughs:
Have a glass of hot infusion of evening primrose or sage leaves twice a day.

For colds, coughs and chest problems:
Have a glass of hot infusion of sunflower seeds sweetened with honey 2 times a day.

For colds, asthma and sinusitis during pregnancy:
Have a glass of celery juice extracted from the fleshy petioles once a day.

For colds and asthma in children:
Get the children to inhale the vapour of chamomile flowers or add a drop of chamomile oil to hot water and make them inhale the vapour.

For colds with abdominal pain:

- Season food with fennel seeds, mustard seeds and ginger on a regular basis.
- Grind a teaspoon of black pepper and fry it in a teaspoon of olive oil. Add 2 cups of water, a few curry

leaves and a pinch of salt. Bring it to the boil. Drink or eat this with steamed rice.

HAY FEVER

This is an allergic disease of the respiratory tract. It is caused by the action of allergens on the oversensitive mucous membrane. Allergens are usually airborne, pet hair or food particles. Pollen from plants is the most common allergen. Continuous sneezing, headaches, distress, depression and red, watery eyes with irritation are the effects of hay fever.

The best form of treatment for hay fever is to avoid the allergens that cause it. One has to find out the real allergen with patience. Stick to a low mucous-producing diet with vitamin C and garlic.

Recipes
- Have a few comfrey leaves in your daily diet.
- Add a teaspoon of orange peel to food or have a glass of infusion of orange peel 2 times a day.
- Gargle with the juice of coriander seeds 3 times a day.

Asana Routine
- Simhasana [Lion]
- All the Pranayama

SINUSITIS

Cavities in the cheek bones below and above the eyes, bones between the nasal cavities and the orbits of the eyes, the bones of the face, and the floor of the skull are called sinuses. These are lined with mucous membranes that connect to the nasal passage. If there is congestion in the passage or if an inflammation develops due to pus-producing germs in these sinuses, sinusitis develops. It can also be due to an allergy. The affected area will be tender and painful. A moderate fever develops, as well as a dull ache and the feeling of heaviness around the nose. Pressing along the eyebrows causes pain in the front bone while pressing the prominence of the cheeks causes pain if it is due to an infection. Severe nasal

congestion leads to loss of the sense of smell. Nasal congestion with a mucous discharge is a symptom of allergic rhinitis. It can cause sinusitis or headache. If a person is allergic to dust, cat fur and moulds, there will usually be recurring sneezing and watering of the nose associated with irritation in the eyes.

Increase the intake of food that clears inflammations and prevents mucous production like ginger, turmeric, cumin, coriander, fenugreek, fennel seeds and asafoetida. Avoid raw fruits and juices.

Recipes
To clear sinus:
- Have a clove of garlic and a glass of warm water 3 times a day. This prevents sneezing and clears a stuffy nose.
- Have black pepper soup with ginger and salt once a day.

Infusion
Have a glass of infusion of orange peel twice a day for 2 weeks.

Inhalation
Inhale the vapour of turmeric powder sprinkled on hot water.

Recipes
To prevent nasal congestion and sneezing:
- Have soup made from lemon balm or peppermint leaves with soya bean curd and ginger once a day.
- Have a raw horseradish in the mornings and drink a glass of warm water with honey thereafter.

Applications
To clear nasal congestion:
- Apply lemon balm or lemongrass oil diluted in base oil to the nose.
- Make a paste from calamus roots and water. Apply this to the bridge of the nose and the forehead once a day for 2 days.

Inhalation

To clear nasal congestion and sinusitis:

Mix a drop of lavender oil, 2 drops of pine oil, 2 drops thyme and 4 drops of eucalyptus oil together. Inhale the vapour of this mixture in hot water 2 times a day.

Asanas

Yoga helps, including all the Pranayama, especially Bhastika Pranayama, which is particularly beneficial. Refer also to Asanas for colds.

THROAT AND AIR PASSAGE COUGHS

A cough is more a symptom of diseases like bronchitis or pulmonary problems or pneumonia than a disease. Common cough due to a simple cold may last a week, but if it persists, consult a doctor. Causes include irritation or pressure on the trachea, pneumonia, tuberculosis, emphysema, bronchitis, heart failure, etc.

Ginger and caraway seeds must form an essential part of the diet. Other types of food, such as almonds, asafoetida, asparagus, blackberries, cabbages, carrots, comfrey, evening primrose, fern, grapes, grapefruit peel, honey (for dry coughs), lemons and pears (for coughs with mucous), marjoram, mustard leaves, okra, olives (for coughs with blood), onions, oranges, parsley, peaches, peanuts (for dry coughs), pears, pumpkins, radishes, raspberries, saffron, spearmint, strawberries and sweet mangoes, also help in preventing coughs. Avoid eating an excess of soya sauce as it causes coughs. Cinnamon too triggers coughs.

HOMEMADE COUGH SYRUP

- Dice some green onions and cook them over low heat for about 2 hours in half a cup of honey. Strain the liquid and store in a container at room temperature. Take a teaspoon of this liquid 2 times a day.
- Boil lemon juice with honey to make a jelly. Take a tablespoon of this 2 times a day.

Recipes

To clear coughs:

- Add a drop of the oil of fennel to a teaspoon of honey. Have this thrice a day.
- Take a teaspoon of grated garlic with 2 teaspoons honey twice a day for 30 days to clear coughs with phlegm. Not to be taken during sore throat.
- Have soup made from fresh peppermint, soya bean curd and fresh ginger twice a day.
- Use 1 part ginger powder to 5 parts natural brown sugar. Add a teaspoon of ghee. Have this in the mornings for a week.
- Have a starfruit before meals to treat coughs and fever from cold.
- Drink almond milk. Refer to recipes for relief from colds.

Juice

- Have a glass of hot water with a teaspoon of lemon juice and honey twice a day.
- Take a teaspoon of onion juice sweetened with honey once a day.
- Have a glass of fresh pear juice 3 times a day.
- Take 2 tablespoons of radish juice with an equal quantity of honey before breakfast.
- Take a teaspoon of syrup made from red cabbage juice.

Infusion

- Have a cup of infusion of basil with honey or an infusion of bilberry leaves or caraway seeds or comfrey leaves or coriander seeds or herb hyssop 3 times a day after meals.
- Have a glass of infusion of sarsaparilla root bark with milk and sugar.

Decoctions

- Add a tablespoon of the decoction of old ginger to a glass of hot milk. Add a teaspoon of sugar and drink this 3 times a day.
- Take a teaspoon of the decoction of betel nuts mixed with honey once a day.
- Take a tablespoon of the decoction of marshmallow roots or horseradish with honey once a day.

- Take a teaspoon of the decoction of evening primrose for coughs that develop with common colds.
- Take a teaspoon of milk decoction of clove flower buds and rock sugar or marshmallow and thyme mixed in equal proportion or the decoction of mullein leaves before going to sleep.

Inhalation
Inhaling an infusion of eucalyptus leaves gives relief.

The following measures help clear chronic coughs:

Recipes
- Steam a few olives or peaches in rock sugar. Take a teaspoon of this 3 times a day.
- Have a steamed ripe papaya (one slice) once a day.
- Have 3 strawberries soaked in a solution of rock sugar 3 times a day.
- Fry a clove of garlic in a teaspoon of olive oil. Add sugar to taste and mix well. Have this once a day.
- Have black pepper soup once a day.
- For children, make them drink the fresh juice of lemon balm or its infusion with sugar 2 times a day.

Infusions
- Take a tablespoon of the infusion of comfrey rootstock 3 times a day for coughs with bronchial ailments.
- Have a glass of the infusion of comfrey leaves just before going to bed if coughs are caused by allergies.

Decoction
Take a tablespoon of the decoction of dried mulberry leaves twice a day.

Application
Apply a hot fomentation to the throat and chest.

The following measures help clear dry coughs:

Recipes
- Core and peel an apple. Add honey to taste. Leave it to steam until it becomes a jelly. Take 2 teaspoons of the jelly 3 times a day.

- Steam 2 figs and 2 dates. Add a teaspoon of honey. Let it steam until it becomes a jelly. Take 2 tablespoons of the jelly 2 times a day.
- Steam a grapefruit with its skin in rock sugar and a small piece of fresh ginger. Take 2 tablespoons of the concoction 2 times a day.
- Have dry roasted or fresh peanuts after meals.

Juice
Have fresh raspberry juice with honey once a day to clear a dry cough with a cold.

Infusion
Have a glass of infusion of basil leaves with honey or peppermint leaves or strawberry leaves or thyme leaves once a day before meals for a week.

WHOOPING COUGHS

This is an infectious respiratory disease caused by germs.

Recipes
- Have the water of cooked sword beans with honey 3 times a day.
- Pour a glass of water into a pot and add 3 cloves of crushed garlic. Bring it to the boil. Add 2 tablespoons of brown sugar to make a syrup. Take a tablespoon of the syrup 3 times a day.
- Sprinkle 4–5 drops of the essential oil of cypress on the pillow before sleeping.
- For children, boil a carrot and dates in one glass of water. Give them the water to drink.

Juice
- Add 2 teaspoons of garlic juice to a glass of any fruit juice. Have this 2 times a day.
- Add a teaspoon of betel leaf juice to a spoonful of freshly prepared onion juice. Add a pinch of asafoetida and honey to taste. Have this 3 times a day.
- Have a glass of the juice of black currant berries or the juice of peach leaves before meals for a week.

Infusions

- Take 2 tablespoons of the infusion of dried basil leaves with honey thrice a day
- Take 2 tablespoons of the infusion of marigolds with honey thrice a day.
- Have a glass of the infusion of crushed comfrey roots mixed with a glass of milk twice a day.

TONSILLITIS AND ADENOIDS

Tonsils are at the base on both sides of the tongue. Adenoids are on the upper back of the throat. They get enlarged due to infection in order to produce lymphocytes during a sore throat, thereby causing obstruction. This interferes with breathing and the swallowing of food.

A painful throat, fever and difficulty in swallowing are common symptoms. Tonsillitis is often accompanied by chills, as well as aches in the back and limbs. There may be coating on the tongue, the entire throat may appear red and hearing may become defective.

Avoid an excess of toffee and sweets as they can lower the body's resistance to infections.

Recipes

- Have a cup of the infusion of agrimony and raspberry leaves mixed in equal parts 3 times a day.
- Add a quarter teaspoon of fresh lime juice, a pinch of salt and a teaspoon of honey to a glass of warm water. Sip a tablespoon of this to clear inflamed tonsils.

Gargles

- Gargle with an infusion of agrimony and raspberry leaves mixed together in equal proportion or with an infusion of geranium or hyssop herbs 3 times a day.
- Soak a few plum fruit in cider vinegar for 6 hours. Boil them in water and add a pinch of salt. Use this as a gargle 3 times a day.
- Add half a teaspoon of black pepper powder, a clove of crushed garlic and half a teaspoon of salt to water (a glass). Bring it to the boil. Use this as a gargle 3 times a day.

LARYNGITIS

This is an inflammation of the mucous membrane of the voice box. Causes include overusing the voice, sore throat, measles, allergies, acute colds, influenza or eating excess irritating foods (like chillies, ginger, etc.). Symptoms are a sore throat with a hoarse voice, which eventually lead to the loss of voice and breathing difficulty.

Recipes

- Have fresh radish juice mixed with ginger juice to clear a hoarse voice.
- Have a glass of the infusion of dry guava fruit (or an infusion of its leaves) twice a day for a week.
- Have a radish mixed together with 1 teaspoon of lemon juice once a day for 2 weeks.
- Inhale the vapour of the essence of cajuput oil once a day.

Gargles

- Soak a plum in cider vinegar. Boil this in water and add a pinch of salt. Use this as a gargle 3 times a day.
- Gargle with the warm infusion of sage leaves as many times as possible.
- As a preventive measure, gargle with salt water as many times as possible.

The following measures are for loss of voice:

Recipes

- Take 2 tablespoons of the juice of radish and ginger mixed together in equal proportion with honey 2 times a day.
- Take a teaspoon of honeysuckle syrup twice a day.
- Chew a ginger as it increases the production of saliva and gives relief.

Infusions

- Have a glass of the infusion of liquorice roots (or gargle with liquorice roots) 3 times a day.
- Have a glass of infusion of marjoram herbs 2 times a day.

Gargles

- Boil a teaspoon of peppermint leaves in a cup of water and add salt. Filter for a clear solution and gargle with this twice a day.
- To a cup of hot water add a pinch of baking soda and a teaspoon of fresh lime juice. Gargle with the solution twice a day.
- Warm a teaspoon of eucalyptus oil and apply a little to the throat. Add the remaining oil to warm water and use it as a gargle.

SORE THROAT

This is a common condition, usually caused by a virus or bacteria. Causes include local irritation of the pharynx due to drinking irritants, viruses, measles, tuberculosis, syphilis, cancer, smoking, the use of antiseptic gargles, food allergy, etc.

The most effective treatment for sore throat is a simple gargle with a weak salt solution. Suck the juice of some preserved or fresh olives. Avoid garlic, cinnamon bark and black pepper in excess while having a sore throat.

Recipes

- To soothe a painful throat, sip honey and lemon juice mixed together in equal proportion.
- To clear itchiness in the throat, take a teaspoon of honeysuckle syrup twice a day.
- To clear phlegm and irritation in the throat, chew two clove buds with a pinch of salt.
- Steam fresh figs and dates in honey. Take a teaspoon of this twice a day for a week.
- Have an onion in apple cider vinegar.
- Have strawberry juice every day for a week.
- Increase the intake of barley, ginger, blackcurrant, juniper berries, watermelons, chickpeas, cucumbers, castor beans, walnuts, pineapples, cabbages and fenugreek in your daily diet.

Infusions

- Steep red rose petals in distilled vinegar. Drink this once a day for a week.

- Have a glass of the infusion of amaranth leaves twice daily to clear throat irritation.
- Have a glass of the hot infusion of blackberry leaves or fig roots or rose petals with honey or an infusion of raspberries twice daily.

Gargles

- Gargle with a warm infusion of angelica roots, peppermint or lemon, or with an infusion of marjoram stems and leaves or with an infusion of marshmallow leaves 3 times a day.
- Gargle with an infusion of amaranth leaves or barberries or pomegranate seeds if there is throat irritation.

PHARYNGITIS

This is an acute sore throat. Acute colds can cause the beginning of an inflammation. Reasons for pharyngitis include lack of sleep and exercise, as well as breathing polluted air, among others.

Besides soft foods and plenty of fluids, have fresh cherries, radishes and lemon salad daily as they give relief to people with pharyngitis at an early stage.

Juice

- Have freshly squeezed lemon juice and honey in warm water daily.
- Have fresh starfruit juice twice a day.

Infusion

Have a glass of infusion of marigold flowers or dry guavas twice a day for a week.

Gargles

- Add a few plums soaked in vinegar to boiling water. Add a pinch of salt. Use this as a gargle.
- Add a quarter teaspoon of salt and baking soda to a glass of warm water. Mix well. Have this thrice a day.

Application

Apply hot fomentation to the throat three times a day.

Asanas

Simhasana [Lion] keeps the throat clear from infections. Other Asanas for the throat include:

- Ujjayi Pranayama [Abdominal Breathing]
- Sheetali Pranayama [Cooling Breath]
- Jalandhara Bandha [Chin Lock]
- Uttanasana [Legclasp Migraine Pose]
- Ushtrasana [Camel variation]
- Paschimottanasana [Backstretch]
- Sarpasana [Snake Pose]
- Shalabasana [Locust Pose]
- Nadi Shodana Pranayama [Alternate Nostril Breathing]
- Yoga Mudra

Strep throat or septic sore throat results when the tonsils are chronically enlarged and infected. It is an infectious disease that spreads through contaminated milk and milk products. In addition to the sore throat, if rashes appear on the skin, the person may be having scarlet fever. The rashes result from the toxins put out by the streptococcus germs. There will be a sudden chill with fever followed by nausea and vomiting. The tongue becomes fiery red. Treatment for this is similar to that for acute sore throat.

ASTHMA

This is a chronic respiratory disorder. The lining of the bronchi becomes congested and swollen, with the muscles adjoining the walls of the bronchi sometimes contracting. Causes include excess mucous, an allergy to dust and pollen, and consuming food with artificial colouring, additives, animal fur and moulds.

Asthma can be secondary to some cardiac or renal diseases already present in an individual. It can be inherited or the result of drugs, ineffective endocrine glands, exposure to temperature, severe weather conditions or emotional disturbances. It also occurs due to reasons of a psychological nature.

It is more common among women. Childhood asthma is linked to eczema and hay fever. Chronic bronchial asthma strikes suddenly, with low wheezing on slight exertion, restlessness, itching in the nose and coughing (this may sometimes not be experienced).

Eat little during an attack and only consume easily digestible foods. Have warm water and include plenty of fluids in the diet. Soft vegetables and fruit should form the main part of the diet. Instead of yoghurt, have buttermilk with a pinch of turmeric. If you do take milk, add saffron, a few black peppercorns and a little ginger and boil it.

Honey is an absorbing agent and fights germs, as does vinegar. Both are essential to the diet. Almonds are very good for lung and chest problems. They, however, should not be eaten alone as they are difficult to digest. Mix them with raisins or milk instead. Season food with asafoetida regularly. It is interesting to note that breastfed children seldom suffer from asthma.

Avoid raw tomatoes as they cause an immediate attack. Also avoid bananas, oils, cold and cooling foods, wind-producing and difficult to digest food, sweet pumpkins, refined sugar, raw foods, rice, seeds, beans, cashew nuts, groundnuts, durians, jackfruit, dates, lemons, and all other fruit except papayas.

Recipes

For asthma and the respiratory system:

- Simmer a few cloves of garlic and a small onion in a glass of water. Drink this as a soup or eat it with brown rice.
- Simmer over low heat a few unpeeled potatoes, an onion, a few cloves of garlic and an unpeeled carrot until the water (3 glasses) reduces to half the original volume. Add salt and drink the soup with meals for 2 weeks. The soup is good for developing the resistance
- Take 2 tablespoons of steamed ash gourd (winter melon) with honey 3 times a day to improve an asthmatic condition. Ginger may be added to the mixture to make a soup.
- Have soya bean curd regularly.
- Have a few comfrey leaves daily for 21 days.
- Have steamed peaches with rock sugar once a day.
- Have a fresh horseradish with honey and raw sugar for 2 weeks.
- Have plenty of almond milk. Refer also to recipes for relief from colds.

Infusion

Have a glass of infusion of aniseed or lemon balm or comfrey leaves or parsley leaves and its seeds 3 times a day after meals for 2 weeks.

Decoction

Take 2 tablespoons of the milk decoction of hippali (piper longum) once a day.

Inhalations

- Inhale the vapour from eucalyptus leaves by putting them in boiling water. This helps to clear bronchial complaints and asthma.
- Pound celery seeds, wrap them in a cloth and inhale the vapour.
- The ether of garlic dissolves the mucous in sinuses. It is useful for people with asthma and hay fever. Pound garlic in water, wrap it in a cloth and inhale the vapour or place the crushed garlic in boiling water and inhale the vapour.
- For children, add a drop of chamomile oil to a pot of hot water and make them inhale the vapour.

The following measures are for asthmatic wheezing:

Recipes

- To ease wheezing and lung spasms, mash some cranberries and strain the juice. Drink a cup of the juice diluted in a cup of water whenever you feel an attack coming. This helps to open up the bronchial tubes.

Applications

- Apply the juice of boiled onions to the soles of the feet at night for 2 weeks.
- Take a crushed garlic clove, a few lavender flowers, parsley leaves, sage leaves and thyme flowers and put them in a pot of boiled water. Keep the pot covered for a few hours. Store the liquid in a glass bottle and use it for a hand and foot bath.

Asanas

All Asanas that encourage deep and relaxed respiration from the chest and abdomen are good. The breathing exercises aim at increasing the use of the diaphragm and abdominal breathing. They also help reduce the frequency, severity and duration of an attack.

- Ujjayi Pranayama [Abdominal Breathing]
- Eka Pada Uttanasana [Single Leg Stretch Breathing]
- Tarasana [Star Pose]
- Yoga Mudra
- Ushtrasana [Camel Pose]
- Simhasana [Lion]
- Paschimottanasana [Backstretch]
- Sarpasana [Snake Pose]
- Shavasana [Deep Relaxation]
- Nadi Shodana Pranayama [Alternate Nostril Breathing]
- Jalandhara Bandha [Chin Lock]

BRONCHITIS

Also known as a chest cold, bronchitis is an inflammation of the bronchial tubes. If inflammation develops in the lungs, it can cause pneumonia. Pain in the chest, fatigue and coughing are common symptoms.

Acute bronchitis is a common disease among children. It usually develops as a complication after a cold, enlarged adenoids and infected tonsils. Allergy and low resistance are other causes. Bronchitis can be a common complication of measles, influenza, exposure to toxic gases like chlorine and infectious diseases. The effect can bring about a fever, chill, hoarseness of voice and wheezing.

Acute bronchitis sometimes leads to chronic bronchitis. This can destroy lung tissues. Heavy discharge of mucous interferes with the breathing and causes shortness of breath and wheezing. Coughing is a prominent symptom, with fever and pain in the middle part of the chest. Dry coughs become worse in the mornings.

Eating mainly fruit and vegetables helps. Sour fruit tend to dissolve mucous. Aniseed, comfrey, hyssop, mullein and thyme help clear sputum and soothe inflamed tissues. Fresh grape juice clears mucous and phlegm. Honey destroys germs due to its moisture absorbing property. Garlic and thyme help fight infections.

Include in the daily diet all types of berries, fresh pineapples, tomatoes in moderation (care should be taken if bronchitis is associated with asthma), lemons, lemon balm, oranges, squashes, asafoetida, celery, fenugreek, fennel, onions, primrose, radishes and saffron. Take angelica herb for bronchitis associated with vascular deficiency. Have plenty of water and fresh sweet orange juice, with some plums and grapes once daily.

Avoid all mucous-forming and fried foods, meat, pastries, sweets, excess starch, and food that has excess seasoning. Also, avoid breathing in dusty air.

Recipes

- Have squash soup without adding any salt once a day.
- Add honey to a pear and eat it once a day.
- Add a thread of saffron and honey to a glass of milk and boil it. This helps to clear mucous.

Juice

Have a glass of radish juice with honey once a day.

Infusions

- Have a glass of infusion of comfrey, thyme or evening primrose. This gets rid of mucous.
- Have a glass of infusion of lemon balm or marigold flowers 3 times a day.
- Add 4 slices of green onions and 4 cloves of garlic to Irish moss jelly. Let this simmer for 30 minutes. Add 4 ounces of honey. Take 2 teaspoons of this every 2 hours. In chronic conditions, it is good to (slowly) sip a teaspoon of plain honey hourly in between doses. This is good for bronchial complaints with an inflamed throat.

Decoctions

- Take a tablespoon of the decoction of celery plant with water 3 times a day.
- Take 2 tablespoons of the decoction of fenugreek seeds in a glass of water. Sweeten this with a teaspoon of honey mixed with either a drop of peppermint oil or a teaspoon of lemon extract. Have this 3 times a day.
- Take a tablespoon of the decoction of dried grapefruit rind with water 3 times a day.

Inhalations

- Inhale the vapour of eucalyptus, either its leaves or its oil, on hot water twice a day.
- Mix a drop of lavender oil, 2 drops of pine oil, 2 drops of thyme oil and 4 drops of eucalyptus oil together. Inhale the vapour of this mixture on hot water two times a day.

Bath

Add to warm water in a bathtub a glass of the decoction of juniper berries or 5 drops of juniper oil. Soak yourself in this for 20 minutes once every other day.

Application

Make a paste from freshly chopped comfrey roots in hot water. Spread paste onto cloth and apply it to the chest and back. Repeat this twice a day.

Asanas

Refer to the Asanas given under asthma.

LUNGS

To prevent problems related to the lungs, herbs with diaphoretic property are very beneficial.

Infusion

Have a glass of the infusion of basil leaves, elecampane with honey, comfrey rootstock and elecampane mixed together in equal proportion or elecampane and marshmallow mixed together in equal proportion once a day after meals.

EMPHYSEMA

This is a disease of the lungs in which the walls of the air sacs are damaged, creating more air spaces, thereby reducing the efficient functioning of the lungs. It is caused by chronic bronchitis and excessive smoking. Common symptoms are difficulty in breathing on exertion, wheezing, severe coughs and "barrel chest".

Recipes

To restore normal breathing:

- Cook 3 or 4 cloves of garlic in milk (a glass). Drink this daily for 7 days.
- Take unsweetened, undiluted fresh grape juice twice a day for 2 weeks. Grapes are good for weak lungs, pleurisy and laboured breathing.
- Grind 10 grams of basil leaves. Add them to a glass of fresh milk. Drink this every morning for 7 days.

Inhalation

For breathing difficulty due to a congested respiratory tract, add crushed garlic and ginger to a pot of boiling water. Cover pot and let it simmer for 2 minutes. Remove the pot from heat and inhale the vapour deeply for a few minutes.

LUNG CONGESTION

When pus in the lungs is unable to escape through the air passages, it accumulates to form abscesses. The major reason for congestion is mucous in the diet.

Add agase, saffron, mustard leaves, mangoes, nutmeg, oranges, fresh fruit juice and the greens of beetroot to the diet. Having cowpeas frequently can clear mucous from the chest. Avoid food that builds up catarrh and causes congestion like dairy products, eggs, sugar, turnips, potatoes, and grains like wheat, oats and barley.

Recipes

For congestion in the lungs and respiratory tract:

- Have a glass of hot almond milk once a day for 5 days before going to bed. Refer to recipes for relief from colds.
- Stir-fry a quarter of a cabbage with a pinch of mustard seeds and a pinch of turmeric. Have this once a day for relief from chest pain.
- Orange peel acts as an antihistamine. Cut the peel into small strips. Soak them in cider vinegar for several hours. Drain off excess liquid and cook peel in honey for a few minutes. Take a teaspoon of this once a day to clear stuffiness in chest and clogged air passages.

- Boil 2 cloves of garlic and ginger in some water. Add a teaspoon of lemon juice and honey. Sip a glass of this slowly.
- Fry a few lemon balm leaves with cumin seeds and some black peppercorns. Leave it aside for a while to cool. Blend well with yoghurt. Add a pinch of salt. Have this with hot steamed rice for a week.

Inhalations

- Inhale the vapour of crushed garlic and ginger on boiling water.
- Into a vapourizer pour 2 tablespoons of vinegar in boiling water. Inhale the vapours 3 times a day for a week.

Application

Apply a hot compress of angelica leaves to the chest twice a day.

The following measures are for phlegm congestion:

Recipe

Mix a few basil leaves, 2 betel leaves, a clove flower bud and a pinch of salt together. Have this twice a day after meals.

Decoction

Have a glass of decoction of the leaves of fenugreek. Add one teaspoon of ginger and honey. Have this twice a day.

LUNG INFECTIONS

Viruses or bacteria usually cause lung infections. Allergies or chronic rhinitis with or without coughs may be a sign of an infection of the lungs or heart.

Common symptoms are coughs with yellowish or greenish phlegm, chest pain and sore throat. For children, the lungs are affected together with the pancreas, resulting in poor digestion.

Drinking plenty of fluids helps to flush out most lung infections. Have cucumbers, celery, comfrey rootstock, eucalyptus leaves, ginger, horseradish, peppermint and kidney beans regularly as they are good for the lungs and prevent inflammation.

Recipes

Cook asparagus in water and liquefy it. Make a drink by diluting the mixture in water. The drink is good for those with lung diseases like Hodgkins disease.

Juice

- Have okra juice with its mucous once a day.
- Grapes are good for weak lungs, pleurisy and those with breathing difficulty. Have a glass of undiluted and unsweetened black grape juice whenever possible.

Infusion

Have a glass of the infusion of elecampane roots or marshmallow 3 times a day.

Decoction

To a decoction of fenugreek seeds and dates add honey. Take a teaspoon of this twice a day. Do not take the decoction if you have a headache or a fever.

Inhalation

Add 2 tablespoons of vinegar to boiling water and mix well. Pour it into a vapourizer. Inhale the vapour 3 times a day for a week. This is effective even for lung infections with pus.

PNEUMONIA

An infection caused by germs or viruses, pneumonia is a disease of the lungs. Delicate lung tissues are seriously affected. Alcoholism, malnutrition, exposure to extreme temperatures, lung injury and inhaling the infected mucous are some of the many causes. Consult a doctor in the early stages of the disease. In inflammation of the lungs caused by germs like pneumococcus, there is a sudden onset of fever with violent chills. There will also be chest pain and weakness, as well as coughs with thick yellow or greenish sputum. Sometimes, the sputum may contain traces of blood. If it is caused by germs like the staphylococcus, the illness usually develops secondary to some other illness like influenza or measles. Some type of pneumonia often follows the common cold. Dry cough develops, and this becomes serious. Aches and pains are felt in the joints and muscles, accompanied by fever and fatigue. Viral pneumonia not caused by bacteria results in coughing with mucous from the lower air passage and fever without much sputum (common in new born babies).

Have plenty of warm fluids. When the patient is well enough to have proper food, a diet rich in protein and vitamins is advised. Add garlic to the diet and avoid cold drinks and exposure to cold weather.

Juice

Add 1 part garlic juice to 9 parts water. Take a tablespoon of this every 4 hours.

Inhalation

Sprinkle turmeric powder into a bowl of boiling water. Keep face well above the water to prevent steam from affecting facial tissue. Inhale the vapour twice a day.

Asana Routine

- Suryanamaskar [Salutation to the Sun]
- Supta Vajrasana [Backward Bend]
- Ushtrasana [Camel Pose]
- Hasta Uttita Pranayama [Complete Breath Standing]
- Lolasana [Scale Balance Pose]
- Matsyasana [Fish in Lotus]
- Padmasana [Lotus]
- Sarvangasana [Shoulderstand]
- All Pranayama

Refer also to Asanas under asthma.

PULMONARY OEDEMA

The lungs become waterlogged from fluid accumulation in the air sacs. Pulmonary oedema is usually caused by a weak heart, kidney disease or acute infectious diseases. Toxins or irritating fumes can also cause this problem.

Symptoms are the sensation of chest pain, with breathing difficulty associated with coughs. A frothy fluid is expelled from the lungs through the nose and mouth. Keep warm with several pillows under the head and shoulder for easier breathing. Avoid all fluid foods.

INFLUENZA (FLU)

This is a contagious disease caused by a virus. The upper respiratory tract becomes red or swollen usually because of an infection or an illness. Common symptoms are fever, chills, muscle aches, fatigue and headaches.

Prevention is the most effective measure. As long as the symptoms persist, a liquid diet with a lot of citrus fruit is beneficial. Herbs like lavender, primrose or rosemary should be added to the diet.

Recipes

- Mix black pepper soup with hot rice and have it as a porridge twice a day. Drink freshly made orange juice half an hour after the porridge.
- Have lemon juice in warm water 3 times a day.
- Add 2 drops of eucalyptus oil to a tablespoon of warm water. Have this mixture at the early stage of influenza.
- Mix 5 drops of chamomile with a tablespoon of honey. Drink this 3 times a day before meals.
- Powder 1 gram of cinnamon, 10 grams of clove flower buds and 30 grams of ginger. Boil it in 1 litre of water for 15 minutes. Have 2 ounces of this liquid every 3 hours.

Infusions

- Boil some basil leaves and ginger in half a litre of water until it reduces to half the original volume. Have a glass of this twice a day after meals for 5 days. The infusion helps to get rid of aches in muscles and joints.
- Have a glass of infusion of diced onions between the main meals of the day and again before going to bed. Do this for 2 weeks.
- For children, give them a cup of infusion of coriander seeds in milk followed by a glass of fresh orange juice 3 times a day.

Decoction

For children, give them a tablespoon of the decoction of black pepper and basil leaves with milk 3 times a day after meals.

Inhalation

Refer to the inhalation given under sinusitis.

Application

For children, apply a ginger compress to the chest once a day. This is good for those with bronchitis, coughs and influenza.

TUBERCULOSIS

This is generally believed to be a disease of the lungs and can affect any part of the body. It is an infectious disease caused by the tubercle bacillus in some organ or tissue, but more often in the lungs. These bacteria can multiply easily in a dark, warm and moist environment. Unlike pneumonia, tuberculosis is a painless infection. There are no symptoms in the early stages. Tiredness, weight loss, poor appetite, fever and persistent coughs with blood and sputum appear at the later stages.

Many patients feel better after a good rest. Although the symptoms disappear soon because of a reduction of activity by the germs, it is necessary to continue to rest for a complete recovery. As the surroundings play a part in the recovery process, the place of rest should be bright and airy.

The diet should include plenty of milk, one or two eggs, vegetables like drumsticks, cabbages, potatoes, fresh fruit, cod liver oil, fenugreek and easily digestible foods. Garlic and raisins have been known to treat tuberculosis successfully.

Avoid overfeeding the patient with excessive meat and fried foods. Do not subscribe to the mistaken notion that exercise helps cure the person already suffering from tuberculosis. It may only help to prevent it, not treat it. Some exercises like Pranayama or breathing exercises, however, do benefit the patient. He or she can perform them while resting in bed.

Recipes

For pulmonary tuberculosis:

- Steam dried figs or dates in water until they become soft. Add sugar and cook until it becomes a jelly. Have a teaspoon of this 2 times a day. It is also good for emphysema.
- Have a clove of garlic 3 times a day followed by a glass of water in which a tablespoon of raisins have been soaked. Eat the raisins a while later.

Recipe

For tuberculosis of the lymph nodes:

Have a glass of the infusion of fig roots 2 times a day.

HICCUPS

A contraction of the diaphragm, hiccups occur as a result of an irritation in either the respiratory tract or the digestive system or by eating and drinking too quickly.

Chew caraway seeds during a hiccup for relief. Sipping water slowly, holding the breath, applying a cold towel to the back of the neck, keeping a teaspoon of sugar in the mouth and swallowing it slowly also provide relief. Other ways to stop the hiccups include taking a deep breath, blowing out your cheeks and then holding the breath for as long as possible. Breathing into a paper bag also helps because the high carbon dioxide content in the bag helps the diaphragm to contract regularly.

Juice

Have a glass of juice of the leaves of pomegranate with sugar 3 times a day.

Infusion

- Sip an infusion of peppermint leaves 3 times a day.
- Add a teaspoon of the juice of pomegranate to an infusion of basil leaves and wheat grass (or barley grass) mixed in equal proportion. Have this after meals.

PLEURISY

Caused by an infection, this is an inflammation of the pleura, the membrane that covers the lungs. It can appear on the surface of the diaphragm with no signs. Fluids may form in the space between the lungs and the chest wall. It sometimes occurs as a result of injury to the ribs, in which case pain is felt when breathing in and out, but not when the breath is held in. If the injury causes pleurisy on the diaphragm surface, pain may be felt in the abdomen, the pit of the stomach or shoulders.

Increase the intake of demulcents in the daily diet.

Juice

Have a glass of okra juice to reduce the chances of inflamed lung membranes that cause pleurisy.

Infusions

- Have a glass of infusion of angelica roots with any herb belonging to the pectoral group to clear pleurisy associated with a fever.
- Have a glass of infusion of borage or elecampane rootstock 3 times a day.

Applications

- Apply a paste of comfrey herbs in warm water to the chest and back 3 times a day.
- Chillies can be used as a poultice for inflammation and pleurisy.
- Stir 3 tablespoons of flaxseeds in boiling water to form a paste. Spread the paste uniformly over cloth and apply it to the whole chest area. Make sure the paste is hot but to your comfort while applying. Adding a pinch of mustard powder to the paste increases the effectiveness of the application.

Asana Routine

For the chest and for better breathing:

- Sarvangasana [Shoulderstand]
- Supta Vajrasana [Backward Bend]
- Marjariasana [Cat Pose]

- Ushtrasana [Camel Pose]
- Uttita Lolasana [Dangling]
- Dwikonasana [Chest Expansion 1]
- Matsyasana [Fish in Lotus]
- Bhujanga Tiryaka [Swinging Cobra]
- Nadi Shodana Pranayama [Alternate Nostril Breathing]
- Bhastika pranayama [Dynamic Breathing]

For general toning and strengthening of the chest:

- Suryanamaskar [Salutation to the Sun]
- Ekapada Jatara Parivartanasana [Legover Single Leg]
- Supta Vajrasana/Matsyasana [Backward Bend/Fish in Lotus]
- Ushtrasana [Camel Pose]
- Chakrasana [Back Pushup]
- Dwikonasana [Chest Expansion 1]
- Lolasana [Scale Balance Pose]
- Dhanurasana [Bow Pose]
- Natarajasana [Shiva's Pose]
- Bekasana [Frog Pose]

17

The Urinary System

The kidneys are vital organs of the body. Their functions are to filter the fluid portion of the blood that regulates the composition and volume of body fluids and to dispose waste. The presence of excess amounts of salt, sodium glutamate, chemicals and drugs can strain the kidneys. This, in turn, strains the heart. The balance between acidity and alkalinity of body fluids is maintained by eliminating appropriate amounts of hydrogen ions through the urine. Uremia results when the kidneys are unable to eliminate waste due to excess waste production. High blood pressure can cause kidney failure. The kidneys stop producing urine due to sudden damage, and this is called kidney failure.

COMMON SYMPTOMS OF KIDNEY DISORDERS

- Increasing frequency and urgency to urinate
- Anuria: inability to produce urine
- Dysuria: burning sensation during urination.
- Oliguria: reduced production of urine.
- Haematuria: blood in the urine.

For healthy kidneys, avoid salt, excess protein, celery, juniper berries, saffron, chillies, parsley, black pepper, fat, alcohol, sugar, barley and wheat.

Painkillers contain phenacetin or acetaminophen. These irritate the kidneys and bladder; therefore, their use should be monitored.

Recipes

To stimulate the proper functioning of the kidneys:

- Ash gourd jam is good for normalising the kidneys. Steam grated ash gourd and cook over low heat with some rock sugar until it becomes a jelly. Have 2 teaspoons of this 2 times a day with half a glass of milk.
- To some water add unpeeled potatoes, carrots, diced onions and garlic until the water reduces to half the original volume. Have the soup with meals for 2 weeks.
- Mix a teaspoon of wheatgerm and brewer's yeast into glass of fresh orange juice. Add some fresh strawberries. Have the drink during breakfast for 14 days.
- Blend 5 red dates that have been soaked in water with red rock sugar. Add 50 grams of dry ginger juice and steam the mixture until it looks like a pudding. Take a teaspoon of the mixture 3 times a day for 5 days.
- Add sugar to a watermelon, cook it over low heat until the sugar dissolves and strain. After a couple of days, the juice becomes thick like honey. Take 1 tablespoon of this 2 times a day for 2 weeks after meals.

Infusion

For healthy kidneys:
Have a glass of hot infusion of dried apple peel with honey daily.

Decoction

For healthy kidneys:
Have 2 tablespoons of bean pod decoction diluted in water 3 times a day.

Bath

For kidney problems:
Boil 500 grams of oat straw in 4 litres of water for an hour. Add the mixture to bath water and soak yourself in it for about 20 minutes.

OTHER TYPES OF FOOD AND HERBS FOR THE KIDNEYS

Asparagus contains asparagine, which is reportedly used to relieve kidney dysfunctions. It also contains the protein, "histones", which control cell growth.

Other types of food and herbs that are beneficial for the kidneys include agrimony, alfalfa, aloe, angelica, bananas, bean pods, beetroot, blackcurrants, black soya beans, black sesame seeds, blackeyed peas (hulls), borage, cabbages, caraway, cherries, chestnuts, cinnamon bark, clove flower buds, coconut pulp, Indian corn, cranberries, cucumbers, dandelions, dill, fennel, garlic, ginger, goldenseal, grapes, kidney beans, grapefruit peel, lemongrass, lima beans, marshmallow, oats, papayas, peaches, pears, peppermint, pomegranates, radishes, raw onions, red dates, starfruit, star anise, string beans, sweet potatoes, sword beans, walnuts and yarrow.

NEPHRITIS

Nephritis is an inflammation of the kidneys, which mainly strikes a person during childhood or adolescence. When the filtering mechanism of the kidneys does not function properly, the large protein molecules may not get filtered. Waste will accumulate in the blood, resulting in high blood pressure and oedema. In addition, the urine will contain some of the large protein (albumin) and blood cells.

Acute nephritis is caused by infectious diseases such as typhoid, malaria and septic sore throats. It can also be caused by certain chemicals like turpentine. Chronic nephritis develops gradually; it takes time to realise the full extent of its damage to the kidneys. In order to make the kidneys filter and remove waste materials the blood pressure increases. The blood pressure compensates for kidney damage. If not treated in the early stage, it may lead to stroke or heart failure.

In the early stages, acute nephritis results in the swelling of the face and eyes. The urine becomes scanty, coloured and turbid with or without blood. There will be albumin and pus as well. Pregnant women will experience severe headaches, while children will suffer from nausea and vomiting. Chronic nephritis will result in weight loss, fever, urine that is very coloured, puffiness of the feet, nausea, shortness of breath, poor eyesight, high blood pressure and pain in the kidney region, which will extend to the uterus.

To prevent nephritis, drink plenty of water. (If you have oedema, reduce it.) The diet should mainly consist of green vegetables and fruit. Try to stick to a low protein and low fat diet.

Magnesium deficiency generally causes kidney problems, so increase your intake of magnesium. Sources of magnesium are brewer's yeast, wheat bran, wheatgerm and raw greens. Vitamin B, which is necessary for the proper functioning of the kidneys, is found in brewer's yeast, wheat bran, wheatgerm, raw mushrooms, raw broccoli, raw cauliflowers, squashes, strawberries and sweet sword beans. Increase the intake of fibre, water and vitamin B6.

Avoid salt, food rich in protein, vegetables containing large quantities of oxalic acid like spinach and rhubarb as well as juniper berries, chocolates and cocoa. Avoid perspiring profusely.

Recipes

To keep kidney inflammation at bay:

- Fast for 7 days by having only carrot and cucumber juice. Follow up with an all-fruit diet — apples, grapes, oranges, pears, peaches and pineapples — for 5 days. Later introduce a diet that includes milk, cereals and potatoes.
- Boil Indian corn in water until it becomes reddish brown. Drink it as a soup.
- Have grapes daily as it clears any inflammation.

Other than the recipes above, you can also massage your back with diluted lemon balm or lemongrass oil. Alternatively, use the herbs during baths. Follow the recipes for the proper functioning of the kidneys as well.

KIDNEY STONES

These are a collection of minerals and chemicals like calcium and oxalic acid. Salts in the urine — phosphates and urates — precipitate and form stones. These stones are caused by kidney infection or stagnation of urine in the kidneys due to difficulty experienced in answering the call of nature.

Common symptoms include increased frequency of urination and pain in the upper back and side of the trunk. If the ureter is blocked, the pain becomes unbearable. Urine may have traces of blood in it.

A poor diet and insufficient intake of water favour the formation of kidney stones. Include in the diet food and herbs that prevent the formation of stones and dissolve them, such as starfruit, pears, cucumbers, watermelons, walnuts, lemons, lemongrass, asparagus and parsley.

Antilithics help to reduce or suppress kidney stones and may even dissolve them. Common herbs that act as antilithics are barberries, mountain cranberries and ground ivy leaves. Milled cereals, refined wheat flour and fruit juice are also beneficial.

Avoid eating anything that causes stones as a result of its rich oxalate and phosphate content like highly refined foods, animal protein, dietary calcium and salt. Tomatoes, fish, crabs, jackfruit, cabbages, knoll-kol and onions are rich in both oxalates and phosphates while whole cereals are rich in phosphates. Tea, coffee, chocolates, peanuts, spinach, beetroot, alcohol and some green leafy vegetables are rich in oxalic acid and calcium. Milk is rich in calcium and phosphates.

It is best to consult a doctor before trying out the recipes that follow. If the stone is large, it can do more damage in the urinary tract.

Recipes

To prevent the formation of stones:
Blend cucumber and yoghurt in water. Add parsley and curry leaves for flavour. Drink the mixture once daily.

The following measures help reduce the size of stones:

Recipe

Boil fresh starfruit in water with honey. Eat the boiled fruit and drink the water once a day. The fruit and drink will eventually help eliminate kidney stones.

Juice

- Cook asparagus and blend it with water. Have the drink once a day.
- Have 4 tablespoons of asparagus juice twice a day to break up the oxalic acid crystals.
- Blend cooked asparagus. Have it once a day.
- Have 1–2 glasses of lemon juice a day so that large stones formed by excess uric acid reduce in size.

Infusion

Drink half a glass of hot infusion of parsley seeds or fresh parsley leaves every hour.

Recipe

To remove stones in the urinary tract:
Fry a few walnuts in olive oil. Add a little sugar and some water (enough to make a syrup). Let the mixture boil until it turns syrupy. Take 2 tablespoons of this freshly made syrup 2 times a day

Applications

- Add 2 drops of juniper oil and 2 drops of ginger oil to warm water in a bathtub. Sit in it for 10 minutes.
- To relieve pain due to kidney stones, prepare a hot ginger fomentation. To do this, boil grated ginger in water until the mixture turns yellow. Dip a towel into the yellow water and apply it to your back.

Asana Routine for kidneys

- Supta Vajrasana [Backward Bend]
- Shashankasana [Baby Pose]
- Marjariasana [Cat Pose]
- Shashanka Bhujangasana [Striking Cobra]
- Vyghrasana [Tiger Pose]
- Trikonasana [Triangle]
- Matsyasana [Fish in Lotus]
- Paschimottanasana [Backstretch]
- Ardha Matsyendrasana [Half Twist]
- Uddiyana Bandha [Abdominal Lift]
- Meditation

OEDEMA
(WATER RETENTION OR DROPSY)

This is swelling due to water retention, particularly in the ankles and feet. There are many causes for this problem. Persistent water retention is an early indication of heart problems. When blood circulation slows down due to an inefficient heart, some fluid from the blood is forced out of the small blood vessels into the surrounding tissues. This results in swelling. The most common places are ankles and legs.

Severe varicose veins sometimes cause oedema around the ankles and legs. Oedema may appear during pregnancy. Abdominal pains just before the start of menstruation — due to uterine contractions and emotional disturbances — can result in oedema as well. The presence of oedema also indicates that the adrenal glands and/or kidneys may be weak, that is, not functioning to their optimum. Sudden fluid retention suggests an allergy, again indicating the weakness of the adrenal glands. This is sometimes due to a high intake of salt or a result of nutritional deficiency. The first sign of fluid retention is puffiness under the eyes, on the legs and around the ankles.

Herbs that are natural diuretics have a beneficial effect on people with oedema. Avoid food rich in salt and sugar, comfrey, liquorice, honey and glucose. Try out the following:

- Have a milk and wholemeal bread diet with a raw onion for 2 weeks.
- Apply either the cooked plant or the decoction of geranium for oedema of the legs.

Recipes

To prevent abdominal swelling that results from kidney or bladder problems:

- Have cooked sword beans or yellow soya beans once a day for a week.
- Cut the pith of banana stems into small pieces. Remove the fibre and cook them together with mung beans. Add a dash of salt and ginger. Have this with meals twice a week.
- Have soup made of fresh asparagus once a day for a week.
- For babies suffering from swelling due to kidney problems, grind cucumber seeds and apply paste around their navel area once a day after their baths. Do this until the swelling reduces.

The following measures help reduce swelling due to accumulation of fluids in the tissues:

Recipes

Besides adding ash gourd, cucumber, grapes, mung beans and pineapples to the diet, try the following:

- Have 2 tablespoons of decoction of old ginger once a day for 2 weeks.
- Have the water of a tender coconut daily for 2 weeks.
- Have soup made of broad beans or horse beans with ash gourd once a day for a week.
- Have soup made from kidney beans, garlic and sugar (a little) once a day for a week.

Juice

- Have carrot juice or soup daily.
- Blend a ripe cucumber with a carrot to make a juice. Have a glass of this twice a day.
- Add 2 parts raisins and 1 part ginger to one glass of water. Bring it to the boil. Have this twice a day to treat nutritional oedema.
- Have juice extracted from a celery petiole, a carrot and an apple mixed in equal proportion 3 times a day.

Infusions

- Cut the stem and leaves of lemongrass. Put them in a vacuum jar, pour in boiling water and cover with lid.

Drink 3 glasses of this hot infusion daily before meals.
- Have a cup of infusion of alfalfa leaves or dandelion roots 3 times a day for 2 weeks.
- Have a cup of infusion of parsley leaves and seeds with marshmallow 3 times a day.

Also refer to recipes that promote urination.

THE BLADDER

The bladder may be infected by germs that travel with the urine or enter through the urethra. For a healthy bladder, increase the intake of food that is rich in diuretics.

Recipe

For bladder infections:

Have a fresh horseradish with honey once a day for a week or have 3 teaspoons of grated fresh horseradish with cider vinegar and grape sugar 3 times a day before meals. Do not take radish if you have diarrhoea.

Infusions

For a healthy bladder:

Have a glass of infusion of bean pods or bean pods mixed with an equal quantity of bilberry leaves or bean pods, bilberry leaves and dandelion roots mixed together in equal proportion 3 times a day.

CYSTITIS

This is an inflammation of the bladder. In women, it can be due to kidney infection or bacteria travelling up the urethra to the bladder after sexual intercourse. In men, it can be the result of an infected kidney or the inflammation of the prostate gland. During urination, there will be a burning sensation. There will also be a feeling of urgency to empty the bladder.

Drink plenty of water. Include in the diet starfruit, honey, horseradish, cider vinegar, grape sugar and food rich in vitamin A. Avoid juniper berries and parsley in excess.

Recipes

- Swallow a chopped clove of garlic with water 3 times a day for 5 days.
- Have a glass of water in which kidney bean pods have been cooked as they are a good diuretic.
- Eat a few watermelon seeds daily to prevent bladder problems.
- Drink a glass of infusion of agrimony, of corn silk or of unripe okra 3 times a day.
- For children, give them 2 tablespoons of infusion of corn silk 3 times a day. A hot fomentation of sandalwood paste on the lower abdomen also gives relief.

BLADDER STONES

Bladder stones are more common in men than in women. Inflammation of the bladder and partial obstruction in the urethra increase the chances of stones forming in the bladder.

An enlarged prostate gland can cause obstruction, thereby resulting in the formation of stones in the bladder. Common symptoms are frequent and painful urination. The urine will also have traces of blood and pus.

Recipes

To prevent the formation of stones in the bladder:

- Boil three starfruit with 2 teaspoons of honey. Eat the fruit and drink the juice once a week. In the early stages of the formation, this may also help dispel the stone.
- Have a glass of hot infusion of 1 part corn silk to 2 parts fennel seeds 3 times a day after meals.

URINE

Light or colourless urine indicates protein deficiency. Dark coloured, smelly urine indicates a high intake of uric acid. If the urine is too frothy, this suggests the presence of proteins. It may also indicate the possible presence of stones or infection of the urinary tract. In men, if there is a weak stream of urine, this indicates an enlargement of the prostate glands. If this symptom is associated with pain, it suggests an inflammation of the prostate gland.

Include in the daily diet carrots, corn, grapes, green onions, lettuce, oranges, pears, pine buds, polished rice, strawberries, string beans and watermelons. Avoid cinnamon if the urine is too yellow or red in colour.

Recipes

For urinary tract infections:

Boil 25 grams of raisins in 250 ml of water until water reduces to half the original volume. Have the mixture twice a day with sugar.

Infusions

- Have a glass of infusion of dandelion plant or roots or pine buds twice a day for 2 weeks.
- Have a glass of barley water 2 times a day for 2 weeks.
- Have a glass of infusion of fresh kidney bean pods without the beans once every 2 hours for 2 weeks. The urine becomes clear and bleeding in the urinary tract stops.

Recipes

To promote urination:

- Cook soya beans that have been soaked in water with 10 cloves of garlic. Have this once a day before meals.
- Boil maize or corn silk or barley over low heat until water reduces to a third of the original volume. Drink half a glass of this 2 times a day with or without milk.
- Have cooked asparagus once a day for 3 days.
- Drink ash gourd soup once every other day for 2 weeks.
- Add to the diet alfalfa leaves, asparagus, cabbages, cherries, cucumbers, dandelion plant or roots, garlic, ginger, kidney beans, lotus roots, mung beans and starfruit. Consuming any of these regularly is beneficial.

Application

Apply a decoction of onions (or applying a poultice of onions to the abdomen) once a day.

The following measures are for Anuria (difficulty experienced in urinating):

Recipe

Soak celery in boiling water and get the juice. Drink a glass of this once a day for 3 weeks.

Infusion

Have a glass of the infusion of alfalfa or black coffee every day for 2 weeks for relief.

The following measures help ease painful urination:

Recipe

Fry a teaspoonful of cucumber seeds and sesame seeds in a teaspoon of ghee. Powder them together. Add a teaspoon of the mixture to a glass of milk. Drink this once a day.

Juice

- Add an equal amount of warm water to a freshly made juice of grapes. Drink it once a day for 3 days.
- Have a glass of the fresh juice of pears, cabbages or fresh strawberries in cold water twice a day for 2 weeks.

Infusions

- Have a glass of infusion of goldenseal roots, lemongrass or eucalyptus leaves - on their own or in combination — with honey every hour for relief from pain in the urinary tract. This is also good for those who experience difficulty in urinating.
- For scanty urination, drink a glass of milk with a teaspoon of sarsaparilla root powder.
- For turbid urine, bladder irritation and irritation during urination, have an infusion of corn silk.

  For children who experience pain during urination, try out the following. Add 2 tablespoons of cooked barley and 1 teaspoon of ginger juice into a glass of water sweetened with sugar. They should drink this once a day or cook mung beans with sugar or honey and serve as a sweet pudding. You can also make a paste from cucumber seeds and apply it to their abdominal region around the navel for an hour. This clears any urinary blockage.

The following measures relieve painful urination and blood discharge:

Recipe

For painful urination with blood discharge, cook eggplants with yoghurt. Eat this twice a day until the bleeding stops.

Juice

- Have a tablespoon of celery juice twice a day until the bleeding stops.
- Have the juice of fresh starfruit mixed together with some cold water 3 times a day.
- Have a glass of juice — 1 part fresh grapes to 2 parts lotus roots — 3 times a day.
- Have fresh watermelon juice once a day for a week to clear urine that is too yellow in colour.

Infusions

- Have a glass of water in which kidney beans have been cooked or the infusion of kidney bean pods for 2 weeks.
- Have a glass of infusion of comfrey roots 3 times a day for a week.

The following measures help reduce frequent or excessive urination:

Recipes

- Have a tablespoon of baked carrot peels daily for 2 weeks.
- Have concentrated black cherry juice 3 times a day for 2 days.
- Fry some black sesame seeds, powder them and mix with jaggery. Have a teaspoon of this twice a day for 7 days.

Infusions

- Have a glass of infusion of neem bark 3 times a day for a week.
- Have a glass of water in which kidney beans have been cooked or a glass of the infusion of kidney beans pods for 2 weeks.

BEDWETTING

This is not a problem but a symptom. The defective control pattern of the brain or the incapacity of the bladder in proportion to the general growth of the body can lead to bedwetting. It can also be due to a blockage in the urinary tract. Do not punish the child or restrict the water he or she wants to drink. Encourage the child to hold the urine as long as it is possible during the day.

The following measures help control bedwetting:

Recipe

Have oats and a glass of infusion made of barberries or fennel seeds on a regular basis.

Infusion

Have an infusion of either St. John's wort or horsetail after dinner.

Application

Apply the warm leaves of lemon balm or garden balm to the lower back twice a day.

Bath

Boil 500 grams of oat straw in water for half an hour. Add it to bath water. Soak yourself in it for 20 minutes.

18

The Reproductive System
❦

The female sex organs are the breasts, uterus, vagina and vulva.

THE BREASTS

CANCER OF THE BREASTS
Women are well aware of the seriousness of having lumps in their breasts. However, not many know that not all lumps are cancerous. If the lump is benign, only the affected tissue in the region is removed; if is malignant, then the entire breast might have to be removed. One symptom of cancerous lumps is deformity in the breasts or nipples. For post-menopausal women, any discharge from the nipples, especially if there is blood, indicate the beginning stages of cancer. Most cancers are painless in the early stages. If there is a lump and it is painless, it is possible that the lump might be malignant. Early self-examination or examination by a doctor may help prevent the illness from worsening or even cure it.

CHRONIC CYSTIC MASTITIS
Sometimes, fluid-filled cavities develop in the breasts. They feel tender to the touch, move and are similar to the cancerous lumps. If there is any lump, have it examined. Try out the following to treat non-malignant lumps:

- Pound the dried seeds of a mandarin orange and boil them in rice wine. Have the juice 2 times a day to soften lumps in the breasts.

- Have a glass of infusion of dandelion plant or roots 2 times a day.

Applications
To eliminate non-malignant lumps:

- Apply grated potato poultice to the breasts to clear up tumours or cysts. Leave it on until it dissolves. Get your breasts checked for the malignancy of the lumps before application.

- Apply castor oil or olive oil to the breasts first. Then rub a piece of white clay on a clean stone with a few drops of water to make a thick milky paste. Add a pinch of turmeric and apply paste to the affected area.

- On a clean stone, rub an elephant's molar tooth with a few drops of water until a milky paste forms. Apply this paste to the breasts once daily.

Application
For cracked nipples:
Grind a few clove flower buds. Add olive oil and mix well until it becomes a paste. Apply the paste to nipples once a day.

INFLAMMATION OF THE BREASTS
The most common breast problem is inflammation. Cracks to nipples and injuries to breasts cause inflammation. Generally, the nipples and the surrounding region are affected first, after which the infection spreads to the entire breasts. Symptoms include tenderness, pain and swelling.

Recipes

To reduce swelling of the breasts:

- Add a teaspoon of cider vinegar to a glass of water. Add a pinch of salt. Mix well. Drink this 2 times a day for 2 weeks. Repeat if necessary.
- Have a few cooked radish leaves regularly to relieve swelling.
- Boil a teaspoon of malt in a glass of water and drink this twice a day for a week.

Applications

To clear congestion in the breasts:

- Boil orange seeds until they turn soft and grind them. Apply the paste to the breasts to soften the lumps. Have also a glass of infusion of orange seeds 3 times a day.
- Apply to the breast a poultice made from the fresh leaves of fennel to the breasts.
- Apply to the breasts either a poultice made from the plant of geranium or a decoction made from the same plant.

Asanas

For healthy development of the breasts:

- Bhuja Valli Shakti Vikasaka and Bahu Shakti Vikasaka [Arm Strengthening Exercises]
- Nauka Sanchalana [Rowing the Boat]
- Chakki Chalana [Churning the Mill]
- Namaskar [Salutation]
- Matsyasana [Fish in Lotus]
- Lolasana [Scale Balance]
- Gomukhasana [Posture Clasp]
- Chakrasana [Back Pushup]
- Dwikonasana [Chest Expansion]
- Parshvottanasana [Back Namaste]
- Sarvangasana [Shoulderstand]
- Meditation

VAGINAL PROBLEMS

ITCHING SENSATION (PRURITUS VULVAE)

An infected discharge from the vagina causes vaginal problems. In some cases, it can be due to skin diseases in the region surrounding the vagina. Diabetes or jaundice may also cause vaginal itching.

Sarsaparilla is one of the best herbs to use for problems in the urino-genital tract. Refer also to recipes listed under Leucorrhoea.

The treatment prescribed for vaginal itching varies depending on the cause As a rule of thumb, avoid all processed and refined foods. Cleanliness is the best preventive method.

Applications

To prevent vaginal itching:

- Apply lemon oil mixed with an equal quantity of glycerine in and around the vagina.
- If itching is due to uterus discharge, take a cold hip bath.

LEUCORRHOEA

More of a symptom than a disease, leucorrhoea is a normal, physiological vaginal discharge that results from excitement, nervousness and debility. Overeating refined foods and stress are other causes. Leucorrhoea is common among pregnant women.

It is normal to have more vaginal discharge than usual before and after the menstrual cycle. The discharge should be thin, light and white or colourless. There is also the abnormal discharge of mucous, otherwise known as "whites", for which there are many causes.

It is good to consult a gynaecologist before using drugs to cure any abnormal discharge. If the discharge is milky yellowish, has a yeast smell, and causes itchiness and soreness around the vagina, the causes can be chronic infection of the cervix, sexual contact with an infected man, contamination from the anus or chemical changes in the vagina.

If the discharge is frothy, greenish-white or yellowish with a bad smell, causes irritation and redness around the vagina and vulva, and makes sex uncomfortable, then the causes are probably sexual contact with or sharing towels with an infected person.

Generally, if the discharge has a bad smell, then this can be the result of an abortion or cancer. If the discharge occurs before puberty, this can be due to the presence of a foreign body, threadworm or pinworm. Scratching the vagina with dirty nails or wearing dirty linens are other causes.

In the pre-menopausal period, the causes can be uterine fibroid, uterine cancer and ulcers, or genital prolapse. In the post-menopausal period, the causes can be cancer of the genital tract, genital prolapse or endometriosis. Vaginal discharge after menopause should be examined for carcinoma, a malignant tumour in the cavity.

To prevent white discharge, make sure your diet consists of mostly antifungal foods. Avoid raw foods. Soak vegetables and fruit in salted water for a short while before consuming them. Look out for moulds on fruit, vegetables, etc. Make yoghurt part of the daily diet.

Avoid corn or corn silk, cheese, all wheat products, celery, cauliflowers, cucumbers, bean sprouts, broccoli, green pepper, lettuce, guavas, coffee, tea, dried fruit, peanuts, butter, margarine and eggs.

The following measures are for white discharge:

Recipes

- Add a pinch of cinnamon powder to a glass of water. Drink this twice a day.
- Fry a tablespoon of shredded white hibiscus flowers in a teaspoon of ghee. Add this to a glass of milk and mix well. Have the drink twice a day.
- Mix a teaspoon of honey with a teaspoon of gooseberry juice. Drink this once a day.
- Mix a teaspoon of gooseberry juice with a banana and a tablespoon of rock sugar. Have the mixture once a day for 21 days.
- Add winter cherry to a glass of milk. Add some sugar. Have the drink in the mornings and evenings.
- Drink soup made of okra to eliminate irritable sensation in the vagina.

Douche

- Boil water with a few neem leaves. Let it cool to a comfortable temperature. Douche 2 times a day with this. Neem water heals by destroying bacteria and fungi.
- Pound the rind of amaranth roots with 25 grams of water in a mortar. Use the strained liquid to douche twice a day.

- Douche with freshly-made yoghurt mixed with water 3 times a day.
- Douche with the infusion of yarrow, leaves of lady's mantle, comfrey leaves, the rind of a pomegranate or lavender flowers 3 times a day.
- Douche with an infusion of raspberries and the resin of myrrh mixed in equal proportion 3 times a day.

Applications

- Apply cocoa butter inside the vagina two times a day.
- Apply freshly-made yoghurt directly into the vagina twice a day.

Try out the following applications for white discharge associated with other problems described below:

- Douche with warm water, to which vitamin E and calcium have been added. This relieves hot flushes and dryness in the vagina.
- Boil some radish leaves with salt in water. Wash the vagina region with the solution to eliminate itchiness.
- To relieve itching in the genital region, boil a few cloves of garlic in water. Wash the region with it.
- If the opening of the vagina is red and there is pain or itch in addition to discharge, insert into the vagina a clove of garlic that has been wrapped in clean cotton wool and dipped in olive oil. Leave this on overnight.

Bath

Have a pelvic bath regularly. Immerse the pelvic region first in cool water and then in hot water alternately a few times. This increases blood circulation and thus strengthens the reproductive glands.

OTHER PROBLEMS

INFERTILITY

Inability to conceive may be due to underdeveloped sex organs, nervous tension, hormonal imbalance or any obstruction in the reproductive parts.

Yoga Therapy for Infertility

Yoga therapy helps in the following ways:

Asanas that act directly on the endocrine gland help stabilise some of the disturbing features of the reproductive system to an extent. Hormones that most directly influence menstruation are produced in the ovaries, but the pituitary and thyroid glands also play an important role in correcting infertility.

Yoga relaxation, with its soothing and energy charging breathing system, is equally important in overcoming tension.

Special Asanas for the pelvic area increase flexibility without hardening the muscles, promote healthy blood circulation to the reproductive organs and tone the muscles of the vaginal region. These exercises are especially beneficial when sexual activity is hindered (because perineal tissues are not relaxed enough), when preparing for pregnancy, during pregnancy and after childbirth.

Asana Routine for Infertility

Perform the following Asanas:

- **Headstand** to stimulate the pituitary gland to produce hormones, which help compensate the weakening of ovaries. Glandular balance is restored.
- Shoulderstand to stimulate the thyroid gland.
- Fish, Cobra, Locust and Bow poses to strengthen and promote healthy adrenal glands.
- Spinal Twist and Uddiyana Bandha for stomach contraction and the stimulation of abdominal organs.
- Balancing poses and cross legged poses to improve the mobility of joints.
- Relaxation to improve sleep and overall mental well-being.
- Pranayama or breathing exercises to develop a healthy breathing capacity. Your breathing is closely linked to the mind. In Hatha Yoga, the practice of deep breathing is a prelude to meditation. Meditation on breathing helps turn the mind inwards. By focusing your attention on breathing, you experience a deeper state of consciousness.
- Meditation to put an end to internal debates or conflicts.

URETHRITIS

This is an inflammation of the urethra. In women, it is manifested by venereal infection. It mainly results from sexual contact with an infected person. People with urethritis experience pain and have urethral discharge during urination.

Avoid alcohol, coffee and casual sexual.

OVARIAN DISORDERS

OVARIAN CYSTS

There are several types of ovarian cysts. Causes include malfunctioning of physiological processes or a pathological condition, in which case, they may be malignant. Common symptoms are abdominal pain (similar to pain caused by appendicitis), obesity, abnormal hair growth, dysmenorrhoea, infertility or disruption of the normal menstrual cycle.

Have a glass of warm infusion of yarrow and marigold flowers mixed in equal proportion. You can also apply a warm horsetail poultice to the pelvic region. Keep the region warm for 2–3 hours.

MENOPAUSE

This is not a disease but the final session of monthly cycles. It is the end of the reproductive stage but is not the end of sexual urge or capacity. Many people think that menopause often causes mental and physical distress. This is not true. It is the imagination, the false notion about menopause and the inability to relax and cope with the new situation that cause menopause to be distressful. The highly-strung and so called "modern" women suffer the most during this period as many hormonal adjustments take place. Much of the physical and mental stress that accompany menopause can be avoided by correcting the menstrual problems beforehand and by maintaining good health.

During menopause, the ovaries — the main sources of oestrogen and progesterone — do not produce these hormones in the right amounts. Lack of oestrogen causes thinning of the skin. It also causes the genital tissues to atrophy. This leaves the lining of the vagina and uterus unlubricated, thereby making it more susceptible to bacterial infection. There will also be a loss of glandular tissue in the breasts. Demineralisation of bones takes place, resulting in an increased risk of fractured bones.

During this time, most women perspire a lot and

generally feel uneasy. For many women, there are no symptoms whatsoever. On the other hand, for those with severe symptoms, skilled hormonal treatment may prove successful. However, too much therapy may inadvertently increase the chances of uterine cancer. It is therefore best to avoid sex hormone therapy unless it is absolutely necessary for fear of addiction, which in turn makes you more susceptible to depression later on.

Post-menopausal sex depends more on psychological factors than physiological needs. In most cases of unsatisfactory sexual relations, the basic cause is psychological rather than physical. Hot flushes, excessive perspiration, nervousness, hyperirritability, palpitations, and tingling or numbness in the hands will be experienced.

Recipes

- Take lemon balm or sarsaparilla or passion flowers or rosemary as tea or add them to food as flavouring.
- Take evening primrose to maintain the balance of fatty acids. Do this over a period of 6 months to a year.
- Have an infusion of chamomile flowers to calm the mind.
- Have powdered soya beans and ground sesame seeds with honey in warm water daily to help overcome frigidity.
- Take vitamin E and calcium together to relieve hot flushes and dryness in the vagina.

Bath

Take cold hip baths with local self massage.

Avoid pungent, sour and salty foods, tea and coffee in excess, ginger, brinjal, clove flower buds, tomatoes, and radishes.

Asana Routine

- Suryanamaskar [Salutation to the Sun]
- Bumi Pada Mastakasana [Headstand Modified]
- Sarvangasana [Shoulderstand]
- Karna Peedasana [Plough 3]
- Supta Vajrasana [Backward Bend]
- Paschimottanasana [Backstretch]
- Bhujangasana [Cobra Pose]
- Dhanurasana [Bow Pose]
- Shavasana [Relaxation]
- Uddiyana Banda [Abdominal Lift]
- Maha Mudra [Great Seal]
- Shanti Mudra [Invocation of Peace Seal]
- Siddha Yoni Asana [Female Accomplished Pose]

UTERINE DISEASES

Herbs that help keep the uterine healthy are chamomile, raspberries, roses and jasmines.

Recipes

For a healthy uterine:

- Have an infusion of 1 part raspberry to 3 parts of shatavari (Asparagus racemosus) or 1 part angelica root with a pinch of ginger once a week.
- Douche regularly with the infusion of raspberries mixed with an equal amount of myrrh.
- Jasmine is a good herb for uterine bleeding. Have an infusion of jasmine flowers or apply diluted essential oil of jasmine to the lower abdominal area.

MENSTRUAL PROBLEMS

Apart from accidents, infectious diseases and inherited problems, the main causes of all menstrual problems are toxin accumulation in the body after high dosages of medication, unhygienic habits and lack of proper exercise.

Irregular periods are also due to the lack of proper dietary habits (consuming wrong or odd combinations of food with no nutritional value), as well as an excess of coffee, tea, refined foods and sour foods. Emotional disturbances like sorrow, fear, anger and worries contribute to menstrual problems. Physical ailments like anaemia, swelling in the womb and displacement of the womb can also cause menstrual irregularities.

Before menstruation starts, you will experience laziness or tiredness, giddiness, loss of appetite, pain in the urinary tract and headaches. You will also be in an irritable mood, experience pain in the abdominal region of the ovary or uterus, have deep pelvic pain, which is often worst during bowel movements, as well as experience pain during sexual intercourse and pain before and during the menstrual cycle. This pain is mainly due to endometriosis, a disease where the endometrium, the lining of the uterus, begins to grow in the other parts of the pelvic region and abdominal cavities.

During the menstrual cycle, if the egg is not fertilised, the presence of endometrium is deemed useless and should therefore be expelled through the menstrual flow. If the uterus and cervix muscles are not healthy enough to expel endometrium easily, it is pushed backwards through the fallopian tubes into the pelvic cavity, where it can implant itself on the ovaries and in between the uterus and rectum. If not controlled, endometrium can reach the abdominal region.

The best treatment for menstrual disorders is to regularise menstrual flow (too much menstrual flow, for instance, can lead to anaemia). You achieve this by keeping the muscles healthy through proper exercise. It is also essential to have a nutritious and cleansing diet. Antibiotics do not work if taken for this problem.

A salt-free diet with bananas, greens of beetroot, sweet basil, buttercup, spearmint, saffron, lemon balm, parsley, carrots, celery, ginger, lotus roots, dates, caraway seeds and rock sugar give adequate nutrients. It is also essential to have at least 1,500 milligrams of calcium supplements per day. Hot water bottle fomentation, massage and rest also have beneficial effects.

The following measures normalise the menstrual cycle:

Juice

Have a glass of fresh red or black grape juice first thing in the morning.

Infusions

- Have a glass of infusion of rose petals and hibiscus mixed in equal proportion once a day.
- Have a glass of infusion of angelica roots with some saffron once a day.
- Have a glass of infusion of elecampane roots. Add a small piece of ginger to it depending on your preference.

- To a glass of infusion of lemon grass, add a pinch of black pepper powder. Drink this twice a day.

Besides the above infusions, you can also have a decoction of shepherd's purse (2 tablespoonful) 3 times a day.

Asana Routine

To normalise the cycle:

- Bhujangasana [Cobra Pose]
- Shalabasana [Locust Pose]
- Dhanurasana [Bow Pose]
- Paschimottanasana [Backstretch]
- Chakrasana [Back Pushup]
- Ushtrasana [Camel Pose]
- Inverted Asanas in general
- Meditation

MENORRHAGIA

This is excessive or increased frequency of menstrual flow. A short or increased frequency of a menstrual cycle can be caused by fibroid tumours, inflammation, a tipped uterus, uterine swelling, ovarian cysts, endocrine gland imbalance, general debility and poor circulation of blood.

To prevent menorrhagia, include in your diet fruit juice, particularly pomegranate juice, yoghurt, wheat and wheat products, lettuce, gooseberries, milk, boiled vegetables, coconut water, bananas, peppermint, rosemary, garlic, carrots, and celery. Avoid cinnamon if there is an excess of menstrual flow.

The following measures help control menorrhagia:

Recipes

- Make a paste from one clove of garlic and some curry leaves. Add a pinch of turmeric. Have a quarter teaspoon of the mixture once a day for 3 days before the period starts.
- Grind a few white hibiscus flowers. Add the mixture to a glass of milk. Mix well and have the drink once a day for 2 weeks before the period starts.
- Have a glass of fresh pineapple juice twice a day.
- Have wheat porridge for breakfast daily.

Infusion

Have a glass of infusion of comfrey rootstock, carrots, celery, ginger, parsley, peppermint, rosemary or amaranth leaves daily for 2 months.

Decoction

Boil 5 grams of powdered coriander seeds in a litre of water until it reduces to half the original volume. Have a glass of this warm and sweetened with sugar once a day until the symptom clears.

AMENORRHOEA

This is the absence of menstruation. It is not a disease but a symptom. Causes include anaemia, tuberculosis, obesity, sexual frigidity, obstruction in the cervical canal and anxiety.

Have food rich in protein, black beans, wheat vermicelli, garlic, eggplants and tomatoes, all of which are heaty. Others include ginger, pineapples, papayas, almonds, walnuts, lettuce, all gourds, milk, yoghurt, sprouts of mung beans, wheat flour, cucumbers, apples, spinach, rosemary, basil and lemon balm.

The following measures promote menstruation:

Recipes

- Stir-fry equal quantities of celery and lotus roots in peanut oil. Add a pinch of salt. Have this once a day for 21 days. This is good for regulating menstrual flow.
- Have a teaspoon of jelly made of ginger, dates and rock sugar with meals.
- Take 50 grams each of seeds of carrots, white radishes and fenugreek. Powder them together. Add 10 grams of the mixture to a glass of water and mix well. Drink this once a day.
- Grind 10 grams of the seeds of carrots with a tablespoon of water. Have the drink once a day.

Juice

- Have a glass of carrot juice or soup regularly.
- Have two tablespoons of celery juice once a day.

Infusions

- Have a glass of infusion of sweet basil leaves, caraway seeds, rosemary, spearmint, parsley, pennyroyal leaves and ginger powder with a teaspoon of honey and saffron or lemon balm 3 times a day on a regular basis.
- Have a glass of warm water with half a teaspoon of ground cinnamon bark sweetened with honey once a day.
- Have a glass of infusion of chamomile flowers, fennel seeds, chrysanthemums or parsley mixed with marshmallow 2 times a day before meals.
- Have a glass of infusion of anise.

Other than the infusion above, have a glass of chicory decoction.

Baths

- Add a warm infusion of lemon balm to bath. To make this add 12 teaspoons of chopped lemon balm leaves to 6 cups of boiling water.
- Take an alternate cold and hot hip bath daily for a week.

DYSMENORRHOEA

This is menstruation that is painful, and pain may be felt either before, during or after the flow. Blood clots or a retention of blood flow cause dysmenorrhoea. Other causes are anxiety and constipation.

A nutritional diet with plenty of rest prevents dysmenorrhoea. Your daily diet should include some herbs like sweet basil, spearmint, saffron, lemon balm, chamomile flowers, buttercup, parsley, spinach, radishes, lentils, dates, oranges, guavas, bananas, carrots, gooseberries, almonds, grapes, apples and figs. Avoid cold water and fruit, and tightfitting clothes. Free your mind of worries.

The following measures ease painful urination:

Recipes

- Add a teaspoon of gooseberry juice and a teaspoon of honey to a mashed banana. Have a tablespoon of this once a day to ease the pain. This recipe is also good for preventing white discharge.

The Reproductive System

311

- Add half a teaspoon of unhusked powdered sesame seeds to a glass of water. Have the drink twice a day.

Infusions

- Have a glass of infusion of chamomile flowers daily before meals. Chamomile flowers mixed with ginger is good for relief from pain due to menstrual cramps.
- Have a glass of infusion of motherwort.
- Have a glass of infusion of parsley or aniseed after meals.
- Have a glass of infusion of lemon grass with a pinch of black pepper powder.

In addition to the above, once menstruation starts, place a hot water bottle on the feet and abdomen and rest for an hour.

PRE-MENSTRUAL SYNDROME (PMS)

A wrong diet and calcium deficiency during menstruation can bring about much discomfort. Symptoms include anxiety, depression, migraines, headaches, dizziness, abdominal bloating, constipation, sugar craving, cramps, acne, pain in the joints and swelling.

Include the following in your daily diet:

- Vitamin B6 found in brewer's yeast, potatoes, salmon and stone ground whole grains.
- Calcium and magnesium found in milk, cheddar cheese, soya beans, whole grain, green vegetables, and beet tops help relieve discomfort.
- Zinc found in poultry, eggs, milk and whole grains.
- Potassium found in bananas, oranges and sun dried fruit.
- Vitamin E found in wheatgerm, vegetable oils, nuts, whole grain and cereals.
- Tryptophan found in wheat bran, wheatgerm, cooked soya and raw mushrooms.
- Essential fatty acids found in safflower, corn, soya beans, sesame oil, brazil nuts, peanuts and sunflower seeds.

Others to be included are legumes, fresh fruit and vegetables and evening primrose oil. Avoid sugar, tea, coffee, cola drinks, chocolates, alcohol and fried fatty foods.

The following measures help ease PMS:

Recipes

- Add a teaspoon of sugar to milk and mix well. Add a pinch of asafoetida to the milk. Have this drink twice a day.
- Have a teaspoon of ground seeds of white radishes mixed with buttermilk once a day.
- If there is swelling in the limbs due to PMS, have a ripe banana mixed with a quarter teaspoon of soya oil before meals.
- Have 2 gooseberry fruit or the juice with honey daily for a month.

Refer also to recipes for normalising menstruation.

Infusions

Have a glass of infusion of any of the following herbs 3 times a day for a week:

- Chamomile flowers (for anxiety),
- Ginger (for cramps)
- Dandelions or burdock (for acne)
- Sarsaparilla (for tenderness in the breasts)
- Parsley (for bloating in the abdomen)
- Raspberries with rose petals or hibiscus flowers (for pain in the abdominal region)

Asana Routine

These Yogasanas help relieve pain.

- Shashankasana [Baby Pose]
- Shavasana [Deep Relaxation]
- Chakrasana [Back Pushup]
- Dhanurasana [Bow Pose]
- Upavishtakonasana [Backstretch Seated Angle]
- Vrukshasana [Tree Pose]
- Shalabasana [Locust Pose]

Do not perform any inverted Asanas.

Asana Routine

To relieve abdominal cramps:

- Vajrasana [Sitting Thunderbolt]

- Marjariasana [Cat without Sucking and Snapping of the Abdomen]
- Shashankasana [Baby Pose]
- Ujjayi Pranayama [Abdominal Breathing]

Asana Routine

Perform only these Asanas during menstruation to normalise it and to strengthen the pelvic region:

- Upavishtakonasana [Backstretch Seated Angle]
- Badha Konasana [Knee and Thigh Stretch]
- Janu Sirasasana [Alternate Leg Pull]
- Paschimottanasana [Backstretch]
- Marjariasana [Cat without Sucking and Snapping of the Abdomen]
- Padahastasana [Legclasp]
- Setu Bandasana [Bridge Pose]
- Sarpasana 1 [Snake 1]
- Shavasana [Deep Relaxation]
- Nadi Shodana Pranayama [Alternate Nostril Breathing]

ENDOMETRIOSIS

Membranes like tissues get attached to the lower part of the colon, ovaries or uterus. During menstruation, these tissues undergo changes and cause pain and hæmorrhaging.

Amaranth leaves help relax the uterine muscles while caraway seeds relieve uterine cramps. Motherwort and oats are tonics for the uterine muscles.

THE UTERUS

Coital pain may result from weak back muscles, poor spinal health, chronic constipation or haemorrhoids. Pain may also stem from the displacement of the uterus, inflammation of the vagina, urethra, uterus or ovaries, or from ovarian cysts.

DISPLACEMENT OF THE UTERUS

The problem arises when the uterus displaces in two ways. One displacement is the backward tipping accompanied by a downward sag. The other is the prolapsed uterus. In this, the uterus is displaced downward and is sometimes accompanied by the cervix protruding from the vulva. This is found in extreme cases. Possible causes are the laxity of supporting muscles, ligaments and tissues.

Other important causes are prolonged labour, lack of rest and a proper diet in the post-natal period, as well as frequent deliveries. Menopausal atrophy may precipitate. Displacement of the uterus may be one of the reasons why some women find it difficult to conceive. A feeling of something coming down through the vagina, a sense of fullness in the region of the bladder and rectum, a dragging discomfort in the abdomen, lower backaches, heavy flow of menstruation and a mild vaginal discharge are common symptoms. There is also an increase in the frequency of urination, but, at the same time, an inability to empty the bladder. These symptoms become pronounced before and during menstruation. The condition may also result in difficulty in normal sexual intercourse, sometimes even sterility.

The displacement can be corrected surgically. However, recent trends suggest that proper exercises, particularly Asanas that can tighten the muscles in the region can prevent the displacement of the uterus. The best way to prevent it is by doing proper antenatal and postnatal care exercises. A sensible diet is advised.

A proper diet includes having apricots, beetroot, black sesame seeds, black and yellow soya beans, cabbages, carrots, celery, figs, grapes, guavas, honey, horse beans, kidney beans, milk, olive, peanuts, potatoes, pumpkins, radishes, saffron, sunflower seeds, and sweet potatoes. Patients should avoid lifting heavy objects and standing for too long. Before performing any Asana, consult a doctor.

Ayurvedic juice therapy suggests a five-day all-fruit diet. There should be 3 meals every day consisting of oranges, apples, pineapples and grapes at 5-hour intervals. The all-fruit diet should be repeated for 3 consecutive days at monthly intervals until you are cured. After the fruit diet, gradually introduce, a balanced diet consisting of seeds, nuts, whole grains, vegetables and fruit.

The following measures are for a displaced uterus:

Application

Carrots have proven most useful in treating a prolapsed uterus. Place pulped carrots in a clean muslin bag and insert bag into the vagina. Repeat this again after 12 hours. This heals and strengthens the reproductive parts and prevents further disorders of the reproductive system.

Baths

- A hot epsom bath twice a week is beneficial. Stay in hot water for not more than 15 minutes. Drink a lot of water before having the bath and take the necessary measures to avoid catching a chill. Keep warm afterwards.
- Have an alternate hot and cold water hip bath regularly.

Asana Routine

In practising Yoga to correct a prolapsed uterus, avoid all movements involving sudden contractions of the stomach muscles or stress on them. There should not be any discomfort while performing the Asanas as well as after completing them. There are two alternative groups of Asana routines. Try out both and stick to the one you are more comfortable with.

Group 1

- Vipareeta Karani Mudra [Shoulderstand Variation]
- Matsyasana [Fish in Lotus]
- Halasana [Plough 1]
- Bhujangasana [Cobra Pose]
- Shalabasana [Locust Pose]
- Janu Sirasasana [Alternate Leg Pull]
- Paschimottanasana [Backstretch]
- Ushtrasana [Camel Pose]
- Nadi Shodana Pranayama [Alternate Nostril Breathing]
- Uddiyana Bandha [Abdominal Lift]
- Yoga Mudra
- Meditation

Group 2

- Sarvangasana [Shoulderstand]
- Poorva Uttana Padasana [Fish simple]
- Padahastasana [Legclasp]
- Chaturanga Dandasana [Strengthening of the Whole Body Step 1]
- Padma Parvatasana [Traction]
- Baddha Konasana [Knee and Thigh Stretch]
- Ujjayi Pranayama [Abdominal Breathing]
- Ushtrasana [Camel Pose]
- Nadi Shodana Pranayama [Alternate Nostril Breathing]
- Uddiyana Bandha [Abdominal Lift]
- Yoga Mudra
- Meditation

THE MALE SEX ORGANS

IMPOTENCE

Impotence is the inability to initiate or maintain an erection. It is a problem that affects men suffering from diabetes mellitus (see chapter 14). It also has a psychological cause, in which case sympathetic counselling can result in normalcy. If impotence is a result of damage to the nerves, nothing much can be done to remedy the situation. Another meaning for impotence is frigidity.

To help prevent impotency, add to your diet food like avocados, celery, fenugreek, garlic, jasmine, onions and bitter gourd.

The following measures help prevent impotence:

Recipes

- Add a quarter teaspoon of powdered basil seeds to a teaspoon of jaggery. Add a little pure ghee. Have this twice a day.
- Add 3 grams of basil seeds to a glass of 50 grams of fresh milk. Boil the mixture. Have the drink twice a day.
- Add 5 grams of ginger juice to a glass of 10 grams of onion juice. Mix well. Add a teaspoon of honey and a tablespoon of fresh milk. Have the drink twice a day.

Infusion
Drink a glass of the infusion of celery root or add 6 drops of celery oil to a cup of warm water and drink this twice a day.

Other than the infusion, have 2 tablespoons of milk decoction of nutmeg once a day to prevent premature ejaculation.

Asana Routine
- Moola Bandha [Perineum Retraction Lock]
- Maha Bandha [Great Binding Lock]
- Maha Mudra [Great Seal]
- Vajrasana [Sitting Thunderbolt]
- Meditation

Perform Asanas given under the Anxiety group (see chapter 20) as well.

STERILITY
Sterility is the inability of a man to effect a pregnancy in a normal woman. It can be due to abnormal testes (mumps can damage testes), improper spermatozoa, obstruction in the ducts, excess intercourse resulting in producing immature spermatozoa and poor nutrition. Anthelmintic and antiparasitical herbs belong can weaken the tissues and may reduce the production of sperms if used in excess.

URETHRITIS
This is inflammation of the urethra. In males, it is manifested by urethral discharge with increasing pain during urination. Urethritis results mainly from sexual contact with an infected person.

PROSTATE GLAND
A defective prostate gland can cause lower backaches, blood in the urine, frequent erections, impotence, premature ejaculations, restricted bowel movements and loss of control over urination.

Zinc is a major ingredient that helps to prevent a defective prostate gland. It is found in brewer's yeast, nuts, eggs, rice bran, onions, chicken, beans, peas,

lentils, wheatgerm, gelatine and sunflower seeds. Corn oil, wheatgerm, garlic, soya bean oil, peanuts, almonds and sesame seed oil help rejuvenate the prostate gland. Also include garlic and pumpkin seeds in the diet as they help cure prostate problems and even impotence. Avoid all refined foods.

To maintain youthfulness, milk, butter, honey and gooseberries are recommended. Rest and proper meditation are equally important. Garlic, yoghurt and sediment found at the bottom of a beehive (pollen) bring about the same effect. Oats is an excellent food for problems of the prostate gland, particularly for children.

Recipe
For Healthy prostate glands:
Add 2 tablespoons of wheatgerm and half a cup of cooked cow peas to a glass of milk. Blend well. Have this once a day.

Asana Routine
The following Asanas for the general toning of the reproductive system, are suitable for both men and women:
- Suryanamaskar [Salutation to the Sun]
- Marjariasana [Cat Pose]
- Shashanka Bhujangasana [Striking Cobra]
- Vyghrasana [Tiger Pose]
- Siddhasana [Male Accomplished Pose]/Siddha Yoni Asana [Female Accomplished Pose]
- Trikonasana [Triangle Simple]
- Utthanasana [Squat]
- Shalabasana [Locust Pose]
- Setu Bandasana [Bridge Pose]
- Sarvangasana [Shoulderstand]
- Pada Angushtasana [Legclasp Gorilla Pose]

Asana Routine
The following Asanas, for a healthy reproductive system, are also suitable both for men and women. Not all the Asanas are to be performed in one session. Select the ones that you are most comfortable with and perform them in the right order. Pregnant women can perform

the following Asanas for the first 3 months of their pregnancy (for Asanas for varicose veins see chapter 15):

- Suryanamaskar [Salutation to the Sun]
- Siddha Yoni Asana [Female Accomplished Pose]: this has a direct effect on the nerve plexuses of the reproductive system. People suffering from sciatica or sacral infections should avoid the Siddha Yoni Asana.
- Supta Vajrasana [Backward Bend]: this aids blood circulation in the back, stretches the intestines and abdominal organs, and promotes deep respiration.
- Bumi Pada Mastakasana [Headstand Modified]: this increases blood flow to the pituitary, which helps to rectify the nervous and glandular systems.
- Shashankasana [Baby Pose]: this tones the pelvic muscles, relaxes the sciatic nerve and regulates the adrenal glands.
- Sarvangasana [Shoulderstand]: this stimulates the thyroid and tones up the legs, abdomen, spine, neck, and reproductive organs.
- Halasana [Plough 1]: this stretches the back muscles, stimulates the nerves, and activates the abdominal organs and the thyroid gland.
- Chakrasana [Back Pushup]: this promotes hormonal secretions, relieves varied ailments of the female reproductive system and massages the abdominal organs.
- Shavasana/Makarasana [Relaxation/Crocodile Pose].
- Marjariasana [Cat Pose]: this brings flexibility to the neck, shoulder and spine, relieves pelvic cramps, and strengthens the pelvic region.
- Supta Badrasana [Knee and Thigh Stretch Lying down]: this increases the flexibility of the thigh joints and strengthens the pelvic muscles.
- Yoga Mudra: this acts on the adrenal glands and massages the abdominal organs.
- Utthanasana [Squat]: this strengthens the uterine muscles, inner thighs, knees and ankles.
- Tadasana [Stretch Pose]: this strengthens the rectus and abdominal muscles, and stretches the intestines.
- Trikonasana [Triangle Simple]: this relieves nervous depression and massages the spinal nerves.

- Uttita Lolasana [Dangling] or Pada Angushtasana [Legclasp Gorilla Pose]: these relieve tiredness by stimulating the spinal nerves as well as stretch the hamstrings, hip and visceral organs.
- Ushtrasana [Camel Pose]: this stretches the stomach and intestines. It is particularly good for those with backaches and lumbago.
- Paschimottanasan [Backstretch] or Upavishta-konasana [Backstretch Seated Angle]: these activate the kidneys, liver, pancreas and adrenal glands, and tone up the pelvic region.
- Udarakarshana Asana [Abdominal Massage Twist]: this stretches and contracts the abdominal muscles.
- Shashanka Bhujangasana [Striking Cobra]: this tones up the reproductive organs, liver and visceral organs, and strengthens the disc region.
- Naukasana [Variation of Saucer Pose]: this strengthens the rectus muscles and activates the gonads.
- Shalabasana [Locust Pose] or Paripoorna Shalabhasana [Swan]: these tone up the intestines, pancreas, kidneys and gonads.
- Vayu Nishankasana [Gas Releasing Pose]: this benefits the nerves of the thighs, knees, shoulders and arms. It also relieves gastric problems.

19

Pregnancy

⸎

A prospective mother must be well-prepared, both physically and mentally, to handle the birth of a child, as well as the responsibilities that come with raising the child. She should learn the basic facts about pregnancy, delivery, and nutritional management for herself and the baby both during and after delivery.

A healthy woman without any serious illness, emotional disturbance or defective hormonal secretions does not miss her period. Once she conceives, the first symptom is that she misses her monthly period. The next few symptoms are morning sickness, nausea and vomiting, which normally disappear in a healthy mother-to-be after the third month of pregnancy. Later, she experiences tenderness in her breasts as well as an increase in their size due to hormonal changes taking place in her body. Frequent urination is experienced due to the pressure exerted by the growing uterus. After the fourth month, the movement of the child can be felt. Most expectant mothers describe this feeling as thrilling. Some mothers may not have such an experience, and this does not mean that the growth of the foetus is in danger.

During pregnancy, many changes take place in the body of the expectant mother. Muscles of the uterus stretch for the foetus to grow and start producing hormones that inform the endocrine glands to change their pattern of activity. This promotes the growth of the foetus and breasts in preparation for the production of milk. The expectant mother will experience an increase of about 4 kg in weight by the end of five months and another 4 kg to 8 kg by the end of 9 months. Towards the end of 9 months, the pituitary produces hormones to stimulate contraction of the uterus muscles in preparation for delivery and milk production. From conception to delivery, it takes about 266 days, and from the last menstruation to delivery, it takes about 280 days.

The expectant mother must go for thorough medical checkups as these are important in detecting and preventing possible complications that may occur either during the pregnancy or later on. The visit should be once a month for the first 6 months, once in 2 weeks for the 7th and 8th months, and every week thereafter.

Any discomfort, even a minor one, must be explained to the doctor. Some symptoms during pregnancy for which immediate action must be taken are frequent headaches, dizziness, morning sickness even after 3 months, discomfort in the lower abdomen, difficulty in urinating, blood in the urine and swelling, especially in the feet.

The development of a healthy baby depends on the food the mother eats. So, diet should be nutritious and rich in natural vitamins and minerals. Unless there is serious illness and provided the diet is nutritious, there is no need for other supplements. An extra protein diet is required only after six months of pregnancy.

In addition to a healthy diet, Yogasanas help build better health by promoting blood circulation. They also help in maintaining healthy tissues of the body and in developing good discipline. Further, they help clear the emotional imbalance of the mind to cope with the new situation. The way the structure of the body and its functions change to meet the new demands of pregnancy and return to normal once the baby is delivered is remarkable.

NUTRIENTS REQUIRED DURING PREGNANCY

The foetus receives its nourishment and oxygen from its mother's blood. So, eating wisely during pregnancy is important for its growth and health. The right diet maintains the health of the mother as well. There is no need to eat for "two" during pregnancy but the mother should eat well. Remember that it is not the quantity but the quality of the food that is important.

- Vitamin A prevents a cleft lip and abnormalities of the eyes. Rich sources of vitamin A are eggs, dairy products, liver, fish liver oil, carrots, green leafy vegetables and yellow coloured vegetables.
- Vitamin B1 (thiamine) prevents stillbirth and underweight babies. Rich sources of vitamin B1 include whole grain cereals, peanuts, brewer's yeast and vegetables.
- Pantothenic acid, another member of the vitamin B group, prevents deformities in the embryo. Although meat is the main source of pantothenic acid, the required quantity is also available in whole grains, wheatgerm, green vegetables, nuts, eggs and brewer's yeast.
- Vitamin B6 (pyridoxine) prevents problems like low tolerance to glucose and seizures. This can be obtained from liver, eggs, milk, cabbages, whole grains, wheatgerm and brewer's yeast.
- Folic acid prevents malformation of the throat and mouth, as well as anaemia in babies. It is found in greens like spinach, brewer's yeast, wheatgerm, lentils, carrot, eggs, pumpkins, beans, whole wheat and whole rye.
- Vitamin B12, folic acid and iron, when taken together, prevent anaemia. They can be obtained from soya beans. It is recommended that vitamin C, found in citrus fruit and green vegetables, be taken along with vitamin B12 so that the iron is better absorbed into the system.
- Vitamin C prevents miscarriages and underweight babies. Rich sources of vitamin C include citrus fruit, berries, potatoes, tomatoes, cabbages and other fresh vegetables.
- Vitamin D is needed for the development of bones.
- Iodine prevents mental retardation and improper physical growth. It is found in edible seaweed like kelp, as well as in vegetables like brinjal and mushrooms.

- Magnesium prevents damage to the placenta and prevents miscarriages. Kelp, millet, whole grains, green vegetables, nuts, seafood, seeds, apples and figs supply magnesium in abundance.
- Manganese is needed for proper development of the brain and muscular coordination, as well as for skeletal growth. It is found in whole grains, beetroot, green vegetables, eggs, peas and nuts.
- Potassium is necessary for preventing kidney abnormalities in the baby. Rich sources of potassium are green leafy vegetables, whole grains, sunflower seeds, spearmint leaves, oranges and bananas.
- Zinc prevents malformation of the brain, learning problems, dwarfism, allergies, club feet and a poor immune system. It is found in brewer's yeast, eggs, liver, mushrooms, pumpkin seeds and seafood.

Keep clean and bathe regularly. After the 4th month, have a glass of warm milk with a saffron thread once a week. This prevents the baby from having any liver problems.

PRENATAL MANAGEMENT

- As anaemia results in a lower supply of oxygen to the placenta, it is essential to consume food rich in protein, dried apricots and spinach. Supplement with vitamin B, vitamin B12, vitamin C and iron tablets.
- Keep clean to prevent infection, particularly in the vagina. Wash the area with water and a non-perfumed soap during each visit to the toilet. Garlic and vitamin C have a natural antibiotic effect to prevent infection.
- Do not lie down in the bathtub while bathing (lying down helps only when you have a contraction but it is not advised).
- Protein in the urine may be a sign of placenta failure and may cause premature labour. Cut a few dried bean pods into small pieces and place them in a large bowl of water. Let it boil until the water level reduces to a third of its original volume. Drink this warm with honey if needed thrice a day.
- Prepare your breasts for breastfeeding by gently applying (do not rub or massage) almond oil on them. Do not use soap on nipples as it is drying.
- Avoid problems associated with constipation through a diet rich in fibre and through Yogasanas.

- If you get cramps in the feet or legs, stretch your heels and at same time, point your toes towards the body and rub the area vigorously.
- Have light meals in the beginning of labour.
- Have some form of sugar every now and then. A teaspoonful of honey in boiling water is recommended.
- Swelling of ankles and fingers during late pregnancy is a sign of fluid retention. Do not cut down on salt or fluid intake. To reduce swelling, lie down and place your legs against the wall. Keep them apart. Drink plenty of lemongrass tea or barley water.
- Have several small meals rather than one big one as such meals help prevent heartburn during pregnancy. Have some plum juice daily.
- Vaginal infection causes pain in the bladder, resulting in frequent visits to the toilet. Dab some fresh yoghurt into the vagina.
- An infusion of raspberries eases labour pains and promotes milk secretion.
- Vitamin E alleviates leg cramps during pregnancy.
- From the beginning of pregnancy, add squashes, buttermilk and lemon juice to your diet and herbs like comfrey and primrose as these are beneficial for an easy delivery.
- If you experience pain or a burning sensation during urination, have tender coconut water or okra.
- If you have been diagnosed with albumin in the urine, have a decoction of bean pods 3 times a day for 3 days.
- If you lose your appetite during pregnancy, have a few cardamom seeds with a teaspoon of sugar.
- If you experience discomfort in the abdomen or have back pains during pregnancy, have an infusion of 6 grams of ginger in 750 ml of water. Add fresh milk to it. Drink this before meals for 3 days.

Avoid certain types of food during pregnancy like highly spicy, refined or canned foods, a high intake of gas-producing and fried foods, as well as sweet drinks. The following is a useful list of food and things to avoid:

- Aloe, barberries, goldenseal, juniper berries, nutmeg, raspberries, angelica, pennyroyal, sage leaves, fennel and ajowan (due to its high content of thymol). Use turmeric, fenugreek, asafoetida and saffron sparingly in food.
- Food that results in constipation.
- Drugs unless prescribed by the doctor, and stay away from cigarettes and alcohol. Rest and exercise should be done in moderation.
- Crowded public places to avoid contagious or infectious diseases like measles, especially German measles.
- Lying back in bathtubs. Do not use essential oils in baths like lavender and jasmine as they can induce labour.
- High-heeled shoes as they can cause back pain.

Asana Routine

Expectant mothers benefit from certain types of physical exercises. While Yogasanas and walking in moderation ensure a healthy pregnancy, performing any type of meditation will ensure a more successful pregnancy. Most of all, pregnant women must ensure that they have enough rest. A happy mother gives birth to a happy child.

The following Asanas can be performed for the first 3 months of pregnancy:

- Nauka Sanchalana [Rowing the Boat]
- Chakki Chalana [Churning the Mill]
- Druta Hastasana [Chopping the Wood]
- Shashankasana [Baby Pose]
- Marjariasana [Cat Pose]
- Shashanka Bhujangasana [Striking Cobra]
- Vyghrasana [Tiger: first position]
- Janu Sirasasana [Alternate Leg Pull]
- Upavishtakonasana [Backstretch Seated Angle]
- Paripoorna Navasana [Diamond Pose 1]
- Dwikonasana [Chest Expansion 1] moderate position only

The following Asanas can be performed for up to the first 6 months of pregnancy:

- Tadasana [Stretch Pose]
- Utthanasana [Squat]
- Setu Bandasana [Bridge Pose: first position]
- Supta Vajrasana [Backward Bend: first position]
- Supta Mushumna Shakti Vikasaka [Pelvic Tilt Lying down]

These Asanas can be performed until delivery time:

- Padanguli Asana [Toe Exercises]
- Gulpasana [Ankle Exercises]
- Janu Shakti Vikasaka [Knee Cranking]
- Supta Bhadrasana [Knee and Thigh Stretch Lying down]
- Utthanasana [Squat]
- Vajrasana [Sitting Thunderbolt]
- Setu Bandasana [Bridge Pose: first position]
- Druta Grivasana [Neck Movement]
- Ujjayi Pranayama [Abdominal Breathing]
- Keep the legs up against the wall while lying down on the floor.
- Paryanaka [Fish in Vajrasana]

CARE AND REMEDY

During pregnancy, some expectant mothers have problems such as vomiting, constipation, backaches, diarrhoea, high blood pressure, oedema and protein in the urine. If you have any of these problems, consult your doctor immediately.

Some preventive measures for specific ailments (besides performing proper Asanas) are as follows:

ABDOMEN

If you experience discomfort in the abdomen and have back pains during pregnancy, have an infusion of 6 grams of ginger in 750 ml of water with fresh milk before meals for three days.

ANAEMIA

Have food rich in protein, dried apricots and spinach. Vitamin B, vitamin B12, vitamin C and iron tablets are other required supplements.

APPETITE

Loss of appetite during pregnancy can be restored by having a few cardamom seeds with a teaspoon of sugar. Grapefruit juice also helps to restore a poor appetite.

BACKACHES

Backaches are common due to change in posture (pregnant women, for instance, tend to walk, sit and sleep in ways that are different from the usual). They can be corrected by proper Asanas. Massaging the back with fresh lime juice also helps.

BLEEDING THROUGH THE VAGINA

Consult your doctor immediately.

BLEEDING IN THE ANUS

There will be some bleeding in the anus if the veins enlarge, a result of pressure from the uterus. This can be rectified by a proper diet. Also, do not strain yourself when evacuating your bowels.

CONSTIPATION

Avoid problems associated with constipation through a diet rich in fibre and through Yogasanas. Castor beans, although good for preventing constipation, is bad for the stomach and should not be used.

CRAMPS

Leg cramps may result from poor blood circulation. Cramps may also result from deficiency in calcium or other specific vitamins in the diet.

If extending legs against wall while lying back on the floor does not help relieve the pain, consult a doctor. For cramps in the feet and legs, extend your heels simultaneously, bring your toes towards your body and rub the area vigorously.

Vitamin E alleviates leg cramps during pregnancy. During this period, consuming saffron in small amounts promotes general health. Saffron improves your blood circulation, especially after childbirth.

HEADACHES AND DIZZINESS

Have a glass of warm infusion of lemon balm 3 times a day.

HEARTBURN

The later part of pregnancy may cause symptoms similar to heartburn. This may be a result of the uterus exerting too much pressure against the digestive tract. You can prevent such pain by consuming food that does not require long hours for digestion and drinking some simple herbal infusions. Have plum juice or celery juice extracted from the fleshy petioles, which is excellent for controlling heartburn, especially during pregnancy. Have several small meals rather than one big one.

INFECTIONS

Garlic and fresh orange juice (vitamin C) have a natural antibiotic effect to prevent infections, so add them to your diet. As vaginal infections can cause pain in bladder, thereby resulting in frequent urination, dab some fresh yoghurt into the vagina. Always wash yourself clean after each visit to the toilet.

MORNING SICKNESS

Vomiting during pregnancy occurs during the second and third months. It is mainly due to psychological reasons and hormonal changes. This is sometimes associated with nausea. Apples, basil, curry leaves, grapefruit, olives, peppermint and bean pods in the diet help prevent morning sickness. Avoid heavy meals, as well as fried and fatty foods. Have a peach for breakfast and season food with a lot of curry leaves.

Recipes

- Steam a grapefruit (do not remove its peel) with olives. Add a pinch of salt. Have the mixture as pudding once a day.
- Grind to a paste equal quantities of coriander seeds, cumin seeds and dry gooseberry paste. Have a teaspoon of the mixture with milk and sugar twice a day.
- Have cooked eggplant with buttermilk.

Juice

- Nausea and dizziness can be cured by having the grated rind of lemon or lemon juice with ice every morning.
- Dilute a quarter teaspoon of fresh ginger juice in half a teaspoon of hot water. Add honey to taste. Have a teaspoon of this every morning.
- Add a pinch of clove flower buds powder to pomegranate juice. Have the drink on an empty stomach.
- Have a glass of apple juice every morning.

Infusions

- Have a glass of infusion of red raspberries.
- Have a glass of infusion of grapefruit peel, peppermint, chamomile flowers or hops 3 times a day before meals. Drink this while it is warm.
- Steep a teaspoon of dried basil leaves in half a cup of water. Have the drink twice a day. Sweeten with honey if desired.

MISCARRIAGES

This is generally due to weak uterine muscles. You can help prevent a miscarriage by doing Asanas that strengthen the uterine muscles. Practise the ones suggested for the first 3 months of pregnancy. It is recommended that you start performing the Asanas from the time you plan to have a baby. Alcohol stops contraction and can be used to prevent a threatened miscarriage but use with care. Consult the doctor on the intake of alcohol.

The expectant mother should also add bioflavonoids, vitamin C, a teaspoon of wheatgerm oil, folic acid, and cooked green and yellow coloured vegetables to her daily diet. Bioflavonoids (contribute to the health of the capillaries in the womb) and vitamin C are constituents of all the cells in the body and are necessary for producing healthy cells. The recommended diet can help ensure the baby's health as well as minimise complications for the mother up until childbirth.

Recipe

Cook an eggplant and mix it with buttermilk. Eat this to prevent miscarriages.

Infusion

Have a glass of infusion of red raspberries. This prevents miscarriages and eases labour pain regularly after confinement.

OEDEMA

Swelling of ankles and fingers during late pregnancy is a sign of fluid retention. Women who are anaemic are hardest hit. Do not cut down on salt or fluids without consulting a doctor first. The following is a useful list of ways to prevent oedema:

- Lie down on the back and keep your legs apart against the wall.
- Drink 2–3 glasses of barley water daily.
- Have a glass of infusion of lemongrass or corn silk for a few days.

POISONING

Known as toxemia, the symptoms are swelling of feet, hands and face, accompanied by headaches, dizziness or blurred vision. A high amount of protein in the urine and high blood pressure are other symptoms.

Cut down on salt in your diet, have enough rest and consult a doctor for proper treatment. If there is protein or albumin in the urine, this may be a sign of placenta failure, which may lead to premature labour.

Recipe

Cut some small dried bean pods and boil them in a large bowl of water until the water reduces to a third of its original volume. Drink this warm thrice a day. Add honey to taste if desired.

STRETCH MARKS

Red patches may appear in the abdomen and breasts due to the stretching of the skin. An increased intake of protein in the diet and food rich in vitamin E and pantothenic acid help prevent these stretch marks. Remember that almond oil massaged gently onto the areas where stretch marks are likely to appear will help nip the problem in the bud.

TIREDNESS

Exhaustion is common during the first 3 months of pregnancy. It can be avoided by having enough rest and a nutritious diet.

URINE

If you experience pain or a burning sensation during urination, have tender coconut water. Eating okra also helps.

VAGINAL DISCHARGE

Vaginal discharge is common but if it causes a burning or an itching sensation, consult a doctor immediately.

VARICOSE VEINS

Varicose veins appear due to pressure on the veins. Resting with feet and legs elevated brings about some relief. Never sit with legs crossed and avoid wearing tight garters.

LABOUR

Birth is a natural occurrence. A healthy expectant mother can expect a healthy baby and a not too difficult delivery. Sometimes, however, complications that endanger the life of the mother or baby do occur. Some problems include bleeding before labour, toxemia, chronic illness, acute anaemia, diabetes, heart trouble, hernia, baby's (wrong) position in the womb, narrow hips and not being in labour even though the water bag has broken, as well as the mother having fever.

Preparation

- Go for walks during labour, especially during early labour.
- During an intense contraction, a light fingertip massage over the lower abdomen is soothing. Make a gentle half circle movement over the lower abdomen from one side to the other.
- If labour progresses fast, kneeling on all fours can help you maintain control. Breathe in and out slowly. If labour is slow, walking outdoors helps. Squatting will intensify labour.

VITAL SIGNS

A few days before labour, the baby moves to a lower position in the womb. This allows the mother to breathe more easily. You may need to urinate more frequently due to increased pressure from the new position. Some time before labour, jelly-like mucous will be discharged from the vagina. Sometimes, this may be stained with blood. Do not worry as this is quite a common occurrence.

The contraction — a sudden tightening of the womb that becomes regular — soon becomes stronger and more frequent. This confirms the beginning of labour. Your water then break. Every mother-to-be experiences pain at the peak of contractions. Often, a very strong contraction is followed by milder ones. The pain is unlike the pain caused by injuries. Many mothers describe the entire process as a life-giving experience and derive pleasure between contractions.

During pregnancy and labour, the body produces hormones called endorphines, which are natural painkillers. Another hormone, oxytocin, serves to stimulate the contractions. Hormone secretion depends on the emotional make-up of an individual. Tension impedes it. For this reason, trust and confidence in people are important.

There are 3 stages in labour:

• The drawing up and widening of the uterus neck opening.
• The passage of the baby through the pelvis and birth canal.
• The expulsion of the placenta after birth.

In the first stage, the upper part of the uterus shrinks. It becomes thicker and harder, and presses the baby down against the lower part of the uterus. Keep your cool. Fear and anxiety cause rigidity in the uterus muscles, thereby causing exhaustion. The endocrine glands will take over by producing extra hormones to fight any type of emergency, including shock. In this stage, while the cervix is dilating, it is usually best to stand upright and walk.

In the second stage, an active person who had exercised regularly during pregnancy will feel a sense of participation and achievement. The temptation to push hard or fast must be curbed. The muscles round the vagina must be stretched naturally (the baby's head stretches the muscles) and not by force. With each contraction, the baby's head is pushed against the tissues of the vaginal opening.

On the way through the pelvic area, the baby has to pass a jointed ring of bone. If the ring is stiff, the baby may be harmed. If the pelvis has been kept supple through exercises, the baby's transit will most likely be quick and easy. In this stage, supported squatting during contractions seems to assert the greatest pressure on the pelvic cavity with minimum muscular effort.

In the third stage after the delivery, the reproductive organs gradually resume their correct size and position. Careful exercises help speed up the process. It is important to ensure that there are no clots or congestion in the uterus or veins. If there are, you may suffer from postnatal backaches, constipation, varicose veins and bad posture.

POSTNATAL CARE

Have nutritious food. In the first week after delivery, instead of getting into a hot bathtub, go for sponge baths. Add tumeric powder to water and make sure water is warm before sponging yourself. A month-long rest is essential.

Many Indians have traditionally made *lehya* or jelly from herbs. This is given to the mother after delivery to strengthen her entire system. It also promotes general health.

Recipe for Lehya

Ingredients

125 grams of dry ginger

250 grams of winter cherry paste (aswagandha)

200 grams of ghee (made from cow's milk),

1 kg jaggery

225 grams of honey

Method

In a frying pan, stir-fry dry ginger and winter cherry paste in ghee. Add to the pan water in which 1 kg of jaggery or natural brown sugar has been dissolved and cook over low heat. Stir constantly until a thick jelly forms. Add honey, allow the mixture to cool and store it in a container. One teaspoon of lehya twice a day with milk for a period of 3 months gives you strength and restores your health.

Other than trying out the above recipe, remember to include herbs like lemon balm, raspberries, fenugreek, ginger, turmeric, black pepper, ajowan, and juniper berries in your diet. Avoid celery, horseradish, mistletoe and cinnamon.

Ways to ease rheumatic pain or colds:

- Fry 500 grams of black soya beans over low heat until they become half burned. Add 350 millilitres of rice wine and leave to marinate overnight. Strain and drink half a glass 3 times a day.
- To a hot bath, add 5 glasses of infusion of grapefruit, including its peel and use it in bath every 3 days for relief from cold sensation.
- Bathe with old ginger that is crushed in hot water for relief from cold symptoms.
- To relieve itch in the genital area, common after childbirth, boil a few cloves of garlic in water. Use this to wash the area.
- Dust turmeric powder on the body after a warm bath. This gives added heat to the body and keeps it from getting cold symptoms after childbirth.
- Apply poultice of corn for relief from rheumatic pain.
- To prevent cold feet, have a foot bath using an infusion of oat straw.

Ways to prevent excessive bleeding:

- Drink an infusion of bamboo shoots. Add to this a teaspoon of molasses or natural brown sugar. The infusion stops excess bleeding after delivery and aids in the complete removal of the placenta.
- Mix together 3 grams of cumin seeds, 3 grams of coriander seeds and 2 grams clove flower buds. Boil the mixture in a litre of water until the water reduces to half the original volume. Have half a glass of the mixture twice a day.

For pain in the abdomen:

- Grind a clove of garlic. Add a pinch of asafoetida and a teaspoon of ghee. Have this twice a day for 3 days.
- Have a glass of infusion of fennel seeds twice a day for 5 days.

Fever:

This is usually due to an infection after childbirth. If you have fever with chills, headaches, lower back pain, and bloody or smelly discharge from the vagina, consult a doctor immediately. Add one-eighth of a teaspoon of powdered dry ginger into half a glass of boiled goat's milk. Drink this twice a day.

EXERCISES

Perform deep breathing exercises. Since the mother is usually propped up in bed after delivery to drain fluids and waste from the uterus, breathing exercises can be done while lying down. After birth, the pelvic region, uterus and vaginal area have to be normalised, while the waist and abdomen have to be firmed up and strengthened.

Asana Routine

The following stretching Asanas are to be performed for a period of 6–12 months after delivery (Some mothers may return to normalcy much more quickly):

- Bhuja Valli Shakti Vikasaka and Bahu Shakti Vikasaka [Arm Strengthening Exercises]
- Padanguli Asana [Toe Exercises]
- Janu Shakti Vikasaka [Knee Cranking]
- Supta Mushumna Shakti Vikasaka [Pelvic Tilt Lying down]
- Vayu Nishankasana [Gas Releasing Pose]
- Shashankasana [Baby Pose]
- Urdhva Hastottanasana [Side Bend Both Arms]
- Druta Grivasana [Neck Movement]
- Janu Sirasasana [Alternate Leg Pull]
- Bhujangasana [Cobra Variation]

Other Asanas for Specific Purposes

- Vyghrasana [Tiger Pose]

Do the first part, that is, until the part where you raise your legs. Alternatively, place your leg apart against the wall while resting your back on the mattress. This stretches the inner thigh, as well as strengthens the back, upper chest and shoulders. It also prevents varicose veins, haemorrhoids and promotes the healing process of the pelvic region.

- Supta Badrasana [Knee and Thigh Stretch Lying down]

This bring about suppleness to hip joints. It tones the pelvis and gets the uterus back into shape. It also increases blood circulation to the pelvic region.

- Setu Bandasana [Bridge Pose]

This strengthens the lower back and thighs, as well as tightens the pelvic floor.

- Siras Angushta Yogasana [Chest Expansion 3]

This increases the flexibility of the ankles, knees and back of legs.

- Shalabasana [Locust Pose]

During this Asana, stretch the abdomen muscles and extend the spine at the same time. This tightens the pelvis and strengthens the lower back.

- The gradual introduction of Cat, Spinal or Abdominal Twist, Shoulderstand and Plough, Fish in Veera or any other relaxation Asanas are beneficial.

CARING FOR THE NEWBORN

Make sure the freshly cut umbilical cord does not become infected. It should be kept clean and dry so that it falls off quickly. The baby should be kept warm (but not too warm). Relatives and friends with infectious problems should not be allowed near the baby. Keep the baby away from smoke. Infection in babies are hard to detect. Often, they go without fever.

LACTATION

Begin breastfeeding the baby from the day it is born. For the first few days, the mother may produce very little milk. If she nurses the baby more often, she will produce more milk (the baby's sucking on the nipples helps to produce more milk).

The need for every mother to breastfeed her baby cannot be overemphasised. Breastfeeding helps in the proper growth of the child and in the development of the mother-child relationship. Breast milk has a better balance of nutrients that the baby needs. The temperature of breast milk is best suited for the baby. Breast milk protects the baby against infection and allergic reactions. Breastfed babies are never overfed and chances of obesity are lower. Breastfeeding also helps the uterus to contract to its normal size. What is more, during breastfeeding, the mother's extra fat is used up. However, if the mother has any illness, she may indirectly transmit the problem to the child when she nurses it, so do not breastfeed when ill.

Milk secretion should not be scanty. Before nursing the baby, she should wipe her nipples with cotton soaked in boiling water. Avoid using boricated water; it can even intoxicate the baby.

The following help promote milk production:

Herbs

Dill seeds, peanuts, asparagus, black sesame seeds, small red beans, figs, basil leaves, caraway seeds, fennel seeds, lavender flowers, dandelion roots, chrysanthemum petals, parsley, barley, orange seeds, papayas, raspberries, wheat, brown rice, soya bean curd, brown sugar and ginger.

Recipes

- Have a cup of barley water boiled with fennel seeds.
- Have a half ripe papaya that is cooked daily.
- Roast 50 grams of peanuts (with their skin). Mix the nuts with red or brown rice and cook well.
- Add shredded wheat and brown rice to your diet on a regular basis.
- Add 150 grams of soya bean curd and brown sugar into a pot of water (3 cups) and boil for 10 minutes. If preferred, add 50 millilitres of rice wine. Drink this once a day for 5 days.
- Blend tender corn in milk, add honey and drink this once a day.
- Have cooked asparagus.
- Crush some dried pips of mandarin oranges and boil them in rice wine. Have the drink 2 times a day.
- Boil watercress seeds in milk. Add natural brown sugar. Have this once a day.

Infusions

- Have a glass of infusion of cumin seeds with milk and honey daily.
- Have a glass of infusion made from the seeds of either a squash or a sweet pumpkin with sugar before breakfast for 5 days.
- Have an infusion of fenugreek seeds 3 times a day after meals. Add some aniseed if desired.
- Have an infusion of fennel seeds with barley water once a day for 10 days.
- Have a glass of infusion of aniseed, fenugreek or dandelion roots once a day after meals.
- Mix together aniseed, dill seeds and sweet marjoram. Have a hot infusion from this mixture.

Decoctions

- Have 2 tablespoons of decoction of chrysanthemum 2 times a day.
- Into half a glass of sweetened milk, add a tablespoon of decoction of caraway seeds. Have this twice a day after meals.
- Have a decoction of dill seeds in combination with coriander or fennel seeds to promote the flow of milk. The decoction gives the best benefit when taken in combination with aniseed, coriander, fennel and caraway seeds mixed in equal proportion.
- Simmer 500 grams of papaya and 30 grams of old ginger in 500 millilitres of rice vinegar over low heat for 40 minutes. Have a cup of this twice a day. It Increases milk secretion and also relieves lochiostasis.

Ways to stop lactation:

- Have walnuts 3 times a day.
- Make a poultice from the crushed leaves or flowers of jasmine without water (only by crushing). Apply it on the breasts.

THE MOTHER AND BABY

For a day or two after delivery, breast milk sometimes fails to appear. This is usually due to excitement or tension on the part of the mother. Once the mother has had enough relaxation, milk production becomes normal. A large amount of milk is produced as soon as the mother starts nursing the baby. Within 2 weeks, both mother and child get accustomed to nursing. It is best to consult a doctor for other complications that lead to inadequate production of milk.

It is sometimes a challenge for the mother to find out the real need of the baby. There will be doubts over feeding the baby on demand or by the clock. It is very important to feed the baby on demand at least for the first few weeks. Later on, a routine can be set. Unless the child is sick, the pattern of demand for milk will be adjusted to the schedule set, which should not be too rigid. Working mothers can set a pattern of feeding through bottle and breast feeding according to convenience. Then comes the question of whether to feed the child with cow's milk or artificial feeds. Cow's milk contains more protein, calcium, potassium and sodium than mother's milk. If cow's milk is given, dilute 2 parts of milk with 1 part of water. Add a pinch of unrefined sugar. Cow's milk has less vitamin A and C and no vitamin D. There is no cause for worry as every healthy baby's liver stores vitamin A and D that will last for a few months. For vitamin C, fresh orange juice (though some children may be allergic to this) or tomato juice can be given as early as 3 months. Start with 1 teaspoon of orange juice diluted with 1 teaspoon of water and gradually increase it to 2 ounces. If tomato juice is given, double the dilution. After breastfeeding stops, introduce egg yolk mixed with milk into the diet (egg white only after the baby is a year old) as well as wheatgerm and molasses (supplies iron). Give them plenty of water to drink. Gradually introduce cereals, fruit and vegetables.

DIET FOR CHILDREN

For infants, breast milk is the best since it has all the nutrients. A mother should, therefore, have nutritious food. Solid foods should never be introduced until the baby is 6 months old. After that, pureed fruit and vegetables of all kinds are to be introduced to develop the baby's taste for all flavours. Adding barley water to dilute cow's milk prevents the formation of hard masses of curd in the baby's stomach.

After 18 months, introduce other nutritious food besides milk. Refined sugar and other processed products should not be given to the child at this stage. It is, however, good to give supplements, such as cod liver oil, if there is a shortage of nutrients in the child's diet. The following is a list of nutrients to include or exclude:

- Take care not to feed the child with an excess of food containing salicylates (chemical similar to aspirin) as these tend to develop hyperactivity in him or her. They also reduce the vitamin C and vitamin B complex and the minerals calcium, potassium and iron in the child's brain. Food containing salicylates is as follows: apricots, blackberries, cherries, grapes, oranges, peaches, plums, raspberries, cucumbers and tomatoes. Add vitamin supplements to the child's diet to compensate for the loss caused by salicylates.

- Avoid a diet rich in carbohydrates as this results in iron deficiency. It may also lead to lack of motivation, learning disability and memory loss.

- A diet rich in fibre should be avoided as it blocks the absorption of vital minerals and vitamins required for the proper functioning of the brain.

- Food with additives is not good for the brain and can cause a slow deterioration of its effectiveness. Cerebral allergens can have a similar effect by diminishing the brain's supply of vitamins and minerals. Common allergens are bread, corn, lentils, peas, and potatoes. Supplements that overcome this problem are vitamin B6 and vitamin C and the minerals calcium, zinc, iron, magnesium, phosphorus, and to some extent selenium and chromium.

Do not completely avoid the types of food mentioned above. They are actually very helpful as long as they are taken in moderation and balanced with either counteracting food or supplements.

FOOD FOR BRAIN DEVELOPMENT

Eggs, fish (well-cooked), buttermilk, milk, plain yoghurt, non-processed cheese, barley, millet, wheatgerm, rice, walnuts, almonds, raisins, peanuts*, dried beans, sunflower seeds, guavas, mangoes, oranges*, papayas, lemons, pineapples, strawberries*, apples*, apricots*, dates, figs, pears, grapes, plums, raspberries*, cauliflowers*, green peppers, peas, potatoes*, sweet potatoes, carrots, cucumbers*, mushrooms, cabbages (cooked), spinach (cooked), onions, pumpkins, radishes, bitter gourd, safflower oil, sunflower oil, unsalted butter, coriander seeds, garlic, ginger, mustard greens, cumin seeds, fenugreek and black pepper.

*Adverse effects when consumed in excess.

FOOD TO AVOID

The following types of food are considered dangerous for the development of the child's brain: pies, pastries, alcohol, chocolate milk, coffee, soft drinks (including herbal teas), ham, sausages, canned foods, chilli sauce, fried foods, sweets, chocolates, coconut oil, palm oil, raw cabbages, coconuts, raw spinach, raw green vegetables, potato crisps, peanuts in excess, glucose and sugar.

The brain is made of protein and though it is best to avoid a high protein intake during pregnancy, the child's brain requires a certain amount of this. It may seem surprising, but a certain amount of food high in fat and cholesterol is necessary for children to aid the healthy development of the brain.

Nowadays, obesity is common among children. It is a common form of malnutrition and may continue into adult life. Knowledge of the nutrition to be taken at this age is beneficial and is a permanent preventive measure from sickness later on in life.

After the age of thirteen, children grow rapidly. At this point, the amount of nutrients required is greater than usual. It is, therefore, necessary to add calcium and protein-rich foods, such as cheese and milk to the diet. Vitamin B complex should be increased to counterbalance the high consumption of carbohydrates.

At the time of puberty and menstruation, it is important to increase the intake of food rich in iron, such as blackstrap molasses, milk, yoghurt and eggs. Along with these, it is good to add food rich in vitamin C like fresh oranges to prevent anaemia and to convert Fe^{+++} to Fe^{++} in green vegetables so that iron is absorbable.

Instilling a good pattern of eating habits in teenagers will benefit them in their later years.

20

The Neuro-Psychological System
☙

Two aspects of the neuro-psychological system considered in this chapter are disorders of the nervous system, in which the nervous system is affected, resulting in abnormalities, and mental disorders, in which an abnormal personality results from an individual's inability to adjust to a new situation. Common causes of nervous disorders are as follows:

- Congenital faults of development such as enlargement of the head due to the accumulation of cerebrospinal fluid — the clear, colourless fluid that surrounds the brain and the spinal cord — within the brain.
- Inflammation of the brain or inflammation of the membranes that cover the brain and spinal cord.
- Toxins produced by germs such as tetanus or lockjaw, diphtheria or botulism, resulting in damage to the brain or other tissues.
- Accidents that cause haemorrhage in the brain or poor circulation of blood to the brain due to vascular diseases or tumours in the brain and spinal cord.
- Deficiencies in the diet and lack of vitamin B, affecting the nervous system.

The symptoms of nervous disorders are as follows: a decrease in the ability to use the muscles of the body, the inability of the muscles to respond to voluntary commands, stiffness, uncontrolled movement of certain muscles, poor coordination between muscles, disturbance in speech, difficulty in swallowing, abrupt jerky movements resulting in convulsions, slow loss of sensation of touch (pain and temperature), frequent abnormal sensations like pins and needles, headaches, dizziness, misleading vision, fainting spells and delusions.

The holistic approach to healing sees any disease of the body as a combination of emotional, mental, physical and environmental factors.

Meditation alters the brain chemistry by increasing the alpha and beta waves. Also, biogenic amines in the urine and cerebrospinal fluid are altered for the better. Meditation also lowers the heartbeat and body temperature, as well as reduces the secretion of noradrenaline and metabolites (neurotransmitters). An experiment in which subjects performed vigorous physical exercises after a period of monitored meditation revealed an increase in plasma noradrenaline but no corresponding increase in heartbeat or blood pressure. This is an important indicator — that Yoga brings the body's autonomic functions under voluntary control.

For nervous disorders, include the following in the daily diet:

- Almonds, apples, avocados, blackberries, dates, oats and raisins. They are the best-known nutrients for nerve tissues.
- Spinach juice, which is an excellent tonic for tired nerves.
- Chamomile flowers, carrots, hops, hyssop, lavender, lime blossoms, mistletoe leaves, rosemary, St. John's wort, as they are good relaxants for the nerves.
- Allspice, peppermint, olives, pomegranates, prunes and walnuts, as they good stimulants for the nerves.

Avoid using excess saffron, camphor, sedatives, drugs and tranquillisers.

Recipe
Add a teaspoon of the decoction of basil leaves and marjoram herbs mixed together in equal quantities to a glass of the infusion of lime blossoms. Add sugar to taste. Have this after meals 3 times a day.

Asana Routine
For a feeling of relaxation, attempt the following:

- Dwikonasana [Chest Expansion 1]
- Grivasana [Neck Roll]
- Paschimottanasana [Backstretch]
- Ananda Madirasana [Intoxicating Bliss Pose]
- Jyestika Makarasana [Head Twist]
- Bhujangasana [Cobra Pose]
- Shavasana [Corpse Pose]
- Shanti Mudra [Invocation of Peace Seal]
- Nadi Shodana Pranayama [Alternate Nostril Breathing]

ALZHEIMER'S DISEASE (PRESENILE DEMENTIA)
This represents the different types of degenerative diseases of the brain. In later life, if specific brain cells become knotted in tangles and deteriorate, senile dementia may result. One of the causes of this is the lack of acetylcholine. Unreasonableness and impaired judgement are just some of the effects. Memory fades, and recent events cannot be recalled, but those that occurred in early life can be recalled. There will a lso be a progressive deterioration in the physical appearance.

Include the following the daily diet:
Choline prevents brain ageing. The richest source of this is lecithin, a soya bean product. Lecithin is also found in egg yolk, green leafy vegetables, legumes, brewer's yeast and wheatgerm.

Recipe
Mix 4 tablespoons of lecithin, a quarter teaspoon of brewer's yeast and a tablespoon of wheatgerm together with any seasonal green vegetable. Add a glass of your favourite fruit juice to this. Blend well. Drink this mixture an hour after breakfast on a daily basis.

ANGER
Anger is a psychological disturbance. Under stress, one loses the power of sound analysis and can misinterpret things. In some circumstances, an emotional outburst may appear as anger, more as a self defence to protect the personal ego. Whatever may be the situation, anger creates more stress and can endanger harmony of the physical systems, resulting in more stressful conditions. To keep calm under all circumstances is a virtue, and this can be achieved by developing self awareness through Yoga. Both Asanas and meditation help control emotional disturbances. They work on the endocrine glands and the nervous system.

Asana Routine
To control anger, try out the following:

- Shashankasana [Baby Pose]
- Yoga Mudra
- Paschimottanasana [Backstretch]
- Karna Peedasana [Plough 3]
- Moola Bandha [Perineum Retraction Lock]
- Nadi Shodana Pranayama [Alternate Nostril Breathing]
- Brahmari Pranayama [Humming of Bee Breathing]
- Sheetkari Pranayama [Hissing Breath]
- Bhoochari Mudra [Gazing At Nothing Seal]
- Meditation

ANXIETY

Induced by an intolerable situation, anxiety is the feeling of uncertainty, apprehension or fear. Although everyone experiences feelings of anxiety at one point or another, and although these feelings usually last only a short while, sometimes, they are frequent, thereby affecting normal behaviour. Anxiety, in fact, produces more anxiety. Its accompanying effects include muscular tension, tremors, perspiration, frequent urination and diarrhoea. There will also be a sensation of "energy loss" due to emotional stress, poor blood circulation or accumulation of waste products in the muscles.

The best way to fight the problem is to learn to relax through Yogasanas. In addition, include in the daily diet nerve relaxants, such as grapes, raisins, hawthorn, St. John's wort and evening primrose.

The following measures prevent anxiety:

Recipe

Add 2 drops of lavender oil and a teaspoon of honey to a glass of water and drink.

Infusion

Have a glass of the herbal infusion of chamomile flowers or lemon balm or the mixture of the equal parts of skullcap and valerian, or marjoram herbs 3 times a day before meals.

Bath

Soak yourself in a bath where a few drops of lavender oil or lavender flowers have been added.

Asana Routine

The Asanas that follow help deal with depression, fatigue, hysteria, mental disorders, migraine, nervousness, stress and strain. The point of concentration is discussed with each Asana for a better understanding of the Asana as well as for better results.

- Suryanamaskar [Salutation to the sun) — breathing
- Bumi Pada Mastakasana [Headstand Modified] — the pituitary glands
- Sarvangasana [Shoulderstand] — the thyroid gland
- Paryanaka [Fish in Vajrasana] — the chest and adrenal glands
- Shashankasana [Baby Pose] — the adrenal glands
- Yoga Mudra — breathing or the adrenal glands
- Ananda Madirasana [Intoxicating Bliss Pose] — breathing
- Dhyana Veerasana [Relaxation Hero Pose] — the pituitary glands
- Paschimottanasana [Backstretch] — breathing
- Karna Peedasana [Plough 3] — the adrenal glands
- Bhujangasana [Cobra Pose] — the gonads
- Advasana [Reversed Corpse Pose] — breathing
- Sarpasana [Snake Pose] — the gonads
- Shalabasana [Locust Pose] — the thyroid gland
- Halasana [Plough 1] — the thyroid or adrenal gland depending on the individual's position
- Shavasana — relaxation
- Nadi Shodana Pranayama [Alternate Nostril Breathing] — breathing or the pituitary glands
- Bhoochari Mudra [Gazing At Nothing Seal]
- Trataka [Candle Concentration] - trinity flame, vapour of gas and wax — flame
- Meditation

CEREBRAL PALSY

This is the inability to control muscle movements coupled with stiffness. Causes include non-progressive brain damage resulting from injury and an insufficient supply of oxygen to the brain. Cerebral palsy can also be inherited. The condition causes stiffness and spastic paralysis of the arms and legs with jerky movements. There may be convulsions, speech impairment and mental deficiency.

Speech training and muscle re-education are essential. Food rich in wheatgerm oil (take a teaspoon of wheatgerm oil daily), including protein, vitamins, minerals and manganese, in particular, help restore the condition at an early stage. Massaging with essential oil using nervines brings about some progress, but this takes time. Avoid fatty foods, food wrapped in aluminium or camphor and menthol.

CERVICAL RIB

In some people, an extra rib develops just above the first rib in the lower part of the neck. This results in nerves and arteries being squeezed. When you lift a heavy object or while keeping your arms raised above your head for a considerable period of time, you may experience some discomfort, which may cause pain, numbness, coolness and a tingling sensation in the forearms. Similar symptoms are experienced for several other problems, when the roots of those nerves that run down the arms are affected. Sometimes, pain also results from pressure from the structure of these ribs.

A gentle hot and cold fomentation on a daily basis gives relief. Performing Asanas to release pressure on the nerves also helps.

CONVULSIVE DISORDERS/EPILEPSY

Recurring convulsions are called epilepsy, which results from uncontrolled nerve activity. There are different types of seizures depending on which part of the brain is affected. Generalised seizures affect the entire body and are known as grand mal. Causes include birth injuries, severe head injuries, meningitis, an insufficient supply of blood to the brain and deficiencies in sodium, sugar and calcium in the body.

Grand mal results from discharges in the brain and is usually hereditary. A tendency to bite the tongue, breathing difficulty and spontaneous urination result. Focal epilepsy involves only a part of the brain and may result from an accident. This can cause periodical amnesia, rage and incoherent speech. Petit mal usually begins in childhood and may disappear along the way. There may be sudden unconsciousness with spasms.

In children, high fever and holding the breath for long periods of time may bring about convulsions. People with low blood sugar or low calcium levels or more than the necessary level of alkalinity in the blood can also get convulsions. In addition, brain tumours, tetanus, injury and so on bring about convulsions.

Have a diet rich in vegetable protein and magnesium. Avoid yoghurt, buttermilk, food wrapped in aluminium, camphor and menthol.

Recipes

- Add 2 tablespoons of vitamin-rich brewer's yeast to every meal.
- Have 3 to 4 cloves of garlic daily with or without honey early in the morning.
- Homemade ghee is considered a tonic for the brain and nervous system. Add a teaspoon of ghee to a glass of hot milk. Have this after meals on a daily basis.

Infusion

Have a glass of the infusion of drumstick roots 3 times a day to cure palsy and epileptic conditions. Refer also to infusion under nervous disorder.

Inhalation

Inhale black pepper powder to prevent epileptic seizures.

Application

Wrap a clove of garlic in cotton wool soaked in olive oil. Place this in your ears to strengthen the nerves. Do this every night before going to sleep.

Asanas suggested for anxiety are also recommended for epileptic conditions.

FACIAL PARALYSIS/BELL'S PALSY

In this a person loses the function of the face muscles on one side. This is due to the lesion of the facial nerve, which is caused by exposure to a cold breeze. Difficulty in closing the eyes, drooping of the mouth and inability to wrinkle the forehead are some effects.

Application

To treat facial paralysis:
Massage using garlic oil or black pepper oil as liniment. A gentle heat treatment in the form of a fomentation and exercising the facial muscles are useful in restoring muscle tone, thus preventing permanent deformity.

Asana Routine

- Pawanamuktasana series for arms
- Simha Grivasana [Lion Neck Movement]

- Simhasana [Lion]
- Netra Shakti Vikasaka [Eye exercises]
- Meditation

FAINTING

Inhalation

To prevent fainting and to decrease its frequency:
Inhale crushed fennel seeds wrapped in a small towel.

Application

To prevent fainting and to decrease its frequency:
Apply lavender oil on the forehead, temples and neck.

GIDDINESS/DIZZINESS

This is a general term representing a variety of symptoms, such as vertigo, light-headedness and disorientation. Dizziness that results from standing up suddenly is associated with an insufficient supply of blood flow to the brain, low blood pressure and excess intake of medication. When the semicircular canals of the ear are disturbed, misleading nerve impulses are produced, causing dizziness. Giddiness can also result from overusing the eyes (for example, sitting in front of a computer for hours), epilepsy, migraine, etc. Other causes of dizziness include head injury or brain tumour, which is associated with ringing in the ears.

There is no direct treatment for giddiness. Instead treat the conditions that will eliminate the problem. For instance, have your eyesight and spinal alignment checked.

Bitter foods are good for nausea and dizziness, so include them in the daily diet. Also include tryptophan, which is found in milk, cheese, meat products and egg yolk, in the diet. Avoid cigarettes, drugs and alcohol.

The following measures help treat giddiness:

Recipes

- Grate half a lemon rind. Mix it with salad or any savoury food and eat.
- When symptoms of giddiness appear, take a teaspoon of sugar mixed together with two drops of lavender oil.

Juice

- Have fresh lemon juice in hot water in the morning before your meals.
- Mix fresh celery juice with honey to taste. Take this as a drink to clear dizzy spells, headaches and shoulder pain associated with hypertension.
- Add a teaspoon of honey to a teaspoon of the fresh juice of raisins or currants. Drink it 2 times a day to clear dizziness associated with headaches and nervousness.

Infusion

Have a glass of the infusion of lavender leaves, peppermint or lemongrass 3 times a day.

Application

Apply lavender oil (or rose oil) behind your ears and forehead. Gently massage, moving towards the temple area for relief.

Asana Routine

- Balancing Asanas
- Netra Shakti Vikasaka [Eye exercises]
- Shashankasana [Baby Pose]
- Shashanka Bhujangasana [Striking Cobra]
- Trataka [Candle Concentration]

DEPRESSION

This is a state of mind that results from some sort of disappointment. Nowadays, this condition is more common among the young. Physically, pain may be experienced in different parts of the body, especially in the chest in the form of heart pain, ringing in the ears, cramps and headaches. Other symptoms are an increase or decrease in the appetite with a corresponding increase or decrease in weight, oversleeping or insomnia, fatigue, self-reproach and pensiveness.

Rest and relaxation with Yogasanas involving deep breathing are the best means of treating the symptoms. Refer to Asanas given under Anxiety. Avoid all kinds of pep pills and hot or pungent herbs like cayenne.

Infusions
Have a glass of the infusion of rose petals or basil leaves 2 times a day after meals. You can also have the infusions of peppermint, lemon balm, rosemary, lavender or lime blossoms. Adding a clove flower bud to herbal infusions is good for emotional upliftment.

Decoction
Drink a cup of the decoction of fennel seeds or milk decoction of nutmeg before going to sleep.

Application
Apply sandalwood paste to the forehead.

HEADACHES
A common symptom associated with many problems of the body, the main causes of a headache are prolonged bad posture, general stiffness and stress. For these, refer to the Asanas under backaches. Other causes include constipation, sinusitis, irregular menstrual flow, high blood pressure (results in throbbing headaches), hormonal changes due to tension, eye strain and sinus that feel like a tight band on the forehead, reaction of chemicals used in food or pollution.

Headaches that last for days or those that frequently reappear are associated with mental disturbances. Those that come on suddenly with severe pain and are associated with fever and stiff neck and those that occur in specific locations accompanied by fainting, bleeding or weight loss are the ones to pay special attention to. Early consultation with a specialist is required.

Take a prescribed daily dose of vitamin C, vitamin E, vitamin B complex, calcium and iron, increasing the dosage slightly during menstruation. To prevent headaches altogether, include naturally grown tomatoes, cabbages, cucumbers, guavas, horseradish, and radishes in salad regularly in the diet. Also, take a teaspoon of cider vinegar in water daily.

The following measures are for relieving headaches:

Recipes
- Drink soup made of spearmint leaves regularly for relief from chronic headaches.

- Take a tablespoon of honey once the symptoms of a headache appear.
- Have cooked celery with vinegar for relief from headaches and hypertension.
- For headaches that result from common cold, use basil leaves as seasoning on food or sniff the dried powdered leaves for some time.
- For headaches associated with cough and cold, mix together 1 part ginger powder, 1 part ghee and 5 parts jaggery. Take a teaspoon of the mixture in the morning.
- For headaches due to neuralgia, dry-fry sword beans until they turn brown. Do not use any oil. Grind the beans into powder. Take 4 grams of this powder with rice wine 3 times a day.

Infusions
- For headaches associated with depression, have a glass of the infusion of lavender flowers.
- Have a glass of the infusion of dried basil leaves in a glass of water with honey and any one of the following herbs everyday 3 times: lemon balm, sage leaves, thyme, leaves of violet, ginger, chamomile flowers, peppermint leaves, lime flowers, elder flowers, ground ivy leaves or rose petals.

Decoction
When the symptom of a headache appear, take a tablespoon of the decoction of chrysanthemum flowers.

Applications
- Sniff the dried leaves of marjoram for relief.
- Use the infusion of lemon balm as a poultice on the forehead and temples or in the bath for relief from headaches and migraine.
- Apply lavender, peppermint, borneol or thyme oil to the forehead and temples in a circular motion for relief. If the headache is associated with neuralgia, avoid borneol.
- Apply to the forehead and temples lime juice mixed together with cinnamon powder, the paste of ginger in water, edible camphor mixed together with milk or calamus and ginger ground in buttermilk for relief.

Asana Routine (Curative)

- Nadi Shodhana Pranayama [Alternate Nostril breathing]
- Brahmari Pranayama [Humming of Bee Breathing]
- Netra Shakti Vikasaka [Palming the Eye]
- Grivasana [Neck Roll]
- Netra Shakti Vikasaka Eye Exercises, particularly Palming the Eye
- Matsya Kridasana [Flapping Fish Pose]
- Jalandhara Bandha [Chin Lock]
- Sheetali Pranayama [Cooling Breath]
- Shavasana [Relaxation]
- Meditation

Asana Routine (General)

- Nadi Shodana Pranayama [Alternate Nostril Breathing]
- Hasta Netra Shakti Vikasaka [Palming the Eye]
- Brahmari Pranayama [Humming of Bee Breathing]
- Uttanasana [Legclasp Migraine Pose]
- Paschimottanasana [Backstretch]
- Grivasana [Neck Roll]

HYPERACTIVITY

This is not a specific disease. It refers to a group of abnormal behaviour and is common among children. There is no scale to measure hyperactivity as research is based mainly on comparative studies. Hyperactivity can result from accumulation of heavy metals or from hyperthyroid activity. There are certain close associations with eczema and asthma. Symptoms are restlessness, impulsiveness, aggressiveness, low tolerance to stress and short attention span.

The most important step to consider is to increase the intake of natural foods, that is, food without any synthetic chemicals or additives. All Asanas for relaxation and the development of concentration are beneficial.

HYSTERIA

This is a subconscious act in which an individual's intense anxiety or frustration shows up in the form of abnormal behaviour. Asanas for relaxation and meditation are beneficial. Refer also to Asanas for anxiety.

Recipe

Have 2 to 3 dates regularly after food.

Infusion

Have a glass of the infusion of lemon balm leaves or drumstick roots 2 times a day.

INSOMNIA

This is the chronic inability to sleep. It is not a disease but a sign of an emotional or physical problem, which prevents the normal functioning of the body. An overactive mind and the inability to relax are causes.

Herbal relaxants are very beneficial. Avocados, chamomile flowers, dandelion roots and leaves, dates, dill, hawthorn, hops, lettuce, peppermint, saffron, etc., help relax the mind and body. Add in the daily diet calming agents that promote sleep, such as lettuce, dates and onion white heads. Tryptophan, which is found in dairy products, such as milk and cheese, together with other amino acids, stimulates the production of the body's own sleep chemical, serotonin.

Avoid sugary foods and alcohol before bedtime. Sleeping pills cannot induce a natural state of sleep. It is best to avoid them. Instead, perform Asanas, especially those for relaxation, in the evening.

The following measures help control insomnia:

Recipes

Have the following before going to bed:

- Have a glass of warm milk without sugar.
- Boil 2 dates with an onion white head.
- Have freshly picked lettuce leaves for a couple of weeks.
- Add a few seeds of aniseed to a glass of boiled fresh milk and drink.

Infusions

Have a glass of the infusion of star anise, basil leaves, dill seeds, orange peel, lemon balm, rosemary, German chamomile, hawthorn, spearmint, elder flowers, hops or lime flowers 2 times a day for a week. You can also mix together one or more of these infusions.

Decoction
Have a decoction of the roots of valerian. This is good but can become a habit.

Application
For a good night sleep, have a herbal bath with chamomile flowers, two drops of chamomile oil, lime blossom flowers, pre-soaked valerian roots or lemon balm leaves.

Asana Routine (Curative)
• Sarvangasana [Shoulderstand]
• Supta Vajrasana [Backward Bend]
• Paschimottanasana [Backstretch]
• Utthanasana [Squat]
• Padanguli Shakti Vikasaka [Dancers 3]
• Nadi Shodana Pranayama [Alternate Nostril Breathing]
• Shanmuki Mudra [Psychic Source Seal]

Asana Routine (General)
• Yoga Anandasana [Animal Relaxation Pose]
• Paschimottanasana [Backstretch]
• Padanguli Shakti Vikasaka [Dancers 3]
• Padahastasana [Legclasp]
• Bhujangasana [Cobra Pose]
• Shalabasana [Locust Pose]
• Sarvangasana [Shoulderstand]
• Supta Vajrasana [Backward Bend]
• Shavasana [Relaxation]
• Bumi Pada Mastakasana [Headstand Modified]
• Matsya Kridasana [Flapping Fish Pose]
• Nadi Shodana Pranayama [Alternate Nostril Breathing]
• Shanmuki Mudra [Psychic Source Seal]
• Deep Relaxation
• Trataka [Candle Concentration]
• Meditation

For insomnia that results from a nervous problem, refer to Asanas under anxiety.

MEMORY/CONCENTRATION
To control emotions and for clearer thoughts, include tryptophan in the diet. Tyrosine helps as well and is found in milk, ghee, yoghurt, raisins, cheese and egg yolk. Nutrients for the brain are found in dried prunes and walnuts, almonds, asafoetida, cabbages, Indian corn or corn silk, dates, olives, onions, parsley, plums, pomegranates, raisins and tomatoes. Include these in the daily diet. Avoid food wrapped in aluminium or cooked in aluminium utensils as aluminium is a destroyer of nerve cells.

Recipes
The following measures help improve memory and concentration:
• Drink almond milk once a week.
• Have raisins and almonds in combination with milk, apples, cashew nuts, cow peas and ghee. Have this in moderation regularly.
• Soak raisins in water overnight. Drink the water and eat the raisins before breakfast.

Infusion
Have a glass of the infusion of basil leaves with honey once daily. This gradually improves the power of retention.

Asana Routine
• Inverted Asanas
• Pranayama
• Nadi Shodahana Pranayama
• Bhastika Pranayama
• Ujjayi Pranayama
• All Mudras including Hasta Mudras
• Trataka
• Meditation
For improving mental development, try out the following:
• Buddhi Tatha Dharti Vikasaka [Mind and Will Power Breathing]
• Smarana [Memory Breathing]

The ideas, suggestions, herbal remedies and diet contained in this book are not intended as a substitue for consulting with your doctor. All matters regarding your health require medical supervision.

- Medha Pranayama [Intellect Breathing]
- Shambava Mudra [Vision and Concentration Seal]

MENINGITIS

This is the inflammation of the membranes that cover the brain and spinal cord and is more common among children. It can develop secondarily to infections like tuberculosis, fungous infections or even when there is no apparent infection. If it is due to infections like tuberculosis, symptoms are irritability, drowsiness, headaches, loss of appetite, vomiting and fever. The vision and hearing can also be affected. In fungous infection, the same symptoms appear but suddenly and progress rapidly with dizziness, vomiting, and stiffness in the neck.

Apart from taking medicinal drugs, stick to a diet that is low in cholesterol with no fat. The diet must be high in vegetable protein as well as include milk and eggs.

MIGRAINE

This is a severe, recurrent headache. There is sudden constriction and subsequent relaxation of the blood vessels of the brain, resulting in a disorderly supply of blood and oxygen to the brain. It afflicts one side of the head. Throbbing or piercing pain is experienced. When the adrenal hormone production is low, blood vessels are more prone to dilation. Thus, a migraine headache is generally triggered in the evening and rarely in the morning. Stress, chemical stimuli, change in atmospheric pressure, hormonal imbalance and diet can contribute to the problem.

Among women, an attack mostly occurs during hormonal changes. Women suffer more than men mainly due to these hormonal changes. Chemicals found in food, pollution and constipation are other contributory factors. Migraine is also one of the most common side effects of using contraceptive pills. Sometimes, it is accompanied by blurred vision, dizziness, diarrhoea, nausea and intolerance to light and sound, distortions of the cognitive functions, disturbed sleep and mood swings. During pregnancy, women do not generally get migraine.

Include basil, cabbages, chamomile flowers, cucumbers, cumin, fennel, goldenseal roots, honey, lemon balm, primrose, radishes or tomatoes in the daily diet. Fish oil brings about relief. Avoid food that can trigger migraine, such as greasy food like cheese, chocolates and chicken liver. Also, avoid caffeine, yeast, food additives and an excess of bananas, figs and citrus fruit. In addition, avoid fasting, and do not stay hungry for long periods of time.

Recipes

Refer to recipes given under headaches.

Infusions

- If the migraine is associated with nausea, have a glass of the infusion of aniseed after meals.
- Have a glass of the infusion of peppermint leaves or spinach 2 times a day for a week.
- Have an infusion of rose petals once a day.

Refer also to recipe given under nervous disorders.

Applications

- Apply a cold compress to the forehead and nape alternatively for relief.
- Apply lavender, peppermint, borneol or thyme oil to the forehead and temples in a circular motion for relief. If the headache is associated with neuralgia, avoid borneol.
- Apply to the forehead and temples lime juice mixed together with cinnamon powder, ginger paste in water, edible camphor mixed together with milk or calamus and ginger ground in buttermilk for relief.
- Apply a thin layer of the paste of mustard seeds to the abdomen or use it in foot bath. At an early stage of the migraine, this gives relief by drawing the blood away from the head.
- Make a paste from the mixture of camphor, cardamom seeds powder and cinnamon in sesame seed oil. Apply this to the temples.

For Asanas to treat migraine, refer to those under anxiety and headaches.

MULTIPLE SCLEROSIS

This is a slow progressive disease involving the central nervous system. Difficulty in talking, double vision, tremors, lack of coordination are some common symptoms.

Manganese is useful in preventing multiple sclerosis. Evening primrose oil, which is rich in polyunsaturated fats, helps rebuild the nerve sheaths. Avoid white bread and other white flour products, as well as food wrapped in aluminium or cooked in aluminium utensils.

Asanas are beneficial, if not more beneficial than physiotherapy to restore normalcy and to prevent deformity of the weakened parts.

Recipes

- Add a teaspoon of vinegar to a teaspoon of honey. Mix well. Have this 2 times a day for tremors.
- Take 2 drops of evening primrose oil in half a glass of warm water once a day.
- Soak a tablespoon of raisins in a glass of water overnight. Drink the water and eat the raisins in the morning.
- Buckwheat, which is rich in manganese, helps clear muscle jerks, tremors and lack of coordination. Take 2 tablespoons of this with every meal.

Infusion

Have 3 cups of the infusion of mistletoe leaves for the first 6 weeks, then reduce it to 2 cups a day. This is also good for paralysis, particularly after a stroke.

Applications

- Use thyme oil and St. John's wort oil to massage the affected area.
- Sleep on a pillow filled with fern leaves (without the stems).
- Comfrey leaves tone up paralysed areas. Use them as poultice or in the bath. Soak the leaves of comfrey in hot water for 20 minutes. Wrap the warm leaves in a towel, and apply to the affected region.
- Mix together the essential oils of chamomile flowers, basil leaves and thyme in equal proportions. Add 1,000 parts almond oil as base oil. Mix well. Use this to massage the affected area.

For Asanas, refer to those under the Pawanamuktasana and Shakti Vikasaka group.

NAUSEA

This is the condition of feeling sick accompanied by the impulse to vomit. There are many causes. For instance, increased pressure inside the skull, a head injury, brain tumour or haemorrhage, may affect the blood supply to the area of the brain that corresponds to vomiting, resulting in nausea.

For nausea with vomiting, include the following in the daily diet: asparagus, barley, coconuts, fennel, grapes, grapefruit, green pepper, kidney beans, lemon balm, lavender, malt, mushrooms (button), nutmeg, orange peel, black pepper, peppermint, pineapples, string beans or sugar cane. If nausea is accompanied by the vomiting of blood, include saffron strands, radishes or vinegar in the daily diet.

Recipes (General Nausea)

- Whenever you feel nauseous, chew a few cardamom seeds.
- Soak a tablespoon of raisins in a glass of water overnight. Drink the water and eat the raisins in the morning.

For relief from vomiting:

- Add 2 drops of clove oil to a glass of water. Drink this to control vomiting.
- Cook grapefruit and fresh ginger together. Eat it with rice.
- Take a teaspoonful of sugar with two drops of lavender oil. Alternatively, you can drink the decoction of lavender leaves with a little sugar for relief.
- Boil a piece of ginger with a quarter teaspoon of black pepper powder in 3 cups of water until the volume of water reduces to a third of the original. Drink this 3 times a day for relief from vomiting that results from an upset stomach.
- Pour a glass of water into a pot. Add about 1 teaspoonful of caraway seeds, a quarter spoonful of cinnamon and a quarter spoonful of dried ginger powder to the water. Bring it to the boil. Add a dash of salt. Drink this as a soup.

Juice (General Nausea)

- Take a teaspoon of the grated rind of a lemon or take a teaspoon of lemon juice with ice.
- Take 2 tablespoons of the fresh juice of curry leaves with lemon juice once a day.
- Take 2 tablespoons of the juice of asparagus before breakfast.
- Take a tablespoon of bitter orange juice 2 times a day.

For relief from vomiting:
Add 2 teaspoons of fresh ginger juice to a glass of fresh orange juice and drink.

Infusions (General Nausea)

- For sickness associated with travel, have an infusion of basil leaves before the journey.
- Whenever you feel nauseous, have a cup of the infusion of aniseed, lemon balm (unsweetened), caraway seeds, ginger, clove flower buds, cinnamon bark or peppermint (unsweetened).

For relief from vomiting:
Have the infusions of any of the following: Two tablespoons of the infusion of dried basil leaves with honey 3 times a day after meals; a glass of the infusion of cinnamon bark 3 times a day to relieve vomiting due to acids in the stomach; or a glass of the infusion of raspberries 2 times a day.

Inhalation (General Nausea)

Cut a lemon or lime in half and inhale.

NERVES

Nerves are insulated within tubes of a greasy material called myelin. Defects in myelin can cause many nervous system disorders.

Include in the daily diet food that are calmative, antidepressant, nervine and sedative. Apple has a high phosphorus content, which assists in rebuilding lecithin in the brain and spinal cord and is, thus, a good nerve food. Lime helps treat brain fever, mental problems caused by high pressure in the brain and nerve problems. St. John's wort is an excellent remedy for spinal and nervous problems, such as neuralgia, sciatica and fibrositis. Food beneficial for the nerves are allspice, almonds, blackberries, carrots, celery, cinnamon, cumin, dates, grapes, hawthorn, jasmine, lavender, oats, onions, bitter oranges, pumpkins, raisins, rosemary and thyme.

Avoid food wrapped in aluminium or cooked in aluminium utensils. Aluminium is believed to be responsible for destroying nerve cells. Avoid heaty tropical fruit, such as durians, jackfruit, mangosteen, rambutans and longans, as well as angelica, borage, camphor and saffron in excess.

Recipes

- To prevent spasmodic nervous conditions, season food with asafoetida.
- Simmer in a glass of water a clove of garlic with salt and black pepper to taste until it is cooked. Crush the garlic in egg white. Cook this and eat it 2 times a day with meals.

Infusions

- Have a glass of the infusion of lemon balm 2 times a day for a month.
- Have a glass of the infusion of peppermint leaves 2 times a day for a week.
- Add honey to the infusion of red rose petals. Drink this once a day.
- Have an infusion or decoction of the roots of drumstick or herb marjoram 3 times a day.
- For children, give them 2 teaspoons of the infusion of lime flowers (or Roman Chamomile or German Chamomile) with honey 3 times a day.

For other nerve problems:

- Have a cup of the infusion of olive leaves. This has a tranquillising effect on the nerves and aids in sleep.
- Make an infusion of dried German chamomile flowers with boiling water. Take 3 tablespoons of this nerve tonic 3 times a day.

Asana Routine

For nerve problems:

- All Bandhas

- Nadi Shodhana Pranayama [Alternate Nostril Breathing]
- Bhastika Pranayama [Dynamic Breathing Standing]
- Yoga Mudra
- Shanti Mudra [Invocation of Peace Seal]
- Vipareeta Karani Mudra [Shoulderstand Variation]
- Maha Mudra [Great Seal]
- Shanmuki Mudra [Psychic Source Seal]

NERVOUS TENSION

Recipe

Add 2 drops of the extract of oats to a glass of cold water. Mix well. Have this 2 times a day.

Infusions

- Have a glass of the infusion of 1 part basil leaves and 2 parts sage leaves 3 times a day after meals.
- Have a glass of the infusion of angelica roots, vervain, lemon balm sweetened with honey, hops, chamomile flowers or evening primrose 3 times a day.

Decoction

Take 2 tablespoons of the decoction of celery seeds 3 times a day.

Bath

- Use angelica roots or pre-soaked valerian roots in the bath.
- Add 4 teaspoons of cut lemon balm leaves to water and bring it to the boil. Mix it with warm water in the bathtub. Soak yourself in the bath for 30 minutes.

Asana Routine

- All Pawanamuktasana [Energy Releasing Exercises]
- Matsya Kridasana [Flapping Fish Pose]
- Chakrasana [Back Pushup]

Avoid all forward bending Asanas.

NEURALGIA

More common among women, this is more a symptom than a disease. Neuralgia is a series of attacks of acute pain from a particular nerve. The pain feels like a lightning stab in the face or neck and lasts for a few seconds. The usual types of neuralgia are trigeminal neuralgia, glossopharyngeal neuralgia and causalgia. A sensory nerve, the trigeminal nerve, has three branches. One towards the skin of the forehead and eyes, one towards the skin of the sides of the face between the eye and mouth, the third towards the skin of the jaw and lower lips. Touching, washing, exposure to cold and even talking can trigger the attack.

The right diet, Yogasanas and massage, help deal with this problem. Avoid alcohol, narcotic painkillers, cold drinks, meat and fried foods, prawns and other types of seafood, as well as herbs like camphor and goldenseal roots.

Recipe

Dry-fry sword beans until they turn brown. Grind them into powder. Take 4 grams of this powder with rice wine 3 times a day for relief from intercostal neuralgia associated with headaches.

Infusion

Take 3 tablespoons of the infusion of dried German chamomile flowers, passion flowers, St. John's wort, basil leaves, fennel seeds, sarsaparilla or ajowan 3 times a day.

Applications

- Apply a poultice made of fenugreek seeds to the affected area for relief from pain.
- Massage with the oil made from chamomile flowers, basil and thyme, with wheatgerm oil as the base.
- Apply either a decoction or a poultice of geranium as a facial mask for facial neuralgia.
- Apply a liniment made by mixing together rosemary, lavender flowers and St. John's wort oil to ease the pain.
- Crush allspice leaves. Add them to water to make a paste. Apply this to the affected region for 30 minutes 3 times a day.
- Grind the seeds or bark of avocados. Mix them with either diluted rosemary or St. John's wort oil. Apply the paste to the affected region 2 times a day.

- Mix mustard seeds powder with water to make a paste. Apply a very thin coat to the affected area. Do not apply too much of the paste as it can cause irritation and inflammation. The area feels warm. Leave the paste on for a few minutes and then clean the area. For sensitive skin, mix with rye flour.

Bath
Use crushed chestnuts in the bath. Alternatively, you can also use the decoction of crushed chestnuts in the bath.

Asana Routine
All Asanas and Bandhas , as well as those below tone the nerves:

- Nadi Shodhana Pranayama [Alternate Nostril Breathing]
- Bhastika Pranayama [Dynamic Breathing]
- Yoga Mudra
- Shanti Mudra [Invocation of Peace Seal]
- Maha Mudra [Great Seal]
- Shanmuki Mudra [Psychic Source Seal]

Refer also to the relaxation group.

PARALYSIS
Temporary paralysis or polyneuritis results from a virus and causes the white blood cells to attack the nerve tissues. Obstruction or bleeding in the brain as a result of high blood pressure or blood stickiness are some causes. Blood clots from either the heart or in the major blood vessels of the neck can also cause obstruction. There may be a sudden weakness or numbness in the arms or legs or on one side of the face.

For paralysis, spasmodic nerves and other nerve problems, the best cure is mind power. This can be done through strong visualisation and positive thinking. Create a mental approach to communicate with the inner mind by analysing and associating yourself with the positive way of life. Once the inner mind is told of the necessary steps to take to relieve the problem, the mind will find its own way and make the body react accordingly. For example, if there is some form of obstruction, visualise a healing finger gently removing it. As far as diet is concerned, have food rich in salicylates on a regular basis.

For partial paralysis, one of the most important food supplements is soya beans. Soya beans contain lecithin, an unsaturated fatty acid. This prevents brain clots, as well as the paralysis of the hands, arms and legs.

Potassium is important for the transmission of nerve impulses. It also helps in the intake of nutrients and in the removal of waste from cells. Aspirin reduces blood stickiness. Include in the daily diet mistletoe leaves, comfrey, oat straw, cherries, thyme, St. John's wort, basil and chamomile flowers. Avoid food wrapped in aluminium or cooked in aluminium utensils. Also avoid all types of fatty foods as well as food that may cause obstruction in the flow of blood.

Recipes
- Banana, rich in potassium, is very beneficial. Eat at least 3 to 5 ripe bananas once a day.
- Add 45 grams of garlic to 3 grams of fried asafoetida, rock salt, hippali, black pepper, ginger and cumin seeds. Mix them well to make a paste. Have 5 grams of this mixture 2 times a day for 84 days.

For partial paralysis:
- Take 2 tablespoons of soya bean lecithin at breakfast daily. This is very effective, especially when taken together with vitamin B complex, vitamin A and vitamin C.
- Use 2 tablespoons of soya oil or safflower oil as salad dressing with 4 tablespoons of wheatgerm. Have this once a day. You can mix the oils together for a better effect.

For temporary paralysis:
Take 1 teaspoon of sunflower oil 3 times a day to improve temporary paralysis.

Infusion
Refer to the recipes given under stroke (see Chapter 15). Also refer to recipe under nervous disorder.

Applications
- Sleep on a pillow filled with fern leaves (without the stems).

- Boil 500 grams of oat straw in 4 litres of water. Add this to the water in the bath. Soak yourself in it for 20 minutes.
- Make a comfrey leaf poultice to tone up the paralysed areas. Pour hot water on the leaves. Place the leaves on a towel, and apply this to the affected area. Alternatively, you can have a bath with comfrey leaves.
- Use thyme oil to massage (Even thyme oil mixed with an equal proportion of St. John's wort oil with a base oil can be used). Alternatively, you can use the oils of chamomile flowers, thyme and basil mixed together in equal quantities, with a base oil. The effect of the healing, in this case, may be slow.

PARKINSON'S DISEASE

This is a chronic, progressive disorder of the nerves. The slowing down of movements, rigidity, involuntary tremors, particularly in the arms, and weakness in the arms are common symptoms. The muscles of the face become immobile, and it becomes difficult for the eyes to blink. In advanced cases, saliva may drool out of the mouth. While walking, the person may lean forward and take short, shuffling, confused steps. The arms become flexed with repeated tremors at the tips of the fingers.

Have a balanced diet, and perform Asanas to activate the nerves. At the early stage, treat this disorder by massaging the affected areas using *Narayaneeya Tailam* or basil oil and chamomile oil mixed together with almond oil as the base oil.

PERSPIRATION

As far as diet is concerned, asparagus and cinnamon induce perspiration, thereby reducing the intensity of a fever. Fresh peach prevents excessive perspiration.

Infusion

To promote perspiration, have a glass of the hot infusion of ginger, marjoram, thyme or lemon with honey.

SHINGLES

This is a virus infection involving the nerves. (It is the same virus as in chicken pox.) Tiny blisters filled with water develop with a red base. They dry up and take on a crust-like appearance after a week or two. Usually, one side of the body is affected.

Recipes

- Take a teaspoon of safflower tincture 3 times a day.
- Add half a teaspoon of desiccated liver to half a cup of milk. Add 2 tablespoons of molasses. Let it stand for a while. When the liver grains become soft, drink the mixture. This helps relieve pain.
- Dissolve some powder of the roots of goldenseal in water. Apply this to the affected area several times a day for 2 weeks. In addition, have the infusion of goldenseal roots with hot water before meals. Take only a small quantity of the herb. If the herb is in powder form, take only a teaspoonful of it once a day.

Applications

- Apply either a decoction or a poultice of geranium as a facial mask.
- Apply a hot compress or use the decoction of chamomile flowers in the bath.
- Apply vitamin E oil liberally. Also take vitamin B and vitamin E supplements daily.

STRESS

In general, this is an emotional disturbance. At the onset of stress, the pituitary secretes the hormones ACTH and STH. These hormones are carried to two small glands above the kidneys, the adrenal glands, and cause the outside of these glands, the cortex, to produce cortisone. The centre portion produces adrenaline. These prepare the body to deal with emergencies. Proteins are at first drawn from the thymus and lymph glands and are broken down to form sugar for energy. The blood sugar soars and the remaining sugar is stored in the liver as glycogen. The blood pressure increases, minerals are drawn from the bones, fat is mobilised and salt is retained and so on. There will be a chain reaction like this. If the stress continues, the body repairs itself by rebuilding with the raw materials at hand.

When the diet is adequate, stress can be tolerated. Should the diet be inadequate, disease develops. To regain health, there should be an adequate intake of food. If stress prolongs after the thymus and lymph proteins are exhausted, proteins from the blood plasma, liver and kidneys are used. Ulcers are produced not just because of the excess secretion of hydrochloric acid but also because the protein from the stomach walls has been used up. This literally eats away the lining of the walls.

Pantothenic acid is essential to every cell in the body. A lack of it often prevents the normal production of cortisone. The deficiency is known as adrenal exhaustion.

Disease itself is sometimes nothing more than the body's reaction to stress. An adrenal hormone desoxcortisone (DOC) counterbalances the effect of cortisone. It helps to fight the infections, protects the body by setting off inflammation around bacteria and toxic substances, and prevents the inflammation from spreading. This hormone causes blood and tissue fluid to be drawn to a damaged area. White blood cells are drawn in, and although swelling, pain, and fever result, the rest of the body is protected. The reaction to stress becomes a disease itself. Examples of such diseases are arthritis, bursitis, colitis, nephritis and allergic reactions. If too little cortisone is produced and DOC is not held in check, the inflammation goes out of hand. On the other hand, too little DOC can be produced, and if cortisone is given as medication, the body becomes susceptible to infections, inflammations, and damage from toxic substances.

Another adrenal hormone, aldosterone, holds salt (sodium) and water in the body, thus preventing dehydration. If it is produced in excess, too much water may be retained such that the hands, ankles, and eyes become puffy. Excess potassium will be lost in the urine. Such a condition can cause high blood pressure and may become a major problem with kidney and heart diseases. Restricting the salt intake at such stages causes aldosterone to be excreted and prevents loss of potassium. The adrenal glands, exhausted from prolonged stress, are unable to produce enough aldosterone. As a result of excess salt and water loss, the blood pressure usually falls and potassium is withdrawn from the walls, in which case sodium is required. Should ACTH or cortisone be given, the doctor carefully weighs in on the advantages and disadvantages. These decrease natural hormone production, inhibit the synthesis of antibodies and white blood cells to fight infection and increase the need for every body's requirement, as well as urinary losses of amino acids, calcium, phosphorus, potassium, vitamin A, vitamin C and all types of vitamin B.

People who are given ACTH or cortisone often develop stomach ulcers, severe spontaneous bruising, nose bleeding, and haemorrhages, and if the sugar formed is not used for energy, it is changed to fat, which partly accounts for the gain in weight. To meet the demands of stress, the starting point is to obtain all the nutrients to produce sufficient pituitary and adrenal hormones. Large quantities of proteins, pantothenic acid, vitamin C should be taken. Vitamin B2 (essential for the synthesis of adrenal hormones), taken together with vitamin B6, increases the benefits. Both must be taken in equal quantities. In the acute stages, as much as 130 mg of protein, 500 mg of vitamin C, 100 mg of pantothenic acid and 2 mg of vitamin B2 and vitamin B6 in fortified milk are to be taken once every 2 hours. When the symptoms decrease, the dosage should be reduced. For mild cases take half of the above 6 times a day.

Without exception, every drug is toxic to some extent. Drugs produce dietary deficiencies by using nutrients, increasing their excretion or chemically taking their place. Aspirin — a simple and the least toxic of all drugs — interferes with digestion, formation of starch, production of tissue proteins and the ability of the cells to absorb sugar, slows down clotting, increases the need for oxygen and nutrients, and activates the urinary losses of calcium, potassium, vitamin C and vitamin B.

Include the following in the daily diet: liver, especially pork liver, brewer's yeast, wheatgerm, kidneys, soya flour, cereals, vitamins A, D and E. The pulp of green leafy vegetables is also beneficial. Research shows that people who are ill should take as much of these types of food as possible.

Perform Asanas involving breathing or Pranayama as well as meditation regularly. Refer to the Anxiety Group and Relaxation Group.

Infusion

Have a cup of the infusion of lemon balm, lavender flowers, lime blossoms or chamomile flowers 3 times a day to calm the mind, thereby reducing the effects caused by stress.

Application

Massage the forehead and temples with the oils of chamomile flowers, basil and thyme mixed together in equal proportions, with almond oil as the base oil.

TINGLING PALMS

People on high blood pressure medication will normally shake and tremble. Potassium and Vitamin B6 in the right proportion reduce the shaking. Trembling is a sign that the person is a step towards Parkinson's Disease. During pregnancy, the mother may get tingling palms. This normally disappears after childbirth.

Recipe

Mix together 2 tablespoons of soya bean lecithin, 2 teaspoons of soya bean oil or olive oil with tomato juice and 2 teaspoons of wheatgerm. Have the mixture with every meal. In addition, take a recommended dosage of vitamin B complex, vitamin A and vitamin C. This is good for tremors, stroke, blood clots due to hardening of the arteries and general heart problems.

VERTIGO

Avoid food wrapped in aluminium or cooked in aluminium utensils. Shashankasana and Trataka, along with all balancing postures, are beneficial.

21

The Skeleto-Muscular System
∾

The bones and joints in our body are designed to withstand a great deal of stress. There are many diseases (there are more than seventy-five diseases of the joints alone) that affect the parts related to the bones and joints, such as the muscles, tendons and ligaments. Some of them are the result of congenital defects while others are caused by wear and tear over the years. Causes of skeletal birth defects may be hereditary. If the expectant mother is exposed to radiation, X-rays, to disease or had indulged in taking drugs during the course of the pregnancy, the child can turn out "defective". Some of the common skeletal birth defects are an extra rib, toe or finger, or missing ribs, a fused spine, etc.

Note that all the nutritional therapies mentioned in this chapter may sometimes not be suitable for everyone. In a few cases, the recommended food may actually trigger arthritic conditions. It must be stressed that each individual responds in a unique way to each therapy. It is up to the individual to persevere until he or she hits upon a diet that offers the best relief.

JOINT DISEASES

ARTHRITIS

This is the inflammation of the joints and is probably the most common disabling disease. It affects people of all ages and is particularly common among those living in temperate climates. It starts with various problems and most of them are related either directly or indirectly to a faulty diet. Fundamentally, arthritis is caused by overloading the body with poison-toxemia. The main culprit is junk food. Excessive consumption of refined sugar, white flour, cereals, alcohol, beef and pork result in the production of too much uric acid. Consuming such types of food over a long period of time can bring about certain allergic reactions and, thus, poison the normal functioning of the body. Stress and strain due to physical exertion and hormonal imbalance are other factors.

Overcooking vegetables destroys the alkaline mineral salts essential to neutralising excess acid in the system. The uric acid is carried around in the blood until it eventually deposits itself between the joints, on the bones or in the muscles. When the uric acid collects in the joints a stabbing pain is felt, and the joints can become locked. In some cases, the joint makes a grating sound (creptis) as it moves on the hard acid deposits. The latter can also wear off the synovial membrane, and very often, the actual joints themselves are worn out. When this happens, the situation cannot be reversed.

If arthritis forms in the spine, the whole body will be affected. If it forms in the cervical column, headaches, migraine, nervousness, insomnia, high blood pressure, neuralgia, vertigo, earache, eye problems, pimples, acne, a stiff neck, pain in the upper arm and a defective thyroid condition will result.

If arthritis affects the thoracic region, chest pains, a defective heart condition, bronchitis, pleurisy and pains, especially in the lower arms and hands will result.

If it affects the lumbar region, constipation, ruptures, hernia, appendicitis, varicose veins, menstrual problems and particularly knee pains, sciatica, lumbago and backache will appear.

Note: When arthritis affects a joint, it is possible for other joints to be similarly affected, although this may initially go unnoticed.

Care and Preventive Measures

There are various medications that control inflammations and joint damage. Unfortunately, the side effects of these medications can cause new problems. With a properly balanced diet containing the required nutrients, as well as well-planned exercises and rest, it is possible to burn up the excess acid, dissolve the deposits, alleviate the pain and halt further damage.

A proper diet (see below) is necessary to maintain the health of the skeletal system. The body's retention of the nutrients for building bones, particularly the minerals phosphorus and calcium depend upon vitamin D. In addition, other essential minerals are to be supplied in sufficient quantities. However, it is not enough to simply adhere to the chosen diet. The joints must also be exercised. While moving the joints is painful, not moving the joints destroys them. Incorrect movement damages them, while intelligent movement of the joints heals.

Whenever acid is produced in the body, sodium is withdrawn from the stomach and then from the joints to neutralise the acid. When sodium is removed from the joints, calcium is deposited and uric acid builds up. If, however, enough sodium is present in the joints, there will be little chance for the waste acids to accumulate. Sodium, besides being a neutraliser, also helps in the elasticity and limberness of joints.

Those suffering from arthritis, besides drinking lots of water, should include at least a few of the following in their daily diets.

Alfalfa, sarsaparilla and **black currants** — rich in iron and other nutrients — prevent anaemia.

Amino acids, like phenylalanine, are not produced by the body. They are available only as supplements or from a proper diet. They serve to protect the pain relievers or endorphines of the body and are found in dried non-fat milk, peanuts, cheddar cheese, turkey, chicken, walnut, oatmeal, shredded wheat, cod fish, peas, corn or corn silk and lima beans.

Black molasses, made from unsulphured cane sugar, is beneficial for the cells. It is rich in nutrients, potassium, pantothenic acid and inositol. In addition, it contains iron, copper, magnesium and B vitamins.

Cherry is one of the best cleansing agents and helps to eliminate acids. It also helps to smoothen out deformities and bumps of the joints.

Cider vinegar — rich in calcium, vitamin D, vitamin A and vitamin C — has the ability to dissolve acid deposits, which can then be easily eliminated through the kidneys.

Cod liver oil and **bone meal** help combat arthritis as they control further deposits of calcium.

Evening primrose oil, when taken with vitamin C, vitamin B6, vitamin B3, zinc and fish oil, helps to relieve the arthritic condition.

Garlic, especially fresh garlic, is well-known as a cure for any inflammation of the lining of the joints as it promotes circulation.

Honey is a natural antibiotic. It contains pollen, which is rich in vitamin C, calcium, copper, silica, iron, magnesium, chlorine, potassium, sulphur, phosphorus, sodium, manganese, nitrogen and dextrine. The actual composition of pollen depends on the types of flowers and the nature of the soil.

Magnesium is an element that soothes and prevents pain. It is found in brewer's yeast, wheat bran, wheatgerm, green leafy vegetables, especially beet green, nuts, brown rice and soya beans.

Natural sodium is best found in plants grown in sunlight and fruit and vegetables ripened by sunlight. Cabbage, celery, cottage cheese, goat's milk, strawberry juice and whey water are good sources of sodium. The mineral is also found in apples, asparagus, brussels sprouts, carrots, cauliflower, dried prunes, dried figs, horseradish, lettuce, okra, onions, potato peels, squashes and sweet almonds.

Shave grass and buchu leaf help eliminate uric acid.

Soya lecithin helps dissolve calcium deposits.

Tryptophan prevents pain. It is found in milk and peanuts.

Zinc helps relieve joint tenderness. It is found in almond nuts, carrots, garlic, ginger, oats, parsley, peanuts, potato skins, raw milk, rye, soya lecithin, split peas and whole wheat. Zinc, together with vitamin C, has an anti-inflammatory effect on the body.

In addition to the above, have fresh fruit and vegetables that are organically grown, yoghurt, apples, bananas, grapes, wheat, rye, grapefruit, sesame seeds, millet, raisins, raw sunflower seeds, cottage cheese, plenty of wholemeal cereals and grilled or steamed fish. Chew 2 cloves of garlic daily.

Avoid an animal protein diet. Also avoid alcohol, baking soda, string beans, pasteurised milk; prawns, red meat, refined flour and its products, excess salt, saturated fats, soda pop, tomatoes, white sugar and white bread. These include fried foods, processed foods, packed foods, canned foods, including soft drinks, sugar products, chemical and preservative-rich foods, coffee, tea and frozen fruit.

Caution

- Some people develop an intolerance to wheat, which results in an irritable bowel problem.
- Cider vinegar is not suitable for people suffering from acute ulcers or for those with kidney stones.
- Phenylalanine should not be taken by children under fourteen years of age or by pregnant or breastfeeding women.
- Vitamin C, when taken in high doses, increases the excretion of uric acid but can cause kidney stones or precipitate gout. Many people think that taking large doses of vitamin C is good, but they are unaware that there is a limit on how much can be consumed, and the limit is less than 4 grams a day. Beyond this limit, it can cause kidney stones or precipitate gout. There are only two instances when a heavy dosage of vitamin C is recommended — for leukaemia and the prevention of miscarriages. If an individual has no evidence of

kidney damage or stones, then the recommended limit for vitamin C is around 500 milligrams to 1,000 milligrams.

- Patients with arthritis due to allergic reactions should avoid food that contains solanine, which is known to trigger arthritic conditions. Solanine can destroy enzymes, cause stiffness of the joints and restrict muscle movement. It is found in tomatoes, potatoes, cucumbers, eggplant and red peppers.

THE THREE STEPS

(i) Stick to a proper diet, which eliminates the poison causing irritation in the joints, muscles and nerves.

(ii) Perform simple Asanas that activate the affected region. This, in turn, increases the circulation of blood and provides an abundant supply of oxygen to rejuvenate the body. It is also the best way to relax.

(iii) The third step is a combination of the first two. Maintain the health of the affected region and prevent it from becoming infected or inflamed again by controlling the diet and performing proper Asanas.

Yoga's multifaceted approach to health aids in the internal healing process and creates the healing power, which develops a "positive state of mind".

Juice

- Take a tablespoon of lemon juice mixed with an equal quantity of honey 2 times a day.
- Take half a teaspoon of the juice of basil leaves mixed with half a teaspoon of raw turmeric juice once a day after meals.

Infusions

- Have a cup of the infusion of horsetail half an hour before breakfast and half an hour before dinner. Besides this, drink half a cup of tea made of stinging nettle to which a tablespoon of Swedish bitter has been added 3 times a day.
- Have a glass of the infusion of the fresh shoots of stinging nettle or celery seeds or dandelion roots once a day.

Bath

- Wash with the decoction of sarsaparilla after a shower.
- Use the decoction of juniper berries or thyme leaves in the bath.
- A bath (do not use boiling water) with baking soda or epsom salts or herbal salts help eliminate acid. Sand walking and massaging the affected region with specific oils have been found to be helpful.

Application

- Apply a paste of calamus roots in water to relieve pain.
- Apply a poultice of cayenne to the affected region once a day.
- Apply a hot compression with the decoction of juniper berries.
- Apply a teaspoon of onion juice mixed together with a teaspoon of mustard oil after a shower.

Asana Routine

Exercise the joints without overstraining yourself. Before doing the exercises, it is better to apply a massage oil or soak the affected region for a few minutes in warm salt water to encourage circulation. Having a positive frame of mind is important. Cultivate this through Yoga relaxation and Asanas, such as the following: Pawanamuktasana, Shakti Vikasaka and Matsya Kridasana. Follow up with a meditation of your choice.

RHEUMATOID ARTHRITIS

This is more like a group of joint troubles. Rheumatoid arthritis is an inflammation of the joint membranes, which undergo a morphological change and affect all the joints. When the synovial membranes and connecting tissues get inflamed, swelling results. While the joint cartilage thins, the joint fluid increases in the area. There will be loss of calcium from the bone ends. In severe cases of inflammation, the tendons become short, while the muscles lose their normal balance. This results in deformity. Destruction of the joints, tissues and lymph nodes occurs, and, as a result, certain organs like the heart, kidneys and liver will be affected. People who suffer from shock, injuries and exposure to dampness are easily affected.

Rheumatoid arthritis usually appears in people before they turn forty and is most common among women. The destruction of joints occurs because of infection, malnutrition, maladjustment to life, a disorder of the endocrine glands, viruses and toxins produced by bacteria. It can also be hereditary. Emotional upsets, venereal diseases, tuberculosis, rheumatic fever and psoriasis are associated with this problem.

Food allergy can also be a cause. Some types of food often responsible for rheumatoid arthritis are wheat, oats, eggs, chicken, coffee, tea, yeast-containing foods, beef, pork and milk. People who go on high fibre diets can develop arthritic symptoms. At first, mild fever with fatigue, soreness, and itchiness or stiffness in the joints are experienced. The knees and fingers are affected first, followed by the shoulders, wrists, ankles and elbows. Eventually, every joint may be inflamed. Swollen joints appear red, tender and warm. Later, the joints begin to swell, and there may be an increase in the quantity of joint fluid. When calcium becomes rarefied, the joint cartilage becomes thin. Anaemia, which is caused by using pain relieving medicines, and loss of weight are common effects. Pain and stiffness are felt more in the morning and during cold spells. In children, skin rashes and swelling of the lymph nodes, joints and muscles are observed, along with fatigue.

There is so much individual variation from case to case that it is not easy to give a definite general plan of treatment for rheumatoid arthritis . The most effective medicines often contain the greatest hazards. Cortisone-type of drugs help but generate most undesirable side effects. In the early stage, tissues are destroyed.

Treatments for prevention or reducing the damage and to help prevent the adjoining tissues from shrinking and weakening include proper relaxation, pain relieving massages, therapeutic Asanas, and a well-balanced diet.

No arthritis can be properly managed without a corresponding change in lifestyle.

A well-balanced diet, which includes an adequate amount of protein, calcium and other essential nutrients as a preventive measure against loss of bone tissue, is essential.

Food rich in certain metals, such as selenium, copper, manganese and zinc, is essential, while food rich in salicylates helps relieve pain. Increase the intake of calcium, vitamin D, vitamin A, vitamin C and iron, such as alfalfa, apples, bananas, black soya beans, cherries, cider vinegar, cinnamon, dried figs, fennel, garlic, ginger, grapes, millet, okra, papayas, parsley, prunes, raisins, raw sunflower seeds, rye, sesame seeds, soya lecithin, wheat and yoghurt. Also increase the intake of water.

Avoid an animal protein diet. Also avoid alcohol, baking soda, beans, canned foods, citrus fruit, coffee, monosodium glutamate, oranges, pasteurised milk, prawns, red meat, refined flour products, excess salt, saturated fats, soda pop, tea, tomatoes and white sugar.

Do not eat fruit immediately after meals as the digestive powers for the two are different. Give a break of at least an hour after meals before eating the fruit or have them half an hour before meals.

General Recipe for People with Rheumatoid Arthritis

Breakfast

Unsweetened grapes or prune juice or mixed fruit or bananas with milk. Oats, wheatgerm, muesli, and honey may be added to the juice.

Lunch and Dinner

Fruit juice, mixed green salad with olive oil and cider vinegar dressing and recommended vegetables with milk. Non-vegetarians can have lightly sauteed fish or traditionally reared chicken without the skin and brewer's yeast.

Recipes

- Take 2 tablespoons of cod liver oil with milk before going to bed every night.
- Take a tablespoon of pure sea water daily. This is available in health shops.
- Peel potatoes and simmer peel for 20 minutes in water. Strain. Drink at least 3–5 glasses of the potato peel broth.
- Boil a piece of cinnamon stick or twig with ginger in 2 glasses of water until water is reduced to half its original volume. Drink a cup of this 3 times daily.
- For arthritic conditions involving the back and legs, have a banana with brewer's yeast, wheatgerm and avocado.

- For shoulder and knee conditions, take the maximum dosage allowed for vitamin E and calcium.

To get rid of creaking joints, take a tablespoon of cider vinegar in a glass of warm water with honey just before meals 3 times a day.

To reduce swelling of the joints:
- Take cod liver oil 3 times a day and gradually decrease the dosage to once a day.
- Have 2 dried figs or a glass of the infusion of leaves of the fig plant 2 times a day before meals.
- Cut a lemongrass stem and leaves into small pieces, put them into a thermos flask and pour in boiling water. Keep the flask closed. Drink this as hot tea 3 times a day.
- Place a few slit okra (good for arthritis and rheumatism) on rice that has just been cooked. The okra get steam-cooked this way. Have them with any recommended spice daily.

Infusion
For arthritis in the back, have a glass of the infusion of alfalfa leaves or sarsaparilla.

Baths
- Mud baths to the affected joints can restore movement.
- Have a warm herbal bath once every 2 days with herbs like chamomile flowers, juniper berries, dock, peppermint, oat straw, horsetail, red clover, alfalfa leaves, fennel seeds or rose hip on their own or in combination.

Application
Apply a cabbage leaf that has been warmed on a hot plate or wok to the swollen area. Wrap it with a towel.

OSTEOARTHRITIS
This is the breakdown of the cartilage and other joint tissues. The smooth layer of the shiny cartilage, which covers the joints, degenerates, resulting in uneven wear and tear. While there will be degeneration in some parts of the joints, there will be an overproduction of bony tissue in other parts. The overproduction is characteristic of osteoarthritis. The disease mostly affects women and while it is most commonly affects the hip joints, it can also affect the other joints.

Some people develop osteoarthritis due to a food allergy. This can go undetected. Another cause is obesity. An overweight person suffering from osteoarthritis should try to reduce his or her weight by avoiding fatty and protein-rich foods. Impaired circulation and exercises of the wrong type or no exercises at all are other causes. Nutritional imbalance, hormonal imbalance during menopause, hyperthyroidism, diabetes, vitamin C deficiency or excess adrenal cortical hormones can also cause osteoarthritis.

Although unpleasant, the disease is not dangerous unless it affects the spine. First, there will be stiffness and then the overgrowth of bones due to pressure on the blood vessels of the lower part of the brain. This leads to dizziness when the head is turned sideways or backwards. Also, weakness may be experienced in the arms and legs. In the hands, it usually affects the bones of the fingers, producing lumps on either side of the furthest joint. The thumb is also affected. Movement causes pain in the joints. In the feet, pain is felt at the base of the big toe. Osteoarthritis rarely occurs in the ankles and shoulders. In the knees, the pain is not severe but knock knees are formed. In the hip, pain is common while walking. In the neck region of the spine, movement is restricted and can cause blackouts or pain in the arms and legs. In the elbows, pain is usually felt while resting and numbness can be felt in the arms. Osteoarthritis in the posterior margins of the vertebrae may press on the sciatic nerve and cause sciatica.

Care and Preventive Measures
Improvement in blood circulation in general and in the joints in particular is the main treatment for osteoarthritis. Increase the intake of calcium and anti-oxidant vitamins A, B, and E but this is best administered by a doctor. Increase in the diet food rich in essential minerals such as iron, zinc, copper, selenium and manganese or their supplements. Do not prescribe them on your own.

People who develop osteoarthritis due to a food allergy should avoid animal fats. Abstain from food that absorbs essential minerals from the body, such as alcohol, tea, coffee, bran and wholemeal bread. Also exclude from the diet the solanaceae group of vegetables, such as tomatoes, eggplant (aubergines), green or red peppers, paprika, potatoes and tobacco. Take care not to injure or over-strain the affected region.

Recipes

- Take a tablespoon of polyunsaturated fatty acids, such as cold pressed linseed oil or gingily oil daily.
- For swelling, drink freshly made lemongrass as often as possible.

The following are suitable for both osteoarthritis and rheumatoid arthritis (a type of arthritis that causes the joints to swell up and become painful):

- Boil a handful of small dried bean pods that are cut in a pot full of water until the volume reduces to a third of the original. Drink it as tea to relieve uric acid accumulation.
- In a food processor, blend several cloves of garlic with honey. Take a teaspoon of the syrup twice a day for relief.

Application

Apply ginger oil and juniper oil mixed together in equal proportion for the pain.

GOUT

This is arthritis with excess uric acid in the blood and urate crystal accumulation in the joints. A metabolic disease, gout usually appears in one joint. Although it is most common in the big toe, it can also occur in the joints of the arms and legs.

Kidney stones are a frequent complication of gout. More men than women suffer from the disease, although women after menopause are susceptible to it. Untreated gout may result in deformity.

There are two types of gout: primary and secondary gout. The former is associated with a hereditary defect in metabolism. Secondary gout is related to the failure of the kidneys to excrete uric acid, which is one of the by-products of the digestive process and usually gets eliminated by the kidneys. In some people, it is not eliminated due to kidney problems and will be present in the body's fluid at a higher than normal level. This can be triggered by crash diets used in weight reduction, wearing wrong sized shoes, eating food rich in fat, exposure to chills, use of drugs like diuretics, emotional anxiety, as well as consuming excessive alcohol, protein-rich foods, creamy dairy products, coconut dishes, sugar products and citrus fruit. Little or no exercise can also be a cause. Painful inflammation may develop suddenly in any joint following an injury or illness or eating the wrong type of food. The patient may feel feverish with swollen red tender joints. The skin turns red, hot and shiny.

Care and Preventive Measures

Having alkaline foods, performing proper Asanas to improve the circulation of blood and learning to relax are the best ways to combat gout.

Include in the diet food that helps the adrenal glands produce cortisone, such as brewer's yeast, wheatgerm, yoghurt and green leafy vegetables. Have celery as it prevents and eliminates uric acid. Black currants are rich in copper, manganese and iron, which are useful in treating gout. Other types of food to include are asparagus, bananas, black mustard, burdock, chilli, comfrey rootstock, dandelion roots, horseradish, muskmelons, oats, sarsaparilla, cauliflower, broccoli, watercress, watermelons and cabbages. The only protein foods that can be taken but in moderation are yoghurt, soya and tofu. Drink plenty of fluids.

Avoid food rich in uric acid like meat, shellfish and chicken. Also avoid food rich in protein, including red meat and string beans, coconuts, dairy products, alcohol, prunes, aerated drinks, chemicals, citrus fruit, tropical fruit and refrigerated foods. The patient should be given a diet low in purine, the substances in cell nuclei from which uric acid is formed. However, avoiding purine totally can result in vitamin B and vitamin E deficiencies. Use garlic, ginger and onions in moderation. They are warm and promote acidity in the body when used in excess.

Recipes

- Have raw walnuts before each meal for a week. Avoid all oily foods during the week.
- Have a fresh uncooked radish once a day with chilli and salt if desired.

Juice

- Add a tablespoon of lemon juice to a glass of water. Add honey to taste. Drink this once a day.
- Have a glass of cherry juice 3 times a day.
- Have celery juice 2 times a day.

Infusions

- To reduce swelling drink freshly made lemongrass tea as often as possible.
- Have a glass of the infusion of asparagus or fennel roots or horseradish or juniper berries or black currants 3 times a day after meals for relief.
- To the infusion of ginger and castor roots, add asafoetida and salt. Drink this once a day.

Decoction

Take a tablespoon of the decoction of cabbage 3 times a day to clear the swelling.

Bath

- To an infusion of ground ivy leaves or fresh herbs, add hot water and soak your feet.
- Use walnut leaves or its decoction in the bath once every other day.
- Boil oat straw in water for an hour and use the infusion either as a foot bath or in the bathtub.

Application

- Apply a poultice of fenugreek seeds after a shower twice a day.
- Massage the affected area with juniper oil and nutmeg oil mixed together in equal proportion.
- To 1 part chamomile flowers add 5 parts olive oil. Mix well and heat under pressure. Add 1 part camphor to the filtered solution and massage.
- To 1 glass of hot water, add half a teaspoon of ground ginger or 2 drops of ginger oil. Mix well. Immerse the affected region in this once a day for 10 minutes. Follow up with a massage with oils (see chapter 24) for maximum benefit.

Asana Routine

- Pawanamuktasana [Energy Releasing Exercises]
- Matsyasana [Fish in Lotus]
- Sarvangasana [Shoulderstand]
- Halasana [Plough 1]
- Chakrasana [Back Pushup]
- Shashanka Bhujangasana [Striking Cobra]
- Meditation

SEPTIC ARTHRITIS

This occurs due to a bacterial infection in the joints and affects the knees. Gonorrhoea is one of the common causes. People with tonsillitis, decayed teeth, sinus infection or intestinal infection are susceptible to the disease. It is more common among young men. It can begin with various problems. It can be a complication due to rheumatic fever, typhoid fever, bacillary dysentery and several others. Most of the problems that cause it are related either directly or indirectly to a faulty diet.

The most important cause of septic arthritis is overloading the body with poison-toxemia. Hormonal imbalance, stress and physical overactivity are other causes of the disease. There will be a sudden increase in the body temperature and one or more joints will swell with pain, particularly when the affected joint is moved. The joint appears red, tender and warm to the touch. The following will also be experienced: loss of appetite, thirst, perspiration with a sour odour and constipation. The urine will be acidic.

Care and Preventive Measures

In the early stages, ice compression and hot fomentation help. To reduce the swelling, have freshly-made lemongrass tea as often as possible. If you have a fever, have a liquid diet and plenty of fruit juice. Avoid exposure to the cold, meat and food rich in protein.

OSTEOARTHRITIS OF THE HIPS

In osteoarthritis of the hips, pain is felt in the hips, groin and knees. Stress on the hips is the main cause. Bending, climbing steps and sitting down become a painful process. Treatment is similar to that outlined under osteoarthritis.

=Asana Routine

The following Asanas are suitable for the pelvis and hips:

- Suryanamaskar [Salutation to the Sun]
- Siddha Yoni Asana [Female Accomplished Pose]
- Supta Vajrasana [Backward Bend]
- Shashankasana [Baby Pose]
- Setu Bandasana [Bridge Pose 1st position]
- Eka Pada Sarvangasana [Shoulderstand Single Leg]
- Chakrasana [Back Pushup]
- Marjariasana [Cat Pose]
- Supta Bhadrasana [Knee and Thigh Stretch Lying down]
- Eka Pada Utthanasana [Squat Single Leg]
- Tadasana [Stretch Pose]
- Tiryaka Tadasana [Swaying Palm Tree Pose]
- Uttita Lolasana [Dangling]
- Udarakarshana Asana [Abdominal Massage Twist]
- Shashanka Bhujangasana [Striking Cobra]
- Naukasana [Variation of Saucer Pose]
- Shalabhasana [Locust Pose] or Paripoorna Shalabhasana [Swan]
- Vayu Nishankasana [Gas Releasing Pose]

JUVENILE RHEUMATOID ARTHRITIS

Also known as Still's disease, juvenile rheumatoid arthritis affects the knees and elbows of mainly children. In addition to rheumatoid symptoms, there may be high fever, rashes, pleurisy and enlargement of the spleen. Treatment for juvenile rheumatoid arthritis is the same as that for rheumatoid arthritis.

TRAUMATIC RHEUMATOID ARTHRITIS

This occurs as a result of an acute injury to a joint. There may be bleeding in the joint or effusion of joint fluid.

Application

- Apply an ice pack and then moist heat. Rest the joint for a while.
- Apply ginger and juniper oil to the affected region.

REITER'S SYNDROME

Mainly caused by a virus or bacterial infection, this type of arthritis occurs only on one side of the body and is common among young people. The eyes and urethra become inflamed, accompanied by skin lesions and fever. The heel becomes painful.

Juice

Have plenty of fruit juice rich in vitamin C.

Application

To castor oil and olive oil mixed together in equal proportion, add a few drops of lavender oil. Apply this to the heels.

ANKYLOSING SPONDYLITIS

This is an arthritis of the spine. Inflammation causes fusion of the lower spine and sacroiliac joints and this gradually spreads to the upper spine. Men are more susceptible to this disease and it can be due to hereditary factors. There will be a sensation of backache in the lumbar area followed by stiffness, which spreads over the back. Once it starts spreading, it can affect breathing. Asanas related to the back and pelvis provide relief.

NEUROGENIC JOINT DISEASE

This is caused by an illness of the nervous system, which is associated with syphilis, diabetes and a defective spinal cord. It usually occurs at the hips, knees or feet.

Application

Apply ginger oil and juniper oil mixed together in equal proportion after a wet, hot fomentation. This gives relief.

SYNOVITIS

This is an inflammation of the membrane lining the joint cavity. Injury causes swelling because of the excessive secretion of lubricating fluid. Blood may force itself into the cavity. Other than injury, inflammation may otherwise be due to rheumatoid arthritis or tuberculosis. Simple synovitis is common after a sprain and usually happens in the knees. The kneecap may be felt rubbing against the bone underneath it when the leg is straightened.

Performing simple exercises regularly and applying a hot fomentation are beneficial.

Infusion
Drink 2–3 glasses of infusion of lemongrass daily.

Application
Apply juniper oil and ginger oil mixed together in equal proportion and massage.

STIFF JOINTS
This can occur for no apparent cause. Have cheddar cheese and soya bean tofu in any form for relief from body stiffness.

Juice
Have a glass of celery juice 2 times a day until the stiffness reduces.

Infusion
Have a glass of the infusion of dandelion roots or lemongrass to help clear the swelling.

Decoction
Have a glass of the decoction of cabbage.

Application
- Apply the juice of mistletoe berries or dandelion stems.
- Apply sesame seed oil mixed together with an equal proportion of camphor for relief from pain in the bones.
- Apply juniper oil and ginger oil mixed together in equal proportion. Juniper oil readily penetrates when applied to the affected area and relieves pain. Its effect is enhanced with ginger.

TENNIS ELBOW
This is a strain on the forearm muscles on the outer side of the elbows. Causes include unnatural movement of the arms while playing or exercising, unexpected jerky movements, shock or overusing the arms.

Asana
Massage the affected region to release the immobilised muscle fibres. Try out the arm exercises in the Pawanamuktasana series as they are beneficial.

TORTICOLLIS
Also known as stiff neck or wry neck, this is the spasm of the neck muscles. It brings about difficulty in turning and tilting the head. Causes include draughts, colds, anxiety or nerves trapped in the muscles or cervical vertebrae.

Application
Massage the stretched muscles with the diluted oil of lavender, basil or chamomile flowers.

Asana
Perform the Pawanamuktasana series of exercises for relief from the spasms.

DISEASES OF THE CONNECTIVE TISSUES AND MUSCLES

SCLERODERMA
This affects the skin, causing it to become thick, tight, smooth and shiny. Movement, thus, becomes uncomfortable. If scleroderma spreads to the connective tissues of the internal organs, it will disrupt the normal functioning of the respective organs. This, in turn, will cause various problems.

Exercise the affected region carefully without damaging the tissues through active movement (as in the continuous movement involved when performing an Asana) and passive movement (the slow motion involved in reaching a position and holding it for a while). Prevent injury to the affected region.

ACHILLES' TENDON CONTRACTURE
The calf of the leg and the arch of the foot become tender and painful. This disorder is more common among women than men due to the former's constant wearing of high-heeled shoes, which causes the Achilles' tendon to shorten.

Application

Apply castor oil or olive oil to the affected region and stretch the foot forward and backward a number of times.

Asana

All asanas that help strengthen the ankle are beneficial.

RHEUMATISM

This is painful inflammation and stiffness of the muscles, joints or connective tissues. There are many bacteria associated with arthritis and rheumatism. These organisms infect the joints or muscles, causing spasms and swelling. If the muscular sheath of the lower back is affected, this is called lumbago. There will be tender and painful nodules or cords in the muscles. If the affected muscles are located at the back of the neck, a headache continues for a long time. If it is at the side of the neck, a stiff neck results. Pain is usually aggravated by tension or overexertion or exposure to cold.

Application

Besides performing simple exercises related to the region followed by an application of heat and massage, as well as referring to the applications under gout, mix 1 drop of garlic oil together with 2 drops of camphor. Apply this to the length of the spine and then over the adjoining muscles. This strengthens the spine.

FIBROSITIS (MUSCULAR RHEUMATISM)

This is the inflammation of the white fibrous tissue that tendons, ligaments, joint capsules, coverings of the bones, sheaths surrounding the nerves and whole muscles are made up of. The inflammation results in the formation of tender and painful bands or nodules in the muscles or surrounding areas. Allergy and lack of exercise are the main causes.

Take food rich in tryptophan, which prevents pain and is found in milk and peanuts. Increase in the daily diet food and herbs like asparagus, barberries, black soya, cayenne, celery, cherries, cinnamon, gooseberries, grapes, muskmelons, mustard, oats, raw walnuts, sarsaparilla, watermelons and wheat. Have dried figs and papayas regularly in the mornings to ease the pain. Take cheddar cheese and tofu for relief from body stiffness.

Recipes

- Crush a clove of garlic and add a teaspoon of honey. Have this twice a day.
- Drink a glass of hot milk with a crushed clove of garlic for relief from rheumatism.
- Add a teaspoon of cider vinegar to horseradish. Have this once a day.
- Take 2 tablespoons of cod liver oil with milk before bedtime.

Juice

- Drink a glass of radish juice once a day.
- Have celery juice and apple juice for gout and rheumatism. This may not suit some people, so add okra.
- In a food processor, blend a cucumber, carrot and beetroot and extract the juice. Have a glass of this juice once a day for relief from rheumatism due to an excess of uric acid.
- Take 2 tablespoons of lemon juice directly or to a glass of hot water and honey (to taste), add 2 tablespoons of lemon juice. Have the drink 3 times a day.

Infusions

- Have a glass of the infusion of bean pods 3 times a day.
- Have a glass of the infusion of figs for numbness due to rheumatism.
- As a diuretic for rheumatism, make an infusion from the leaves of yarrow. Have this 3 times a day.
- Have a glass of the infusion of coriander leaves 3 times a day. The infusion can be administered externally for joint pains and rheumatism.
- Make an infusion from the fresh green shoots of stinging nettle, which are rich in many minerals. Have a glass of this 3 times a day.
- Have a glass of the infusion of ginger and rosemary mixed together in equal proportion. Add a teaspoon of the infusion or fresh juice of lemon balm.
- Have a glass of the hot infusion of parsley, ginger, alfalfa leaves, German chamomile flowers, dandelion roots and leaves or juniper berries individually or in combination regularly to prevent rheumatism.

Bath

- Have a hot bath with the decoction of walnut leaves once in 2 days.
- Add the decoction of juniper berries to hot water and soak in the bathtub for 15 minutes.
- Add the decoction of oat straw to bath and soak in bathtub for 15 minutes.

Application

Apart from the treatment under gout (minus the baths), the following are beneficial:

- Apply fennel oil to the affected area.
- Apply juniper oil mixed together with nutmeg oil in equal proportion twice a day or use the decoction of juniper berries in the bath.
- Make a paste from a teaspoon of powdered mustard seeds and water. Apply a thin coat to the affected area in moderation (excess can cause irritation and inflammation). The area will feel a little hot. Leave it on for a few minutes, then wash the area (for sensitive skin, add 1 teaspoon of rye flour to powdered seeds and water).
- Apply the warm water in which a coriander plant has been boiled. This relieves the itch and pain.
- Apply the poultice of allspice (a good muscle relaxant) or its infusion.
- Apply a poultice of chillies for rheumatism, especially if rheumatism is associated with inflammation.
- Apply a poultice of horseradish mixed together with vinegar.

BACKACHE

One of the symptoms of backache is discomfort in the back. Causes of back pain originate from skeletal and muscular structure. Obesity is a common cause of backache, resulting from poor postural habits. Backache also results from problems like a slipped disc, tuberculosis, kidney problems and arthritis. It is when weights are lifted with a bent back or when work is done with a sagging back that backache is felt. Obese people who rest more and work less are liable to get backache more often. It can be a referred pain from the structures within the pelvis during menstruation and pregnancy.

General backache, besides being due to poor postural habits, also results from nervous tension, disorder of the joints and ligaments, chills, cold, menstrual problems and general stiffness. Common symptoms are persistent backache, which is prominent in the morning and fades off as the day unfolds, and sudden sharp pain. If there is no obvious cause for the backache, performing Yogasanas for the back brings about relief. Eating a cooked papaya or a fresh ripe fruit daily is beneficial. Season food with black mustard as often as possible.

Recipes

For lumbago (lower back pain), the following will be beneficial:

- Fry dill seeds and grind them. Add 1 teaspoonful of the powder to a glass of rice wine and drink daily.
- Dry-fry star anise or fennel seeds and grind. Add 1 teaspoon of the powder and a pinch of salt to a glass of warm water. Have this before every meal.

Infusions

- Have a glass of the infusion of castor roots and cumin seeds mixed together.
- Have a glass of the infusion of German chamomile flowers 3 times a day.

Decoction

Boil a small piece of cinnamon in water. Have the decoction before sleeping for relief from numbness in the skin, fingers and muscles.

Bath

As a bath for lumbago, boil 500 grams of oat straw in 4 litres of water for an hour. Use the water in a bathtub.

Applications

To relieve back pain:

- Rub lime juice or a cut lemon to the affected region.
- Apply a poultice of geranium or its decoction.
- Apply lemongrass oil mixed together with twice the quantity of coconut oil.
- Mix cooked oats together with a teaspoon of mustard powder. Apply the mixture to the affected region as a poultice.

MUSCLE CRAMPS

A combination of energy from the food and oxygen within the muscle produces muscle power. This is mainly disturbed by the poor circulation of blood.

Obesity, anaemia, poor nutrition, varicose veins and heart problems may reduce the supply of blood to the muscles. Nutritional interference, inadequate oxygen or the inability to get rid of carbon dioxide at the normal rate of the muscles results in muscle cramps.

Calcium, phosphorus and sodium, in particular are necessary for the muscles to function normally. Have plenty of milk in the daily diet as it contains calcium. Supplement this with vitamins B, C and D.

Infusion

Have a glass of the infusion of fennel leaves, chamomile flowers, motherwort, peppermint or lemon balm.

Bath

Have a warm bath followed by hot and cold showers to improve circulation. For other types of baths, refer to those under muscular rheumatism.

Applications

- Place a hot water bottle on the lower back. This relieves leg cramps by increasing blood circulation.
- Massage with ginger oil and basil oil mixed together in equal proportion with lavender oil or neem oil as the base.

Asana

All Asanas that improve blood circulation are beneficial.

MUSCULAR DYSTROPHY

In this disease, the fibres of muscles weaken and degenerate. The main cause is hereditary. At an early stage, vitamin E helps to stop the break down of the muscles. However, the advanced stage of muscular dystrophy is irreversible. If the child walks on toes, the hip joints get weaker and the calf muscles may look enlarged. In adults, it will start with weakness in the shoulders, face and then arms, gradually spreading to the back.

Wheatgerm oil (rich in vitamin E), when taken together with vitamins C, A and B6, helps to develop strength in the muscles to a certain extent and may prevent them from deteriorating further.

Infusions

- Have 4–6 cups of infusion made from the leaves of lady's mantle daily.
- Have a glass of the infusion of cinnamon once a day to tone the muscles.

Application

Soak finely chopped shepherd's purse in either juniper or rye spirit for a week. Rub the muscles with the liquid twice a day.

MUSCULAR PAIN

Medication, in particular analgesics, eases the pain but the pain comes back again. Phenylalanine is a natural protein, which is capable of easing the pain.

Have a balanced diet rich in phenylalanine. Magnesium is another element that soothes and prevents the pain. It is found in brewer's yeast, wheat bran, wheatgerm, green leafy vegetables, nuts, brown rice and soya beans.

Recipes

In a food processor, blend green leafy vegetables with 1 teaspoon of brewer's yeast, 1 teaspoon of wheat bran, 1 teaspoon of wheatgerm, 1 tablespoon of almonds or any mixed nuts, and water or any permitted fruit juice. Drink this once a day.

Infusion

For muscular pain with spasms, have a glass of the infusion of nutmeg once a day.

Application

Apply comfrey rootstock paste to the affected area. Do this after the bath once a day.

Asana Routine

For muscles and tendons (general toning of muscles and tendons):

- Bhuja Valli Shakti Vikasaka [Arm Strengthening Asanas]
- Katichakrasana [Cork Screw Pose]
- Uttita Lolasana [Dangling]
- Nauka Sanchalana [Rowing the Boat]
- Baradwajasana [Twist in Veera]
- Shashankasana [Baby Pose]
- Matsya Kridasana [Flapping Fish Pose]

INFLAMMATIONS

A burning sensation in any part of the body due to inflammation of the tissues.

Recipe

Boil a glass of milk with a few ground almonds and saffron threads. Drink this with honey.

Infusion

If the whole body experiences a heaty sensation, have a glass of infusion of onions.

Applications

- Apply aloe mixed together with butter.
- Apply a crushed cucumber to the area for relief.
- Apply juniper oil, lavender oil or rosemary oil if there are aches and pains in the muscles.
- Apply the paste of comfrey leaves mixed together in water if the pain results from pulled tendons.

MUSCULAR SPRAIN

Pulled muscles, tendons and ligaments are sprained mainly due to accidents.

Bath

Have a hot herbal bath as it improves blood circulation. For other types of baths, refer to those under muscular rheumatism.

Applications

- Apply the paste of comfrey leaves mixed together in water.
- Dilute the essential oils of thyme and rosemary with witch hazel oil and apply.

MYASTHENIA GRAVIS

This is the development of muscular weakness, which affects the muscles around the eyes, face, limbs as well as the muscles involved in swallowing. Abnormalities of the thymus or tumours are sometimes associated with myasthenia gravis. Have a diet rich in protein, vitamin E, vitamin B complex and manganese.

Asana

Asanas related to the muscles help prevent further deterioration.

OSTEOPOROSIS

This is a condition in which the bone substance throughout the skeletal frame decreases. It usually occurs in the immobile regions of the body due to a plaster cast, malnutrition, diabetes or vitamin C deficiency. It also occurs when there is a hormonal imbalance, for example, during menopause.

Pain in the bones, easy cracking of bones (fracture), and kyphosis are common symptoms. Increase the intake of calcium and other nutrients.

Asana

Asanas that help activate the major muscles to stimulate movement are beneficial.

CURVATURE OF THE SPINE

There are three types. Those with a hunchback suffer from kyphosis. A curvature that forms a hollow towards the back with the shoulders jutting back is lordosis. Curvature to the side that causes the lowering of one of the shoulders is scoliosis. Most of these problems are caused by postural defects, poliomyelitis and malformation.

Asana

Besides gentle massage, performing Asanas regularly will improve the posture and correct the problem. Refer to Asanas for toning the back.

SLIPPED DISC

Due to pressure, substances of the intervertebral discs may deteriorate and part of the disc substance may push itself against the roots of a spinal nerve, causing nerve injury. This is known as a slipped disc. If the nerve involved is the sciatic nerve, the pain will be felt down the leg along the path of the nerve. The pain will be aggravated by sneezing, coughing, etc. Muscular spasms will result.

Refer to recipes for Sciatica.

Asana

Besides applying heat and massage, the following Asanas help relieve the pressure on the nerve: Padma Parvatasana [Traction] and Utkatasana [Imaginary Chair].

SCIATICA

The sciatic nerve is the single thickest nerve in the body, as thick as the little finger. Sciatica can begin with frequent attacks of lumbago, followed by inflammation of the root of the nerve. It can happen suddenly or gradually. There will be a sharp shooting pain, which will begin from the buttocks and run down the thigh, calf and even ankle. This may be accompanied by tingling and numbness in the little toes. Include garlic to food rich in vitamin B1 like beans, dried peas, nuts, milk and eggs.

Recipes

- Have 10 grams of port wine with 1 teaspoon of elder berry juice.
- Boil a handful of small bean pods that are dried and cut in a litre of water until the volume reduces to a third of the original. Have the drink 3 times day.

Bath

Boil 6 teaspoons of crushed mustard seeds in water and add the decoction to a bathtub. Soak in the warm bath for 15 minutes.

Applications

- Apply the poultice made from fenugreek seeds.
- Make a paste from powdered mustard seeds and water. Apply a thin coat to the affected area in moderation (excess can cause irritation and inflammation). The area will feel a little hot. Leave it on for a few minutes, then wash the area (for sensitive skin, add 1 teaspoon of rye flour to powdered seeds and water). Good for treating bruises, sciatica and ganglions.

Asana Routine

A person suffering from sciatica requires some help from the instructor because in the beginning, it will not be possible for him or her to do them alone. Certain variations are required as well, depending upon the nature of the pain and the mental attitude of the person. Select only those Asanas that can be performed without strain. Do not perform the extreme position.

Try out the following Asanas:

- Pawanamuktasana [Energy Releasing Exercises], particularly the toe exercise and knee cranking.
- Natarajasana [Shiva's Pose]. This can be replaced with Vyghrasana [Tiger Pose] but do this with the help of another person, in which case perform it after Gomukhasana [Posture Clasp]. Follow up with Grivasana [Neck Roll]
- Utkatasana [Imaginary Chair]
- Pada Angushtasana [Legclasp Gorilla Pose] without bending forward too much.
- Gomukhasana [Posture Clasp]
- Supta Bhadrasana [Knee and Thigh Stretch Lying down]
- Janu Sirasasana [Alternate Leg Pull]
- Setu Bandasana [Bridge Pose 1st position]
- Sarvangasana [Shoulderstand]
- Uttana Padasana [Inverted Dog]
- Naukasana [Saucer Pose]
- Paripoorna Shalabhasana [Swan]
- This can be replaced by Bhujangasana [Cobra Pose], Shalabasana [Locust Pose] or Shashanka Bhujangasana [Striking Cobra]

- Jatara Parivartanasana [Legover Both Legs] with help only
- Matsya Kridasana [Flapping Fish Pose]
- Makarasana [Crocodile Pose]

The following is an alternative Asana routine for sciatica:
- Pawanamuktasana [Energy Releasing Exercises]
- Mushumna Shakti Vikasaka [Pelvic Tilt Lying down]
- Utkatasana [Imaginary Chair]
- Pada Angushtasana [Legclasp Gorilla Pose]
- Gomukhasana [Posture Clasp]
- Shashankasana [Baby Pose]
- Supta Bhadrasana [Knee and Thigh Stretch Lying down]
- Janu Sirasasana [Alternate Leg Pull]
- Naukasana [Saucer Pose]
- Paripoorna Shalabhasana [Swan] (Alternatively, Sarpasana [Snake Pose] and Shalabasana [Locust Pose] can be performed)
- Matsya Kridasana [Flapping Fish Pose]
- Nadi Shodana Pranayama [Alt Nostril Breathing]

Note: Do not attempt forward bending Asanas (except Pada Angushtasana and Janu Sirasasana, which should be done under supervision).

BUNIONS
A bunion is a painful swelling of the joint tissue, including the bone. It occurs on the side of the foot at the base of the big toe. Causes include wearing small or narrow or pointed or wrong-sized shoes.

Applications
- Massage the area with natural turpentine.
- Apply lemon juice twice a day for a couple of weeks.
- Rub a mixture of olive and castor oils daily. Place a thin slice of garlic over the foot and bandage. Leave it on overnight. This may soften and even dissolve the bunion in the early stages.

BURSITIS
The fluid-filled sacs located in the muscles near the joints lubricate joints. When these sacs are infected, the joints become painful. The shoulders, knees and hips are usually affected the most. Calcium deposits in the tendons, also known as calcification of bursa, leads to a more painful joint. This includes miner's elbow, housemaid's knee and bunion. The best treatment technique is to clear the inflammation (refer to the treatment under arthritis).

Application
Apply alternate hot and cold compresses to the painful area 2 times a day.

Asana
If the shoulders are affected, the following Asanas will be beneficial:
- Pawanamuktasana [Energy Releasing Exercises]
- Uttita Lolasana [Dangling]
- Urdhva Hastottanasana [Side Bend]
- Gomukhasana [Posture Clasp]

HEEL SPUR
Calcaneal spur or heel spur occurs due to the strain of weight. Try to reduce putting on weight on the heels. Increase the intake of vitamin C.

Bath
To increase blood circulation, have a hot foot bath in salted water, followed by a massage with an oil made the following way: mix a teaspoon of castor oil together with a teaspoon of olive oil, add 6 drops of lavender oil and 6 drops of chamomile flowers oil.

Application
Apply a poultice of millet flour mixed together with castor oil once every night.

SPRAINS
This is a forcible wrenching or twisting of a joint with partial rupture or other injuries to its attachments without dislocation.

Applications

- Apply an ice pack as first aid to the area immediately.
- Mix a teaspoon of warmed coconut oil together with a clove of crushed garlic. Apply the oil after a hot water fomentation.

ASANAS FOR SPECIFIC AREAS OF THE SKELETO-MUSCULAR SYSTEM

These are therapy exercises for general toning, muscular weakness and nerve stimulation. Make sure the spine is erect in all the sitting and standing exercises. Do not strain yourself while performing the exercises. Gentle movements and not jerky or quick movements strengthen the back. Any holding should always be comfortable. If there is any strain, come out of the posture. Relax between repetitions and between exercises.

Asana Routines

For the arms:

- Skanda Tatha Bahu Mula Shakti Vikasaka [Shoulder Blade]
- Bhuja Bandha Shakti Vikasaka [Upper Arm]
- Kaphoni Shakti Vikasaka [Elbows]
- Mani Bandha Shakti Vikasaka [Wrists]
- Kara-Prushta Shakti Vikasaka [Back of the Palms]
- Kara Tala Shakti Vikasaka [Palms]
- Anguli Mula Shakti Vikasaka [Finger Joints]
- Bhuja Valli Shakti Vikasaka [Arms]

For the neck and shoulders:

- Bahu Shakti Vikasaka [Arm Exercises]
- Hasta Grivasana [Hand and Neck Pose]
- Druta Grivasana [Neck Movement]
- Gomukhasana [Posture Clasp Variation]
- Jalandhara Bandha [Chin Lock]
- Shavasana [Relaxation]
- Uttita Parshva Trikonasana [Triangle Stretched Knee 1]
- Dwikonasana [Chest Expansion 1]

- Bhu Namanasana [Spinal Twist]
- Paschimottanasana [Backstretch]
- Jyestika Makarasana [Head Twist]
- Sarpasana [Snake Pose]
- Makarasana [Crocodile Pose]
- Bhoochari Mudra [Gazing at Nothing Seal] or Shanmuki Mudra [Psychic Source Seal]
- Yoga Mudra

For toning the back:

- Padanguli Asana [Toe Exercises]
- Gulpasana [Ankle Exercises]
- Janu Shakti Vikasaka [Knee Cranking]
- Badha Konasana [Knee and Thigh Stretch]
- Katichakrasana [Cork Screw Pose]
- Tadasana [Stretch Pose]
- Dwikonasana [Chest Expansion 1]
- Shashankasana [Baby Pose]
- Mushumna Shakti Vikasaka [Pelvic Tilt]
- Pada Angushtasana [Legclasp Gorilla Pose]
- Chakra Pawana Mukta Jatara Parivartanasana [Back Pushup Legover]
- Paschimottanasana [Backstretch]
- Naukasana [Saucer Pose]
- Paripoorna Shalabhasana [Swan] or Sarpasana [Snake Pose], Shalabasana [Locust Pose] or Shashanka Bhujangasana [Striking Cobra]
- Nadi Shodana Pranayama [Alternate Nostril Breathing]

Alternative Group

- Mushumna Shakti Vikasaka [Pelvic Tilt]
- Trikonasana [Triangle Simple]
- Santulana Asana [Balance Posture]
- Pada Angushtasana [Legclasp Gorilla Pose]
- Utkatasana [Imaginary Chair] or Padma Parvatasana [Traction]
- Gomukhasana [Posture Clasp]
- Vajrasana [Sitting Thunderbolt]
- Ardha Matsyendrasana [Half Twist]

- Janu Sirasasana [Alternate Leg Pull]
- Naukasana [Saucer Pose]
- Shashanka Bhujangasana [Striking Cobra]
- Chakrasana [Back Pushup]
- Jatara Parivartanasana [Legover Both Legs]
- Yoga Mudra
- Advasana

For the displacement of the disc:
(If the condition is not too serious, try out the following Asanas with the help of someone)
- Vrukshasana [Tree Pose]
- Padahastasana [Legclasp]
- Utkatasana [Imaginary Chair] or Padma Parvatasana [Traction]
- Ushtrasana [Camel 1]
- Shashankasana [Baby Pose]
- Uttana Padasana [Inverted Dog]
- Sarpasana [Snake Pose] or Bhujangasana [Cobra Pose]
- Shalabasana [Locust Pose]
- Bhu Namanasana [Spinal Twist]
- Vayu Nishankasana [Gas Releasing Pose]
- Chakrasana [Back Pushup]
- Naukasana [Saucer Pose]
- Adhomuka Swanasana [Strengthening the Whole Body step 2]
- Vyghrasana [Tiger Pose]
- Gomukhasana [Posture Clasp]
- Matsya Kridasana [Flapping Fish Pose]

Specific Asana routine for the displacement of the disc:
- Mushumna Shakti Vikasaka [Pelvic Tilt]. If this is too difficult, perform it lying down. Refer Supta Mushumna Shakti Vikasaka [Pelvic Tilt Lying Down]
- Pada Angushtasana [Legclasp Gorilla Pose]
- Ushtrasana [Camel 1,2,3]
- Uttana Padasana [Inverted Dog]
- Bhujangasana [Cobra Pose]

- Shalabasana [Locust Pose]
- Supta Badrasana [Knee and Thigh Stretch Lying down]
- Chakra Pawana Mukta Jatara Parivartanasana [Back Pushup Legover]
- Gomukhasana [Posture Clasp]
- Matsya Kridasana [Flapping Fish Pose]
- Nadi Shodana Pranayama [Alternate Nostril Breathing]

Performing the following Asanas for over a period of time is beneficial:
- Jyestika Makarasana [Head Twist]
- Makarasana [Crocodile Pose]

Note: Do not perform any forward bending Asanas. Relax yourself in Advasana.

22

The Sense Organs

∽

The sense organs — eyes, ears, skin, nose (see chapter 16) and tongue (see chapter 13)— are the link between the body and the surroundings. This chapter discusses the problems associated with the eyes, ears and skin, as well as the recipes and treatment necessary to cure them.

EAR PROBLEMS

Most of the problems related to the ears and nose start from the mucous membrane. Some may come about as a result of microbes, which are considered in this section.

Common anti-microbial herbs are garlic and indigo. Others include onions, peanuts, cider vinegar, olive oil, oranges, peppermint, chamomile flowers, fennel, marjoram and agrimony.

DEAFNESS

There are two common types of deafness: conduction deafness or nerve deafness. Conduction deafness, if caused by foreign bodies like water, insects or wax in the external ear, is easy to treat. If conduction deafness is a result of pus from the middle ear, this too can be treated provided the treatment begins at an early stage. If it is due to pressure change, cold or enlarged adenoids, the performance of certain Asanas will help cure it. If deafness is due to a degenerated nerve centre, then this results in permanent deafness.

Avoid aspirin in excess. For instance, people who have been treated for arthritis with aspirin have experienced hearing loss and other ear problems. A low-fat diet helps temporary hearing loss. Unpeeled dry peanuts help clear partial deafness.

Applications

For temporary deafness:

- Take a thin gauze or cotton and wrap it around a clove of garlic. Gently push it into the ear canal and leave it on overnight. Repeat this every night for 14 days to clear the pressure or infection.
- Put a drop of warm soya oil in the outer ear canal. Soya oil helps to clear temporary deafness and ringing in the ear.

EARACHE

This can be a symptom of inflammation of the middle ear. Congestion in the nose or violent blowing of the nose can cause earache.

Infusion

Have a cup of infusion of mullein leaves or mullein flowers or chrysanthemum flowers once a day.

Applications

- Warm a teaspoon of olive oil. Put a few drops of the oil into the ear.
- Place a piece of cotton wool soaked in the oil of cajuput in the ear. Leave it on overnight.
- Make a fresh thin wick of gauze or cotton. Wet it with 5 percent phenol in glycerine or entrops. Gently place it in the outer ear canal.

EAR INFECTIONS

Applications

- Cut a clove a garlic and wrap cotton around it. Place it gently in the ear canal once a day for 5 days. The vapour kills the germs.
- Mix equal quantities of garlic juice and olive oil. Apply 1–2 drops of the mixture in the ear or dip a wad of cotton into it. Place the cotton in the outer ear. Leave it on overnight for relief from pain and infections.

STUFFINESS

This is a blockage that results from colds or pressure change in the ears.

Recipe

Orange peel is antihistaminic (antihistamine neutralises or inhibits the effect of histamine in the body. It is used mainly to treat allergic disorders and colds). Cut the peel into small strips and soak them in cider vinegar for several hours. Drain off and cook them in honey for a few minutes. Eat this regularly to clear stuffiness or clogged air passages.

EARWAX

Earwax is secreted by sweat glands in the ear. Excess wax can cause noises similar to ringing in the ear, deafness or earache.

Applications

- Put a few drops of peppermint juice in the ear to help clear the wax.
- Put a few drops of either the strong infusion of marjoram leaves or the weak infusion of agrimony leaves in the ear.
- Make a long roll (like a drinking straw) with a piece of paper. Place one end firmly (but not too deep) in the ear. Light the other end of the straw and allow it to burn at a safe distance from you (if possible, get someone to help you do this). Extinguish the flame quickly. The heat creates a vacuum that helps to dislodge as well as draw out the wax.

INFLAMMATIONS

Application

For inflammation of the middle ear:
Put a few drops of the warm infusion of chamomile flowers, fennel leaves or fennel seeds in the ear 3 times a day.

Avoid swimming or any activity in which water may enter into the ears.

RINGING IN THE EARS (TINNITUS)

Inflammation of the middle ear is a common cause for ringing in the ears or tinnitus. Other causes include high blood pressure, nervousness, diseases of the auditory nerves, anaemia and excess use of quinine or salicylates. Find out the cause and treat it accordingly to cure ringing in the ears.

MENIERE'S DISEASE

Symptoms are dizziness, nausea, vomiting and ringing in the ear. There may not be any fever or pain. Causes include emotional disturbance, allergies, metabolic changes or arteriosclerosis (an arterial disease).

The following measures are for ringing in the ears and Meniere's disease:

Recipes

- Crush 30 grams of sunflower seeds. Add 30 grams of rock sugar and mix well. Bring it to the boil. Drink this when it is in a semi-liquid form twice a day. Continue doing this for 2–3 weeks.
- Refer to recipe 2 under temporary deafness.

Application

For ringing in the ear, place a wad of cotton soaked in onion juice in the ear or put 2 drops of freshly made onion juice directly in the ear 3 times a day for ringing in the ear.

EYE PROBLEMS

CATARACT

This is the gradual clouding and opacity of the lens of the eyes. It usually develops as a result of old age or illness. If left untreated, it will lead to vision loss. In the early stages, there will be a reduction in the acuteness of vision. As the cataract worsens, the ability to see reduces until the person can just about differentiate between light and dark. Calcium deficiency causes cataracts.

Beans, beet greens, mustard greens, parsley, turnip greens, broccoli, wheatgerm, peanuts and brewer's yeast are essential to prevent cataract. Vitamin B2 prevents cataract from worsening.

CONJUNCTIVITIS

This is the inflammation of the moist membrane that lines the inner surface of the eyelids and covers the whites of the eyes. There will be a burning sensation, as well as redness and swelling of the conjunctiva. There will be watery discharge in the early stages and mucus at a later stage.

Recipe

Have soya bean curd regularly to clear red eyes.

Applications

- Mix a drop of diluted chamomile oil together with white clay. Apply it to the eyelids.

• Put 2 drops of fresh loofa juice into the eyes. This is particularly good for children.

Wash

Wash the eyes with the infusion of fenugreek seeds or chamomile flowers 3 times a day. Refer also to point 5 under eyewash for eye irritation.

GLAUCOMA

This is a disease of the eye, which, if left untreated, can lead to loss of vision. In glaucoma, the eyeballs suffer increased pressure. Vitamin C helps to lower eye pressure. Supplement your diet with vitamin C or have food rich in vitamin C.

Recipe

Have carrots boiled in water and drink the water as well without adding any seasoning.

DULL, RED OR YELLOW EYES AND OTHER EYE PROBLEMS

Dullness of the eyes suggests a general lack of energy. Redness of the whites of the eyes shows an inflammatory condition. It also suggests a nutritional deficiency. Yellowness of the whites of the eye suggests a malfunction of the liver. It is also indicative of a person with jaundice.

Carrots are essential to healthy eyes. It helps to absorb iron from other types of food and prevents night blindness. Other essential food types are amaranth, apples, beans, beet greens, bitter gourd, chamomile flowers, cornflour, cucumbers, drumstick leaves, fennel, gooseberries, hyssop, jasmine, mung beans, mustard greens, oats, papayas, parsley, rose petals, sarsaparilla, sunflower seeds, verbascum and vervain.

Have sun dried sunflower seeds regularly to prevent deterioration of long-sightedness. Thiamine (vitamin B1) helps to improve your eyesight (garlic helps to boost the absorption of thiamine in the body), as does having cooked drumstick leaves as soup regularly.

Applications

For healthy eyes:

• Mix a teaspoon of almond oil with a teaspoon of honey. Add a pinch of the powder of liquorice roots and a teaspoon of rose oil with white wax as a base. Make it into a paste and apply to the eyelids 2 times a day.

• Apply eyetex made from frangipani flowers, jasmine flowers or white buttercup flowers to the lower eyelids regularly. Get the juice by rubbing any of the above-mentioned flowers on one side of a clean tile made of clay. Place the tile over a lighted wick dipped in castor oil so that the layer of juice is on the outer side. Cover the tile and wick with a clean cane basket to prevent dust and other particles from getting in. Leave it to stand like this for a day. When the entire juice gives a soot-like appearance, remove the powder gently and mix it with castor oil or diluted chamomile oil to get a fine paste. You are now ready to apply the eyetex to the eyes.

Recipe

For blurred vision:

Powder dried mulberry leaves and mix them with sesame seeds in equal proportion. Add honey to taste. Have 10 grams of the mixture for 30 days. Drinking parsley juice regularly is also beneficial for blurred vision.

The following measures are for eye irritation:

Applications

• To soothe the eyes apply a lotion of chamomile flowers, hyssop flowers, vervain leaves or verbascum flowers.

• Apply a paste of chamomile flowers or white clay to which a drop of chamomile oil has been added to the eyelids.

Wash

• Wash the eyes with a decoction of fennel seeds.

• Wash the eyes with an infusion of rose petals. To do this, steep a few rose petals in a cup of hot water, filter and use the clear solution as a wash or apply it as a compress on the eyes 4 times a day.

- To a teaspoon of aloe jelly add 2 teaspoons of boric acid and 500 millilitres of warm water. Wash the eyes with the clear solution. This is good for tensed, itchy and red eyes.
- Wash the eyes with the infusion of fenugreek seeds. To do this add a teaspoon of fenugreek seeds to boiling water. Let this stand for 10 minutes. Filter the water and wash the eyes with the filtered solution.

The following measures are for wrinkled eyelids and tired eyes:
Applications
Place a slice of freshly cut cucumber on the eyelids for half an hour.

Wash
Soak a gauze in freshly-squeezed orange juice and apply it to the eyelids. After half an hour, wash them with cold water.

The following are for inflammations, styes and other eye problems:
Wash

- Wash the eyes with an infusion of marigold flowers, the juice of mulberry leaves or the hot decoction of comfrey roots twice a day.
- For black eyes wash the eyes with the infusion of hyssop stems or St. John's wort.

Applications

- Apply a cold tea bag for 15 minutes to the eyelids. This is also good for tired eyes.
- For styes, apply a warm lotion of chamomile flowers, hyssop flowers, vervain leaves or verbascum flowers.
- Put a drop of rose water into the eyes before sleep to prevent eye infections.
- For relief from watery eyes and blurred vision, apply a bandage of crushed apples to the eyes. Leave it for a few hours.
- Puffy undereye circles are due to temporary fluid accumulation in the tissues under the facial skin. Splash the eyes with cold water first thing in the morning. This helps to keep the skin around the eyes firm and relaxed.

Refer to chapter 2 for Asanas that strengthen the eyes. In addition, perform Prana Mudra, a Hasta Mudra.

SKIN PROBLEMS

More than half the skin disorders are influenced by psychological factors. Stress is one of the major causes. The neck, jaws, chin and the skin around the mouth are common areas affected by stress. For example, the skin becomes pale when you are frightened, congested when you blush and sweaty as a result of perspiration when angry. These are just temporary changes. If you suffer constantly from tension and it affects you seriously, then this is projected as a disease. Changes in climatic conditions or medicines can also cause skin diseases.

Exercises that help release stress as a result of the beta endorphines secreted by the brain give a sense of well-being. Relaxation and meditation are equally important in relaxing the mind and body. In addition, essential nutrients that help overcome stress such as calcium, vitamin B complex and magnesium are necessary.

When treating skin diseases, if you see an increase in the signs of irritation, this is indicative of going overboard with the treatment. It may also be indicative of an allergic reaction to the treatment. The types of food listed below may cause allergic reactions in some people, so it is better to watch out for signs and supervise treatment from the very beginning.

Take food that has acidophilus as this helps in the growth of healthy bacteria as well as plenty of fibre as this helps to minimise stress; food that heals external wounds and stops bleeding like aloe, comfrey rootstock and turmeric powder; food that increases blood circulation to the skin in general and the affected area in particular like sarsaparilla, burdock and goldenseal; food that acts as an antiseptic like turmeric, papayas, thyme and indigo; and antibacterial herbs like basil. Chlorophyll has a deodorising effect on the body. Barley grass, wheat grass and alfalfa leaves are the best source of nutrients for healthy skin.

Sarsaparilla, turmeric, hibiscus flowers and neem juice are excellent for clearing skin problems. Other types of foods that are beneficial include the following:

barberries, celery, cucumbers, juniper berries, kidney beans, lemons, muskmelons, neem leaves, oats, olive, peppermint, primrose, rose petals, apples, millet, sprouts, asparagus, black sesame seeds, lemon balm, elder flowers or berries and marigold flowers.

There is also a need to eliminate caffeine, cigarettes, alcohol, a diet rich in protein and stimulants like coffee, etc., as they magnify stress.

As far as applications for skin problems are concerned, aloe is a good choice. It has a wide application for skin problems as it soothes and softens the skin. The fresh juice of aloe is applied to heal wounds, sunburn, insect bites and minor cuts. It also prevents infections.

Bath

For healthy skin:

A hot water bath with the decoction of walnut leaves or angelica roots or chamomile flowers or the infusion of juniper berries or juniper leaves or neem leaves gives wonderful results.

Skin Tonics

- Vinegar, being acidic, is an ideal skin tonic. To make a vinegar tonic mix half a cup cider vinegar together with half a teaspoon of the powder of clove flower buds. Add 2 drops lavender oil, 2 drops rosemary oil, a tablespoon rose petals and 4 cups rose water. Leave the mixture to stand for a week. Give it a good shaking shake 2-3 times daily. After a week, strain the liquid and apply it to the skin at night after a bath.

- Heat a slice of orange, half a lemon and 2 tablespoons of castor sugar in a cup of milk until it nearly boils. Allow it to cool and strain. Apply it to the skin as a lotion after a bath.

- The infusions of rosemary, chamomile flowers, elder flowers, peppermint, spearmint, comfrey, parsley or fennel seeds help heal and firm the skin. The infusions also clear spotty skin, patchy skin and wrinkles.

INFLAMMATORY AND ALLERGIC DISEASES

ACNE

This is an inflammatory disease that affects the skin of the face, chest, shoulders, upper back and neck. It is most common during the adolescent age.

The number one cause of acne is excess iodine due to eating too much seafood, shellfish, salted fish and red meat. People with acne should build up their resistance to diseases and take measures to prevent the problem from worsening.

Increase the intake of essential fatty acids as they are highly beneficial. They are found in the oils of flaxseeds, evening primrose, borage and linseed. Avoid medicated soaps and cosmetics, fried foods, nuts, excess sugar, chocolates, iodised salt, cola drinks, and pastries. Avoid washing your face too often and situations that cause undue anxiety and tension. Have kidney beans and strawberries on a regular basis.

Rinse your face with the liquid made from a freshly mashed cucumber in cool water. This is very nourishing for the skin. An oil bath, besides being good for all types of skin, is also relaxing.

Applications

- Apply a warm infusion of elder flowers, leaves of lady's mantle and thyme leaves mixed in equal proportion to the affected area.

- Apply a warm compress of the decoction of burdock roots or the decoction of marshmallow.

- Apply a poultice of hops, marshmallow or thyme leaves and flowers twice a day.

- Apply an ointment of marigold petals or marshmallow roots twice a day.

- Instead of a soap, use yellow dhal flour (also called besan) on the skin. Mix a cup of besan with a tablespoon of turmeric powder. Apply this to the entire body like soap.

- Apply a little yoghurt to the affected area. Leave it on for 20 minutes and wash clean. Repeat this twice a day.

- Shred horseradish and cover it with cider vinegar. Leave this aside for a day. Apply the mild juice (wet it with cold water before applying) to the area, and leave it on for 5–10 minutes. Wash clean. Repeat this 2 times a day.
- Mix equal quantities of lemon oil and glycerine and apply.

Asana Routine

- Sarvangasana [Shoulderstand]
- Halasana [Plough 1]
- Paryanaka [Fish in Vajrasana]
- Tadasana [Stretch Pose]
- Tiryaka Tadasana [Swaying Palm Tree Pose]
- Katichakrasana [Cork Screw Pose]
- Tiryaka Bhujangasana [Swinging Cobra]
- Udarakarshana Asana [Abdominal Massage Twist]
- Pranayama (all types)

SKIN ALLERGIES

A number of diseases that afflict people are caused by allergies. In such cases, almost every body tissue may show some allergic reactions. The reactions may take different forms. Common allergens are pollen, hair, pet animals, furs, feathers, milk, egg, fish, shellfish, pork, fowl, wheat, oranges, strawberries, cereals and butter. Orange peel is a good antihistamine. Papayas and lemon balm also help.

Recipe

Dice 2 medium-sized unpeeled potatoes, an onion, 2 cloves of garlic and a carrot. Add water just enough to submerge them. Bring it to a simmer over low heat until the water reduces to half the original volume. Have 2 cups of this as a soup before every meal.

Infusion

Have a glass of infusion of coriander seeds 3 times a day.

Applications

- If the allergy is due to poison ivy, cut a lemon and apply to the infected area.

- If the allergy is due to animal protein and poison in the body, wash the affected area with a clove of garlic crushed in a glass of water and half a teaspoon of salt. Apply turmeric powder. Add 1–2 drops of lavender oil to 2 teaspoons of neem oil, and apply this to the area. Dust the whole area with medicated or turmeric powder.

ANGIONEUROTIC OEDEMA

Caused by skin sensitivity to some external allergens, angioneurotic oedema is the sudden swelling of the lips, eyelids or ears. It is usually associated with itching, a burning sensation and stiffness in the region of the lips, eyelids or ears. Never allow the swelling to persist and reach the larynx.

Wash

- Wash the affected area with water used to rinse rice.
- To starch water add a teaspoon of baking soda. Wash the area with the solution 3 times a day.

CELLULITE

This is the lumpy orange-coloured skin on the thighs, hips and buttocks, and is common among women. It occurs as a result of hormonal and dietary imbalance.

Applications

- Apply a poultice made from a teaspoon of lemon balm or origanum mixed with hot bran or take 2 tablespoons of flaxseed or linseed cooked in a glass of water like a porridge once a day for a week.
- To a bucket of warm water add a glass of decoction of cypress leaves and shoots. Soak your feet in this for 20 minutes. Continue doing this for a week.

CHILBLAINS

This is an inflamed area on the skin (feet, hands, face or ears) with either a dark red or purple coloration. It is caused by frequent exposure to the cold and poor blood circulation. There will be an itching and burning sensation. Avoid exposure to cold places, as well as avoid rubbing the inflamed skin and consuming tobacco in any form.

Recipe

To improve blood circulation refer to recipes and Asanas given in Chapter 15.

Infusion

Have a glass of infusion of stinging nettle or elder flowers with honey 2 times a day.

Applications

- Apply diluted garlic juice or stinging nettle juice.
- Apply an ointment made from glycerine and cayenne in equal proportion.
- Boil water with a clove of garlic and wash the area with this. Now apply lemon juice.
- Apply a compress of fresh onion juice.

Wash

- Wash the affected area with an infusion of oat straw for relief.
- Wash the area with chamomile oil and then dry yourself. Apply dried bean pods meal to clear the itch.

CONTACT DERMATITIS

This is skin irritation that occurs as a result of chemicals or develops as an allergic reaction to certain substances, resulting in red or swollen skin on contact.

Many people show allergic reactions to certain soaps, detergents and many household things (fur, carpet, etc.). Those who work in industries show signs of allergic reactions to a lot more substances. Some common metals like nickel and chromium used in jewellery and tanning leather goods cause allergic reactions.

Furthermore, modern technology uses various types of chemicals in manufacturing fabrics. Some people may be allergic to certain fabrics and the dyes used in making them. Even natural things like the leaves of poison ivy or poison oak are allergens to some. Find out the cause of your allergy and treat it accordingly.

Bath

Use the decoction of chamomile flowers in the bath or apply it as a compress.

FRECKLES

These are small, yellowish or brownish spots that appear due to local accumulation of melanin. These cells enlarge in sunlight. Fair-skinned people are affected most. Once freckles appear, they are almost permanent.

Application

Apply a few drops of salted lemon juice mixed with 1 glass of buttermilk to the face to clear freckles. Or apply a lotion of tansy.

ECZEMA

The causes of eczema are mainly allergic reactions, stress and nervous tension. Other factors are extreme changes in the temperature, excess intake of saturated fats, as well as a diet deficient in essential fatty acids and vitamin B. Vitamin B2 deficiency can cause eczema, which normally appears on the scrotum for men. The red scaly areas may spread. There will be redness, as well as an itchy and burning sensation.

Increase in the daily diet foods that are a rich source of vitamin B2. Include essential fatty acids, brewer's yeast, raw carrots, liver, lemons, lemon balm, wheatgerm (some people may develop signs of allergic reactions to wheat products) and yoghurt.

Avoid chocolates, orange juice, fish, prawns and other types of seafood. Also avoid using chemical soaps and cosmetics.

Recipes

- Add 3 drops of primrose oil to a glass of warm water. Drink this once daily.
- If eczema occurs due to a lack of fatty acids like linoleic acid, take 3 tablespoons of safflower oil daily.

Wash

- Wash with the decoction of geranium or apply the poultice of the geranium plant.
- Wash the area with diluted garlic oil. Now apply a mixture of wheatgerm oil and turmeric powder.
- Boil a spoon of ground black pepper in 2 litres of water. Use the liquid to wash the affected area 2 times a day.

- Boil fresh guava leaves in a cup of water to make a decoction. Wash the area with the decoction 3 times a day.

Applications

- Mix basil leaves with salt and apply to the affected area. This may be painful but it is very beneficial.
- Apply a poultice of oatmeal or use its infusion in the bath.
- Mix the sap of the fresh roots of burdock with petroleum jelly. Apply this 3 times a day.
- Apply a compress of marigold flowers. Leave it on for as long as an hour daily.
- Mix half a blade of aloe, 15 drops of kyolic (garlic extract), 15 drops of basil oil, 5 tablespoons camphor and a pinch of turmeric together. Apply this as a cream.
- For dry eczema steep lavender flowers in warm olive oil overnight. Strain and apply.
- Wash the area with an infusion of chamomile oil. Dry the area and apply dried bean pods meal. Do this 3 times a day to treat moist eczema. You may also use a decoction of chamomile flowers in the bath.
- Wash the area with garlic water. Use a towel to dry. Wash again with salt water to which a pinch of turmeric has been added. Now apply a mixture of the fresh juice of lemon balm leaves and basil leaves. After half an hour, apply sandalwood paste to the area. Sandalwood paste can be used for poison ivy or poison oak when the skin is thickly covered with tiny blisters.

Psoriasis

This is a serious relapsing skin disease that makes the skin appear like silvery scales. The usual parts of the body affected are the elbows, knees, back and buttocks.

The eczema-like appearance on the skin occurs as a result of poor metabolism of fats. There will usually be a high level of cholesterol in the blood and skin.

Increase the intake of lecithin. Avoid fats and animal protein in the diet. Include hepatics to improve the functioning of the liver.

Recipe

Eat chutney made from lemon balm and cumin seeds. To do this, dry fry cumin seeds and lemon balm leaves. Put the cumin seeds and balm leaves into a blender.

Add a tablespoon of grated coconut and a pinch of salt and chilli. Blend well. Have the chutney with rice or bread.

Juice

Have at least 5 glasses of the fresh juice of either red or black grapes daily.

Wash

Boil a teaspoon of black pepper corns in a kettle of water. Allow it to cool and wash the area with it. After half an hour, wash the area with freshly made coconut milk.

Application

Apply or wash with the decoction of either burdock or sarsaparilla roots or leaves.

Rashes

Rashes appear due to an allergy to drugs like penicillin, phenolphthalein, quinine, salicylate, etc. They are difficult to diagnose.

Nettle rash or urticaria (also known as hives) appears as red skin and itches a lot. Causes include insect bites as well as allergic reactions to drugs or food. The rash worsens when exposed to heat, sunlight or water.

Antihistamine drugs are useful in treating rashes. In general, a gentle massage over the area using a body massage oil helps. A low-fat, salt-free diet and regular exercise also helps. Avoid asafoetida.

Recipe

Add a tablespoon of ground dried orange peel to a glass of boiling water. Let it stand for 10 minutes and drink the water. You may add honey to taste.

Wash

- Wash the affected region with the decoction of coriander seeds once a day.
- Boil chamomile flowers in water to make a decoction. Wash the affected area with the decoction or use it during your bath. It helps to clear rashes, including inflammations.

Applications

- Apply a compress of agrimony.
- Apply evening primrose oil twice a day.
- Apply honey to chicken pox scars at the early stage (the first or second day) of the disease. This clears them up.

SCABIES

This is an infectious disease that makes you want to scratch a lot. It is caused by parasitic mites.

Applications

- Apply a hot fomentation with the decoction of elecampane roots twice a day.
- Mix a drop of garlic oil and 2 drops of camphor or borneol and apply.
- Mix equal quantities of cinnamon oil, thyme oil, rosemary oil and pine oil with wheatgerm oil as the base oil and apply.

SUNBURN

Sunlight alters the natural collagen fibres that give skin its elasticity. Fair-skinned blue-eyed individuals are more sensitive to sunlight than dark-skinned persons. As far as possible, avoid going under the hot sun without any protection. Use sunscreen.

Applications

- Apply an ointment of marigolds, honeysuckle or elder flowers to the affected area.
- Apply a compress of burdock leaves, angelica roots or elder flowers.
- Apply fresh yoghurt. Leave it on for about 20 minutes.
- Make an infusion of lettuce leaves, stinging nettle or chamomile flowers and apply.

BACTERIAL DISEASES

BOILS, ABSCESSES AND CARBUNCLES

- Boils are red painful swellings. Never squeeze a boil as the germs may cause blood poisoning.
- Abscess is the collection of pus in a body cavity formed by the degeneration of tissues. Abscess can be easily inflamed.
- Carbuncles are more than boils and are accompanied by general illness.

Boils and carbuncles are caused by the same kind of germs. They occur due to the body's low resistance to infections. Poor dietary and hygienic habits are other reasons.

Applications

Before applying the following pastes or poultices, wash with diluted garlic infusion to which a pinch of turmeric powder has been added.

- Apply a poultice of powdered fenugreek seeds to dissolve an abscess.
- Apply the tincture of echinacea rootstock or the decoction of yarrow to clear abscess.
- To draw out the pus apply a paste of asafoetida in water.
- To get rid of deeply embedded abscess apply baked onion.
- To get rid of a whitlow or boil on the tip of a finger bore a hole in a lemon and stick the affected finger into it for a day or two.
- Mash a few clean inner cabbage leaves gently. Apply the poultice 5 times a day.
- Roast sarsaparilla leaves and grind them to make a paste. Add a few drops of olive oil and apply the paste twice a day.
- Boil 5 grams of marshmallow roots in 1 glass of water. Add sarsaparilla roots. Grind the mixture and apply the paste. The water in which the roots are boiled can be drunk as tea.
- Roast a fresh fig and cut it in half. Apply this as a poultice.
- Apply the paste made from sarsaparilla leaves and marigold flowers to clear carbuncles.
- Grind a few neem leaves. Add a teaspoon of turmeric powder. Apply the paste.
- For carbuncles, apply the poultice of sweet pumpkin or the poultice of coriander seeds mixed with barley meal.

FUNGAL DISEASES

More often than not, fungal diseases affect the skin. Many types of fungus are enemies of many disease-producing bacteria, including the bacteria found in the intestines or vagina of a healthy person.

Most antibiotics are not useful in treating fungal diseases. They may instead help pave the way for their progress. Antibiotics taken over a long period of time can destroy good bacteria and, with a few exceptions, lead to more problems.

CANDIDIASIS

Candidiasis of the skin may affect the mucous membrane of the digestive tract or vagina. Obese people and diabetics are more susceptible to getting the disease. Refer to obesity (chapter 23) and leucorrhoea (chapter 18) for ways to treat candidiasis.

RINGWORM

Ringworm of the beard, also known as barber's itch, is a contagious disease. Small nodules first appear at the hair follicles and then spread to the surrounding area. Ringworm of the body is mildly contagious. A word of advice is to keep the affected area dry and clean.

Applications

- Apply a small raw papaya slice or the fresh milky juice of papayas to the affected area. Leave it on overnight. Continue doing this for a week.
- Grind a teaspoon of the seeds of white radish with yoghurt to get a paste. Apply the paste once a day for a week.
- Add 1 teaspoon of turmeric powder to some water to make a paste. Mix well. Add a little honey and apply the paste.
- Mix a teaspoon of orange peel powder together with neem oil. Apply this once a day.
- Add turmeric powder to the juice of neem leaves and apply.
- Mix lemon grass oil together with twice the quantity of coconut oil and apply.

OTHER SKIN PROBLEMS

BRUISES AND SPRAINS

Applications

- Boil or steep grated ginger until the water turns yellow. Dip a towel into the water and apply it warm to the affected area.
- Apply the crushed leaves of comfrey or hyssop directly to bruises.
- Apply the crushed leaves of parsley or St. John's wort to sprains.
- Apply a cold compress of the infusion of witch hazel, marigold or wintergreen or a cold poultice of burdock leaves or the oil of St. John's wort to sprains, joints and lower back pains for relief from pain. Applying a cold and hot compress alternatively also helps.
- Add a few drops of sesame oil to 1 teaspoon of grated ginger juice. Apply this to sprains and bruises.
- Apply a poultice of fennel leaves 3 times a day after cleaning the affected area with garlic water.
- Mix lemon grass oil together with twice the quantity of coconut oil and apply.

BURNS

Applications

- Apply honey immediately to the affected area to treat hot water burns.
- Apply potato juice, barley, honey, iguana fat, cucumber juice, fresh aloe jelly or the juice of aloe plant.
- Apply the oil of peppermint or marigold.
- Apply apple cider vinegar to fire, hot metal or hot oil burns.
- Add a teaspoon of honey to a teaspoon of the juice of fresh betel leaves and apply.
- Apply sesame oil mixed with an equal quantity of olive oil.
- Apply soya sauce to prevent the burn from worsening.
- Apply lemon oil mixed with an equal quantity of glycerine.
- Clean the burnt area with diluted saline water or entrops oil. Now apply the paste of fresh orange peel (do not bandage).

- Apply iguana fat, emu oil or peacock fat. Leave it on for 20 minutes, then apply wheatgerm oil. Repeat this for 2 more days after which apply only wheatgerm oil and take vitamin B6 supplement. Do this for a week.

CORNS AND CALLUSES

Corns and calluses, which protect the sensitive tissues of the foot from friction or pressure, are patches of toughened or thickened outer skin.

Corns, which are cone-shaped with tips, occur as a result of wearing the wrong-sized shoes. Hard corns are usually found on the top of the toes or on the ball of the foot. Soft corns, which are moist, form between toes. Calluses generally form on the weight-bearing flat surface of the foot. They do not have any tips.

People who are diabetic should not self-medicate.

Applications

- Apply Roman Chamomile oil.
- Blend olive oil or castor oil with lemon juice and apply.
- Bake a clove of garlic and apply to the corns. Take care not to apply to the unaffected area.
- Wrap a poultice of cooked hot rice or millet spread on a banana leaf around the region. Leave this on for half an hour.
- Apply a wad of cotton dipped in 40 percent salicylic acid to the affected foot at night. The next morning soak the foot in a solution of Epsom salts and warm water for about 10 minutes. Dry the foot with a towel. Apply castor oil and cover the foot in a plastic bag for an hour.
- Wrap the affected area with a moist towel. Put on your socks so the moisture can be retained for several hours. After this, soak the foot in salted hot water for 20 minutes. Repeat this for a few more days. It will then be easy to remove the corn or calluses without strain.

Cancer of the Skin

Hiding behind beauty marks, blemishes and sores may be the early warning signs of skin cancer. Overexposure to the ultraviolet rays of the sun produces solar keratoses, which aid in the development of skin cancer. Moles that appear after four years of age should stay small. If they do not, consult a doctor for proper medical advice.

A 1980 study at Japan's National Cancer Centre showed that vegetables reduce the risk of cancer. Onions, cabbages and carrots are some of the most effective vegetables cited in the study. The fibrous inside of loofa or angle gourd when dried and used as a bath-time sponge may also help reduce the risk of cancer. Another study in China found that loofa, carrot, turnips and some seed sprouts contain interferon inducers, which are useful in treating cancer.

Food rich in silica is found to be beneficial. Not taking animal protein, meditation is believed to prevent the spread of cancerous growths.

Juice

Have a glass of raw carrot juice daily.

Infusion

Have a glass of infusion of the mixture of the leaves of ground ivy and agrimony in equal proportion twice a day.

CUTS AND ABRASIONS

Clean the area with warm water with a pinch of turmeric powder or a drop of garlic oil.

Wash

Wash with lemon juice. Apply geranium leaves or the thin membrane between onion layers to aid in the healing process.

Applications

- Apply the powder of marigold roots.
- Add a pinch of turmeric powder or a drop of garlic oil to warm water. Clean the affected area with this.
- Soak a wad of cotton in an infusion of agrimony or yarrow or comfrey leaves or marigold petals and apply.
- For abrasions, apply an ointment made from lady's mantle or comfrey leaves.

DRY SKIN

Oils found in the skin are unsaturated and unless vegetable oils are taken, the skin becomes dry. Food rich in vitamin A, vitamin C, linoleic acid, and vitamin B helps remedy the problem. Adding 5–10 milligrams of vitamin B2 to the daily diet is also beneficial.

Infusion

Apply an infusion of the leaves of borage as a lotion for dry skin.

INFLAMMATION OF THE SKIN

Recipe

Mix 8 ounces of milk together with a tablespoon of wheatgerm and a tablespoon of wheat bran. Blend the mixture well and drink it daily.

Applications

- Apply vitamin E oil to clear inflammations.
- Apply a cut lemon for inflammations caused by poison ivy.
- Make a poultice from 1 tablespoon of barley flour, 1 tablespoon of vinegar, 2 figs and honey. Apply the poultice to the affected area for relief from hard inflammations.
- Erysipelas or red patches on the skin (a form of skin inflammation) can be cured by applying barley flour mixed with honey and ghee or sandalwood oil and lemon juice or aloe or crushed cabbage.
- For gangrene in the feet, soak feet in a bag of honey for a couple of hours.

INSECT BITES AND STINGS

Applications

- Apply the juice of aloe vera or the juice of parsley leaves to the affected area. Alternatively, an ointment of thyme and summer savoury may also be applied.
- For bites caused by sandflies, apply the mixture of salt and turmeric in hot water. Leave this on for about 10 minutes. Apply garlic extract or oil and then apply yoghurt mixed with 3 drops of thyme.
- Apply a poultice made from echinacea or lemon balm.
- For stings, rub the area with a cut raw onion for immediate results.
- Apply the raw leaves of plantain or wheatgerm oil to relieve the pain from wasp and hornet stings. For wasp stings, the juice of witch hazel may also be applied. For hornet stings, honey may also be applied.

SKIN IRRITATIONS

Avoid buttercups, figs and sage as they cause irritation.

Applications

- Rub the juice of cucumber for relief from skin irritations, inflammation, burns and bedsores.
- Apply the juice of aloe or evening primrose oil.
- Apply a poultice of fenugreek seeds or lemon balm.
- Grind a teaspoon of cumin seeds with 2 teaspoons of coconut milk. Apply the mixture to the affected area half an hour before taking a shower. This helps to get rid of bedsores or sores that result from perspiration.

ITCHY SKIN

Wash

Wash the area with the juice or infusion of cucumbers, chamomile flowers, goldenseal roots, marigold flowers, St. John's wort or coriander.

Applications

- Apply bean pods meal.
- Give a hot fomentation with the decoction of elecampane roots twice a day.

PIMPLES

Blackheads, yellow spots and red spots are usually caused by a malfunction of the kidneys, liver or bowels. Hormonal imbalance is another cause. Find out the cause and treat it accordingly before treating the pimples.

Applications

- Apply yoghurt to the pimples. Leave it on for 20 minutes, then wash with cold water.
- Cut a lemon in half, sprinkle sugar and warm them on a hot pan. When the sugar dissolves, apply the cut lemon in a patting motion to the pimples. Do not press or squeeze.

RED-COLOURED BLOOD VESSELS ON THE SKIN/ SPIDER VEINS

Increase the intake of citrus fruit, green peppers, cabbages, turnip greens and rosehips (for bioflavonoids).

STRETCH MARKS

Overweight people and women who give birth within short intervals of time get these marks. A diet deficient in protein causes these marks.

Increasing protein in the diet and adding food rich in vitamin E and pantothenic acid help prevent these stretch marks.

SKIN ULCERS

Ulcers may sometimes be cancerous. Check with your doctor before it is too late.

Wash

- Wash the area with a decoction of comfrey roots, calamus roots, goldenseal roots or marshmallow.
- Wash with the decoction of juniper wood, particularly for lingering ulcers.

Applications

- Apply the juice of onion to get relief.
- Apply a poultice of carrots or Indian corn to the cancerous ulcers for relief.
- Soak the rind of lemon in vinegar and marinate it for a week. Apply the solution 2 times a day.

TUMOURS UNDER THE SKIN

Check with your the doctor for the malignancy or otherwise of the tumours.

Applications

- Crush garlic in lard and apply.
- Roast fresh figs, cut them into two and apply to the region to soothe the pain.
- Apply a ripe custard apple mixed with salt to hasten suppuration.
- Apply a poultice from the crushed leaves of lemon balm or fenugreek seeds or cooked barley or fresh fennel leaves.
- To reduce the swelling of a hardened tumour, apply the whole plant of cayenne steeped in milk.
- To dissolve small fibroids and cysts in the pelvic cavity as well as to promote blood circulation in the region, apply a poultice of grated raw cabbages.

WARTS

Warts occur due to viral infections. Include lymphatic cleansers like garlic and vitamin C in the diet.

Applications

- Apply vitamin E oil.
- Apply the juice of white cabbages or the milky juice of the stem and leaves of the fig plant.
- Rub the affected area with a cut garlic and then apply white clay.
- Mix aloe gel, turmeric powder, the juice of lemon balm leaves and basil leaves, and a drop of garlic oil together to make a paste. Apply the paste every night for a week.
- Apply the juice of onions mixed with a little sea salt (or rock salt) and white clay.
- Bake a clove of garlic and apply. Take care not to apply to the unaffected area.

WRINKLES AND THE COMPLEXION

Wrinkles occur as a result of skin becoming loose. Also, insufficient oil production dehydrate the cells and tissues and cause wrinkles.

Sweet potatoes, milk, carrots, winter squashes, cheese and eggs help prevent wrinkles. Vitamin A helps increase blood circulation and stimulates the fibroblasts (skin cells).

Improve the complexion by consuming extra vitamin C (up to 1 gram). Food and herbs that improve the complexion are green peppers, broccoli, oranges, grapefruit, strawberries, lemons and limes.

The following measures help improve the complexion:

Tonic

Blend 8 ounces of milk, 4 ounces of carrots and 2 teaspoons of zucchini squash. Drink this once a day.

An oil bath is generally good for all types of skin. It is also relaxing.

- For a rosy complexion, clean and rub the face with egg white regularly.
- To nourish the skin, rinse the face with freshly mashed cucumbers in cool water.
- For smooth skin devoid of excess oil, rub the skin with a cut lemon.

- For a clear and smooth skin, apply yoghurt on the face. Leave it on for a while, then wash with cold water.
- To treat dry skin, apply olive oil to the face daily.
- To restore the natural feeling (devoid of anxiousness, etc.) back to the hands, rub them with lemon juice. To soften the hands, rub them with the mixture of lemon juice, glycerine and eau de cologne mixed in equal proportion.
- Apply an infusion of chamomile flowers to remove wrinkles.

Asana Routine
To prevent wrinkles by increasing blood circulation:

- Simhasana [Lion]
- Sarvangasana [Shoulderstand]
- Asanas for relaxation

WOUNDS
Wash

- For an open wound, wash with the infusion of Roman Chamomile.
- Wash the wounds with water and apply the decoction of eucalyptus leaves or lady's mantle leaves or dried herb or chamomile flowers or comfrey or fenugreek or St. John's wort.

Applications

- Apply a teaspoon of crushed betel leaves directly.
- Mix the juice of basil leaves together with turmeric powder or its paste and apply.
- Mix turmeric powder with guava leaves or neem leaves and apply as a poultice.

BLEEDING WOUNDS
Wash
Wash with the mixture of diluted lavender oil and thyme oil mixed in equal proportion.

Applications

- Apply a compress of agrimony to aid the healing.
- Apply papaya sap, its leaves or skin to the wound directly.

- Apply blackberry leaves, lemons, onions, turmeric powder or guava leaves to the wound.
- Dissolve half a teaspoon of aloe in a cup of water and apply.
- Mix a drop of lavender oil with 10 drops of olive oil and wash the affected area.
- Apply the fine membrane between the layers of an onion to the wound. Cover the wound with gauze. The membrane acts as an antiseptic and aids in the healing process.

SWEATING DISORDERS
Food and drugs give a characteristic odour to sweat. Foul smelling sweat results from fermentation, bacterial infection or some chemical change that may be taking place in the sweat. Sluggishness of the autonomic nerves causes insufficient sweating. It is common with vitamin A deficiency. The main causes of excessive perspiration, on the other hand, are nervous tension or fear. Cleanliness is the best method of treatment.

Bath

- Have a foot bath with 20 grams of cypress herb boiled in a litre of water.
- Have a hot water bath with the decoction of walnut leaves once in 2 days.
- Add to hot water the decoction of lemon balm. Soak your legs in this.

HAIR PROBLEMS
HAIR LOSS
Hair is made of protein, so an adequate amount of it is necessary for healthy hair. This comes from milk, yoghurt, soya beans and cheese (vitamin A prevents coarse hair). A lack of inositol, which is found in wheatgerm, brewer's yeast and molasses, can lead to hair loss. An excess of iron, copper and iodine may also contribute to hair loss as well as premature greying. Apple cider vinegar helps to improve the strength and condition of the hair and nails.

Applications

For hair loss:

- Apply a mixture of coconut oil and lime water regularly.
- Apply the juice of amaranth for soft hair.
- After shampooing, rub the scalp vigorously with the pads of your finger until it tingles to activate the sebaceous glands.
- Apply 10 gooseberries boiled in half a litre of coconut oil or the juice of gooseberry with an equal quantity of lime juice regularly as a shampoo.
- To prevent hair loss due to vitamin deficiency apply a mixture of lettuce and spinach juices. In addition, drink the juice of lettuce, carrots or alfalfa.
- For hair growth shampoo hair with cooked black beans and fenugreek seeds or massage hair roots with coconut milk. Applying coconut oil regularly also helps.

Application

For patchy loss of hair:

Apply the paste made from the seeds of limes and black pepper in water (this causes skin irritation for some people) to areas experiencing patchy loss of hair. The paste stimulates hair growth by increasing blood circulation to the affected area.

DANDRUFF

This occurs when the epidermal cells die at different rates in different places. Some causes include bacterial infections, hormonal imbalance, indigestion, stress and tension. Dandruff most often appears on the scalp. In other parts of the body, the eruption looks like oily crusts with the skin beneath it inflamed.

Massaging the scalp daily for five minutes is one of the best ways to nip the problem in the bud. Avoid starchy and fatty foods, and products made from sugar and white flour.

Wash

- Wash hair twice a week with the paste of green gram powder and yoghurt.
- After rinsing hair with shampoo, rinse it again with a teaspoon of lime juice.

Applications

- Apply lemon juice with the rind to the scalp.
- Apply the decoction of 1 tablespoon of beetroot in 1 glass of boiling water.
- Add a few drops of rosemary oil to olive oil and apply to the hair after shampooing it.
- Soak 2 tablespoons of fenugreek seeds in water overnight. Blend and apply paste to the scalp. Rinse hair with shampoo after 1 hour.
- Apply any of the following on the scalp: warm olive oil or linseed oil, cider vinegar diluted with water, lemon juice with warm water, the juice from freshly-grated ginger mixed with olive oil or sesame oil. Follow with a gentle massage. Finish a non-oily treatment by rinsing with fresh warm water and an oily treatment with a good herbal shampoo wash.

23

The Endocrine Glands and Lymphatic System
∽

The ductless glands secrete hormones into the blood, and these hormones are responsible for the proper growth of the body and bodily functions. They regulate blood circulation to help the body cells either absorb or prepare waste for elimination, depending on need. Mental activity, including intelligence, and proper physical growth depends to a great extent on the healthy secretion of these hormones.

The most important endocrine glands, which function in coordination with one another, are the pituitary, parathyroid, thyroid and adrenal glands, islets of Langerhans in the pancreas and sex glands. Often, the disease of one endocrine gland affects the function of the other. The main defect of the endocrine glands is the production of either excess or insufficient hormones.

THE ROLE OF THE GLANDS

- The pituitary controls the growth and function of the adrenal, thyroid and sex glands.
- The thyroid controls the rate of the body's chemical activity (metabolism).
- The adrenal glands monitor the metabolism and control the sex glands.
- Male gonads, or testicles, besides producing sperms, are responsible for the development and maintenance of secondary sex characteristics and impulse.
- Female gonads, or the ovaries, in addition to producing the ovum, contribute to the menstrual cycle and the changes that take place during pregnancy.
- The parathyroid regulates the bone metabolism.

THE PITUITARY

The pituitary gland, the master gland of the entire body, is situated just below the central part of the brain. It produces a number of hormones like the thyrotropin, which regulates the thyroid as well as the adrenocorticotrophic hormone (ACTH), which controls the activities of the adrenals.

In excess, the ACTH stimulates the adrenal glands. The effect is similar to taking excess cortisone. If there is an overproduction of the growth-promoting hormone in early childhood, gigantism results. If the overproduction occurs during adulthood, the hands, feet, lips, nose and the ridges of the eyes enlarge. This is usually due to a tumour in the pituitary gland.

If the anterior lobe does not produce enough hormones, other endocrine glands are affected. In the early stages, this results in premature ageing. Later, weakness, low blood pressure, low blood sugar and low body temperature result. If the pituitary gland releases an insufficient amount of antidiuretic hormone (ADH), diabetes insipidus results. Diabetes insipidus also results if there is hypopituitarism.

Asana Routine

- Suryanamaskar [Salutation to the Sun]
- Shirasasana [Headstand]
- Yoga Mudra
- Matsyasana [Fish in Lotus]
- Padahastasana [Legclasp]
- Brahmari Pranayama [Humming of Bee Breathing]
- Shambava Mudra [Vision and Concentration Seal]
- Meditation

THE THYROID

There are many thyroid diseases, but it is beyond the scope of this book to discuss all of them. The thyroid produces three hormones and thyroxin is the principal one. The hormones are responsible for the proper metabolism of the body. Both the overactive and underactive thyroid cause problems. Bitter foods, oats and kelp keep the problems at bay.

HYPERTHYROIDISM

When the thyroid is overactive, excess hormones are produced. This, in turn, increases the rate of the tissues functions in the body, resulting in nutritional problems and heart failure. One such problem is Grave's disease, which is prevalent among women. This occurs due to a defective immune system. Food burns faster and the appetite increases despite overeating. Weight loss, nervousness, intolerance to any changes, rapid heartbeat, breathing difficulty, weakness in muscles, enlargement of the thyroid gland and bulging eyes are common symptoms.

Have a low animal protein diet without any fat. Perform Asanas in combination with relaxation massage and meditation. Evening primrose, together with kelp, helps in normalising the thyroid to a great extent. The best way is to prevent it altogether with the help of proper nutrition.

Recipe

Make herbal tea from the mixture of bugleweed (Lycopus virginicus), stinging nettle, valerian roots or chamomile flowers and yarrow mixed together in equal proportion. Drink this 3 times a day for 21 days.

Application

Apply calamus roots with chamomile oil to the thyroid region for relief.

HYPOTHYROIDISM

This is when the thyroid produces an insufficient amount of hormones. A common symptom is enlargement of the thyroid. An underactive thyroid causes lethargy, weight gain and depression.

If the hormone deficiency starts with the expecting mother, the child will not grow symmetrically and the brain will not develop fully. The skin becomes thick, teeth will only form at a later stage and the voice will become hoarse. If not treated at an early stage, the child may become a dwarf.

In adults, the heartbeat and breathing will become slower if the production of the hormones falls below normal. Perspiration will become scant. The body appears fat with puffy skin. The voice will become hoarse.

The best way to prevent it is through proper nutrition.

GOITRE

This is when the thyroid enlarges. It can result from iodine deficiency, which causes swelling around the neck. In non-toxic goitre, the thyroid enlarges but does not produce enough hormones. This may again be due to iodine deficiency, drug intake, which disrupts the mechanism of the thyroid, or due to enzyme imbalance. Toxic nodular goitre, which is due to the overproduction of hormones, stems from a complication of non-toxic goitre. In this, the eyes do not bulge. Include iodine in the diet daily. A rich source of iodine is seaweed, especially bladderwrack and kelp.

Asana Routine

To promote activity of the thyroid:

- Sarvangasana [Shoulderstand]
- Halasana [Plough 1]
- Matsyasana [Fish in Lotus]
- Siras Angushta Yogasana [Chest expansion 3]
- Simhasana [Lion]
- Grivasana [Neck Roll]
- Bhujangasana [Cobra Pose]
- Jalandhara Bandha [Chin Lock]

THE PARATHYROID

The parathyroid, which has four glands, produces hormones that regulate the calcium and phosphorus levels in the blood. Hypoparathyroidism occurs when low levels of calcium and high levels of phosphorous are present in the blood serum. It is one of the side effects of removing the parathyroid surgically.

If the disease develops in early childhood, the child's mental development will be retarded. Teeth will be deformed and growth will not be normal. If the problem is not rectified, abdominal muscle cramps, breathing difficulty, sensitivity to light and convulsions may occur. The brain may eventually be damaged.

Treatment requires the administration of calcium salts and vitamin D. Avoid dairy products as they contain high amounts of phosphorus.

Hyperparathyroidism, a high level of calcium in the blood and urine, is more common. It may cause the development of kidney stones. Apart from the hormonal imbalance, a major cause is tumour. Excessive thirst or urination, pain in the joints and loss of appetite are some symptoms. Treatment is the same as for hyperthyroidism.

THE ADRENAL GLANDS

These glands are located just above each kidney. The outer cortex and inner medulla are two distinct parts. The adrenal cortex produces thirty or more steroids. Of these, three hormones are very important: the aldosterone (regulates the salts potassium, sodium and water distribution in the body), cortisone and hydrocortisone (regulate glucose, amino acids and fat metabolism, and control the immunity and inflammatory reactions of the body), and sex hormones. The medulla produces adrenaline, which has an influence on the heart muscles and the walls of the blood vessels. This helps vary the blood pressure as required by the body. The hormone is responsible for stimulating the sympathetic nerves, for raising the level of blood sugar by liberating stored energy from the cells of the liver and for the sudden response to changes in the external environment.

With healthy nutrients and exercise, it becomes possible to renew the defective adrenal glands. Cortical hormones of the adrenal glands and the hormones

(ACTH) of the pituitary should work in harmony to get the best results for tissue nutrition and general body vigour.

When the adrenal cortex produces excess hormones, fragile bones, diabetic tendencies, a swollen face, neck and trunk, and an increase in blood pressure result. This condition is known as Cushing's syndrome.

Deficiency of the cortex hormones, which is usually due to damage of the cortex walls, produces fatigue, low blood pressure, poor appetite, nausea and vomiting with diarrhoea. This condition is known as Addison's disease. To rectify the problem have plenty of water with salt.

Many plants have natural chemicals similar to adrenal hormones. They include borage, liquorice and wild yam.

Asana Routine
- Marjariasana [Cat Pose]
- Shashanka Bhujangasana [Striking Cobra]
- Ushtrasana [Camel Pose]
- Paschimottanasana [Backstretch]
- Bhujangasana [Cobra Pose]
- Shalabasana [Locust Pose]
- Dhanurasana [Bow Pose]
- Yoga Mudra
- Meditation

THE SEX GLANDS

TESTES AND OVARIES
The function of the testes' secretion is to develop male sex characteristics. This works well only with the coordination of the adrenal and pituitary hormones. Ovarian functions are associated with the thyroid and pituitary glands. There must be harmony among the adrenal, pituitary and thyroid glands for good health.

Asanas
- Suryanamaskar [Salutation to the Sun]
- Marjariasana [Cat Pose]
- Shashanka Bhujangasana [Striking Cobra]
- Vyghrasana [Tiger Pose]

- Siddhasana [Male Accomplished Pose]
- Siddha Yoni Asana [Female Accomplished Pose]
- Shalabasana [Locust Pose]
- Chakrasana [Back Pushup]
- Sarvangasana [Shoulderstand]
- Padahastasana [Legclasp]
- Moola Bandha [Perineum Retraction Lock]
- Maha Bandha [Great Binding Lock]
- Maha Mudra [Great Seal]

ISLETS OF LANGERHANS

These secrete the hormone insulin, which helps to control the metabolism of carbohydrates. Otherwise, diabetes mellitus results.

THE LYMPH GLANDS

It is through the lymphatic system that the major cleansing of tissues and organs take place. In addition, it is in the lymphatic glands that anti-microbial is partially located. There are several organs made of tissue cells called lymphocytes. Some of these organs are the spleen, thymus and lymph nodes. The circulating white blood cells are also called lymphocytes. Other lymphoid tissues are the tonsils, adenoids and the appendix. The lymph nodes are present in the neck, armpits, groin, central chest cavity and abdominal cavity.

The lymph, a fluid tissue, moves through the lymph channels, finally entering into the blood stream. As it passes the channels, it checks on foreign bodies, germs, unwanted cells and prevents them entering the blood stream. The lymph is responsible for producing antibodies that help control viral, bacterial and fungal infections. It also regulates the healing process of damaged tissues. Malfunction of this system results in allergy, as well as diseases of the joints, kidneys, lungs and the skin.

The diseases affecting the lymphatic system produce swelling. These swellings disappear as the infections subside. Sore throat, bad cold, infection of the tonsils or in the middle of the ear result in swelling of the lymph nodes on the sides of the neck and below the jaws.

Infection in the arms swells the nodes in the armpits. In the scalp, the lymph behind the ear and back of the neck swells. Infections in the legs affect the lymph gland of the groin.

Food and herbs beneficial for healthy lymphatic glands are beetroot, figs, oranges, grapes, apples, fresh green vegetables, white fish, marigolds, goldenseal and cleavers. Two of the best cleansers of the lymphatic system are echinacea and jasmine. Herbs beneficial for the inflammation of the lymph glands are garlic, onions, pine, rosemary and sage leaves. Include them in the daily diet.

Application

Apply 1 clove of garlic crushed in 1 teaspoon of any type of fat to the inflamed gland for relief.

GLANDULAR FEVER

This is an infection of the lymph nodes, in particular the neck. It may be caused by a virus. There will be swelling in the neck and it will be tender to the touch. Symptoms include fever, sore throat, skin rash, enlargement of the spleen and inflammation of the liver.

The following measures are for swollen glands:

Bath

A hot water bath with the decoction of walnut leaves once in two days is beneficial.

Application

Apply a hot fomentation to the tender area with chamomile flowers infusion. Do this 3 times a day.

THE SPLEEN

It is a ductless organ that produces red blood cells in infancy and modifies the blood composition. Food and herbs that tone up the spleen are dates, evening primrose, barberries, barley, beans, horse beans, polished rice, potatoes baked in their jackets, string beans and yellow soya beans.

Recipes

- For an enlarged spleen, have an onion cooked in cider vinegar 2 times a day.
- Mix 25 grams of asafoetida together with 10 grams of rock salt. Add 10 grams of ginger juice and mix well. Have a teaspoon of this mixture 2 times a day with meals.
- Boil in a litre of water a teaspoon of fresh aloe gel together with a pinch of salt and a tablespoon of rock sugar. Let it boil until the volume decreases to a quarter of the original volume. Take a tablespoon of this once a day for 5 days.

Juice

Take 2 tablespoons of the juice of chicory leaves 2 times a day.

Infusion

- Powder the tender bark of the drumstick tree. To 10 teaspoons of this powder add a teaspoon of asafoetida. Infuse a teaspoon of this mixture in boiled water. Drink a cup of the infusion twice a day for a week.
- Drink a glass of the infusion of dandelion roots 3 times a day. It not only prevents the formation of gall stones but is beneficial for the inflammation of the liver and the enlargement of the spleen.

Decoction

For an enlarged spleen, have a glass of the decoction of chicory flowers, seeds and roots 3 times a day.

OTHER PROBLEMS

PREMATURE AGEING

For a youthful look, include milk, butter, honey and gooseberries in the diet. Have adequate rest and meditate frequently. Garlic, yoghurt and the sediments found at the bottom of the beehive (which is nothing but pollen) are also beneficial. Anti-oxidants, rejuvenative and emmenagogue prevent or slow down the ageing process. Sources include vitamin A, beta carotene, vitamin C, vitamin E, selenium and zinc.

Include the following regularly in the daily diet:

amaranth leaves, lotus seeds, liquorice roots, hibiscus flowers, shatavari, jasmine, saffron threads and food rich in iron. Eating an onion — cooked or raw — daily promotes muscular strength. Avoid refined foods and bitter foods in excess as they exacerbate the ageing process.

Recipes

- Make a soup from a carrot, spinach and lotus roots in equal proportion in water. This helps to maintain good blood.
- Cube the flesh of a mature coconut. Add 1 teaspoon of brown cane sugar to the cubes. Store this for 2 weeks in a jar at room temperature and leave it aside. Have 2–3 cubes of this 2 times a day. This relieves weakness and prevents premature ageing.
- Fry a clove of garlic, a few black peppercorns and a piece of ginger in sesame oil. Sprinkle a little salt, brown sugar, cider vinegar and onion for general well-being. Add tomato juice and wheat flour to thicken if necessary.

Bath

Have a bath regularly with comfrey rootstock to prevent premature ageing.

FEVER

An infection or inflammation produces toxins, which when they reach the hypothalamus (heat regulating region) in the brain, disturb the balance, resulting in a rise in body temperature. However, not every rise in the temperature is due to toxins and so, not every rise in the temperature is the sign of a fever. Fever occurs when the white blood cells have to fight against foreign bodies.

During a fever, an individual feels flushed, may sweat, has a headache, and if there is muscular contraction, may shiver. The symptoms depend on the region or organ that has been affected. The illness is generally accompanied by dry hot skin, rapid pulse, chills, aches and pains in the muscles and joints. While dehydration during a fever reduces the flow of urine, a high fever sometimes causes delirium and convulsions. A pale face, irritability, loss of appetite and drowsiness are some symptoms of the illness among children.

If the temperature rises rapidly, control it with a cold compress on the forehead using a towel dampened in water and vinegar. Sometimes, sponging the entire body also helps. For children the sponging should be done using tepid water, and not cold water. Sweating should be induced only when the temperature is in the safe range. When the sweating stops, there may be trouble ahead as the patient may be heading towards hyperpyrexia (delirium).

With children, do not take any chances when they have a fever. A slight delay can result in convulsions. There is a chance that the child may become epileptic after several convulsions. During a convulsion, make the child lie on its stomach with its mouth turned to one side so it does not choke on its vomit. To prevent it biting its tongue stuff a spoon or cloth between its teeth. Immediate medical attention is extremely crucial.

Lemon juice and fruit juice are beneficial during a fever, while infusions of basil leaves and peppermint relieve the effects of a fever. Others include olives, passion flowers, sandalwood and sarsaparilla. The caloric requirement of a patient suffering from fever is higher than of a normal person. Also, a higher quality of protein is required as tissue protein is lost during fever. Do not give the patient any fatty foods; in many cases, the patient may not relish any food. As soon as the fever subsides, feed him or her at regular intervals. Remember to feed the patient easily digestible protein, such as milk, and carbohydrates in the form of glucose, such as fruit (sugar) juice. Increase the quantity of cereals, carbohydrates and starchy foods, bland fluids, such as barley water, fruit juice and water. Have more types of food that are febrifuge and refrigerant. Avoid cinnamon, asafoetida and massage, as well as an excess of fat, cream and eggs.

Recipes

- Boil 1 ounce of oats in 3 pints of water until the water reduces to a third of the original volume. Strain and add a tablespoon of lemon juice, some raisins and sugar to taste. This is a nutritious drink for a fever.
- Drink barley water mixed together with an equal amount of milk. To do this wash the barley thoroughly in water. Cook the washed barley in a frying pan filled with a glass of water. Throw away the water. Using plenty of

fresh water, cook it again until the water reduces to half. Strain, add milk and drink the water 3 times a day.

- Tea made from fenugreek seeds brings down a fever, especially if the fever is associated with poor digestion. To do this soak fenugreek seeds in water overnight. Bring it to the boil. Add a teaspoonful of honey and drink a glass of this 2 times a day.

- For relief from a fever accompanied by vomiting, have a glass of sweetened lemon juice or drink a glass of water in which a slice of lemon has been infused.

- For a child with a fever, try this: add 1 drop of evening primrose to a tablespoon of water. After the child takes this, give him or her plenty of fresh sweet orange juice to drink.

Infusions

- Have an infusion made from the equal quantities of basil leaves and dry ginger 2 times a day.

- Have a glass of the infusion of lemon grass. Add a pinch of ginger and cinnamon mixed together with sugar. Have this 2 times a day.

- Mix half a teaspoon of ginger powder together with 1 teaspoon of honey. Add 1 cup of boiling water. Let it stand for 10 minutes and then drink the infusion.

- Drink a glass of infusion of any of the following 3 times a day: young leaves of borage (to reduce the intensity of a fever); lemon with a little honey (to induce sweating and reduce fever); lotus (to treat fever with excessive thirst); the cold infusion of hibiscus flowers; eucalyptus leaves (without boiling); chamomile flowers; neem; jasmine; grapefruit; tea of olive; and sarsaparilla roots.

- For a child with a fever, give him or her 2 teaspoons of the infusion of chamomile flowers or spearmint leaves 3 times a day.

Decoctions

- Take 2 tablespoons of the decoction of olive leaves 3 times a day.

- Grate dried ginger and boil it in water with a teaspoonful of coriander seeds, a few black pepper corns and a teaspoonful of cumin seeds. To a strong decoction of this add milk and sugar to taste. Drink this 2 times a day during the course of a fever.

Applications

- Apply a paste made from calamus roots to the forehead.

- To soothe aching pains and for relief from a fever, apply a few drops of lemon juice mixed together with 1 teaspoon of coconut oil to the affected joints.

- To bring down the fever, apply the juice of basil leaves to the forehead and eucalyptus oil to the soles of the feet.

TYPHOID FEVER

During typhoid fever, the water balance will be upset. The intestinal walls will become highly inflamed. So, avoid protein foods. Also avoid consuming milk in excess. After convalescing, increase the intake of protein gradually.

Infusion

Have an infusion of bilberry leaves or blueberries. Drink this 3 times a day until the fever subsides.

MALARIA

Malaria is caused by a tiny parasite plasmodium. Intermittent fevers that return repeatedly are due to this serious disease. The liberal inclusion of unnatural foods such as white sugar, white flour, etc. in the daily diet lowers the effectiveness of the immune system. Diet plays an important role in treating malaria.

Recipe

Grapefruit contains natural quinine. Boil a quarter of the fruit in a glass of water and strain the pulp. Drink the juice 3 times a day.

Juice

Extract the juice of tulsi (basil) leaves. To a tablespoon of this juice add a quarter teaspoon of black pepper powder. Have this mixture twice a day.

Infusion

Have an infusion of basil leaves after meals daily.

Decoctions

- Add 2 tablespoons of barberry root decoction to a glass of water. Drink this 2 times a day.

- Powder cinnamon bark and boil a teaspoon of the powder in a glass of water. Add a pinch of pepper powder and a teaspoon of honey. Have the decoction 2 times a day.

OBESITY

Obesity causes extra strain on the heart, kidneys and liver, as well as on the weight bearing joints like the hips, knees and ankles. Overweight people are susceptible to such diseases as thrombosis, heart failure, high blood pressure, diabetes and arthritis. Weight gain is not always a simple case of overeating but is also an indication of a general imbalance in metabolism.

The only sensible way to lose weight is to follow a carefully planned dietic treatment together with suitable Yogasanas. A diet rich in complex carbohydrates is beneficial. Dates can be consumed in abundance by people suffering from obesity. Herbs that provide low calorie nutrition are wheat and barley. Fennel seeds, sprouted rice, sprouted barley, and senna help detoxify stagnation and help in the assimilation of food. Avoid fried foods, sesame seeds and comfrey, and do not snack.

The following types of food help prevent obesity:

- **Apples** are one of the best sources of pectin, which breaks down fat in food.
- **Asparagus** has asparagine, which stimulates the kidneys to break down fat.
- **Beetroot** has iron, which cleanses fat cells, and choline, which clears fat in the kidneys, liver and gall bladder.
- **Cabbages** are rich in sulphur and iron, which clear fat from the gastrointestinal areas.
- **Carrots** have beta carotene, which accelerates the rate of metabolism.
- **Celery** is concentrated in calcium and energises the endocrine glands.
- **Citrus fruit** reduce the effects of fats by liquefying them.
- **Cranberries** are both diuretic and acidic and this dual function helps to dislodge fat.
- **Cucumbers** have magnesium (see chapter 10) and alkaloids (see chapter 11).
- **Eggplant** creates glandular hormonal reactions and helps to control the appetite.

- **Parsley** contains vitamin A and enzymes to break down fatty tissues.
- **Soya beans** are rich in lecithin, which is a defence mechanism for adipose cells.
- **Tomatoes** with vitamin C and diuretic properties speed up the metabolic process.
- **Watermelons** have vitamins A and C, as well as a mineral rich liquid, which breaks down fatty deposits.
- **Cider vinegar** helps dissolve fat. Take 2 tablespoons of this with fruit juice daily.

Recipes

- To a glass of ice water add a lemon slice. Drink this before meals.
- To a glass of vegetable juice, add a clove of garlic. Drink this before meals. It helps you eat less and yet feel full.

Infusions

Some herbal infusions, such as the following, are useful since they promote sweating and urine discharge:

- Have a cup of the infusion of corn silk, fennel seeds, peppermint and dandelion roots, followed by lemon juice before each meal.
- Pour a glass of boiling water over 2–3 chamomile flower heads. Add a lemon slice and allow it to macerate overnight. Strain and drink the solution first thing in the morning.

Asana Routine

Certain Yogasanas are important for any weight reduction programme. Not only do they break up fat deposits or redistribute them, they also strengthen the flabby areas of the body.

The following Asanas work on the glands, improve blood circulation and induce proper breathing:

- Sarvangasana [Shoulderstand]
- Dhanurasana [Bow Pose]
- Chakrasana [Back Pushup]
- Naukasana [Saucer Pose]
- Vajrasana [Sitting Thunderbolt]
- Yoga Mudra
- Trikonasana [Triangle Simple]

- Jatara Parivartanasana [Legover Both legs]
- Meditation

HOW TO SHED WEIGHT

Start by having a juice therapy for 7 days. Have the juice of lemons, grapefruit, oranges, pineapples, cabbages and celery. After the juice therapy, go on an all-fruit diet for 2–3 days. After this, stick to a low calorie diet with whole grains, vegetables and fruit. Repeat this regularly at two monthly intervals.

A Typical Menu

Breakfast

Have a glass of fresh orange juice or grapefruit juice, dry toast and a cup of black coffee.

Lunch

Have a large salad with olive oil and vinegar, with lots of garlic.

Dinner

Have a healthy proportion of protein, tomatoes with garlic and a baked potato.

TIPS ON LOSING WEIGHT

- Try not to have meals at irregular times of the day.
- Use vegetable cold pressed monosaccharide oils.
- Have oranges, grapefruit, apples, pears, watermelons, bananas, figs or pineapples before every meal to kill the appetite. Taking these fruit raw or in the form of juices or slightly steamed regularly, in addition to a sensible healthy diet, gives good results.
- Eat nothing in between meals and avoid high-fat foods like butter, cheese, chocolates, red meat, fried foods, legumes, sugar and its products, soft drinks and alcohol. Also, avoid high calorie foods such as nuts, avocados, pears and yoghurt.
- Iodised salt is not good for overweight people. Avoid kelp, which is the richest source of iodine.
- Get into the habit of taking a herbal salt bath once a week (drink plenty of fluids before and after the bath. The duration of the bath should not exceed 15 minutes.)

- Above all, the mental attitude of the obese person plays an important role in his or her losing excess fat. The relaxation therapy is highly beneficial.

24

Essential Oils and Massage
∽

This chapter discusses some treatments that can be done in the privacy of your home. More often than not, careful application of common non-toxic agents bring about great relief to certain ailments. The believer in natural therapy for simple ailments should, however, bear in mind that all ailments cannot be treated by home remedies and that he/she should be able to identify when to call or seek the help of a physician.

Among some of the drug-free methods of treatment, the application of essential oils is one of the most important and popular. Essential oils are the essence from various flowers, leaves, barks, roots and berries by different methods of extraction. They contain the active ingredients of the plant and are in a concentrated form.

In Ayurveda, essential oils and massage are used for healing both physical and mental ailments. Traditional books on Ayurveda list many formulas on the various combinations of herbs and oils extracted from flowers, leaves and other parts of plants for treating specific ailments. These act on the body and mind by activating and encouraging the flow of energy from the Chakras.

According to Yoga therapy, the energy known as *Prana* flows through specific energy pathways or meridians, and so special attention is given to identifying and releasing these energies. A patient responds to the healing process better when he or she is relaxed.

Aromatherapy cannot, on its own, contribute to the healing process. It becomes holistic in approach only when complemented by a nutritious diet and relaxation through Yoga. A person's lifestyle and emotional problems are also important factors that influence the healing process. Aromatherapy, when combined with a simple massage and Yogasanas, has proven successful in the treatment of stress and stress-related diseases. Aromatherapy massage, in fact, is perhaps the best-known and most important application of essential oils.

Researchers have discovered that plant essences exert an influence on the mind and body and that these essences are linked to the properties and nature of the plants. Essential oils are highly volatile and contain active substances of the plants they are extracted from. Some may have the consistency of water, but mix well with vegetable oils.

Essential oils are often confused with herbal or floral oils. They are, in fact, very different. Although herbal oils have various cosmetic uses and are good for massage, they lack the ethereal and concentrated nature of essential oils. They, therefore, cannot be a substitute for essential oils.

The aromatic molecules of essential oils can enter the bloodstream, where they have a physiological effect. With a nutritious diet, therapeutic Yogasanas and the application of the correct essential oils, many problems of the mind and body can be prevented and even cured.

Essential oils are not recommended for internal use and they are not to be applied directly as they are too strong. Children under 18 months should not be treated with these oils. Pregnant women or nursing mothers should avoid basil, cedarwood, sage, hyssop, juniper, marjoram, myrrh, pennyroyal, rosemary and thuja.

COMMON ESSENTIAL OILS

There are several essential oils. The commonly used ones are listed below. All the herb names given here are oils extracted from those herbs.

ALLSPICE

The oil obtained from the leaves and fruit of allspice is yellowish in colour. Dilute this with water before applying.

Note: Allspice contains eugenol, which causes skin redness or irritation when applied directly.

ALMOND (BITTER)

There are 2 types of almond oils. One is bitter and the other is sweet. Sweet oil (from sweet nuts) does not produce any essential oil. Bitter almond oil is nourishing for the skin and eyes, and helps relieve muscular pain and spasms. It is used mainly used as a base oil.

Note: Bitter almond oil contains cyanide and benzaldehyde, which are toxic when used in excess.

AMBRETTE SEEDS

The oil obtained from the seeds is pale, yellowish-red and is non-toxic. Age the oil before using for the best results. It mixes well with sandalwood and rose.

ANGELICA ROOTS

A colourless oil is obtained from the seeds and roots. The root oil is phototoxic. It is best known for bronchitis associated with vascular deficiency.

Note: It should not be used during pregnancy or if you are suffering from diabetes.

ANISE STAR (ILLICIUM VARUM)

A pale yellow sweet-smelling oil is extracted from the fruit and leaves. It is warming, stimulates the digestive system, as well as helps cure or prevent respiratory problems and rheumatism.

Note: In large quantities, star anise disrupts the circulatory system and causes cerebral disorders.

ANISEED (PIMPENLLA ANISUM)

A colourless or light yellow, spicy sweet warming oil. In excess, it is narcotic and slows down the circulation.

ARNICA

Oil from the flowers is orangey-yellow in colour. It has a bitter flavour and smells like radish. It is one of the best oils for bruises.

Note: The oil is highly toxic and should not be applied to broken skin.

BASIL SWEET (OCIMUM BASILICUM)

This is used widely in Ayurvedic medicine. Its essential oil is a stimulant and an excellent nerve tonic. A colourless oil, which has a calming yet uplifting effect on an individual, is obtained from the whole herb. It acts as an antidote for poisons, helps treat individuals suffering from insomnia and respiratory problems, improves blood circulation and the digestive system, and is a skin refresher. It is also used for the nerves and skin and is usually mixed with hyssop and bergamot.

Note: It should not be used during pregnancy.

BERGAMOT

A light greenish-yellow oil is obtained from the rind of the fruit. It has a wide range of applications and has an uplifting effect on individuals. It is used mainly for mouth, skin, respiratory and urinary tract problems. Because it acts as an anti-depressant, it is also used for refreshing in the bath.

Note: The application makes the skin sensitive to ultra violet light.

BLACK MUSTARD (BRASSICA NIGRA)

The essential oil from black mustard seeds is oral toxin, dermal toxin, irritates mucous membrane and should not be used like other essential oils.

BLACK PEPPER (PIPER NIGRUM)

A pale olive-coloured warm oil is extracted from pepper corns. This oil was used in India 4,000 years ago for treating and dilating the blood vessels. It is very beneficial to the aches and pains of the muscles, and stimulates the digestive, circulatory and lymphatic systems.

Note: It should be well diluted before use.

BORNEOL

It is also known as Borneo camphor and is a good substitute for camphor. It is extracted from camphor wood. It was used to treat the plague. It is very useful in treating infections and is a tonic for cardiac problems.

CAJUPUT

A green-tinged yellow oil is obtained from leaves and twigs of *kayu puthe* or white wood. It is a warming oil that is excellent for colds and coughs, and for relieving toothache. A few drops of cajuput in the bath reduces the intensity of a fever. It is used mostly as inhalation for respiratory problems, chronic laryngitis and bronchitis. It also stimulates the pulse rate.

CALAMUS

A thick pale yellow oil is extracted from the rhizomes. It is used mainly for abdominal disorders like indigestion, characterised by heartburn, nausea, pain in the upper abdomen, gastritis and gastric ulcers. It is also a tonic for fever, nervous complaints, vertigo, and headaches.

CAMPHOR

This is a white oil distilled from the wood. It stimulates the heart, improves blood circulation and clears chest congestions.

Note: Brown and yellow camphor contain safrol, which is toxic and carcinogenic. Avoid using them. In its crude state, brown and yellow camphor are poisonous in large doses. Pregnant women and those suffering from nervous disorders should avoid camphor.

CARAWAY

The oil, which is non-toxic, is extracted from caraway seeds. It is used to treat flatulence and to promote the production of milk in nursing mothers.

CARDAMOM

Cardamom produces a colourless oil, which is extracted from the steam distillation of seeds. It is a warming, non-toxic oil used to treat problems of the digestive and nervous systems.

CARROT SEEDS (DACUS CAROTA)

The dried fruit seeds produce the essential oil, which is yellow with warming property.

CEDARWOOD

The oil, which is deep amber in colour and non-toxic, is distilled from the wood. It is one of the oldest known oils that is used mainly for skin problems.

Note: Pregnant women should avoid this.

CELERY SEEDS

A pale yellow oil, which is non-toxic, is extracted from the seeds. It is used to treat rheumatoid arthritis.

Note: Pregnant women should avoid this during pregnancy.

CHAMOMILE

Chamomile blue, also known as German chamomile (Matricaria recutica), has the same properties as Roman chamomile (Chamaemelum nobile), except that it works better for inflammations. This is because it has a higher percentage of azulene. The oil from the German variety (obtained from the flower heads) has the colour of blue ink, while the Roman variety is pale blue to yellow in colour. Both the German chamomile and Roman chamomile are two of the best anti-inflammatory oils. They are soothing and have a calming effect on the nerves. They also act as a sedative. A bath in any one of these is relaxing. They are used for many common problems, such as stomach cramps, period problems, skin irritation and vomiting during pregnancy.

CINNAMON

Its yellowish oil, which is warming, is obtained from the leaves of the cinnamon tree. It is one of the best stimulants. Dilute it well before use.

Note: The oil from the leaves, and not the bark, is safe to use.

CLOVE

The pale yellow, sweet, spicy oil from the clove bud is least toxic. The oil from the leaves is dark brown, while the oil from the stem is pale yellow, with a strong spicy flavour. A strong stimulant for the mind and body, clove oil is excellent for relief from any pain. The oil is used to relieve toothache.

Note: Dilute it well before use; otherwise, it becomes an irritant.

CORIANDER

Coriander oil is colourless and extracted from the seeds. It is non-toxic when used in moderation. It is used mainly for problems of the digestive system.

CUMIN

Cumin oil is pale yellow in colour and extracted from the seeds. It is used to treat digestive problems.

CYPRESS

The needles and twigs of the cypress tree produce a green olive oil. The oil is useful for treating problems of the urinary system and for loss of fluids due to perspiration or menstrual problems. It is also used for treating varicose veins, haemorrhoids and broken capillaries.

DILL

A colourless oil is obtained from seeds and herb. The commercial oil, which is also produced from the seeds, has a different composition. The essential oil is used for gastrointestinal and endocrinal problems.

ELECAMPANE

Elecampane oil is obtained from dried roots. It is used mainly for respiratory problems.

EUCALYPTUS

The colourless oil, which is warming, is obtained from the fresh leaves. It is mainly used in steam inhalation for the treatment of respiratory ailments. Another variety has a lemon flavour, is not so warming and is refreshing.

FENNEL

The crushed seeds produce a colourless oil. It is excellent for digestive problems, arthritis and gout. It is also good for liver, spleen and gall bladder problems. It is one of the ingredients in gripe water.

Note: Pregnant women and epileptics should avoid using the oil.

FRANKINCENSE

The gum resin produces a pale yellow warm oil. It is used to treat rheumatism, and respiratory and urinary tract infections. It is calming and helps to slow down breathing, and so aids in the relaxation process.

GARLIC

The colourless oil, obtained from fresh bulbs, has a strong odour and its use as a medicinal herb has been acknowledged for thousands of years. It is used for respiratory and urinary infections, heart diseases, high blood pressure, diarrhoea, tuberculosis, hepatitis, skin eruptions and ringworm. Due to its unpleasant odour, however, it is seldom used. The curative property of garlic lies in its pungent flavour.

GERANIUM

A green oil is extracted from the leaves of the geranium. It is a cooling and calming oil and is used for treating anxiety and depression. It also stimulates the lymphatic system, and is used as a remedy for wounds and tumours.

GINGER

A pale yellow oil, which is warming, is extracted from the unpeeled root. It strengthens the body's immunity to diseases. It is also the most important oil for treating rheumatism, the calcification of joints and muscular pains due to cold rheumatism. It induces labour and is used to treat impotence.

GRAPEFRUIT

A greenish-yellow oil is obtained from the fresh peel. The oil cannot be stored for long as it gets oxidised. It has a detoxifying property.

JASMINE

A dark orange oil, best known as an uplifting oil, is extracted from jasmine flowers. A relaxant, it is used to treat urinary infections, respiratory problems and menstrual cramps.

JUNIPER

Juniper berries produce a pale yellow oil. It is a good carrier of other essential oils. It is used mainly for expelling toxic fluids from the body and for treating cystitis.

Note: Pregnant women and people with kidney diseases like nephritis should avoid it.

LAVENDER

A colourless oil, one of the most widely used essential oils, is extracted from fresh flower tops. A diuretic and a sedative, lavender oil promotes the flow of bile. The oil is also normally used for therapy.

An embrocation of the stems and flowers is used to treat muscular pain and stiffness. A compress of the infusion of flowers and stems on the forehead relieves headaches and giddiness. An infusion of flowers added to water relaxes and refreshes the body.

Lavender oil has a marvellous effect when it comes to relieving fatigue, palsy and nerve problems. It can also be used on skin for relief from bee stings and insect bites.

LEMON

A pale greenish-yellow oil is extracted from the fresh peel. A good antiseptic, lemon oil is a "cure all" for infectious illness. It is used to treat insect bites, warts, corns and verrucae, as well as boils and broken capillaries.

LEMON BALM/MELISSA (MELISSA OFFICINALS)

A pale yellow oil is extracted from part of the fresh leaves and flowering tops. It is a calming oil that has an uplifting effect. The oil or juice is used externally to treat eczema, allergic reactions and bee stings. Lemon balm is used widely to treat dyspepsia and depression. It is used in abundance because it is non-toxic.

Note: Pregnant women should avoid lemon balm oil or juice during their pregnancy.

LEMONGRASS

An anti-bacterial, amber-coloured oil is obtained from fresh lemongrass leaves. It is used as a diuretic. It is used to treat open pores, acne, sinusitis and fluid retention.

LIME

A pale yellow oil with a (citrus) fruity scent is extracted from whole ripe fruit. It is non-toxic.

LINALOE

The essential oil from the whole plant is non-toxic. It is used to treat problems of the skin and the nervous system.

MARIGOLD (CALENDULA OFFICINALIS)

The extract, obtained from marigold flowers, contains calendulin, resin, wax and volatile oil. It is non-toxic.

MARJORAM

A pale amber-coloured oil is obtained from the herb. It is warming and relaxing. It is used to treat pre-menstrual pain and to improve blood circulation.

Note: Pregnant women should avoid this.

MYRRH

A pale amber-coloured sticky oil is obtained from crude myrrh. It is used to treat arthritis, weak gums, ulcers, and menstrual and respiratory problems.

Note: Pregnant women should avoid this.

NEROLI (CITRUS AURANTIUM VAR AMARA)

A very relaxing oil, it is used as an ingredient in eau de cologne. It is used to treat anxiety, depression and insomnia.

NUTMEG

The oil from the fruit (red) is used to treat rheumatism, cramps, sprains, bruises, asthma and coughs. The oil from the seeds (white) is used to treat painful bones, swelling, gastritis, arthritis and rheumatoid arthritis.

ORANGE (BITTER)

The rind of a ripe fruit produces a dark yellow liquid, which is good for strengthening the heart and reducing the coagulation of blood, palpitation, jaundice and heartburn. It can be taken internally in a diluted form.

PALMAROSA

A pale yellow oil is obtained from the fresh dried grass. It is a good stimulant for the digestive and circulatory systems.

PARSLEY

A yellow amber oil is obtained from the seeds while a greenish-looking one is obtained from the herb. Both oils are mildly toxic. They are diuretic and are used to treat problems of the urinary tract. They are also used to treat dyspepsia and intestinal colic.

Note: Pregnant women should avoid this.

PATCHOULI (POGOSTEMON CABLIN)

The oil extracted from the dried leaves has a sweet, earthy flavour and is non-toxic. The aged oil has a better effect.

PEPPERMINT

Peppermint is a pale yellow oil from the herb. Highly penetrating, it is cooling and refreshing on the skin. It is used for all types of digestive disorders and prevents morning sickness during pregnancy.

PINE

The oil from the needles of the Scotch pine is widely used. It is a colourless and powerful antiseptic. It is used to treat pneumonia, colds, bronchitis and influenza. It is also used in a bath for aches and pains.

ROSE

It is a widely used ingredient in Eastern medicine. A pale yellow oil is extracted from fresh petals. It has antiseptic qualities. It is also a sedative, an antidepressant and an anti-inflammatory. It is good for dry and sensitive skins, and has aperient and astringent qualities. Petals contain malic acid and tartaric acid. These help dissolve gall stones. Red rose has some medicinal value. Its infusion is good for headaches, dizziness, nerves, mouth sores and the heart.

ROSEMARY

A colourless oil, with antiseptic qualities, is extracted from fresh flowering tops. The oil relieves or prevents spasms, encourages the flow of bile, and menstrual discharge, and is a stimulant for the liver and bladder. It is used to treat depression and cardiovascular weaknesses. It has a refreshing and stimulating effect on circulation. It sharpens the mental faculties and strengthens the heart. It gives relief from rheumatic and bronchial problems, and gives lustre and tone to dark hair. An infusion of rosemary, besides acting as a painkiller, is used to treat rheumatism, eczema, bruises, headaches and wounds. Fresh leaves are applied for relief from insect bites and bee stings.

Note: Pregnant women should avoid this, as should epileptics. It is not to be taken internally as it can cause poisoning.

SAGE LEAVES (SALVIA OFFICINALIS)

The pale yellow oil is oral toxic, abortifacient.

Note: Epileptics should avoid it.

SANDALWOOD

The roots and heart of the wood produce a pale yellowish-brown, non-toxic oil. The oil is used to treat urinary and respiratory infections. It is also used to treat dry, itching and inflamed skin.

SPEARMINT

The flowering tops produce an olive-coloured warming oil. The oil is used to treat digestive problems.

SWEET ORANGE (CITRUS SINENSIS)

The yellow or orange coloured liquid with a sweet fruity scent is extracted by cold expression and is non-toxic. The distilled oil oxidises easily and is photo toxic. Sweet orange oil, from the rind of sweet orange, is used to treat sluggish digestion.

TEA TREE

The oil is extracted from the leaves. It is an excellent germicidal and antifungal oil, and has a wide range of uses.

THYME

A reddish-brown oil from the fresh leaves and flowers becomes a clear oil on further distillation. It is warming and has an invigorating effect. It is a strong antibiotic, eases muscular pains and clears many types of infections.

Note: Thyme can irritate the mucous membrane and can cause skin irritation. Pregnant women should avoid it.

TURMERIC

A yellow oil from the rhizomes. Used for treating problems of digestion and circulation.

Note: Should be used in moderation. The presence of tumerone, a ketone, makes it toxic when or if taken in excess.

WHEATGERM

This makes an excellent base oil and contains vitamin E. It protects the delicate area around the eyes and removes scars on the skin.

YARROW

The dried herb produces a dark blue oil. It is used mainly for treating menstrual problems and for treating thrombotic conditions with hypertension.

Note: Take this in moderation.

YLANG YLANG

A pale yellow oil from the fresh flowers is good for calming the nerves.

Note: When used in excess, it causes headaches.

PROPERTIES OF ESSENTIAL OILS

ALTERATIVES

Help correct disorderly functions of the body.

Example: elecampane.

AMOEBICIDAL

Destroys amoebae.

Example: garlic.

Causes loss of feeling.

Examples: allspice, almond bitter and spearmint.

ANALGESIC
Lessens any pain.

Examples: allspice, bergamot, black pepper, borneol, cajuput, chamomile (both German and Roman), coriander, eucalyptus, ginger, hops, jasmine, lavender, lemon balm, marjoram, nutmeg, peppermint, rosemary and turmeric.

ANAPHRODISIAC
Decreases sexual desire.

Example: marjoram.

ANTHELMINTIC
Expels intestinal worms.

Examples: almond bitter, bergamot, calamus, camphor, cajuput, carrot seeds, cinnamon, clove, eucalyptus, garlic, onion and thyme.

ANTI-ANAEMIC
Helps to get rid of anaemia.

Examples: chamomile and lemon.

ANTI-ARTHRITIC
Helps to control arthritis.

Example: turmeric.

ANTIBIOTIC
Inhibits or kills other organisms.

Examples: clove, garlic and horseradish.

ANTI-CONVULSANT
Prevents convulsions.

Examples: calamus, lavender and linaloe.

ANTIDEPRESSANT
Alleviates depression.

Examples: basil, bergamot, borneol, geranium, jasmine, lavender, lemongrass, lemon balm, patchouli, rose, sandalwood and ylang ylang.

ANTIDIARRHOEAL
Combats diarrhoea.

Example: cinnamon.

ANTIDOTE
Neutralises the effect of poison.

Examples: cinnamon (especially for food poisoning.)

ANTI-EMETIC
Reduces the occurrences of vomiting and nausea.

Examples: clove, nutmeg and patchouli.

ANTIHAEMORRHAGIC
Combats bleeding.

Examples: geranium and marigold.

ANTIHISTAMINE
Helps treat allergies.

Examples: caraway, clove and lemon balm.

ANTI-INFLAMMATORY
Clears inflammations.

Examples: arnica, camphor, fennel, geranium, jasmine, linaloe, marigolds, myrrh, patchouli, peppermint, turmeric, yarrow and ylang ylang.

ANTIMICROBIAL
Destroys micro-organisms.

Examples: black pepper, cajuput, caraway, cinnamon, fennel, garlic, lavender, lemon, lemongrass, peppermint, parsley, mustard, myrrh, onion, patchouli, rosemary and thyme.

ANTINEURALGIC
Reduces nerve pain.

Examples: cajuput, chamomile, clove and eucalyptus.

ANTI-OXIDANT
Delays cell deterioration and tissue damage.

Examples: allspice, celery seed, clove, coriander, cumin, ginger, lemongrass, marjoram, nutmeg, rosemary, thyme and turmeric.

ANTIPHLOGISTIC
Prevents inflammations.

Examples: chamomile, peppermint, myrrh, rose, and sandalwood.

ANTIPRURITIC
Prevents itching.

Example: peppermint.

ANTIPUTRESCENT
Prevents putrefaction.

Examples: cinnamon and thyme.

ANTIRHEUMATIC
Prevents and relieves rheumatism.

Examples: celery seed, clove, coriander, cypress, eucalyptus, juniper, lavender, lemon, lime, nutmeg, onion, parsley, rosemary, thyme and yarrow.

ANTISCLEROTIC
Prevents hardening of the tissues.

Examples: lemon and onion.

ANTISCORBUTIC
Helps treat scurvy.

Examples: lemon and lime.

ANTISEPTIC
Destroys microbes and prevents their growth.

Examples: ajowan, allspice, star anise, aniseed, basil, bergamot (for pulmonary and genito-urinary problems), black pepper, borneol, cajuput (for pulmonary, genito-urinary and intestinal problems), calamus, camphor, chamomile, caraway, carrot seed, celery seed (for urinary problems), cinnamon, cardamom, clove, cumin, costus, cypress, eucalyptus, fennel, garlic, geranium, ginger, grapefruit, horseradish, jasmine, juniper, lavender, lemon, lemongrass, lime, linaloe, marigold, marjoram, mustard, myrrh, onions, palmarosa, parsley, patchouli, peppermint, rose, rosemary, sandalwood (for urinary and pulmonary problems), thyme (intestinal, pulmonary, urinary), yarrow and ylang ylang (for pulmonary and genito-urinary problems).

ANTISPASMODIC
Prevents spasms.

Examples: almond, angelica, aniseed, asafoetida, basil, bergamot, borneol, cajuput, cardamom, celery sees, cinnamon, coriander, cumin, costus, cypress, dill, eucalyptus, fennel, ginger, jasmine, juniper, lavender, lemons, marigold, marjoram, lemon balm, nutmeg, peppermint, onion, rose, sandalwood, thyme and yarrow.

ANTITOXIC
Is an antidote.

Examples: bergamot, black pepper, cumin, garlic, grapefruit, juniper, lavender, lemon, patchouli and thyme.

ANTITUBERCULAR
Prevents the spread of tuberculosis by destroying bacteria or by inhibiting their growth.

Example: Rose

ANTITUMOUR
Prevents the formation of tumours.

Example: garlic

ANTITUSSIVE
Relieves coughs.

Examples: ginger and thyme.

ANTIVIRAL
Prevents viral growths.

Examples: borneol, camphor, clove, costus, eucalyptus, garlic, limes, marjoram, peppermint, onion, patchouli and rose.

APERITIF
Increases the appetite.

Examples: black pepper, caraway, celery seed, coriander, fennel, ginger, lime, mustard and thyme.

APHRODISIAC
Increases sexual desire.

Examples: black pepper, cardamom, cinnamon, clove, coriander, cumin, ginger, jasmine, juniper, nutmeg, patchouli, rose, rosemary, sandalwood, thyme and ylang ylang.

ASTRINGENT

Contracts organic tissues.

> Examples: caraway, cinnamon, cypress, geranium, grapefruit, juniper, lemon, lemongrass, marigold, peppermint, myrrh, parsley, patchouli, rose, rosemary, sandalwood, thyme and yarrow.

BACTERICIDAL

Destroys bacteria.

> Examples: black pepper, calamus, camphor, chamomile, coriander, cumin, costus, dill, garlic, ginger, grapefruit, lemon, lemongrass, lime, linaloe, marjoram, lemon balm, onion, palmarosa, patchouli, rose, sandalwood, thyme and turmeric.

CARMINATIVE

Relieves flatulence.

> Examples: ajowan, allspice, angelica, star anise, aniseed, asafoetida, basil, bergamot, black pepper, borneol, cajuput, chamomile, caraway, carrot seed, cinnamon, cardamom, celery seeds, clove, coriander, cumin, costus, dill, fennel, garlic, ginger, horseradish, jasmine, juniper, lavender, lemon, lemon balm, lemongrass, marjoram, peppermint, myrrh, nutmeg, onion, parsley, patchouli, rosemary, sandalwood, thyme and yarrow.

CEPHALIC

Remedies disorders of the head.

> Examples: cardamom, ginger, marjoram, peppermint and rosemary.

CHOLAGOGUE

Increases bile production.

> Examples: chamomile, celery seed, garlic, lavender, marigold, peppermint, rosemary and turmeric.

CICATRISANT

Promotes healing by the formation of scar tissues.

> Examples: chamomile, eucalyptus, geranium, jasmine, juniper, lavender, lemon, marigold, myrrh, palmarosa, patchouli. rose. rosemary, sandalwood, thyme, and yarrow.

DECONGESTANT

Clears congestions.

> Example: eucalyptus.

DEPURATIVE

Clears impurity in the blood stream.

> Examples: angelica, carrot seed, celery seed, coriander, cumin, eucalyptus, fennel, garlic, grapefruit, juniper, lemon, onion and rose.

DIAPHORETIC

Causes perspiration.

> Examples: angelica, black pepper, cajuput, calamus, cypress, garlic, ginger, juniper, lavender, lemon, marigold, marjoram, lemon balm, peppermint, rosemary and yarrow.

DIGESTIVE

Aids digestion.

> Examples: angelica, basil, bergamot, black pepper, chamomile, cardamoms, celery seed, cinnamon, coriander, cumin, costus, dill, nutmeg, onion, palmarosa, patchouli, rosemary, turmeric and yarrow.

DIURETIC

Promotes urination.

> Examples: angelica, aniseed, bergamot, black pepper, camphor, caraway, carrot seed, cardamoms, celery seed, cumin, cypress, eucalyptus, fennel, garlic, geranium, grapefruit, horseradish, juniper, lavender, lemon, marjoram, onion, parsley, patchouli, rosemary, sandalwood, thyme and turmeric.

EMETIC

Induces vomiting.

> Example: mustard.

EMMENAGOGUE

Induces menstruation.

> Examples: angelica, basil, chamomile, caraway, celery seed, carrot seed, cinnamon, cumin, dill, fennel, juniper, lavender, marigolds, marjoram, lemon balm, peppermint, myrrh, nutmeg, parsley, rose, rosemary and thyme.

EXPECTORANT

Removes mucous from the respiratory system.

> Examples: angelica, star anise, aniseed, asafoetida, basil, caraway, clove, costus, eucalyptus, fennel, garlic, ginger, horseradish, jasmine, marjoram, peppermint, myrrh, onion, sandalwood, thyme and yarrow.

FEBRIFUGE

Reduces the intensity of a fever.

> Examples: angelica, basil, bergamot, black pepper, cajuput, chamomile, eucalyptus, garlic, ginger, lemon, lemongrass, lemon balm, lime, marigold, peppermint, mustard, palmarosa, parsley, patchouli and yarrow.

FUNGICIDAL

Prevents fungal infections.

> Examples: coriander, garlic, geranium, lemongrass, marigold, marjoram, myrrh, onion, patchouli, rosemary, sandalwood and thyme.

GALACTAGOGUE

Increases the secretion of milk.

> Examples: aniseed, basil, caraway, celery seeds, dill, fennel, jasmine and lemongrass.

GERMICIDAL

Destroys germs.

> Example: ajowan.

HAEMOSTATIC

Stops bleeding.

> Examples: cinnamon, geranium, lemon, rose and yarrow.

HEPATIC

Tones the liver.

> Examples: chamomile, carrot seed, celery seed, cypress, peppermint, rose and rosemary.

HYPERTENSIVE

Raises the blood pressure.

> Examples: rosemary and thyme.

HYPNOTIC

Induces sleep.

> Example: chamomile.

HYPOCHOLESTEROLAEMIC

Lowers the cholesterol level in the blood.

> Examples: garlic and onion.

HYPOGLYCAEMIC

Lowers the blood sugar.

> Examples: eucalyptus, garlic and onion.

HYPOTENSIVE

Lowers the blood pressure.

> Examples: asafoetida, calamus, costus, dill, garlic, lavender, lemon, marjoram, lemon balm, onion, parsley, turmeric, yarrow and ylang ylang.

LARVICIDAL

Prevents or kills larvae.

> Examples: caraway, clove, coriander, cumin, and nutmeg.

LAXATIVE

Promotes the evacuation of bowels.

> Examples: bergamot, black pepper, fennel, ginger, marjoram, parsley, rose and turmeric.

LEUCOCYTOSIS

Increases the production of white blood cells to fight diseases.

> Examples: garlic, lavender and rosemary.

LIPOLYTIC

Causes fats to split.

> Example: coriander.

MUSCLE RELAXANT

Relaxes tensed muscles.

> Examples: allspice and carrot seed.

NARCOTIC

Induces sleep.

> Example: almond.

NERVINE

Tones the nerves.

Examples: celery seed, cumin, juniper, lavender, lemongrass, marjoram, peppermint, patchouli, rosemary, thyme and ylang ylang.

PARTURIENT

Aids in childbirth.

Example: jasmine.

PROPHYLACTIC

Prevents infections.

Examples: basil, eucalyptus and patchouli.

RESTORATIVE

Strengthens and revives the body system.

Examples: basil, coriander, limes, myrrh and rosemary.

RUBEFACIENT

Causes redness of the skin.

Examples: black pepper, eucalyptus, ginger, horseradish, juniper, lavender, lemon, mustard, rosemary, thyme and turmeric.

SEDATIVE

Is a calming agent.

Examples: chamomile, celery seed, jasmine, juniper, lavender, lemongrass, lemon balm, marjoram, myrrh, rose, sandalwood and ylang ylang.

SIALOGOGUE

Stimulates the production of saliva.

Example: cardamom.

SPASMOLYTIC

Is an antispasmodic.

Example: clove.

STIMULANT

Quickens the physiological functions of the body.

Examples: basil (for the adrenal cortex), black pepper (for the circulatory, digestive and nervous systems), borneol (for the adrenal cortex), celery seed (for the uterine), cinnamon (for the circulatory and cardiac and respiratory systems), coriander (for the cardiac, circulatory and nervous systems), fennel (for the circulatory system) and geranium (for the adrenal cortex).

USING ESSENTIAL OILS

Bath

This is one of the easiest ways of using essential oils. Add 5–10 drops of any essential oil mixed with base oil to a warm bathtub. Chamomile and lavender are good for stress-related problems while rosemary and pine are good for rheumatic aches and pains in the joints.

Compress

This is used mainly to reduce inflammations.

Hot compress

Make a hot compress by filling a bowl with hot water. Add 5 drops of essential oil. Dip a hand towel or flannel into the bowl, squeeze out excess water and place it on the affected area for a while. Repeat this for a couple of times. A hot compress is used for treating backache, rheumatism, arthritis, abscess, earaches and toothache.

Cold compress

Follow the method for hot compress but use ice-cold water instead. A cold compress is good for headaches, sprains, strains and swollen parts.

Inhalation

Add 3 drops of any essential oil to a bowl of steaming water. Cover head and bowl with a large towel and inhale for a few minutes. Repeat after a short break. Inhaling vapour is good for sinusitis, and throat and chest infections.

Douche

Add 5 drops of tea tree oil to a litre of warm water and douche, which is good for genito-urinary infections like thrush. Douching after childbirth aids in the healing process. The oils used for this purpose are either lavender or cypress.

Application

Mix any essential oil with any suitable base oil to get a 1–3 percent concentration and apply to the affected area. All oils cannot be applied directly to the skin. Only certain oils like the following can be applied directly: lavender oil for burns and insect bites; and tea tree oil for spots. Depending on their concentration, lemon oil can be applied on warts and sandalwood oil or paste on acne.

Massage

Freshly-mixed essential oils with any base oil always have a relaxing effect. The essential oils are mixed with base oils like almond oil, wheatgerm oil, soya oil, grape seed oil or coconut oil. Usually 6–10 drops of essential oil are mixed with 2 teaspoons of base oil. Physical ailments like rheumatism and indigestion require a higher concentration. Emotional and nervous conditions require oils of a lower concentration.

After massaging the affected area, do not expose the area to draught. Cover the area with a cloth so that the oil is fully absorbed. The oils take as long as 12 hours to take effect. So after the massage, do not wash the area for at least 12 hours.

TREATING CERTAIN AILMENTS WITH ESSENTIAL OILS

Note: The oils in italics are the most beneficial.

ABSCESS
Compress, bath or application.

> Examples: *bergamot, chamomile, lavender, tea tree*, eucalyptus, lemon and thyme.

ACNE
Massage, compress, bath, inhalation or application.

> Examples: *bergamot, chamomile, geranium, lavender, rosemary,* camphor, clove, grapefruit, juniper, lemon, peppermint, sandalwood, spearmint and tea tree.

ACHES/PAINS
Massage, compress or bath.

> Examples: *chamomile, coriander, eucalyptus, ginger, lavender, marjoram, pepper, rosemary,* aniseed, basil, cajuput, camphor, peppermint, nutmeg, pepper, spearmint, thyme and turmeric.

ALLERGY
Massage, bath, application or inhalation.

> Examples: *coriander, chamomile, lavender* and *lemon balm.*

AMENORRHOEA
Massage or bath.

> Examples: *marjoram, myrrh,* basil, carrot seed, celery seeds, cinnamon, dill, fennel, juniper and parsley.

ANXIETY
Massage, bath or inhalation.

> Examples: *bergamot, lavender, lemon balm, ylang ylang,* basil and juniper.

APPETITE LOSS
Massage.

> Examples: *bergamot,* caraway, cardamom, ginger, myrrh and pepper.

ARTHRITIS
Massage, compress, bath or application.

> Examples: *chamomile, eucalyptus, ginger, marjoram, black pepper, rosemary,* allspice, angelica, cajuput, calamus, camphor, carrot seed, clove, coriander, juniper, lemon, myrrh, nutmeg, parsley, sarsaparilla, thyme, turmeric and yarrow.

ASTHMA
Massage or inhalation.

> Examples: *elecampane, lavender, peppermint,* asafoetida, cajuput, clove, eucalyptus, lemon, lemon balm, marjoram, myrrh, rosemary, tea tree and thyme.

ATHLETE'S FOOT
Application.

> Examples: *lavender, myrrh, tea tree,* clove, eucalyptus, lemon and lemongrass.

BLOOD PRESSURE (HIGH)
Massage or bath.

> Examples: *garlic, lavender, marjoram, yarrow, ylang ylang,* lemon balm and lemon

BLOOD PRESSURE (LOW)
Massage or bath.

> Examples: *coriander, eucalyptus, ginger, pepper, rosemary,* borneol, cinnamon, cumin, **cypress,** geranium, lemon, nutmeg and thyme.

BOILS

Compress.

> Examples: *bergamot, chamomile, lavender, tea tree*, black pepper, eucalyptus, lemon and thyme.

BLISTERS

Application.

> Examples: *bergamot, chamomile, lavender, tea tree.* eucalyptus, lemon and thyme.

BRONCHITIS

Massage or inhalation.

> Examples: *borneol, elecampane, eucalyptus, marjoram, myrrh, sandalwood,* asafoetida, basil, cajuput, camphor, caraway, clove, lemon, lemon balm, peppermint, orange (bitter), rosemary, tea tree and thyme.

BRUISES

Compress or application.

> Examples: *arnica, fennel, lavender,* borneol, clove, geranium and thyme.

BURNS

Compress or application.

> Examples: *lavender, sesame oil* and *olive oil* (mixed together), aloe, chamomile, clove, eucalyptus, geranium and tea tree.

CALLUS

Massage, bath or application.

> Examples: *fennel, geranium, grapefruit, juniper,* lemon, parsley, rosemary and thyme.

CATARRH

Massage or inhalation.

> Examples: *eucalyptus, lavender, peppermint, tea tree, thyme,* cajuput, elecampane, ginger, lemon, myrrh and black pepper.

CHICKEN POX

Compress or bath.

> Examples: *lavender, tea tree*, bergamot, chamomile and eucalyptus.

CHILBLAINS

Application.

> Examples: *lemon, marjoram, pepper* and chamomile.

CHILLS

Massage or bath.

> Examples: *cinnamon, ginger, pepper,* camphor, grapefruit and orange.

COLD

Massage, bath or inhalation.

> Examples: *borneol, eucalyptus, tea tree, thyme,* basil, bergamot, cajuput, camphor, caraway, cinnamon leaf, clove, coriander, ginger, grapefruit, juniper, lemon, marjoram, peppermint, orange, rosemary and spearmint.

COLIC

Massage.

> Examples: *chamomile, lavender, marjoram, peppermint,* caraway, cardamom, carrot seed, clove, coriander, cumin, dill, fennel, ginger, melissa, parsley, pepper and rosemary.

CONSTIPATION

Massage, compress or application.

> Examples: *Black pepper,* cinnamon leaf, fennel, marjoram, nutmeg, orange and turmeric.

CORNS

Application.

> Examples: *lemon, tea tree* and cinnamon.

COUGHS

Massage or inhalation.

> Examples: *elecampane, eucalyptus, marjoram,* basil, borneol, cajuput, camphor, caraway, ginger, lemon balm, myrrh, black pepper, rosemary, sandalwood and tea tree.

CRACKED SKIN

Application.

> Examples: *myrrh* and *sandalwood.*

CUTS

Application or compress.

Examples: *chamomile, lavender, tea tree, yarrow,* borneol, clove, eucalyptus, geranium, lemon, linaloe, myrrh and thyme.

CYSTITIS

Compress, bath or douche.

Examples: *bergamot, chamomile, lavender, sandalwood,* eucalyptus, parsley, tea tree and thyme.

DANDRUFF

Application.

Examples: *lavender, rosemary*, eucalyptus, lemon and tea tree.

DEPRESSION

Massage, bath or inhalation.

Examples: *bergamot, lavender, sandalwood, ylang ylang,* basil, grapefruit and lemon balm.

ECZEMA

Application or bath.

Examples: *bergamot, chamomile, lavender,* juniper, myrrh, rosemary and thyme.

FEVER

Compress or bath.

Examples: *eucalyptus, peppermint, rosemary, sandalwood paste, tea tree, yarrow,* basil, bergamot, borneol, ginger, juniper, lemon, lemongrass, spearmint and thyme.

FRIGIDITY

Massage, bath or inhalation.

Examples: *jasmine, orange blossom, ylang ylang,* nutmeg, parsley, pepper and sandalwood.

GASTRIC SPASMS

Massage or compress.

Examples: *allspice, ginger, lavender,* caraway, cardamom, cinnamon, coriander, cumin, peppermint and black pepper.

GOUT

Massage or application.

Examples: *angelica, carrot seed, juniper, rosemary,* basil, celery seeds, coriander and thyme.

HAEMORRHOIDS

Application or bath.

Examples: *juniper, myrrh, yarrow,* coriander and geranium.

HEADACHE

Massage, compress or inhalation.

Examples: *chamomile, lavender, peppermint,* cumin, eucalyptus, grapefruit, lemongrass, marjoram, rosemary, spearmint and thyme.

HEARTBURN

Massage.

Examples: *cardamom* and *black pepper.*

HERPES

Application.

Examples: *aloe, bergamot, eucalyptus, sarsaparilla* and *tea tree.*

INDIGESTION

Massage.

Examples: *allspice, caraway, cardamom, chamomile, fennel, lavender, marjoram, peppermint, orange,* basil, celery seed, cinnamon, clove, coriander, cumin, dill, ginger, lemon balm, lemongrass, nutmeg, parsley, black pepper, rosemary and thyme.

INFLAMED SKIN

Application.

Examples: *chamomile, lavender, myrrh,* angelica, camphor and yarrow.

INSECT BITE

Application.

Examples: *chamomile, lavender, lemon balm, tea tree,* basil, bergamot, cajuput, cinnamon, eucalyptus, lemon and thyme.

INSOMNIA
Massage, bath or inhalation.

> Examples: *chamomile, lavender, lemon balm,* basil, sandalwood, thyme and ylang ylang.

LACTATION (TO IMPROVE)
Application.

> *Fennel,* celery seed and dill.

LABOUR PAINS (TO RELIEVE)
Compress or bath.

> Examples: *jasmine, lavender, nutmeg* and cinnamon.

LARYNGITIS
Inhalation.

> Examples: *lavender, sandalwood* and *thyme.*

LEUCORRHOEA
Bath or douche.

> Examples: *bergamot, lavender, myrrh, rind of pomegranate, sandalwood,* cinnamon, eucalyptus, marjoram, raspberry with myrrh and rosemary.

LIVER (TO TONE)
Massage.

> Examples: *rosemary,* carrot seed, celery seeds and turmeric.

MEASLES
Bath.

> Examples: *eucalyptus, tea tree,* bergamot and lavender.

MENOPAUSE
Massage or bath.

> Examples: *geranium, rose,* cypress and fennel.

MENSTRUATION (EXCESS)
Massage or bath.

> Examples: *cypress, rose and* chamomile.

MENSTRUATION (PAINFUL)
Massage, compress or bath.

> Examples: *chamomile, lavender, marjoram,* basil, lemon balm and rosemary.

MIGRAINE
Compress.

> Examples: *lavender, sesame oil* with *camphor, cinnamon, cardamom,* basil, chamomile, coriander, marjoram, peppermint and spearmint.

MUSCLE CRAMPS
Massage, compress or application.

> Examples: *allspice, lavender, marjoram, black pepper, rosemary,* coriander, cypress, grapefruit and thyme.

MUSCLE TONING
Massage, bath or application.

> Examples: *grapefruit, marjoram, black pepper, rosemary,* allspice, borneol and ginger.

NAUSEA
Massage or inhalation.

> Examples: *chamomile, fennel, lavender, peppermint,* basil, cardamom, clove, coriander, lemon balm, nutmeg, pepper, sandalwood and spearmint.

NERVOUS FATIGUE
Massage, bath or inhalation.

> Examples: *angelica, basil, peppermint, rosemary,* borneol, cardamom, cinnamon, coriander, cumin, eucalyptus, ginger, grapefruit, lavender, lemongrass and thyme.

NEURALGIA
Massage or bath.

> Examples: *chamomile, lavender, marjoram, rosemary,* basil, celery seed, coriander, eucalyptus, geranium, peppermint, nutmeg and thyme.

OBESITY
Massage or bath.

> Examples: *fennel,* juniper, lemon and orange (bitter).

OEDEMA

Massage or bath.

> Examples: *angelica, carrot seed, fennel, grapefruit,* cypress, geranium, juniper, orange (bitter) and rosemary.

PALPITATION

Massage.

> Examples: *ylang ylang* and orange (bitter).

PRE-MENSTRUAL SYNDROME (PMS)

Massage, bath or inhalation.

> Examples: *chamomile, lavender,* geranium and marjoram.

PSORIASIS

Bath or application.

> Examples: *angelica, bergamot, lavender,* carrot seed and chamomile.

RASHES

Application, compress or bath.

> Examples: *chamomile, lavender,* carrot seed, sandalwood, tea tree and yarrow.

RHEUMATISM

Massage, compress or application.

> Examples: *chamomile, cypress, eucalyptus, lavender, juniper, marjoram, rosemary,* allspice, angelica, basil, black pepper, borneol, cajuput, camphor, celery seed, cinnamon leaf, clove, fennel, ginger, lemon, nutmeg, thyme and turmeric.

RINGWORM

Application.

> Examples: *lavender, myrrh, tea tree,* geranium and spearmint.

SCABIES

Application.

> Examples: *cinnamon, lavender, peppermint, spearmint.* bergamot, lemongrass, rosemary and thyme.

SCARS

Application.

> Examples: *lavender* and *sandalwood.*

SCIATICA

Massage or bath.

> Examples: *chamomile, lavender, marjoram, rosemary,* borneol, celery seed, coriander, eucalyptus, geranium, spearmint and nutmeg.

SINUSITIS

Inhalation.

> Examples: *eucalyptus, peppermint, tea tree,* basil, cajuput and ginger.

SORE THROATS

Inhalation.

> Examples: *thyme,* bergamot, cajuput, eucalyptus, ginger, myrrh, sandalwood and tea tree.

SPRAINS

Compress.

> Examples: *chamomile, lavender, marjoram,* borneol, camphor, clove, eucalyptus, ginger, black pepper, rosemary, thyme and turmeric.

STRESS

Massage, bath or inhalation.

> Examples: *bergamot, chamomile, lavender, lemon balm, marjoram, rose, sandalwood, ylang ylang,* basil, borneol, cardamom, cinnamon, geranium, juniper, lemongrass, linaloe, peppermint, orange, rosemary and thyme.

TONSILLITIS

Inhalation.

> Examples: *thyme,* bergamot and geranium.

TOXIN CLEANSER

Massage, bath or application.

> Examples: *angelica, carrot seed, fennel, grapefruit, juniper,* celery seed, coriander, cumin and parsley.

ULCERS IN THE MOUTH
Application.

> Examples: *fennel, myrrh,* bergamot, cinnamon, orange (bitter) and thyme.

VAGINAL ITCHING
Douche.

> Examples: *bergamot, lavender, myrrh,* juniper and tea tree.

VARICOSE VEINS
Compress or application.

> Examples: *cypress, yarrow and* lemon.

VERTIGO
Inhalation.

> Examples: *lavender, peppermint, sesame oil* with *cardamom, camphor, cinnamon* and lemon balm.

WARTS
Application.

> Examples: *lemon, tea tree* and cinnamon.

WHOOPING COUGHS
Massage or inhalation.

> Examples: *lavender* and *tea tree.*

WOUNDS
Application, compress or bath.

> Examples: *chamomile, eucalyptus, lavender, myrrh, tea tree, yarrow,* bergamot, cypress, geranium, juniper and linaloe.

WRINKLES
Massage, application or bath.

> Examples: *rose,* fennel, lavender, lemon balm, sandalwood and ylang ylang.

Apart from the essential oils mentioned above, there are certain oils and ointments that are prepared according to the Ayurvedic herbal systems. They are available at Ayurvedic herbal clinics. The oils used for massage (and the ailments they help treat) are as follows:

AMRUTHANJAN
Respiratory, abdominal, muscular and joint problems.

BALA THAILAM
Rheumatism, heart, tetanus, etc.

CHESOL
Contains abrus precatorious, brassica campestris, capsicum annum and aloe barbadensis. Good for muscular pain and sciatica.

DHANVANTHARAM THAILAM
Rheumatism and menstrual disorders.

EMBROCATION
Contains belladonna, bryonia, arnica, rhuxtox. It is used for treating sprains and joint inflammations.

EMU OIL
Relaxes the muscular tissues.

ENTROPS
Contains phenol, eucalyptus and camphor. This is one of the best anti-inflammatory oils.

HIMASAGAR
Rheumatism, blood pressure, headaches and insomnia.

IGUANA FAT
Relaxes muscles and heals torn tissues.

KARPOORADHI THAILAM
Camphorated oil with other herbs for rheumatic and respiratory problems.

KSHEERABHALA THAILAM
Rheumatism, paralysis, epilepsy and uterine complaints.

NEEM OIL
For healing. It is also a disinfectant agent for skin diseases and an anti-inflammatory agent for joint and muscular pains.

VALIYA PRASARANI THAILAM
Arthritis, nerves and uterine problems.

MASSAGE THERAPY

Massage therapy dates back to ancient times. The Egyptians, Persians, Chinese and Indians were well aware of its usefulness as a healing force and a physical therapy for maintaining the body.

Massage is both relaxing and nourishing because of the feeling of touch. The oils used during this treatment are effectively absorbed by the skin and the bloodstream.

It is beneficial to practise self-massage on areas that cause discomfort. A system of remedial manipulations of body tissue, massage is a method preferred by aromatherapists in treating many problems.

The procedures for the treatment of certain diseases or injuries are too complicated; therefore, it is not advisable to do a massage without proper training. Engage the expertise of a well-qualified masseur.

Though much depends on the mastery and technique of massage, equally important is an intuitive observation of the posture, breathing and responses of an individual and his or her mannerisms. This traditional eastern technique is based on the idea that the body is a bio-energy system.

Massage involves the expenditure of energy by the therapist. The friction produces heat and this, in turn, causes a looser atomic structure. The body relaxes and the tissues soften. Eventually, the energy concentrated in the region is released.

IMPORTANT ELEMENTS IN MASSAGE THERAPY

The most important element in massage therapy is the sense of touch. There is a close link between physical touch and emotion. The healing power of touch is instinctive.

The second element is *Rajas* or "energy". According to Yogic massage therapy, the vital force — *Prana* — flows through *Nadis* or "channels" and *Chakras* or "energy centres". The main channel absorbs vital force from the breath. In a healthy individual, the force is balanced between the positive and negative polarities (similar to yin and yang forces).

In addition to the above, the three *Gunas* or "qualities", *Tamas* or "inertia" and *Satva* or "intelligence" are present in the body; they have to be balanced. Orthodox medicine, however, does not see eye to eye with Eastern medicine on this. But recent studies

through holograms provide an explanation for this three-dimensional image.

The third important element is awareness of the body.

SPECIALISED FORMS OF MASSAGE THERAPY

Japanese Shiatsu disperses blocks of energy.

Ampuku is used on the abdominal area. It is used for treating abdominal disorders, tensions and sexual problems.

Chinese Tui Na involves kneading and pinching the body.

The key element in massage therapy is compassion; in Yoga, the Anahatha Chakra ("heart centre") is associated with the sense of touch. The masseur must be able to feel the patient's physical and emotional problems and find a way of channelling the energy flow or the vital force to the specific areas in order to relieve his or her problems. Massage combined with sympathetic counselling is very beneficial. Many people think that receiving a massage is just a one-way process. This is wrong. Massage in association with body awareness helps to ensure that the mind is used constructively to support the healing process. The masseur or the therapist, once he or she receives feedback from the patient, adjusts the massage technique to suit the individual. He or she also takes into account the emotional and psychological state of the individual.

The Yogic Chakra System identifies seven primary energy points situated within the hollow central channel of the spine. These Chakras can be activated to varying degrees. When not functioning properly, the Chakras are dull and sluggish instead of pulsating harmoniously. Ailments of the body due to an imbalance in the Chakras can be rectified through massage and Yogasanas.

A knowledge of body language is another important asset for the therapist. A body can portray many things. There is, however, no rigid rule to be followed. The same physical gesture may mean different things under different circumstances. Body language can give a good insight while communicating with people. A few examples follow:

- A pale colour indicates weakness of the skin.
- Dullness in the eyes reveals a lack of enthusiasm.
- The area directly over the heart, the heart Chakra, is the region associated with emotions. By placing a finger here and asking the patient to concentrate on his or her breathing, tension due to emotional feelings can be released.
- Cold and tense hands reveal resentment.

For a Yoga therapist, an awareness of these processes is an added advantage in handling emotional problems; thus, the holistic approach can be applied successfully.

By experiencing the way the massage is done, the body functions better and more efficiently. This, however, is a long term process as the massage does not heal ailments directly but promotes bodily conditions that are favourable to self-healing.

During massage, avoid sensitive areas like lumps, sores, skin eruptions and prominent veins. People with a heart condition, clots and serious infections should avoid being massaged. Pregnant women too should avoid massage as it can injure the foetus.

Practical hints for massage:

- Ensure the place is warm. The body loses heat during a massage.
- The masseur must have short fingernails.
- Jewellery may be a hindrance, so avoid wearing any.
- Select the right oil for the right problem.

SELF-MASSAGE TECHNIQUES

For general well-being, it is beneficial to practise self-massage on specific areas like the face, neck, hands and legs. Self-massage will help you experience the sensation of touch. It gives an idea as to how the application works and how it relaxes the area massaged. When it is performed slowly and gently in a rhythmical manner, it can drive away tension experienced in that area.

First practise the Sense of Touch Meditation to awaken tactile awareness. Choose some object for touching and feeling.

Sit comfortably and close your eyes. Pick up the object and start feeling it using the fingers of both hands. For 10 minutes, fix your attention on its quality, texture, shape and temperature. Your attempt at this stage is to merge with it. Once you have practised this, try out the following:

SHOULDER

The possible problems are stiff neck, aching shoulders and headaches.

Shoulder to Elbow

- Sit comfortably with the spine erect.
- Place 4 fingers of the right hand on the left shoulder and the thumb by the base of the neck. This helps the second finger fall on one of the main pressure points.
- Mould hand to the curve of the shoulder and gently tap the area for about a minute.
- Gracefully glide hand towards the shoulder joint and down the upper arm to the elbow. As you move the hand, look out for any point of discomfort. If there is one, stop moving and gently stroke the area with your fingers.
- Repeat the entire process 3–5 times.
- Now stroke the other side.

Back of Neck

- Place fingertips of both hands on either side of the spine (cervical region).
- Make circular movements, applying very little pressure.
- Make the area move with the fingers; do not rub.
- Slowly glide fingertips from the base of the skull down the whole of the neck.
- When fingertips finally reach shoulder tops, squeeze and release the flesh on the shoulders.
- Do this for 5 times, each time slightly lower than the previous time.

Shoulder

- Place the base of the right palm on the left shoulder. Keep the wrists loose and fingers folded.
- Pat the shoulder in a rhythmical manner. Do this for a minute on each side. It helps to improve circulation in the area.

Temples to Elbows

- Place first 3 fingers on the temples on either side of the face and the thumbs behind earlobes.
- Gently press the area behind the earlobes with the thumbs. At the same time, softly roll and move fingers over the temples in a circular manner, moving forward from the top of temples and going round from the bottom of the temples towards the ear. Do this

continuously for 2 minutes. Glide fingers gently towards the chin.

- Repeat the movement 2 or 3 times. The thumb need not be in same place during this movement.
- Slide hands from the chin down to the neck in front and cross them so that each hand is on the opposite shoulder.
- Continue down the opposite arms to the elbows. Repeat this several times.
- Finally, clasp each lower arm and perform abdominal breathing slowly.

ARMS

- Arm massage can relieve pain in shoulder, so stroke the entire arm.
- Knead all the way down the arm, squeezing and releasing the flesh.
- Pat gently all around the arm.
- First with palm, then with the thumb and fingers, apply gentle but firm circular pressure all around the elbow, paying particular attention to the hollow areas.
- Make circular rotations with the palm on the forearm.
- Finally, stroke the entire arm.

HANDS

- Stroke the back of the hands and squeeze them by pressing between the palm and the fingers.
- Using the thumb, squeeze each finger. Apply circular pressure to the joints.
- Stroke tendons on the back of the hands with the thumbs. Alternate this between the right and left hands.
- Place fingers on the back of the hand and the thumb at the centre of the palm. Apply pressure with the thumb and make a static circular movement.
- Shift thumb all over the palm and do the same. Perform the same with the wrist.
- Gently apply stroking and squeezing movements to the palms. Start at the fingers and end at the base of the palms. The movement is like pushing.

FACE

Use a fine face oil as a lubricant before a massage.

- Place both hands on the face, with fingers on the forehead and the base of palms on the cheeks. Hold the position for a while.
- Move the hands downward and gently glide fingers out towards the ears, running them over temples. Imagine a magnetic force drawing tension away.

- Tilt the neck to one side. Using the back of the hands, stroke gently, starting from the collar bone towards the chin. The stroking should be firm for increased circulation but it should not hurt.
- Tilt the neck to the other side and repeat.
- Using the thumbs, move the hands along the jawline, starting from behind the earlobes. Keep the thumbs close to the bone.
- Using the back of the hands, slap gently under the chin. While doing this, curl the tongue back in the mouth.
- Keep the mouth open to form a circle. With two fingers move round it, applying circular pressure to the teeth.
- Move the palms from the corners of your mouth to your ears.
- Move the palms down the forehead, from the hairline to the bridge of your nose.
- Using a finger and a thumb, gently press muscles between the eyebrows.
- Stroke firmly along the eyebrows, starting at the bridge of nose and ending with increased pressure on the temples.
- Pinch the eyebrows, moving from the centre towards the temples.
- Apply gentle pressure to the tiny indentation in the bone under the eyebrows at the bridge of nose.
- Perform Netra Shakti Vikasaka (iv) (see chapter 2).

ABDOMEN

- Lie on your back.
- Using the fingers, stroke the navel region. Increase the radius each time, making circles in the clockwise direction a couple of times.
- Use the entire surface of the hand to make circular movements. Do not apply pressure.
- Knead the abdominal region, starting from the top of navel. Move down in a circular motion.
- Turn over to one side and gently stroke the sides of the abdomen. Repeat on the other side.
- Cup hands over the navel for a few minutes. Feel the heat and lift hands upward.

HIPS

Gentle pummelling is the best method of massaging this area.

LEGS

Leg massage relieves aches that result from standing for a long period of time, relaxes tired muscles and stimulates circulation.

- Starting from the thighs, gently stroke each leg 2 times.
- Knead the thighs rhythmically with both hands, squeezing and releasing the muscles.
- Gently stroke each thigh with both hands. Compare the difference between energetic kneading and smooth-flowing strokes.
- To enrich blood circulation, pummel (with a gentle bouncy movement) the front and outside of the thighs with clenched fists. Do not repeat the kneading or stroking after this.
- Using all fingers, gently rub all around the knees.
- Apply circular pressure around the kneecap.
- Pressing the kneecap at the sides near the top with the thumbs, softly stroke behind the knees.
- Move kneecap gently with the hands. Check whether you experience a fluid or spongy sensation.
- Knead calf muscles with both hands.
- Squeeze muscles away from bone, releasing gently.
- Gently stroke the area.
- Fold the palms of both hands and give a gentle shake to the calf muscles.

FEET

Bad posture, backache and weariness can all stem from unnoticed foot problems. The following is an effective foot massage:

- Place one foot on the opposite thigh.
- Place one hand over the top of the foot and other on the sole of the foot. Gently stroke the entire area, from toes to ankle.
- Support foot with one hand, pressing thumb on the centre of the sole.
- Using the thumb and fingers of the other hand, squeeze and roll round each joint. Stretch each toe with a gentle pull.
- Place one thumb over the other and applying comfortable pressure, run down sole starting from the balls of the toes. Make a line (direction for massage) at the centre and two on the sides.
- Using one thumb, apply pressure with a circular movement on the arch and ball of the foot. Make a knuckling movement all over the sole.
- Now "hack" (like chopping firmly, but gently) sole with the edge of the palm.

- Gently stroke feet using your fingers, moving from ankles down to the toes.

MASSAGE TECHNIQUES FOR CERTAIN AILMENTS

It is always better to learn how to massage before making the effort by just reading the notes. This technique requires practical learning. Consult an expert before massaging.

ARTHRITIS

Apply olive oil mixed with an equal quantity of nutmeg oil to the affected area. Expose the area to the early morning sun for 10 minutes. Have a hot bath to work up a sweat. Later massage body with any of the following liniments:

- Mix a teaspoon of winter green oil, eucalyptus oil and camphorated oil together with half a teaspoon of turpentine. Shake well and apply.
- On a low flame, fry 20 cloves of garlic and 10 dry chillies with seeds in a cup of pure coconut oil. Fry until they turn brown. Let the oil cool and apply it to the affected area.
- Mix in a cup of boiling water mullein, granulated slippery elm bark, lobelia and cayenne in the ratio of 2:3:1:1 to make a paste. Spread the paste as a poultice on a cabbage leaf and cover the affected area with it after your bath. The swelling and pain will reduce.

ASTHMA AND HAY FEVER

- Gently massage the chest and back with camphor oil. Make outward strokes from the centre of the body. Now apply gentle pressure to the area around the collar bone.
- With gentle pressure, massage the thumbs of each hand and the next 3 fingers, including the web between them until tender spots (soft and sensitive to the touch) are no longer felt in the area.
- After the massage, soak feet in hot water containing crushed garlic. Add a drop of either thyme or lavender oil (thyme or lavender leaves may be used instead of the oil).

BACKACHE (GENERAL)

- Using a combination of juniper oil, ginger oil and camphor in equal proportion with wheatgerm as the base oil, massage the lumbar region (a drop of clove oil may be added to the above if the backache is unbearable). Move slowly towards the pelvic area.

- From the buttock region move up until you reach the sides of the hip joint.
- From the upper portion of the buttocks, move outward. Now turn towards the centre of the buttock linings with a semi circular movement.

CHILBLAINS

Massage the chest and back using cream or ointment made from either elder flowers or horseradish roots.

COUGHS AND COLDS

- Using camphor oil, gently apply pressure to both sides of the spinal column between the shoulder blades. Continue applying the pressure and move downward until you feel the pelvic bone. Increase the area of massage on either side of the spine each time.
- Using the thumbs, apply a gentle pressure near the centre of the chest and move down along the rib cage.
- Apply pressure just above the armpits in front of the shoulders and the sides of the navel region.
- Massage the entire arm, moving downward.

CONSTIPATION

- Massage firmly with deep kneading starting from the lowest part of the right side of the abdomen.
- Continue to move upward towards the ribs. Move horizontally across the abdomen to the left side, after which move down towards the lowest part of the left side of the abdomen.

HEADACHES

This can be done as a self-massage, but it is best done by someone who knows how to do it properly. The following can help clear a severe headache when done correctly:

- Sit in a comfortable position.
- Lower the head and chin.
- Place the index and second fingers on the temples and the thumbs at the corner of the jawbone right under the earlobes.
- Gently massage the temple area in a circular motion. While doing this, move the thumb up and down behind the ear occasionally.

HEART

- Gently massage the left foot under the third, fourth and fifth toes until tenderness disappears. Similarly massage right below the last two fingers of the left hand.

- Later soak feet and hands in warm water containing garlic and a drop of chamomile oil.

KIDNEYS

- Massage the sole of each foot at the centre by pressing and rolling.
- Move down the inner edge of the feet towards the heels. Repeat this several times.

NECK AND SHOULDERS

People sometimes awaken with stiff wrists and numb fingertips. These are symptoms of an affected neck, shoulders and arms. The main cause is disorder in the cervical vertebrae or cartilaginous discs.

The disorder exerts pressure on the blood vessels and nerves. Light pressure on the neck in the area of the cervical vertebrae produces pain.

- Warm neck by using a dry hot towel or by applying gentle strokes with the palm. Use basil or camphor or chamomile oil or a mixture of all three
- Using all fingers, gently press the area, starting from the base of the skull and move outward to the area behind the ears. Turn downward towards the base of the neck.
- Starting from behind the ears, move down slowly, pressing gently towards the neck and end pressure near the front of neck at the Adam's apple.
- Move slowly from the base of the skull towards the centre of the neck. Massage downwards, stopping near the collar bone on the shoulder. Repeat the process a couple of times.

PLEURISY

- Massage the chest and back using a mixture of camphor and basil oils.
- Massage the fingers by pressing between the fingers (webs). Also, gently massage the pads of your fingers.

RHEUMATISM

- Apply gentle pressure and massage the affected area with downward strokes using a mixture of juniper, ginger and nutmeg oils (a mixture of juniper, lavender and rosemary oils may also be used).
- Massaging the affected area with lavender oil also helps.

STROKE

Apply a cold compress intermittently to the forehead and face.

TONSILLITIS

- A warm fomentation to the chest and spine helps, especially if you are developing a cough.
- A hot foot bath twice a day helps clear the congestion in throat and neck.

VARICOSE VEINS

- If swelling or varicose ulcers are present, use alternate hot and cold foot baths for 20 minutes. Start with a 2-minute hot and a 30-second cold bath, and gradually increase the time for the cold bath until both are 2 minutes each.
- Without rubbing, dry the area immediately.

Although massage is soothing there are occasions when it can be dangerous. Do not massage during the following instances and always consult the doctor when in doubt:

- When there is a fever, an infection or a contagious disease like tuberculosis.
- When there is acute back pain, do not massage the spine directly.
- When pain shoots down the arms as the back is being massaged.
- When there is a skin infection.
- When the pectoral muscles are covered by lymphatic fatty tissues.
- When there is thrombosis, which is the formation of a blood clot in a blood vessel. Never massage or rub in acute thrombophlebitis, which is the formation of a blood clot in the wall of an inflamed vein, as it may cause part of the clot to pass on to other parts of the body, causing serious damage or death.
- During pregnancy.
- When there are varicose veins, do not massage directly on them.

Index

ASANAS

Some of the Asanas mentioned in this book and their English names

422